REGULATORY DELIVERY

This ground-breaking book addresses the challenge of regulatory delivery, defined as the way that regulatory agencies operate in practice to achieve the intended outcomes of regulation.

Regulatory reform is moving beyond the design of regulation to address what good regulatory delivery looks like. The challenge in practice is to operate a regulatory regime that is both appropriate and effective. Questions of how regulations are received and applied by those whose behaviour they seek to control, and the way they are enforced, are vital in securing desired regulatory outcomes.

This book, written by and for practitioners of regulatory delivery, explains the Regulatory Delivery Model, developed by Graham Russell and his team at the UK Department for Business, Energy and Industrial Strategy. The model sets out a framework to steer improvements to regulatory delivery, comprising three prerequisites for regulatory agencies to be able to operate effectively (Governance Frameworks, Accountability and Culture) and three practices for regulatory agencies to be able to deliver societal outcomes (Outcome Measurement, Risk-based Prioritisation and Intervention Choices). These elements are explored by an international group of experts in regulatory delivery reform, with case studies from around the world.

Regulatory Delivery is the first product of members of the International Network for Delivery of Regulation.

Volume 10 in the series Civil Justice Systems

Civil Justice Systems

Series General Editor: Christopher Hodges, Director, Swiss Re/CMS Research Programme, Centre for Socio-Legal Studies, University of Oxford

This series covers new theoretical and empirical research on the mechanisms for resolution of civil disputes, including courts, tribunals, arbitration, compensation schemes, ombudsmen, codes of practice, complaint mechanisms, mediation and various forms of Alternative Dispute Resolution. It examines frameworks for dispute resolution that comprise combinations of the above mechanisms, and the parameters and conditions for selecting certain types of techniques and procedures rather than others. It also evaluates individual techniques, against parameters such as cost, duration, accessibility, and delivery of desired outcomes, and illuminates how legal rights and obligations are operated in practice.

Regulatory Delivery

introducing the

Regulatory Delivery Model

*A guide for those charged with implementing regulations who believe
that outcomes of protection, prosperity and efficiency matter*

by

Graham Russell

Chief Executive of the Office for Product Safety and Standards

and

Christopher Hodges

Professor of Justice Systems and Head of the Swiss Re Research
Programme on Civil Justice Systems, Centre for Socio-Legal Studies,
University of Oxford

Supernumerary Fellow of Wolfson College, Oxford

with

Helen Kirkman, Head of Regulatory Delivery Strategy,
Office for Product Safety and Standards

Jenny Nobes, Head of Strategy, Office for Product Safety
and Standards

Including case studies and contributions from 34 authors
in 10 countries

HART PUBLISHING

Bloomsbury Publishing Plc

Kemp House, Chawley Park, Cumnor Hill, Oxford, OX2 9PH, UK

HART PUBLISHING, the Hart/Stag logo, BLOOMSBURY and the Diana logo are
trademarks of Bloomsbury Publishing Plc

First published in Great Britain 2019

A catalogue record for this book is available from the British Library.

Library of Congress Cataloging-in-Publication data

Names: Russell, Graham, MBE editor, contributor. | Hodges, Christopher J. S., editor, contributor.

Title: Regulatory delivery / Christopher Hodges and Graham Russell.

Description: Oxford ; New York : Hart 2019. | Series: Civil justice systems; volume 10 |
Includes bibliographical references and index.

Identifiers: LCCN 2019029552 (print) | LCCN 2019029553 (ebook) | ISBN 9781509918584 (hardback) |
ISBN 9781509918607 (Epub)

Subjects: LCSH: Administrative agencies—Great Britain. | Administrative agencies. |
Trade regulation—Great Britain. | Trade regulation.

Classification: LCC KD4882 .R44 2019 (print) | LCC KD4882 (ebook) | DDC 342.41/06—dc23

LC record available at https://lccn.loc.gov/2019029552

LC ebook record available at https://lccn.loc.gov/2019029553

ISBN:	HB:	978-1-50991-858-4
	HB:	978-3-406-74843-1 (CH Beck)
	HB:	978-3-8487-6139-5 (Nomos)
	ePDF:	978-1-50991-859-1
	ePub:	978-1-50991-860-7

Typeset by Compuscript Ltd, Shannon
Printed and bound in Great Britain by CPI Group (UK) Ltd, Croydon CR0 4YY

To find out more about our authors and books visit www.hartpublishing.co.uk.
Here you will find extracts, author information, details of forthcoming events
and the option to sign up for our newsletters.

FOREWORD

Regulatory delivery – namely the downstream, enforcement side of regulatory policy – has at times been called the unknown child of better regulation. Over the course of the last 20 years, OECD member countries have all made significant investment in the institutions and tools that governments use to design high-quality regulation. However, good regulatory outcomes depend on more than just well-designed rules and regulations. Regulatory delivery has been overshadowed by these 'design' initiatives in most OECD countries to date.

Regulatory enforcement and inspections is therefore a relatively new and understudied element of better regulation. Only a few OECD member countries have introduced significant cross-cutting reforms in this area. The United Kingdom has been a pioneer in this regard. Building on the wisdom of the 2005 Hampton review and the innovative work of the Office for Product Safety and Standards and its predecessors, the UK has developed and applied enforcement strategies that deliver the best possible outcomes by achieving the highest possible levels of compliance, while keeping regulatory costs and administrative burdens as low as possible. A number of other OECD countries are currently considering some reform initiatives and are seeking guidance and good practice examples.

In this book Graham Russell, who has been at the forefront of the UK's innovation for some years, and Christopher Hodges, who has more latterly brought academic rigour to the discipline, provide a model to enable regulators to explore their understanding of the topic. Building on previous work and fundamentally extending the international community's knowledge, they provide important insights into how governments can ensure that businesses willingly comply with the law – because they understand the protections it provides rather than the costs that it imposes. This approach rightly acknowledges that enforcement and inspections are a critical component of the policy process because they ensure that objectives enshrined in legislation are put into practice.

The book recognises that enforcement and inspection authorities must therefore be integrated into the regulatory policy cycle. It makes the case that the feedback they offer should be part of the review process of regulations – providing the critical link between the design of regulations and their monitoring and implementation. This is particularly important in a 'post-truth' environment where well-grounded evidence is becoming increasingly critical to policy making in the public interest.

In our response to this new field, OECD developed key principles and guidance for organising and reforming enforcement and inspections in all countries. The 2014 'OECD Best Practice Principles for Regulatory Enforcement and Inspections' is a set of common values that are relevant for all organisations and sectors where inspections take place. The Principles include planning and better targeting inspections, communicating with regulated subjects, preventing corruption, and promoting ethical behaviour, as well as the organisation of inspections and the governance of inspection authorities. The 2017 OECD Regulatory Enforcement and Inspections Toolkit further extended this work, presenting a checklist to help officials, regulators and stakeholders assess the level of development of the inspection and enforcement system in a given jurisdiction and to identify strengths and weaknesses, and potential areas for improvement.

Better regulation is a key pillar not only to support good policy-making, but more generally the rule of law and ultimately representative democracy. So strengthening our regulatory delivery agenda has never been more important than today. The Regulatory Delivery Model, introduced in this book, provides a new and valuable framework to guide and assess this.

Nick Malyshev
Head of Regulatory Policy Division
OECD

CONTENTS

PART ONE
WHY DELIVERY?

PART TWO
THE REGULATORY DELIVERY MODEL

Prerequisites: Governance Frameworks

Prerequisites: Accountability

Prerequisites: Culture

Practices: Outcome Measurement

Practices: Risk-based Prioritisation

Practices: Intervention Choices

PART THREE
INTERNATIONAL BEST PRACTICE EXAMPLES

PART FOUR
REFLECTIONS

ABOUT THE CONTRIBUTORS

Graham Russell, Chief Executive, Office for Product Safety and Standards
Graham Russell is Chief Executive of the Office for Product Safety and Standards (OPSS) in the UK Government Department for Business, Energy and the Industrial Strategy (BEIS). Graham's career and experience has been as a regulator since qualifying as a Trading Standards Officer in Staffordshire County Council in 1990. In 21 years with the local authority he led a number of regulatory services and created new regulatory functions responsible for animal health and welfare, at the local level, and for controlling the activities of claims management businesses at the national level.

After working with government teams supporting the Hampton, Macrory, Rogers and Anderson reviews (see Annex 1), which collectively marked a step change in UK thinking on the modernisation of regulation, Graham was appointed the first chief executive of the Local Better Regulation Office (LBRO) and established LBRO as a pioneer of the concept of regulatory delivery. Working with the Chair, Dr Clive Grace, Graham led a range of initiatives to test new approaches to the effective delivery of regulation at a local level. Graham continued to lead the organisation through expansion of remit as the Better Regulation Delivery Office in 2012, Regulatory Delivery in 2016 before the creation of the Office for Product Safety and Standards in 2018, a new national oversight body for product regulation which also continues work on good regulatory delivery.

Graham is a Fellow of the Chartered Trading Standards Institute.

Professor Christopher Hodges, Professor of Justice Systems and Head of the Swiss Re Research Programme on Civil Justice Systems, Centre for Socio-Legal Studies, University of Oxford
Prof Chris Hodges is Professor of Justice Systems at Oxford University, where he is also Head of the Swiss Re Research Programme on Civil Justice Systems at the Centre for Socio-Legal Studies and Supernumerary Fellow of Wolfson College. He spent the first 25 years of his career as a corporate lawyer in the City of London advising multi-national businesses on resolving disputes and complying with regulation across Europe. Having written a PhD in European regulation of consumer product safety in his spare time, he then escaped back to Oxford in 2004 and started critical research into what actually makes people obey laws, or behave in certain ways, and how systems can best achieve delivery of regulation and dispute resolution.

He has written widely on effective and emerging models of regulation and dispute resolution. His seminal work Law and Corporate Behaviour, for the first time drew together from a range of disciplines the importance of adopting a fresh approach. He has developed this further with Ruth Steinholtz to recognise the importance of aligning the cultures of regulated and regulators to improve outcomes through Ethical Business Practice and Regulation.

Florentin Blanc, Business Inspections Reform Specialist – World Bank Group
Florentin came to inspection reform from a background in education and with NGOs. His work with the World Bank and as a consultant has established his position as a leading expert on risk-based regulation across the world. His PhD research on the efficacy of inspection has gone a long way to answering the questions that sit at the heart of our understanding of what makes a difference to business behaviour and regulatory outcomes. Reformers working to change their context who have had the privilege of Florentin's input will understand the unique contribution that his passion, knowledge, experience and drive bring to the table.

Giuliana Cola, BMTI (Italian Online Commodity Exchange)
Giuliana has a background in humanities and social sciences focused on development cooperation and sustainability. She gained experience in administrative burden assessment as research assistant for a reform project led by the World Bank. Giuliana combines international education in Italy, France and Japan with knowledge in public policies and better regulation which she applies to the agri-food, agro-energy and industry.

Jigjidmaa Dugeree, Senior Private Sector Specialist, International Finance Corporation
Without Jiji's personality, drive, understanding and insight the reform journey that Mongolian regulators have taken over the last ten years would probably not have happened and would certainly not have attracted the worldwide interest that it has. Jiji understands the domestic consequences and the political environment extremely well but also has a clear sense of vision and purpose and the ability to connect the journey that she has led, with other reform journeys in many parts of the world.

Ariel Francisco Faraon, Procurement Compliance Manager, Universal Robina Corporation & Consultant on Regulatory Management
Mr. Faraon was the Project Manager of Project Repeal: the Philippine Red Tape Challenge, a whole-of-government initiative to cut red tape through a programmatic approach of repealing burdensome laws and regulations. While managing a project in the Department of Trade and Industry (DTI), he represented DTI in the development of the country's medium-term development plan for 2017–2022. With a combined six years of service in the government holding various positions as Project Manager, Supervising Labour and Employment Officer, Planning, and Monitoring and Evaluation Officer, Mr. Faraon leveraged his expertise in helping regulatory agencies implement their respective regulatory reforms. He is now busy managing the corporate procurement group of the country's biggest business conglomerate.

Nestor Ian Favila Fiedalan, Senior Trade & Industry Development Specialist, Government of the Philippines
A graduate of Political Science and Law, Mr. Fiedalan has worked with the Philippine Department of Trade and Industry as Senior Trade and Industry Specialist for Supply Chain and Logistics. Together with Mr. Faraon, he spearheaded the implementation of Project Repeal, the Philippine Red Tape Challenge specifically in logistics and transportation sector. During his stint in the government, he actively participated in the lobbying of the Ease of Doing Business and Efficient Government Services Delivery Act of 2018.

He assisted the Department of Agriculture and the Maritime Industry Authority in their regulatory reforms initiatives. He is presently employed in one of the country's biggest business conglomerates.

Matt Gantley, Chief Executive of UKAS
Matt Gantley is the Chief Executive of UKAS, the UK's national Accreditation Body. Matt has over 20 years' experience in conformity assessment and prior to joining UKAS he was the Managing Director of NQA Certification and held senior Directorship positions in certification, training and consulting enterprises. His key achievements include strategic and commercial development alongside international management in emerging markets. Matt is passionate about corporate and business strategy and served as a visiting MBA lecturer at Manchester Business School. Matt has also fulfilled Non-Exec roles for Elmhurst (Energy Training/Certification), was a Board Director of SSIP (Safety Schemes in Procurement) and was the Chairman of the Association of British Certification Bodies.

Dr David Snowball, Health and Safety Executive
Joseph Januszewski, Health and Safety Executive
Mike Calcutt, Health and Safety Executive
Michael Bone, Health and Safety Executive
The Health and Safety Executive's scientists bring a deep commitment to scientific testing which underpins the study of regulation. This not only provides confidence in individual products but has created an evidence base for approaches that can change the way inspectors work. Their work on premises-specific data-sharing has enabled HSE and other UK regulators to cross divides and perceived barriers to the use of data enabling precision, consistency and proportionality to the targeting of premises.

Duncan Johnson, Office for Product Safety and Standards
Having led teams in a range of regulatory practices in Birmingham City Council, Europe's largest municipality, Duncan is well placed to advise on the way that regulatory delivery reform can be implemented. In addition to that he brings a creativity and development capability that has been fundamental in shaping the UK's Primary Authority product, enabling UK regulators and businesses to create better outcomes and drawing the interest of regulators from around the world.

Giedrius Kadziauskas, Inspection Reform and Better Regulation Consultant
Giedrius has shaped the regulatory reform approach in Lithuania, which is noted for its energetic innovation, and brought the fruits of that experience to the benefit of reformers around the world. In both cases the combination of sharp insight, clear communication and patient encouragement have enabled impact that goes beyond the immediate and is also producing long term benefits.

Helen Kirkman, Office for Product Safety and Standards
Helen started her work in the area of regulation as a frontline Trading Standards officer and then as a consultant to regulatory agencies across the UK and now with responsibility for regulatory approaches across the Office for Product Safety & Standards. In all of these roles Helen's grasp of the strategic imperatives and the detail on the impact of individuals, whether that is business, consumers or inspectors themselves, has ensured a clear, compelling approach to implementation of risk-based regulation with an outcome focus.

Paul Leinster, Professor of Environmental Assessment, Cranfield University
Professor Paul Leinster has over 40 years of practical experience in environmental management, policy development and regulation. Paul joined Cranfield University in 2015 as Professor of Environmental Assessment. Prior to this he was Chief Executive of the Environment Agency and before that Paul worked in the private sector for over 20 years. He has a particular interest in translating research into effective policy, regulatory, operational and governance measures and in natural capital and ecosystem service approaches to environmental management. He is a member of the government's Natural Capital Committee and chairs the Bedfordshire Local Nature Partnership and the Institute of Environmental Management and Assessment.

Tom Ling, Senior Research Leader and Head of Evaluation, RAND Europe
Tom Ling has over 20 years of experience in designing, managing and delivering complex impact evaluations. He is a senior research leader at RAND Europe and head of evaluation with over 20 years' experience contributing to research projects with the European Commission, Save the Children, UK government departments, the National Audit Office, the Health Foundation in the UK and many others. He has published widely on evaluation, accountability, and related topics. He leads evaluations and applied research focused on the key challenges facing organisations in health, well-being, and development. Before re-joining RAND, Ling was head of Impact Innovation and Evidence at Save the Children where his responsibilities included ensuring that evaluations contribute to policy and change in the challenging environment of international development. Prior to Save the Children, Tom spent ten years at RAND Europe as director for Evaluation and Performance Audit following four years as senior research fellow at the National Audit Office in the UK.

Nick Malyshev, Head of Regulatory Policy Division, OECD
Under Nick's leadership the OECD Regulatory Policy Committee has developed a broad remit including work on the regulatory policy peer review of impact assessments and use of other tools, but also contributing to developing thinking on International Regulatory Co-operation and regulatory delivery. This has helped to ensure the countries within the OECD network have a broad approach in their thinking about regulation from policy to delivery, impacts on business and outcomes for beneficiaries.

Srikanth Mangalam, President of Public Risk Management (PRISM) Institute, Ontario, Canada
In his journey from front line regulation to consultancy, Srikanth has brought a sharp focus on the value and use of risk in prioritising resource allocation but also in shaping enforcement practices and dialogue with business. His knowledge of, and involvement in, shaping of Canada's delegated administrative authority model has assisted those interested in regulatory delivery around the world to challenge their assumptions and contemplate an alternative approach.

Giuseppa Ottimofiore, Regulatory Consultant
Giuseppa Ottimofiore has a PhD in Law and is a consultant on regulatory delivery, primarily working with the World Bank Group on inspections, licensing assessment and regulatory reform projects in Portugal.

Marcelo Pacheco dos Guaranys, Deputy Minister, Ministry of the Economy, Brazil

Marcelo's position as Deputy Minister in the Ministry of the Economy and prior to that in the Presidential Office in Brazil and as the President of the Brazilian Civil Aviation Agency enables him to understand the breadth of strategic challenges facing a country of enormous scale and complexity. His recognition that within that, the role of delivery of regulation as a shaper of economic and business environments and builder of confidence in domestic and international markets, has brought a fresh insight and a vivid communication approach which not only tells the story about Brazil's reform but also opens up new horizons of those interested in the strategic impact of regulation.

Professor Simon Pollard, Pro-Vice-Chancellor, School of Water, Energy and Environment, Cranfield University

Simon leads Cranfield University's School of Water, Energy and Environment. His career spans senior appointments in academia, consulting and government. He is an environmental engineer and Fellow of the Royal Academy of Engineering. His scholarship seeks to reconcile society's unease about pollution with organisational and regulatory responsibilities for its safe management. Recent papers examine organisational competencies in risk management in the international water sector, as it responds to calls for sustained service levels under constrained access to finance, climate change and water scarcity.

Kathryn Preece, Office for Product Safety and Standards

Prior to joining the civil service Kathryn spend 20 years as an Environmental Health Officer within a variety of local authorities including gaining significant enforcement experience at a large city authority, leading on food safety at a new unitary authority and as Head of Service being responsible for the reorganisation of the Environmental Health and Licensing functions into a high performing service in a busy district authority. Kathryn's ability to recognise opportunities for regulatory excellence and innovation and desire to develop successful working relationships led to the creation of the blueprint for the Better Business for All programme which has been instrumental in reshaping the way in which regulatory support is delivered.

Phil Preece, Office for Product Safety and Standards

As an experienced health and safety inspector who has worked in local authorities and the UK's national regulator the Health and Safety Executive, Phil brings his expertise in this regulatory area to the breadth of regulation. Whilst he has a special expertise in the use of risk, his investigatory skills and leadership have been widely recognised in his work in setting up the Product Safety enforcement team in the Office for Product Safety and Standards, focusing on long standing issues around the safety of white goods.

Marcus Rink, Chief Inspector, Drinking Water Inspectorate

Marcus Rink is the Chief Inspector at the Drinking Water Inspectorate. As Chief Inspector he provides independent scrutiny of the water industry ensuring the safety and quality of water and public confidence through a robust regulatory framework. The role encompasses a range of statutory and non-statutory functions, discharging the duties of the Secretary of State and the Welsh Government to: ensure companies meet their regulatory requirements; local authorities take action in respect of private supplies; the provision of UK data to the European Commission and membership of the European Drinking Water Directive committee.

Richard Sanders, Office for Product Safety and Standards
Richard's long experience and deep knowledge of the UK's legal metrology system has enabled the UK to play a major role in domestic, European and global fora for development of confidence in measurement systems. Now in his championing of BSI and UKAS across government, Richard is ensuring that the roles of standards and accreditation are well understood and effectively deployed.

Dr Paul Sanderson, Research Associate, Centre for Business Research, Cambridge Judge Business School, University of Cambridge
Paul brings the disciplines of a research economist and social theorist to the practice of regulatory delivery. His deep knowledge of governance issues across the private and public sectors has shaped thinking on the prerequisites of the Regulatory Delivery Model.

Erica Sheward, Office for Product Safety and Standards
In a disparate career spanning from writing a book on food safety for airlines to setting up a high street food premises and lecturing on food safety at post graduate level, Erica has managed to maintain a robust approach to understand regulatory delivery problems whilst also challenging peers and stakeholders alike to rethink their accepted practices. Now in a new role with Leatherhead Food Research, Erica is bringing her experience of reform to the benefit of clients around the world.

Mariam Shkubuliani
Mariam was an MSc student at University of Greenwich and completed her MSc dissertation on consumer understanding of the FHRS under Erica Sheward's supervision.

Scott Steedman, Director of Standards, BSI
Scott Steedman joined BSI in January 2012 and was appointed to the Board in October 2012. An engineer by background, he started his career at the University of Cambridge before moving to industry where he spent over 20 years as a consultant working in the Built Environment sector. He was a Non-Executive Board Member of the Port of London Authority from 2009 to 2015 and served as Vice-President (Policy) for the European Committee for Standardization from 2013 to 2017. He is currently Vice-President (Policy) of the International Organization for Standardization.

Ruth Steinholtz, Founder, AretéWork
Following a varied and exciting international legal career in various industries, Ruth Steinholtz founded AretéWork in 2011. The firm assists organisations globally in managing risk and improving results by fostering strong ethical cultures based upon values. Previously, as General Counsel and Head of Ethics at Borealis AG, Ruth developed a values-based approach to ethics and compliance – employing ethics ambassadors throughout the company. Organisations around the world have adopted this approach.

Martin Traynor, Business Consultant
There are not many hotel managers who have turned their hand to policy making and regulatory reform and Martin stands unique for his contribution locally through the Leicestershire Chamber of Commerce and the Local Enterprise Partnership and also nationally where his contribution to the UK Regulatory Policy Committee has been outstanding. Martin is now the UK Government's Small Business Crown Representative. Alongside all of that he has helped shape a national programme in the UK called Better Business for All which has

enabled local authorities across the country to develop new tools for new challenges. He has a unique ability to speak and think as an experienced entrepreneur in ways that policy makers and regulators alike can hear.

Christian van Stolk, Vice President, RAND Europe; Research Group Director, Home Affairs and Social Policy
Christian van Stolk is vice president at RAND Europe and director of the Home Affairs and Social Policy research group. He has wide experience in evaluation and performance having been the client manager for RAND Europe's strategic partnership with the UK National Audit Office. He has a particular interest in assessing the performance of regulatory agencies, central government and the civil service. He has undertaken projects for the UK government, European institutions, World Bank and OECD.

Rob Velders, Owner at Velders & Novák Consultancy on Enforcement
The Netherlands is rightly regarded as a leading nation in development of both regulatory policy and regulatory delivery. In terms of delivery Rob through his work as an international inspections reforms consultant, inspector and with the Dutch Inspectors Council, has been responsible for bringing many innovative practices to fruition. He is renowned for his understanding of the ways that inspectors work, the ways they can work together and the ways the fruits of that co-operation can reduce burdens for business whilst also improving outcomes through better use of data.

Chris Webb, Executive Director – Regulatory Practice and Strategy at EPA Victoria
Chris Webb is the Executive Lead for Legislative Transformation at EPA Victoria. As the architect of a world first preventative duty model of legislation for environmental regulation, he is now focussed on helping reshape the organisation to be ready to deliver when it comes into effect in 2020. He has worked across all aspects of regulation, and has built high performing teams with innovative approaches, as well as contributing to the community of practice across Australia. Prior to working as a regulator Chris' background has included risk, safety and environmental management in the oil industry and major events such as the Australian Formula 1 Grand Prix. With this strong practical industry grounding, and experience across regulators, Chris has the firm belief that one of the secrets to unlocking great regulatory practice is understanding the connection that internal culture has with the external experience of the regulator, and the critical role it plays in delivering effective outcomes.

LIST OF ABBREVIATIONS

BBfA	Better Business for All
BEIS	Department for Business, Energy and Industrial Strategy (UK)
BRDO	Better Regulation Delivery Office (UK, see also Annex 1)
BSI	British Standards Institution
DWI	Drinking Water Inspectorate (regulates water quality in England and Wales)
EA	Environment Agency (UK)
EBP	Ethical Business Practice
EBR	Ethical Business Regulation
EHO	Environmental Health Officer
EPA Victoria	Environment Protection Authority in Victoria (Australia)
FHRS	Food Hygiene Rating Scheme (UK)
FSA	Food Standards Agency (UK)
GASI	General Agency for Specialised Inspections (Mongolia)
HSE	Health and Safety Executive (UK)
INDR	International Network for Delivery of Regulation
ISO	International Organisation for Standardisation (Geneva, Switzerland)
LAs	Local Authorities (UK)
LBRO	Local Better Regulation Office (UK, see also Annex 1)
LEPs	Local Enterprise Partnerships (UK)
LGUs	Local Government Units (Philippines)
OECD	The Organisation for Economic Cooperation and Development (Paris, France)
OPSS	Office for Product Safety and Standards (UK)
OSH	Occupational safety and health

PRO-REG   Programme for Strengthening Institutional Capacity for Management
             in Regulation (Brazil)

UKAS   UK Accreditation Service

WHO   World Health Organisation (Geneva, Switzerland)

LIST OF FIGURES, TABLES, BOXES

Figures

Tables

Boxes

PART ONE

Why Delivery?

Introduction

GRAHAM RUSSELL

I. Take Three Envelopes – A Regulatory Parable

The Chief Executive sat nervously in his new office.

It was his first day as head of the regulatory agency and the thrill he had felt when first offered the position was now tempered with caution – daunted by the prospect of the challenges ahead. His imagination began to run wild. He pictured himself as a high-wire artist. Was this how Blondin had felt? Staring at the tightrope stretched across the Niagara Falls, aware of the drop beneath him, the calls to 'keep your balance' from either side rising above the crashing of the water onto the rocks far below?

With these images filling his mind, he was relieved to find three plain envelopes, left by his predecessor – tucked away in his desk on the day she left office. Having appreciated her advice when they had met a few weeks ago, he was pleased that she had left him some encouragement for his new challenge.

The envelopes were numbered, and the first was marked 'Open after one year' so he felt able to relax a little.

Those early weeks, his honeymoon period, rushed past. Buoyed up by the enthusiasm of staff and stakeholders alike, he sailed along on a tide of goodwill: making decisions, allocating responsibilities, reporting progress. But as weeks turned into months, that tide begin to ebb away. Problems turned into crises, resources were never enough, and he seemed to face equal criticism from those he should be protecting and those he was regulating.

It was with some relief that he reached the first anniversary of his time in post and opened the first envelope. What wise words would his predecessor offer to guide him through these stormy waters? He opened the envelope and took out a single sheet of paper bearing just three words:

'Blame your predecessor'

While he was a little surprised, he was delighted with the authorisation provided by this clear instruction and responded straight away! Every criticism of the broken state of the agency, the lack of resources, demoralised workforce and flawed processes was quickly justified as a consequence of the misadventures of the previous Chief Executive. He explained that he was working to correct her errors, put right the wrongs of the past and steer the ship in a new direction.

This seemed to quell the concerns being expressed, in the short term at least. Government ministers recognised that he needed time to make his own mark; business voices were persuaded that the changes they looked for would happen and staff redoubled their efforts to ensure it was their voice that would determine the future direction.

However, even with skilful management of the news agenda there was a limit to how long his narrative could last. Well before the end of his second year, it was clear that something more radical had to be done. As the next anniversary approached, he was starting to ask fundamental questions about the shape, scale and scope of the organisation he had been asked to lead. So, he was reassured when he opened the second envelope, marked 'Open after two years', to discover the next three wise words:

'Announce a reorganisation'

That's exactly what I thought, he mused, as he stared at the words prepared for him ahead of time by his farsighted predecessor. Immediately he took out a blank sheet of paper and drew a new organisational chart – one that would move the more troublesome voices further away whilst ensuring that only those who shared his insights would have access to the key decisions.

The confusion of reorganisation had its impact. Everyone became busy, shuffling jobs and responsibilities. With all the power struggles that ensued, it was quite a while before any internal voice could be heard above the noise. Externally the appearance of activity was sufficient to distract stakeholders from the ongoing failure to make an impact on long-term outcomes or focus priorities on the areas of greatest risk.

Once again, the words of advice had granted some respite. But the Chief Executive knew that restructuring in itself could not solve all of his problems. As the reorganisation progressed, deeper questions about purpose and values were being asked and remained unanswered.

Inevitably these questions surfaced when a major review was announced by the responsible minister. The prospect of external scrutiny caused the Chief Executive some sleepless nights and the third anniversary of his time in office arrived just in time. Remembering how well his predecessor's guidance had served him before, he rushed into the office desperate to discover a solution.

Tearing open the final envelope he read three final, fatal words:

'Prepare three envelopes'

Whilst this story is not unique and can be found on the internet dating back to at least 2003 in a range of contexts, it is particularly relevant for the challenges of regulatory delivery. Having set up and run agencies to deliver regulation covering various disciplines from Trading Standards, Food Safety, Animal Health and Welfare to Community Safety, Claims Management and now Product Safety and Standards, I am acutely aware that each one is different. There are no universal guides and *Regulation for Dummies* hasn't yet been written! Without a map to guide progress, or at least chart the territory, planning is frustrating, successes are tactical rather than strategic, best practice is seldom shared, and painful lessons are frequently repeated. The loudest voices, rather than those that most need attention, or perhaps might facilitate valuable change, claim the most attention.

The Regulatory Delivery Model explained in this book is borne out of these experiences – witnessed in the UK and around the world. While delivering regulation isn't easy, there is an abundance of established good practice, more is being developed and there is plenty to learn from others. The model provides a guide for leaders and framers of organisations charged with delivering regulation. Regulatory delivery is a complex territory and a map is an essential tool.

II. Historical Context

In the UK when I trained as an inspector in Trading Standards in the 1980s, traditional risks in metrology and food standards were managed through routine, time-scheduled inspections (unannounced in that businesses were not advised that an inspection was coming but scheduled sufficiently tightly that one business responded to our arrival with the words: 'I was expecting you yesterday!'). Areas seen as more novel, which at that time included consumer credit and trade descriptions, were more likely to be addressed through investigation of complaints – sometimes linked to withdrawal of authorisation to trade.

Historically, delivery of regulation has utilised some variation of these three principal ways in which regulatory agencies assess and control the behaviour of the regulated: pre-entry authorisation (licensing); in-service supervision (inspections); and post-event assessment (investigations).[1] The origins of this thinking, and its development in several states, is explored by Florentin Blanc in his review of regulatory history.[2] My experience, in the UK and more recently in other jurisdictions, has been that while there is significant variation in allocation of effort to these options between contexts and countries, there is limited appetite to explore that variation (which seems to arise as much from risk appetite in the local culture as it does from the scale or nature of the risk). Operators of regulatory systems don't necessarily wish to identify the reasons for their system, to justify its design, to change the local shape or to explore alternative options.

We will return to this analysis in chapter twenty, but back then, as a newly qualified officer, I can recall questioning whether more was expected of me than simply fulfilling my quota of routine inspections. Like many new entrants to a career in public services, I was keen to make an impact and motivated to serve those members of society who most needed protection. Having studied for three years and satisfied the examiner in numerous exams, I had been given the authority to enforce the law, and I had a warrant card to prove it – surely, I should use these powers for some purpose?

GRAHAM JOHN RUSSELL

is employed by

Staffordshire County Council

and is authorised to represent

THE TRADING STANDARDS
DEPARTMENT

County Trading Standards Officer

**41a EASTGATE STREET
STAFFORD ST16 2LZ**
Telephone: STAFFORD 223121

Signed

Authorisation as a newly qualified Trading Standards Officer (1990)

[1] See ch 20 and in particular fig 20.1.
[2] Florentin Blanc, *From Chasing Violations to Managing Risks: Origins, Challenges and Evolutions in Regulatory Inspections*, (Cheltenham, Edward Elgar Publishing, 2018).

However laudable these aims may have been, they were hardly unique. I read recently of an officer appointed to his first inspector's post back in the 1950s who was able to persuade his deputy Chief Officer that, if he completed all his routine inspections ahead of time, he could take half a day a week to carry out more interesting proactive investigatory work![3] Neither did new thinking start in the UK, not even in 2005 with the much-quoted Hampton Review.[4] As Blanc has pointed out,[5] eighteenth-century guilds regulated for prosperity as well as protection, and when the UK Government set up the Health and Safety Executive in 1974, it restructured several predecessor inspection agencies around a common purpose and gave the new agency an expectation that risk assessment would be built into its ways of working.

I was fortunate to join a team of like-minded individuals in Burton-on-Trent working for Staffordshire County Council.[6] We worked hard and investigated and prosecuted more offences than ever before, including the first prosecution for weights and measures offences for 30 years! While this gave a certain sense of satisfaction (and may have annoyed colleagues for its Stakhanovite pretensions), did it contribute to the outcomes for which we were set up?

My father certainly didn't think so. As the owner of two small retail shops, he took a dim view of me working as a Trading Standards Officer and loved to recount the story of the day two officers came into his shop in Walsall. They took away a sample of erasers on the basis that they might be mistaken for sweets by young children. Months later they returned with test results which showed that the items were in fact 'dangerous'. They demanded to seize the stock, which had long since been sold, and accused my father of various heinous crimes with accompanying threats. He reasoned that while he was occasionally frustrated by the behaviour of his customers, harming them didn't form part of a sustainable business model and that if highly qualified Trading Standards Officers took three months to decide the erasers were dangerous, how was he supposed to know?

Experience showed us that time spent with a business – for example assisting a small food producer to think through provisions for checking the weight of packages; providing training in understanding the outputs of complex weighing machines and introducing quality assurance methods – is not only likely to be more agreeable to the business than formal interviews under caution but also more likely to inculcate long-term change. While compliance depends on the intent of the regulated entity, and criminality should always be punished, creating and embedding a sustainable change in behaviour is much more likely to happen when the regulatory agency engages with the business than when they rap on the door, however large the stick. The UK's Food Standards Agency demonstrated this with its Safer Food, Better Business approach.[7] More recently, research comparing the impact of different approaches by four municipalities in Staffordshire (discussed more fully in

[3] CTSI, College of Fellows, Newsletter Issue 77, 17.
[4] Philip Hampton, *Reducing Administrative Burdens: Effective Inspection and Enforcement* (HM Treasury, 2005).
[5] Blanc, *Chasing Violations* (2018).
[6] It was my privilege to be part of a great team led by Tony Shore. I learnt so much from working with them (and my snooker improved immensely). My thanks to them all including Ron Cheeseman, Jane Curran, Paul Miles, Susan Ironside, John Grief and the late and much missed Dave Huckerby.
[7] Safer Food Better Business is a business information pack approach that is tailored to the needs of different businesses. See www.food.gov.uk/business-guidance/safer-food-better-business.

chapter thirteen), has evidenced the impact that a supportive approach can have on business survival as well as compliance.[8]

Reviewing the lessons of that period reminds me that we made many mistakes and false starts, but it does seem to point to two conclusions. Firstly, that even though the range of interventions formally available (licensing, inspection and investigation) was very narrow, in practice officers were using a wider range of options to achieve regulatory outcomes. But secondly, and crucially, that in the absence of a secure authorising environment, the selection of these tools lacked the organisation, intent, assessment and impact that a professional would want in their work.

As I moved on, working with valued colleagues leading services across the West Midlands (including Sarah Smith, then the youngest Head of Service in the country at Solihull Council and 20 years later still provoking me to improvement as Deputy Chief Executive), we saw the impact that transparency could have on internal culture and the importance of the citizen as a beneficiary of regulation and as an actor for improvement. But we also saw the extent to which established practice tended to drive resource allocation.

In reviewing files recommended for prosecution, I was struck by the way we considered it valuable and constructive to spend as many as 150 officer-hours putting together a report to prosecute the owner of a small shop for selling alcohol, cigarettes, videos or solvents to a young person, but much less valid to spend even a third of that time training the shop owner and their staff to avoid making such sales in the future. This was despite our instinct and experience, which told us a prosecution could not equip the retailer with the knowledge or skill to avoid a repeat offence even if that was their intention. Today we are perhaps more aware of the limits of deterrence[9] and the efficacy of alternative interventions, 'nudge'[10] and behavioural insights. Simply making statements about the amount of time spent on an activity compared with the outcomes achieved began to change the culture of our own operation.

Through painful experience we learnt that businesses need certainty before they will make changes in their behaviour, but regulators preferred to caveat their advice with phrases such as 'only the courts can decide'. Later this would lead to the development of Primary Authority.[11] Again my father had an anecdote to suit the occasion – after buying his first minibus and anxious to do the 'right thing', he asked a police sergeant what speed limits he should follow. After much head-scratching and consultation of manuals, the officer announced that he had no idea what speed limits applied, but my father could be sure that if he exceeded them, he would be prosecuted!

Looking at our internal processes revealed the benefits of empowering staff, as well as empowering consumers and businesses. Empowerment begins with understanding the power of data and encouraging transparency in its use. When officers advising consumers were given access to information about the work they were doing (showing, for example,

---

[8] Staffordshire University, 'Measuring the Impact of Regulation', study for Stoke-on-Trent and Staffordshire Enterprise Partnership (forthcoming).

[9] See ch 22 on Ethical Business Regulation.

[10] Richard Thaler and Cass Sunstein, *Nudge: Improving Decisions about Health, Wealth, and Happiness* (Yale, Yale University Press, 2008).

[11] See ch 9.

how long cases took, how often complaints were linked to registered premises and the amount of redress obtained) and, importantly, were authorised to make changes, they were ready and able to adjust their behaviour – improving outcomes and raising consistency across their teams.

Transparency can have a similar impact on business behaviour. Like most authorities, we in Staffordshire had our share of regular complainants who presented us with their own take on the woes of the world. Occasionally, one produced something more compelling – including a complaint that the use by suppliers of breakfast cereal of over-sized boxes was misleading as well as wasteful. Investigation showed he was right – some boxes contained more air than product! But prosecution was an uncertain and ill-targeted way to tackle a widespread pattern of detriment which caused no physical harm. In the end, with the help of a supportive journalist, and after informing the businesses, we published a league table of the worst offenders in the national press.[12] Daytime television picked up the story and within six months the whole industry had changed its approach.

In a pre-millennial, more paternalistic society, local authorities and national regulatory agencies were only beginning to see the potential and power of consumers, what Secretary of State Eric Pickles would later call an army of armchair auditors.[13] Stephen Butterworth, arriving as a new Director at Staffordshire County Council, introduced Consumer Watchdogs – citizens trained, informed and empowered to identify concerns and take action on a range of issues from firework noise nuisance to the health impacts of the diets of ethnically distinct communities.

'Nudged' ourselves by businesses who were displaying any receipt or other document we gave them after an inspection as a way to advertise their compliance, we began to produce Inspection Certificates, showing the results of inspections that businesses could display to customers.

Gradually we saw both the impact and the limits of these approaches and began to differentiate the areas where beneficiaries were motivated and capable of acting (such as selecting the retailer of a regular purchase) from those where, however well informed, their motivation (eg in relation to counterfeit goods) or their capacity (when tied into long-term contracts for supply or employment) meant that our intervention was required. While the average consumer is willing to look at the number of stars a regulatory agency gives to a restaurant before they choose where to eat, the same information is less likely to motivate a change in an employer or utility supplier[14] and does not always persuade hard-up parents that the genuine football shirt is worth twice the price of a fake (see chapter twenty for further assessment of these differences).

In 2007, I was fortunate to be offered the opportunity to set up the Local Better Regulation Office (LBRO). With significant statutory powers to guide the behaviour of 400 local regulatory agencies, this role presented great potential to test alternative approaches and to seek an evidence base for the contention that there might be a better way of delivering regulation. Although our size was limited by Parliament to 'some 25 people', we were able to

---

[12] 'Consumer Affairs: Breakfast cereals just a lot of puff', *The Independent*, 9 January 1998.
[13] 'Eric Pickles "shows us the money"', UK Government news story available at www.gov.uk/government/news/eric-pickles-shows-us-the-money-as-departmental-books-are-opened-to-an-army-of-armchair-auditors.
[14] State of the Energy Market 2018 Report (Ofgem, 2018).

assemble a great team (17 of whom have been so passionate about the task that they are still working in the Office for Product Safety and Standards today!).

As we explored these opportunities, working with local and national partners in innovative pilots and seeking to engage citizens and businesses in alternative solutions, it became clear that we lacked an organising frame for the many initiatives we were testing. When Dr Clive Grace, as chair of LBRO, asked for a strategy to deliver our mandate, which was 'to secure the more effective performance of local authority regulatory services in accordance with the principles of better regulation',[15] we knew we had to do more than marshal a collection of good ideas.

We were so keen to be focused on outcomes, we had ours printed on the office mugs!

III. Developing the Model: The Practices

As the leaders of a new and uniquely commissioned organisation, we wanted LBRO to make an immediate impact. But I was also conscious that long-term change would require a focus on the embedded barriers that inhibited that change – the barriers that seemed to restrict many regulatory agencies. A key conversation was with Adrian Levett, then recently retired as Chief Trading Standards Officer in Warwickshire, who had significant experience with pilots of alternative delivery approaches including Crossing the Boundaries[16] and the Retail Enforcement Pilot.[17] Together, we identified that sustainable change required a new understanding of attribution that could unlock greater confidence in decision-making and resource allocation. This confidence would come through the use of better tools for risk assessment and outcome measurement. Without it, regulators found it hard to move away

---

[15] *Principles of Good Regulation* (Better Regulation Taskforce, 2003).
[16] The Crossing the Boundaries pilot brought together local authority led partnerships with the aim of promoting best practice and consistency of enforcement through cross border service delivery.
[17] Alan Page, Michael Hewitt and Shaun Lundy, *Review and Assessment of the Lessons Learnt from the Retail Enforcement Pilot* (DARM, Middlesex University, 2010).

from the traditional activities of inspection, licensing and prosecuting which, because they are easily measured, provide funders with a sense of assurance that 'something is being done' even when there is scant evidence that what is being done is well targeted or effective.

The result of these deliberations was the commissions that led to RAND Europe's development of the Impacts and Outcomes Toolkit (see chapter fourteen) and Matrix's work on National Threats.[18] The first tackled the question of attribution when the intended impacts of regulatory activity are long term and shared. Under Rebekah Eden's careful sponsorship, RAND produced a powerful tool which is now used around the world. The second commission looked at the challenge of risk-based prioritisation within and between agencies. Where regulatory agencies have a place-based mandate, the agency best placed to mitigate a risk may not represent or be funded by the population who will benefit. Regulators may be delivering environmental benefits for those downwind or downstream of the activities they police. Matrix looked at the example of product safety inspection at UK ports and found that, where inspections are justified on a risk basis, checks are up to 39 times more effective if carried out once, before the items are dispersed through the supply chain. This report, subsequently taken forward by UK National Trading Standards, has led to additional resources for local authorities charged with work at ports and borders in the UK and illustrated the need for broader thinking on regulatory risk.

Evidence that this was not solely a local problem had come from the Hampton Report, which concluded that 'Risk assessment – though widely recognised as fundamental to effectiveness – is not implemented as thoroughly and comprehensively as it should be' and from analysis of the Hampton Implementation Reviews of UK regulatory agencies which showed that understanding outcomes and embedding a risk-based approach were continuing challenges for many regulatory agencies.[19] From these roots, thinking around the twin challenges of outcome measurement and risk-based prioritisation was further developed and they would go on to be identified as two of the three elements that constitute the practices domain of the Regulatory Delivery Model.

Identification of a third practice quickly followed. One of the most significant limiters to improving regulatory delivery is adherence to a limited range of interventions (typically, as discussed above, licensing, inspection and/or investigation).[20] A responsive approach is required for the different contexts, capabilities and motives of the regulated. Shaped in part by Ayres and Braithwaite on *Responsive Regulation*[21] and significantly influenced by Malcolm Sparrow's imagining of the toolkit and the toolbox in *The Regulatory Craft*,[22] we worked to create a wider range of brushes and the capability to select from a broader palette. We paid particular attention to co-production approaches[23] and consumer empowerment tools as we sought to equip ourselves and our partners with additional ways to make effective intervention choices.[24]

---

[18] Matrix Insight, *Addressing National Threats Through Local Service Delivery* (Local Better Regulation Office, 2009).

[19] 'Regulatory Quality: How Regulators are Implementing the Hampton Vision' (National Audit Office, 2008).

[20] See ch 20 and in particular fig 20.1.

[21] Ian Ayres and John Braithwaite, *Responsive Regulation: Transcending the Deregulation Debate* (Oxford, Oxford University Press, 1992).

[22] Malcolm Sparrow, *The Regulatory Craft: Controlling Risks, Solving Problems, and Managing Compliance* (Washington DC, Brookings Institution Press, 2000).

[23] See ch 20 and in particular fig 20.2.

[24] See examples in *Regulation and Growth* (Local Better Regulation Office, 2012).

IV. Developing the Model: The Prerequisites

In time these three practices would form one domain within the Regulatory Delivery Model. Kate Fletcher, who leads on reform strategy for the Office for Product Safety and Standards, designed many of these approaches and has been the true architect of the model. From 2010, she and I began working, often with IFC/World Bank colleagues, to support emerging, fragile and post-conflict states seeking to establish a business environment in which businesses could flourish and consumers and international investors could have confidence.[25] This experience evidenced the need to further develop the model as it became clear that the practices could not be established, or once established sustainably achieve impact, without the right context.

To some extent this reflects the fact that it is necessary to improve both design and delivery – the challenge of whether bad regulation can be well enforced is always there and the tools of regulatory policy, including impact assessment, remain important. Every country has its version of the Dangerous Dogs Act[26] – legislation that, however well intentioned, is incapable of achieving its purpose. But it was clear that the design of delivery was in itself a major inhibitor in almost every context in which we worked. So, for example, while the governance framework may be a given for the regulatory agency, we have recognised the importance of engaging those in central ministries who make design decisions if the agency is to be given a clear mandate and commensurate powers. Even within established agencies, we have often found that confusion at this level, or a lack of self-awareness in mapping the landscape, was inhibiting improvement. As we developed tools in this area we were increasingly confronted with the need not only to understand the governance framework within which the agency works – its purpose, structure, position and powers – but also to develop the tools to challenge that framework where it was inappropriate for the expectations placed upon the agency or the agency's own sense of place.

The second issue that we saw functioning as a prerequisite is accountability. In Nepal and Ethiopia we saw the potential of new approaches to engagement with business. Reformers recognise that their initiatives require an authorising environment for success, and therefore accountability to those regulated was often an established work area in regulatory reform programmes – normally under the heading of public/private dialogue. But the scale, sophistication and scope of the reform seemed insufficient for the significance of effective accountability for regulators. This argument is developed further in chapter seven so a couple of examples will suffice here. When regulatory agencies seek to improve their accountability, they face competing criticisms – those seeking to build relationships with those they regulate can be accused of regulatory capture whilst those proposing a role for the beneficiaries of regulation may be seen as neglecting their statutory role. In another direction, while good practice is generally said to involve a regulatory agency being independent from government, an organisation that derives its mandate and resourcing from government can scarcely be described as independent from it. As we delved further into

---

[25] 'Inspection Reform Approaches in Fragile and Post-Conflict States – Liberia case study', presented at Better Regulation Delivery Office and World Bank Group conference, 'Inspection Reform: Breaking Down Barriers to Trade and Investment' (unpublished, 2014, available from author).

[26] For further explanation see Anthony King and Ivor Crewe, *The Blunders of our Governments* (London, Oneworld Publications, 2013).

these questions, we saw the need for an approach to accountability which was sufficiently nuanced to handle competing demands from beneficiaries, regulated entities and sponsors; in which regulatory agencies proactively build the capacity of all those to whom they were accountable; and where the reality of being accountable to those over whom you hold coercive power is embraced by an agency that owns the necessity of accountability.

For a period, it seemed that these two elements were sufficient: Governance Frameworks and Accountability providing the pull and the push, the yin and yang, prerequisites for success. But the further afield we worked, as we tested the model with regulators in Kyrgyzstan and Brazil, it was clear that the energy of sustainable change is not contained solely within governance or accountability and we reflected further on the importance of regulatory culture as an agent of change.

At LBRO we understood that our new organisation, even with significant statutory powers of direction and instruction, could not externally instil sustained change in 400 local authorities. In practice we chose not to use most of our forceful, formal, statutory measures, preferring to rely on approaches that would build the capability of local regulators – developing their own culture to utilise their existing discretion effectively.

In the UK we explored approaches to culture through the work of local and national regulators on a Common Competency Framework, reassessing the importance in initial training and continuing professional development of skills and judgement alongside technical knowledge. More recently we have taken this forward by leading the development of an apprenticeship for frontline regulators,[27] returning to the belief that culture is absorbed more than it is taught, that behaviours matter more than knowledge and that soft skills have the most long-term impact. This has been sharpened further with an emphasis on values as we have considered the need for a regulatory agency to understand what they bring to relationship-based regulation, including through work on Primary Authority (see chapter nine); Better Business for All (see chapter eight); and Ethical Business Regulation (see chapter twenty-two).

V. Using the Model

Together, and in this form, it is these three elements that are the prerequisites. They are a separate domain, acting alongside the practices that emerged earlier, which we have brought together in the Regulatory Delivery Model. Since formalising the model in this way, we have had opportunity to work with keen collaborators including in the UK, India and Chile to explore the way the model can be used for internal and peer review and to identify priorities for reform.

As we have developed the model, engagement with academics has helped to sharpen our thinking. Working on this book with Professor Christopher Hodges has clarified the mapping function of the Regulatory Delivery Model. Whilst offering a tool to analyse the state of a regulatory agency, it principally operates as a guide to thinking about regulatory delivery. As we set it out here, the Regulatory Delivery Model is a map to guide the

---

[27] See Regulatory Compliance Officer apprenticeship standard available at www.instituteforapprenticeships.org/apprenticeship-standards/regulatory-compliance-officer.

traveller, both in the preparation (the prerequisites) and in the undertaking of the venture (the practices). In this book we seek to illustrate the map with examples of organisations around the world who have embarked on their own journeys.

Early discussions with Professor Paul Sanderson at Cambridge University explored an expectation that models should also have predictive capability – anticipating a given outcome from a change in inputs. We will suggest that the Regulatory Delivery Model's predictive value comes from its dynamic use – the tension within and between the domains and between the elements – and we will explore some examples of this in chapter two. At this point it is sufficient to say that the elements are not isolated land masses on a map; they influence and shape each other.

Whether used as a map, a diagnostic tool or a predictive model, I hope that the Regulatory Delivery Model offers enough for it to find its place amongst emerging thinking about regulatory delivery. For those who, like me, have been and still are on a journey of discovery, I hope that by setting out the model and telling some of the story of how it has been developed, we will give others the opportunity to shape their futures in ways that are more fruitful than the experience of the hapless new Chief Executive at the start of this chapter.

Inevitably when writing a book, a line must be drawn, and interesting and important areas in the development and use of regulatory delivery have had to be left out.

Changes in technology are foremost in the thinking of many regulatory agencies. Advances in the products we buy (shifting rapidly from LPs to CDs to downloads, or from gas-guzzling cars to ride-sharing apps to driverless, rechargeable vehicles) and in the way we buy them (from high-street shops to online sales platforms to 3-D printing) have given regulatory agencies new challenges. The same technological shifts are creating new opportunities. Increasing interconnectivity, with the Internet of Things allowing connected fridges to be as responsive as phones, and new ways to manipulate huge quantities of data, offer regulators alternative solutions. These challenges and opportunities herald the dawn of *innovation regulation*.

Elsewhere, the challenges are more contextual. In Peru environmental regulators wrestle with the need to protect a unique and irreplaceable eco-system whilst enabling a diverse population to share the benefits of their natural resources. In fragile and post-conflict states, including Liberia and Somalia, we have worked with reformers seeking to use regulatory delivery to bring stability and confidence to domestic and international audiences – protecting people whilst increasing economic activity and foreign investment.

It has been our privilege to meet amazing regulators who are creating their own solutions, utilising the powers of delivery. The journey of reform continues, and we offer this book, and the Regulatory Delivery Model it elaborates, to them all – to those full of optimism as well as those who are more gloomy – in the hope and belief that it will help all regulators to adapt and thrive.

1

The Rationale for Regulatory Delivery

GRAHAM RUSSELL AND CHRISTOPHER HODGES

I. Introduction

Well-designed and delivered regulation plays a vital role in all modern societies, but whilst much attention has been paid to the design of regulation as the focus for effective regulatory reform, authors and policy-makers have historically overlooked the importance of regulatory delivery mechanisms in securing desired outcomes. Effective regulatory delivery focuses on securing these outcomes: protection for those at risk and prosperity for those who comply, with efficient use of state resources.

This book examines approaches to the delivery of regulation through the concept of the Regulatory Delivery Model. It is based on the understanding that the success of regulation arises as much from its successful implementation, or delivery, as it does from its design.

We all depend on effective regulation: from the basics of the cleanliness of the air we breathe and the water we drink to our capacity to engage in long-term purchase decisions, whether in property, investments or education. Since Adam Smith begrudgingly accepted the need for 'a regulatory framework that prevents ruthless selfishness, greed and rapacity from leading to socially harmful outcomes'[1] we have recognised the benefits that come from a well-ordered regulatory environment.

If the first aim of regulation is protection, it follows that to be successful regulation must protect. It must do more than state its purpose: it must be delivered effectively. At its inception, all regulation has a policy objective. Normally this is a societal aim, to resolve a perceived market or behavioural failure. Too often this arises from mounting pressure to act – risk-reflex reactions can overwhelm the measured approach of evidence-based policy.[2] But the law, once enacted, is intended to fulfil that objective. Both impact assessments and post-implementation reviews are predicated on the view that this purpose can be defined and progress towards it can be tracked. However, these outcomes seldom follow from simply passing a new requirement into law. If change in behaviour is required, some action will be necessary to achieve that purpose even if, at the minimum threshold,

---

[1] Heinz Kurz, 'Adam Smith on Markets, Competition and Violations of Natural Liberty' (2016) 40 *Cambridge Journal of Economics* 615.

[2] 'Response with Responsibility: Policy-making for Public Risk in the 21st Century' (Risk and Regulation Advisory Council, 2009).

it is as simple as communicating the change to the relevant people. Regulatory delivery is about defining, implementing and assessing that action.

Seen in this way, regulation is a tool for governments to improve the way that markets work: protecting consumers, employees and citizens; supporting sustainable business growth, trade and investment; and improving societal and environmental outcomes. The basic proposition is that regulation exists for a purpose – governments intervene in markets to solve policy problems – and so regulatory policy focuses on how to create rules to address market failures. As this policy has developed, those with an interest in regulation have begun to recognise that the challenge of operating a regulatory regime that is both appropriate and effective is wider than just the question of enacting well-designed legislation. Questions of how laws are received and applied by businesses and others whose behaviour they seek to control, and the way they are enforced (together, *regulatory delivery*) are seen to be of equal importance if progress is to be made towards desired regulatory outcomes.

In striving for 'good regulation', regulatory reformers have until recently focused their attention on regulatory simplification tools. The idea of regulatory delivery, which this book aims to explain and illustrate, relates to the agencies tasked with ensuring that legislation can be effective in achieving the desired societal outcomes. In these terms, securing strategic regulatory outcomes relies on taking a 'whole lifecycle approach' to regulatory reform, where regulation is used as a tool for government to achieve societal objectives by controlling not just the design of regulation but also its implementation. The OECD's development of best practice principles for both regulatory governance and regulatory enforcement marks a shift towards this approach for reformers,[3] as does the work of the World Bank Group on Good Regulatory Practices.[4]

Traditional 'enforcement' is but one aspect of achieving desired outcomes. Delivery of regulation requires attention to the conditions that determine whether the agency charged with implementation can operate effectively such as the way an agency is set up and operated, its external relationships, internal values and behaviours, and its authorising environment. It also requires consideration of the practices of the agency such as how it prioritises, how it selects interventions and how it measures progress towards outcomes.

To date, the absence of a normative framework against which the design of regulatory delivery regimes can be developed, implemented and evaluated has led to a disparate range of approaches to regulatory delivery being taken by reformers in their efforts to secure effective regulatory outcomes. The development of the Regulatory Delivery Model, by Graham Russell and his team in the UK Government, provides reformers with an opportunity to consider their approaches to the design, implementation and review of regulatory delivery in a structured, consistent, robust and transparent way that can be aligned with their approaches to reform at other stages of the regulatory lifecycle. The model is unique in that, for the first time, regulatory delivery has been conceptualised in a rigorous and transparent

---

[3] 'Regulatory Enforcement and Inspections', OECD Best Practice Principles for Regulatory Policy (OECD, 2014) and 'The Governance of Regulators', OECD Best Practice Principles for Regulatory Policy (OECD, 2014).

[4] 'Good Regulatory Practices' (Washington, DC, World Bank Group, 2017), available at http://documents. worldbank.org/curated/en/753291501065430312/pdf/117750-BRI-PUBLIC-GGPTACJointOfferingo nGoodRegulatoryPractices.pdf.

way, enabling the consistent evolution of regulatory practice by setting out a framework to steer improvement. It comprises three prerequisites for regulatory agencies to be able to operate effectively (Governance Frameworks, Accountability and Culture) and three practices that agencies need in order to deliver societal outcomes (Outcome Measurement, Risk-based Prioritisation and Intervention Choices). In essence, the model (explained in chapter two) encourages and supports a holistic approach to the design and practice of regulatory delivery.

A. The UK Context

The UK's journey of regulatory reform is not unique, but it serves to illustrate the impact of the tools of better regulation policy. Since the 1940s, reformers have prescribed bonfires of red tape and developed tools now utilised globally – from impact assessment, standard cost modelling and post-implementation review to consultation techniques and business-led challenge tools. More recently, the UK has also been among the early adopters of a focus on the second aspect of this two-stage journey: delivery alongside design. The Principles of Good Regulation[5] and then the Hampton Report of 2005[6] were seminal in drawing together emergent thinking and setting a template for future thought seen, for example, in Sir Philip Hampton's conclusion that 'The enforcement of regulations affects businesses at least as much as the policy of the regulation itself'. See Annex 1 for key dates in the UK's regulatory reform journey.

The Regulatory Delivery Model has been developed predominantly from experience of business regulation, including regulation of food and non-food products, occupational safety and health, construction and fire safety, and environmental and consumer issues. These areas are somewhat distinct from economic regulation (including of energy and utilities), sector regulation (including of aviation and nuclear), financial regulation (including of loans and banking), and public sector regulation (including of education and health). While the model has been used in some of these areas, its application to them remains to be fully assessed.

Similarly, most of the model's development has been in the UK. In formalising the Regulatory Delivery Model and testing its applicability, we have benefited from regular exposure to regulatory delivery in other countries in a variety of settings, including inter-governmental reviews and the biennial Office for Product Safety and Standards International Inspection Reform conference.[7] We will argue that the approach is inherently generic as it provides a set of principles which can be applied to any regulatory context. The authors of the case studies included in this book, drawn from 10 countries, illustrate some ways they have applied those principles.

---

[5] 'Principles of Good Regulation' (Better Regulation Taskforce, 2003).

[6] Philip Hampton, *Reducing Administrative Burdens: Effective Inspection and Enforcement* (HM Treasury, 2005).

[7] 'Inspection Reform. The Change that Matters. Conference Report' (Better Regulation Delivery Office, 2013), available at https://webarchive.nationalarchives.gov.uk/20130705015825/http://www.bis.gov.uk/assets/brdo/docs/intcon-2012/international-conference-report.pdf. Note: the Better Regulation Delivery Office is a predecessor organisation to the Office for Product Safety and Standards.

II. Why Delivery?

In presenting a book about regulatory delivery, it is reasonable to ask why there has been an increasing focus on the delivery of regulation. Or to put it another way, why has the improvement of regulatory policy not been sufficient? In this section we will ask why delivery matters, consider some of the drivers for this new focus and go on to ask whether there is anything about regulation that makes delivery challenging.

The first observation is that delivery matters in any policy area. To some, Tony Blair has become synonymous with attention to this topic. He drew attention to the contrast between the ability of government to shape policy responses and its apparent inability to implement those solutions. As he has written, 'in government, where "doing" is what it's all about, the gap is suddenly revealed as a chasm of bureaucracy, frustration and disappointment.'[8]

Around the world, it is noticeable both how frequently this challenge is experienced and how often Tony Blair-style 'delivery units'[9] have been established as the solution. In Canada, Pakistan, Peru and Sierra Leone, their ubiquity demonstrates the appeal of having a central unit to drive delivery of the government's top priorities.[10]

Of course, the focus on delivery did not start in the twenty-first century. In the UK, the creation of Executive Agencies in the 1980s was an earlier response to a similar challenge, but we can go back much earlier. Perhaps in 1170, King Henry II was frustrated that his 'policy' was not being 'delivered' when he is said to have cried

'Will no one rid me of this turbulent priest?'[11]

Today, delivery is recognised as a critical part of the policy cycle. Standard diagrammatic representations, such as that shown in Figure 1.1, show it as 'implementation' or similar.

However, despite this acceptance in theory, in practice reform of regulation has tended to be focused on policy levers, and in many places that is still the case. There is a variety of possible reasons for this. One is that policy-makers see regulation as *their* instrument and therefore take it as *their* responsibility to rectify any problems it causes, utilising the tools with which they are familiar. Another is based on the widespread, perhaps instinctive, belief that you cannot implement bad law well and that you should therefore focus on improving the law. A third possible reason notes the significance of the role of the courts as arbiters of disputes and suggests that their focus on interpretation rather than application will tend to highlight the content of the rules rather than their delivery. Alternatively, perhaps it is because the improvement tools – from impact assessment to post implementation review – are the tools of the economist policy-maker rather than of the regulator. Finally, we might ask whether delivery has received less attention because it is a frontline, person-centred activity remote physically, philosophically and academically from the centres of power and intellectual analysis.

---

[8] Tony Blair, *A Journey* (London, Arrow Books, 2010) 18.

[9] The Prime Minister's Delivery Unit was created in June 2001 in the Cabinet Office. See *Civil Service Reform in the Real World: Patterns of Success in UK Civil Service Reform* (Institute for Government, 2014).

[10] Michael Barber, *How to Run a Government: So that Citizens Benefit and Taxpayers Don't Go Crazy* (London, Penguin Books, 2016).

[11] Elizabeth Knowles (ed), *The Oxford Dictionary of Quotations* (Oxford, Oxford University Press, 1999) 370.

Figure 1.1 Policy cycle as shown in the UK Government Green Book on policy-making (2003)[12]

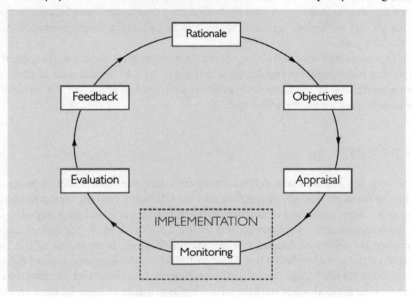

Whatever the reason, experience, not just in the UK but apparently worldwide, is that modernising regulation has been taken, at least initially and sometimes solely, to mean improving policy-making – seeking to perfect the 'rules' rather than improve their delivery.

III. What are the Drivers of Regulatory Delivery?

A more promising line of enquiry is to ask why the new focus on delivery of regulation has emerged at this time. Understanding the drivers for this change will help us to see both the causes of the problem and the shape of the solution.

Numerous, often diverse and occasionally conflicting, drivers can be seen in modernisation journeys. In analysing the rise of delivery as an aspect of regulatory reform, these drivers can be grouped into three categories which, for the convenience of those schooled in the Oxbridge disciplines of PPE,[13] can be labelled prosperity, protection and efficiency.[14]

Modernisation of the delivery of regulation seeks to improve the impact of the regulatory activity (effectiveness) whilst minimising its cost to the state (efficiency). While the principal impacts of effectiveness must be on the originating policy objectives (protection), effective delivery will also promote benefits for the regulated (prosperity) both directly

---

[12] *The Green Book: Appraisal and Evaluation in Central Government* (HM Treasury, 2003).

[13] Philosophy, Politics and Economics, a generalist degree long favoured by aspiring politicians and public servants.

[14] The characterisation of the outcomes of regulatory delivery as 'Prosperity and Protection' was created by Clive Grace when chair of LBRO to signify the multiple benefits regulatory agencies should deliver. The addition of efficiency recognises the public sector benefit.

through reducing costs and indirectly by improving confidence and control. Aims to improve outcomes in at least two, and often all three, of these areas can be seen in operation in the case studies of this book, including in Canada, Lithuania, the Netherlands, Australia, Brazil and Mongolia.

Problems identified with delivering objectives in these three areas have become the drivers for reform of the way that regulation is delivered. We will look at each of these areas in turn to understand why the focus on regulatory delivery has arisen, why it has arisen now and some aspects of its nature and scope.

A. Prosperity

We start with the last of these drivers, prosperity, because historically at least, the first driver for the focus on delivery of regulation in the UK came from the concerns of business. This has often been described in solely negative terms: enterprise being impeded by inefficient, disproportionate enforcement. Just as the UK's drive for better policy beginnings were marked by pejorative language when Harold Wilson, as President of the Board of Trade, ignited the first 'Bonfire of Red Tape' in 1948,[15] so the language around delivery has focused on 'unnecessary inspections', 'disproportionate sanctions' and 'bureaucratic licensing processes'. Expressed solely in these terms, the arguments become focused on balancing costs or measuring burdens.

That language inevitably sets prosperity and protection as alternatives in which 'wins' for the regulated must be 'losses' for the intended beneficiaries. A more nuanced position is achieved if we consider the potential for effective delivery of regulation to encourage, or at least allow, growth – the hypothesis that properly delivered regulation can have an outcome of prosperity as well as protection and that a focus on outcomes and competitive markets will ensure that all the benefits of a good regulatory environment are achieved.

In 2004, when Gordon Brown, as the UK's Chancellor of the Exchequer, asked Philip Hampton to review the impact of inspections on business, he was responding to continued business concerns.[16] Despite a prolonged and evidentially successful programme of bearing down on the cost of regulations (through impact assessment, standard cost modelling and policy controls), the perception of business was that the impact of regulation was not changing.[17] In this view, routine inspections, characterised by high cost and low value, continued regardless of risk or impact, unaffected by Whitehall task forces, ministerial pronouncements or the measurement activity of economists.

By tasking the chair of one of Britain's largest supermarkets with leading the review, Gordon Brown was consciously calling the retailers, seen as the loudest source of complaints about inspections, to propose their own solution – to 'put up or shut up' – with the knowledge that the remedy they proposed would have to gain public confidence. The fact that the Hampton Review[18] has had an enduring impact and is widely referred to,

---

[15] *Hansard*, HC (series 5) Vol 457, cols 112–20 (4 November 1948).
[16] 'Budget 2004', HM Treasury, ch 3, para 57.
[17] Philip Hampton, *Reducing Administrative Burdens: Effective Inspection and Enforcement: Interim Report* (HM Treasury, 2004).
[18] Hampton (2005).

not just in the UK but around the world, is testimony to its timeliness and the proportionality brought to bear by its author and his team of civil servants and experts. Jitinder Kholi and Sir William Sargent, as Chief Executive and Chair of the Better Regulation Executive, presided over the development and implementation of the report which, in a short period of time, changed the focus of the debate, legitimising the voice of business and renewing the focus on outcomes.

A parallel insight into why the tools of better regulatory policy have not always shifted the dial of business perceptions can be obtained through survey data. Recognition of the legitimacy of business views, as an aspect of accountability, will be considered further in this book but, as a starting point, investment in surveying business views delivers evidence of changes over time as well as identifying areas for further research.

The UK's Business Perceptions Survey[19] has tracked perceptions of regulation since the publication of the Hampton Report. This period, which has been marked by a greater focus on delivery, alongside improvements in policy and reductions in red tape, has seen business perceptions of the obstacles presented by regulation starting to change, as illustrated in Figure 1.2.

Figure 1.2 'Proportion of UK businesses that agree that the overall level of regulation in the UK is an obstacle', UK Business Perceptions Survey 2018[20]

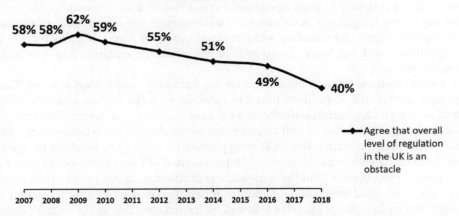

But numbers do not tell us everything. Often the most usable insights come from entrepreneurs themselves. Work in the West Midlands in 2004 gathered views from hundreds of business people to understand the impact of Trading Standards services and to explore why inspections did not have the impact hoped for.[21] This research drove a range of learning and many of the delivery tools in use today – including certificates for compliance, trade-led guidance, transparent risk frameworks and new approaches to officer competency – were piloted in that period. But the strongest message, and a clearly stated driver for the focus on

---

[19] OMB Research, 'Business Perceptions Survey 2018, BEIS Research Paper Number 14' (Department for Business, Energy and Industrial Strategy, 2018).
[20] ibid.
[21] Helen Kirkman, *Improving the Assessment of Business Needs* (unpublished report prepared for MidCOTS, a regional group of Trading Standards services in the West Midlands, 2004).

delivery of regulation, is summed up in a 2007 quote from the owner of a small business in the North of England:

> I have to comply with thousands of regulations across a dozen themes. Scrapping two or three burdensome regulations here and there is great, but it doesn't make a great difference to me. What makes a difference is the attitude of inspectors. Being able to sleep at night because I know I have got it right and don't fear an inspector knocking on the door.[22]

This echoed the desire expressed by businesses, in the earlier West Midlands work, for a more helpful and collaborative approach, with one business explaining: 'We would like the department to work in partnership with us, to uphold the law, on a regular basis'.[23]

It is worth noting here that the aspiration of business, expressed in views like this, is not to find an excuse not to comply, or a space free from regulatory constraints. They are asking for support to achieve compliance; confidence that their efforts will be recognised and protection from unfair competition from those who don't invest in compliance.

Policy work to improve legislation, eliminating some requirements and streamlining others, does not necessarily change the impact of regulation on regulated entities. Indeed, there is evidence that the rate of change, whether increasing or decreasing the requirements, has more impact than the requirements themselves[24] so even a reduction in administrative burdens can increase the cost. What impacts more on regulated entities, particularly in the view of small businesses that lack the capacity to internalise the costs, is the way in which regulation is delivered.[25] This thinking is elaborated further, in a practical case, in chapter eight, dealing with the development of Better Business for All. This programme, which has been created by frontline officers, is uniquely shaped to address this mismatch.

Guided by these insights, inspections are not necessarily understood as a cost. Heavy-handed, unexpected inspections timed to coincide with the busiest period – whether 2am in a nightclub, Sunday afternoon in a care home or just before Christmas in a supermarket – will never be well received. But we might also ask whether such activity has much effect. Inspection viewed as an opportunity for an expert regulator to provide a regulated entity with targeted, accessible input on areas of risk, current performance and actions for improvement (plus the consequences of failure to change) can be both an effective and a welcomed intervention. *Inspection* is best used to describe an intervention with a regulated entity which is intended to assess, understand and change the entity's *likelihood of compliance*, and should be organised with that in view. Interaction which is undertaken solely to assess a compliance state at a point in time, whether through test-purchasing, sampling or so-called *unannounced inspection*, has its own purpose but it cannot have the same impact as a well-framed inspection. The mistake many commentators make is to assume that such activity will influence the behaviour of the regulated entity – as our predecessors knew, 'you don't fatten a pig by weighing it'!

---

[22] Feedback from informal conversations with small business owners in the early days of LBRO.

[23] Kirkman (unpublished).

[24] Jigsaw Research, 'Business Perceptions Survey 2014' (National Audit Office and Department for Business, Innovation and Skills, 2014). Proportion of businesses agreeing that keeping up to date with new regulations is a burden (2009 – 72%; 2010 – 69%, 2012 – 65%, 2014 – 63%).

[25] OMB Research, 'Business Perceptions Survey' (2018).

i. Austerity

The question of whether the delivery of regulation can, in pragmatic or legitimacy terms, be seen as a facilitator of growth came into sharp focus in the UK and other economies impacted by the economic crash of 2008. When the UK's coalition Government, elected in 2010, made growth the lens through which all policy should be assessed, the question for regulatory agencies became 'what, if anything, do we offer?'.

Initial answers were polarised. Business associations, if not businesses themselves, amplified by parts of government, were talking about regulatory agencies solely as barriers to growth and calling for 'inspection holidays', moratoria on sanctions and regulators 'staying away' until growth returned.[26] For their part, many regulators were equally negative, denying that they could (in practice) or should (by law) do anything to facilitate growth. The widely held view that regulatory agencies were established to protect consumers and that consumers are more vulnerable than ever in austere times was used to justify distance from the growth agenda.[27]

The Local Better Regulation Office (LBRO) proposed an alternative in 2009[28] in which local regulatory agencies could be part of the recovery solution and followed this in 2010 with a publication[29] that encouraged regulatory agencies to recognise the business experience of regulation. Faced with their own challenges and severe resource constraints, regulators initially made an unwilling audience. However, practical examples began to tell a different story. LBRO's 2012 publication 'Regulation and Growth' pointed to regulatory agencies, both locally and nationally, choosing options that enabled growth.[30]

Box 1.1 Enabling growth whilst delivering protection: an example

As an example of an intervention choice that enables growth whilst delivering protection, we can consider a regulatory agency that identifies a business supplying unsafe food. At the simplest level they have two choices. Closing the premises down will protect the public by ensuring that the supply of unsafe food ceases. It will, however, also remove a source of supply, restricting choice and potentially increasing transport and environmental costs. It reduces employment and could impact adversely on local prosperity. The alternative approach, working with the business to improve its compliance so that it produces safe foods, avoids these disbenefits and may equip the business with skills and the confidence to grow. This was one of the findings from the UK Food Standards Agency's 'Safer Food, Better Business' programme, which rolled out a step-by-step handbook on how small businesses could put food safety management procedures in place alongside training and

---

[26] For example, this view was expressed at a meeting of Scottish businesses. See also 'From the Business End of the Telescope. Perspectives on Local Regulation and Enforcement' (Local Better Regulation Office, 2010).

[27] For example, this view was expressed in a meeting between the Better Regulation Executive, LBRO and the chairs of UK national regulatory agencies, under the Chatham House Rule.

[28] 'Supporting Businesses Towards Recovery' (Local Better Regulation Office, 2009).

[29] Local Better Regulation Office, 'From the Business End of the Telescope' (2010).

[30] 'Regulation and Growth' (Local Better Regulation Office, 2012).

advice from inspectors. Forty-five per cent of small to medium enterprises felt that having a food safety management system made their business more profitable,[31] and compliance improved from 30 per cent in 2002 to 48 per cent in 2007.[32]

B. Protection

While the proposition that better delivery of regulation can improve protection has entered the debate more slowly than suggestions that it can enable growth, it is equally imperative. This slow adoption has been, in part at least, because modernisation of regulation has been characterised as prioritising the needs of the regulated over those of the beneficiaries. It perhaps also reflects an assumption about the impact of regulation: that it will, by its mere presence, provide protection.

In the UK, the Regulators' Code and the Growth Duty (described in more detail in chapter five) enable and require regulatory agencies to think about the success of the regulated community but both are equally clear that the actions of the regulatory agency must effectively secure the policy and statutory purpose for which they are established. For some, that inevitably means a zero-sum game – a balancing act in which more effective enforcement inevitably means less business opportunity and vice versa. This is an assumption – a worldview – that, while pervasive, can and should be challenged. The thesis of this book, and the narrative behind the reform of regulatory delivery, is that protection is non-negotiable and must be achieved, but that is most effectively and sustainably achieved when it is delivered in ways that respond to differences in approaches to compliance among regulated communities.

Regulation is a tool of social policy – one of the five levers by which government seeks to impact society.[33] By prescription and with statutory and often criminal force, regulation sets out a required change in the behaviour of the regulated. Regulators are tasked with ensuring that change occurs. The success of regulatory agencies in achieving that behavioural change and moving towards the societal outcome for which the legislation was designed is therefore a legitimate measure of the agency's performance. Improving the delivery of regulation so that it is effective in achieving those protection outcomes has become an increasingly significant driver in focusing on the delivery of regulation.

We must therefore ask whether regulation has delivered the outcomes for which it is created. Are consumers, workers and other intended beneficiaries well protected? The answer seems to be, at best, 'sometimes'. Concern about whether traditional enforcement tools, traditionally used, can ever be wholly effective has been evident in the literature for some time.[34] Regulatory enforcement that is not responsive to the conduct of regulated

---

[31] 'Food Safety Management Evaluation Research Report' (Food Standards Agency, 2007).
[32] 'Food Standards Agency Annual Report 2007–08' (Food Standards Agency, 2008).
[33] Martin Stanley, *How to Be a Civil Servant* (London, Biteback Publishing, 2016).
[34] See eg Ian Ayres and John Braithwaite, *Responsive Regulation: Transcending the Deregulation Debate* (Oxford, Oxford University Press, 1992); Keith Hawkins, *The Uses of Discretion* (Oxford, Clarendon Press, 1995); Bridget Hutter, *Regulation and Risk: Occupational Health and Safety on the Railways* (Oxford, Oxford University Press,

entities has been identified as resulting in lower effectiveness – and efficiency – of the regulatory delivery system[35] and of its outcomes – understood as the mitigation of regulatory risks.

In exploring this area, we should recognise that use of traditional delivery tools is rooted in confidence of their effectiveness. We must tread carefully here as, in common with many market systems (including, for example, banking and insurance), regulatory delivery 'works' because it is believed to work and the actors in the system participate on that basis. Some of the most prevalent beliefs, which perhaps have the characteristics of myths, are that everything is inspected, that fear of being caught impacts behaviour and that inspections and enforcement actions are effective in improving compliance.[36] Because these myths are at least in part unfounded, reform of regulatory delivery needs to identify and engage with more effective approaches. Let's take a moment to examine these three beliefs in more detail.

i. Coverage – Is Everything Inspected?

Finite resources mean that regulatory activity can never be universal. Choices have to be made and are made, however implicitly. At a strategic level decisions are made about:

- whether a given activity should be subject to regulation (excessively low pay, made illegal in some nations, is regarded as poor practice or a market phenomenon in others);
- whether prescriptions should be actively enforced (many countries have labour market regulators while others rely on self-enforcement through civil actions by workers or their representatives);
- whether interventions should prevent access (licensing); monitor activity (inspection) or deal with breaches (investigation); and
- which regulatory areas should receive the most resources, relatively as well as absolutely.

Tactical decisions – about how many activities should be inspected and which ones should be targeted – are more widely recognised as part of a regulatory agency's function. In both cases the question of scarcity of resources should not be the only factor. As we will see effectiveness is more important

Risk-based prioritisation, explored further in chapter sixteen, is the necessary tool for choices to be made. Protection will be achieved if scarce resources are focused on the area of greatest need. Risk is the currency that allows comparisons to be made and prioritisation to be effective. But in many countries, long-standing blockages prevent those choices being made.

In central Asian, post-Soviet economies this has been seen in statutory requirements – for example that every consumer complaint must be followed up with an inspection – and in a regulatory culture that deems 100 per cent inspection as necessary, without too much

---

2001); Keith Hawkins, *Law as a Last Resort: Prosecution Decision-Making in a Regulatory Agency* (Oxford, Oxford University Press, 2002).

[35] John Braithwaite, 'Responsive Regulation and Developing Economy' (2006) 24 *World Development* 884.

[36] See for example Alan Terry and Philip Cullum, *Measuring Up: Consumer Perceptions of Weights and Measures Legislation* (National Consumer Council, 2007).

regard for its impact.[37] In practice, inspectors know that this is unachievable and live with the tension created by this failure. Even in closed processes where 100 per cent inspection can be achieved (such as slaughterhouse production lines) experience shows that it does not lead to complete or even better compliance.[38] Persuading inspectors that they could be more effective if they targeted their effort requires a change in culture – in their understanding of their role – as well as in the rules by which they operate.

In the UK, an equivalent example has been seen in reluctance to de-prioritise. Local authorities tasked by 12 or more national ministries and agencies to deliver hundreds of pieces of legislation were understandably reluctant to 'choose which to enforce'. Work to prioritise that list, initially led by Paul Connolly in the Local Authority Better Regulation Group and then through the Rogers Review,[39] identified the unwillingness of central government departments to set priorities (a request for the top three priorities for local enforcement produced an initial list of 800!). Legislation[40] was required to ensure central agencies made choices, informing the resultant Priority Regulatory Outcomes[41] set out by LBRO, and enabling frontline regulators to act upon them.

Malcolm Sparrow, in *The Regulatory Craft*[42] and subsequent books, has identified creating space and using it to make choices as a key determinant of the professionalisation of regulators that, at the same time, empowers them, enables them to make an impact and allows them to ensure this impact becomes known.

ii. Impact – Does Deterrence 'Work'?

In his 2015 book,[43] Christopher Hodges identifies the fallacies in the thinking that deterrence drives behavioural change and therefore that the tools of deterrence (imposing sanctions) are necessarily effective in affecting human behaviour. This belief is found widely over time and in diverse cultures to the point where, in public discourse at least, it is seldom questioned. It can seem that every news bulletin includes some item describing corporate misbehaviour which could be ended at a stroke if fines were doubled, prison sentences introduced and enforcement resources multiplied. The question of why these simple solutions have failed to work in the past, or why their adoption now would have radically different outcomes, is seldom asked.

In his survey of the enforcement policies of UK regulatory agencies, also reported in that book, Hodges shows that many UK agencies have grappled with this question and adopted more responsive and supportive practices and policies. His descriptions with

---

[37] For example, Tajikistan and Kyrgyzstan. See also ch 25.

[38] 'A Review of Meat Cutting Plants and Cold Stores. Final report October 2018' (Food Standards Agency and Food Standards Scotland, 2018).

[39] Peter Rogers, *National Enforcement Priorities for Local Authority Regulatory Services* (The Stationery Office, 2007).

[40] Regulatory Enforcement and Sanctions Act 2008, s 11.

[41] 'Priority Regulatory Outcomes: A New Approach to Refreshing the National Enforcement Priorities for Local Authority Regulatory Services' (Local Better Regulation Office, 2011).

[42] Malcolm Sparrow, *The Regulatory Craft: Controlling Risks, Solving Problems, and Managing Compliance* (Washington, Brookings Institution Press, 2000).

[43] Christopher Hodges, *Law and Corporate Behaviour: Integrating Theories of Regulation, Enforcement, Culture and Ethics* (Oxford, Hart Publishing, 2015).

Ruth Steinholtz of Ethical Business Regulation[44] (explained further in chapter twenty-two) point towards an emerging way forward based on behavioural psychology and empirical evidence on how humans behave, rather than on philosophical and economic theories. The Ethical Business Regulation model focuses on encouraging and recognising systemic ethical business practice by businesses, based on a body of consistent evidence, that can be the foundation for trust that the business is controlling its own activities and risk through adopting an ethical culture throughout the organisation, and on which a more collaborative engagement between regulatory agencies and business can be founded.

None of these means that proportionate sanctions should not be used in response to non-compliance that passes evidential and public interest tests[45] – deterrence is only one of the reasons for sanctioning. But the assumption that increasing penalties will increase the impact on future behaviour has been undermined by recent evidence and the need for public protection demands a better approach.

iii. Results – Does Inspection 'Work'?

Although regulatory agencies around the world conduct hundreds of thousands of inspections every year, it is easier to count the number than it is to measure their impact. When we contemplate whether inspections work, we ask why they are carried out. For some they are 'what inspectors do' – the clue is in the name. While there might be discussion about who to inspect or how, debate about whether to inspect at all is unlikely if you are addressing a group of inspectors. When agencies in the UK addressed the question, they discovered that other methods of engagement are more fruitful and even that non-specialists are better at gathering generic information than qualified officers.[46] If the purpose of inspection is defined more widely, in terms of guiding the behaviour of regulated entities and providing evidence-based confidence, then there are more examples of success.[47] However, all too often inspection rates are the focus – mandated externally, sometimes in law with changes calculated for effect, whether by virtue of signalling the quantity of inspections or the size of the reduction. In this context any initiative which focuses solely on numbers is too narrow. Demanding fewer inspections through 'inspection holidays', small business exemptions and other moratoria makes little more sense than intentions to inspect every business, follow up every complaint or check every consignment.

Florentin Blanc has provided a valuable reference point with ground-breaking research which, for the first time, quantifies the impact of different delivery approaches in terms of outcomes (see chapter fifteen). He concludes that labour enforcement in his native France, involving a relatively high number of control visits and arising from limited use of tools

---

[44] See Christopher Hodges and Ruth Steinholtz, *Ethical Business Practice and Regulation: A Behavioural and Ethical Approach to Compliance and Enforcement* (Oxford, Hart Publishing, 2017) and Hodges (ibid).

[45] 'Code for Crown Prosecutors' (Crown Prosecution Service, 2018).

[46] See for example, information on the Business Compliance Service operated by local authorities in Greater Manchester, available at www.businesscomplianceservice.org.uk. The Business Compliance Service uses a 'regulatory triage' approach, deploying Business Compliance Assessors who are not authorised regulatory officers to visit lower-risk businesses, gathering information across a range of regulatory functions that is fed back to specialist regulators.

[47] Local Better Regulation Office, 'Regulation and Growth' (2012).

and risk-based methods and a rather coercive approach to enforcement, results in mixed effectiveness compared to other EU Member States. The research by Staffordshire University discussed in chapter thirteen, suggests that neither compliance (protection) nor survival (prosperity) are enhanced by an inspection-led approach.[48]

iv. Evidence of Impact

All three 'myths' suggest that regulatory delivery is in need of attention, and reform, to ensure deliver of protection outcomes. Further evidence of the need for effective delivery to ensure the desired social policy change can be seen by comparing the changes that occur. Fifty years ago, in the UK, legislation to require equal pay for men and women and legislation to require riders of motorcycles to wear helmets was introduced. Today, the debate about equal pay continues and new legislation aimed at transparency of pay was introduced in 2016. Conversely, little is heard about the issue of motorcycle helmets and compliance is high. The reasons for such differences are varied but start with societal acceptability. The principle is that delivery of regulation – what happens after the law is passed – matters and attention should be given to what works.[49]

This difference in the impact of different pieces of legislation is not simply a matter of good policy-making. Legislation which could never be actively enforced can still have an impact. Rule changes that should be straightforward to implement are sometimes ignored. Examples abound, but one of each will suffice. Legislation across Europe banning smoking in public places has changed behaviour considerably, but would have been difficult to enforce in the absence of widespread public acceptance.[50] In Myanmar, legislation releasing entrepreneurs from the requirement to deposit significant bonds before starting to trade had little impact – this appeared to be because the business community did not believe that inspectors would change their behaviour and they continued to deposit the bonds even when told they were not required.[51]

More positively, there is a growing number of examples of the impact effective delivery can have on protection and we will examine a number of them in this book. Looking forward, research, including in fields of behavioural insights, is showing that behaviour can be understood, and regulated entities encouraged to change by adoption of a range of more effective tools. The UK's Behavioural Insight team has shown[52] how data that improves predictability of negative outcomes can be accessed, without inspection. New technologies including the Internet of Things offer the potential to improve safety as products become more intelligent, whilst others have pointed to effective means of inculcating sustainable change (see chapters twenty and twenty-two).

---

[48] Staffordshire University, 'Measuring the Impact of Regulation', study for Stoke-on-Trent and Staffordshire Enterprise Partnership (forthcoming).

[49] For example see What Works networks, a collaboration between government, academia and the research councils, available at www.gov.uk/guidance/what-works-network.

[50] 'A breath of fresh air smokefree workplaces 10 years on' (Local Government Association, 2017), available at www.local.gov.uk/sites/default/files/documents/22.4%20Smoke%20free%20-%2010%20years%20on_V13_Web.pdf.

[51] Informal conversations between Graham and businesses in Myanmar during a visit to Naypyidaw in December 2014.

[52] 'Using Data Science in Policy. A report by the Behavioural Insights Team' (Behavioural Insights Team, 2017).

C. Efficiency

The third driver of our regulatory PPE is efficiency. Whilst the global financial crisis drove a search for the purpose of regulation it also, through public sector austerity, drove fresh thinking about what works and how it could be resourced. Doing 'more for less' may have been a mocked mantra but it also unleashed creative thinking.

The very act of being forced to consider the efficiency of current practice is a driver for change. Cuts of 70 per cent in the resources available to some UK regulatory agencies[53] have been, if not a burning platform, at the very least a motive for change.

Of course, a motive to change is not in itself a driver of improvement. Thinking about delivery does not always improve the outcomes of regulation. Whilst some agencies have innovated, and this book highlights some outstanding examples, others have retrenched,[54] de-prioritising advice and support in favour of a focus on sanctioning and deterrence.

Reducing the number of inspections is a very crude indicator of delivery reform. However, it can be instructive. In some places it has been a direct result of reduction in resources, in others it has been a political imperative, sometimes as part of a wider reform package.[55] Where work has been done to study the impact of fewer inspections it seldom indicates a flourishing of non-compliance, despite apocalyptic concerns.[56] Blanc has shown that, if replaced with more effective delivery methods, reducing the number of inspections whilst targeting and improving those that remain can be highly effective (see chapter fifteen). Data gathered by the UK's Food Standards Agency illustrates this point, showing that a reduction in staffing levels and in the number of food safety inspections by local environmental health services, in the context of a continuing trend of switching activity to higher-risk businesses, resulted in both an increase in the number of businesses found to be achieving broad compliance and an increase in the number of formal enforcement actions, such as licence suspensions, cautions, written warnings and prosecutions.[57]

In other economies, where regulation has become a source of income for municipalities and regulatory agencies, the need to increase efficiency is a driver for reform. Without it, the reliance placed upon these income sources acts as a barrier to any other reform. In some places this has driven illicit activity, with people reportedly paying to become border guards in Georgia because it could be so lucrative.[58] In others it is a much more legitimate

---

[53] The UK's Chartered Trading Standards Institute conducts an annual workforce survey. In 2016, the survey report identified that one local authority Trading Standards Service had lost 73% of its budget in the two years to 2016. In 2017, the survey report identified that one service had seen a 61% fall in its budget over a single year. Survey reports, available at www.tradingstandards.uk/news-policy/vision-and-strategy-1/workforce-survey.

[54] Based on conversations Graham and colleagues had in 2011/12.

[55] 'Inspections Reforms: Do Models Exist?' (Washington, World Bank Group, 2010) 21.

[56] For example, Steve Tombs, '"Better Regulation": Better for Whom?', Centre for Crime and Justice Studies Briefing 14, April 2016, reported in Environmental Health News, available at www.ehn-online.com/news/article.aspx?id=15507&utm_campaign=7066764_EHN%20Extra%2005%2F05%2F16&utm_medium=email&utm_source=Chartered%20Institute%20of%20Environmental%20Health&dm_i=1RSV,47GR0,B872UT,FBL3X,1; and Carina Bailey, 'Mind the Cracks' (2017) 10 *Trading Standards Review* 18.

[57] Reported in *Environmental Health News*, available at www.ehn-online.com/news/article.aspx?id=5772&LangType=2057&terms=less%20inspection.

[58] In 2003, prior to reform efforts, payments of up to $10,000 were reported. See World Bank Group, *Fighting Corruption in Public Services: Chronicling Georgia's Reforms* (World Bank Group, 2012), 37.

source of concern. However, early experience, including from Nairobi, Kenya, has been that replacing complex costly permit requirements with simpler cheaper Single Business Permit approaches not only reduces costs to business but also reduces administrative costs for regulatory agencies and, by encouraging simpler compliance, reduces the attractiveness of the grey economy and so increases overall income to the state.[59]

IV. What is the Challenge?

We have looked at the three drivers for extending regulatory reform to implementation and thus the development of *regulatory delivery*. We have seen that the delivery of regulation is important to the regulated, to beneficiaries and to the public purse. Increasing expectations for rising levels of prosperity, protection and efficiency have driven the reform programme and made this a pressing question for today. Regulatory delivery is seen to be both sufficiently important and sufficiently in need of reform for some focus to be given to its improvement. The consequent question is whether it has any characteristics that make its reform challenging. Is there anything about regulatory delivery that makes it particularly or distinctively difficult?

This book will, in proposing a model for improving delivery, discuss these challenges within the six elements of the Regulatory Delivery Model, explained in detail in chapter two. For this introduction it will be sufficient to sketch out the dimensions of the challenges within the two domains of the model: prerequisites and practices.

A. Prerequisites

Prerequisites deal with the fundamental descriptors of a regulatory agency: governance frameworks; accountability; and culture. Brief consideration of the characteristics of an agency charged with regulatory delivery demonstrates the need for special attention. Regulatory agencies exercise the coercive power of the state, almost always based on statutory powers. This, in itself, gives them a complex relationship with those they regulate – at the same time depending on them for their success whilst needing their failures to sustain their resources; instructing them in their behaviour and yet requiring feedback if they are to improve. This complexity, which can also be seen in relationships with government sponsors and those for whom they act (beneficiaries), requires attention to both governance and accountability. While ensuring effective governance is acknowledged as an issue for regulatory agencies, accountability – in terms of it being a proactive responsibility of the agency – is less recognised. Accountability, particularly to the regulated but also to sponsors and beneficiaries, does not necessarily fit well with the 'parent' role allocated to (or taken up by?) regulatory agencies. In our experience there is limited acceptance of a requirement to build external capacity which will hold them to account.

All of this is shaped by, and shapes, the culture of the organisation. The complex mix of skills required at the personal level, the necessity of integrity in the face of opportunities for

---

[59] Nick Devas and Roy Kelly, 'Regulation or Revenues? An Analysis of Local Business Licences, with a Case Study of the Single Business Permit Reform in Kenya' (2001) 21 *Public Administration and Development* 381.

corruption and the significance of leadership are all challenges for a regulatory agency. The culture of a regulatory agency is not always explained or explored but it significantly influences the way that the agency behaves and therefore the capacity to deliver outcomes (see chapter twelve).

Many of these characteristics of regulatory agencies are seen in other public sector bodies and are not individually unique to regulators. The absence of competitive and market forces often requires other constraints on behaviour, positioning and scope. Many bodies, public and private, achieve their success through the behaviour of others, and culture is widely recognised as the determinant of long-term sustainable achievement.[60] So, what is different about regulatory agencies? In addition to the availability of coercive power, it is the ubiquity of these factors, their overwhelming strength in determining the authorising environment and their inter-relationship, that uniquely define the challenges of regulatory delivery. As we will consider further in chapter two, it is also the inter-relationships, the dynamics between these factors, that is both essential to the ability of a regulatory agency to achieve its purpose and the key to solving the challenges of regulatory delivery.

B. Practices

The practices of a regulatory agency – its use of risk, its ability to monitor outcomes and its capacity to use the appropriate tools – have been more widely considered, although often in isolation.[61] Experience shows that they remain problematic, both independently and in concert. A regulatory agency is unlikely to succeed without a thoroughgoing understanding of what it seeks to achieve; how it should allocate scarce resources; the full range of tools and their likely impact (coupled with an ability to use them); and a means of assessing whether progress is being made towards outcomes.[62]

Each of these issues requires an approach which goes beyond the traditional understanding of what a regulator is and does, at both the agency and the individual level. Without this understanding the behaviour of the agency, and consequently its impact, will be significantly skewed. To give two examples: while measurement of outcomes is challenging for any public service, the particular difficulties inherent for regulatory agencies (including plurality of ownership and long timeframes for impact) have driven reliance solely on input and output measures. Seeking public recognition, if not approval, in such a complex environment can have a perverse impact on the activity of regulatory agencies,

---

[60] eg recently expanded requirements on company directors and boards to ensure that their organisation's culture is aligned with the business's purpose and based on ethics and integrity, to ensure long-term sustainability: 'The UK Corporate Governance Code' (Financial Reporting Council, 2018); 'The Wates Corporate Governance Principles for Large Private Companies' (Financial Reporting Council, 2018).

[61] For example, see Julia Black and Robert Baldwin, 'Really Responsive Risk-Based Regulation' (2010) 32 *Law & Policy* 181; 'What is the Value in Regulators Sharing Information: Research Results' (Better Regulation Delivery Office, 2013); Cary Coglianese, *Listening. Learning. Leading: A Framework for Regulatory Excellence* (Alberta Energy Regulator and Penn Program on Regulation, 2015); 'Better Business Compliance Partnerships: Programme Evaluation' (Department for Communities and Local Government, 2016); *Performance Measurement by Regulators* (National Audit Office, 2016); Cary Coglianese, 'The Limits of Performance-Based Regulation' (2017) 50 *University of Michigan Journal of Law Reform* 525.

[62] 'Implementing Hampton: from Enforcement to Compliance' (HM Treasury, Better Regulation Executive and Cabinet Office, 2006).

for example targeting lower risk but easier to inspect premises or prosecuting simpler cases. Second, there is the challenge of communicating risk in the face of public and media perception of the role and potential of regulatory agencies. Work by Rick Haythornthwaite, Donald Macrae and others on the UK's Risk and Regulation Advisory Council,[63] taken forward by the Dutch Government, has described the challenge of 'risk-reflex' reactions; the need for evidence-led responses; the importance of taking time to separate issue and response; and the importance of influencing multiple risk actors. While this work outlined ways forward, for many its implementation remains an aspiration.

V. What is the Answer?

Driving effective change in regulatory practice requires that the design of regulatory delivery is given equal attention alongside the design of regulatory policy. Regulatory practitioners are increasingly recognising the vital connection between the design of regulatory requirements and the design of regulatory delivery initiatives (the implementation). This is something which has generally escaped the scrutiny of governments and policy-makers, as well as academic thinking. Simple practical questions to ask when contemplating a regulatory regime or individual rules – but questions of fundamental importance – include: how those subject to the regime or rule will comply with it; the extent to which this is likely and how it will be measured; how they can be helped or motivated to comply; and how non-compliance will be identified and tackled.

While it may be possible to identify good practice that is near-universally relevant, it is unlikely that it could be defined in detail due to important differences in contexts. Taking into consideration a specific context not only means that the relative importance of different aspects of regulatory delivery varies; it also implies that the way to address a given issue will differ. As capacity, priorities, legal systems, institutions and cultures diverge, inspiration may be taken from practices elsewhere, but it will not be necessarily easy or advisable to copy them as they are.[64] Their respective importance – and relevance – will vary depending on the most salient problems in a given country.

Some regulators may be looking for a model prescribing a methodology for regulatory delivery in much the same way that models of risk assessment provide tools for enumeration.[65] The challenges of delivery are contextual and nuanced and cannot be reduced to a set of formulas. In developing the Regulatory Delivery Model we aim to provoke interest in the need to think about delivery, to provide a shape which can guide that thinking and predict likely outcomes, and to offer some prompts as to what effective delivery may include. In this book the model is supplemented with some great examples of how agencies around the world have delivered improvements within that framework.

---

[63] The UK's Risk and Regulation Advisory Council led a short-term experimental offensive against the poor handling of public risk. Information is available at http://webarchive.nationalarchives.gov.uk/20100104183913/ http://www.berr.gov.uk/deliverypartners/list/rrac/index.html.

[64] See 'Assessment of Institutional and Technological Models Supporting Integrated Inspection Functions' (World Bank Group, forthcoming).

[65] See for example 'Enforcement Management Model' (Health and Safety Executive, 2013) available at www.hse. gov.uk/enforce/enforcement-management-model.htm.

VI. Contributors and Primary Audience

This book has been written principally by and for practitioners of regulatory delivery. It takes a practical rather than a theoretical or academic approach. Those who have contributed the case studies offer substantive experience of the challenges of real-world implementation and expertise in regulatory delivery reform.

The book is intended to be useful primarily for strategy leads in regulatory agencies around the world. Its practical focus provides a structured way of thinking about how regulatory agencies can act effectively to achieve their purpose and is supported by case study examples from a diverse range of regulators and other key players. The book should also be of interest to others within agencies and to regulatory policy-makers. It offers insights for academics and others with an interest in regulatory delivery, governance and public policy, who should find that the practical focus and case studies provide insight into regulation from the perspective of the regulator.

VII. Outline of this Book

The structure of this book follows the six main elements of the Regulatory Delivery Model. After an overview of the model from Graham Russell in chapter two, each section begins with an exposition by Graham and Helen Kirkman of the meaning of that element, its implementation in practice, its challenges and limitations and its dependency on other elements. Each element of the model is then supported by case studies illustrating particular examples from practice which illustrate that theme and develop the interdependencies with the other elements as follows.

Governance Frameworks (chapter three) is followed by contributions from Srikanth Mangalam, explaining the delegated Administrative Authority model in Ontario, Canada; Helen Kirkman and Paul Sanderson, reporting on the UK's use of a code-based approach to changing regulator behaviour; and Giedrius Kadziauskas, describing the Lithuanian experience of reforming the regulatory framework to deliver improvements in accountability.

Accountability (chapter seven) contributions follow from Martin Traynor and Kathryn Preece, reporting their experience of the development of the UK's Better Business for All programme; and Duncan Johnson, on how the Primary Authority scheme has changed the relationship between business and local regulators.

Culture (chapter ten) contributions follow from Rob Velders, highlighting the important work of the Inspection Council in the Netherlands; and Chris Webb, describing the cultural transformation of the Victoria Environment Protection Agency.

Outcome Measurement (chapter thirteen) contributions follow from Christian van Stolk and Tom Ling, introducing the tool that RAND Europe developed to support regulatory agencies in mapping their progress towards outcomes; and Florentin Blanc and Giuliana Cola, examining the question of whether inspection makes a difference to outcomes.

Risk-based Prioritisation (chapter sixteen) contributions follow from Paul Leinster and Simon Pollard, considering the use of different regulatory tools in the area of environmental regulation; a team from the UK Health and Safety Executive and Phil Preece describing the development of an IT tool to inform risk-based targeting; and Marcus Rink, reporting on progress towards a more evidence-based approach in the regulation of drinking water quality.

Intervention Choices (chapter twenty) contributions follow from Erica Sheward and Mariam Shkubuliani, considering the empowerment of consumers as a means of improving regulatory outcomes; Christopher Hodges and Ruth Steinholtz, setting out emerging thinking on how regulatory agencies can more effectively regulate businesses that are able to demonstrate ethical and compliant behaviour; and Scott Steedman, Matt Gantley and Richard Sanders, describing UK approaches to using standards and accreditation as an intervention choice.

The book then provides some examples of reforms in particular countries that are at different stages of their reform journey, illustrating the application of the model in diverse contexts. Marcelo Pachecho dos Guaranys describes the Brazilian experience, moving from the reform of regulatory policy towards regulatory delivery reform; Jigjidmaa Dugeree, Giuliana Cola, Florentin Blanc and Giuseppa Ottimofiore report on Mongolia's consolidation of multiple regulatory agencies and the experience of reforming the working practices of the newly established single agency; and Ariel Francisco Faraon and Nestor Ian Favila Fiedalan describe the challenges and context for regulatory reform in the Philippines. Finally, Christopher Hodges reflects on the concepts and examples set out in the book. He notes their place in the evolution of thinking about regulation, its context and its practice. He then suggests a number of steps that seem important to take next, notably the creation of national and international communities of practice on regulatory delivery such as the International Network for Delivery of Regulation, and to focus on the culture of regulatory and regulated organisations.

2

The Regulatory Delivery Model

GRAHAM RUSSELL

I. What is the Regulatory Delivery Model?

In the Introduction to this book, we set out the context in which the Regulatory Delivery Model was developed, describing how we came to understand the importance of the six elements and to identify the relationships between them. In this chapter we set out our thinking on the model and how it can be used. Each element of the Regulatory Delivery Model is considered in more detail in the six overview chapters that make up the framework of this book.[1]

The Regulatory Delivery Model has two domains: prerequisites and practices. The prerequisites describe the three elements that define the potential of a regulatory agency to fulfil its mandate and to continue to do so in a changing environment. The three practices cover the operational activity of a regulatory agency and its ability to plan, deliver and describe whether it is achieving the outcomes for which it exists.

The model is divided into these two domains because of key differences between the elements in the two groups. In part this is temporal, in that prerequisites come first in the establishment of an agency, but it is also a difference of function and authorisation. Initially, the prerequisites have a sense of being given to the organisation, by those setting it up or implicit in its creation, whilst the practices are products of decisions taken, however intentionally, by the agency. Over time these distinctions may become less pronounced – as for example the regulatory agency builds its approach to accountability beyond the foundations set out in the governance framework while risk-based prioritisation becomes hard-wired into its operating psyche. However, significant distinctions remain, even in very mature agencies. This has frequently been seen when we have sought views on the relative strength of a regulatory agency in terms of the two domains or in terms of each element. Policy-makers will say that the weaknesses lie in governance, accountability or sometimes culture and want to address this as the priority while those from operational teams are equally sure that an initial emphasis on risk, outcomes or interventions will be of most value.

Within the two domains the elements operate as distinct features but interact with each other. The diagrams that follow lay out the model as an overview – the prerequisites in

---

[1] Chapter 3: Governance Frameworks; ch 7: Accountability; ch 10: Culture; ch 13: Outcome Measurement; ch 16: Risk-based Prioritisation; ch 20: Intervention Choices.

Figure 2.1 and the practices in Figure 2.2 – and begin to explore how the interactions work in practice.

Figure 2.1 Prerequisites in the Regulatory Delivery Model

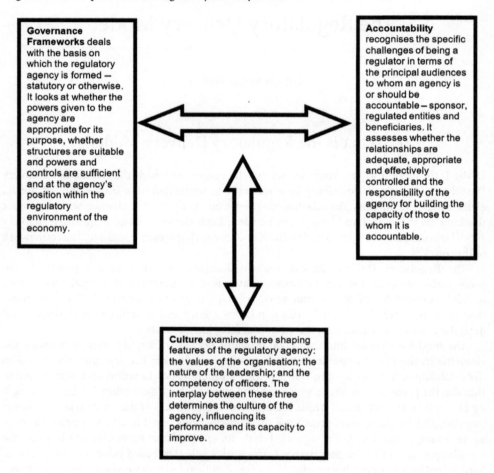

Governance Frameworks deals with the basis on which the regulatory agency is formed — statutory or otherwise. It looks at whether the powers given to the agency are appropriate for its purpose, whether structures are suitable and powers and controls are sufficient and at the agency's position within the regulatory environment of the economy.

Accountability recognises the specific challenges of being a regulator in terms of the principal audiences to whom an agency is or should be accountable — sponsor, regulated entities and beneficiaries. It assesses whether the relationships are adequate, appropriate and effectively controlled and the responsibility of the agency for building the capacity of those to whom it is accountable.

Culture examines three shaping features of the regulatory agency: the values of the organisation; the nature of the leadership; and the competency of officers. The interplay between these three determines the culture of the agency, influencing its performance and its capacity to improve.

II. Use of the Regulatory Delivery Model

The Regulatory Delivery Model can be used as a map, a diagnostic tool or a predictive model, as discussed in the Introduction.

As a map the model operates to describe, analyse and assess a regulatory agency. Used in this way, all six elements in both domains are important and whilst the analysis can start at any point in the model, we have found it helpful to work through it in the order laid out here. This ensures a thorough assessment of the agency's potential as well as its practices and seeks to determine the causes as well as the symptoms. It avoids any bias introduced by the preferences of those leading reform for one domain over the other (as noted above, typically policy-makers will favour or focus on prerequisites while

Figure 2.2 Practices in the Regulatory Delivery Model

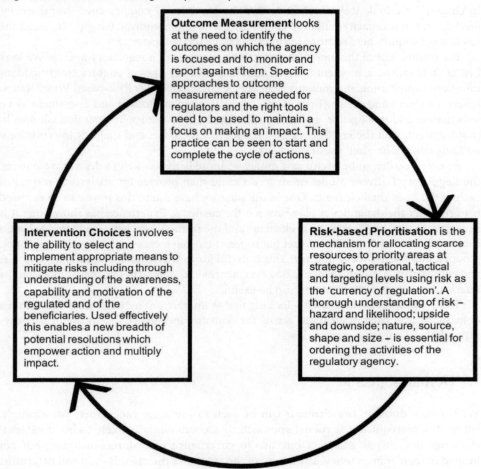

Outcome Measurement looks at the need to identify the outcomes on which the agency is focused and to monitor and report against them. Specific approaches to outcome measurement are needed for regulators and the right tools need to be used to maintain a focus on making an impact. This practice can be seen to start and complete the cycle of actions.

Intervention Choices involves the ability to select and implement appropriate means to mitigate risks including through understanding of the awareness, capability and motivation of the regulated and of the beneficiaries. Used effectively this enables a new breadth of potential resolutions which empower action and multiply impact.

Risk-based Prioritisation is the mechanism for allocating scarce resources to priority areas at strategic, operational, tactical and targeting levels using risk as the 'currency of regulation'. A thorough understanding of risk – hazard and likelihood; upside and downside; nature, source, shape and size – is essential for ordering the activities of the regulatory agency.

more operationally minded people will be drawn to the practices). A clear and systematic sequential understanding of the issues which the regulatory agency faces can prevent over or under emphasis on either domain or any of the elements.

We have developed a set of key lines of enquiry in respect of each element of the model, providing a series of questions that can be used to assess and understand the regulatory agency. These questions are not intended to comprehensively explore each element but should provide a good starting point. Exploration of these questions will give a sense of where strengths and weaknesses lie and highlight potential for improvement. This approach has proved useful as a diagnostic tool but also as a way for the regulatory agency to bring forward its own evidence, giving the agency and any external reviewer confidence that the good practice and the foundations already in place can be used in reform.

The key lines of enquiry are grouped at the end of each of the overview chapters. Under the prerequisites we look first at Governance Frameworks (chapter three) and the key lines of enquiry consider purpose, structures, landscape and powers and responsibilities. In chapter 7 we look at Accountability and the key lines of enquiry cover transparency, mechanisms and capacity-building. Culture is the final prerequisite (chapter ten) and the key lines of enquiry here relate to leadership, values and competency.

The second half of the model deals with the practices of a regulatory agency. We look first at Outcome Measurement (chapter thirteen) with key lines of enquiry covering identification, contribution and measurement. The second practice is Risk-based Prioritisation (chapter sixteen) and the key lines of enquiry relate to identification and assessment; data; information and intelligence; and using risk. Finally, we consider Intervention Choices in chapter twenty and the key lines of enquiry address the range and shape of interventions; building compliance; and use of sanctions.

As noted earlier, to be useful as a model with predictive as well as descriptive powers, the Regulatory Delivery Model needs to do more than provide for analysis in respect of each of the individual elements. One of the ways we have found this power to be accessed is to consider the dynamics at play between the elements. Experience has shown that it is necessary to work on both specific elements and the relationships between them to shape a successful reform programme. As set out so far, the six elements are arranged in sequence, grouped into two domains of three. This is useful for formal assessment, avoidance of bias and comparison between agencies. However, alternative approaches, focusing more on the interactions between the elements, can be useful.

Three examples we have used – looking first at interactions between elements within a domain, then at pairs of elements across the domains and finally at purposeful pathways through the elements – are as follows.

A. Domain-Specific

Within each domain, the elements can be seen to influence each other. For example, within the prerequisites, a robust approach to accountability is likely to build external challenge not only to practices but also to governance procedures, including but not limited to their transparency. The nature of the culture of the organisation will determine whether that challenge is embraced as a source of improvement or resisted. Indeed, it is the culture of the organisation that will have driven that search for greater accountability whilst the existing governance framework will have enabled it, and so an upward spiral is created.

One way of understanding the inter-relationship between the three prerequisites is to consider the governance framework of a regulatory agency and the accountability to which it is subject as two pressures which, if held in tension and constantly monitored, can hold the organisation in place and prevent it falling. We sometimes illustrate this by having two people push a large beach ball. If they both push in opposite directions with equal force, the beach ball will remain above the ground in a stable position – even though they are individually unstable, leaning inwards, towards one another. But what about when stability is insufficient? Improvement is necessary to meet rising expectations, address diminishing resources or respond to technological or societal change. To make the beach ball rise, a third force is required – acting from beneath to push it upwards. This force is culture and its effects on the regulatory agency's governance and accountability can be seen in many ways.

For example, an organisation with an open culture will want to be accountable and to build the capacity of those holding it to account.

Within the practices domain, a desire to use a wider range of intervention choices, appropriately empowering beneficiaries whilst robustly enabling earned recognition, necessitates wide-ranging and confident use of risk assessment at strategic and operational levels. Continued authorisation of these delivery options depends upon measurement of outcomes and communication of real improvement and is likely to have been driven by a desire to focus on the agency's most important outcomes.

To help people think through these interactions, and the way they are at work in their regulatory agency, it can be helpful to have groups create narratives starting at different points in the cycle. Those who start with identification of outcomes will see the need to prioritise scarce resources, and therefore the importance of risk, and the need to deploy effective interventions. Taking risk as a starting point will generate a debate about the agency's role in mitigating risk, directly and indirectly, through different interventions and the need to measure progress towards those outcomes. Using intervention choices as the basis for a narrative tends to broaden the discussion about the role of beneficiaries and intermediaries with risk and outcomes becoming respectively the drivers and evaluation points for the wisdom of those choices.

It is therefore possible to focus attention on one or other domain in isolation when establishing a reform programme. This allows exploration of the ability of elements to cross-fertilise each other within domains, developing understanding across the domain that engages with and empowers both policy and delivery users whilst preserving space for further reform initiatives.

B. Matched Pairs

While the six elements in the model are separate from each other, they are not independent. Particular linkages can be drawn between pairs across the domains. To illustrate this point we will describe three particular pairings that, in our experience, have proved useful in a variety of contexts.

Governance Frameworks and **Risk-based Prioritisation.** Both speak to the selection of the organisation's activities – choices made by it and for it. They address the reality that there are things a regulatory agency will not be responsible for, as well as areas it will prioritise. Effective governance is likely to empower good use of risk assessment whilst inconsistent use of risk, particularly in strategic areas, will undermine the sense of purpose and confuse others in the same landscape. Without the clear sense of purpose and position that arises from a strong governance framework, a regulatory agency is unlikely to have the means or motivation to prioritise risks to its outcomes.

Accountability and **Outcome Measurement** draw upon the benefits/costs the agency can offer/impose and the interests of stakeholders in those outputs and outcomes. Effective delivery of change is likely to drive interest, appreciation and accountability. Whilst poor delivery of outcomes may drive challenge, it is too often accompanied by limited articulation of outcomes and together these drive towards disengagement. If accountability is weak, a regulatory agency may lack the motivation to identify or measure its outcomes with the rigour required.

Culture and **Intervention Choices** are closely linked by the necessity of competency for the safe exercise of discretion, but they also both address the ownership a regulatory agency has, or should have, of its purpose. Often expressed initially though leadership, a willingness to own the challenges the organisation faces, and a strong set of values will enable an agency to make choices and is more likely to incentivise beneficiaries to exercise their potential. An agency with a culture that doesn't value the competency necessary to exercise discretion can be expected to find itself using blunt instruments and incapable of making good intervention choices.

C. Purposeful Pathways

When an agency faces criticism, it can be difficult to get beyond the symptoms to identify and focus on the causes. Comments may be expressed like this:

'(This agency) lacks impact.'

'Relationships with (this agency) have broken down.'

'There is a problem with the structure of agencies within (this area)/across government.'

'There is no sense of value from (this agency's) work.'

Getting beyond these symptoms and understanding causes requires a diagnostic that is objective and is structured outside of the immediate context. The Regulatory Delivery Model has, in our experience, been able to provide this approach, operating as a structured and sequential way of understanding a regulatory agency and the factors in its prerequisites or practices that may contribute to the reported perceptions.

The symptoms described above each speak to a condition, or set of conditions, that can be addressed by focusing on the elements in an intentional order. For example, a perceived lack of impact should start with consideration of purpose and other aspects of governance leading to inward activity on outcome measurement and confidence in the use of intervention choices which can be outwardly expressed through existing and developed accountability mechanisms.

By contrast, a concern about the inter-agency relationships under which an agency operates might also start with the governance framework, focusing now on structures, but is more likely to look at use of risk-based prioritisation, both individually for the agency and in sharing of profiles and interventions, and the culture of the organisation in terms of openness and cooperation.

Finally, concerns about the value an agency offers, and its effective use of resources should start with its strategic use of risk and look at the cultural values it displays and its internal governance structures which will enable a better assessment of outcomes and more confident engagement with those holding it to account.

III. Summary

In the first two chapters we have set out our thinking on why regulatory delivery matters, including why its importance has come to the fore in recent years, and given an overview of the Regulatory Delivery Model. By providing some examples of the ways in which the six elements that make up the model can be used in sequence, within domains, as matched pairs and to provide purposeful resolution, we have begun to suggest ways in which the model can be used: as a map; as a diagnostic; and as a predictive tool to guide regulatory agencies in their work. In the rest of the book we will deal with each element in turn, starting with the prerequisites.

PART TWO

The Regulatory Delivery Model

Prerequisites: Governance Frameworks

3

Governance Frameworks

GRAHAM RUSSELL AND HELEN KIRKMAN

As explained in the previous chapter, the first domain of the Regulatory Delivery Model sets out three prerequisites that are considered, both individually and collectively, to determine whether the right conditions are in place for good regulatory delivery. The first of these prerequisites relates to the 'Governance Frameworks' within which a regulatory agency operates.

In this chapter we explore why governance is at the heart of good regulatory delivery – and therefore central to the Regulatory Delivery Model – and consider what we mean when we talk about governance frameworks in connection with regulatory agencies, thinking about their purpose; their structures; their relationships in the regulatory landscape; and their powers and responsibilities. We also consider the interactions between Governance Frameworks and the other elements considered in the Regulatory Delivery Model, in particular, the remaining prerequisites: Accountability and Culture.

I. Defining Governance Frameworks

Governance can be defined[1] as the manner in which *control* is exercised; the *influences* over a person or organisation; or – particularly with respect to government or state institutions – the ways in which policies are delivered. Governance is considered within the Regulatory Delivery Model as the collective set of rules and relationships that define the regulatory agency. These rules and relationships, both external and internal, establish a framework within which the regulatory agency operates.

A regulatory agency's governance framework has multiple external constituents. They are concerned with the regulatory agency's authorisation, such as the law that establishes it; its outward-facing role; and its defined relationship to others, including the relationships through which it is held accountable by the state, for performance and financial control. These are part of establishing an effective authorising environment, which is further strengthened by aspects of accountability.[2,3] A principal ingredient in its 'licence to operate'

---

[1] *Oxford English Dictionary* (Oxford, Oxford University Press, 2018).

[2] Robin Holt and Terry McNulty, 'Securing the Licence to Act: a Foundational Capability' (2008) 1(1) *Journal of Strategy and Management* 72.

[3] 'Social Licence' (Institute for Research on Public Policy, 2014), available at http://policyoptions.irpp.org/magazines/technology/licence-to-act.

is the extent to which the regulatory agency establishes confidence and then trust amongst beneficiaries and regulated entities that it will deliver outcomes with equity, consistency and predictability.

While these constituents of governance are created outside of the regulatory agency, and are therefore categorised here as 'external', there is a need for the regulatory agency to internalise them as part of its decision-making processes, for example in its Board, in order for them to become an effective part of its approach to governance. The internal constituents of the regulatory agency's governance framework determine how it works – through its strategies, policies and procedures.

II. The Importance of Governance Frameworks for Regulatory Agencies

In establishing a regulatory agency and giving it responsibility for implementing regulation, government is authorising that body to exercise the power of the state; awarding it the ability to take action in ways that can have a significant impact on those subject to the requirements. The regulatory agency has a powerful role in public life; tasked with ensuring that regulated entities meet the standards set by regulation. It usually has significant discretion as to how it goes about this task, in terms of what it chooses to do, how it chooses to do it, and the choices it makes about what it will not do.

The public sector is generally less impacted by the forces, including the profit motive and competition, that act in the private sector to maintain service levels and drive change and improvement. Regulatory agencies are particularly insulated from these forces for change by their requirements for independence of action.

This separation from market influences and risks, in conjunction with the ability of the regulatory agency to exercise the coercive power of the state and the discretion that it is usually afforded in doing this, brings with it multiple challenges and risks. These challenges and risks may operate at an organisational level or at the level of a team or individual regulatory officer. They range from inappropriate, overly zealous or ineffective use of regulatory powers to corruption or regulatory capture. Dysfunctional relationships with regulated and beneficiary communities and an absence of trust are symptomatic of such behaviours.

The proposition put forward in the Regulatory Delivery Model is that good regulatory delivery – that properly addresses the challenges and risks identified here and ensures that the power of the state is exercised appropriately – is reliant on a robust governance framework operating in conjunction with effective accountability mechanisms (see chapter seven) and an appropriate organisational culture (see chapter ten).

The regulatory agency's governance framework is central to the Regulatory Delivery Model because it gives the foundation for the regulatory agency to act and defines the boundaries of what the regulatory agency can do; how it goes about doing it; and who it interacts with. The governance framework supports and shapes the regulatory agency's culture and establishes the rules of play that provide transparency and accountability to the regulated community and others with an interest. A robust governance framework is at the heart of good decision-making, and essential to an effective, credible regulatory agency that is respected by those it regulates; those that the law seeks to protect; and others in the landscape.

The topic of regulatory governance has been the focus of increasing interest over the past decade. For example, its importance was recognised by the OECD through its development, in the wake of the global financial and economic crisis, of principles for regulatory policy and governance. The OECD's 2012 publication on this topic[4] notes that 'It is important to consider how governance arrangements of a regulatory agency will influence public trust'.

Regulatory agencies can face significant external pressures, for example through political and media interest. Deservedly or not, they are often first in the spotlight when a significant incident occurs relating to their area of control. As highlighted by Malcolm Sparrow in his book[5] examining the 'craft' of delivering regulation, regulators

> face a range of demands, often contradictory in nature:
> - be less intrusive – but be more effective;
> - be kinder and gentler – but don't let [them] get away with anything;
> - focus your efforts – but be consistent;
> - process things quicker – and be more careful next time;
> - deal with important issues – but do not stray outside your statutory authority;
> - be more responsive to the regulated community – but do not get captured by industry.

For a regulatory agency faced with managing these contradictory demands, there is no single answer. Effective governance is the key to achieving a solution that maintains the credibility of the law and the agency. A recent review[6] of regulatory agencies in the UK noted that the commonality, for a diverse range of regulatory agencies, is

> the need to maintain their integrity through independence – both from government and those they regulate – avoiding undue influence and ensuring the decisions they make are fair, well-reasoned and evidence-based. It is a complex space to negotiate and a difficult path to tread.

Governance provides clarity and promotes transparency. It establishes and embeds the rule of law and authorises desired behaviours. Where the regulatory agency has an appropriate governance framework in place, this is evident in both its relationships and its performance. The agency's external relationships will be characterised by well-founded cooperation with partners and the trust of stakeholders. Internally, the agency's ways of working will be clearly set out, with empowered staff who are confident in the boundaries of their responsibilities. This will be apparent in the agency's effective prioritisation of its resources; its achievement of outcomes; and its financial probity.

It is instructive to compare the governance of regulatory agencies with the governance of private organisations (referred to as 'corporate governance'). There has been a great deal of discussion and reform of the latter, especially since the economic crisis of 2008 that revealed serious inadequacies in the governance of commercial corporations and banks. The OECD defined the purpose of corporate governance as 'to help build an environment of trust, transparency and accountability necessary for fostering long-term investment,

---

[4] 'Recommendation of the Council on Regulatory Policy and Governance' (OECD, 2012).
[5] Malcolm Sparrow, *The Regulatory Craft: Controlling Risks, Solving Problems, and Managing Compliance*. (Washington DC, Brookings Institution Press, 2000).
[6] 'Striking the Balance: Upholding the Seven Principles of Public Life in Regulation' (Committee on Standards in Public Life, 2016).

financial stability and business integrity, thereby supporting stronger growth and more inclusive societies.'[7] Corporate governance is achieved, in part at least, through structures and communications requirements that are aimed at holding the organisation externally accountable for its actions. Such structures and requirements are seen in, for example: transparency in the appointment of directors; criteria that apply to directors, and their statutory responsibilities; reporting requirements of companies to shareholders in relation to financial and operational matters and policy; auditing; and, any requirements for reporting to or involvement of external or internal stakeholders, such as staff councils or consumer panels.

The UK significantly upgraded its Corporate Governance Code in 2018. The Code, a set of principles with which companies must either comply or explain divergence, places significant emphasis on the purpose of the organisation as being the fundamental driver of its activities (and hence the focus of governance and accountability), pointing to the importance of aligning values and culture with that purpose,[8] as further discussed in chapter ten.

The mature regulatory agency will want to consider the suitability of its governance framework in light of developing thinking from across a range of sectors, including corporate governance, taking care to apply best practice principles appropriately to the unique context and responsibilities of regulatory delivery.

III. Aspects of Governance Frameworks

In the Regulatory Delivery Model, Governance Frameworks are considered in terms of four aspects: the regulatory agency's purpose; its structures; the landscape in which it operates; and the rules that determine what it can do – its powers and responsibilities. Exploring key questions in these four areas can improve understanding of the current position and enable identification of improvement that is needed.

Consideration of the relationship between Governance Frameworks and other elements of the Regulatory Delivery Model is also beneficial. These relationships are particularly important in respect of the other prerequisites: Culture and Accountability. For example, there is a dynamic interaction between Governance Frameworks and Accountability which will be explored further in chapter seven. One aspect of this interaction is the way that governance frameworks create, and are then shaped by, transparency in accountability. A transparent approach to the regulatory agency's governance framework – its role and responsibilities; its delegation of decision-making responsibilities and the decisions it takes – can create the conditions for effective accountability and confidence in the regulatory agency. Transparent approaches may arise through the culture of the regulatory agency but can also be mandated through its governance framework. For example, chapter five describes the UK Government's use of code-based approaches to embed transparency and

---

[7] 'G20/OECD Principles of Corporate Governance' (OECD, 2015). See also 'Corporate Governance and Business Integrity. A Stocktaking of Corporate Practices' (OECD, 2015).

[8] 'The UK Corporate Governance Code' (Financial Reporting Council, 2018), Principle B; see also 'Guidance on Board Effectiveness' (Financial Reporting Council, 2018); and for large private companies 'The Wates Corporate Governance Principles for Large Private Companies' (Financial Reporting Council, 2018).

chapter six explores the use of legislative measures in Lithuania to drive improvements in transparency across its regulatory agencies.

A. Purpose

In establishing or tasking a regulatory agency, government should be clear about the intent of the law and the role and purpose of the agency. Having done this, it is important that the purpose is transparently communicated and that steps are taken to ensure it remains relevant and that the agency is equipped to fulfil it.

Setting a clear purpose is necessary for establishing the regulatory agency in law but also in practice. Its 'authorisation to act'[9,10] starts with this founding purpose, even though – as we will see – that authorisation is developed, nurtured and sustained by the impact of its activities, the coherence of its behaviour and the response, in terms of confidence expressed and trust offered, of those with whom it works. In different legislative traditions the positioning of the agency in law will be more or less important and the relative weight of de facto and de jure considerations will vary but, in all cases, as a creature of the state and a wielder of the state's authority, the regulatory agency depends upon a clear and secure statutory purpose. Because the regulatory agency's purpose is therefore normally found in statute, it can be seen as being external to the regulatory agency and is also likely to be perceived as being fixed over time.

Government is able to refine or amend the role or purpose of a specific regulatory agency over time, in the light of its developing priorities, by amending its statutory purpose. For example, the UK's Maritime and Coastguard Agency has its foundations over 200 years ago in the establishment of the precursor organisation to Her Majesty's Coastguard, with a clear purpose at that time of combatting the threats to the country's economy and security posed by smuggling.[11] The Coastguard's purpose was amended by statute in the mid-nineteenth century to encompass a responsibility for safety at sea and in the twentieth century in response to concerns about pollution control at sea so that the agency now has a broader mandate and purpose.

Alternatively, government may refine or amend the statutory role or purpose of all regulatory agencies. As an example, many of the long-standing regulatory agencies in the UK were established with statutory purposes focused solely on protection. In 2017, legislation was implemented to require existing regulatory agencies 'to have regard to the desirability of promoting economic growth'[12] when exercising their regulatory functions. This redefining of the statutory purpose of regulatory agencies as 'prosperity and protection' reflects the UK Government's commitment to building a regulatory environment that works well for business and its belief that this is compatible with delivering the high levels of protection required.

The fact that purpose is largely externally set, and often perceived as fixed, can create in the agency a sense of a lack of control and of malleability, and this may affect how the

---

[9] Holt and McNulty 'Securing the Licence to Act' (2008).
[10] 'Social Licence' (n 3).
[11] 'A Short History of HM Coastguard' (blog, January 2014), available at http://hmcoastguard.blogspot.com/2014/01/a-short-history-of-hm-coastguard.html#!/2014/01/a-short-history-of-hm-coastguard.html.
[12] Deregulation Act 2015, s 108.

regulatory agency and its staff feel about their statutorily defined purpose. This can, in turn, impact on the way in which the regulatory agency feels able to respond to changing contexts and new risks and the agency should be clear about how and when it can challenge its authorisation.

To enable it to maximise its impact, the regulatory agency should always be clear about the current role and purpose defined for it by government and about the scope of its authorisation. It should equally be clear about the boundaries of its role and any barriers that exist to it acting in specific ways or developing new approaches to delivering its purpose.

The regulatory agency's own vision of its role, purpose and objectives – what it aims to achieve – needs to be clearly articulated within the organisation, to provide certainty for its staff. They should also be communicated externally, to the regulated community, partners and other stakeholders. This transparency of role and purpose provides clarity and acts as a basis for confidence in the regulatory agency. Chapter twelve highlights the importance of this clarity of role and purpose for Victoria's Environment Protection Authority, as it set about a cultural transformation programme that aimed to address a loss of confidence in the regulatory agency. By agreeing and communicating a simple statement or purpose – 'we are an effective environmental regulator and an influential authority on environment impacts' – the agency was able to signal the importance that it placed on both its enforcement role and its role as a credible scientific voice in creating solutions to environmental issues.

B. Structures

Some aspects of the structure of the regulatory agency – its overall size and shape, its position within government and its distance from it, the role of non-executives and often the composition and shape of the senior executive team – are normally determined externally to the agency. Government will have made the decisions that determine the organisation's nature – whether as a ministerial department with a regulatory function or as an independent agency. In the case of an independent agency, policy-makers will also have addressed the question of leadership, whether by a Board, an individual, or in some other way. Similarly, the formal relationships within which sponsorship accountability occurs (see chapter seven) will have been determined by government and will often be defined through reporting requirements, budget allocation processes, etc.

However, structures are never wholly externally determined. Within an established framework, the regulatory agency's internal structures and its inward-facing policies, procedures and decision-making processes, which play a significant part in the way in which the agency operates and makes decisions, will be set internally. For example, when we look at the importance of establishing a 'risk appetite' for discretion, discussed in chapter ten, the role of setting an appropriate hierarchy, and ensuring the competency of those within it, will be seen to be vital in ensuring that the chosen approach can be delivered.

Whether set externally or internally to the agency, ensuring that these arrangements are carefully established and maintained is important. Decisions should be made with reference to existing domestic and international good practice and guidance, for example good practice in relation to the governance arrangements for independent regulatory agencies is explored in the OECD's 2014 guidance,[13] which sets out principles for decision-making and governing body structure. The agency's sponsor (normally but not always government) must establish the agency carefully and ensure that its appropriateness is maintained as the context, in the sector and across the economy, changes. At the same time, the agency has a responsibility to take actions within its remit and to flag necessary action for others. In chapter four, Srikanth Mangalam explores both of these responsibilities, within the particular governance arrangements that have been developed for delegated administrative authorities in Ontario.

The development of good practice in governance structures for regulatory agencies starts with the significant body of work on corporate governance set out above.[14] Its adaptation for regulatory agencies must recognise the particularities of being a regulator. So, for example, if a representative approach is taken to selection of non-executives, care will be required to ensure separation of regulatory decisions (such as licence approval or sanctioning). If independence and separation from government is selected, then structures will need to be sufficiently robust not only for operational and strategic decision-making but also to articulate the need for sustainability through funding review cycles.

C. Landscape

In contrast to its role in determining the purpose and structures of regulatory agencies, government may play a less explicit or intentional role in determining the regulatory landscape or environment. Its decisions on the establishment of new regulatory agencies or the allocation of regulatory responsibilities to existing agencies determine the landscape but they are usually made sequentially over time, often in response to events, rather than proactively or strategically. The resultant landscape seldom looks 'designed', can be complex and is likely to involve individual regulated entities interacting with multiple regulatory agencies. Chapter twenty-six provides an overview of the landscape in the Philippines which demonstrates this complexity for regulatory delivery generally and specifically for food law enforcement and the impact of complexity on all three outcomes – reducing protections, inhibiting prosperity and affecting efficiency.

Inspection reformers in many countries have, in recent years, addressed themselves to the question of complex regulatory landscapes and three possible responses tend to emerge.

The first is to explore whether the regulatory system can be simplified and improved by reconfiguring its structures, for example through consolidation of agencies. The consolidation of multiple regulatory agencies into a smaller number of agencies has been well explored.[15] At the extreme this can be into one regulatory agency, although consolidation around broad themes is more common – the OECD Best Practice Principles for Regulatory Enforcement and Inspections identify ten themes[16] and the UK's Hampton Review made

---

[13] 'The Governance of Regulators', OECD Best Practice Principles for Regulatory Policy (OECD, 2014).

[14] See also 'The UK Corporate Governance Code' (n 8).

[15] 'How to Reform Business Inspections. Design, Implementation, Challenges' (Investment Climate Advisory Service, World Bank Group, 2011).

[16] Food safety; Non-food products safety and consumer protection; Technical and infrastructure/construction safety; Public health, medicines and health care; Occupational safety and health; Environmental

radical proposals to reduce 31 national regulators to seven thematic bodies.[17] In practice consolidation has not been widely or thoroughly implemented. The 'single inspectorate' model is not common. Despite dramatic innovations, most notably the experience of Mongolia in establishing a single consolidated agency with a broad regulatory remit (described in chapter twenty-five), it is seen as radical and introducing internal challenges of organisation and culture. Less dramatic consolidations are still perceived as bureaucratic and cumbersome, subject to reversal for political reasons and sometimes obstructed by the personal agendas of entrenched leaders.

The second possible response to complexity is to establish a 'lead agency' model – in which one regulatory agency takes some or all responsibility in relation to a particular sector or particular regulated entities, coordinating the interactions of other regulatory agencies. These are solutions that appeal to regulated entities and are frequently recommended in the reviews, including those assessing Hampton implementation in the UK,[18] but tend to be less appealing to regulators who see their power base, their freedom to act and their direct contact with regulated entities being eroded. In practice, lead agency arrangements are seen as difficult to implement and legal, cultural and practical reasons (including IT) may be cited. Where arrangements are sustained, they tend to have a specific legal mandate to overcome these challenges (see, for example, the case study on Primary Authority in chapter nine and the legal mandate given to the Peruvian environmental regulator to coordinate the planning activities of national and local regulators).

The third option, which involves building a model in which regulatory agencies have a high degree of collaboration, is seen as simpler, more realistic and flexible and therefore more achievable. Examples (including the Netherlands' Inspection Council, introduced by Rob Velders in chapter eleven) have shown considerable impact but their sustainability can be dependent on individual leadership and cooperative cultures. Solutions to provide longevity beyond the span of the initial leaders seem to focus on generating a degree of formality through the development of Terms of Reference and Memoranda of Understanding, as seen in some examples from the UK.[19] Going a step further, the Food Safety Regulation Coordinating Board, established in the Philippines and discussed in chapter twenty-six, is statutorily established with a mandate to coordinate.

These and other examples portray complex regulatory landscapes in which regulated entities – even the very smallest businesses – are likely to fall within the scope of multiple regulatory agencies. Sometimes these agencies are concerned with regulations that are unconnected, perhaps relating to different aspects of the business or different areas of its operations. All too often, they are concerned with regulations that impact on the same areas of operation of the regulated entity and, as a consequence, the regulated entity can experience multiple, uncoordinated inspections or other regulatory interactions. For example,

---

protection; State revenue; Transportation safety; Banking, insurance and financial services supervision; Nuclear safety. 'Regulatory Enforcement and Inspections', OECD Best Practice Principles for Regulatory Policy (OECD, 2014).

[17] Philip Hampton, *Reducing Administrative Burdens: Effective Inspection and Enforcement* (HM Treasury, 2005).

[18] 'Regulatory Quality: How Regulators are Implementing the Hampton Vision' (National Audit Office, 2008).

[19] See eg Terms of Reference for the Market Surveillance Co-ordination Committee at Annex C of 'The General National Market Surveillance Programme for the United Kingdom December 2012–2013' (Department for Business, Innovation and Skills, 2011); 'MoU between CQC, Health and Safety Executive and Local Authorities in England' (2017); 'MoU between the Office for Nuclear Regulation and the Environment Agency on Matters of Mutual Interest in England' (2015).

in the UK, a small catering business may be regulated by different officers in relation to food safety, occupational health and safety, fire safety, consumer protection measures, etc. This multiplicity is of concern not only because it gives rise to the possibility of inconsistency and increased administrative burdens for the regulated entity, but also because it generates inefficiencies for the state and has the potential to damage protections. Inadvertently or with more malicious intent, a regulated entity that experiences interventions from two or more regulatory agencies can delay or obfuscate its response or even play one agency off against the other by exploiting differences or perceived conflicts in their regulations.

In this context, it is critical that each regulatory agency has a clear understanding of the regulatory landscape within which it operates and its relationship to other public bodies, whether regulatory or otherwise, that are operating in the same sphere and whose activities overlap or impact on its own. The regulatory agency's understanding of its own role and responsibilities is shaped, to a greater or lesser degree, by its understanding of the role of these other bodies and the position and nature of the boundaries between them.

The Local Better Regulation Office, when it was first established (see Annex 1), recognised the complexities of the UK regulatory landscape for local authorities and the regulated community and commissioned work to map this landscape. This work, which was updated in 2009,[20] identified that 433 local authorities, 58 fire and rescue authorities and 152 port health authorities were delivering regulation at that time under nearly 200 pieces of legislation, for which policy responsibility was held by a dozen central government departments. In doing so, local regulators were interacting with, and often taking direction from, eight national regulatory agencies. The report noted that 'the sheer number of bodies in this landscape creates complexity and a multitude of interactions'.

The use of a mapping tool can assist a regulatory agency and its staff to move to a better collective understanding of their regulatory landscape, providing them with greater clarity around their role, where they sit, and who they need to work with. Mapping exercises have been used to great effect as part of the Regulatory Delivery Model, as a first step towards simplification, helping organisations to identify where there are gaps in their knowledge or understanding that require further clarification.

A good understanding of the landscape, the regulatory agency's own role and responsibilities, and those of complementary regulatory agencies is a precursor to the necessary step of dedicating resources to working well within the landscape. This involves establishing the right coordination mechanisms to work well with partner organisations, including other regulatory agencies, so that duplication of effort is minimised or eliminated and gaps in the regulatory landscape are filled. As mentioned above and elaborated in chapters eleven and twenty-six, the Inspection Council established in the Netherlands and the Philippine Food Safety Regulation Coordinating Board offer examples of mechanisms for cooperation and for the coordination of activities by different regulatory agencies.

Bilateral and multilateral partnership working can be beneficial for the regulatory agencies involved, in terms of reducing duplication of effort, improving targeting of their resources and addressing inconsistency. However, it can also deliver significant benefits for those that they regulate – reducing the administrative burdens associated with being regulated. By improving targeting, for example, through sharing data, and identifying and

---

[20] 'Mapping the Local Authority Regulatory Services Landscape' (Local Better Regulation Office, 2009).

addressing regulatory gaps, partnerships can also better tackle regulatory risks, thereby delivering benefits for those that the law is intended to protect. Chapter nine explains how the UK has established a statutory framework to address some of the challenges associated with delivering national regulation through multiple local authorities by implementing a 'lead agency' approach, referred to as 'Primary Authority'. In doing so, it has improved the effectiveness of the regulatory system.

D. Powers and Responsibilities

Where the powers and responsibilities of a regulatory agency are appropriate to its role and purpose, the right conditions are created for effective delivery. Where these powers and responsibilities are also clear and well-communicated, this reduces opportunities for malpractice or corruption and gives confidence to beneficiaries and to the regulated community by acting as an enabler for effective accountability mechanisms.

Clarity of powers and responsibilities also raises the confidence of the regulatory agency and its officers. Where officers are equipped with a good understanding of the boundaries of their powers and responsibilities, they are better able to properly exercise professional discretion within these boundaries, making informed, proportionate and consistent decisions. They are protected from allegations of over-zealous enforcement or, conversely, from the criticism that they have failed to 'act tough' and are reassured that their decisions will be respected as fair and legal.

In addition, clarity of powers and responsibilities means that the regulated community can understand what to expect of the regulatory agency and can recognise and challenge deviations from the expected behaviour. For example, full transparency of officer powers enables regulated entities to identify and challenge any overstepping of those powers. The importance of mechanisms to effectively enable challenge is explored in detail when we examine Accountability, the second prerequisite in the Regulatory Delivery Model, in chapter seven, but challenge is only possible if there is a clear statement of the standards that can be expected. For example, in the UK, section 2 of the Regulators' Code,[21] an extract of which is included in Box 3.1, requires all regulatory agencies to make mechanisms available for complaints, appeals and feedback (see chapter five for further information on the Regulators' Code).

Box 3.1 Extract from section 2 of the Regulators' Code

2.3 Regulators should provide an impartial and clearly explained route to appeal against a regulatory decision or a failure to act in accordance with this Code. Individual officers of the regulator who took the decision or action against which the appeal is being made should not be involved in considering the appeal. This route to appeal should be publicised to those who are regulated.

---

[21] 'Regulators' Code' (Better Regulation Delivery Office, 2014).

2.4 Regulators should provide a timely explanation in writing of any right to representation or right to appeal. This explanation should be in plain language and include practical information on the process involved.

2.5 Regulators should make available to those they regulate, clearly explained complaints procedures, allowing them to easily make a complaint about the conduct of the regulator.

2.6 Regulators should have a range of mechanisms to enable and regularly invite, receive and take on board customer feedback, including, for example, through customer satisfaction surveys of those they regulate

Both the legislative framework and the environment in which the regulatory agency operates will influence its internal governance arrangements – the inward-facing policies, procedures and decision-making processes that determine responsibilities and standards of behaviour. These need to be clear and well communicated to all staff and the regulatory agency should ensure that their operation is monitored through effective oversight arrangements.

The regulatory agency's defining legislation – for example, the statute that establishes the body or that tasks an existing body with a new regulatory role – will often set out specific powers and associated responsibilities. An example is given in Box 3.2 of some of the specific powers afforded to UK officers in relation to consumer protection regulation, and the responsibilities that are associated with the use of these powers. However, powers and responsibilities may also be established by generic rules – in laws or codes that govern the behaviour of all public bodies, or that apply specifically to regulatory agencies. Similarly, the regulatory agency's use of its powers will usually be constrained by provisions in the legislation it enforces but may also be constrained by generic rules, setting boundaries for the regulatory agency and its officers.[22]

Similar considerations apply to the existence and applicability of sanctioning powers. Whether those powers, the processes followed by the regulatory agency and the courts and the range of sanctions available are set out in the statutes founding the agency or in more general legislation, it is important that they are proportionate and that they are accessible. In many jurisdictions each regulatory agency will be just one user of a common set of powers, sanctions and procedures. Courts will be independent, and sanctions will be decided by them. In some contexts, all sanctioning decisions are separated from the enforcer, even if still within the regulatory agency. However, increasing use of civil sanctions, restorative justice and penalty notices are, if not blurring that distinction, at least broadening the range of options. Provided transparency is maintained and governance is firmly matched by accountability, this need not be a problem and can be an additional opportunity in the regulatory agency's toolkit. Like many recent developments, it is how it is understood, utilised, communicated and challenged that determines its value.

---

[22] UK examples include the Police and Criminal Evidence Act 1984 and the Regulation of Investigatory Powers Act 2000.

In the UK, the Macrory report[23] set an ambitious target for a wider use of civil sanctions within an accountability framework which has probably still not been fully realised after 13 years.

Box 3.2 Summary of enforcement powers, Consumer Rights Act 2015

Powers

- to require the production of information specified in a notice, for the purpose of ascertaining whether there has been a breach;
- to purchase products;
- to observe carrying on of business;
- to enter premises without a warrant or, in certain circumstances, with a warrant;
- to inspect products;
- to take copies of records or evidence;
- to test equipment;
- to require the production of documents;
- to seize and detain goods;
- to decommission or switch off fixed installations;
- to break open containers or access electronic devices;
- to require assistance from persons on premises.

Associated responsibilities

- to give notice of the testing of goods;
- to pay compensation, in certain circumstances, in respect of loss or damage caused by the seizure or detention of goods.

Associated rights of regulated entities

- to access seized goods and documents;
- to appeal against detention of goods and documents.

The design of the legislative framework within which regulatory agencies operate can be used to embed desired values and regulatory behaviours and can equally be used to control or prohibit unacceptable practices.

Many examples exist of rule sets being developed to require or authorise desired regulatory behaviour. These include the code-based approaches used by the UK, Australia,[24] Liberia,[25] Ontario[26] (see Table 10.1 in chapter ten), and others. Chapter five explores how

---

[23] Richard Macrory, 'Regulatory Justice: Making Sanctions Effective' (Cabinet Office, 2006).
[24] See www.cuttingredtape.gov.au/sites/default/files/documents/regulator_performance_framework.pdf.
[25] See www.moci.gov.lr/doc/MoCI.General.Inspection.Guide.021315.pdf.
[26] 'Regulator's Code of Practice: Integrity in Pursuit of Compliance' (Government of Ontario, 2011).

the UK Government has sought, through a code-based approach, to establish rules on practices and approaches that cut across regulatory agencies. It provides an insight into the UK's experience of influencing the behaviour of regulatory agencies by establishing a framework of principles that regulatory agencies are required to internalise by incorporating them into their own processes; training their staff in relation to the principles and their application; and being transparent to stakeholders about their approach to meeting the principles.

Where the legal framework, in custom or practice, demands a statutory basis for reform of regulatory practices, several countries have gone down the route of developing 'inspection laws', often with the support of the World Bank Group, which advocates this approach[27] in a report on its experience of business inspection reform projects:

> Reforming the framework for inspections is necessary whenever a lack of clarity in the rules governing the planning, execution and follow-up of inspections leaves excessive power and discretion in the hands of individual inspectors. Experience suggests that successful inspections reform almost always involves a substantial element of framework reform, and that framework reform is an effective way to achieve some rapid improvements, to root out the most obvious abuses, and to lay the foundation for sustainable reform.

The report notes examples of inspection reform laws from several countries, over a 20-year period, including:

* Mexico – Federal Administrative Procedure law, 1995
* Georgia – On Control of Entrepreneurial Activity law, 2001
* Tajikistan – On Inspection of Economic Activity of Business Entities law, 2006
* Ukraine – On State Control over Business Activity law, 2007

Further examples are explored in this book in chapter six, which describes the Lithuanian experience, and chapter twenty-five, reporting on the reform journey in Mongolia.

IV. Key Lines of Enquiry

As discussed in chapter two, we have developed key lines of enquiry in respect of each element of the Regulatory Delivery Model that can be used to assess and understand the current picture in respect of that element. These questions, presented in Box 3.3, in respect of Governance Frameworks, are intended as a starting point upon which a regulatory agency or a third party can build in order to give a sense of where strengths and weaknesses lie and to highlight potential for improvement.

Box 3.3 Key lines of enquiry: governance frameworks

Purpose

* Has the government been clear about the purpose of the regulatory requirements and of the regulatory agency?

---

[27] World Bank Group (2011).

- Is the purpose sufficiently well understood and agreed to give the agency an adequate authorising environment?
- Does the agency clearly communicate its role, purpose and objectives, both internally and externally?
- Is the agency clear about the strength and scope of its authorisation and when and how it can be challenged?

Structures

- Is the shape of the regulatory agency, its decision-making capability and its relationship to government appropriate for its purpose?
- As purpose changes, has the design been realigned to changing purposes (whether articulated or not)?
- Are the agency's internal structures and policies, procedures and decision-making processes appropriate? Do they reflect domestic and international good practice?

Landscape

- Does the regulatory agency have a clear understanding of the position of other regulatory agencies in the regulatory system – both horizontal (peer regulators) and vertical (international/network, national, regional and municipal regulators)?
- Are responsibilities clear and not overlapping? Is simplification possible?
- Does the agency have appropriate arrangements to work collaboratively with other regulatory agencies?
- Does the agency have a clear understanding of the other significant bodies in the regulatory system, governmental, stakeholders (regulated and beneficiaries) and how they interact?
- Is the agency's understanding of the landscape mapped in a way that is useful to the agency and others?

Powers and responsibilities

- Does the regulatory agency have powers appropriate to its role and purpose?
- Are those powers established in law in accordance with local requirements and systems?
- Are those powers, and any responsibilities that accompany their use, clearly communicated and understood?
- Does the agency have clear and effective internal rules determining use of its powers, and is their operation monitored through appropriate oversight arrangements?

V. Summary

This chapter has set out why governance is at the heart of good regulatory delivery and therefore central to the Regulatory Delivery Model. We have explored what we mean when we talk about governance frameworks in connection with regulatory agencies – thinking about their purpose; their structures; their relationships in the regulatory landscape; and their powers and responsibilities. We have also considered some of the interactions between governance and other elements of the Regulatory Delivery Model, which we will explore in more detail in later chapters.

The next three chapters illustrate various aspects of the themes that we have touched on in this chapter although the experience of the authors, and therefore our learning from them, goes well beyond solely questions of governance.

In chapter four, Srikanth Mangalam explains a particular approach to governance in the delegated Administrative Authority model, which deliberately extends independence from government to maximise stakeholder engagement. In chapter five, Helen Kirkman and Paul Sanderson report on the UK's use of a code-based approach to changing regulatory agency behaviour. In chapter six, Giedrius Kadziauskas, describes the Lithuanian experience of reforming the regulatory framework to deliver improvements in accountability.

4

The Delegated Administrative Authority Model, a Radical Alternative Governance Framework from Ontario, Canada

SRIKANTH MANGALAM

I. Background

Canada's Constitution Act (1867) divides the responsibilities of the Government into federal and provincial/territorial jurisdictions. It also allows provincial governments to delegate some responsibilities to one or more municipal government(s). The Federal Government has responsibilities such as defence, criminal law, trade regulation, taxation and banking, transportation and citizenship.

Provincial and territorial governments in Canada (currently numbering 10 and three respectively) typically have responsibilities including family law, health law, labour standards, environment and natural resources, education, consumer protection, public safety, social services and housing. There are several instances of shared responsibility between the provincial and federal governments. Municipal governments are given their authority by the provincial government and are typically responsible for property taxes, property standards, public health, fire and emergency services, zoning, business licences, and local by-laws.

There are over 700 pieces of consolidated law with several thousand corresponding regulations in Ontario province, covering many of the above-mentioned responsibilities and administered by governmental and non-governmental authorities and agencies. Over the years, governments of Ontario have attempted to cut unnecessary red tape, reduce burdens on businesses and create efficient and effective regulatory systems and continue to try new and innovative approaches as envisioned in the recently promulgated Burden Reduction Act of 2017.[1]

One of the earliest introductions of burden reduction initiatives happened in 1995. The Progressive Conservative Party of Ontario under the leadership of Mike Harris formed the provincial government with a campaign platform that was entitled The Common-Sense Revolution.[2] Key points within this platform included: (a) spending cuts, including

---

[1] Burden Reduction Act SO 2017, c 2 – Bill 27.
[2] 'Ontario's Environment and the 'Common Sense Revolution': A First Year Report' (Canadian Institute for Environmental Law and Policy, 1996).

a civil service freeze, to reduce the deficit; (b) a review of privatising government assets; (c) abolishing the Employer Health Tax; (d) 'workfare', requiring welfare recipients to work for their benefits; and (e) a 30 per cent income tax cut.[3]

One of the outcomes of the privatisation of government assets involved the creation of an alternate service delivery model called the administrative authority. Existing agencies and government departments primarily focused on consumer protection and public safety were 'moved' out of government into these administrative authorities with three primary objectives: (a) reduce red tape and burdens on businesses; (b) improve efficiency and effectiveness in the operations of regulatory agencies; and (c) enhance public safety and consumer protection.

Based on the model of the Ontario New Home Warranty Programme, which was established in 1976,[4] and similar alternate service delivery models in Alberta and in other jurisdictions including the United Kingdom and New Zealand, Ontario established its first administrative authority in 1996 through the Safety and Consumer Statutes Administration Act. The administrative authorities were established with an intent to create a viable alternative approach to administration of public policies and regulations through the creation of private, not-for-profit corporations wherein services are provided on a cost recoverable, fee-for-service basis. There are 14 such administrative authorities currently operating in Ontario, most of which involved moving government departments and agencies. The more recent administrative authorities were primarily created to either address existing gaps in the regulatory system or consolidate multiple portfolios lying within or outside government. Similar models are also being developed and implemented in other provinces of Canada including British Columbia, Manitoba and Saskatchewan. The public sector governance continuum is illustrated in Figure 4.1.

Figure 4.1 Public sector governance continuum in Canada[5]

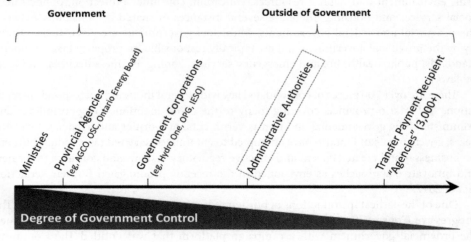

[3] 'A Common Sense Look at the 'Common Sense Revolution', Ontario Libertarian Party Newsletter 17(3), Winter 1995, available at www.libertarian.on.ca/bulletin/v17n3a.htm.

[4] Elaine Todres and Associates for the Minister of Small Business and Consumer Services, 'Delegated Administrative Authority Model Review' (2009).

[5] 'Designed to Deliver' (Ontario Treasury Board Secretariat, 2009).

When Ontario delegated the administration of several statutes to delegated administrative authorities in 1997, it was achieved through the Consumer Statutes Administration Act. The Ontario administrative authorities are now responsible for the day-to-day administration of provincial licensing and regulatory regimes as set out in Table 4.1.

Table 4.1 Ontario administrative authorities and their responsibilities

Name of organisation	Mandate
Ontario Motor Vehicle Industry Council	Motor vehicle dealers and salespersons
Real Estate Council of Ontario	Real estate brokerages, salespersons and brokers
Travel Industry Council of Ontario	Travel retailers and wholesalers
Technical Standards and Safety Authority	Technical standards and safety of technical systems, devices, equipment, products and related professions
Electrical Safety Authority	Master electricians, electrical contractors and electrical safety standards
Vintners Quality Alliance Ontario	Integrity of Ontario wine appellations and enforcement of winemaking and labelling standards
Bereavement Authority of Ontario	Funeral homes
Condominium Authority of Ontario	Advice and protection of condominium-owners
Tarion	Home warranty protection
Condominium Management Regulatory Authority of Ontario	Oversight of condominium managers and management firms
Ontario Film Authority	Licensing of film distributors, retailers and exhibitors and oversight of film classification activities
Resource Productivity and Recovery Authority	Producers of products generating waste that can be recovered, recycled or reused
Ontario One Call	Contact centre for coordinating and managing excavation requests across services
Retirement Homes Regulatory Authority	Oversight of retirement homes

II. Model Governance and Accountability

The administrative authorities have been established as not-for-profit corporate structures that derive their authority from government through administrative agreements.[6] Under this model, the Ministry responsible for the administrative authority retains overall responsibility for setting and controlling the governing legislation and regulations, providing governance oversight of the administrative authorities with respect to the legislation, and ensuring that they are accountable to the public on their performance and effectiveness.

---

[6] 'Administrative Authority Model and Governance: Presentation to UK Delegation' (Ontario Ministry of Government and Consumer Services, 2017), available from author.

While the Government is responsible for designing, making and monitoring the legislation and regulation, the administrative authority is delegated the responsibility to administer legislation in accordance with the law and an administrative agreement with the Government. The governance of the administrative authorities is illustrated in Figure 4.2.

Figure 4.2 Governance of administrative authorities in Ontario

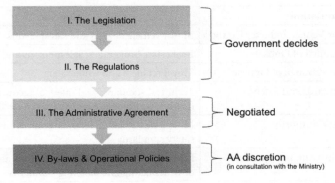

The administrative agreements set out the details of the relationship between an administrative authority and the ministry, including: planning and performance monitoring (eg business plan, annual report, performance scorecards); sharing of information with government; and governance requirements (eg minister's approval of board composition). The by-laws and operational policies typically vary across the administrative authorities but may include further clarification on roles of the board, committees, chief executive/executive director, registrar and other staff.

The administrative authorities are identified as the operational arm of the ministry with the responsibility for administering their legislative mandates along with the fiduciary responsibilities, financial health and the day-to-day delivery of regulatory services. In order to achieve this, the minister responsible for the administrative authority has a number of formal and informal tools that include appointment of directors to administrative authority boards; requirement of annual reports, business plans and audited financial statements; the right to order a number of operational, legislative and regulatory reviews; and, control over legislation and regulations. The accountability framework is shown in Figure 4.3.

The ministry takes the lead in developing and recommending legislative and regulatory changes in consultation with the administrative authorities. The ministry negotiates and establishes the terms of delegation, roles and responsibilities of the ministry and the administrative authority (eg the fee-setting process) in an administrative agreement. The ministry provides oversight and ensures administrative authorities are carrying out their delegated duties which includes monitoring performance to ensure public interest is protected (eg by reviewing annual reports).

While the administrative authorities are responsible for electing a majority of board members and the board's chair, the minister may choose to appoint a minority of members to the board of directors of the administrative authorities. The administrative authority appoints persons to carry out statutory functions under the delegated legislation (eg registrar, inspectors and statutory directors).

Figure 4.3 Accountability framework of administrative authorities in Ontario[7]

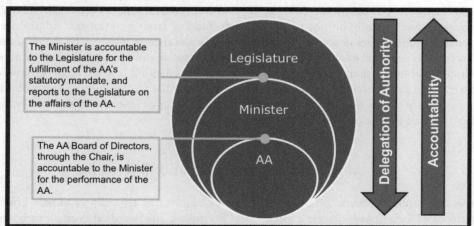

The Minister is accountable to the Legislature for the fulfillment of the AA's statutory mandate, and reports to the Legislature on the affairs of the AA.

The AA Board of Directors, through the Chair, is accountable to the Minister for the performance of the AA.

III. Model Description

The administrative authorities themselves are set up as private, not-for-profit corporations managed by an independent board of directors. The administrative authorities are positioned at arm's length and not considered as agencies of the province. Despite being designated by legislation they are self-financed and operate independently.

The administrative authorities are responsible for the day-to-day administration of the designated legislation and the regulatory functions of the administrative authority typically include those shown in Figure 4.4. In addition, some administrative authorities also have the authority to adjudicate disputes.

Figure 4.4 Regulatory responsibilities of administrative authorities in Ontario[8]

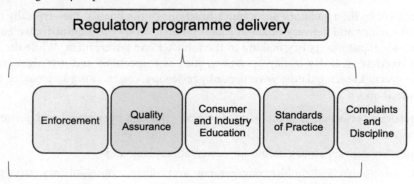

Regulatory programme delivery

Enforcement | Quality Assurance | Consumer and Industry Education | Standards of Practice | Complaints and Discipline

---

[7] ibid.
[8] ibid.

The administrative authority is responsible for managing its financial and operational affairs. Administrative authorities are financed by fees from industry members or for services rendered, and typically do not receive ongoing funding from government. Administrative authorities set fees in accordance with processes and criteria approved by the minister. Oversight is provided by the ministry, who conduct reviews and may comment on administrative authorities financials. The administrative authorities are considered to be outside government public accounts (not a 'controlled entity'). While most administrative authorities currently cannot be audited directly by Ontario's Auditor-General, that model is being modified and legislation is being put in place to change it.

IV. Model Implementation and Operation

The independent boards of the administrative authorities typically represent cross-sections of society with diverse expertise and portfolios. The boards also establish board committees, which are typically structured based on their responsibilities and oversight functions.

The boards of the administrative authorities have two oversight functions: corporate governance; and regulatory governance.[9]

The corporate governance of each board is focused on their fiduciary responsibilities including:

- review and adoption of strategic and business plans;
- enterprise risk management;
- financial management including major infrastructure investments;
- succession planning and appointments of the chief executive or head of the administrative authority;
- oversight of stakeholder management and communications; and
- management of internal controls and management information systems.

With respect to the regulatory governance functions of the boards, they typically oversee the performance and delivery of key regulatory functions by the administrative authority and provide input into policy making to the minister and government. While the boards cannot interfere with day-to-day operations such as inspections and investigations, they provide oversight on regulatory governance by reviewing, commenting and making recommendations on:

- regulatory performance demonstrated typically through operational and performance reports;
- regulatory delivery strategies and implementation plans; and
- consumer/public/stakeholder engagement and other non-regulatory strategies to manage risk to public interest determined by the administrative authorities' mandates.

---

[9] Todres et al, 'Delegated Administrative Authority Model Review' (2009).

The administrative authorities themselves are structured differently from each other, generally reflecting the nature of the businesses and sectors being regulated and styles of the different boards. In most instances, the statutory regulatory powers within the administrative authorities are also situated differently. For example, in some cases the chief executive of the organisation may also be the registrar with statutory powers, whereas in other cases those designated in legislation with the authority to administer regulations may report into the senior leadership and/or the chief executive who may not possess any statutory powers.

Administrative authorities typically interact with and receive feedback and advice from external stakeholders and the public/consumers through stakeholder advisory councils. Council members representing a cross-section of the regulated businesses, impacted customers, consumers and the public provide inputs into:

- fee-setting;
- policy-making;
- regulatory delivery methods;
- strategic and business plans; and
- challenges and opportunities in stakeholder engagement including compliance and enforcement.

Due to the flexibility provided, particularly from the fee structure and being considered independent of government public accounts, the administrative authorities are able to invest smartly in resources and infrastructure for the purposes of delivering their mandates. Most of the administrative authorities are able to use advanced risk-based approaches to guide their inspection and enforcement efforts ranging from allocation of internal resources, making decisions on fees including licensing fees, administering non-compliance penalties and enforcement activities.[10] Availability of funding also assists the administrative authorities in undertaking several activities that are not traditionally seen as enforcement, such as consumer-awareness campaigns, training and education programmes for regulated stakeholders, public education and internal staff training.[11]

Apart from meeting oversight expectations such as those listed in administrative agreements and by-laws, many administrative authorities have established fairly advanced and innovative performance reporting frameworks that are based on strong evidence and analytics, and are outcome-focused. Most of these performance reports are available for public consumption and provide significant information on trends in the regulated sectors, performance of the regulators and the regulated parties, and strategic direction taken by the administrative authorities.[12,13] Some administrative authorities also provide very specific details of performance and non-compliances of the regulated stakeholders through the use of public registers providing consumers with a clear idea of the

---

[10] ibid.

[11] ibid.

[12] 'Reports and Policies' (Toronto, Technical Standards and Safety Authority, no date), available at www.tssa.org/en/about-tssa/reports-and-policies.aspx.

[13] 'Corporate Reports' (Electrical Safety Authority, no date), available at www.esasafe.com/about-esa/reports-and-stats.

performance of individual stakeholders.[14] These reports are in addition to mandatory ones including financial statements, strategic and business plans, ministers' scorecards, and corporate annual reports.

V. Administrative Authority Reviews

Several external reviews of the administrative authorities and their performance have taken place over the past 20 or more years since their inception. These have included broad reviews across all administrative authorities,[15] some of which have been scathing, others have been supportive and highly encouraging. The report of the Commission on the Reform of Ontario's Public Services from 2012[16] recommended that the Ontario Government should be setting up several more administrative authorities as they had been found to reduce costs to taxpayers, improve regulatory outcomes and efficiency, retain government oversight and increase industry engagement.

In addition, reviews of specific administrative authorities have also taken place as a result of major events such as catastrophic incidents or corporate failures.[17] These reviews have led to recommendations, some of which have brought significant changes to legislation governing those administrative authorities and have resulted in structural changes to governance, accountability and operations. In addition, there have been audits of the ministries responsible for the oversight of the administrative authorities conducted by the Auditor-General of Ontario.[18] These audits have also resulted in findings that have led to changes and improvements being made to the functioning of the administrative authorities, including investments in areas such as information infrastructure and governance.

Despite several such reviews, none of these studies have necessarily yielded any findings or assessments objectively and quantitatively demonstrating the true impact of the administrative authorities on the very purpose of their creation, ie, increased efficiencies, reduced burden on businesses and improved public interest outcomes. This does not necessarily mean that they haven't performed effectively, but perhaps indicates a need for a comprehensive scientific review of the performance of the model.

VI. Model Assessment and Conclusions

As the previous section suggests, the lack of a formal academic assessment of the administrative authorities and the model itself prevents the author from providing an objective

---

[14] 'Public Register' (Retirement Homes Regulatory Authority, no date), available at www.rhra.ca/en/search-the-public-register.

[15] See, eg: Todres et al (n 4); Don Drummond, 'Public Service for Ontarians: A Path to Sustainability and Excellence' (Commission on Reform of Ontario's Public Service, 2012); M Lio and S Bulhoes, 'Improving the Effectiveness of Consumer & Public Representatives On Delegated Administrative Authorities' (Consumers Council of Canada. 2006); 'Ontario's Environment and the 'Common Sense Revolution': A First Year Report' (Canadian Institute for Environmental Law and Policy, 1996), available at www.cielap.org/cat_other.php.

[16] Drummond, 'Public Service for Ontarians' (ibid).

[17] Douglas Cunningham, 'Final Report: Review of the Ontario New Home Warranties Plan Act and the Tarion Warranty Corporation' (Consumer Protection Ontario, 2015), Michael Birk and Susanna Katz, 'Report of the Propane Safety Review' (Ministry of Consumer Services, 2008).

[18] 'Annual Report of the Auditor General of Ontario' (Office of the Auditor General of Ontario, 2009).

representation of the benefits and limitations of the model. However, a combination of evidentiary sources and deductive reasoning of aspects such as governance and operating structures can lead to identification of potential advantages and disadvantages of the model. For example, the findings of the Propane Review[19] and the response from the Government through the amendments to the Technical Standards and Safety Act suggest that there are gaps and limitations in regulatory governance and oversight. The most effective way to address these gaps either through legislation or other alternative means have not been assessed.

The clear separation between policy-making and regulatory delivery provides the platform for independence in decision-making which is seen as an important criterion for regulatory best practices.[20] An inherent desire on the part of several of the administrative authorities to avoid creating perceptions of conflict of interest with regulated businesses who provide their revenue drives several innovative initiatives. However, the ability to address this perception in a transparent manner is reliant on good evidence and appropriate measurement methods. Similarly, conflicts between the financial sustainability of the administrative authorities and addressing the expectations in the mandate have led to perceived questioning of the model.

The flexibility of the operating model, particularly due to the independent fee structure, provides great opportunities for innovation and smart decision-making. There are several examples of innovative practices and methods originating from the administrative authorities that have been cited in literature and have attracted the attention of other agencies and jurisdictions globally.[21] These innovative approaches have helped the administrative authorities use science and evidence to characterise the behaviours and performance of their regulated sectors and make informed decisions on regulatory delivery. In addition to publications, many of these administrative authorities undertake peer reviews to identify opportunities for improvement, invest in new and smart methods for data collection[22] and influencing behaviour change.[23] Mandate boundaries may prevent governments from acting. The delegated administrative authority model has allowed some of the administrative authorities to look beyond administering a regulatory mandate, but focusing on actual outcomes, reduction in harm, for example.[24]

As regulators and policy-makers become exposed to more external challenges including the emergence of disruptive technologies, global trade agreements and pressures to create competitive business environments, they are starting to examine alternate models that provide them with flexibility in capacity-building and delivery. Third-party models such

---

[19] Michael Birk and Susanna Katz, 'Report of the Propane Safety Review' (Ministry of Consumer Services, 2008).

[20] 'The Governance of Regulators', OECD Best Practice Principles for Regulatory Policy (OECD, 2014).

[21] See, eg: Srikanth Mangalam, 'United States of America Patent No US 8,463,635 (United States Patent and Trademark Office, 2013); Arun Veeramany and Srikanth Mangalam, 'Application of Disability-adjusted Life Years to Predict the Burden of Injuries and Fatalities due to Public Exposure to Engineering Technologies' (2014) 12 *Population Health Metrics*; Supraja Sridharan and Srikanth Mangalam. 'Carbon Monoxide Risks and Implications on Maintenance-intensive Fuel-burning Appliances – A Regulatory Perspective' in *2017 Annual Reliability and Maintainability Symposium* (Institute of Electrical and Electronics Engineers, 2017); Sarah Thorne, Joel Moody and Laurel Austin, 'Using Mental Modelling In Risk Management: Understanding Electrical Occupational Safety Behaviour' (Decision Partners, 2016).

[22] 'Internet of Things: The New Government to Business Platform' (The World Bank, 2017).

[23] Thorne, Moody and Austin, *Using Mental Modelling* (2016).

[24] Public Risk Management Institute, 'Risk Based Regulatory Delivery – Review and Toolkit of Modern Practices, Prepared for Transport Canada and Community of Federal Regulators', available at http://prism.institute/wp-content/uploads/2018/08/Study-on-Modern-Regulatory-Practices-Final-Report.pdf.

as administrative authorities that include instruments such as cost-recovery schemes and powers to establish 'soft' policies, and look beyond traditional compliance and enforcement tools to gain compliance assurance are becoming more attractive options for consideration.[25]

A forthcoming national guideline[26] identifies principles that define acceptable practices of risk informed decision-making by regulators. Some of those principles may be appropriate indicators for an objective assessment of the model and individual administrative authorities. In addition to measuring their effectiveness, the approach would also allow for comparing and benchmarking against government-controlled regulators and other jurisdictions.

---

[25] ibid.
[26] 'Guideline for Managing Risks to the Public Interest in a Regulatory Context: Public Comment Document' (Underwriters Laboratories, expected 2019).

5

Code-based Approaches, the Use of Codes to Change the Behaviour of Regulators in the UK

HELEN KIRKMAN AND PAUL SANDERSON

I. Background

In striving for 'good regulation', regulatory reformers in the UK have, since the early 1990s, focused their attention on regulatory simplification tools, making sure that new regulatory measures are necessary, well-designed and capable of delivering the desired protections, and reviewing existing regulatory measures to the same end. A significant proportion of the regulation that has an impact on UK business has been derived from the implementation of European Union Directives and in 2005 the EU launched its own programme to simplify EU law and reduce administrative burdens on business associated with regulation.[1]

Significant progress has been made in ensuring that regulations are clear and appropriate and that they are well communicated, so that both regulatory agencies and regulated communities have a high level of awareness and understanding of the regulations, and of the outcomes that they are intended to promote. Equally, progress has been made in the measurement of regulatory impact and of simplification programmes.[2]

Whilst regulatory simplification has been welcomed by business in the UK, a growing voice from the business community over the years has advocated the importance of considering, in parallel, the way in which regulations are enforced by the regulatory agencies tasked with their implementation. The UK Government has taken an active approach to inviting business views on their experience of 'being regulated' and how different approaches to delivering regulation affect them. A wealth of information has been gathered

---

[1] 'Implementing the Community Lisbon programme: A Strategy for the Simplification of the Regulatory Environment', Communication of the Commission to the European Parliament, the Council, the European Economic and Social Committee and the Committee of the Regions, 2005.

[2] The UK's Regulatory Policy Committee scrutinises impact assessments for regulatory proposals (see www.gov.uk/government/publications/costs-and-benefits-of-new-regulation-regulatory-policy-committee-opinions-since-may-2015); deregulatory proposals; and regulatory agencies' submissions in respect of the government's Business Impact Target.

on the cross-cutting issues arising from the regulatory practices that most trouble regulated communities.[3] These have included:

- poor communication with individual regulated entities and with regulated communities;
- insufficient understanding, on the part of regulatory agencies, of the sectors and businesses they regulate;
- a failure to provide clear guidance and advice on what the regulatory agency expects;
- regulatory activity that is not proportionate to the potential harm;
- a lack of regulator focus on the most serious risks;
- overly burdensome regulatory processes, such as information requests;
- a lack of consistency, both in relation to a single regulatory agency and across regulatory agencies; and
- inadequate and poorly explained complaints and appeals mechanisms.

Having accepted that changes in the culture and practice of regulatory agencies were desirable, the Government took the view that its intervention was essential in order to effect such change. The UK now has over 20 years' experience of addressing itself to this challenge and different approaches have been developed, over this period, with the aim of influencing the behaviour of regulatory agencies in the UK. Periodic evaluations have assessed the impact of the approaches taken.

The UK approach has been rooted in the concept of establishing a rule set for regulatory agencies that expresses a common view of what good regulatory delivery looks like. The intention is that this should provide clarity for all regulatory agencies as to government's expectations, thereby driving changes in regulator behaviour, supporting improvement and raising the practices of all regulatory agencies above a minimum standard. The use of rules to establish a minimum standard also has the effect of providing regulated entities with a framework against which they can hold regulatory agencies accountable.

II. Context

Responsibility for the delivery of regulation in the UK is spread across a large number of regulatory agencies. At the national level, more than 60 regulatory agencies – both independent and ministerial agencies – hold responsibility for discrete areas of regulation, with examples being the Food Standards Agency, tasked with ensuring that food is safe, and the Health & Safety Executive, with responsibility for workplace health and safety. Regulation is also delivered by a large number of local bodies. A 2009 report[4] identified that 433 local

---

[3] The UK Government's Focus on Enforcement programme, launched in 2012, and the parallel Business Focus on Enforcement initiative, identified cross-cutting issues and opportunities for improvement, for example in relation to regulatory appeals processes. Further information available at http://webarchive.nationalarchives.gov.uk/20160106103937 and http://discuss.bis.gov.uk/focusonenforcement.

[4] 'Mapping the Local Authority Regulatory Services Landscape' (Local Better Regulation Office, 2009).

authorities, 58 fire authorities and 152 port health authorities were responsible for enforcing an extensive range of legislation at the local level.

The number of regulatory players in the UK, their different responsibilities and the relationships between them have evolved over a lengthy period. This has created significant complexity, elevating the scale of the challenge of effecting a systematic change in culture across the regulatory landscape.

It has been important for the UK, acknowledging this diversity of regulatory agencies, to recognise that prescriptive detail that might work well for one regulator is unlikely to work equally well for all. The approach taken has therefore relied primarily on the establishment of general principles that are capable of being implemented by a broad range of regulatory agencies.

A code-based approach has been used to establish these principles and expectations of behaviour, acknowledging the power of codes in regulating behaviour. An individual rule can be considered a schema, a guide to behaviour, constraining the choices of regulated actors. A code or set of rules, however, works at a deeper level. It becomes more than the sum of its parts. This becomes apparent when one considers for instance reports of corporate governance non-compliance by large companies. A report in the media of the failure of a company to conform to a rule regarding the composition of its board tends to suggest a lower level of misconduct than a report that states the company has failed to comply with the requirements of the UK Corporate Governance Code. Regulated entities therefore have a greater propensity to comply when a rule is embedded within a code – even when conformance with that code is completely voluntary, containing 'rules of conduct, which in principle have no legally binding force but which nevertheless may have practical effects'.[5]

This is especially so when the rules within a code are themselves considered by regulated entities to be the codification of best, or even, accepted practice. Research on the use of codes in the UK has found that positive conformance with codes depends on factors such as the extent to which:

- regulated entities are engaged in the formation and revision of the code, and thus feel a sense of ownership;
- monitors exist and are effective;
- the rules are consistent with existing workplace norms and best practices;
- regulated entities are familiar with the use of codes to provide guidance and constrain sub-optimal behaviour.[6]

These findings are not inconsistent with the development and content of the code-based approaches detailed below, particularly with regard to levels of engagement and consistency of enforcement practice.

---

[5] Francis Snyder, 'Soft Law and Institutional Practice in the European Community' (European University Institute, Law Working Paper 93/5, 1993).

[6] Paul Sanderson, David Seidl, John Roberts and Bernard Krieger, *Flexible or not? The Comply-or-Explain Principle in UK and German Corporate Governance*. (Cambridge, University of Cambridge: Centre for Business Research, 2010).

III. Promoting a Voluntary Code

The mechanisms used to establish general principles for the behaviour of regulatory agencies have evolved over the past three decades, with a trend from voluntary measures to statutory obligations. These statutory obligations have, for the most part, been introduced as part of the wider legislative framework – applying to most regulatory agencies. In the case of some recently established regulatory agencies, they have been incorporated into founding statutes.[7]

As early as 1994, the government introduced legislation[8] that marked a new focus on how enforcement practices could be improved, authorising Ministers to require regulators to provide certain information to businesses, in the interests of improving *'fairness, transparency and consistency'*. In practice, this Ministerial power was not used to impose requirements on regulators, although its inclusion in legislation appeared to influence the behaviour of some regulators, who adopted certain practices on a voluntary basis.[9]

The government subsequently developed a voluntary code, the Enforcement Concordat,[10] articulating a view of what constituted good practice in delivering regulation. The Enforcement Concordat aimed at tackling perceived weaknesses in the UK's regulatory enforcement regime by setting out principles for good enforcement policy. Its development was informed by the views that the business community had been expressing to government over a period of time and by consultation with business, regulatory agencies, the voluntary sector and consumer groups.

The Enforcement Concordat encouraged partnership working between regulatory agencies and the businesses that they regulate, as a means of achieving higher levels of compliance. It set out general principles, including in relation to:

- setting clear standards;
- clear and open provision of information;
- helping business by advising on and assisting with compliance;
- well-publicised effective and timely complaints procedures;
- proportionality in relation to enforcement action; and,
- consistency of enforcement practice.

Regulatory agencies were encouraged to improve communication with regulated entities, with the Enforcement Concordat setting out a commitment that regulated entities should receive clear explanations of what they need to do and by when, should have opportunities to resolve differences before enforcement action is taken (unless immediate action is needed), and should receive a clear and timely explanation of their rights of appeal.

---

[7] The Human Tissue Act 2004 established the Human Tissue Authority, requiring it to 'have regard to the principles of best regulatory practice (including the principles under which regulatory activities should be transparent, accountable, proportionate, consistent and targeted only at cases in which action is needed)'.

[8] The Deregulation and Contracting Out Act 1994, s 5, superseded by the Regulatory Reform Act 2001, authorised ministers to set out a code of good practice in enforcement.

[9] 'Twenty-Eighth Report of the House of Lords Select Committee on Delegated Powers and Deregulation' (1999).

[10] 'Enforcement Concordat' (Cabinet Office, 1998).

The Enforcement Concordat was promoted to regulatory agencies by Government, and in the first 18 months after its introduction around a third of local regulators and half of those operating at a national level signed up to the voluntary code.[11] Effort was put into encouraging regulatory agencies to sign up, gathering varied examples of established and developing good practice, and sharing these with regulators.[12] These examples focused, in particular, on the development of good partnerships between regulatory agencies and businesses, and the effective provision of support to help businesses comply with regulations, by making information, guidance and advice readily available through different routes. Regulatory agencies were also encouraged to monitor their own performance in applying the principles set out in the Enforcement Concordat, through self, peer or independent assessment, consultation and other feedback mechanisms.

By 2001, the Concordat had been adopted by 96 per cent of local authorities in England and Wales, by all the local authorities in Scotland and by the vast majority of central government agencies.[13] However, the Government's evaluation of the impact of the Concordat a few years later was that while it had

> brought some clarity into the UK regulatory enforcement regime, it was only partially successful in its aims of changing regulatory culture and practice. This was due to two main factors:
>
> - First, although the Enforcement Concordat was adopted by virtually all regulatory bodies with enforcement functions, its implementation was patchy and inconsistent across the country, which caused difficulties for those regulated, and
> - Secondly, the Enforcement Concordat did not place sufficient weight on risk-based enforcement, a key necessity to ensure that enforcement activities are proportionate and targeted.[14]

This view of the Enforcement Concordat had been informed by the seminal work of the Hampton Review team in 2004/05. Hampton was tasked with considering 'the scope for promoting more efficient approaches to regulatory inspection and enforcement while continuing to deliver excellent regulatory outcomes'.[15] The recommendations of the review team's report[16] (the 'Hampton Principles') shaped the UK's approach to improving regulatory practice over subsequent years and continue to do so.

Box 5.1 The Hampton Principles

I. Regulators should recognise that a key element of their activity will be to allow, or even encourage, economic progress and only to intervene when there is a clear case for protection.

II. Regulators, and the regulatory system as a whole, should use comprehensive risk assessment to concentrate resources in the areas that need them most.

III. Regulators should provide authoritative, accessible advice easily and cheaply.

---

[11] Twenty-Eighth Report (1999).

[12] 'Enforcement Concordat Good Practice Guide for England & Wales' (Small Business Service, 2003).

[13] 'Government Capacity to Assure High Quality Regulation. OECD Review of Regulatory Reform in the United Kingdom' (OECD, 2002).

[14] 'A Code of Practice for Regulators – A Consultation' (Cabinet Office, 2007).

[15] 'Reducing Administrative Burdens: Effective Inspection and Enforcement Interim Report', Annex A (HM Treasury, 2004).

[16] 'Reducing Administrative Burdens' (ibid).

IV. No inspection should take place without a reason.

V. Businesses should not have to give unnecessary information or give the same piece of information twice.

VI. The few businesses that persistently break regulations should be identified quickly and face proportionate and meaningful sanctions.

VII. Regulators should be accountable for the efficiency and effectiveness of their activities, while remaining independent in the decisions they take.

IV. Establishing a Statutory Code

The lessons learned through the experience of the Enforcement Concordat suggested that, while progress had been made, further voluntary arrangements would not have the necessary weight to effect a real change in regulatory behaviour. There was an acceptance that, while the act of commitment involved in 'signing up' to a voluntary code has benefits, its voluntary status means that it remains, in the eyes of some regulatory agencies and particularly regulated entities, a less powerful driver for change than a statutory obligation.

In 2006, the Government introduced legislation that marked a significant shift in the UK's approach to changing the behaviour of regulatory agencies, providing a statutory basis for principles that had previously been adopted on a voluntary basis.

The UK's Principles of Good Regulation,[17] that had been well established with its policy-makers since 1997 as a pillar of the regulatory simplification programme, were placed on a statutory footing[18] for a large number of existing regulatory agencies at both national and local level. The effect of this step was to require the regulatory agencies to act in a manner that is proportionate, accountable, consistent, transparent and targeted. This duty was applied to regulators at all levels at which they exercise their regulatory functions – from setting their policies, procedures and guidance to individual decisions as to whether or not to inspect a particular business, or what action to take in respect of a specific breach.

At the same time, the Legislative and Regulatory Reform Act 2006 authorised ministers to issue a statutory code of practice[19] that regulators would be required to have regard to at their general level functions of, for example, policy-making and standard-setting. The first statutory code[20] took effect in 2008 and at around this time, certain regulatory agencies were also placed under a duty not to impose or maintain unnecessary burdens in the exercise of regulatory functions.[21] Four years later, the first statutory code was replaced by its current iteration, the Regulators' Code.[22]

---

[17] 'Principles of Good Regulation' (Better Regulation Task Force, 2003).

[18] Legislative and Regulatory Reform Act 2006, s 21.

[19] Legislative and Regulatory Reform Act 2006, s 22.

[20] 'Regulators' Compliance Code: Statutory Code of Practice for Regulators' (London, Department for Business, Enterprise and Regulatory Reform, 2007).

[21] Regulatory Enforcement and Sanctions Act, ss 72, 73(3)–(6).

[22] 'Regulators' Code' (Better Regulation Delivery Office, 2014).

The Regulators' Code is rooted in the Principles of Good Regulation and brings forward much of the good practice previously recognised in the voluntary Enforcement Concordat, in respect of: assisting businesses to comply; good communication with business; proportionate responses to breaches of regulatory requirements; and provision of access to complaints and appeals processes. At the same time, it takes forward key aspects of the good practice identified through the Hampton review. It builds, for example, on the Hampton principle that regulators should concern themselves with economic progress, only intervening where there is a clear case for protection. It also addresses criticism of the Enforcement Concordat by placing significant emphasis on the importance for regulatory agencies of assessing risks to their regulatory outcomes and using this risk assessment to inform their decisions.

The Regulators' Code sets out government's expectations of good regulatory delivery in clear, simple terms, establishing six broad principles for regulatory agencies with underpinning detail. The six principles are explored here.

Box 5.2 Regulators' Code – the first principle

'Regulators should carry out their activities in a way that supports those they regulate to comply and grow.'

A key priority for the Government during the period in which the Code was being developed, and since then, has been to promote growth in the UK economy. It is well accepted in the UK that the regulatory climate is an important factor in business decisions to invest and their ability to grow and that the way in which regulation is delivered at the frontline is a significant aspect of this. The importance of proportionate regulatory activity and support for those businesses that wish to comply had been recognised in the Hampton Principles.

The Code's first principle establishes a supportive role for regulatory agencies, emphasising that the ways in which a regulatory agency behaves can have beneficial impacts on the businesses regulated. The Code represents a shift away from previous messaging on the impact of regulatory delivery, which had focused on the importance of avoiding the imposition of unnecessary regulatory burdens on business. While this remains important, the Code also points to the ways in which regulatory agencies are able to impact positively on markets and individual businesses. For example, where regulation is open to different interpretations, businesses can experience uncertainty which impacts adversely on their confidence and willingness to invest. The Code points regulatory agencies to the ways in which they are able to 'support or enable economic growth for compliant businesses' by providing greater certainty. This might be achieved, for example, by providing advice and guidance to regulated entities that is assured by the regulatory agency, giving the business confidence. Business confidence and certainty are also at the heart of the Code's emphasis on the importance for the regulatory agency of ensuring that it has competent regulatory officers. Regulatory competence is framed in terms of the officers' technical knowledge and skills, their understanding of those they regulate, their understanding of the principles of good regulatory delivery, and their understanding of the regulatory agency's approach.

The importance of considering economic growth and proportionate regulatory activity had been clearly expressed in the first iteration of the statutory code in 2008. Nevertheless, it became evident, following the introduction of the code that some regulatory agencies were not properly articulating their important role in enabling growth against their duty to deliver protections.[23] In parallel with the 2012 revision of the Code, government considered the need to strengthen the rule set in this area, taking account of evidence indicating that, despite the statutory code, some regulatory agencies continued to see economic factors as being inconsistent with their existing duties, while others felt constrained from giving proper consideration to economic growth because they felt that they did not have a clear authorisation to balance growth with the protection duties explicitly set out in their founding statutes.

A clear and unequivocal duty was established separately, in statute, that regulatory agencies should 'have regard to the desirability of promoting economic growth'[24] and this duty took effect in March 2017, applying to most non-economic regulators in the UK. Statutory guidance on how to comply with this duty[25] operates in parallel to the Regulators' Code, providing more detailed guidance for regulatory agencies. It emphasises the importance for regulatory agencies and their staff of having a thorough understanding of the business environment, the markets or sectors in which they are regulating, and the individual regulated entities that they deal with. This understanding ensures that they are well-equipped to act proportionately, making well-informed decisions.

Box 5.3 Regulators' Code – the second principle

'Regulators should provide simple and straightforward ways to engage with those they regulate and hear their views.'

The second principle of the Code sets expectations in terms of the accountability mechanisms that a regulatory agency should have in place. These are expressed at two levels: first, in terms of the regulator's accountability to those it regulates and to the intended beneficiaries of regulation; and secondly, in terms of the individual regulated entity.

The Code stresses the importance of wide engagement, to enable the regulatory agency to understand the views of those it regulates, citizens and other interested parties. Good engagement allows the regulatory agency to establish strong two-way relationships within which it can gather information and views – ensuring that it is better informed about how the regulation is working and about the impact of its own approach, or proposed changes to its approach – and disseminate information. These relationships enable the regulatory agency to ensure that its approach is appropriate and to build confidence in the approach.

---

[23] 'Consultation Paper: Non-economic Regulators: Duty to Have Regard to Growth' (Better Regulation Delivery Office, 2013), and associated 'Government Response' (Better Regulation Delivery Office, 2013).
[24] The Deregulation Act 2015, s 108.
[25] 'Growth Duty: Statutory Guidance' (Department for Business, Energy and Industrial Strategy, 2017).

The message that consultation is important, as a means of enabling the regulator to understand whether proposed approaches will work, is woven throughout the code, with an expectation that regulatory agencies will consult on the design of risk frameworks and on guidance that they develop.

In relation to individual regulated entities, the Code focuses on the importance of good communication and on ensuring that the regulated entity is readily able to provide feedback on their experience of being regulated; to comment or complain about the behaviour of the regulatory agency or its staff; or to appeal regulatory decisions.

Box 5.4 Regulators' Code – the third principle

'Regulators should base their regulatory activities on risk.'

The third principle of the Code sets an expectation that regulatory agencies will follow risk-based approaches (see chapter sixteen). By considering risk at every stage of their decision-making processes – from prioritising the areas on which they will focus their efforts to choosing the most appropriate interventions, targeting checks on compliance and determining proportionate responses to breaches – regulatory agencies are able to ensure that they make the most effective use of their resources and that the cost to regulated entities of 'being regulated' is proportionate.

The Code requires an evidence-based approach to determining risk which draws on all available data on compliance. This allows regulatory agencies to properly recognise the compliance record of those they regulate and to make well-informed assessments of the regulatory risk presented.

The Code emphasises the importance of evaluating the effectiveness of the regulatory agency's activities (see chapter thirteen) and adjusting the approach being taken by the regulator where evaluation indicates that this is appropriate.

Box 5.5 Regulators' Code – the fourth principle

'Regulators should share information about compliance and risk.'

Most regulated entities are regulated by multiple regulatory agencies and this, in itself, can create difficulties, for example in relation to duplication or inconsistent expectations being placed on a business by different regulators. The Code focuses on the importance of collaboration between regulatory agencies, recognising that such collaboration can be a means of minimising problems but can also deliver wider benefits both for the regulated entity and for the regulators. The fourth principle sets an expectation that regulatory agencies will collaborate in respect of the collection of relevant data and information from businesses, and the use of such information and data. This collaboration enables regulatory bodies to minimise the administrative burdens that can be associated with providing information to regulatory agencies. It also enables regulatory agencies to draw on a wider data set when assessing risk and improves their targeting.

The Code acknowledges that there are legal constraints on the sharing of information and data and emphasises that data sharing should take place only where the law allows and through secure mechanisms.

During the development of the Code, it was acknowledged that data-sharing would be one of the most challenging areas for regulatory agencies to make progress in, but one in which significant gains could be made. A recent survey of UK businesses[26] identified that 60 per cent of businesses agreed, or strongly agreed, that completing paperwork for government was a burden, while a further 66 per cent found having to provide the same information more than once was a burden. Overcoming the practical, cultural, technical and legal barriers to improving sharing of data between regulatory agencies was seen as a way of reducing this burden while at the same time leading to 'better targeting of regulatory resources, and an improvement in the way operational and resourcing decisions are taken'.[27] Chapter eleven describes the approach taken in the Netherlands, where the Inspection Council created an IT facility to connect data from all regulatory agencies and chapter eighteen provides an example of a data-sharing project developed by local regulators in the UK[28] which delivered benefits in terms of improving risk-based targeting of inspections and reducing the risk associated with local regulators not being aware of new businesses.

Box 5.6   Regulators' Code – the fifth principle

'Regulators should ensure that clear information, guidance and advice is available to help those they regulate meet their responsibilities to comply.'

The fifth principle of the Code is firmly rooted in the belief that, in most areas of business regulation, the majority of businesses are generally willing to comply and, amongst this group, failures are most likely to result from a lack of awareness or knowledge of the requirements, a lack of understanding of the requirements or of how they can be met, or a lack of attention to achieving or maintaining compliance on an ongoing basis. In most areas of business regulation, only a small proportion of businesses wilfully breach their regulatory obligations, demonstrating what can be referred to as 'criminality'.

Where compliance failures can be attributed to a lack of knowledge or understanding, the provision of clear regulatory information, guidance, advice and other support is the most effective means of improving compliance levels. To a certain extent, their provision

---

[26] IFF Research, 'Business Perceptions Survey 2012' (National Audit Office, Better Regulation Delivery Office, Better Regulation Executive, 2012).

[27] 'Consultation Paper: Data Sharing for Non-economic Regulators' (Department for Business, Innovation and Skills, 2014).

[28] 'Evaluation Report of Data Sharing through the Intelligent Regulatory Information System (IRIS)' (Health and Safety Laboratory, 2015).

can also be an effective means of tackling non-compliance that results from a lack of attention.

The Code emphasises that information, guidance and advice should be readily available and easily accessible to regulated entities.

The Code acknowledges that regulated entities can be fearful of seeking advice from their regulator, particularly in circumstances where they know that they have a compliance issue and places a responsibility on regulatory agencies to take active steps to address this issue, so that regulated entities feel able to seek advice when they need it.

As with data collection and use, the Code recognises that collaboration between regulatory agencies is particularly beneficial in relation to the provision of advice and guidance. Businesses in the UK have, in the past, reported how challenging they find it when following the advice or guidance of one regulatory agency means that they fall foul of the expectations of another. This can arise where both regulatory agencies are enforcing the same regulatory requirements or where they are enforcing different regulatory requirements that both impact on the same business activity. In these cases, the Code establishes a clear expectation that responsibility for the resolution of any differences or inconsistencies should lie with the regulatory agencies rather than with the regulated entity.

Box 5.7 Regulators' Code – the sixth principle

'Regulators should ensure that their approach to their regulatory activities is transparent.'

The final principle of the Regulators' Code is an overarching principle that aims to deliver improvements in transparency, as an enabler of greater accountability. It is underpinned by requirements as to the types of information that a regulatory agency should make available, and how it should do this. There is an expectation that regulatory agencies will publish a wide range of information, including:

- clear information on how the regulatory agency communicates with regulated entities, and how it can be contacted;
- clear information on the regulatory agency's approach to providing information, guidance and advice;
- an explanation of the approach taken to checking compliance, including details of the risk frameworks used;
- the regulatory agency's enforcement policy, setting out how it will respond to compliance failures;
- details of any fees and charges;
- clear information about how to provide feedback to the regulatory agency or to complain or appeal; and
- details of the regulatory agency's performance.

The Code does not explicitly require regulatory agencies to publish information about their compliance with the provisions of the Code. However, following publication of the Code a number of regulatory agencies in the UK chose, in the interests of transparency, to share their own compliance assessment.[29]

V. Implementing the Regulators' Code

The Office for Product Safety and Standards is responsible for the Regulators' Code, and the approach taken to the implementation has been broadly similar to the approach that would be expected of a regulatory agency that has responsibility for implementing regulatory requirements, though without the enforcement powers or sanctions. This has involved using a suite of interventions to support compliance, comprising: awareness raising activities; provision of information, guidance and advice; the creation of tools to support compliance; and working with regulatory agencies to understand their compliance issues.

The Office for Product Safety and Standards has worked to raise awareness of the statutory principles of good regulation, the Regulators' Code and the statutory 'growth duty' amongst regulatory agencies and frontline regulatory officers through a proactive approach: making information, resources and good practice case studies available; presenting at events and conferences; running workshops for individual regulatory agencies and groups of regulators; and dissemination of updates via social media.

Further support has been provided to help regulatory agencies to improve their practices through a range of measures, including:

- developing tools, such as a template enforcement policy that local regulators can adapt to suit their own needs;

- supporting regulatory agencies to review their current practices and identify where changes might be needed;[30]

- facilitation of networks such as Expert Panels that bring together regulatory agencies and representatives of the regulated sector to address regulatory issues in a collaborative manner.

Considerable effort has also been committed, since 2014, to raising the profile of the statutory code in the business community and improving understanding that businesses are entitled to challenge poor behaviour by regulatory agencies. The Government views the Regulators' Code as a key tool in improving the accountability of regulators to regulated entities and citizens. Where businesses are willing to challenge the regulatory agencies, poor practices are exposed with consequent improvements.

---

[29] They include, for example, the Office of Nuclear Regulation, which published an assessment in 2015 and an updated assessment in 2018, available at http://news.onr.org.uk/2015/09/onr-demonstrates-compliance-with-regulators-code and www.onr.org.uk/documents/2018/onr-regulators-code-self-assessment%20report-2018.pdf; the Marine Management Organisation, available at www.gov.uk/government/publications/regulators-code-action-plan; and the Human Tissue Authority, available at www.hta.gov.uk/about-us/how-we-do-it/hta-self-assessment-against-regulators%E2%80%99-code.

[30] See for example www.assembly.wales/laid%20documents/gen-ld10285/gen-ld10285-e.pdf.

The Regulators' Code thus acts as a frame of reference that regulated entities can use. Where a regulated entity considers that the provisions of the Regulators' Code are not being met by its regulator, it is able to raise this through the formal complaints process that the regulatory agency is required, by the Code, to make available and accessible. Where the regulatory agency's own complaints processes do not deliver satisfaction, the regulated entity has recourse to an independent ombudsman who is able to consider the complaint, using the Regulators' Code as a frame of reference. For example, complaints about local regulators are considered by the Local Government Ombudsman, who has committed to taking account of the Regulators' Code.[31]

VI. Lessons from the UK Experience

A post implementation review by the Government in 2012 considered the impact of the statutory code,[32] gathering evidence around the principles of the code from a range of stakeholders. The review found that regulatory agencies had broadly adopted the principles of the code and had reflected its introduction in their policies. However, there was evidence that the code had been considered at the point of its introduction but was not being used, as had been intended, as a reference for ongoing challenges and improvement. It was evident that awareness and understanding of the statutory code was poor amongst the business community and some frontline regulatory officers. The review also found considerable variation across regulatory agencies in terms of meeting the transparency requirements of the statutory code.

These findings were addressed in the 2013 revision of the statutory code[33] and the subsequent launch of the current Regulators' Code, with its stronger emphasis on transparency and accountability. The Office for Product Safety and Standards' resourcing of an ongoing implementation programme has raised the profile of the statutory code and created a focal point for considering how it is working in practice.

More recent research and discussions on the efficacy of the Regulators' Code conducted with a number of large and small UK regulatory agencies found that all regulators agreed the Regulators' Code provided an effective framework for regulating.[34] Even some agencies not required to follow the code used it as guidance and several had made changes to their practices based on the contents of the code.

However, translating generic guidance into operating standards can be resource-intensive. While larger agencies were overwhelmingly positive about the benefits provided by the guidance in the code, some smaller agencies found the code burdensome. In general,

---

[31] See for example www.lgo.org.uk/decisions/environment-and-regulation/other/14-016-211.

[32] 'Regulators' Compliance Code: Statutory Code of Practice for Regulators' (Department for Business, Enterprise and Regulatory Reform, 2007).

[33] 'Consultation Paper: Amending the Regulators' Compliance Code' (Regulation Delivery Office, 2013) and associated 'Government Response' (Better Regulation Delivery Office, 2013).

[34] Paul Sanderson and Sarah Taverner held a series of meetings with UK regulators to discuss lessons learned from research to date on optimising compliance with regulatory codes (supported by the University of Cambridge: Economic and Social Research Council Impact Acceleration Account and the Better Regulation Delivery Office, 2016).

agencies with smaller budgets struggled to devote sufficient resources to implementation leaving them aware of the potential for their actions to be non-compliant. They expressed a preference for: (i) clearer and simpler guidance that outlined the absolute minimum levels of compliance necessary; and (ii) illustrations of best practice to assist them in designing both rules for their own regulated entities and their working arrangements with co-regulators. On the other hand, some of their larger counterparts were concerned, despite the principles-based nature of the code, that it placed unnecessary requirements on them to demonstrate compliance with rules and practices they had established for themselves some time ago, suggesting perhaps that while 'one size fits all' codes are both desired, and desirable, the level of detail they set out is inevitably a compromise.

Nonetheless, extensive engagement and consultation in relation to the development of the Regulators' Code, the Growth Duty and associated measures have meant that, in general, there is a good degree of buy-in to the purpose and content of these measures. As a governance tool, the Regulators' Code goes a long way in terms of setting minimum standards across a wide range of regulatory agencies and it is changing expectations of regulatory behaviour, on the part of both regulators and those they regulate. Chris Hodges' study of enforcement policies published by regulatory agencies in the UK has shown that many are articulating a supportive and proportionate regulatory approach.[35]

However, experience continues to show that the effectiveness of the Regulators' Code in changing the behaviour of an individual regulatory agency is highly dependent not just on the size and capacity of the regulatory agency but also on its values and the strength of the accountability mechanisms that are in place. Whilst many regulatory agencies have engaged actively with the spirit and content of the Code, some have shown less commitment.

Businesses have, in some instances, called for a 'stronger Code' that applies to individual decision-making by regulators.[36] They have also voiced concerns that, in the absence of active compliance monitoring and specific sanctions for non-compliance, some regulatory agencies will continue to fail to take proper account of the Code.

---

[35] See Christopher Hodges, *Law and Corporate Behaviour: Integrating Theories of Regulation, Enforcement, Culture and Ethics* (Oxford, Hart Publishing, 2015); and Figure 10.1 in Christopher Hodges and Ruth Steinholtz, *Ethical Business Practice and Regulation. A Behavioural and Values-Based Approach to Compliance and Enforcement* (Oxford, Hart Publishing, 2017).

[36] 'Government Response to the Consultation on Amending the Regulators' Compliance Code' (Better Regulation Delivery Office, 2013).

6

Transparency Approaches, Changing the Role of Supervisory Institutions in Lithuania

GIEDRIUS KADZIAUSKAS

I. Introduction

Lithuania is a country of three million people located at the eastern shore of the Baltic Sea. It has been a member of the European Union and NATO since 2004. The main sectors of the economy are agriculture, food production, manufacturing and provision of services and the main trade partners are European Union countries – Latvia, Poland, Germany – and also Russia.

There are 60 municipalities in the country, but most of the business supervision functions are centralised and delivered by central government from the capital or through local branches. In recent years the number of local branches of central institutions has decreased, as budget pressures increase and more services are handled online.

There are 56 business supervisory institutions in Lithuania. The term 'business supervision' includes all the activities that a regulatory agency – or 'business supervisory institution'[1] – uses to achieve its goals. The term was introduced in Lithuania to emphasise that a physical inspection is not the only tool. The term 'business supervision' has a similar meaning to 'regulatory delivery', except that it emphasises the application to businesses, rather than to all duty-holders. The number of business supervisory institutions is high, as it includes all governmental agencies that have any powers to inspect businesses, even those with minimal impact on the economy. For example, the Lithuanian Service of Technological Security of State Documents supervises the printing of official documents such as passports and have only four businesses to supervise in their remit. The Lithuanian Tourism Board has a legal power to inspect tourist guides, but they do not exercise it. Both institutions are placed in the list[2] of business supervisory institutions besides the behemoths: the State Tax Inspectorate; State Food and Veterinary Service; State Labour Inspectorate; and others. It is estimated that the 10 biggest inspectorates account for more than 80 per cent of all inspections. It was intentional to create one list of all institutions

---

[1] Business supervisory institution is used together with the term 'inspectorate' to describe governmental institutions with inspection powers.

[2] The list of business supervisory institutions is provided in Government Decree 511. It is described in more detail later in the text.

with inspection powers to convey that all institutions are covered by the horizontal rules on inspections and also to demonstrate that there is significant burden on businesses merely from the number of institutions.

II. Main Goals and Instruments of the Reform

The reform of business supervisory institutions was started by the Government in 2009 as a part of broader business environment improvement efforts. Initially a lot of attention was paid to reducing their numbers by consolidation and increased cooperation in planning and performing inspections. However, consolidation in 2009/10 did not bring major changes – the legal consolidation process was slow and the cooperation among inspectorates did not bring tangible results for businesses. Therefore, the reform took a broader approach that aimed to improve the practices of business supervisory institutions, including their attitudes and interactions with businesses.

The goals of the later reforms were twofold – decreasing the inspection burden on businesses, and increasing effectiveness of business supervisory institutions in delivering regulatory outcomes – ensuring safety for consumers, citizens, the environment and work-ers, fairness of trade, collection of state revenue, and others.

The key transformation that was required from the supervisory institutions was a shift of focus to compliance promotion activities, and an obligation to be proactive with provision of advice rather than keep using inspections as the primary method of exerting influence on businesses. Those priorities were chosen because regulatory delivery was not considered transparent and business-friendly. Businesses were constantly complain-ing about the lack of clarity on inspection planning, about the conduct of inspections by inspectors and about the sanctions imposed. It was widely discussed that some businesses used connections in regulatory agencies to fight competitors. Inspection itself was consid-ered more a process of luck depending on the benevolence of the inspector rather than on clearly established procedures to establish non-compliance. There were inspectorates that stood out and were already using business-oriented approaches, but those were excep-tional cases and there was no horizontal management of regulatory delivery on behalf of the Government.

It was clear that it was important not only to decrease the inspection burden on busi-nesses but also to help businesses to comply with legislation to improve safety and attain other key interests. Regulatory agencies are well placed to assist businesses in navigating the often complex legislative requirements. Previous governments in Lithuania have carried out various deregulation projects, for example, the Sunrise Commission,[3] which aimed to repeal different provisions that put unsubstantiated and disproportionate burdens on busi-nesses, but even if some provisions were amended, regulations repealed, or licences revoked there was no systemic and tangible impact for the majority of businesses.

---

[3] The Sunrise Commission was set up by the Government to reduce red tape in the periods 1999–2003 and 2009–2012. The Commission asked the business community to identify, discuss and find alternatives to individual permits, licences and obsolete regulatory requirements.

The Government of 2008–2012 realised that inspection reform with the aim of changing the role of business supervisory institutions from solely inspection activity to being able to support businesses to comply could act as a major and systemic change that could have a positive impact for the majority of businesses. Business supervisory institutions are in a unique position in the government administration – after the registration and acquisition of licences and permits needed for operation, inspectors are the frontline public servants that businesses meet. Those encounters form how the Government administration and ultimately the state is perceived by businesses and citizens.

The main instruments used during the reform addressed both structural issues and the practices of business supervisory institutions. There was consolidation of business supervisory institutions – in the initial stages and later as a secondary priority – and the legal framework was developed to set out obligations to use risk assessment and planning; the use of alternative ways of promoting compliance other than business inspection (physically checking premises), transparency requirements for supervisory institutions, and performance management tools. Performance indicators for business supervisory institutions were also introduced. Changes to the practices of business supervisory institutions were driven through: the introduction of inspection checklists; the development and promotion of hotlines in business supervisory institutions to advise individuals and businesses; the development and promotion of compliance support tools (advice, guidelines, manuals); and the provision of assistance to business supervisory institutions in introducing risk assessment and risk-based planning.[4]

The Law on Public Administration was amended[5] to embed this new approach to inspections. Among other issues, an obligation to provide advice[6] was placed on business supervisory institutions. It was worded as the 'principle of provision of methodological assistance'. This principle means that business supervisory institutions must cooperate with businesses, provide advice to businesses on matters within their competence, implement other preventative measures which help businesses to meet legal requirements, and apply sanctions as a last resort.

This principle does not apply during inspections if its application would hinder the achievement of the goals of supervision of compliance.

The introduction of the main instruments was followed by support and encouragement from the Ministry of Economy and Ministry of Justice to assist supervisory institutions in implementation. Guidelines were adopted for developing checklists, introducing hotlines for provision of advice, implementing risk-based assessment and planning and introducing performance assessment indicators.[7] Business supervisory institutions participating in the reform received guidance from the reform team. Bi-monthly meetings of the heads or

---

[4] More information about the general reforms is available in 'Regulatory Policy in Lithuania. Focusing on the Delivery Side' (OECD, 2015).

[5] Law on Public Administration, 17 June 1999, No VIII-1234. The key amendment on business supervision was enacted by the Law of 22 June 2010, No XI-934.

[6] In the Law on Public Administration and other legal acts and in general usage in Lithuania, the term 'consultation' is used to designate the provision of advice. That terminology is not used here in order to avoid the potential for confusion with the usage of the same term to describe that part of the legislative process when the draft is presented for comment by interested parties.

[7] The last version of guidelines was adopted on 3 July 2015, No 4-432/1R-169. Three guidelines are available in Lithuanian at https://goo.gl/L2TaUB.

deputy heads of the main inspectorates were an effective vehicle to present reform tools, receive feedback from institutions, test various ideas and monitor the implementation of the reform measures.

III. Transparency as a Method to Achieve Better Compliance

Improved transparency was seen as an important tool of the reform that would put inspectors and businesses on an equal footing, allow effective public scrutiny over the functioning of business supervisory institutions, and allow effective comparison between the different business supervisory institutions in charge of the different fields of supervision. The transparency of business supervisory institutions means not only being transparent about their operations, but also the state being transparent about the regulations, about the requirements checked during the inspection process and about the use of enforcement actions, including sanctions.

The aim was to increase:

- the availability of data for public scrutiny;
- trust between supervisory institutions and businesses;
- the transparency of daily operations of supervisory institutions; and
- the accountability of supervisory institutions.

Establishing an equal standing for businesses and inspectors was a key element in the transparency agenda. The reform team believed that there was a need to increase resistance of businesses and inspectors to corruption by eliminating the inspector's power that emanates from an imbalance of information. The supervisory institutions could not always ensure the transparent behaviour of inspectors, therefore the reform aimed at empowering businesses to defend their rights and secure a transparent inspection process. With this aim in mind, different issues that required more transparency and publicity were tackled:

- Information about the rights and obligations of both business and inspectors during the inspection process were clarified and published as a brochure.
- Checklists were introduced which set out the only questions that can be checked during the visit.[8]
- Tools for business to better understand and anticipate the inspections process were created. Risk assessment rules were published, so businesses could better understand their risk status, and inspection plans for each inspectorate were made public.
- An obligation on inspectorates to notify businesses 10 days in advance of an inspection was introduced. This notification must specify the grounds, time limit and subject matter of an inspection to be conducted and includes a preliminary list of documents which the business must prepare for inspection.
- Different feedback mechanisms were introduced to give businesses a stronger voice in protecting their rights and interests during and after the inspection process.

---

[8] There is widespread debate on the status of the legal requirements not included in the checklist.

Box 6.1 Gathering business feedback

In 2014 Lithuania introduced a simple yet efficient method of collecting feedback from businesses that had been inspected. The system is administered centrally by the Ministry of Economy and allows the inspectorates to join the electronic feedback system. The inspectorates need to periodically provide the emails of the firms inspected to the system. Most of the inspectorates use IT systems to manage inspection work so transmission of emails is automatic. The centralised feedback system then sends an electronic letter from the Ministry of Economy together with a short questionnaire about the inspection experience. The questionnaire contains questions on the experience of the business during the inspection:

'Do you agree or disagree with these statements?

- The inspector(s) acted professionally.
- The inspector(s) was polite and friendly.
- The inspector(s) understood your business's interests and needs.
- The inspector(s) responded to questions raised during the inspection.
- The inspection went smoothly.
- Inspection has contributed to improving your company's performance.

Were any irregularities detected during the inspection?

If you answered YES to the previous question, did the inspector(s) explain what risks/consequences are caused by the recorded violation?

Did the inspector(s) request, directly or indirectly, any remuneration?

Would you like the inspector(s) who inspected your company to inspect you next time?'

The positive reception by business can be judged by the figures: out of 56,020 questionnaires sent between the official launch on 8 August 2014 and March 2018, 12,813 answers were received (22.9 per cent). Twenty per cent of filled-in questionnaires contained an answer to an open question, 'Please provide a commentary about your inspection or provide a recommendation'. The responses were positive overall: 94 per cent of businesses agreed with the statement that inspection was a positive experience, bearing in mind that approximately a quarter of the responses related to cases where some violations were found (in 73.3 per cent of cases there were no violations found). A dashboard containing some results is available online.[9]

The system functions without major promotion and investment, but there are still issues to be solved. There is currently too little action by the Ministry of Economy and the

[9] See www.inspect.ukmin.lt.

inspectorates on the feedback received. The results are used only occasionally (in annual reports or some presentations) and there is no periodic review of the results or recommendations from the Ministry of Economy to the inspectorates on areas for improvement based on results. There is also currently no review of the questionnaire and no major promotion efforts taken to increase response rate.

IV. General Legal Background on Transparency

The Lithuanian legal framework ensures access to information available in state institutions. It stems from the constitutional provision in Article 5 stipulating that 'state institutions serve the people'. Key legal acts that entrenched the obligation to be open are the Law on Public Administration[10] and the Law on the Right to Obtain Information from State and Municipal Institutions and Bodies.[11]

Openness requirements for state institutions are interwoven into the fabric of other instruments that provide for openness for information and successfully implement it in practice.

Legislative process is governed by Parliamentary Statute[12] and the main tool for providing transparency in relation to legislative requirements is the Registry of Legal Acts (www.e-tar.lt), where people are able to access and trace all legislation at every stage, from the initial draft prepared by the line ministry and submitted into the system for initial consultation with other state institutions. In addition, all the comments from other state institutions are available, as well as replies by the drafting ministry. Once the Act is submitted to the Government, all the accompanying documents are attached and available to the public – the main draft text, comments by other state institutions, comments by citizens, businesses and non-governmental institutions. The Parliament acts in similarly open manner: drafts originated in the Parliament, opinions by different parliamentary committees and drafts in various stages are publicly available on the Parliament website (www.lrs.lt). All the agendas of parliamentary and governmental sessions are available, parliamentary and government sessions are broadcast online, and verbatim records of parliamentary deliberations are available to the public.

A. Legal Acts with Specific Provisions on Transparency of Business Supervisory Institutions

In the initial stages of the reform, the amendment to the Law on Public Administration was passed which added an additional chapter to the law where new rules pertaining to the functioning of business supervisory institutions were stipulated.[13] The Law covered substantial

---

[10] 'Law on Public administration', 17 June 1999, No VIII-1234.
[11] 'Law on the Right to Obtain Information from State and Municipal Institutions and Bodies', 11 January 2000, No VIII-1524.
[12] 'Statute of the Parliament of the Republic of Lithuania', 17 February 1994 No I-399, 1994 m vasario 17 d Nr. I-399.
[13] In a number of countries that embark on inspection reforms, a separate law detailing the new approach to inspections is quite common eg Slovenia, Tajikistan, Ukraine, Mongolia, Armenia, Greece.

elements of business supervision: provision of advice to foster compliance; carrying out inspections; application of sanctions; and other administrative measures.

The same law embeds the principle of transparency as one of the principles of public administration (Article 3 of the Law on Public Administration). This principle requires that information about the principles, procedures and results of execution of the supervision of business activities, disclosed in a summarised form, shall be available to the public. This principle does not apply if the disclosure of information hinders the achievement of goals of the supervision activities.[14]

The law also introduced the obligation on business supervisory institutions to publish specific supervision related information. Article 36(6) stipulates the list of information which is put into more detail in Regulation 511. The list of essential information to be published on the website is listed in Article 7.17 of Regulation 511 titled 'Information for the client'. The Article reiterates and adds more details to the original list of information referred to in Article 36 of the Law on Public Administration.

B. Types of Information that Business Supervisory Institutions Publish

Business supervisory institutions are required to publish a wide range of information, including: the regulatory requirements that businesses must comply with; any guidance on the regulatory requirements or on their approach to inspection; documents setting out their policies and procedures; information about their structure and activities; performance indicators; information about the businesses in their remit; and feedback received from businesses. This information is explored further below.

i. List of Applicable Acts

A list of the legal acts establishing requirements for businesses, supervision powers and sanctioning powers.[15]

The most significant goal for this obligation is to provide the essential information for businesses about the applicable legal requirements. Even though all legal acts are publicly available in the general legal registry, business supervisory institutions have an obligation to provide the exhaustive list for the businesses in their remit.

The list of legislation must be structured and published in accordance with recommendations approved by the Minister of Justice.

ii. Performance Indicators

The shift from inspection based to a risk-based system was fostered by the introduction of performance indicators for the work of business supervisory institutions. In order to monitor the progress towards objectives, Regulation 511 mandated inspectorates to establish and

---

[14] Specified in para 1 of Art 36 of this law or other requirements of confidentiality set in other legal acts.
[15] 'Regarding Optimisation of the Functions of Supervisory Authorities', Decree No 511, 4 May 2010.

monitor performance indicators. Business supervisory institutions must report on indicators in the following areas at least monthly:

- progress towards the goals of the institution (purpose) – for example, measures related to level of environmental protection, non-food-product safety, food safety, revenue collection or occupational health and safety;
- the share of inspections that are targeting highest risk businesses, economic activities or objects compared to all inspections;
- the proportion of inspections carried out using the control questionnaires (checklists) compared to all inspections;
- the proportion of inspections carried out with advance notice to the business compared to all inspections;
- amount of the business supervisory institution's budget assigned for risk assessment, planning and analysis;
- amount of the business supervisory institution's budget assigned for consultation, information and prevention; and
- the number of staff members involved in refresher courses and training.

The precise wording and calculation method for each indicator can be determined individually by the supervisory institution, taking into account its activities and aggregated data. Indicators and periodic fluctuations in indicator meanings do not affect the assessment of the supervisory institution's activities. The indicators and the meanings of their respective periods or the values of the last three months must be published monthly online.

iii. Provision of Advice and Guidance

Business supervisory institutions are required to publish any guidance for businesses or inspectors in a form which is convenient and understandable to businesses.[16]

Business supervisory institutions not only provide information on the extent of non-compliance or inadequate enforcement of legal acts, but advice on the most relevant issues for businesses. Compliance promotion through provision of advice is one of the most important aspects of the reform. The amendments to the Law on Public Administration stipulated that business supervisory institutions must provide advice to businesses on matters within their competence as well as carrying out preventative actions intended to preclude possible violations of legal acts.[17]

Most of the business supervisory institutions provide advisory materials for different groups of businesses on safety, compliance with legal requirements, etc. Some of the institutions use adapted materials from international practice (for example, the Labour Inspectorate) and others use original content. The quality and quantity of guidelines differ from one institution to another.

The effectiveness of advice and its importance increased through the introduction of a binding power in relation to written or publicly announced advice. The Law on Public Administration stipulates that if a business acts in accordance with written or publicly

---

[16] 'Regarding Optimisation of the Functions of Supervisory Authorities', Decree No 511, 4 May 2010.
[17] The components of supervision according to the Art 36(3) are: (1) provision of advice; (2) inspections; (3) assessment of information about businesses; (4) sanctioning.

announced advice that has been approved by the head of the business supervisory institution, then sanctions must not be imposed on the business, even where the advice that it has acted on is subsequently determined to be inaccurate, for example, by a court decision.

Business supervisory institutions faced the challenge of providing advice on requirements and their implementation, in the knowledge that their advice could later be changed by advice or a decision of the same institution, a superior body or a court. The businesses could rely on advice provided and plan their actions accordingly, and business supervisory institutions were motivated to create internal processes to ensure that advice provided is uniform and aligned with other laws and regulations.

The business supervisory institutions provide advice through multiple channels, for example the State Labour Inspectorate provides advice through training courses, during inspection visits, via a telephone hotline, via the Inspectorate's Facebook page and through answers to written and email enquiries (see Table 6.1 for volumes in 2017).

Table 6.1 Information provided by the Labour Inspectorate on the amount of advice it provided in 2017[18]

Answers to written enquiries	9,588
Telephone hotline	106,202
Labour Inspectorate Facebook page	5,663
Total number of people receiving advice	121,453

Box 6.2 Telephone hotlines

Establishing telephone hotlines that provide information to businesses and citizens was one of the key methods to use the knowledge that business supervisory institutions had accumulated to give businesses and citizens the opportunity to ask for advice on interpretation of requirements in a safe environment (in most cases you are not required to identify yourself when calling). The State Tax Inspectorate is a perfect example of where there was demand for such a service. The government set recommendations for the hotlines:

(1) to direct most of the enquiries to one number;
(2) to designate and train staff to handle calls;
(3) to keep a log of enquiries;
(4) to develop a decision tree of questions and answers (best practice is to make the decision tree public on the web page);
(5) to record the conversations for reference and quality management purposes;
(6) to exercise quality control of the answers provided.

In 2017, the Labour Inspectorate provided 106,202 pieces of advice via telephone hotline; the Food and Veterinary Safety Authority provided 2,897 in 2016; and the State Tax Authority responded to nearly one million enquiries in 2015.

---

[18] State Labour inspectorate. General performance indicators 2017.01.01–2017.12.31, available at www.vdi.lt/PdfUploads/VeiklosSritysBendrieji.pdf.

iv. *Risk Criteria*

Business supervisory institutions are required to publish their rules on risk assessment, eg risk criteria, risk level calculation rules and inspection planning procedure. The publication of risk criteria for assessment of the risk level of businesses, is required unless the publication could undermine the effective execution of business supervision. Even though the formulation of the requirement is quite vague, a number of institutions have published the risk criteria, the weight attributed to each criteria and also the calculation method (eg see Table 6.2, which gives some examples of the State Labour Inspectorate's weighting for different risk criteria).

Table 6.2 Weightings used for different risk criteria in the algorithm to assess risk with regard to workplace accidents (extract of full criteria list)[19]

		Criteria	Weights
Criteria that increase risk	K20	The level of risk of economic sector with regards to the workplace accidents according to the NACE classification	8,28
	K23	Use of flammable, easily combustible substances on site	7,56
	K21	Number of potentially dangerous equipment on site	7,17
	K22	Use of chemical substances on site	6,85
	K24	Dangerous objects	6,44
	K9	Violation of health and safety requirements during last five years, taking into account their importance to accidents at workplace.	5,18
	K16	Lethal accidents at work during last five years	4,76
	Continues...		

The State Tax Inspectorate was one of the proponents of the argument that it was not always helpful to be transparent about all risk criteria. The Tax Inspectorate employs an elaborate risk assessment system where more than 300 risk criteria are used for analysis. Some of the criteria are dynamic and change to reflect the patterns used by businesses for various tax evasion schemes. It is evident that sharing such risk criteria could give signals to businesses about the knowledge of the supervisory institution of unlawful behaviour.

v. *Checklists*

Supervisory institutions are required to publish their rules on checklists – rules detailing structure of checklists, requirements for questions, development process, checklist review procedures, etc.

The introduction of checklists into the inspection process was one of the most widespread tools of the reform. Supervisory institutions gradually started developing checklists for different business groups and using them for inspections. The process commenced with

---

[19] Lithuanian State Labour inspectorate. Description of the risk assessment algorithm and the criteria for occupational health and safety assessment of businesses.

sectors categorised as lower risk with large numbers of businesses in the sector and with a relatively low level of knowledge amongst the businesses about managing risks. For example, checklists for auto repair shops on environmental protection, or small construction sites on occupational health and safety. Institutions were given the right not to develop checklists for sectors with high-risk businesses and those with a high level of knowledge amongst businesses.

Great effort was put into the clarity and brevity of checklists. Guidelines on development of checklists were produced and adopted.

vi. Business and Compliance Information

Business supervisory institutions are required to publish information about businesses in their remit including: a list of businesses, searchable by type and activity; details of permits/licences issued; and the results of inspection, including details of non-compliances and sanctions applied. Both the law and Regulation 511 stipulate that inspectorates shall provide not only the statistical information about non-compliances and incidents, but also an analysis of reasons for failure to comply with legal requirements.

Regulation 511 also recommends publication of a 'white list' of businesses that have a good history of compliance in order to encourage businesses to comply with the legal requirements. Only a few of the business supervisory institutions provide such 'white lists' (former Lithuanian non-food inspectorate, currently State Consumer Rights Protection Authority). Similarly, inspectorates are hesitant to share 'black lists' of businesses with a history of poor compliance, although several institutions do publish them.

vii. Proposals to Amend Unreasonable Regulations

The business supervisory institutions are required to report on proposals they have made to amend regulations which are disproportionate, ineffective or impossible to comply with. There is a duty on the business supervisory institutions to employ a critical approach towards legislative requirements that fall within their area of supervision. When inspecting compliance with legal requirements, the supervisory institution should listen to the business's opinion regarding the reasonableness of the regulation. Where an institution identifies an excessive supervision-related administrative burden, regulatory loopholes or legal requirements that appear unfounded, the institution should not continue to just enforce these requirements but instead has an active obligation to review them and to propose amendments to the relevant authority. Such information should be provided in the annual institutional report.

This requirement was designed to try to eliminate instances where the institution publicly criticises the legal requirements in cases where businesses or the media complain about ridiculous requirements, instead putting the onus on them to remedy the situation.

Information about the implementation of this requirement is also included in the annual report of the institution as well as the list of mandatory performance indicators.

The article also lays out the duty for supervisory institutions to correct information if they provide the media or any third party with inspection-related information that later turns out to be incorrect. The correction must be executed using the same mode as that of its dissemination.

viii. Information about Violations, Sanctions and Fines

Although information about violations and the administrative measures applied is reported and published, the Law explicitly states that numbers of sanctions imposed, the size of sanctions or other indices related to the imposition of sanctions on businesses cannot be the criteria used to evaluate the effectiveness and efficiency of business supervisory institutions and officials. This provision is an important element of the broader quest to transform the goals of inspectorates and change assessment of their performance by superior bodies, politicians and the wider public.

ix. Plans of Inspections

Each business supervisory institution must publish a plan (annual or quarterly) with information about planned inspections. The plan contains details of the business and of the inspection. See Table 6.3, which is an example inspection plan for fire safety inspection.

Table 6.3 The inspection plan of Lithuanian State fire and safety department Kėdainiai territorial unit (2017)

No	Title of the establishment	Address of the establishment	Risk category of the establishment	Date of the planned inspection	Title of the territorial unit carrying out inspection
1	Farm X	Kėdainių regional municipality, Pelėdnagių subdistrict, Kudžioniai	I	May	Kėdainių fire and safety department unit
2	Healthcare centre X	Kėdainių regional municipality, Pelėdnagių subdistrict, Pelėdnagiai, [street]	II	February	Kėdainių fire and safety department unit
3	Farm Y	Kėdainių regional municipality, Pelėdnagių subdistrict, Beinaičiai	II	March	Kėdainių fire and safety department unit
4	Manufacturer X	Kėdainių regional municipality, Pelėdnagių subdistrict, Pelėdnagiai, [street]	II	August	Kėdainių fire and safety department unit
5	Manufacturer Y	Kėdainių regional municipality, Pelėdnagių subdistrict, Pelėdnagiai	III	January	Kėdainių fire and safety department unit
9	Cultural centre X	Kėdainių regional municipality, Josvainių subdistrict, Josvainiai, [street]	I	August	Kėdainių fire and safety department unit

x. Internal Administrative Information

According to the Law on the Right to Obtain Information from State and Municipal Institutions and Bodies, state institutions are obliged to publish the salaries of employees. The information is provided as an average of a group of employees, not personalised. For example, the heads of units received a salary of 1,646 euros before deduction of taxes, and senior specialists (including inspectors) received a salary of 1,079 euros[20] before the deduction of taxes. The actual salary of individual employees would differ because of the various complementary payments, for example additions for the number of years in the public service.

xi. Vehicles Used by the Institution

There is also an obligation on the state institutions to publish the list of the vehicles owned and used by the institution. The underlying reason for this requirement is based on the track record of poor management of vehicles, eg usage for non-work-related travel, and reckless or disrespectful driving. The requirement also requires the name of the institution to be visible on the vehicle. It is believed that public oversight could play a role in disciplining the use of public property.

xii. Legal Documents

Legal documents that control the business supervisory institution's internal procedures and actions, as follows:

- rules on appeals (besides the framework in the Law on Public Administration): business supervisory institutions adopt rules detailing procedures on lodging an appeal against the decision, procedures on internal review;
- rules on complaints by citizens and businesses filed about non-compliance of businesses with the legal requirements: assessment of such complaints, anonymity, follow up on complaints; and
- rules on carrying out inspections: rules prescribing duties and obligations of inspectors during the process, planning and authorisation of inspection process.

xiii. Information about the Activities of the Institution

Activities such as goals, plans of the institution, monitoring, performance management, and different activities carried out and services rendered.

V. Accessibility of Transparency Information to the Public

The use and perception of information depends on its accessibility, user-friendliness and layout. Layout of the information discussed on the web pages of all state institutions is mandated by a government regulation. The decree titled 'General description of

[20] Lithuanian State Labour inspectorate, available at www.vdi.lt, salaries of employees for the third quarter 2017.

requirements for webpages of state and municipal institutions'[21] stipulates that the structure of the business supervisory institution's website must be clear, simple and user-friendly, the menu headings must be accurate, and must not exceed four words.

The institution's website must contain the following sections and areas:

1   Structure and contacts
2   Legal information:

   a   Legislation
   b   Draft legislation
   c   Analysis and research
   d   Violations/non-conformities
   e   Monitoring of legal regulation/implementation

3   Areas of activity of the institution
4   Corruption prevention instruments
5   Administrative information:

   a   Regulations;
   b   Planning documents;
   c   Information about wages of employees;
   d   Incentives and awards;
   e   Public procurement information
   f   Budget execution reports;
   g   Financial statements;
   h   The supervision of businesses;
   i   Vehicles owned or used by the institution.

6   Services provided by the institution
7   Links

The required structure is followed by all institutions, enabling users to navigate with ease.

Business supervisory institutions also use other layouts to give clearer pathways for businesses to find the relevant information. For example, the State Labour Inspectorate and State Food and Veterinary Authority have a 'For Business' box located at the top of the first page. This does not preclude the publication of business-supervision-related information in the structure required by law.

A. Ease of Accessibility

Although a lot of information is provided by business supervisory institutions there are still areas to be improved:

- Simplification of information to make it more accessible. A lot of information could be revised and reformulated for better accessibility, for example through the use of plain language or omission of minor unnecessary details (still mandated by law but irrelevant for the majority of users).

---

[21] Decree No 480, 18 April 2003.

- Moving to a structure based on business processes, different groups/types of businesses that would be more accessible to users than the current layout where information is structured according to law or institutional structures.

- More systematic attempts to constantly monitor user behaviour with the aim of improving access, layout and downloads. There are few proactive attempts to encourage users to provide feedback on the usefulness and ease of use of the websites (eg no pop-up windows, or feedback forms asking 'Did you find the information useful?').

- Better analysis of usage of information by businesses and citizens. Very few institutions track what documents are retrieved from their sites, how users get to the information they want or how users navigate through their websites.

VI. Conclusions

The inspection reform entailed a major shift in the role and tools of business supervisory institutions. A focus on delivering policy objectives rather than merely enforcing legal requirements and a broader understanding of the importance of compliance promotion led to the need to open supervisory institutions to scrutiny from businesses and the public. Tools of transparency empowered businesses to comply and cooperate with inspectors rather than remain passive inspected subjects or objects of observation.

A strong governance framework establishing transparency rules for business supervisory institutions was created. Most of the institutions comply with the framework and indeed have made additional efforts to make more information publicly available and increase the accessibility of this information. There is general consensus amongst inspectorates that business supervisory activities – including legal requirements businesses have to comply with and internal rules that govern the planning and inspection process should be publicly available.

The usability of information and actual use of information that is provided still needs to be assessed and improved. There is little analysis on what is used and needed by businesses. There is a lot of room to learn from the private sector on understanding the needs of businesses, tailoring information for better accessibility and analysing current patterns.

The reform established that all supervisory institutions despite the different fields that they work in – from food to technical safety – share the same core function in the state administration system therefore the rules pertaining to inspections, planning and publication requirements should be similar.

Prerequisites: Accountability

7

Accountability

GRAHAM RUSSELL AND HELEN KIRKMAN

This chapter explores Accountability, one of the three elements considered within the Regulatory Delivery Model as fundamental prerequisites to provide the right conditions for regulatory agencies to operate effectively. Reflection on the accountability of the regulatory agency to government, beneficiaries and those it regulates can improve understanding of the current position and enable identification of improvement that is needed.

In this chapter we first consider what is meant by accountability – addressing the questions of what the regulatory agency should be accountable for and to whom – and highlighting some of the reasons why it is important for regulatory agencies. We then set out the approach taken in the Regulatory Delivery Model to structuring reflections on accountability by reference to three aspects: the transparency that is crucial if accountability is to work well; appropriate mechanisms for interested third parties to hold the regulatory agency to account; and the capacity of various stakeholders to hold the agency to account effectively.

We will also consider the interactions between Accountability and other elements of the Regulatory Delivery Model, in particular Governance Frameworks (see chapter three) and Culture (see chapter ten).

I. Defining Accountability

Accountability, in the context of regulation, can be defined as 'the obligation to account for regulatory activities to another body or person'.[1] It is understood within the Regulatory Delivery Model in terms of the empowerment of stakeholders to participate in the regulatory process and to challenge the regulatory agency. It is important both as a constraint on the behaviour of the regulatory agency and as an enabler – by strengthening the authorising environment through creation of confidence and utilisation of trust.

In defining accountability in respect of regulatory agencies it is important to consider both what the regulatory agency should be accountable for and to whom they should be accountable.

---

[1] Martin Lodge, 'Accountability and Transparency in Regulation: Critiques, Doctrines, and Instruments' in Jacint Jordana and David Levi-Faur (eds), *Politics of Regulation: Institutions and Regulatory Reforms for the Age of Governance* (Cheltenham, Edward Elgar Publishing, 2004).

A. Accountable for What?

This question of what the regulatory agency should be accountable for was addressed in the UK by a House of Lords select committee that conducted a review of regulatory account-ability in 2003.[2] The review concluded that 'Regulators should be accountable for cost effective regulation which meets rational, well-defined objectives'. Fundamentally, they felt that regulatory agencies should be accountable for how they are delivering regulation to achieve the purposes or outcomes of the law.

The same question was addressed by the World Bank Group in its 2006 guidelines for reformers of business inspections.[3] Three areas in which regulators should be account-able were considered and different methods of accountability were identified in respect of each:

- Financial, through review during the annual budget process.
- Policy, through assessment of performance against goals and targets.
- Judgement of quality of inspectorate actions through appeals procedures and review by courts and other due-process mechanisms.

In practice, the question of what the regulatory agency should be accountable for is highly dependent on the perspective of the party wishing to hold them to account, with different parties placing a varying degree of emphasis on the three areas of accountability identified by the World Bank Group.

B. Accountable to Whom?

Traditional views of accountability have often focused, sometimes exclusively, on the rela-tionship between the regulatory agency and the state, looking for example to Parliament or ministers to hold the agency to account. More recently, there has been increasing interest in a broader view of regulatory accountability.

The Regulatory Delivery Model encourages a wide consideration of accountability, with a focus on three parties in particular: the state, referred to here and throughout this chapter as 'government'; the 'beneficiaries' of regulation (referring both directly to those whom the law aims to protect and to those who articulate their concerns – whether that is groups such as trade unions representing workers or people speaking up for the environment and animals); and businesses and others that are regulated, referred to as 'regulated entities'. Figure 7.1 is a simple representation of some of the relationships between these parties.

Accountability in relation to regulatory agencies means different things to government, beneficiaries and regulated entities, and it is important to each for different reasons. Some of these reasons are explored briefly here, before considering the importance, for the regu-latory agency, of responding to and working with the competing forces from each of these parties.

---

[2] 'The Regulatory State: Ensuring its Accountability, House of Lords Select Committee on the Constitution 6th Report of Session 2003–2004' (The Stationery Office, 2004).
[3] 'Good Practices for Business Inspections: Guidelines for Reformers' (World Bank Group, 2006).

Figure 7.1 Accountabilities of the Regulatory Agency

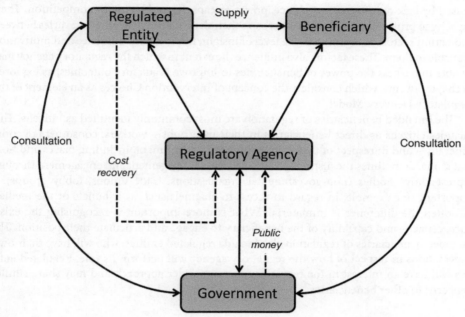

i. Accountability to Government

Government, both as the owner of the policy underpinning the regulatory requirements delivered by the regulatory agency and, in many cases as the provider of public money to the regulatory agency to fund its activities, has a clear interest in the activities of the regulatory agency and what it is achieving. As explored later in this chapter, the relationship between government and a regulatory agency will usually be characterised by formal accountability mechanisms.

In terms of accountability, government also acts as a proxy for the intended beneficiaries of the protections established by regulation – whether these relate to individual citizens as workers or consumers, or more widely, shaping places and safeguarding the environment – who have a reasonable expectation the government will ensure that regulatory agencies perform their role in an effective and efficient manner, making proper use of their resources.

ii. Accountability to the Beneficiaries of Regulation

Regulatory agencies exercise the authority of the state and spend public money to deliver their role. They are accountable to citizens and others for ensuring that the intended benefits of regulation are realised. Whilst this accountability to beneficiaries is delivered, in part, through the regulatory agency's accountability to government, regulators should not overlook their direct accountability to beneficiaries and should consider what accountability mechanisms will work for the particular groups concerned.

Citizens and other beneficiaries depend on regulation to correct imbalances in 'markets' caused by lack of information, choice, power or capacity and by unfair competition. Their capacity to protect themselves, and therefore their dependence on regulators, varies between and within sectors accounting to the level of insight, information, influence and motivation available to them. These factors also influence the extent to which the regulatory agency may be able to harness the power of beneficiaries to improve regulatory outcomes, as explored in chapter twenty, which considers the concept of Intervention Choices as an element of the Regulatory Delivery Model.

The intended beneficiaries of regulation are most commonly identified as 'citizens'. This includes citizens as direct beneficiaries in their own right – workers, consumers or more generally – and in respect of their concern for the environment, including places and flora and fauna. Sometimes the distinction between direct engagement and engagement through representative bodies (non-governmental organisations, trade unions, lobby groups) is important (for example, in regard to access to channels such as tribunals or the media), but often the difference is immaterial. What is more important is recognising the existence, capacity and capability of the beneficiary to engage and articulate their position. The intended beneficiaries of regulation also include regulated entities, who will have their own expectations in respect of how the regulatory agency will perform its role. Regulated entities will have an interest in the regulatory agency's wider approach and may share similar concerns to other beneficiaries.

iii. Accountability to Regulated Entities

Regulation has an impact which can be different from the perspective of an individual regulated entity and from the perspective of 'all those subject to the regulatory requirements', referred to here, for simplicity, as a 'sector'. Similarly, the impact of being regulated by the regulatory agency can be different from the perspective of the individual and that of the sector. It is important therefore that the regulatory agency takes account of these two perspectives when considering its accountability to regulated entities.

The experience of being regulated is inevitably coloured by the nature of the relationship between the regulatory agency and those it regulates. We return therefore to the question, explored elsewhere in this book, of the unique and defining characteristics of this relationship. Regulatory agencies are monopolistic by nature, as are most public bodies, and this means that regulated entities do not, in most cases, have any choice as to who they are regulated by. In addition, regulatory agencies differ from other public bodies in that, in order to deliver their task of ensuring that regulated entities meet regulatory requirements, they are authorised to exercise the coercive power of the state. For example, they may be empowered to require remedial action to be taken or to propose or impose punitive sanctions. This creates an inevitable imbalance of power between the regulatory agency and those subject to the regulatory requirements. Regulatory agencies and their officers are often able to exercise their powers with a significant degree of discretion and this discretion, whilst it is valuable and has the potential to bring benefits, also presents challenges (see chapter ten for discussion on this point), giving rise to risks of arbitrariness, inconsistency, capture or corruption.

Seen from the perspective of the sector or the individual regulated entity, robust accountability mechanisms help to provide the checks and balances necessary to ensure that the regulatory agency exercises its discretion appropriately. The obligation that regulators have to protect those they regulate from the unfettered use of their powers is discharged in part by being accountable to businesses and their competitors. A distinction can be drawn here between relationships between a regulatory agency and regulated community that are sector-based (for example, the regulation of consumer product manufacturers by a product safety regulator) and those that are locality based (such as the regulation of a wide range of businesses in a geographic area by a regulatory agency that has a broad regulatory remit). Both types of regulated communities are likely to have an interest in the regulatory agency's performance and will have an interest in questions of fairness and of whether a level playing field is in operation. However, their key concerns and interest in various issues are likely to differ and engagement methods should be selected to respond to these differences. (See further the discussion of the different purposes of the UK's Business Reference Panel and Better Business for All programmes later in this chapter.)

iv. *The Competing Forces of Accountability*

Whilst a consideration of accountability in relation to each of the three parties – government, beneficiaries and regulated entities – is important, it is critical that they are not solely considered in isolation. An assessment of how the accountabilities to each of the three parties are working relative to each other can identify whether their relative strength is appropriate.

Where there is an imbalance of accountabilities, the regulatory agency may find itself unduly influenced by the wishes or needs of one party, to the detriment of the others, a phenomenon described, at its extreme, as 'regulatory capture'.[4] Regulatory capture can involve a regulatory agency acting in a way that is beneficial to an individual regulated entity or sector at the expense of the protections that it is tasked with delivering. However, a regulatory agency might equally be 'captured' by the interests of a particular group of citizens or, for example, an environmental lobby group. In any case of capture other interest groups lose out. In this example, the resultant focus on particular protections may leave little room for the voice of those regulated to be heard leading to unnecessarily high levels of regulatory burden that can be damaging to economic prosperity.

Where the Regulatory Delivery Model is used as a diagnostic tool this ideally involves the reviewing team having direct conversations with representatives of all three parties as well as with the regulatory agency and its staff. This is important because accountability will tend to mean different things to each of these parties; its mechanisms will inevitably be different, and key concerns will also differ. These discussions can elicit varying perspectives on accountability, providing insights into how accountability mechanisms are working in practice for different parties.

When working with regulatory agencies, we have used a workshop exercise to explore how accountabilities to each of the three parties work relative to each other in practice. The exercise involves a representative from the regulatory agency standing in a plastic hoop which is attached to three ropes. The ropes are then handed to three participants playing the roles of regulated entities, government and beneficiaries. These three participants are encouraged to pull on their rope each time they articulate a means by which they can hold

---

[4] George Stigler, 'The Theory of Economic Regulation' (1971) 2 *The Bell Journal of Economics and Management Science* 3.

the regulatory agency to account. It is only by providing an appropriate level of accountability in all three directions that the regulatory agency can be held in a central position, avoiding mischiefs such as regulatory failure or capture or excessive burdens that arise when the regulatory agency is pulled too close to one of the three parties, at the expense of the other two.

The regulatory agency's accountability to government, beneficiaries and regulated entities can be strengthened or substituted by the existence of effective accountability mechanisms between the regulatory agency and its peers. The benefits that this collaboration brings in terms of accountability are explored in various chapters of this book. In particular, chapter nine examines the way in which the accountability of a lead regulatory agency to its peers provides confidence through the UK's Primary Authority scheme and chapter eleven considers the experience of the Netherlands' Inspection Council, which has established a sense of regulatory agencies acting as co-players in the regulatory system, with the collaboration between them strengthening effectiveness, for example through the sharing of data and good practice.

II. The Importance of Accountability to the Regulatory Agency

As we have seen in examining the different accountability relationships of regulatory agencies, accountability is important to government, beneficiaries and regulated entities in different ways. However, we should not lose sight of the benefits that accountability brings to the regulatory agency itself.

One benefit is in the way people view the agency. Experience shows that where a regulatory agency recognises the importance of accountability and takes a wide view of it, actively encouraging feedback and external challenge from a wide range of stakeholders and ensuring that the feedback received informs their behaviour and actions, this creates the conditions for the regulatory agency to be more credible and trusted. Conversely, where accountability is poor, this tends to result in a mutual lack of understanding and trust which can impact adversely on the effectiveness of the regulatory agency.

Other benefits relate to the agency's outcomes directly. The relationships built through the establishment of robust accountability mechanisms enable regulatory agencies to be better informed, which directly influences their ability to regulate well. Alongside its own actions to mitigate risks, the regulatory agency's task is to change behaviours, using the range of tools at their disposal to ensure that regulated entities comply with the regulatory requirements. The factors that should guide regulatory agencies in choosing the appropriate tools are explored in detail in chapter twenty and also feature strongly in the work of Christopher Hodges and Ruth Steinholtz on Ethical Business Practice and Regulation (see chapter twenty-two). For some purposes and in some contexts, these choices will lead to the regulatory agency taking on the role of encouraging and supporting the majority to comply. The mantra that 'You can't regulate what you don't understand' is commonly used in relation to the risks that regulation seeks to control, often in association with a call for more scientific data. However, it is equally true of regulated entities and this presents regulatory agencies with varying degrees of challenge, depending on the multiplicity of environments in which they may be engaged. A way of understanding this role is to consider the challenge facing a salesman trying to close a deal. The salesman needs to understand what the customer wants or values, what might persuade them to buy a particular product, and equally what might deter them from buying it. Similarly, a regulatory agency taking on the role of selling compliance needs to understand what is important to those it regulates; what might encourage them to comply and what barriers to compliance might be in play. In this metaphor, regulated entities are seen as customers of the regulatory agency and accountability mechanisms enable the agency to listen to the views of regulated entities and understand how their products, messages and methods can be shaped to be most persuasive. Taking the metaphor further, just as a sales manager might get too close to a customer and be rotated by their director to maximise returns, so a regulatory agency selling compliance can lose sight of the purpose of the regulatory requirements and the needs of the beneficiary. Effective accountability holds all parties in parity and shines a light into dark places.

Regulatory accountability is inextricably linked to the other prerequisites of the Regulatory Delivery Model – Governance Frameworks and Culture (see chapters three and ten respectively) – and here too the benefits of good accountability mechanisms are evident.

Governance provides the framework within which accountability operates and can be used to drive transparent behaviour on the part of the regulatory agency, enabling accountability. The use of governance frameworks to drive improvements in transparency and accountability has been well illustrated in chapters five and six, which explore the different approaches taken in the UK and Lithuania. However, the relationship between the regulatory agency's governance and accountability is not one way. The operation of accountability mechanisms acts as an enabler for effective governance by providing feedback and control. It creates the opportunity for stakeholders to input the information, challenge and views that can drive and inform changes to both decisions and decision-making processes. Accountability mechanisms therefore have the potential to strengthen the regulatory agency's governance and its governance frameworks.

Similarly, the interactions between accountability and the regulatory agency's culture are two-way. Where appropriate accountability mechanisms are in place and are working well, they can help to shape the regulatory agency's culture and can be actively used to drive a cultural change. A clear example is provided by Chris Webb in his account of the cultural change programme undertaken by the Environment Protection Authority in Victoria, Australia (see chapter twelve). Equally, the regulatory agency's approach to accountability is shaped by its organisational culture and examples of this have been seen in regulatory agencies that were established with a consumer protection purpose and have consequently developed an organisational culture that has a narrow external outlook, focused on consumers. Such a regulatory agency may see its accountabilities as being to individual consumers, consumer representatives and government (as a proxy for the consumer interest) and may pay insufficient attention to its accountability to those it regulates.

III. Aspects of Accountability

Reflection on accountability is structured, within the Regulatory Delivery Model, by reference to three factors that are recognised as enablers of accountability in relation to all three parties to whom the regulatory agency is accountable. These enablers – transparency, the existence and operation of accountability mechanisms, and the capacity and willingness of the third party to hold the regulatory agency to account – are explored further here.

A. Transparency

Transparency is a key enabler of accountability. Transparency enables stakeholders to understand the expectations, approach and activities of the regulatory agency and this understanding in turn enables informed input by stakeholders and challenge where stakeholders feel that the regulatory agency is not acting appropriately.

The importance of transparency for regulatory agencies is widely recognised, with the incorporation of transparency requirements into the governance framework for regulatory agencies being common where reform of regulatory delivery is underway. This is demonstrated by the UK and Lithuania examples referred to earlier (see chapters five and six) and in the case studies included in Part 3 (chapters twenty-four, twenty-five and twenty-six). A further example is the approach taken by the Australian Government as part of its efforts to improve the performance of its regulatory agencies. It has established key performance indicators that cover active transparency, alongside 'reducing regulatory burden, communications, risk-based and proportionate approaches, efficient and coordinated monitoring and continuous improvement'. Regulatory agencies are required to measure and publicly report their performance in these areas and there is a clear expectation that this will both drive improvements in the performance of regulators and 'give business, the community and individuals confidence that regulators effectively and flexibly manage risk'.[5] This example also illustrates one aspect of the interrelationship between the prerequisites and practices of the Regulatory Delivery Model, with Outcome Measurement (see chapter thirteen) acting as an enabler of greater accountability.

The extent to which a regulatory agency is committed to transparency can be judged, in the first instance, by considering what information it proactively makes available, for example by: publication of its objectives and priorities; written enforcement policies[6] stating how it will respond to non-compliance and the factors that will be taken into account in determining appropriate enforcement action; details of its activities[7] and enforcement actions taken;[8] and details of appeals against its actions. As noted earlier, the discretion afforded to regulatory agencies and their officers can give rise to various risks, and measures are needed to counter those risks, including a transparent approach by the regulatory agency. The regulatory agency may choose to place greater emphasis on transparency on its approach to issues that give rise to particular concerns amongst its stakeholders about the discretionary nature of its powers. For example, by providing clarity about its interpretation in relation to contentious points or about its focus and priorities.[9]

---

[5] 'Regulator Performance Framework' (Australian Government, 2014).

[6] Christopher Hodges, *Law and Corporate Behaviour: Integrating Theories of Regulation, Enforcement, Culture and Ethics* (Oxford, Hart Publishing, 2015) ch 13.

[7] See, for example, 'Enforcement and Market Surveillance Annual Report 2016–17' (Office for Product Safety and Standards, 2018).

[8] See, for example, the lists of enforcement actions published by the Office for Product Safety and Standards, available at www.gov.uk/government/publications/statutory-enforcement-actions.

[9] See, for example, 'Statement from FDA Commissioner Scott Gottlieb, M.D. on FDA Food Safety Modernization Act enforcement discretion guidance' (US Food and Drug Administration, 2018), available at www.fda.gov/NewsEvents/Newsroom/PressAnnouncements/ucm591382.htm.

However, publication of information alone may not achieve transparency; information must be made available in such a way that it is easily accessible and that allows different target audiences to engage with it. This requires the regulatory agency to have an understanding of the needs and preferences of the different parties and to be responsive to these needs by considering how it can simplify and present information in a way that will meet current needs while recognising that these may change over time. We return to this question of understanding different needs later in this chapter, when considering the capacity of different groups to hold the regulatory agency to account.

B. Accountability Mechanisms

The accountability mechanisms between the regulatory agency and the different parties to whom it is accountable can take many forms. A single mechanism is very unlikely to provide effective accountability, and accountability mechanisms will usually be multiple and varied, to meet the diverse needs of different stakeholder groups.

In considering the regulatory agency's accountability to different parties it is important to recognise the significance of proxies in many areas of regulation, in representing the views of those that might not make their own individual voices heard. For example, individual consumers, workers or smaller businesses may be reliant on proxies such as consumer bodies, trade unions or trade associations to hold the regulatory agency to account. Proxies are also important where the intended beneficiary or beneficiaries of regulation, do not have their own voice, which is the case, for example, for animals or the environment.

Accountability mechanisms may be formal – embedded in the regulatory agency's governance framework – or informal. We will consider here both formal and informal mechanisms, in relation to government, beneficiaries and regulated entities.

i. Accountability Mechanisms – Government

Traditionally, formal accountability mechanisms have often been restricted to the relationship between the regulatory agency and government. Government, both as the owner of the regulatory requirements delivered by the regulatory agency and, in many cases as the provider of public money to the regulatory agency to fund its activities, will usually have established formal accountability mechanisms between itself and the regulatory agency, for example through the legislative framework that forms part of governance.

In the UK, the House of Lords identified, in its 2004 consideration of regulatory accountability, three elements of formal accountability mechanisms: 'the duty to explain; exposure to scrutiny; and the possibility of independent review'.[10] Formal accountability mechanisms to government are likely to incorporate all three of these elements. They may cover the regulatory agency's accountability for policy outcomes, compliance with standards, performance and use of public money. Specific requirements may be included in the regulatory agency's founding statute; for example, requirements to provide annual

[10] 'The Regulatory State' (2004).

reports and accounts.[11] Equally, generic provisions may apply, such as scrutiny arrangements applicable to all bodies funded by public money[12] or periodic reviews. In the UK, independent regulatory agencies were subject, from 2011, to substantive reviews at least once every three years. More recently, there has been a move away from these triennial reviews of individual regulators to a thematic approach, with functional reviews of agencies in similar or related areas of government to identify opportunities for improvement.[13]

The extent of accountability to government must be viewed in the context of the value of visible independence of the regulatory agency and this requires careful consideration of the nature and extent of mechanisms such as ministerial oversight. The UK's Committee on Standards in Public Life addressed itself to the challenges faced by regulatory agencies in this area,[14] concluding that

> government has a legitimate, democratic interest in the strategic direction of a regulatory body and in its efficiency and overall effectiveness. However, governments must not be involved in the operational decisions of regulators as this would influence and undermine their judgement and their authority. Clarity and transparency about the interaction between regulatory bodies and the government can go a long way to allay fears of misplaced interference.

The Committee made a best practice recommendation that 'The operational independence of regulators must be upheld. Ministerial guidance on operational aspects may be transparently considered, but should not be treated as binding, unless there are statutory provisions for such guidance'.

The OECD, in considering best practice for the governance of regulators, addressed the question of independence as a means of protecting regulators from undue influence and maintaining trust in their integrity, establishing a principle[15] that:

> Independent regulatory decision-making at arm's length from the political process, is likely to be appropriate where:
>
> - there is a need for the regulator to be seen as independent, to maintain public confidence in the objectivity and impartiality of decisions;
> - both government and non-government entities are regulated under the same framework and competitive neutrality is therefore required;
> - the decisions of the regulator can have a significant impact on particular interests and there is a need to protect its impartiality;
> - the autonomy of regulators (organisational, financial and decision-making) situated within a ministry should be safeguarded by provisions in their empowering legislation.

---

[11] Examples include the UK's Civil Aviation Authority (required to report to Parliament under the Civil Aviation Act 1982) and Gambling Commission (required to report to Parliament under the Gambling Act 2005 and the National Lottery etc Act 1993).

[12] In the UK, the National Audit Office is responsible for scrutiny of public spending. It audits the financial statements of all central government departments, agencies and other public bodies, and reports the results to Parliament. The policy, administration and spending of regulatory bodies can also be subject to scrutiny by Parliamentary Committees.

[13] See, for example, 'Regulatory Futures Review' (Cabinet Office, 2017).

[14] 'Striking the Balance: Upholding the Seven Principles of Public Life in Regulation' (Committee on Standards in Public Life, 2016).

[15] 'The Governance of Regulators', OECD Best Practice Principles for Regulatory Policy (OECD, 2014).

ii. Accountability Mechanisms – Beneficiaries

The regulatory agency's governance framework may establish formal accountability mechanisms in relation to beneficiaries and these are likely to relate to wider engagement, such as requirements to consult on proposed approaches or requirements to maintain engagement mechanisms.

However, accountability mechanisms in respect of beneficiaries are frequently informal and these informal mechanisms vary greatly. Depending on the context, it may be appropriate for the regulatory agency to establish sustained and ongoing mechanisms (such as established citizen panels) or to use ad hoc mechanisms (such as 'one-off' consultation exercises).

Accountability mechanisms need to provide means for the intended beneficiaries of regulation to participate and challenge at multiple levels. At a strategic level, regulatory agencies need to take responsibility for encouraging dialogue, gathering views in relation to their ways of working and taking account of these views. At the individual level, regulatory agencies need to make available good mechanisms for feedback and challenge in regard to actions and decisions.

There is a need for the regulatory agency to consider whether it is, in so far as is possible, gathering representative views and to provide a multiplicity of mechanisms where appropriate. However, it is important to recognise that it can be challenging to gather views first hand, in particular from some groups of citizens. In these circumstances, representative groups or other interested parties – such as consumer associations or social or environmental non-governmental organisations – can act as a useful proxy.

iii. Accountability Mechanisms – Regulated Entities

In relation to regulated entities, formal accountability mechanisms should address both feedback and challenge. Feedback covers the broad range of views the entities may have about the practice and policies of the agency while challenge focuses, in particular, on the rights to appeal against individual enforcement actions taken by the regulatory agency. Challenge mechanisms are particularly important in respect of regulatory actions, decisions and sanctions, as a means of ensuring the regulatory agency's proper use of the coercive power of the state. The OECD[16] recommends that:

> Citizens and businesses that are subject to the decisions of public authorities should have ready access to systems for challenging the exercise of that authority. This is particularly important in relation to regulatory sanctions, i.e. sanctions issued by an authority in virtue of a regulation.

In the UK, the challenge mechanisms are established in the legislative framework, with rights to appeal to a court or tribunal being routinely included in regulations that make sanctions available to the regulatory agency, and an independent backstop being provided in respect of complaints, which may be escalated to an Ombudsman.[17] Nevertheless, views gathered from business[18] identified concerns about the effectiveness of regulatory complaints and

---

[16] 'Recommendation of the Council on Regulatory Policy and Governance' (OECD, 2012).
[17] The Local Government Ombudsman or the Parliamentary and Health Service Ombudsman.
[18] The findings of UK Government's 'Focus on Enforcement' review are reported in 'Small Business Appeals Champions and Non-Economic Regulators: Consultation' (Department for Business, Innovation and Skills, 2014).

appeals systems. The issues complained of were reported to fall into the following broad categories:

- The explanation or advertising of procedures. Businesses have expressed concerns about lack of knowledge and understanding on their part as to how to go about querying, complaining about, or appealing against action taken by a regulator.
- Opportunity for problems to be resolved informally before prohibitively costly formal processes are triggered.
- The operational independence of the person considering the complaint or appeal.
- The publication and collection of data on complaints and appeals that would allow third-party scrutiny of a regulator's performance.

These concerns were responded to, in part, by strengthening guidance to regulatory agencies about their complaints and appeals processes through the Regulators' Code[19] (see chapter five) which requires complaints and appeals processes to be impartial and clearly explained.

Mechanisms for challenging the regulatory agency's actions or appealing against enforcement decisions need to be accessible and well explained and it is important that regulatory agencies recognise the concerns of regulated entities that might consider making a complaint or appeal. These concerns, whether justified or not, are usually rooted in the imbalance of power between the regulatory agency and those it regulates, and are a likely contributor to the experience – common to many regulatory agencies – of very low numbers of challenges and appeals.

The provision of a mechanism for reviewing whether complaints and appeals processes are operating in a fair manner can be one way of providing assurance to regulated entities that they can trust and avail themselves of complaints and appeals mechanisms without fear of retribution.

However, accountability is not just about the rights of appeal. At the individual level, regulatory agencies also need to make available good mechanisms for feedback on routine interactions. Chapter six provides an example of progress in this area in Lithuania, reporting on the introduction of a centrally administered electronic feedback system that gathers feedback from businesses that have been inspected by a range of regulatory agencies (see Box 6.1). The design of this system acknowledges the challenge for regulatory agencies of obtaining honest feedback from businesses, who can be fearful of being seen to criticise their regulator. Research in the UK in 2003 explored solutions to various aspects of this challenge, comparing the results of questionnaires sent directly to inspected business by local regulators with the results of face-to-face interviews by independent researchers and identifying that businesses were more willing to express dissatisfaction to the independent researchers. A further stage of the same research explored some of the issues around a lack of willingness to provide feedback to the regulatory agency. Businesses from four ethnic minority communities were targeted, employing researchers from the same community as the businesses.[20] Honest feedback on the experience of being inspected is valuable to the regulatory agency as it can help it to identify issues on the frontline and

---

[19] 'Regulators' Code' (Better Regulation Delivery Office, 2014).
[20] Helen Kirkman, 'Improving the Assessment of Business Needs' (unpublished report prepared for MidCOTS, a regional group of Trading Standards services in the West Midlands, 2004).

to evaluate whether its inspection programme is effective. It is therefore important for regulatory agencies to seek such feedback and to do so in ways that maximise response rates and address any concerns that businesses might have about being frank about their experience.

Research into why regulated entities don't engage is limited but informal discussions have suggested four avenues for exploration to understand why they tend not to make use of accountability mechanisms, including but not limited to appeals. Some are genuinely scared of retribution and see no basis for trust that they will not suffer consequences. Evidence for the extent of this concern is found in the proportion of queries made under the UK Regulators' Code that call for independent investigation of complaints. Others are too busy with the functions of business to step aside to improve the system. This can be combined with scepticism about the extent of the regulatory agency's commitment and therefore the likely impact of their efforts. Finally, and perhaps most intriguingly, representatives talk about a sense that, in a world of complex rules and regulations, a regulated entity knows they have probably got something wrong and are therefore guilty of some degree of non-compliance. Even if the thing they have been accused of is not true, there will be something else they have failed to do. As a result, they feel guilty and may be concerned that these additional crimes could be discovered. While regulators may explain that each of these concerns is unnecessary and businesses should trust them, if we consider our own responses when interacting as private individuals with agencies that wield the power of the state, such as the police, can we detect traces of similar thinking?

Accountability mechanisms need to build confidence to address these concerns. They also need to provide means for sectors and individual regulated entities to participate and challenge at other levels and these mechanisms are commonly informal. As with beneficiaries, regulatory agencies need to take responsibility for encouraging dialogue with sectors and individual regulated entities at a strategic level, gathering views in relation to their ways of working and taking account of these views. There is, again, a need for the regulatory agency to provide a multiplicity of mechanisms where appropriate and to consider whether it is gathering representative views. Intermediaries that have existing trusted relationships with particular regulated communities can play an important role in representing the views of those communities to the regulatory agency. For example, trade associations that have a good understanding of the views and experience of their members can act as a source of information for the regulatory agency that is particularly valuable in relation to smaller businesses, whose views might not otherwise be heard.

C. Capacity of Third Parties

Formal and informal accountability mechanisms need to be supported, if they are to be effective in holding the regulatory agency to account and driving positive change, by active participation on the part of the third parties to whom the regulatory agency is accountable. This requires an appropriate level of capacity to scrutinise, understand and challenge the agency.

While this level of capacity may usually be assumed to exist in government, the regulatory agency should be mindful of the need to educate its government sponsors in relation to current issues and challenges that the agency is facing. Similarly, a level of capacity can normally be assumed in relation to business sector representatives.

However, the regulatory agency should remain conscious that capacity may be limited in some business sectors and areas of civil society and it is important that the regulatory agency has an understanding of whose voices it is hearing and responding to. Views differ on the question of whether the regulatory agency has a responsibility in such situations to provide support to build the capacity of the groups that are not actively engaging with it. While some consider that this goes beyond the role of the regulatory agency, others point (philosophically) to the power imbalance and the obligation of the powerful to redress the balance; (politically) to the state's responsibility to listen; or (pragmatically) to the benefits to the agency of a balanced, comprehensive understanding of views. Each of these proponents would argue that this responsibility is not limited to circumstances where views are being expressed loudly and clearly but extends to those whose views are not readily expressed or clearly articulated (sometimes expressed as a 'bias to the poor').[21] In the UK, the public sector equality duty[22] requires regulators, as public bodies, to take steps to meet the needs of people from protected groups where these are different from the needs of other people and to encourage their participation in public life or in other activities where this is disproportionately low. A good level of understanding is required in order to meet the expectations set by the equality duty. Mapping the sources of enquiries and complaints in a way that highlights areas of under-representation and seeking to identify the reasons for these can help a regulatory agency to build this understanding.

There can be clear benefits to the regulatory agency in building capacity amongst under-represented groups (which can be regulated entities as well as beneficiaries). By improving their ability to hold the regulatory agency to account and to participate in its development and review of its strategy and policies, the regulatory agency is able to assure itself that it is addressing the outcomes that matter to these groups. In contrast, where the regulatory agency does not take on this responsibility, it risks responding to the views of those best able to protect themselves, further marginalising vulnerable groups.

i. Capacity of Beneficiaries

A consideration of capacity to hold the regulatory agency to account is of particular relevance in respect of beneficiaries. The regulatory agency should take responsibility, particularly where civil society representation is not well established, for developing capacity; for example, by establishing consumer or citizen panels[23] and committing resource to developing these as an effective accountability mechanism. This can also open up the possibility of employing intervention choices that are delivered through beneficiaries (see chapter twenty).

In the UK, recognition of the importance of accountability to the beneficiaries of regulation has led to the establishment of accountability mechanisms in the legislative framework in certain areas. For example, the UK's Communications Act 2003 established the

---

[21] David Sheppard, *Bias to the Poor* (London, Hodder and Stoughton, 1983).

[22] The public sector equality duty, established by the Equality Act 2010, covers nine protected characteristics: age, disability, gender reassignment, pregnancy and maternity, race, religion or belief, sex and sexual orientation.

[23] Examples include the UK's Civil Aviation Authority Consumer Panel (www.caa.co.uk/Our-work/About-us/CAA-consumer-panel) and Financial Services Consumer Panel (www.fs-cp.org.uk).

Communications Consumer Panel[24] to represent the interests of UK consumers in relation to regulation in the communications sector. The panel describes itself as being independent of the regulator and it represents the interests of consumers, citizens and micro-businesses.

Regulatory agencies in the UK have also developed a wide range of non-statutory mechanisms to improve capacity amongst target groups. Some examples, from the West Midlands, dating back to the 1990s, include the development of a Consumer Watchdog scheme (discussed in the Introduction), which recruited and trained volunteers from the community to act as an informed point of contact between Staffordshire Trading Standards and local communities, and the establishment of a text messaging service providing warnings of scams and rogue traders, which aimed to tackle low levels of engagement with young people.

Being accountable means responding to the variability between beneficiaries, in terms of their ability to protect themselves, their dependence on regulators and their preferred means of interacting with the state. Regulators should proactively consider these imbalances and address them. This includes taking responsibility for considering and being transparent about the need for trade-offs between long- and short-term impacts and between sectors and policies.

ii. Capacity of Regulated Entities

Regulatory agencies should also consider what accountability mechanisms will work for those they regulate and, as with beneficiaries, should consider their responsibility to address any lack of capacity.

Engagement with regulated communities through, for example, business panels, can provide regulatory agencies with a forum in which they can build a relationship which will enable good dialogue and allow the regulated to provide honest feedback and share information. Such mechanisms can promote more informed risk assessment by the regulatory agency, enabling it to make better choices and be more effective. Our experience in running a business panel in the UK since 2009 is that there is significant value in sustained engagement through a recognised, high-profile forum that has broad business representation. The UK's Business Reference Panel comprises the regulatory leads from 150 trade associations, business representative bodies and individual businesses with an outreach potential to over 1.5 million businesses, from micro and start-up businesses to large multi-national corporations. It meets four times a year and shapes the agenda around the issues of greatest concern to members. While this mechanism is powerful in creating national dialogue about new policies or issues affecting specific sectors, it is less effective in addressing concerns around localised impacts and delivery methods. For that a different, more local approach is required and an example of productive engagement with regulated communities is provided in chapter eight, which reports on the development of Better Business for All partnerships with local business communities in the UK.

Whether considering beneficiaries or regulated entities, one aspect of capacity, which almost operates as a sub-set, is the use of language. Government creates its own vocabulary and regulatory agencies can be particularly guilty of this, even if this is through custom

---

[24] Further information on the Communications Consumer Panel is available at www.communications consumerpanel.org.uk.

and culture rather than as a deliberate barrier. The effect is to limit engagement and it is surely the responsibility of the party that creates the esoteric language to also provide the dictionary. Having heard policy-makers ask for 'evidence' when businesses or consumers think that their experience should be validated, and regulators talk confidently about 'risk assessments' when householders are wondering whether their products are safe, it is clear why one business person said: 'I could learn Italian quicker than I could understand you'!

IV. Key Lines of Enquiry

As discussed in chapter two, we have developed key lines of enquiry in respect of each element of the Regulatory Delivery Model that can be used to assess and understand the current picture in respect of that element. These questions, presented in Box 7.1 in respect of Accountability, are intended as a starting point on which a regulatory agency or a third party can build in order to give a sense of where strengths and weaknesses lie and to highlight potential for improvement.

Box 7.1 Key lines of enquiry: accountability

Transparency

- Can the regulatory agency show that it has taken measures to increase the transparency of its functions and processes to regulated entities, to beneficiaries and to government?
- Does the agency communicate in ways that are effective for its context – including through publication but also by use of other effective, relevant channels?
- Does the agency's approach reflect domestic and international good practice?
- Can the agency show that this transparency builds confidence and trust?

Mechanisms

- Are there effective mechanisms to enable the regulatory agency to be held to account by regulated entities, beneficiaries and government?
- Does the agency develop its understanding of the needs and preferences of particular audiences and tailor its accountability mechanisms accordingly?
- Does the agency have appropriate mechanisms for feedback, challenge and appeal for those affected by its regulatory activities?
- Are the agency's accountability mechanisms understood and accessible?
- Does the agency use the outcomes of accountability, including ways it has changed, to demonstrate the value of engagement?

Capacity-building

- Does the regulatory agency have a clear map of those to whom it is accountable?
- Does the agency recognise a responsibility to build the capability of those to whom it is accountable? And does it work to build the capability of those who find it most challenging to hold it to account?
- Can the agency provide evidence that its accountability is effective – including examples of changes to its governance, culture or practices arising from accountability?

V. Summary

This chapter set out to explain why Accountability is of key importance in the Regulatory Delivery Model. We have considered the different parties that regulatory agencies need to think about when considering accountability and looked at the enablers of accountability: transparency; effective mechanisms; and the capacity of third parties. We have also discussed some of the interactions between Accountability and other elements of the Regulatory Delivery Model, which we will explore in more detail in later chapters.

The next two chapters illustrate, through their exploration of two very different developments in local regulatory delivery in the UK, some of the themes that we have touched on in this chapter.

In chapter eight, Martin Traynor provides the business perspective on the development of the Better Business for All programme in his local area and Kathryn Preece explains how the Office for Product Safety and Standards has supported the roll-out of the programme across most areas of England. In chapter nine, Duncan Johnson reports on how the UK's Primary Authority scheme, which enables a business and a local regulatory agency to develop a constructive regulatory relationship, is based on a network of robust accountability mechanisms which enable trust in the scheme.

8

Better Business for All, an Approach to Building Local Capability for Collaboration and Accountability

MARTIN TRAYNOR AND KATHRYN PREECE

This chapter tells the story of the development of closer relationships between a local business community and local regulators, enabling closer collaboration and accountability. Martin Traynor has had a long career in the hospitality sector, which in the UK is heavily regulated, and a subsequent role representing businesses as Chief Executive of Leicestershire Chamber of Commerce, as a member of the Regulatory Policy Committee and as the Small Business Crown Representative. This has given him first-hand experience of how regulation, and the way in which it is delivered, can impact on businesses. Martin gives the business perspective on the economic context and cultural challenges to developing a local solution to better collaboration between regulators and businesses. Kathryn Preece is the Programme Manager for the Office for Product Safety and Standards on simplifying local regulatory delivery and gives the government perspective on the development of this initiative and subsequent spreading of good practice across the country.

I. The Economic Context for Change

It has been argued for some time that the recent recession, along with a long period of austerity, has forced many countries, including the UK, to think about the future of society and to examine what services can be realistically afforded in the new economic climate. In turn, this has forced the public, private and third sectors to take a hard look at all the services they provide in a way that has never been experienced in modern times.

Against this very challenging backdrop, the world of regulation and regulatory delivery once again came under the spotlight, as governments searched for new ways to help stimulate their flagging economies.

A comprehensive review of the UK's regulatory environment was by no means a new initiative. Ever since Harold Wilson, President of the Board of Trade in 1947, famously promised to deliver 'a bonfire of regulations' successive governments have committed to reducing the regulatory burden on the UK's business community. Unfortunately, following countless reviews and numerous initiatives there was limited evidence of any significant progress. In fact, this was confirmed by successive business surveys in the UK[1] reporting that 'regulations and red tape' were the single biggest inhibitor to business growth.

As the recession deepened in the UK, both national and local government made a concerted effort to find new ways of easing the regulatory burden on business in an attempt to help stimulate economic growth. In 2008, the Government established the Local Better Regulation Office (LBRO) (now the Office for Product Safety and Standards) to provide a focus for thinking about how the regulatory burden could be addressed, without compromising protections,[2] through improvements to the way that regulation is delivered at a local level.

At the national policy level, all government departments considering new regulations were required to prepare impact assessments, so that decision-makers could fully understand the economic impact that a regulation would have on both the economy and the businesses involved. Targets were also set under the 'one in, one out' rule, where each government department was required to find an equivalent saving to business for every pound of cost imposed by a new regulation. To support this activity and to provide independent scrutiny, the Government established the Regulatory Policy Committee in 2009 (see Annex 1) to oversee the process. The Government demonstrated its commitment to listening to the voice of business by inviting people such as Martin to join the Committee.

In 2011, in response to many years of lobbying by the business community, and recognising the volume of regulations that governed day-to-day life in the UK, the Government acted, introducing the Red Tape Challenge with the aim of engaging with the wider business community, along with other key players across civil society, to review the current stock of regulations (based on their experiences) and to identify outdated and/or obsolete regulations, with the intention of either amending or repealing them. The Prime Minister, David Cameron, announcing the measure, said:

> There are over 21,000 statutory rules and regulations in force, and I want us to bring that number – and the burden it represents – down. Indeed, I want us to be the first government in modern history to leave office having reduced the overall burden of regulation, rather than increasing it.

As part of the review of the UK's regulatory environment, it became apparent that the way in which regulations were being enforced was having a disproportionate impact on many businesses, especially for the four million UK small and medium enterprises. What was also clear, was that to tackle this issue would require some fresh thinking and a real need to find new ways of working.

At the local level, where a significant proportion of regulatory enforcement activity takes place in the UK, a focus was also placed on exploring these new ways of working. The aim was to explore how regulatory services could be delivered in a way that could ultimately provide tangible support to local businesses and to help promote economic growth.

---

[1] UK Chambers of Commerce conduct quarterly economic surveys with their members on a range of topics which include barriers to business growth. Summary results are available at www.britishchambers.org.uk/policy-maker/economic-data/quarterly-economic-survey.

[2] See LBRO reports, including: 'Supporting Businesses Towards Recovery' (LBRO, 2009), 'From the Business End of the Telescope: Perspectives on Local Regulation and Enforcement' (LBRO, 2010), 'Regulation and Growth' (LBRO, 2012).

II. The Cultural Challenge

In many ways, reviewing and replacing regulations is a straightforward exercise. Changing the culture of how regulations are enforced was, and still is, a much bigger challenge. To achieve this would not only require a different form of engagement between the regulators and those being regulated, but a significant change in attitude on both sides.

Local regulatory services had traditionally viewed themselves as responsible for carrying out a defined statutory duty, with the aim of protecting the public. This principal task was achieved through ensuring that regulations were enforced, and the non-compliant were appropriately dealt with. Whilst being aware of examples of previous good practice in the past, personal experience at the time was that officers delivering these important services did not routinely view themselves as a vehicle for providing frontline business advice and support.

For their part, businesses often viewed regulatory services with an element of suspicion. From their perspective, regulatory services were not seen as a source of reliable information and trusted advice, but as a regime that imposed requirements on businesses. Visits – such as inspections – were treated as 'an inspector calls', where the minimum of dialogue would take place in the fear of bringing further sanctions on the business. Instead of asking for advice and support, a culture of fear existed where officers were kept at a distance.

In Leicestershire,[3] local regulators had assumed that businesses knew that regulatory services could be approached to provide advice and guidance. However, when tested this was clearly not the case. The provision of advice and guidance was inconsistent across the county, where little had been done to develop this service.

It was recognised that the expertise and experience of regulatory services officers should not be under-estimated; their regulatory advice and guidance could be a valuable facet of business support. The overt involvement of regulatory services in the provision of business support makes economic sense for both businesses and local authorities.

Regulatory officers have the knowledge, expertise and experience to advise individual businesses on what they need to do to comply with regulatory requirements. In providing this advice, whether it be free of charge or paid for, such as through the Primary Authority scheme (explained in the next chapter) regulatory services can ensure that businesses know what they need to do to achieve compliance. Equally, businesses are able to concentrate on exactly what is needed rather than seeking additional expertise and spending time and money unnecessarily. Having bespoke advice enables a willing business to achieve compliance, allowing regulatory services to then focus their limited resource on those who present the greatest risk, such as the minority who are wilfully non-compliant. The cultural challenge in Leicestershire was to reposition regulatory services as an accepted and valued provider of business support within the local landscape.

---

[3] Leicestershire is a county in the Midlands region of England. There are multiple local authorities in Leicestershire, including the unitary authority of Leicester City, Leicestershire County Council, Leicestershire Police, Leicester Fire and Rescue and seven second-tier district councils.

III. Developing a Local Solution

In taking this initiative forward it soon became apparent that if regulatory services were to play an effective role in business support, they needed to develop a new offer for businesses that would be consistent, transparent, and informed by business needs, whilst still meeting the statutory obligations. The overarching aim had to be to develop an offer where local regulatory services become a trusted source of information and advice, and where officers were able to signpost businesses to the support available to help them grow and prosper.

It was also recognised that to achieve such a goal would require a significant cultural change on both sides. Regulatory services would need to understand what type of service offer businesses in their locality needed and be prepared to change their provision accordingly. The local regulatory system in the UK is complex[4] and navigating this complex regulatory environment was a challenge for business. Addressing this challenge was an essential step to building a relationship between regulators and the businesses they regulate.

In our local area of Leicestershire, we saw from the very outset there was a desire to both stimulate a change and to test new ways of working. This led to the development of a new model for partnership working between regulatory services and local businesses, called a Better Business for All partnership (BBfA).

In developing any new initiative, especially where the two sides are poles apart, it is necessary to create an environment where open and honest dialogue can take place. This environment was created under the leadership of LBRO. As a government agency with no local bias or knowledge, LBRO was able to support business representatives and regulatory service managers in Leicestershire to strike up a meaningful dialogue and identify drivers for change.

Using its influence as a government agency, LBRO was able to encourage a range of partners to become involved. In addition to regulatory services managers from the local authorities in the area, national regulators such as the Environment Agency, the Health and Safety Executive and Her Majesty's Revenue and Customs (HMRC) joined the partnership. Business representation was provided by a range of national and local business support organisations, such as the Federation of Small Businesses, the Leicestershire Asian Business Association, Leicestershire Chamber of Commerce and local town Chambers of Trade. Crucially, the partnership also made an early connection with the Leicestershire Local Enterprise Partnership, recognising that Local Enterprise Partnerships (LEPs)[5] liaise with many leading business groups and provide a quick entry point to the local business community.

---

[4] In England there are 293 local authorities. The structure of local government varies across England – in some areas regulatory responsibilities are divided between a county council (primarily in relation to consumer protection and in some cases fire safety) and a district council (primarily in relation to public health, occupational health and safety, and local licensing). In other areas, there is a single unitary authority which is responsible for most local regulation, other than fire safety. In Wales, Scotland and Northern Ireland all local authorities are unitary.

[5] LEPs are locally owned partnerships between local authorities and businesses. They play a central role in determining local economic priorities and undertaking activities to drive economic growth and the creation of local jobs. See www.lepnetwork.org.uk/the-lep-network.

In the early stages, just sitting down in a room to discuss the challenges each party faced was a significant step forward. Both sides held significant misconceptions about the other, with a real lack of understanding of what each party was trying to achieve and little comprehension of the pressures of running a small business or indeed a hard-pressed public service.

An intensive period of focus was placed on improving understanding, involving: a series of productive meetings; workshops exploring current regulatory culture and how it might need to change; business awareness sessions for regulatory officers, incorporating visits to local businesses to improve understanding of the challenges of running a small business and the impact of regulation and enforcement; and business leaders shadowing officers on inspections. These activities contributed to the development of mutual trust and understanding between local regulators and the local business community.

Regulators soon recognised that the vast majority of businesses actually wanted to be compliant, but either didn't realise they weren't being compliant or just didn't know how to be compliant. In turn, this prompted a discussion on whether regulatory services needed to move away from the more traditional enforcement model, to an environment of supporting compliance, where regulatory services could take a more proactive role in supporting businesses to become compliant. In fact, it was an early recognition that regulatory services already provide an element of frontline business support.

Local businesses started to recognise that regulatory services were not the enemy and could be a trusted source of information and advice. In fact, business started to recognise that a relationship could exist which would be beneficial to them, whilst still recognising the need to comply with regulations.

Practical steps taken by the partnership in Leicestershire during its first year of operation included: establishing a BBfA Charter setting out the behaviours and attitudes expected of partners; establishing a Business Focus Panel to act as a critical friend to the BBfA partnership and also as a consultative group for regulatory services to use to consult with businesses, eg on the development of policies and practices; developing a single point of access within Leicestershire where businesses are able to obtain the advice and guidance they need from regulatory services in one place; developing and disseminating a single regulatory advice pack for start-up businesses; developing an offer of regulatory support for businesses considering relocating to the area; and the development of a pilot for sharing data between regulatory services.

An early emphasis on evidence-based decision-making saw interviews, focus groups and surveys being used to gather information and views from both regulatory services staff and local businesses. The evidence gathered proved useful in informing the partnership's priorities but also provided a baseline against which the impact of the programme would be measured.

IV. The Better Business for All Programme

BBfA, as a concept, was piloted in both Leicestershire and in nearby Birmingham in 2011/12. Following the successful pilots, BBfA was further developed by LBRO and promoted to local regulators across England as a viable model for better collaboration and improved accountability, with a focus on delivering effective regulation whilst reducing both real and perceived regulatory barriers to business growth. LBRO took a role in facilitating introductions between relevant partners, supporting the development of new partnerships, and enabling the sharing of good practice. This involved working closely with local BBfA partnerships, hosting national shared learning days, supporting regional networks of partnerships, recognising good practice through the provision of annual awards[6] and hosting a range of online materials.[7]

The BBfA programme has its foundations in the principles of the UK Regulators' Code (described in chapter five) and is a programme that strives to create the right regulatory conditions to support growth by considering how regulation is both delivered and received. It focuses on the importance of the interaction between business and the regulator, ensuring that the interaction is valuable and effective for both parties. It assumes that the quality of the interaction between a business and those who regulate it will determine the future relationship a business has with the regulatory system and will influence its attitude towards compliance. BBfA recognises that supporting business to comply is not just about providing advice; it is about building relationships between business and regulators, and between different regulators.

BBfA is a principles-based programme, meaning that it can be adapted to local circumstances (see Box 8.1).

Box 8.1 The five principles of BBfA partnerships for local regulatory delivery

Strategic

BBfA partnerships consider what is needed, wanted and valued in a locality and consider how expertise and resources can be shared and allocated to ensure that demand can be met.

Local

BBfA partnerships seek to address how services are delivered at a local level and make changes that suit local circumstances. The programme brings together relevant stakeholders in a defined geographical area. It focuses on the way we do things around here.

Collaborative

BBfA partnerships bring together those services that have an impact on the way business operates. They also bring business organisations to the table, involving them as equal partners, as well as LEPs and Growth Hubs.

---

[6] Annual awards are administered by The Office for Product Safety and Standards and details of shortlisted and winning entries are published, with the aim of recognising and disseminating good practice. See, for example: BBfA Awards 2016: Shortlisted Entries, available at www.gov.uk/government/uploads/system/uploads/attachment_data/file/507635/bbfa-awards-2016-shortlisted-entries.pdf.

[7] Materials explaining BBfA are available at www.gov.uk/government/publications/business-regulation-better-business-for-all.

Practical

BBfA partnerships are designed to ensure any changes made benefit all those involved. They are not a talking shop but are action-focused. Action plans are developed based on local evidence for change or activity to support local priorities.

Growth focused

The focus of BBfA partnerships is to support business to survive, prosper and grow. All improvements and changes made through the programme have this focus in mind. Linking the programme into the LEPs strategic priorities helps to keep the programme focused on growth.

Extracted from training materials used by the Office for Product Safety and Standards

Over the six years that BBfA has been operating, experience has shown that the key determinants of success for a partnership include having the right partners; robust governance arrangements; clear and appropriate objectives and good accountability mechanisms.

A. The Partners

BBfA is a model for collaborative working, and the pilot local authorities and LBRO identified early on that its success in local areas is largely determined by the quality of the partnership that develops in a locality. Success is heavily reliant on the partnership having the right people involved, with the vision, energy and capacity to make things happen. Those attending partnership meetings need to be empowered to make decisions on behalf of their organisations and have the ability to think strategically, enabling them to see the bigger picture and recognise opportunities and hurdles as they become apparent.

In terms of the organisations that make up BBfA partnerships, the programme has predominantly focused on the regulatory functions provided by local authorities through trading standards, environmental health (food safety, health and safety, environmental protection), licensing and fire safety services. National regulators such as the Health and Safety Executive and Environment Agency have an open invitation to attend programme meetings and are considered as virtual partners who become actively involved when programme activities are relevant to their priorities.

The right business representation is critical. It can sometimes prove challenging to sign up individual businesses, particularly the owners of smaller businesses who are time-poor. However, local business organisations and economic partnerships can often provide input and have the reach to both collate evidence and to distribute information to a significant number of local businesses. As in the Leicestershire experience, BBfA partnerships routinely include representatives from local Chambers of Commerce, the Federation of Small Businesses, trade associations and other local business groups.

As the programme has matured, growing recognition of the importance of involving local authority economic development teams has resulted in these services becoming core members of many local BBfA partnerships. Improving the understanding between economic development teams and regulatory services has been fundamental in helping to change the business perceptions of how regulatory services operate in an area as economic development teams have well-established relationships with leading local business groups.

The model recognises that regulatory services are a key business support service and need to be linked to other organisations offering business support. Local business support organisations are often involved in BBfA partnerships. Growth hubs[8] are regarded as essential partners in every programme. Regulatory officers visit thousands of businesses every year across a LEP area and are therefore well placed to signpost businesses to help that is available through local growth hubs and from economic development teams.

B. Governance

LBRO, when it established the programme, did not seek to prescribe a governance model for local BBfA partnerships, as every area is different and many of the key players will vary depending on local circumstances. As these are 'partnerships of the willing' it is for local decision-makers to come together and agree what will work for that area.

However, experience has shown that governance arrangements utilising the LEP structure can be beneficial – particularly in terms of gaining support for the partnership and ensuring an ongoing focus on growth – and this approach has been recommended to new partnerships. A LEP Board member chairing the BBfA steering group ensures that the partnership understands the priorities of the LEP and, importantly, the LEP recognises the role that regulatory services are playing in supporting local growth. Securing LEP Board support has proven to be essential in ensuring the sustainability and profile of the BBfA programme in a local area.

Good governance will ensure that reporting mechanisms are robust without detracting from the purpose of the programme. Reporting of partnership activity has an important role in ensuring that the value of the programme is recognised. Many programmes have relied on their connections to the LEP and associated governance arrangements to support bids for funding.

C. The Objectives

BBfA is rooted in the needs of a locality and as such each programme will have its own distinct objectives and desired outcomes. However, to be considered as a BBfA programme and to have access to the national branding, now owned by the Office for Product Safety and Standards (formerly LBRO – see Annex 1), local programmes must reflect defined key objectives (see Box 8.2).

---

[8] Growth hubs are the central repository of information, advice and support for business within a defined local area. The aim of the hubs is to provide a holistic approach to business support. Through a single point of contact a business will connect to the information, advice or support it requires.

Box 8.2 BBfA key objectives

1 Simplifying the local regulatory system and processes
2 Providing advice and support to business
3 Increasing the business awareness of regulatory officers
4 Effective coordination across the regulatory system
5 Establishing an ongoing dialogue between regulatory services and local business
6 Supporting national and local priorities
7 Building trust through transparency and accountability

Extracted from training materials used by the Office for Product Safety and Standards

---

Local action plans provide the detail as to how the objectives will be achieved. Most local programmes have developed strands of activity around these key objectives which generally reflect the following:

- accessible advice and support;
- culture and competence of officers;
- coordination and communication across the local system; and
- accountable partnerships.

The BBfA programmes are designed to make improvements that will benefit all the parties involved. They are not talking shops but action-orientated partnerships. Business people regard time as very important and expect to see things happen. They are also very willing to try something new, but if it doesn't work, then recognise it, and move on. Though there is still a tendency to be risk-averse in the public sector, current economic circumstances have driven an agenda for change which is more in line with the approach businesses will take in regard to risk and reward.

BBfA action plans are always developed from a local evidence base, where the need for change is clearly defined as well as being linked to local priorities. For example, if there is a local priority around supporting the visitor economy, then the BBfA action plan and programme will aim to deliver some outcomes that can support the local objectives.

D. Accountability

The UK Regulators' Code (see chapter five) requires regulators to ensure their approach to regulatory activity is transparent, enabling greater accountability to stakeholders. The BBfA model provides a mechanism for greater accountability. The dialogue that becomes integral to well-functioning programmes results in a local system that is transparent, with businesses and other stakeholders understanding how their views can be heard, whether through informal information-gathering and consultation or via more formal feedback and complaint mechanisms.

Simplifying the local regulatory system, through enhanced coordination and collaboration between regulators, has demystified much of the regulatory landscape for business.

In addition, the development of joint service standards and enforcement policies by local regulators has provided clarity to business. Many local BBfA programmes have developed local charters which set out the roles and responsibilities of regulators and business, creating the conditions where they can be held accountable for their actions.[9]

V. What is BBfA Achieving?

By January 2018, six years after the initial pilots, BBfA partnerships had been established in 32 of the 39 Local Enterprise[10] areas in England. The significant uptake of the programme has been a testament to the real difference it is making in local regulatory delivery.

At a national level, the Office for Product Safety and Standards has seen indications of a range of benefits arising from the BBfA programme, with participants in the programme at a local level being its greatest advocates and showing pride in its achievements. The benefits seen have been to both the regulatory system and to business communities. One example, is the advice given through the BBfA partnership to a cheese company in Cornwall, which received support to pass food inspections by US regulators, allowing them to start exporting their handmade cheese to the US.[11]

Most strikingly, there has been a change in the perception that businesses have of local regulatory services and the regulatory system. Developing relationships that have been based on understanding and trust has enabled regulatory services to act upon business concerns and address some of the misconceptions businesses may have had. Face-to-face dialogue, confronting difficulties and taking decisive action have been key to this change in perception.

Regulatory officers in areas where BBfA programmes are established now have a better understanding of the role they play in supporting businesses to be compliant and successful, and the links between their role and growth. When businesses have confidence, they are far more likely to make informed investment decisions. Without that confidence they may be reluctant to commit. The provision of accurate and trusted advice that can be relied upon can make a real difference to the decision-making process.

There has also been a shift in emphasis for regulators to be regarded, and to regard themselves, as part of the business support solution. With local regulators interacting with a wider range of businesses than many other local organisations, they are ideally placed as a conduit for business support messages. But the shift has been greater than just other organisations recognising the potential of regulators, regulators themselves, through enhanced training and exposure to business opinion have now come to regard themselves as key delivery agents of business support. Providing advice and guidance to a business to enable it to comply is as much an element of business support as providing financial advice to a

---

[9] The Leicester and Leicestershire BBfA Partnership Charter is available at http://www.llepbizgateway.co.uk/wp-content/uploads/2015/03/BBfA-Partnership-Charter.pdf.

[10] Each LEP area will contain at least two local authorities with many having six to eight, and the largest having 19. Because of overlapping LEP geography some local authorities are covered by two LEPs.

[11] 'Forging our Future: Industrial Strategy – the story so far', Policy Paper (Department for Business, Energy and Industrial Strategy, 2018) available at www.gov.uk/government/publications/forging-our-future-industrial-strategy-the-story-so-far/forging-our-future-industrial-strategy-the-story-so-far.

business. With growth hubs now including regulatory services in their business support providers networks this is evidence that the shift has occurred.

Business now understand how they can access advice and through the establishment of charters and clear service standards, businesses are clear about their responsibilities and those of the regulator, and subsequently the ways they can hold regulators to account against these responsibilities.

BBfA has fundamentally shifted the way in which local regulators shape their service delivery. Preparing service plans in isolation from other regulators and businesses results in activity that not only fails to meet the needs of the business community but can also waste the scarce resources available to local authorities. Designing services that are based on input from business, considering their contribution to local priorities and maximising the resources available results in benefits for all involved in either the delivery or receipt of regulation.

An environment where regulatory services work with business leaders, creates a culture of mutual trust and support. Localities soon gain a reputation as somewhere that is 'a good place to do business', based on this business-focused culture.

VI. Conclusions

Changing the regulatory environment in the UK is an ongoing journey. The introduction of initiatives such as the Red Tape Challenge, the one-in, one-out regime, and the overall review of regulations has clearly had a positive impact on the regulatory burden for UK businesses.

The way in which regulations are being enforced has also impacted on how the business community operates. A new, and far more collaborative approach, is being adopted where compliance is the order of the day. The move away from the very traditional enforcement model has been a journey for many in local regulatory services. However, this positive approach has grown in both acceptance and delivery as the BBfA programme is rolled out across England and there is emerging evidence that businesses are feeling the benefits.

9

Primary Authority as a Mechanism for Strengthening Regulator Consistency and Accountability

DUNCAN JOHNSON

I. Introduction

This chapter describes Primary Authority, a statutory scheme in the UK that holds regulators accountable to business, citizens and government. It originated as a mechanism to address specific challenges in the regulation of national businesses by large numbers of independent local authorities across the UK. The development of machinery to address these challenges has produced an accountability model for regulatory delivery that is of wider relevance to regulators and policy-makers.

II. Challenges in UK Local Regulation

A significant amount of technical regulation applicable across the UK is delivered by 433 local authorities, each serving a geographically defined municipal area. Much of this regulation is principles-based. This delivers well-understood benefits in terms of enabling innovation, but also creates uncertainty and risk of inconsistent interpretation of requirements by regulators.[1] Businesses trading across the UK reported difficulty in operating within this regulatory environment flowing from a number of key issues:

(i) inconsistent interpretation of national regulations between local authorities[2,3] and between individuals within local authorities, resulting in uneven requirements;
(ii) the absence of a single point of accountability within the regulatory system where the interpretation of requirements for an individual business can be agreed;

---

[1] Robert Baldwin, Martin Cave and Martin Lodge, *Understanding Regulation. Theory, Strategy, and Practice* (Oxford, Oxford University Press, 2012).

[2] A third of businesses indicated that advice received from different local authorities was 'fairly inconsistent' or 'very inconsistent'; 'Business Perceptions of Local Authority Regulatory Services: a survey of businesses conducted for the Local Better Regulation Office' (Ipsos MORI, 2008).

[3] 'Government Response to the Consultation on Transforming Regulatory Enforcement' (Department for Business, Innovation and Skills, 2011).

(iii) businesses requiring confidence in their national approaches felt obliged to meet the highest standards demanded for any issue, resulting in 'gold plating' of regulatory requirements; and

(iv) businesses reported that they would be more likely to invest in compliance if they had greater confidence that their approach would be recognised nationally.

It should be noted that in responding to these business concerns the UK Government also needed to consider whether the reported unevenness of requirements might indicate inadequate protection in some areas.

III. Shaping a Solution

The proposed solution was to enable businesses to choose a local authority to become a single point of contact within the regulatory system where they could develop and agree their approach to compliance. This single point of contact would need to have the capacity to engage deeply with the business to understand the specific context within which principles-based regulation applies, enabling it to support the business in choosing an effective approach to compliance. Business confidence would then need to be delivered via a robust assurance mechanism to hold all local regulators accountable for respecting the agreed approach.

Previous efforts had been made to deliver this approach on a voluntary basis through collaborative arrangements amongst local authorities. However, a perceived lack of regulator accountability to respect advice resulted in low business confidence. What was required was a mechanism to deliver assured advice that had appropriate legal underpinning to deliver accountability to business, government, and citizens.

IV. Assured Advice

A key principle in UK law is that only the courts can provide definitive interpretation of legislation. Historically, this has led to some reluctance on the part of regulators to issue assurance and provide certainty that any particular application of regulatory requirements was acceptable. Logically, we might expect this reluctance to be especially prevalent in the local regulatory system where any application that they agreed could be subject to challenge by many other local authorities. For this reason, bespoke advice relating to the adequacy of an approach to compliance within the circumstances of a specific business was relatively rare and would often be accompanied by a disclaimer stating that ultimately only the courts could provide definitive legal interpretation.

Whilst recognising that only the courts can provide definitive interpretation of the law, it is self-evident that regulators routinely derive their own legal application of requirements when conducting their activity. Regulators must reach their own view as to whether compliance has been achieved in deciding whether to require a business to do more, or whether to commence legal proceedings against the business.

Where a regulator is willing to be transparent about its own application of regulatory requirements, it can do so via assured advice. Assured advice requires the regulator to provide its understanding of requirements to the business, and to confirm that it will not subsequently challenge this application, for example, through the courts.

The original driver of assured advice came from the business perceptions of inconsistency previously discussed. However, UK experience shows that assured advice can also deliver wider benefits.

If we consider a simple scenario in which a business operates 10 premises across the UK, each equipped with extensive racking used to store products. The risks arising from racking are well understood by occupational health and safety regulators. Racking may become overloaded or damaged and fail with catastrophic consequences. Individuals have a tendency to climb racking, and on occasion to fall from it.

A business facing these risks will need to ensure that they are properly managed in line with principles-based regulations. These regulations may mandate appropriate training, require reasonable precautions to be taken, and so forth. This provides the business with plenty of scope for flexibility of approach and innovation, but a significant challenge in knowing when compliance has been achieved. Since risk can never be reduced to zero, the business must accept that, irrespective of its approach, an accident may nevertheless occur. Following an accident, the adequacy of its approach is then likely to be reviewed by the regulator, acting with the benefit of hindsight.

An alternative approach would be for the business to bring forward the moment at which the adequacy of its approach to compliance is assessed by the regulator. The regulator could engage with any preferences and innovations that the business sought to explore under the principles-based regime and could work collaboratively to agree a compliance solution. This could then be translated into assured advice. In this example this might include: which staff should be trained and how often; the content of any training; how the business should inspect racking; procedures for taking damaged racking out of use; and so on. Once this had all been agreed and assured advice issued, the business could confidently focus on delivering the required approach. If an accident did subsequently occur then any accident investigation would be equipped with a detailed understanding of what should have been in place, providing a sound basis from which any culpability could more easily be established.

V. How Primary Authority Works

Primary Authority was established under the Regulatory Enforcement and Sanctions Act 2008. This legislation set out a number of key rights and accountabilities for government, businesses and local authorities. It also created mechanisms for the coordination of regulatory effort, as well as providing a framework to underpin assured advice.

Under Primary Authority, a business and a local authority can apply to government for nomination as a legally recognised partnership. The local authority in a partnership (known as the 'primary authority') can issue assured advice to the partner business.

Government[4] issues statutory guidance[5] that establishes the rules of Primary Authority and has a responsibility to provide transparency around the partnerships that exist via a

---

[4] The role of administering Primary Authority was initially the responsibility of the Local Better Regulation Office (see Annex 1) and now sits within the Office for Product Safety and Standards.

[5] 'Primary Authority Statutory Guidance' (Regulatory Delivery, 2017).

public register.[6] Government also considers the suitability of local authorities to form a partnership (for example their capacity) and has the power to revoke partnerships if the primary authority does not meet required standards. Where advice issued by a primary authority is disputed, government undertakes 'determinations' in respect of appeals to establish whether assured advice is 'correct' and 'properly given' and whether proposed enforcement action is inconsistent with such advice. Where advice is found to be correct, and proposed enforcement action to be inconsistent with that advice, the action is blocked. Where advice is not upheld then it falls away and the enforcement action can proceed.

A. Single Point of Contact in the Regulatory System

A primary authority acts as a single point of contact, enabling a business with which it is in partnership to have a more streamlined experience of being regulated. Figure 9.1 shows the relationships in Primary Authority where an individual business is partnered with a local authority and Figure 9.2 shows the relationships where the partnership is established between a primary authority and a 'coordinator', a type of partnership discussed later in the chapter.

Figure 9.1 How Primary Authority works: direct partnerships

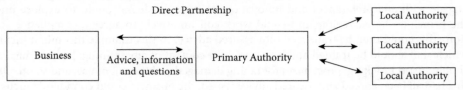

Figure 9.2 How Primary Authority works: coordinated partnerships

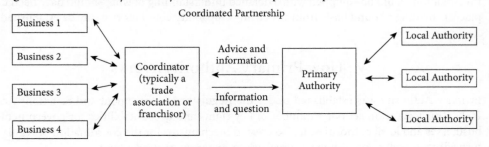

The primary authority, having issued assured advice to the partner business, can block enforcement action (widely defined to include prosecutions and legal notices requiring improvements) proposed by other local authorities if the action is inconsistent with the assured advice. In this way the primary authority can deliver on its commitment that its advice will be respected across the regulatory system. Primary authorities are empowered to recover their costs from the business, enabling their proactive advisory role to be fulfilled while ensuring that scarce regulatory resources can continue to be deployed on the basis of risk.

[6] The Primary Authority Public Register is available at https://primary-authority.beis.gov.uk/par.

All other local authorities that regulate the partner business are legally required to notify any proposed enforcement action in relation to the business to the primary authority and must refrain from proceeding with enforcement action if blocked by the primary authority. In the event that a local authority wishes to contest the primary authority's interpretation of the regulatory requirements, as they apply to the business, it can appeal to government against the blocking of an enforcement action.

Similarly, a business that is acting on the basis of assured advice may appeal to government against enforcement action that it considers to be inconsistent with the advice if this action is not blocked by the primary authority. In this way, the business holds the primary authority accountable for standing by its advice.

The statutory guidance that underpins Primary Authority sets out important provisions to ensure that assured advice operates effectively. These include a requirement that assured advice be reviewed at appropriate intervals to take account of changes in regulation, technology, business practice, or events. The guidance emphasises that this systematic review should include discussion with the business to ensure that confidence can be maintained where any change is necessary.

The statutory guidance also confirms that the business remains accountable for its compliance with the law at all times. Assured advice does not in any way transfer this responsibility or any other legal risk to the regulator who is merely providing clarity as to their position in relation to seeking further interpretation from the courts at a future date.

Most important of all, the statutory guidance states that all parties must be clear as to when assurance is being given, and when it is not.

B. The Importance of the Relationship

The relationship between the primary authority and the business is central to the success of the Primary Authority model. In this model, the business has a new incentive to work collaboratively through the potential to secure assured advice. The primary authority also has an incentive to properly understand risk within the business, as well as the operational realities that the business faces, in order to be able to provide appropriate advice.

These incentives, as well as the shared commitment to long-term partnership and the availability of time for deep close working, typically result in increased trust between regulator and business. Generally, businesses share their own detailed understanding of internal compliance performance against their analysis of risk in a way that is not often seen in regulatory interactions. This in turn enables the regulator to better understand how the regulatory system as a whole should interface with the business. This might enable better targeting of checks across the business; for example, close supervision of a critical area of business improvement.

Whilst the benefits of relationship are clear, it is important to recognise the risk of regulatory capture in these circumstances. Primary Authority has a number of mechanisms in place to mitigate the risk of capture, of the primary authority or its officers:

- The determination role played by government acts as a check on inappropriate advice. Advice may be challenged by any local authority and advice that is found to be incorrect – for example because it is deemed too generous an application of the law – falls away. In these circumstances enforcement action proceeds as normal. It is interesting to note that over the first eight years of the scheme's life there have been only a handful of challenges made against assured advice.

- The statutory guidance draws attention to the risks of regulatory capture and requires local authorities to manage and deliver their primary authority partnerships in a manner that mitigates this risk (see Box 9.1).
- The statutory guidance also establishes a clear expectation that a primary authority that is developing advice will take account of the views of its peers and relevant national regulators. This supports consistency and guards against capture.
- Government may revoke a partnership where there is evidence that the local authority is no longer suitable to act as a primary authority. Evidence of regulatory capture would clearly qualify as a reason to revoke.
- Many primary authorities elect to clearly separate their own regulation of the business, for example inspection of a local outlet, from their partnership under Primary Authority. This increases their own confidence that integrity is being maintained.

Box 9.1 Extract from Primary Authority Statutory Guidance Part D: Guidance to Primary Authorities

18. Managing Primary Authority

18.1 A local authority that provides primary authority services has an ongoing responsibility to ensure that it has effective arrangements in place to resource, manage and deliver partnerships, including suitable oversight and contingency arrangements.

18.2 A primary authority has an ongoing responsibility to ensure that it has effective arrangements in place to ensure that staff that it engages to support partnerships:

- have the skills, knowledge and expertise needed to lead regulation of the business in relation to partnership functions in which it has agreed that it will provide advice;
- have appropriate access to mechanisms that promote consistency including, for example, through Expert Panels, networks and liaison groups;
- are competent in the delivery of primary authority services and are operating in accordance with guidance on Primary Authority and the principles of good regulation; and
- are able to undertake their role with integrity and objectivity, acting at all times in the public interest.

18.3 A primary authority should have regard to the requirements for transparency and accountability, both in terms of the service that it provides to businesses and coordinators and the service that it provides to enforcing authorities.

18.4 A primary authority should recognise that the benefits that can be realised by working closely in partnership with businesses can be accompanied by an increased risk of bias and perceptions of regulatory capture. Primary authorities should be mindful of this risk and should take appropriate steps to maintain their independence and objectivity and that of staff assigned to support partnerships.

C. Accountability within Primary Authority

The accountability model for Primary Authority can be considered as a triangle with the primary authority in the centre. In this model the interests of beneficiaries (citizens, workers and the environment), business and government are each linked to the primary authority. The ability of each of these three parties to hold the primary authority to account is key to maintaining appropriate action from the primary authority as regulator. This is shown in Figure 9.3 below:

Figure 9.3 Accountability model for Primary Authority

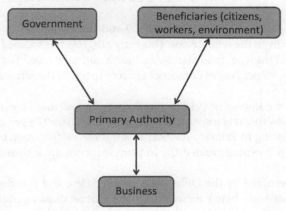

Within Primary Authority, the mechanisms for regulator accountability to each of the three parties are:

(i) Government:

    (a) issues statutory guidance that establishes the behaviours and practices expected of local authorities;

    (b) has the power to nominate and revoke partnerships in line with these rules; and

    (c) deals with appeals in relation to assured advice via its 'determination' process.

(ii) Businesses:

    (a) are entitled to seek a partnership and have access to a 'market' of local authority regulators from which they can choose a partner able to deliver the service and quality standards that they require;

    (b) are entitled to seek assured advice from their primary authority;

    (c) are entitled to transparency around the costs recovered for service provided; and

    (d) can challenge enforcement action that they consider to be inconsistent with advice received from their primary authority by referring to government for determination.

(iii) Beneficiaries – the interests of beneficiaries are mainly represented by other local authorities which can:

    (a) rely upon transparency from government in terms of the partnerships that exist;

(b) demand transparency from primary authorities in terms of the topic areas where assured advice has been issued;

(c) challenge incorrect or overly generous assured advice via the determination process when such advice is used to block their enforcement action. Where such challenge is successful the advice will fall away; and

(d) Report evidence of unsuitability in primary authorities to government for action, for example, inadequate capacity or regulatory capture.

VI. Impact of Primary Authority

Primary Authority was launched in April 2009 and rapidly gained traction with national businesses, especially in the retail sector. This early progress was focused mainly in the regulatory areas of food hygiene, food standards, health and safety, and fair trading regulation. Within a few years, 93 per cent of consumer grocery spend in the UK was in a business with Primary Authority.[7]

Research into the impact of Primary Authority showed that 76 per cent of businesses reported a more positive relationship with regulators (versus 37 per cent in a comparison group not participating in Primary Authority). Of these participating businesses reporting improvement, 78 per cent attributed the improvement partly or directly to the impact of Primary Authority.[8]

Case studies gathered by the Office for Product Safety and Standards[9] illustrate some of the benefits that were being delivered by the partnerships operating under Primary Authority, in terms of improved protections, savings in compliance costs for business and improvements in turnover. Examples included:

- a car retailer that saw a reduction in customer complaints of around 30 per cent as a result of changes to its internal culture and overall approach, brought about through working with its primary authority;

- a food business that worked with its primary authority to strengthen its management of food hygiene across 900 premises and saw a measurable improvement in its Food Hygiene Rating Scheme scores (see chapter twenty-one), positioning it as one of the top-rated operators on the high street;

- a care home group that worked with its primary authority to agree and deliver improvements to its food safety programme across more than 200 care homes, with projected savings in excess of £1 million; and

- a business that secured £2.5 million of sales on the basis of advice from its primary authority that reassured its commercial customer.

The regulatory scope of Primary Authority has been extended, since its introduction, to further technical areas, including fire safety. In addition, new provisions introduced in 2013

---

[7] Kantar Worldpanel Grocery Market Share figures, compared against Primary Authority Register.

[8] 'Review of Primary Authority: Quantitative Surveys' (ACL, 2015).

[9] See, for examples, video case studies available at www.youtube.com/watch?v=ynp-M7nmers and 'Primary Authority and Growth' (Better Regulation Delivery Office, 2015)

and 2017 have enabled groups of businesses to participate via representative groups such as Trade Associations. In this case, the Trade Association can secure assured advice tailored to the needs of a sector, and all members of the association are entitled to rely upon that advice. This has enabled regulators to connect to existing infrastructure that is trusted by business, and where significant expertise in sectoral issues is located. Critically, Trade Association success is defined by their ability to reach businesses in a sector. This means that the establishment of a single point of contact here can result in both the creation of high-quality advice, and its cascade to many businesses that may otherwise be hard for regulators to reach. This approach also benefits from economy of scale with perhaps thousands or tens of thousands of small businesses contributing to the development of effective assured advice tailored to their sector. In some cases, these partnerships have also been able to act as a focal point for regulators and business to commission research to underpin regulatory advice that can support innovative approaches to compliance, again via a mechanism that benefits from economy of scale.

By January 2019 there were 76,000 businesses benefiting from Primary Authority, with an expectation that participation in the scheme would continue to grow.

VII. Accountability as a Driver for Regulatory Change

As already stated, the initial aim of Primary Authority was to improve regulatory consistency. However, it can be argued that the accountability model that underpins Primary Authority has delivered a much wider set of benefits.

Improved regulator accountability has driven a much more robust approach to the provision of advice by primary authorities. Primary authorities know that they will be held accountable to stand by their advice in the future, and to hold others accountable to do so. This places new emphasis on properly understanding the context of a business, and to support the development of realistic and proportionate solutions that nevertheless recognise that risk will never be reduced to zero. This pressure, supported by funding from business partners, has enabled the development of high-quality advice that is delivering real confidence to business partners and regulators alike.

Primary authorities faced with providing assured advice have been encouraged to collaborate with peers from across the regulatory system to ensure that advice across the regulatory system is coherent. Expert Panels have been developed, often focused on a specific sector, bringing regulators and businesses together to build shared understanding of requirements in particular circumstances. For example, the Primary Authority Supermarkets Group brings together representatives of the major UK supermarkets and their primary authority officers. Expert Panels and other informal networks also create opportunity for challenge, helping to address the risk of regulatory capture. Where agreement is reached, multiple primary authorities often go on to issue assured advice that may be tailored to individual business circumstances, but which is underpinned by common interpretation of key issues. This can create de facto industry standards that draw upon both business and regulator insights.

Regulator accountability to business has also driven a much stronger service ethos amongst primary authorities. As paying customers, businesses are empowered to demand advice services that meet their needs. In one example, a food business highlighted that since its manufacturing processes ran 24 hours a day, 365 days a year, it would need regulatory advice with a similar level of availability. Historically, securing this from a local regulator would have been problematic, but cost recovery enables this business requirement to be translated into a local authority service offer that can be costed.

The accountability of all local authorities to stand by assured advice from a primary authority that is being followed by a business has incentivised a more considered approach to regulation at the frontline. Where an inspector discovers something that doesn't appear right, the obligation to act in accordance with primary authority advice has driven new behaviour. It is now more beneficial for the inspector to refer to the single point of contact created under Primary Authority at an early stage to establish what has been agreed, and to properly understand the approach of the business ahead of any formal action. This has also created a much clearer intelligence picture at the single point of contact where, for example, patterns of issues or 'near misses' are being identified. This often results in problems being fixed right across a national business, not just at a single location. In the same way, where a primary authority's advice is reaching hundreds or even thousands of businesses across a sector, through a trade association, the intelligence it receives can assist in identification of issues right across that sector.

VIII. Applying the Lessons of Primary Authority to Regulation in other Contexts

Primary Authority has been outlined here as a response to a specific set of challenges in the UK local regulatory system. However, the business need for consistency and certainty in a world of principles-based flexibility is encountered in many regulatory environments. For this reason, the solutions of a single point of contact, a relationship based on shared under-standing of the business context, and assured advice appear equally relevant within many regulatory situations. The challenges to overcome in ensuring accountability to business, to government, and to beneficiaries are likely to be universal.

Through Primary Authority, UK local regulators have overcome the significant cultural and legal challenges to issuing advice to business for which they will later be held accountable.

Accountability to government has been established through the statutory nature of the scheme, including enabling government to establish the framework of rules via statutory guidance.

In addition, the risk of regulatory capture has been mitigated through the creation of accountability to beneficiaries. In the context of Primary Authority this is achieved through the ability of other local authorities to challenge assured advice that has been issued.

Primary Authority has required significant legal underpinning in order to construct accountabilities across many independent local authority regulators. In the context of a single national regulator, the legal underpinning is likely to be less legally complex, with the concept of the regulator committing itself to respect its own advice likely to be simpler and the implementation easier. However, the question of how to deliver accountability to beneficiaries and to government and avoid regulatory capture in the absence of parallel regulators with the capacity to challenge will need careful consideration.

Prerequisites: Culture

10

Culture

GRAHAM RUSSELL AND HELEN KIRKMAN

This chapter considers the culture of regulatory agencies. 'Culture' is the third of the three elements considered within the Regulatory Delivery Model as prerequisites for good delivery of regulation.

We first consider what is meant by culture and its importance in providing the right conditions for regulatory agencies to operate effectively. We explore influences on culture, setting out the approach taken in the Regulatory Delivery Model to structuring reflections on the regulatory agency's culture by reference to three factors: the agency's leadership; its values; and its approach to competency.

We will also consider the ways in which culture is inextricably linked to the other prerequisites: Governance Frameworks (see chapter three) and Accountability (see chapter seven).

I. Defining 'Culture'

Different definitions of organisational culture abound and the concept can, at times, seem vague and imprecise. Culture is considered within the Regulatory Delivery Model as a collective understanding and purpose that manifests itself in the visible behaviour of the regulatory agency: 'the way things are done around here'.[1,2] Culture is an internal force arising from the internal and external environment of the past and present and shaped by perceptions of the future. It determines how the regulatory agency will respond to the forces of governance and accountability and supports improvement (as discussed in Graham's explanation of the development of the Regulatory Delivery Model – see Introduction).

II. The Importance of Culture for Regulatory Agencies

Culture has a powerful influence on the behaviour and practices of any organisation and of the individuals that make up that organisation. It helps to determine the shape and

---

[1] Terrence Deal and Allan Kennedy, *Corporate Cultures: The Rites and Rituals of Corporate Life* (Boston, Addison-Wesley Publishing Company, 1982).

[2] Edgar Schein at www.cultureuniversity.com/culture-fundamentals-9-important-insights-from-edgar-schein.

performance of the organisation and its ability to form functional relationships with other agencies. These factors impact on the credibility of any organisation and influence public perceptions of it. For example, this is recognised in the UK Corporate Governance Code, which emphasises the importance of aligning culture with the purpose and values of the organisation: 'The board should establish the company's purpose, values and strategy, and satisfy itself that these and its culture are aligned. All directors must act with integrity, lead by example and promote the desired culture.'[3] The Introduction to the Code states:

> To succeed in the long-term, directors and the companies they lead need to build and maintain successful relationships with a wide range of stakeholders. These relationships will be successful and enduring if they are based on respect, trust and mutual benefit. Accordingly, a company's culture should promote integrity and openness, value diversity and be responsive to the views of shareholders and wider stakeholders.

Culture is capable of driving both short-term improvement and longer-term sustainable change in an organisation. However, it is important to recognise that whilst organisational culture can support and drive improvement, it can also act as a barrier to desired behaviours and can inhibit change. For example, research with UK local authorities in 2016 identified that despite widespread agreement that there are benefits to improved data-sharing between regulatory agencies, progress is being inhibited, in part by cultural barriers.[4]

The proposition put forward here is that while culture is important for *all* organisations, there are significant factors that point to culture meriting particular attention in relation to regulatory agencies. The importance of organisational culture in ensuring the practice of desired behaviours by regulatory agencies is increasingly being recognised, including in a recent report[5] on the ethical behaviour of UK regulators and in work on ethical business regulation, which is explored in chapter twenty-two.

A. Public Sector

The first factor of significance is that regulatory agencies, in common with many other public sector organisations, are not generally subject to the commercial influences – such as profitability and competition – that might otherwise act as drivers for improvement. In the absence of these forces for change, organisational culture plays a more significant role in the public sector in ensuring effective delivery and driving improvement.

Improvement in the public sector tends to be discussed in terms of efficiency – the process of turning public money into positive outcomes for individuals and society[6] – and is underpinned by concepts such as an ethos of public service or delivering public good

---

[3] 'The UK Corporate Governance Code' (Financial Reporting Council, 2018), Principle B; see also 'Guidance on Board Effectiveness' (Financial Reporting Council, 2018); and for large private companies 'The Wates Corporate Governance Principles for Large Private Companies' (Financial Reporting Council, 2018).

[4] 'Overcoming Cultural Barriers to Information Sharing within Regulatory Services' (Centre of Excellence for Information Sharing, 2016).

[5] 'Striking the Balance. Upholding the Seven Principles of Public Life in Regulation' (Committee on Standards in Public Life, 1995).

[6] See for example https://quarterly.blog.gov.uk/2016/01/25/improving-public-sector-efficiency-to-deliver-a-smarter-state.

which, whilst they can seem nebulous, are important shapers of organisational culture and a powerful influence on the behaviour of individuals within the organisation.

For example, in 2001, the UK suffered an outbreak of foot and mouth disease that was of an unprecedented nature and magnitude. It lasted 32 weeks and cost the public sector over £3 billion and the private sector more than £5 billion, with the rural economy and parts of the tourist industry being particularly badly affected.[7] A review of the outbreak concluded that 'those involved worked extremely hard to bring the disease under control' and noted that those in the field 'worked punishingly long days in stressful and often distressing conditions'.[8] It was acknowledged in the wake of the outbreak that the public service ethos of animal health regulators and other public servants had been a critical factor in tackling the outbreak and its impact on local communities. For example, evidence to the UK's Select Committee on Public Administration, addressing the concept of a public service ethos, noted the contribution of ADAS, an advisory service for farmers, during the 2001 foot and mouth outbreak:

> Many ADAS staff were called to the frontline to assist with a wide variety of duties. A significant number of staff, whilst struggling to keep up their normal work spent evenings and weekends on Foot and Mouth duties. Even when it was known that no overtime would be given they still felt the need to go and do whatever they could for the industry which they 'served'.[9]

ADAS had a public sector background but had been privatised four years prior to the outbreak. The evidence to the Select Committee pointed to both the importance of ADAS's organisational culture and its resilience:

> [ADAS management have spent the last four years trying to change the public service ethos and replace it with one more suitable to the private sector.] The Foot and Mouth crisis gave a clear demonstration that the public service ethos with regard to the delivery of work is still alive in ADAS even after four years of trying to replace it.[10]

B. Exercising the Power of the State

The second significant factor is that regulatory agencies differ from most other public bodies in that they are authorised to exercise the coercive power of the state. As has already been noted in relation to Governance Frameworks (see chapter three) and Accountability (see chapter seven), the possession of this coercive power magnifies the need for controls on the behaviour of regulatory agencies. Whilst the regulatory agency's governance framework and accountability mechanisms are important in providing such controls, the culture of the regulatory agency determines internally how it will respond to the largely external forces of governance and accountability and therefore plays a crucial role in determining how it will exercise its coercive powers.

---

[7] 'The 2001 Outbreak of Foot and Mouth Disease. Report by the Comptroller and Auditor General' (National Audit Office, 2002).

[8] ibid.

[9] Available at https://publications.parliament.uk/pa/cm200102/cmselect/cmpubadm/263/263ap24.htm.

[10] ibid.

This becomes even more important when we take account of the fact that a regulatory agency may, in exercising the power of the state, have a significant degree of discretion. Discretion plays an important part, in terms of the nature of the broad approach that a regulatory agency chooses to take. However, discretion is also exercised by regulatory agencies when individual decisions are made at an operational level. The discretion afforded to regulatory officers is particularly evident in sanctioning decisions but will often extend to other operational decisions, such as which regulated entities they will inspect and when. It also encompasses the judgment used in interpreting and applying regulation in a particular context, as explored in the Primary Authority case study in chapter nine.

This discretion on the part of regulatory agencies and their officers is valuable and brings with it the potential for significant benefits. However, it also presents challenges, for example, in raising the possibility of unfairness and inconsistency. This possibility can, if not properly managed, reduce the regulatory agency's effectiveness, as a belief that one's competitors are not bearing the same compliance costs can act as a barrier to compliance.[11,12] Recognition of the challenges associated with discretion can elicit very different responses: from a desire to eliminate or fully control discretion to an acknowledgement both that attempts to eliminate it bring different challenges and that there are benefits associated with properly managed discretion. A 2014 international seminar on regulatory discretion explored these issues, reaching the tentative conclusion that:[13]

> [D]iscretion in implementation of regulations is not only unavoidable in practice (there can be no entirely 'neutral' enforcement, there is no rule that does not require some degree of interpretation, maybe no 'facts' that are absolutely beyond discussion on how exactly to characterize them) – but necessary to ensure that implementation of regulations leads to the desired outcomes of regulation. Without discretion, there is a real risk that enforcement is done in a 'tick box' way, with two potential downsides: missing the real threats and risks, and harming the economy without a real positive impact on what the regulation aims to achieve (eg safety). At the same time, it is essential to have safeguards, in particular accountability, as a counterpart to discretion.

Culture is a significant factor in determining the way in which regulatory agencies manage discretion and this is considered further later in this chapter, particularly in relation to the regulatory agency's approach to professional competency.[14]

III. Aspects of Culture

Having established that the organisational culture of regulatory agencies merits attention, we will go on to consider the influences on culture and to set out the framework used within

---

[11] Donald Macrae, 'Compliance and Delivery Analysis' in Claire Dunlop and Claudio Radaelli (eds), *Handbook of Regulatory Impact Assessment* (Cheltenham, Edward Elgar Publishing, 2016).

[12] Christopher Hodges and Ruth Steinholtz, *Ethical Business Practice and Regulation: A Behavioural and Ethical Approach to Compliance and Enforcement* (Oxford, Hart Publishing, 2017). See in particular ch 2: 'The Importance of Fairness in Observing Rules'.

[13] Available at http://ialorg.wpengine.com/wp-content/uploads/2014/01/The-Hague-131205-Summary-and-conclusions1.pdf.

[14] Florentin Blanc, *From Chasing Violations to Managing Risks* Origins, Challenges and Evolutions in Regulatory Inspections (Cheltenham, Edward Elgar Publishing, 2018).

the Regulatory Delivery Model to structure reflection on culture, by reference to three factors: leadership; values; and competency.

A. Influences on a Regulatory Agency's Culture

Culture is subject to multiple influences, both internal and external, and is adaptive. In the early stages of its establishment, the developing culture of a regulatory agency is powerfully influenced by its governance framework – both its establishing statute and the wider legislative framework. These help to structure regulatory culture and will remain an influence on it. In more mature regulatory agencies, culture can still be changed, to an extent, by amendments to the governance framework. Attempts to change culture across multiple regulatory agencies in the UK through amendments to the governance framework are discussed in the case study in chapter five that explores the UK's use of code-based approaches and the case study in chapter nine that examines the way in which its Primary Authority scheme has changed the relationship between local regulatory agencies and regulated entities, with resultant changes in regulatory culture.

However, the regulatory agency's governance framework alone doesn't determine culture. The early development of organisational culture is also heavily influenced by leadership and by the pre-existing culture of the individuals that come together to form the new organisation, bringing with them a range of skills, professional backgrounds and acquired assumptions about ways of working. As the organisation matures, the development of a shared history and narrative becomes an increasingly important internal factor and leadership plays an important part in shaping this shared narrative and using it to influence future development.

The culture of a regulatory agency is also context-dependent, being influenced by a range of external factors. At the outset these are likely to include significant aspects of implicit culture in the wider social system[15] and in the regulatory system. As the regulatory agency develops, its culture will also be increasingly influenced by its relationships with other players in the regulatory system. These include: regulated entities; the beneficiaries of regulation; its peer regulators and quasi-regulators; and other public bodies or non-governmental organisations operating in the same field. Chapter eleven examines the Netherlands' experience of bringing regulatory agencies together, through the work of the Inspection Council, and shaping more of a shared culture. The Netherlands identified the importance, when building collaboration, of understanding different ways of working and addressing misunderstandings that may arise due to different use of language, producing a conceptual framework[16] for common language which defined commonly used wording.

Development of the International Network for Delivery of Regulation (INDR), discussed in chapter twenty-seven, provides a new opportunity for peer support and challenge in a safe space with international colleagues. Interestingly, the INDR's research committee has also identified developing a shared lexicon as a valuable, early step in enabling conversations across different contexts.

---

[15] Errol Meidinger, 'Regulatory Culture: a Theoretical Outline' (1987) 9 *Law and Policy* 355.
[16] Rob Velders and Meindert Brunia, 'Begrippenkader rijksinspecties' at www.rijksinspecties.nl/publicaties/publicaties/2013/01/02/index.

Culture shapes the regulatory agency's approach to its relationships with other bodies and its approach to accountability and our experience is that an examination of these relationships, both from the perspective of the regulatory agency and that of the other party, can provide valuable insights into the cultural forces at play. As explored in chapter seven, there is a symbiotic relationship between culture and accountability. Robust accountability mechanisms are encouraged by a positive, outward-facing organisational culture, in part because such a culture is better able to build the internal and external capacity needed for accountability. Accountability, and the relationships within which it is important, can in turn have a powerful effect on the regulatory agency's culture. The experience of the UK's Drinking Water Inspectorate (see chapter nineteen) provides a clear example of this. Marcus Rink, the Chief Inspector, has fostered a culture of openness, predictability, fairness and consistency and, in order to encourage shared understanding, has introduced a secondment programme that allows staff from the regulated companies to see how the regulator works from the inside.

Further external factors on the culture of a regulator include the nature and direction of political influence, which will directly impact the organisation's sense of purpose, indirectly affect its sense of freedom to act and, in terms of notions of independence, influence external perceptions of validity. Other external factors are court decisions that comment on regulatory behaviour, which might change behaviour but might also inhibit the confidence a regulator has to display its culture overtly, and pressure from observers and commentators, including the media. We will next examine some of the indicators of organisational culture, but it is helpful first to address the question of whether there is such a thing as a 'good culture' or 'the right culture' for a regulatory agency. It appears unquestionable that there are good values that will be common to effective regulatory agencies and, similarly, good behaviours that are likely to be common. However, it would be hard to argue that there is a single, universal 'good regulatory culture'. Each regulatory agency operates in its own context and has its own unique history and its culture is likely to have features that are idiosyncratic to the organisation.

The type of statement which may have universal value as a description of 'good' culture is likely to be at a broad level, for example:

- In order to deliver regulation effectively, the regulatory agency's culture needs to be strong and healthy and must be attuned to its purpose and context, with a commitment to delivering good outcomes that will maintain its relevance.

- A collaborative culture that engenders sharing of good practice can strengthen the regulatory agency.

- To ensure sustainability and the delivery of long-term outcomes, the regulator's culture must be open to challenge yet resilient against negative external forces.

We can be sure that public and political perceptions of risk, pressure from the media and the risk regulation reflex[17] (see chapter sixteen) all tend towards internal, defensive cultures

---

[17] Florentin Blanc (ed), 'Understanding and Addressing the Risk Regulation Reflex. Lessons from International Experience in Dealing with Risk, Responsibility and Regulation' (Dutch Risk and Responsibility Programme, 2015).

which can inhibit the regulatory agency's progress towards significant outcomes; and that there is evidence that a regulatory agency's legitimacy can be important in determining whether it is effective in its role. Perceptions of legitimacy can be affected by the culture of a regulatory agency, as was noted in a recent case study of the Environment Protection Authority in Victoria, Australia[18] (EPA Victoria). The case study notes that, despite a long and proud history, EPA Victoria was faced in the late 2000s by legitimacy problems. Stakeholder concerns about the agency's performance were reflected in the organisation's internal culture, with disagreement and confusion as to its purpose and role being evident. In response, EPA Victoria embarked on a change programme (described in chapter twelve), with a shift in its organisational culture being identified as one of the most important aspects of this transformation.

B. Indicators of Regulatory Culture

Organisational culture is complex and multi-layered. While culture manifests itself at a surface level in the behaviour of an organisation and its staff, it is important to understand the reasons for this behaviour, and extensive work has been done in this area.[19] Schein's well-recognised model of organisational culture[20] identifies organisational behaviour and artefacts as the elements in a culture – such as organisational structures and process – that are visible and can be recognised externally. He proposes that there are two further levels of culture: the organisation's stated beliefs, values and rules of behaviour; and the underlying assumptions that are unconscious, shared, taken-for-granted behaviours, constituting the essence of organisational culture. Experience exploring the relationship between regulators and the businesses they regulate, for example through the development of the Better Business for All partnerships described in chapter eight, shows that businesses respond to their perceptions of regulators, which are, unsurprisingly, influenced more by the regulator's behaviour than by any published values or statements.

In assessing or exploring the culture of the organisation through consideration of its behaviours, the concept of authorisation to act or authorising environment can be helpful. While the culture will impact on the environment, the stronger relationship is the way in which the sense of confidence that the organisation has is demonstrated in its behaviours. A strong culture exhibited in freedom to act will be seen in broad intervention choices, confident decisions and announcements and high levels of proactive transparency.

Reflection on the culture of a regulatory agency can improve understanding of the organisation's behaviour and that of its regulatory officers and this can help to identify underlying issues that may need to be addressed. This reflection is structured, within the Regulatory Delivery Model, by reference to three factors – leadership, values and professional competency – and these are explored further below.

---

[18] Eric Windholz, 'The Evolution of a Modern (and more legitimate) Regulator: A Case Study of the Victorian Environment Protection Authority' (2016) 3 *Australian Journal of Environmental Law* 17.

[19] This work is summarised in Hodges and Steinholtz, *Ethical Business Practice and Regulation* (2017).

[20] Edgar H Schein, *Organisational Culture and Leadership*, 5th edn (New Jersey, John Wiley & Sone, 2017).

i. Leadership

The leaders of an organisation are a primary influence on the development of its culture and are best placed to lead cultural change. The leadership of a regulatory agency often rises from its professional core. It represents fulfilled ambition and models the culmination of a professional regulatory culture which may enable or inhibit change. The phenomena of the impact of promoting professionals within an organisation on the culture of that place is widely noted, from education and the police to the armed forces and social services.[21] Whether firefighters make better leaders than lawyers might be a source of dispute. But professions have to live with the reality that their cultural approach shapes their leaders, who in turn shape the future culture. For a regulatory agency this means that the characteristics of a great frontline regulatory officer – for example independence, self-reliance, negotiating skills and tenacity – can, if over-represented in its leaders, lead to a culture perceived as arrogant, cynical and stubborn.

Regulatory leaders should model and embed appropriate behaviours, values and practices and should challenge examples of undesirable behaviour including corruption, discrimination, short-termism and negativity. By their words and even more by their behaviours, leaders have the capacity to shape an organisation for good, encouraging diversity and protection of the vulnerable. A review of the ethical behaviour of UK regulators commented on the importance of leadership: 'Our evidence demonstrated the importance of visible and engaged leadership for promoting ethical standards within the regulatory agency. Where the Board takes integrity, openness, and accountability seriously, the ethical culture of the regulatory organisation reflects this'.[22]

By establishing clear expectations and standards of conduct for their staff, leaders set the conditions for effective performance management and appropriate incentives. They have a responsibility to ensure that there is clarity across the organisation as to its purpose, role and responsibilities. This includes being particularly clear about the role of frontline officers – because of their direct impact on regulated entities – ensuring that staff understand their role in relation to the outcomes that the regulatory agency aims to achieve. As highlighted by the case study of EPA Victoria discussed above, confusion as to the nature of the regulatory agency's role can be very damaging to its effectiveness. An inquiry at that time into dangerous methane gas leaks from a landfill site was critical of the agency's culture and decision-making processes,[23] identifying them as one of a number of factors contributing to the fact that 'the EPA ineffectively utilised the enforcement tools at its disposal'. Through its transformation programme, EPA Victoria sought to address these issues through a clear commitment to 'a proportionate, risk-based approach that provides the ultimate reassurance that tough action will be taken on those who fail to meet acceptable standards, but still drives environmental improvements and rewards good performance'[24] (see chapter twelve).

---

[21] See for example www.tes.com/news/its-mistake-assume-good-classroom-teachers-will-make-good-headteachers.
[22] 'Striking the Balance. Upholding the Seven Principles of Public Life in Regulation' (Committee on Standards in Public Life, 2016) 54.
[23] 'Brookland Greens Estate – Investigation into Methane Gas Leaks' (Victoria Ombudsman, 2009).
[24] 'Concise Annual Report 2010: Transforming into a Modern Regulator' (EPA Victoria, 2010).

In considering the way in which a regulatory agency is being steered by its leadership, it is helpful to consider the dynamic interactions between culture and the three practices that constitute the second domain of the Regulatory Delivery Model. These three practices of Outcome Measurement, Risk-based Prioritisation and appropriate Intervention Choices are enabled by a regulatory culture that embeds outcome focused behaviours. Leadership plays a key role in this, including through modelling such behaviours and encouraging the challenge 'What are we achieving by doing things in this way?'. The UK report on cultural barriers to data-sharing between regulatory agencies, mentioned earlier in this chapter, discusses the need to 'develop more effective outcome focused leaders' in order to overcome a 'culture of inertia'.[25]

While leadership is a requirement of all organisations, it is a particular focus of attention within the Regulatory Delivery Model partly because establishing effective executive leadership can present significant challenges in the regulatory environment. One reason is contextual: regulatory agencies are often small and many have a narrow field of operation which remains static over time. This can mean that they may not be able to provide the sustained challenge that is needed to develop and retain talented and ambitious leaders. Another relates to the nature of the people being led. Frontline regulatory staff can present specific challenges, particularly in regulatory agencies that value high levels of professional competency. Professional regulatory officers are often characterised as highly independent and self-motivated. They pride themselves on their regulatory expertise and can be resistant to direction or changes in approach where they feel that these present a challenge to their independence and discretion. Finally, it is important to recognise the particular character traits that are required of regulatory leaders in responding to tough regulatory dilemmas and maintaining a well-considered position, sometimes in the face of powerful external influences, such as the political and media pressures referred to earlier.

However, leadership is itself a competency, which can be instilled and developed along with other professional attributes. Shortly after it was established, the Local Better Regulation Office (LBRO)[26] recognised the need, in the UK, for a leadership development programme that was focused on the particular needs of local regulatory leaders. It supported the delivery of a strategic leadership programme in 2008, with its Chair, Clive Grace, noting 'Issues of leadership and culture are critical to successful and modern local authority regulatory services'.[27] LBRO also developed a leadership competency framework as part of its Common Approach to Competency.[28] In the Netherlands the Inspection Council has been developing its focus on building leadership capacity (see chapter eleven) and in the Office for Product Safety and Standards one of our early priorities has been building a leadership development programme for our 39 'heads of function'.

[25] 'Overcoming Cultural Barriers to Information Sharing within Regulatory Services' (Centre of Excellence for Information Sharing, 2016) 11.

[26] Note: the Local Better Regulation Office is a predecessor organisation to the Office for Product Safety and Standards.

[27] The launch of the 'Strategic Leadership in Modern Local Government' was reported by LACORS, available at www.ihsti.com/lacors/PressReleaseDetails.aspx?id=20088. See also 'LBRO Annual Report and Accounts 2008–9' (Local Better Regulation Office, 2009).

[28] LBRO developed core regulatory skills in partnership with local and national regulators which were launched in 2011. The core regulatory skills were subsequently revised and published as 'Core Competencies for Regulators' (Regulatory Delivery, 2016) available from the Office for Product Safety and Standards.

ii. Values

The values of the regulatory agency, both collectively and individually, play an important part in determining its culture and its approach to its role and relationships. The origins of the organisation's values are diverse. They are likely to be heavily influenced by its leadership and key members of staff, who may join the organisation from a range of backgrounds and for different reasons, bringing with them their own particular set of values. They will also draw, particularly at the outset, on commonly held values in the wider society and regulatory community. This might be expected to be particularly true of values that are common to many working in the public sector – the 'public service ethos' referred to earlier in this chapter – and of commonly held values that relate to the behaviours expected of regulatory agencies. For example, traditional approaches to dealing with regulatory non-compliance have often been rooted in the commonly held belief that deterrence through punitive sanctioning is a regulatory agency's most effective tool. As highlighted in the discussion of ethical business regulation (see chapter twenty-two), the findings of behavioural psychology are significantly undermining the theory of deterrence. Nevertheless, it persists and the values of a regulatory agency that has a strong underlying belief in the theory of deterrence will differ significantly from those of a regulatory agency that has developed a more 'responsive'[29] approach. Some regulators have used the designation 'modern regulator'[30] in connection with regulatory approaches in which the regulatory agency works in partnership with regulated sectors to support improvements in compliance, resorting to enforcement action where compliance failures are perceived to be deliberate and calculated or where a supportive approach is ineffective.

A regulatory agency's stated or actual values will be influenced in a number of ways, including by values that are externally dictated through the regulatory agency's governance framework. For example, in the UK, all public officials and public servants are expected to adhere to seven values-based principles:[31] selflessness; integrity; objectivity; accountability; openness; honesty; and leadership. In addition, regulatory agencies are expected to act in accordance with values-based principles around consistency and proportionality.[32] In the Netherlands, three Basic Principles for Good Enforcement were officially adopted by the Government in 2000 – independence, professionalism and transparency – and a further three principles were added in 2005, reflecting the increased emphasis on reducing burdens on business – selective, effective and cooperating (see chapter eleven). In Ontario,[33] the Public Service of Ontario Act establishes the values of professionalism, integrity, accountability and excellence for all public servants and a code provides further organisational values and elements of professionalism for regulatory ministries (see Table 10.1).

---

[29] Ian Ayres and John Braithwaite, *Responsive Regulation: Transcending the Deregulation Debate* (Oxford, Oxford University Press, 1982).

[30] For example see: 'Becoming a Modern Regulator' (Health and Safety Commission meeting paper, 2004) available at www.hse.gov.uk/aboutus/meetings/hscarchive/2004/060404/c53.pdf, and 'Concise Annual Report 2010: Transforming into a modern regulator' (EPA Victoria, 2010).

[31] 'Standards in Public Life, First Report' (Committee on Standards in Public Life, 1995).

[32] Legislative and Regulatory Reform Act 2006, s 21.

[33] 'Regulator's Code of Practice: Integrity in Pursuit of Compliance' (Government of Ontario, 2011).

Table 10.1 Organisational values and elements of professionalism[34]

Organisational values	Elements of professionalism
Trust	Honesty and integrity
Diversity	Objectivity
Creativity	Timeliness
Efficiency	Respect
Fairness	Confidentiality
Excellence	Knowledge
Collaboration	
Responsiveness	

Whilst values that are mandated in this way should have a significant influence on the values of the regulatory agency, they will not necessarily align completely with the organisation's own understanding or expression of its values. Our experience is that the question 'What sort of regulator are we?' elicits a vast range of responses. Whilst some of these responses relate to the regulatory agency's statutory basis or sense of its own identity – 'We are a Ministerial Agency'; 'We are a Licensing Authority'; 'We are an independent environmental protection agency' – many relate to its perceptions of its own values and behaviours; shedding some light on its culture – 'We are a modern, forward-thinking regulator'; 'We are a cooperative regulator'; 'We are tough when we need to be'. The range of these answers demonstrates the importance for the regulatory agency of asking the question and working with its staff to understand and shape the answer.

Many tools are available to assist organisations in identifying their own values and we have used such tools when working with regulatory agencies on implementing better regulation approaches. For example, groups of regulatory officers have been asked to consider where the organisation's attitudes and behaviours lie on the continuum between two opposing terms such as those in Table 10.2, in order to generate discussion about the actual values of the organisation and the values that they feel the organisation would ideally have.

Table 10.2 Examples of contrasting organisational values[35]

Competitive	Collaborative
Outward-facing	Inward-facing
Traditional	Leading-edge
Non-hierarchical	Hierarchical
Risk-averse	Risk-hungry
Team performance	Individual performance

(continued)

[34] Extracted from 'Regulator's Code of Practice' (2011).
[35] Extracted from materials used, as a basis for workshop discussion, by the Office for Product Safety and Standards (developed by R Powell, 2009, based on an adaptation of material from John Seddon. See, for example, Systems Thinking in the Public Sector: The Failure of the Reform Regime… and a Manifesto for a Better Way (Triarchy Press, 2008)).

Table 10.2 *(Continued)*

Top-down leadership	Distributed leadership
Formal	Informal
Listening	Telling
Experimental	Tried and tested
Diverse	Mono-cultural
Customer is always right	Provider is always right

A sense of coherence around the organisation's values is critical to developing and maintaining a strong and healthy organisational culture and it is important for the organisation to recognise where there are significant differences between its stated values and the collective values of its staff. This can be a particular issue where the organisation is undergoing a significant change in its role, purpose or regulatory approach – a lengthy period of adjustment can be needed and should be actively managed.

Equally, differences may arise as a result of gradual shifts in culture over time. For example, a regulatory agency might examine its own behaviours and practices – asking itself what it values – and identify 'collaborative' as a core organisational value. Over time, internal and external factors such as changes in staff and pressure on resources may mean that while the organisation continues to describe itself as 'collaborative', this is no longer borne out in the behaviours that it exhibits. Such shifts, if left unnoticed or unchallenged, can lead to a divergence between the regulatory agency's actual values and its stated values, which will cause confusion and may damage its credibility. The choice here is to accept the shift and to redefine the organisation's values or to reassert the desired value, in this case 'collaborative', and undertake a programme of work to address the issues that led to a shift away from collaborative behaviours and embed its importance.

The Office for Product Safety and Standards has, internally and through pilot work, explored the use of the Barrett Cultural Values Assessment,[36] a cultural measuring tool which enables regulatory agencies and other organisations to gain a valuable picture of their cultural health. Such tools can provide organisations with a clearer understanding on which to base work to drive improvements in their culture and practices, as highlighted in chapter twelve, which notes the important role played by the use of such a tool – in this case the Organisational Cultural Inventory assessment[37] – in tracking the progress of the organisation's cultural transformation programme.

iii. Competency

As noted earlier, culture is significant in determining the manner in which regulatory agencies address the challenges associated with their exercise of discretion. Within the

---

[36] Richard Barrett, *The Values-Driven Organization: Cultural Health and Employee Well-Being as a Pathway to Sustainable Performance*, 2nd ed (Abingdon and New York, Routledge, 2017).
[37] Developed by Human Synergistics International.

Regulatory Delivery Model, particular attention is paid to the way in which these challenges are approached in respect of the discretion afforded to individual officers. At the extremes, the two approaches that can be chosen involve either equipping officers to make the best possible decisions on a case-by-case basis or putting measures in place to minimise the degree of discretion available to individual officers (see Figure 10.1).

The first approach involves accepting a high degree of officer discretion and trusting them to exercise this discretion appropriately, in line with the regulatory agency's processes and values. This approach requires that the regulatory agency values professional competency and commits resource to recruiting and training officers, ensuring that their competency is maintained. Providing transparency around the regulatory agency's approach to competency can provide reassurance to the regulatory agency's stakeholders.[38]

The importance of competency is recognised in OECD guidance:[39] 'Inspectors should be trained and managed to ensure professionalism, integrity, consistency and transparency: this requires substantial training focusing not only on technical but also on generic inspection skills, and official guidelines for inspectors to help ensure consistency and fairness.' The regulatory agency will need to support its officers in making good, consistent judgment-based decisions by providing appropriate processes, mechanisms and decision-making tools. It will also need to pay particular attention to its own quality assurance mechanisms and to ensuring that robust complaints and appeals processes are available to regulated entities (see chapter seven, which explores accountability).

The second approach – that of minimising officer discretion – will usually involve establishing detailed rules to prescribe, for example: which businesses (or other regulated entities) are selected for inspection; what is inspected (including through the use of checklists); and the enforcement decisions to be made in particular circumstances. Whilst such rules can be an appealing solution, the design of fair and appropriate rules, in the face of multiple variables, can prove extremely challenging and tends to lead to the sort of enforcement that is characterised as 'tick box'. The rules may fail to deal properly with complexities and will struggle to keep up with the pace of change. The risks are not just to process. There is a real risk that enforcement will miss the biggest threats to regulatory outcomes as well as causing a disproportionate burden on regulated entities.

Nevertheless, such approaches are widely advocated and can be appropriate where carefully used, particularly while regulatory officers have low levels of competency or where the legitimacy of the regulatory agency is damaged and there is a need to rebuild the trust of regulated communities. The OECD guidance[40] referred to above highlights the benefits of inspection checklists in terms of promoting consistency, supporting business compliance and providing transparency for businesses as to the inspector's expectations.

In practice, most regulatory agencies will end up at some point on the spectrum between these two extremes and our experience is that the most effective approaches are found

---

[38] For example, the UK's Pensions Regulator has published a statement of its competencies, expressing these in terms of their interdependencies to the organisation's stated values: 'Our Purpose, Values and Competencies' (The Pensions Regulator, 2013).

[39] 'Regulatory Enforcement and Inspections, OECD Best Practice Principles for Regulatory Policy' (OECD, 2014).

[40] ibid.

where a regulatory agency has achieved an appropriate relationship between the level of officer competence and the extent to which it prescribes how its officers must behave, with this optimal position being indicated by the white boxes in Figure 10.1 and the less favourable positions being shown by the darker boxes.

Figure 10.1 Relationship between professional competency and rules-based decision-making frameworks

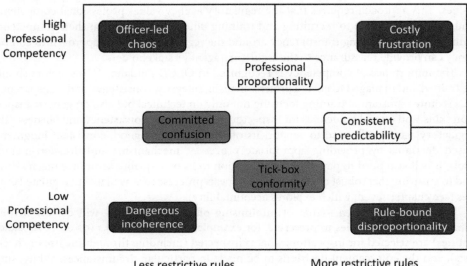

Our work with regulatory agencies in the UK to develop a regulatory competency framework for regulatory officers working in any regulatory area (a summary of which is shown in Figure 10.2) has been underpinned by the belief that frontline regulatory officers, whatever their field of technical expertise, share common core regulatory competencies that are transferable between areas of regulation.[41] These core regulatory competencies are as important as the officer's technical and organisational competencies. They incorporate the generic knowledge and skills needed by all regulatory officers to enable them to:

- understand the context in which they operate and those they regulate;
- work with risk-based approaches;
- check compliance and respond appropriately to non-compliance;
- support improvements in compliance; and
- evaluate the impact of their activities in order to inform future approaches.

---

[41] *Core Competencies for Regulators* (2016), available from the Office for Product Safety and Standards.

Figure 10.2 Diagrammatic representation of the core regulatory competencies and the relationship between them

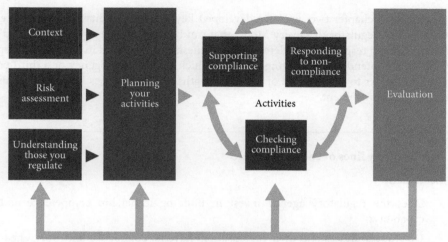

Technical knowledge of the regulation is critical; for example, ensuring that food inspectors have good knowledge of food safety laws. However, where regulatory competency is defined only in terms of technical knowledge, the regulatory skills associated with working with business, carrying out risk assessment, providing advice and investigating complaints can be undervalued and underdeveloped. The Netherlands' experience of establishing an Inspection Academy, explored in the following chapter, is of interest here, as is work done in the UK to establish an apprenticeship to develop frontline regulatory officers working in different regulatory areas, providing them with core skills and knowledge and seeking to embed the key behaviours.[42] The incorporation of core regulatory competencies into, for example, training programmes, job descriptions, performance management arrangements, etc ensures that officers are well equipped to deliver their role.[43]

In working with regulatory agencies to explore their approach to professional competency, we have used exercises to encourage regulatory officers and their managers to explore the relative importance of different elements of competency, including:

- understanding and use of the technical regulation;
- understanding and changing business behaviour;
- understanding the industry; and
- understanding the legal framework.

This exercise has proved useful in beginning a discussion in relation to what aspects of competency are valued and how frontline officers and leaders feel that this could or should change.

---

[42] 'Regulatory Compliance Officer: Details of Standard' (Institute for Apprenticeships, 2018), available at www.instituteforapprenticeships.org/apprenticeship-standards/regulatory-compliance-officer.

[43] For example, in the UK, local fire safety authorities are encouraged to adopt a common Competency Framework for Business Fire Safety Regulators that emphasises core competencies based on the Common Approach to Competency developed by LBRO and its successor organisations. Available at www.cfoa.org.uk/18262.

IV. Key Lines of Enquiry

As discussed in chapter two, we have developed key lines of enquiry in respect of each element of the Regulatory Delivery Model that can be used to assess and understand the current picture in respect of that element. These questions, presented in Box 10.1 in respect of Culture, are intended as a starting point on which a regulatory agency or a third party can build in order to give a sense of where strengths and weaknesses lie and to highlight potential for improvement.

Box 10.1 Key lines of enquiry: culture

Leadership

- Does the regulatory agency invest in building leadership competence and capability?
- Do leaders understand their organisation, have its confidence and work effectively with it?
- Are they modelling appropriate behaviours, values and practices through their words and actions?
- Are they building a culture that focuses on outcomes?
- Do they set clear expectations and standards of conduct?

Values

- What does the regulatory agency value?
- Are those values shared throughout the organisation, across managerial and operational levels and across specialist activities and commands?
- Are those values appropriate to the agency's regulatory task? And do they reflect the sort of regulator it aims to be?
- Are those values clearly communicated, both internally and externally?

Competency

- Does initial and continuing training, learning and development ensure the ability of the staff to deliver the purposes of the regulatory agency?
- Does the assessment and development of competency fully and proportionately address knowledge, skills and behaviours?
- Is the level of discretion afforded to individuals and decision-making units within the agency proportionate to the competency of the people involved?

V. Summary

This chapter set out to explain the importance of the culture of regulatory agencies in enabling them to operate effectively and to explore what we mean when we talk about culture in connection with regulatory agencies. We have considered, in particular, the impact of values, leadership and approach to competency on the behaviour of a regulatory agency. We have also considered the dynamic relationship between Culture and the other prerequisites of the Regulatory Delivery Model: Governance Frameworks and Accountability.

The next two chapters illustrate specific aspects of the themes that we have considered in this chapter, drawing from two particular examples, in the Netherlands and Australia, which, while they touch on many aspects of regulatory delivery, have particular relevance to culture. In chapter eleven, Rob Velders highlights the leadership role of the Inspection Council in the Netherlands in furthering collaboration between regulatory agencies and developing common approaches in areas such as the training of inspectors. In chapter twelve, Chris Webb provides a powerful example of how a regulatory agency has, through work to build a healthy organisational culture, improved public perceptions and its own ability to deliver.

11

Cooperative Approaches: The Work of the Inspection Council in the Netherlands

ROB VELDERS

I. Introduction

This chapter deals with experiences from the Netherlands relating to cooperation between national inspectorates. The process of closer cooperation started at the end of the 1990s and many lessons have been learned. In addition, regulatory delivery and enforcement has a higher profile in the Netherlands than other countries, with lots of social, scientific and political interest driving debate and scientific research over the last 20 years, which is drawn upon in this chapter.

II. Cultural Background of the Netherlands

Before going into detail about the organisation of inspectorates in the Netherlands and how they cooperate, it is helpful to explain something of the Dutch culture and history in order to appreciate the developments better.[1]

The Netherlands – meaning 'the lowlands' – is a country that literally lies low. Big parts (which are the most densely populated) lie lower then sea level. This means that since ancient times there has been a constant threat of flooding. No one party could solve this problem on their own and so farmers, noblemen, townspeople and other citizens needed to work together to address this problem. They had to build dykes and reshape rivers and canals to keep their feet dry, and wet uninhabitable parts of land were turned into habitable land. Such new land is called 'polder' in Dutch; this word is now also used as a verb that means to negotiate, cooperate and find consensus.

At the beginning of the seventeenth century the Netherlands became an important trading country. Ships were sailing out to the Far East and to the New World to conquer pieces of land, but in particular with the aim to trade. Equipping these ships was very costly and the risks were huge. The Netherlands as a unified nation state did not exist until that time; the towns and provinces were in charge and there were constant threats of war with the British, the French and the Spanish. Therefore, it was almost impossible for individuals

[1] Based on the Raiffeisen-lecture of Geert Mak 'De Mercator Sapiens Anno 2004'.

or local governments to organise and fund these expeditions. They had to cooperate. For funding such high-risk operations, cooperation, agreement and trust between the investors was needed. And it worked. During the Dutch 'Golden Age' in the late sixteenth and seventeenth centuries, the Dutch Republic dominated world trade, conquering a vast colonial empire and operating the largest fleet of merchants of any nation. The Province of Holland was the wealthiest and most urbanised region in the world. Between 1590 and 1712 the Dutch also possessed one of the strongest and fastest navies in the world, allowing for their varied conquests, including breaking the Portuguese sphere of influence on the Indian Ocean and in the Orient. It is no wonder that at this time the world's first stock exchange was created in the Netherlands and one could become a shareholder of successful enterprises.

Such a system could only flourish within a context of trust, order and peace – after all, one had to have a guarantee that one could redeem all those valuable papers at any time. Hence, these merchants in Bruges, Ghent, Antwerp, Dordrecht and Amsterdam had developed a culture of tolerance that made it possible to do business with all faiths and cultures, while ensuring that their society was calm and remained ordered.

This short historic background describes the underlying factors for the success of cooperation in the Netherlands. Francis Fukuyama wrote in his book, *Trust: The Social Virtues and the Creation of Prosperity*,[2] about the difference between 'high-trust countries' and 'low-trust countries'. The Netherlands no doubt belongs to the first category. In these countries (which also include Germany and Scandinavian countries) law is respected and in general one can say that promises and informal agreements are kept.

III. Inspectorates in the Netherlands

How is Dutch enforcement organised at the national level? The Netherlands is a parliamentary democracy which means that government is accountable to parliament and ministers have no constituency of their own. Inspectorates are part of the ministries as you can see in Table 11.1. Most heads of inspectorates, the inspector-generals, are a member of the board of the ministry they belong to.

Table 11.1 Netherlands Inspectorates (and Dutch acronym), their number of full-time employees and the ministries[3] they are part of.

Inspectorate	Number of full-time employees	Ministry
The Netherlands Food and Consumer Product Safety Authority (NVWA)	2,335	Ministry of Agriculture, Nature and Food Quality
Inspector-General of the Armed Forces (IGK)	12	Ministry of Defence
Defence Safety Inspectorate (IVD)[4]	25	Ministry of Defence

(continued)

---

[2] Francis Fukuyama, *Trust: the Social Virtues and the Creation of Prosperity* (New York, Free Press, 1996).
[3] The ministries of General Affairs and of the Interior and Kingdom Relations incorporate no inspectorates.
[4] This Inspectorate was established in 2018 after a series of safety incidents within the Dutch army.

Table 11.1 *(Continued)*

Inspectorate	Number of full-time employees	Ministry
Radio Communications Agency (AT)	283[5]	Ministry of Economic Affairs and Climate Policy
State Supervision of Mines (SodM)	80	Ministry of Economic Affairs and Climate Policy
Dutch Inspectorate of Education (IvhO)	580	Ministry of Education, Culture and Science
Cultural Heritage Inspectorate	24	Ministry of Education, Culture and Science
Tax and Customs Administration	28,152[6]	Ministry of Finance
Health and Youth Care Inspectorate (IGJ)[7]	657	Ministry of Health, Welfare and Sport
Human Environment and Transport Inspectorate (ILT)	1,113	Ministry of Infrastructure and Water Management
Inspectorate for Justice and Security (IV&J)	60	Ministry of Justice and Security
Inspectorate SZW (ISZW)[8]	1,132[9]	Ministry of Social Affairs and Employment
Authority for Nuclear Safety and Radiation Protection (ANVS)	120	–[10]

The Dutch national inspectorates cooperate closely. The heads of all inspectorates meet regularly through the Inspection Council, which is the forum for steering and designing cooperation between the inspectorates. Some of the inspectorates, such as the Tax and Customs Administration and the Inspectorate of the Armed Forces, are members of the Council but do not actively participate in the initiatives. The Netherlands Court of Audit also has a standing invitation.

There is a memorandum of cooperation for the Inspection Council which sets out the purpose of the forum and how it operates. The Inspection Council promotes and coordinates the execution of cooperation and knowledge development in accordance with the official Dutch basic principles of good enforcement[11] and other applicable government policies. The inspectorates implement their cooperation in a multi-annual programme and the members of the Council are each responsible for parts of the cooperation. The chair of the Inspection Council is elected every two years and the Council meets about every six weeks.

[5] The Radio Communications Agency has several tasks. About 40% of FTE relates to the enforcement department.

[6] Including 4,290 FTE for Customs.

[7] This inspectorate is a merger of the Healthcare Inspectorate (610 FTE) and the Youth Care Inspectorate (47 FTE). This merger took place in October 2017.

[8] Former Labour Inspectorate.

[9] The inspectorate SZW was rewarded €50 million annually in 2017 to raise the amount of inspections. This is not taken into account in Table 11.1.

[10] The ANVS was established in 2015 and changed from being part of a ministry into an independent body (a so-called independent administrative body (ZBO)) in 2017, due to international rules.

[11] Transparency, independent, professional, result-oriented, selectivity and cooperation; see Ch 12.

The funding for cooperation activities is provided by the inspectorates, proportionate to the number of employees of each inspectorate.

The Inspection Council is supported by a small bureau that prepares documents for the meetings of the Council, coordinates projects and manages the inspection academy.

A. Market Regulators

As well as these inspectorates, there are regulatory agencies that are not part of a ministry. They are independent administrative bodies (in Dutch: ZBOs) and are not part of the Inspection Council,[12] instead cooperating with each other through the Market Surveillance Summit (*Markttoezichthoudersberaad*). However, there is less cooperation than the Inspection Council and cooperation with the Inspection Council is not very intense yet. Table 11.2 shows the Dutch Authorities cooperating in the Market Surveillance Summit in 2016/17.

Table 11.2 Dutch authorities cooperating in the Market Surveillance Summit

Authority	Number of full-time employees
Authority Financial Markets (AFM)	574
Dutch Central Bank (DNB)	588[13]
Netherlands Authority for Consumers and Markets (ACM)	553
Dutch Healthcare Authority (NZa)	431
Netherlands Gaming Authority (Ksa)	69
Dutch Data Protection Authority (AP)	72
Dutch Media Authority (CvdM)	53

There are also some other enforcing bodies in the Netherlands, on a national, provincial and municipal level, as well as the water boards. They will not be further mentioned here. In this chapter we will focus mainly on enforcement at a national level by inspectorates and market surveillance authorities.

IV. History Leading to the Inspection Council

During the 1990s regulatory enforcement moved up the agenda of society and politicians. Decentralisation and privatisation lead to calls for better enforcement. The crash of the El Al plane in Amsterdam in 1992 and the subsequent reports and public anger about this incident, as well as increasing interest in environmental issues, strengthened the call for better and firmer enforcement.

---

[12] Note that the Authority for Nuclear Safety and Radiation Protection (ANVS) is a ZBO since 2017, but is part of the Inspection Council and so is listed in Table 11.1.

[13] Of a total of 1,800 employees.

The debate resulted in the presentation of the Basic Principles for Good Enforcement. In 2000 the first three basic principles of good enforcement were officially adopted by the Government: enforcement should be independent, professional and transparent.

At the end of the last century the inspectorates listed in Table 11.1 started to cooperate on an informal basis as regular meetings of the heads of inspectorates. The aim was to create a platform for exchange of knowledge and to learn from each other, to improve and to facilitate cooperation. There was a particular impetus from the occurrences of several severe incidents that raised serious questions about the lack of cooperation between enforcing bodies.

Another issue that started towards the end of the 1990s was mergers between inspectorates. From the 23 that existed at this time, fewer than half are currently still in place (see Table 11.1). The number of inspectorates was brought down to about one per ministry. While merging the inspectorates the number of staff was also brought down by about 30 per cent.[14] The rationale was that mergers would mean inspectorates could be more efficient and be able to do more with less.

In 2003 the Dutch national Government initiated a programme aiming to achieve a more modern government (*Programma Andere Overheid*). The programme focused on less bureaucracy and fewer regulations while increasing the effectiveness and impact of government actions and building the trust of citizens and business in government. One part of it concerned a project for all national inspectorates aiming to reduce burdens from inspections and increase their effectiveness. A national project manager was appointed with a small team to support better cooperation between inspectorates. The motto was 'less burden, more effectiveness'. Several kinds of cooperation were tested: exchange of information and intelligence (for example, observations by inspectors during their inspections that are not part of their competency but that may be of interest for other inspectorates such as an environmental inspector signalling to the labour inspectorate that he doubts whether a scaffold on a premises is solid enough to hold the people that make use of it); coordination between inspections; joint inspections; (simple) inspections on behalf of other inspectorates; and complete delegation of inspecting activities to other inspectorates.

In 2005, however, pressure on inspectorates to improve performance and in particular to reduce burden for those being inspected became high when Parliament called the Government to merge all inspectorates (except the Tax and Customs Administration) into one inspectorate.[15] However, it was felt that this would not solve the problem of burden, and instead a commitment was made to reduce the burden by 25 per cent and to give businesses that were compliant an inspection holiday, meaning a maximum of two inspections annually by the national inspectorates.[16]

A programme to realise these goals was set up. Until then the meetings of the heads of the inspectorates were still informal meetings. But in order to show that they were serious in meeting the new demands and to be able to be formally ordered by the Government to take responsibility, the meetings were formalised, and the Inspection Council was set up with the Bureau of the Inspection Council as the team to support the programme.

---

[14] In the same period the total reduction of staff of the whole national government was lowered by less than 7%.
[15] See also ch 25 for Mongolia's experiences in implementing a merger of all their inspectorates.
[16] With defined exceptions for high-risk businesses, for EU requirements and when justified complaints have been received. See www.government.nl/topics/reducing-the-regulatory-burden/regulatory-burden-on-businesses.

Also, in 2005, additional basic principles for good enforcement were introduced by the Government, not coincidentally closely related to the reduction of burden. The new principles required good enforcement to also be selective, results oriented and cooperative. The six basic principles also play an important role today in shaping and executing enforcement in the Netherlands.

A. Getting Started on Cooperation: Measuring and Tackling Burden in Priority Sectors

In order to begin to tackle the goal of reducing the burden by 25 per cent, in 2006 the Inspection Council set up a method for measuring burden from inspections. This resulted in consideration of two kinds of burden: qualitative and quantitative.

Quantitative burdens are those that are relatively easy to measure such as the time and money spent by a business that is to be inspected. Quantitative burdens also include the expenses due to preparing for an inspection, the actual time and money that an inspection takes, plus all the work and investment that is required after the inspection. However, there was debate over the question of whether this includes the time (and money) that must be invested in measures to comply with the rules because it would create a difference in burden for compliant and non-compliant businesses.

The qualitative factors are more about determining the mood and perceptions of burden of a business that has been inspected. Table 11.3 shows examples of these qualitative factors.

Table 11.3 The qualitative factors explored as potential inspection burdens, including an example of what is meant for each

Qualitative factors	Example: It is appreciated when …
Expertise of the inspector	… the inspector is sufficiently familiar with the matter or subject of inspection and of the applicable rules.
Attitude of the inspector	… the inspector has an open mind and focuses primarily on advising on the requirements instead of focusing solely on non-compliance.
Working method of the inspector	… the inspector is well prepared, and the inspection is done systematically.
Clarity over the purpose of the inspection	… it is clear what the purpose and goal of an inspection is.
Plausibility of questions asked by the inspector	… the inspector makes clear or can explain why questions are asked and information is needed.
Measures are taken in relation to the risks and legal powers of the inspection	… the measures imposed by the inspector are felt to be reasonable, that is, these measures and the required investments are proportionate to the identified risks and the legal powers of the inspection are applied fairly and proportionately.

(continued)

Table 11.3 *(Continued)*

Qualitative factors	Example: It is appreciated when …
Focus on details	… the inspector focuses on the main issues that are relevant for risks and assesses the details only when necessary.
Learning effect for the companies	… the inspection is conducted in such a way that the business gains new insights that can improve business operations.
Co-ordination with other inspections	… inspections from other inspectorates do not overlap and are aligned. This avoids contradictory or incompatible requirements being imposed and avoids the same information being requested more than once.
Duration of the inspection	… the duration of an inspection is reasonable when considering the aspects being checked.
Timing of the inspection visit	… an inspection is carried out at a time that minimises the negative effect on the performance of a business.
Quality of inspection reports and next steps	… the inspection report is clear and consistent with the inspection performed. Communication with the business about the report is satisfying. Enough clarity has been provided on the recommended follow-up activities.

Cooperation between inspectorates started in specific areas. Some of these areas were a business sector (eg chemical industries), others were looking at a geographical area (eg Port of Rotterdam). For each area, someone from one of the participating inspectorates was appointed as the lead and regular meetings were organised. Areas that were identified at the beginning are as follows:

- Catering
- Port of Rotterdam (harbour)
- Hospitals
- Farms
- Schiphol Airport
- Meat production
- Road transportation
- Recreation
- Industries
- Childcare
- Chemical industries
- Nuclear industries
- Waste

In each area burden was measured by an external consultancy. It turned out that the burden from inspections was not as bad as expected. Most companies were not visited more than twice per year by national inspectorates. A big part of the burden due to inspection visits was caused by local government institutions. The research showed that the burden was caused mainly by the qualitative factors of the inspections. Whilst in general businesses were not so dissatisfied by the inspections (almost without exception they scored the quality of the work of the inspectors positively) it was felt that there were improvements that could be made. Interestingly some people suggested that it was possible that good-quality inspections could even lead to more acceptance over the invested time and costs of companies, although this was not researched further.

In 2014 all inspectorates conducted surveys to investigate customer satisfaction of inspected businesses. Here satisfaction also turned out to be (very) positive. Businesses valued inspections as necessary and valued the quality of the inspections. Nevertheless, the image of inspectorates had not improved, in particular in political debate, and it remained important for inspectorates to improve the way they operated.

It turned out that each of these areas demanded their own specific kind of cooperation depending on the issues. For example, in hospitals one of the products of the programme was creating an annual calendar of inspections that was established by all relevant inspectorates, tackling the problem of burdens from poor timing of inspections. In waste it was more relevant to share information between enforcing authorities because multiple parts of the waste-processing chain needed to be effectively regulated. Joint inspections by food and labour inspectors were considered for the catering sector as was predominant in road transportation. However, in small restaurants and hotels it was found that they preferred not to be inspected through joint inspections. The owners of small restaurants and hotels often felt raided by multiple inspectors and were unable to deal with all inspectors at the same time. In addition, restaurants and hotels were worried that customers could think that something was wrong, and they would lose business. So, for catering it was found to be better to coordinate separate inspections spread out over the year and/or adopt some of the inspection tasks for other inspectors. The food inspectors (after a short training programme) adopted some of the basic inspections with regard to labour, reducing the number of inspections.

B. Need for Common Language between Inspectorates

It is important that misunderstandings due to language and ways of working (ie culture) of the different parties do not undermine the efficiency of the cooperation. In the early cooperation work of the Inspection Council it was discovered that most of the inspectorates had developed their own language and ways of working. To reduce misunderstanding while cooperating, a conceptual framework[17] for common language was produced in 2013. It defined commonly used wording and it was officially adopted by the Inspection Council and used in all documents.

---

[17] Rob Velders and Meindert Brunia, *Begrippenkader rijksinspecties*: www.rijksinspecties.nl/publicaties/publicaties/2013/01/02/index.

V. Exchange of Inspection Information: *Inspectieview*

For cooperation between inspectorates to deliver better regulatory protections, exchange of information is highly important. That is why the Inspection Council decided to create an IT facility to connect data from all the inspectorates. Later it was decided that other organisations, in particular, the police and local environmental enforcing agencies, should be connected as well. The facility that was built was called *Inspectieview* (Inspection View). It is web-based and connects real-time information from all participating inspectorates on individual businesses as well as enabling data to be analysed and supporting the inspectorates in carrying out risk-based inspections. *Inspectieview* itself is not a database so inspectors only need to update their inspectorate's database.

An inspector can log in to *Inspectieview* and search by the name of a business that they plan to inspect. The tool searches all connected inspection systems and within seconds provides a list of all inspections that have taken place during the past five years. By clicking on the inspections, the inspector can see the findings and actions that have taken place. In order to keep inspectors from an overload of information the findings of all inspections are classified in three categories, from serious non-compliance to small administrative violations. This categorisation also reduced juridical problems in the exchange of information. Based on this information it can be decided whether to inspect a business.

Inspectieview also enables data analysis. Analysts can create queries based on different fields such as business sector, regulatory area, history of compliance, etc. Thus *Inspectieview* can be used in support of the analysis necessary for risk-based inspections, using data on compliance from other areas of regulation as well as the area the inspectorate covers.

To safeguard the data within *Inspectieview* a three-step protection was used: username and password for each inspectorate and an extra password that is provided via text message every time an inspector logs into the system. Also, all activities from inspectors that have accessed the system are logged.

For creating and maintaining *Inspectieview*, a team of technicians as well as a helpdesk and a small bureau had to be established. They are accommodated by the Inspectorate for Human Environment and Transport (ILT).

In law, *Inspectieview* is granted a key role in the exchange of information between enforcing bodies concerning the environment.

Although *Inspectieview* is a very promising instrument, in practice it has not always worked as smoothly as one would hope. Every organisation that wants to participate in *Inspectieview* needs to invest in an interface (software that connects their databases to *Inspectieview*). Some inspection bodies, in particular regional enforcement bodies, have had difficulties in financing this.

In addition, business inspection information of the participating inspectorates was not easy to combine because every database has a different way of storing information and so matching records relating to the same business was a challenge. Also, due to the mergers in recent years, inspectorates often have several databases that each need to be connected to *Inspectieview*.

In addition, it is by no means the case that every inspector with access to the system will really use it. Often, they do not know or forget that they have access. In addition, for some it feels like extra work in preparing their inspections. *Inspectieview* clearly has potential to reduce the burden for business by enabling risk-based inspection based on data from multiple relevant inspectorates. However, there remain cultural barriers to overcome in terms of embedding the use of the system by all inspectors, as part of a risk-based way of operating.

VI. Drivers for Further Change

A. Budget Cuts

One other important development that started at the beginning of this century is budget cuts. In addition to the general budget cuts for all ministries of around five per cent every four years, all Dutch inspectorates faced extra budget cuts, spurred on by the slogan 'Do More with Less' and usually also following each merger. This has resulted in a decrease of almost one-third in the number of inspectors over the past 15 years. Several investigation reports after incidents concluded that budget cuts have had too big an impact on the performance of the inspectorates involved. As a consequence, since 2015 extra budget or reduction of budgets cuts have been awarded to the Healthcare and Youthcare Inspectorate, the State Supervision on Mines, the Inspectorate SZW (former Labour Inspectorate) and the Netherlands Food and Consumer Product Safety Authority.

B. Advice from the Netherlands Scientific Council for Government Policy

In 2013 the Netherlands Scientific Council for Government Policy (WRR)[18] published a report 'Supervising public interests. Towards a broader perspective on government supervision'[19] on inspections.

The report concluded that with regard to inspections the emphasis of policies had been on burdens, compliance and on its political and administrative role, which are all legitimate as such. But a unilateral focus on each of them will lead to problems. The report highlighted the difficulty for supervisory agencies in being asked to do more with less although noted this seemed to have resulted in a move towards professionalisation and innovative practices in inspectorates. The report concluded that the (political) perspective on improving enforcement should be broadened to look beyond the incidents[20] of today and avoid the pendulum swing from increasing strictness following an incident where regulation is seen to have failed and reducing supervision in efforts to reduce burdens. The question in that case is what role supervision plays in society and what its value is or could be (supervision here is a similar concept to regulatory delivery).

---

[18] The Netherlands Scientific Council for Government Policy (WRR) is an independent advisory body for government policy. The task of the WRR is to advise the Dutch Government and Parliament on strategic issues that are likely to have important political and societal consequences.

[19] https://english.wrr.nl/publications/reports/2013/09/09/supervising-public-interests.-towards-a-broader-perspective-on-government-supervision (synopsis, English version).

[20] Since 2000 there have been several (near) incidents in industries, childcare, fires in the Netherlands that led to criticism of inspections, more stringent laws and heavier penalties for non-compliance.

Recommendations were:

(1) Review the national government's vision on supervision.
(2) Encourage a culture that focuses on benefits and improve the knowledge infrastructure so that supervision can be properly evaluated and backed by scientific evidence.
(3) Encourage the use of force field analyses when introducing, structuring or exercising government supervision.
(4) Strengthen the reflective capacity of supervisory bodies.
(5) Put firm guarantees in place that allow supervisory bodies to act impartially and, in conjunction with this, to position themselves independently.
(6) See to it that supervisory bodies are held publicly accountable for the capacity and instruments deployed and for the results achieved, and that they have an appropriate accountability relationship with parliament.
(7) Create a realistic relationship between the anticipated benefits of supervision and the available quantitative and qualitative capacity.

So far, the Government's basic principles have not been reviewed and there are no plans to do so. In 2018 the Inspection Council together with some scientists presented a 'Science Agenda' aiming to connect questions that have arisen from supervision to scientific research agendas. It determines three themes to focus on: good supervision in the midst of increasing social complexity; smart supervision in a complex information society; and effectiveness of the supervisory profession. Cooperation with scientists was already a trend within several inspectorates. Some already have scientists in their organisation or have established close cooperation with universities. But this cooperation will be strengthened through the scientific programme.

VII. Accountability of Inspectorates: Annual Reports

In 2016 the prime minister issued an instruction to all ministers about the governance of inspectorates within their ministries. One of the main issues is that there must be complete transparency about the relationship between the ministers and the inspectorates. In particular instructions from the minister to the inspectorates must be published or reported to parliament.

Although some inspectorates were already doing this, all inspectorates agreed to publish annual (or more frequent) 'State of ...' reports. These are reports in which the inspectorates do not report their results but report trends they have encountered or big issues that (may) come up. It turns out that these reports often get much media attention and ignite or contribute to a public and political debate.[21]

Increasing numbers of inspectorates are setting goals of what they want to achieve, when they want to have achieved it and how they want to do that. More and more they involve

---

[21] See, for example, (all in Dutch): State of Labour Safety 2018 – www.inspectieszw.nl/publicaties/rapporten/2018/04/17/staat-van-arbeidsveiligheid-2018; State of Geothermia – www.sodm.nl/actueel/nieuws/2017/07/13/staat-van-de-sector-geothermie-ook-aardwarmte-moet-veilig-gewonnen-worden; State of Education – www.onderwijsinspectie.nl/onderwerpen/staat-van-het-onderwijs/archief.

the public and the objects of their inspections in determining the risks and setting the goals. And publishing inspection results is part of that trend. For example, inspection information about all individual schools, medical facilities, restaurants and chemical industries is published on the internet. And this trend is gaining pace.

VIII. Competency of Inspectors: The Academy for Public Oversight

The Bureau of the Inspection Council has established an Academy for Public Oversight. While the big inspectorates already had their own academies, the smaller ones did not. And during the last few years the overlap has become smaller since awareness grew that inspectorates all need the same training on inspection skills. The role of the Inspection Academy is to provide training on these core skills for inspectors whilst the inspectorates remain responsible for the necessary technical training topics. The Academy has two assignments. It provides training for inspectors of all inspectorates on core skills and it functions as a focal point for knowledge about good supervision practice, for example risk-based inspections.

A. Training for Inspectors

In order to be able to perform an inspection, inspectors need to:

- know about the subject they inspect;
- know about the rules that are applicable; and
- have skills in performing good inspections.

For the first two parts of knowledge each inspectorate is responsible. But the skills for performing good inspections are universal. The Academy for Public Oversight currently provides training in three areas, alongside training for trainees and top civil servants:

- **New inspectors** – In this course the working practices of a new entrant inspector are targeted. Knowledge, behaviour and skills are learned. The participants gain insight and tools to develop a conscious, balanced professional attitude in the supervisory process. The acquired knowledge will be directly useful in the workplace.
- **Strategic enforcement** – Here strategic issues related to modernisation of supervision are the focus. The course provides innovation and cooperation perspectives. It develops relevant competencies for participants, and current issues and strategic developments are discussed. This helps inspectors to stay up to date on the latest developments and knowledge on enforcement.
- **Professionalism and broadening knowledge** – In this course various themes are central such as; risk and risk-based supervision, vertical, horizontal and internal supervision, social security and supervisory benefits and professionalism. Inspectors are expected to participate in inspections with other inspectorates. It is aimed at deepening knowledge of supervision. It provides a better view of the position of enforcement and inspectors in society.

Participants on these courses are always a mix of inspectors from several inspectorates. It is not compulsory, and each inspectorate pays for their inspectors that participate.

IX. Leadership: Evidence, Professional Representation and Disseminating Good Regulatory Practice

A. Scientific Research Programme

In 2018 a Science Agenda for Supervision was drafted at the request of the Inspection Council. Headed by scientists from universities, it focuses on two aspects:

- **Contents** – The agenda provides an overview of the main themes on which scientific knowledge can be of value for supervisory practice. The focus is not on knowledge about specific regulatory areas, but on knowledge about the 'subject of supervision' (similar to regulatory delivery), and the associated administrative and organisational issues. ·

- **Form** – The agenda provides a vehicle for establishing a dialogue between science and supervisory practice. In addition, proposals for shaping a continuous dialogue are being developed and it is used for addressing issues in scientific networks.

B. VIDE – The Professional Association for Enforcers

In 2000 VIDE was created as a membership association for enforcement professionals. VIDE is an independent foundation that aims at professionalism of its members and to contribute to the continuous improvement of supervision, inspections and enforcement. Members are enforcing bodies (and all their inspectors) as well as other individuals. It organises lectures and meetings and it funds a research post at a Dutch university. In addition, VIDE gives an annual prize to the best articles about enforcement issues. Its annual congress has high attendance and is a known place for meeting inspectors from all inspectorates and market surveillance authorities.

C. Linking Enforcement Professionals to Latest Developments

A weekly magazine with an overview of all news, reports, legal judgments and parliamentary issues regarding enforcement has been published since 2007. It consists of around ten pages mainly with news that is relevant for all enforcers.

It is closely connected to the Dutch LinkedIn group for enforcement. The group is only accessible to professionals in enforcement and over 8,000 inspectors are members. Within the group, discussions take place, questions are asked, and job offers can be found.

Since 2010 a scientific journal on enforcement has been published. *Tijdschrift voor Toezicht* is made by, and written for, experts who are professionals in supervision. It aims at bridging the gap between science and practice and facilitates different disciplines to learn from each other. It also looks beyond national borders. The goal is to gather, interpret and disseminate knowledge and information about enforcement. It deals with questions such as what good effective supervision is, it looks critically at the functioning of existing enforcement techniques and pays attention to problems and trends, eg thinking about how regulators can fill an information gap or how can they deal with changing expectations within society.

Also worth mentioning is the Dutch Centre for Crime Prevention and Safety (CCV), which is an independent foundation aiming to maintain safety and quality of life in the Netherlands. It provides knowledge, tools, and tailor-made advice to help to create a safe living environment, work environment and way of living.

One of the most relevant products of CCV is the Intervention Compass (Circle of Nine),[22] which started as the Table of Eleven. It is an online tool, also available in English, that helps supervisors to understand why specific rules are being violated. In addition, it provides inspiration by presenting proven good examples. Enforcers within the Netherlands actively use the tool to apply behavioural insights in policy, implementation and supervision.

For three years the CCV has issued an online magazine about supervision called *ToeZine* (a merger of the Dutch words for supervision and magazine), that publishes background stories on current enforcement topics.

X. Future Trends

The clearest trends within Dutch enforcement at the beginning of 2019 are:

- better (scientific) basis on which inspection plans are made, interventions can be applied, and effects can be monitored;
- setting clear goals on what needs to be achieved, how and when. A better debate is possible on what inspections can achieve and what can be expected from enforcement;
- involvement of businesses that are inspected in the process of determining the goals that inspectorates want to achieve as well as on the means to realise these goals;
- a stronger focus on risks and solving problems instead of on non-compliance;
- publishing inspection results;
- signalling trends and problems for society and political debate;
- a debate on whether to let business pay for enforcement;
- higher penalties for violations; and
- continuing improvement of cooperation with the aim to act as if inspections are one.

[22] www.interventiekompas.nl.

12

Culture as a Transformation Tool, the Experience of the Environment Protection Authority in Victoria, Australia

CHRIS WEBB

I. Background

The Environment Protection Authority in Victoria, Australia (EPA Victoria), established in 1971, is one of the first dedicated environmental regulators in the world. Part of the Victorian state government, EPA Victoria's jurisdiction covers approximately the same area as the United Kingdom, with roughly 10 per cent of the population and industry. Varying in size over time, the regulator currently has around 450 employees in a range of roles including operational, policy and science.

Initially focused on the licensing of emissions from a relatively small cohort of around 1,000 businesses conducting activities with the potential for significant pollution, and the setting of environmental quality objectives, the role of the regulator grew significantly over the decades that followed to encompass a broad range of pollution and waste matters. Since 2010, EPA Victoria has been on a sustained journey of change and improvement to establish its legitimacy as the environmental regulator.[1] Legitimacy can be considered the social licence to operate, as distinct from the statutory basis, and is derived from the support of business, community and government.

While this change programme has taken many forms addressing operational, technical and systems problems, the most fundamental and enduring changes have been driven by a recognition that the organisational culture underpins performance. This chapter provides an assessment of the impacts of internal culture, the diagnosis and design of a programme to change the experience and the positive results it has yielded for the organisation.

II. Signposts for Change (Up to 2010)

Throughout its existence, EPA Victoria has had a reputation for innovative approaches to regulation. In the decade leading up to 2010, there had been a significant programme to

---

[1] Eric Windholz 'The Evolution of a Modern (and more legitimate) Regulator: A Case Study of the Victorian Environment Protection Authority' (2016) 3 *Australian Journal of Environmental Law* 17.

drive 'beyond compliance', which had resulted in a number of initiatives designed to provide an incentive for good performers and highlight those considered best in class. The approach was grounded in the theory that by providing clear signals to business of the benefits of environmental performance, it would establish sustainable environmental performance as part of the 'triple bottom line' of economic, social and environmental performance for business.[2]

Two reports issued in 2009/10 became the catalyst for change at EPA Victoria. The Victorian Ombudsman's report[3] into the handling of the methane impacts from a former landfill on a new housing estate was critical of EPA Victoria's role in the regulation of the landfill, through its closure period and as the methane issue arose, stating that 'the EPA missed numerous opportunities to improve the standard of the landfill'; 'the EPA failed to protect the environment'; and that 'the EPA failed to take adequate enforcement action in relation to the landfill over a number of years' and 'ineffectively utilised the enforcement tools at its disposal'. The second report, from the Victorian Auditor General's Office,[4] examined the regulation of hazardous waste movements in Victoria, and was critical of the role that EPA Victoria had played, concluding:

> The EPA is not effectively regulating commerce and industry's management of hazardous waste. Its monitoring and inspection activities lack coherence, purpose and coordination. This, combined with poor business information because of the EPA's lack of data reliability, poor analysis and reporting and inadequate documentation of its rationale for decisions, means that there is neither sound compliance monitoring nor effective enforcement regimes.

Both reports stated that despite numerous opportunities to intervene in both cases, no actions were taken by the regulator.

Changes in leadership flowed through to the senior executive and a new generation of leaders was marked by the declaration of a Transformation to a Modern Regulator,[5] and the first step was a deep understanding of the culture that underpinned the organisation and its performance as a regulator.

A. Internal Experience

One of the first exercises that the new leadership embarked upon was a series of sessions with staff asking them to share their stories, good and bad, about the experience of working at EPA Victoria. While this was initially viewed warily by some, a substantial cohort took the opportunity and provided a frank assessment of their recent experiences. Within a range of responses some described a fragmented organisation that had lost its primary sense of purpose – as a regulator.

While many saw that the push for innovation and support for good businesses had merit, it was seen as having a cost in terms of the focus on the traditional regulatory and

---

[2] John Elkington, 'Towards the Sustainable Corporation: Win-Win-Win Business Strategies for Sustainable Development' (1994) 36 *California Management Review* 90.

[3] 'Brookland Greens Estate – Investigation Into Methane Gas Leaks' (Victoria Ombudsman, 2009).

[4] Victorian Auditor-General, 'Hazardous Waste Management' (Victorian Government Printer, 2010).

[5] 'Concise Annual Report 2010: Transforming into a Modern Regulator' (EPA Victoria, 2010).

science functions. Frontline operational staff reported that they had felt inhibited from taking regulatory action; some of those involved in issuing licences had felt pressure to 'find a way to say yes' to new applications; and the core science function felt that important evidence was not being used in important decisions. Whether real or perceived, these pressures drove a culture that was felt to vacillate on controversial decisions or simply push them further up the hierarchy and viewed the exercising of remedial and sanctioning powers as a failure on the part of the regulator to have 'helped the business'.

B. External Experience

The two government reports mentioned above provided some immediate areas for scrutiny for the new leadership, but the change programme required a more detailed and specific focus on where the greatest improvements were needed. EPA Victoria commissioned a thorough review of its compliance and enforcement functions by an independent expert, resulting in a significant report[6] detailing 119 recommendations for improvement touching all aspects of the core regulatory functions.

As part of the assessment for this review, a significant consultation exercise was undertaken with community, business and government to determine the experience of EPA Victoria as the environmental regulator, as well as the expectations. As may be expected, the comments differed based on the perspective of the audience, but there were some consistent themes that aligned with the internal views. Regardless of the audience, everyone wanted a 'better regulator'.

Some in the community saw EPA Victoria as 'toothless' and captured by big business; they felt that significant issues were not being dealt with, and decisions did not take community views into account. They wanted more transparency and a willingness to explain and defend decisions that impacted residents. Too often, they felt their environment was not being protected. From a business perspective, some experienced a regulator that took too long to make decisions and was unwilling to provide clear advice on what was required for compliance. They pointed to cases of inconsistent advice from different parts of the regulator and a failure to act on poor performers who were undercutting legitimate operators in a tight economy.

The wider context was a question over the future of the regulator. EPA Victoria is one of only two environmental regulators in Australia that has continually maintained its status as an independent authority. In other states, often driven by regulatory failures, equivalent bodies have been dismantled and reassembled as subordinate departmental regulators. Often these bodies are also allocated additional responsibilities that are seen as related, such as conservation, sustainability and heritage. Historically this model has distracted effort away from core regulation of pollution and waste, and often diluted the effectiveness in these areas through over reliance on policy settings within the department. In a number of instances this has led to further regulatory failures, which has in turn lead to the recreation of an independent authority.

---

[6] Stan Krpan, 'Compliance and Enforcement Review: A Review of EPA Victoria's Approach' (EPA Victoria, 2011).

Against such a backdrop there was a clear need, and a significant mandate, for EPA Victoria to chart a very different course. The leadership recognised that if the external experience of the regulator was to change, then the first priority was to change the internal experience. As stated by the Chairman, culture is the currency of delivery.

III. Actual and Preferred Culture

A. Assessing Culture

Myriad tools exist to assist in the diagnosis of organisational cultures. Whilst the initial engagement of staff and external stakeholders had provided some important informal understanding of the current state, there was a need for some means by which some empirical and meaningful evaluation could be made that would also give insights into what interventions could guide the transformation. The use of such tools also provides a common language that allows simple representation of often complex internal behavioural norms.

In 2007, the organisation had undertaken such an exercise using the Organisational Cultural Inventory or OCI (Human Synergistics 1987–2017) assessment. The tool involves a detailed set of questions that relate to the individuals' experience of the work environment, and by virtue of what is observed, what behaviours are being encouraged or motivated. The behaviours are segmented into constructive, passive-defensive and aggressive-defensive.

These in turn are segmented into subsets as shown in Figure 12.1 (for example 'aggressive-defensive' splits into subsets of 'oppositional', 'power', 'competitive' and 'perfectionistic').

While each of these terms has some level of specific detail in the context of the tool, the dictionary definition serves sufficient purpose to understand how these manifest. Importantly, the passive-defensive and aggressive-defensive should be read as 'negative' behaviours, whereas the constructive is a positive behavioural set. Graphically, the results are presented as a segmented circumplex, with colour-coding according to the scheme in Figure 12.1. Strong constructive cultures are often simply referred to as 'blue' cultures.

The first use of the tool includes both an assessment of the current state, and then poses the same questions in the context of the desired state. Unsurprisingly, this latter exercise almost universally results in a profile that has a large focus on the 'constructive' behaviours, with a very low prevalence of the other two.

The preferred culture results for EPA Victoria in 2007 were in accordance with the expected assessment, but the actual culture results demonstrated a significant challenge. The results showed very limited experience of constructive behaviours, and the common experience was an organisation dominated by avoidance, oppositional and conventional styles (see Figure 12.2). This manifested a culture of blame-shifting and unwillingness to take accountability, constant criticism of others and a strong motivation to conform and make a good impression. This in turn correlated to the reported external experiences of, among other things, protracted decision-making and an unwillingness to provide clear and unambiguous compliance advice.

Given the importance of this existing data, the decision was taken to proceed with this tool as the benchmark. Despite management effort since the 2007 results, a retest in 2011

Figure 12.1 Organisational Cultural Inventory behavioural categories – blue is constructive, green passive-defensive and red aggressive-defensive

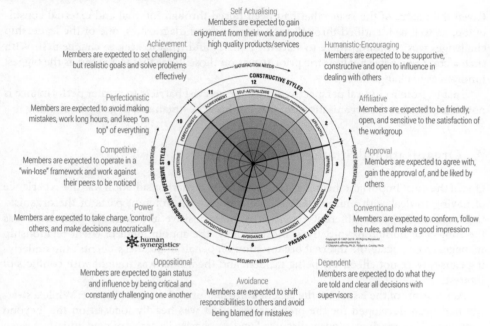

provided a profile that was almost identical and thus a clear message that while the preferred culture remained the same, the organisation had not yet experienced any substantial shift in that direction.

Figure 12.2 Results of Organisational Cultural Inventory assessment conducted by EPA Victoria in 2007 and 2011

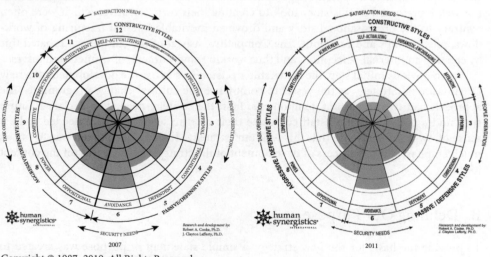

IV. Beginning the Change

Given the nature of the issues that had been raised through internal and external consultation, as well as identified through the use of cultural diagnostics, one of the leadership challenges was choosing where to start the journey and what to seek to change first. With such a comprehensive analysis the priority was on those items that were seen as the biggest hindrances to change itself.

That is, from a cultural perspective one of the greatest barriers to greater performance is not so much what the organisation does, as it is how the organisation goes about doing it.

A. Organisational Strategy Development

One of the most important themes arising from the external consultation was the experience of having to deal with multiple EPAs. Interactions with different parts of the organisation resulted in vastly different experiences, both positive and negative. This issue was the subject of numerous initiatives, most notably: the appointment of client relationship managers to navigate the internal organisation on behalf of business 'clients'; the underlying causes were not effectively being tackled; and the model was fraught with conflicts of interest.

At the heart of the issue was the lack of a singular organisational purpose. While a strategy had been developed for the previous period, it was heavily focused on the 'beyond compliance' approach previously discussed and emphasised a series of new initiatives, such as funding, voluntary agreements and client management. A strong narrative around this approach existed almost to the exclusion of most of the rest of the business including the previously core science, technical and regulatory functions.

It was also evident from an internal perspective that, outside of those parts of the business that were the focus of the direction, the strategy was viewed as the work of a small group who simply launched it upon the organisation. Each of the various parts of the organisation not well represented in this story took to creating their own narratives which were often contrary to the organisational story and drove an inevitable internal fracturing of workflows, relationships and functions. The Competitive aspect of the culture exacerbated this by creating an internal perception, and thus working environment, of winners and losers.

As an obvious initial step, the leadership decision was to use the development of a new Organisational Strategy as the vessel to commence the cultural change programme. The approach had two important components: first, the strategy needed to declare a future state and a pathway that all staff could see their role in; secondly, there needed to be a sense of ownership, a sense that this was 'our' strategy. The approach taken was to put as much emphasis on the process of development of the strategy, as there was on the content itself.

B. Defining Our Purpose

To provide the basis for the new strategy, a simple statement of purpose was created to encompass the two key roles for the organisation: 'We are an effective environmental regulator and an influential authority on environment impacts'. These two streams provided a strong message to the organisation that signalled an important resetting of the organisational priorities. First, as characterised by the Krpan report,[7] the perception internally was that those activities seen as the traditional regulatory functions had fallen out of favour and were not the keys to the future. Secondly, the role of a credible scientific voice in shaping the state's environmental policy had diminished.

The focus on the regulator was seen as critical as a resetting of both internal and external perception of the importance of the core role. Considerable effort was made during the design of the strategy development process to ensure that the internal understanding of the term, and thus the external experience, was reshaped as a positive. The framing of the role of the 'effective' regulator and its evolution from the 119 recommendations from the Krpan report, were critical to the exercise to regain the ownership of the term.

Similarly, the purpose of the influential authority is to recognise that many or even most issues faced by an environmental regulator will often fall into the category of harmful but not necessarily illegal. In this case, rather than simply declare an inability to act, the role of the regulator is to compile the body of evidence, engage with the right participants and create a solution to the problem. In some cases, this will result in the problem being made illegal, and thus regulatable; in other cases, it may become a problem for another regulator or even simply a government policy matter. In the latter case, the ongoing role for the influential authority is to continue to monitor to identify if change is occurring and continue to advocate for improvement.

With these two simple constructs as the basis for a strategy, the next stage was to commence a development programme that built the internal ownership.

C. A Collaborative Approach

Often organisational strategies have a kernel developed by an executive team, and are then farmed out to staff to fill in the detailed level. Done well, and communicated deftly, this approach can provide quick progress and some degree of momentum, but it will generally not be sufficient to win over a disengaged team. The approach to the development task literally commenced with the statement of the organisation's purpose and a blank page.

The philosophy that underpinned this approach, consistent with the principles of deliberative democracy, was that provided with the right information and framed accordingly, the capable and knowledgeable staff would very likely produce a plan that would be equal or superior to any compiled by an executive team. This overt show of faith in the people was a critical juncture in the cultural journey.

Through a series of events, ranging from whole of staff workshops to smaller focused sessions, a series of questions was repeatedly posed in relation to the desired future state, what was most important to get us there, and what was most important to fix first. Throughout the latter stages of 2010 and the first half of 2011, an iterative process of distilling out key themes and retesting with staff occurred. This was interspersed with testing with external stakeholders both for their views on what the priorities should be, and how the developing

---

[7] Krpan, 'Compliance and Enforcement Review' (2011).

strategic narrative was perceived. In both cases there was considerable alignment between internal and external audiences regarding the regulator that the organisation needed to be, and the considerable journey required to achieve that outcome.

As previously stated, given the number of areas under consideration, the choices of which parts to fix first were of secondary importance to having a singular organisational plan that provided a clear, consistent and collegiate narrative that could withstand five years of change. The final strategy in the form of the 5-Year Plan,[8] delivered in time for launch in the commencement of the 2011/12 financial year, achieved these goals with a simple yet compelling picture of the scope and scale of organisational change required.

Externally facing, the strategy provided for three pillars of work to deal with the challenges of legacy contamination from Victoria's industrial past, organisation-wide programmes to tackle current pollution issues, and driving policy changes that would shape the environmental future. Internally, the strategy identified a series of capabilities that were crucial to delivery of this programme and initiated work on building strong partnerships with the authorising environment, sound business operating processes and IT platforms, a reformed science and engineering expertise and finally a significant investment in rebuilding the core regulatory capability.

D. Realigning the Organisation

The next step in the process was to restructure the organisation to best support the delivery of the 5-Year Plan. Based on the level of engagement built through the development of the plan, the executive team took the bold step of turning this task over to the organisation. Again, based on the principles of deliberative democracy, it was envisaged that if the team had truly taken ownership of the plan, then with the right information and leadership they were in the best position to determine the structure required for success.

The process to drive the work commenced with a call for nominations from within the organisation for those who were considered best able to represent the collective views. With these nominations accepted by the individuals themselves, a cohort of around 100 staff then formed 10 teams briefed in the task and given three weeks to consult, develop and present their draft concepts back to the executive. The executive committed to accepting one of the proposals. During this period two teams self-identified that they thought other teams' ideas were superior to their own and withdrew.

At the end of the defined period eight options were presented to the executive team, with each team explaining the logic and reasoning behind the design choices. While there were consistent themes through each of the options, each had unique perspectives and to some degree each was workable. In the end, in line with the commitment, the executive evaluated the options and chose one. There was a slight deviation whereby a small number of unique aspects of the other models were identified as desirable and were able to be accommodated into the chosen option. This too was consulted with the groups, with

---

[8] '5-Year Plan 2011–2016' (Environment Protection Authority Victoria, 2011).

a strong positive response and seen as a genuine sign of the executive's willingness to seek the best outcomes.

The results were communicated to all staff, and whilst the turnaround for designing the new structure had been a matter of weeks, the time saved allowed a more considered approach to the actual structural change which was given six months to come into effect. Again, this was positively received by staff as it allowed the change to occur whilst still maintaining the delivery of the early building blocks of the plan, as well as core regulatory activities.

E. The Immediate Challenge for the Culture

The change to the new structure was scheduled to take place in mid-December 2011. Given that the change was to be significant and extensive internal movements were inevitable, along with advancement opportunities, the decision was made some months out to avoid new appointments or long-term backfills. It was intended that this would all be most effectively addressed post-implementation, and as such on the eve of the change the organisation was carrying a significant number of vacancies.

On the afternoon prior to the new structure going live, the Treasury Department announced the Sustainable Government Initiative. This effectively put a freeze on all new recruitment, and an undefined level of staff reductions over the next two years based on existing headcount. This obviously put at risk all the work of the development of the 5-Year Plan and the restructure, and also had the potential to unravel any cultural inroads made in the process.

The staff, however, took this challenge in a manner consistent with the ownership built over the past year. Notwithstanding that the ultimate result of the announcement was that instead of an organisation of around 420, EPA Victoria would be at around 320 within two years, the team recast plans, reprioritised work programmes and established parity processes to ensure that where vacancies became available they would be moved to the highest priority areas. The deliverables for the plan were not changed; the means by which they would be delivered were the focus.

This response was the strongest indication to the executive that the hard work to establish a new culture had driven some change. The decision was taken to recheck the culture early in 2012 as these changes became reality, and the result was powerful (see Figure 12.3). It was clear that the process of engaging the staff in both articulating and enabling their future state, notwithstanding a substantial disruption to the plan, had provided a significant increase in the experience of working as a constructive culture. Both the extension of the 'constructive' styles (blue) and the retraction of the 'defensive' styles (green and red) were irrefutable evidence that the collective experience had shifted strongly, and positively.

According to the Human Synergistics team working with EPA Victoria, this magnitude of change between two single-year profiles is rarely seen and an incredible achievement. They cautioned, however, that the constructive styles were not yet at a level that would be considered self-sustaining, and that a substantial continued effort would be required to maintain this experience, let alone to take it further.

Figure 12.3 Comparison of Organisational Cultural Inventory Assessment conducted by EPA Victoria in 2011 and 2012

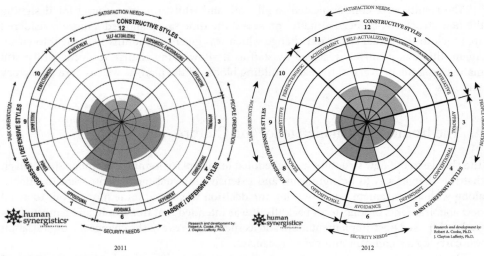

2011   2012

V. Maintaining the Change

A. The Importance of Totems

Of course, whilst these two key streams of work provided the backbone of the change, a number of smaller initiatives also played a role. As the experience of culture is talked about within the organisation as 'the way most of us behave around here, most of the time', it is sometimes the small things – the gestures and the leadership signals – that can have a profound effect on the culture. The journey for EPA Victoria during this time was replete with a number of these, some of which can in hindsight be seen to have had an effect beyond their original intent. These over the short-term, and some enduring still, provided 'totems' for the business; symbolic markers that staff could point towards as either examples of the change, or common aspirations.

B. Compliance and Enforcement Principles

A critical exercise at the commencement of any period of operational change for a regulator is the review and revision of a compliance and enforcement policy. This document provides the basis for internal operational policy settings, which in turn guide the application of law; it also sends a powerful message to the community and business declaring how the regulator intends to go about its role and allowing itself to be held to account. One of the key outcomes of the Krpan report[9] was to produce a policy document that dictated a new risk-based approach to environmental regulation.

[9] Krpan (n 6).

Key to any such policy is the articulation of the principles by which the regulator will undertake the role. There are a small number of principles that are commonly drawn upon for these documents by most regulators, and so the actual ones chosen are less important than the declaration, the meaning bestowed upon each one, and the clear line of sight to how they will be manifested in an operational sense.

For the purposes of the 2011 Compliance and Enforcement Policy,[10] the chosen principles were:

- **Targeted:** Compliance and enforcement activities will be targeted at preventing the most serious harm.

- **Proportionate:** Regulatory measures will be proportional to the problem they seek to address.

- **Transparent:** Regulation will be developed and enforced transparently, to promote the sharing of information and learnings. Enforcement actions will be public, to build the credibility of EPA's regulatory approach and processes.

- **Consistent:** Enforcement should be consistent and predictable. EPA aims to ensure that similar circumstances, breaches and incidents lead to similar enforcement outcomes.

- **Accountable:** To ensure accountability, compliance of duty-holders, enforcement decisions and the conduct of authorised officers will be explained and open to public scrutiny.

- **Inclusive:** EPA will engage with community, business and government to promote environmental laws, set standards and provide opportunities to participate in compliance and enforcement.

- **Authoritative:** EPA will be authoritative by setting clear standards, clarifying and interpreting the law and providing authoritative guidance and support on what is required to comply. EPA will be prepared to be judged on whether individuals and business understand the law and their obligations. EPA will also be an authoritative source of information on the state of the environment, level of compliance with the laws it regulates, key risks and new and emerging issues.

- **Effective:** Enforcement will seek to prevent environmental harm and impacts to public health, and improve the environment. Enforcement action will be timely, to minimise environmental impacts and enhance the effectiveness of any deterrence.

While these are not unique to EPA Victoria, the internal impact of these clearly articulated principles was significant. Up until the publishing of the policy in the public domain, the narrative around the new focus on regulation was to some extent considered to be rhetoric. The symbolism of declaring these principles publicly and detailing how they would translate into actions created an immediate reality of accountability for all staff.

This in turn provided a personal incentive to explore and understand how they would be expected to contribute to the organisational delivery against the principles. As a result, the principles were adopted across a range of other documents and became merged with the broader internal narrative as organisational principles. Whereas they had originally been designed to serve an important but relatively singular regulatory purpose, they became a more fundamental set of principles that were embraced across the organisation

---

[10] 'Compliance and Enforcement Policy' (2011).

and redefined to suit the many and varied contexts, from corporate support to marketing and science.

C. Open Executive Meetings

One of the enduring artefacts from the time that preceded the changed direction for the organisation was a mistrust of the executive. Prior to the exercises in broad engagement around the strategy and restructure, and in some pockets beyond this point, this mistrust was tangible and openly discussed. Whilst reportedly derived from historical management practices whereby staff were summoned to executive meetings, openly criticised, and summarily dispatched, the perception endured that these meetings were secretive affairs.

The issue was discussed by the executive, and to attempt to correct this misperception, the decision was taken to open the weekly executive meetings to all staff. The only topics that were closed were any matters relating to confidential staff or personal matters, which were held at the start of the agenda. All other matters were discussed publicly.

The meeting was moved from the board room to the conference room, and theatre-style seating was arranged. The move proved very successful, and the first few meetings attracted an audience of around 50 observers. Feedback from staff was that they respected the boldness of the move and would equally respect the confidentiality of any discussions held in the room. Over the ensuing months, numbers gradually dwindled as it became evident that the bulk of these meetings focused on budgetary matters, approval of papers that had been developed by the teams, or similarly important but somewhat mundane matters. Following a series of meetings where no observers attended, it was communicated that the intent was to move the meeting back to the board room, and while anyone was still welcome to attend, there would be limited seats.

There were no objections to the move, and no requests to observe were forthcoming. Although this move did not completely rebuild the trust deficit, it dispelled a significant myth.

D. The Gnomies

Recognition of achievement and performance by staff is an intrinsic part of any good organisational culture. Coming from an executive team, this can send strong positive messages, but, given the previously discussed culture of winners and losers, any such programme internally was a fraught path.

A group of staff provided an alternative and powerful option with the proposal to establish achievement awards based on nomination and evaluation by peers. Drawing upon an informal theme of the early stages of the cultural change focus whereby garden gnomes had been used in various communications, the awards were titled The Gnomies. Golden gnomes were sourced and mounted, and a series of categories announced as open for nomination.

The finalists and winners were announced at an all-staff event. While ultimately endorsed and presented by the executive, the recognition by colleagues from across the organisation proved to have a far more profound effect on staff, and the awards were repeated each year throughout the 5-Year Plan.

E. 'Says Who? So What?'

One of the early observations by the incoming CEO was the lack of confidence by operational staff to make important regulatory decisions. On a series of occasions, staff presented significant issues to the executive that appeared to warrant a swift response, but there was a demonstrable lack of will to take those steps. Instead there seemed to be a concerted effort to explain why there was nothing that could be done or that it would set a dangerous precedent – these being clear manifestations of the 'avoidant' cultural norm.

The choice was made to confront this approach constructively but with a clear message. When presented with a case where there was 'nothing we can do about it', the response became 'Says who?'. When this was met further with the list of reasons, and these were considered to lack substance, the further response was 'So what?'. While somewhat blunt, and in the early instances confronting for staff, it quickly gained traction.

The felt experience was that this was an executive that didn't shy away from hard calls, and in fact were openly encouraging staff to bring recommendations to the executives' attention and they would receive support. The words were scribed in large letters on the window of the CEO's office as a constant reminder, and the repeated experience of being encouraged to take action became the new norm. The words have since been erased, but the bias to act still remains a consistent message from the office.

F. The Modern Regulator

At a very early stage in the change, the concept of the 'modern regulator' was introduced as a means of differentiating the historical understanding of the role of the regulator. Although it is a phrase that has been used in various quarters to express differing meanings, this ambiguity allowed it to be redefined and owned. The use of the term by EPA Victoria captures the sense that a regulator has many tools at its disposal, well beyond simply its statutory instruments, and that these should be consciously applied in the appropriate mix to drive improvements in a constantly changing world.

The use of the term allowed the formation of narratives internally that connected field activity with marketing functions, licences with community engagement. It is a concept that allowed continual evolution and reinvention of what it means to be a regulator and helped avoid the compulsion to simply update or modify the existing understanding. While not claiming ownership of the term, EPA Victoria has used it extensively and it has been maintained as a consistent but evolving part of the organisational story.

VI. From the Inside Out

A. The External Experience

The use of cultural diagnostics provides an empirical basis for charting cultural movement, but there is an equally important test that can only be performed through engaging with the authorising environment. The underlying philosophy that drove the focus on culture was that in order to change the external experience, the organisation first had to change the internal experience. With no equivalent external assessment tool, judgement of the effectiveness of the programme in changing the 'felt experience' of the regulator relied on a series of proxy surveys as well as direct consultation.

Although no quantitative dataset has been generated to measure the improvement, there are a number of important observations which, when compared with experiences early in the change programme, demonstrate that significant progress has been made. Importantly, the results of the OCI surveys have been regularly shared with external audiences and feedback sought. In particular, as the results are explained to these audiences, and how they would manifest as behaviours, there is almost universal acknowledgement of the correlation with their experiences, both positive and negative.

For example, when the 2011 results were shared, and the avoidance and oppositional extensions explained, business validated the result with numerous stories about how this was experienced. Similarly, community reported that the 'safe' decisions made, and the corresponding extensions in approval and convention were absolutely their experience and greatest concern.

Further concerted efforts were made during 2013 to understand how progress was being made, with the following observations found to be the most compelling evidence of change.

B. Business

For those businesses that had the most direct involvement with EPA Victoria the consistent observations made were that the regulator had become visibly more active and willing to make decisions. While those subject to compliance action often suggested that it was not necessary, the actions were seen to be proportionate and clear advice and guidance had been provided which was absent in the past. Some credit was given for the efforts to streamline processes and apply a more risk-based approach, but they still saw some room for improvement in ensuring that burden was minimised. Importantly, the regulator was seen to take compliance seriously and would follow through on requirements; again, this was a stark contrast to previous criticisms. Generally speaking, the feedback was that the change seen in the internal cultural indicators was being felt in the outside world.

C. Community

Through its Community Reference Group and a number of issue-based engagement processes, feedback from impacted and interested community members was collected. The overall sense was that there had been a baseline shift from a general assessment of 'no good' to 'not as good as we want you to be'. This was a subtle but significant change. The previous assessment around 2011 was from a community that had all but given up on the regulator. The shift was to a community that recognised that there was a will to change, and they had regained hope, but there was still a way to travel. Similarly, the general assessment was that the internal indicators were a valid depiction of the change they saw.

D. Government

The relationship with government as a key stakeholder is different to business and community, and the signals are accordingly different. The legitimacy of a regulator is often indicated by invitations to participate in decision-making or policy-setting, other regulators seeking advice or opportunities for joint work or, importantly, being held up as exemplar across government. On each of these counts, EPA Victoria experienced the recognition of peers and across government. Most notably, on a number of occasions in public forums the Victorian Auditor General's Office used EPA Victoria as an example of how to respond to investigations and criticism and was among a number of key government agencies that declared the regulator amongst the leaders in the state.

While these observations are largely anecdotal in nature, they form an important evaluation of the progress made in the early years of change and gave confidence in maintaining the trajectory for the long term.

VII. Resilience through Adversity

A. The Test of a Strong Culture

Whilst any organisation can make important gains in its culture, one of the important tests that any culture can undergo is the resilience to change. Whether this change is perceived as a positive or a negative one, the roots of culture in individual perception, behaviour and action, mean that the impact of the change may affect the culture through its people rather than look for a direct effect. Every organisation experiences change, sometimes self-initiated, sometimes externally driven. It is the recognition of the change as it looms or occurs, and the organisational and cultural response that is the measure of the health of the culture.

B. Major Incident Response

In February 2014 a major fire broke out in a large open-cut brown-coal mine in Victoria. The fire burned for 45 days and blanketed the surrounding towns in thick smoke before it was extinguished. As with many other agencies involved, EPA Victoria had no experience in such a situation. Previous involvement in incidents had largely been to provide technical advice on air and water impacts. The situation demanded real-time environmental monitoring and advice, particularly air quality, on an enormous scale – a task that was well beyond any previous expectation, and equally beyond any equipment or personnel at the disposal of the organisation.

Across the incident response approximately 120 personnel, or roughly 30 per cent of the organisation, were directly involved and virtually everyone across the organisation was indirectly impacted by stepping in to support those in response roles. Across all agencies there were thousands of personnel deployed and it is considered one of the largest single incidents ever managed in the state. Considering the enormity of the task, and the need to rapidly build a capability from scratch, the final result was a significant achievement, albeit too slow and insufficient in the eyes of the impacted community.

Those staff involved reported a mixed experience. While the internal assessment was that we had delivered a response far in excess of what we considered our role and capability, and that there were numerous individual and collective achievements of which the team could be proud, the assessment by the community and the media was one of failure.

This presented a cultural and leadership challenge for the organisation. Within the organisation it was important that the achievements were acknowledged and validated, it was equally important as an accountable regulator, that a parallel narrative was accepted that despite this the organisation had fallen short of the expectations of community. It was around this time that a retest of the OCI was undertaken, and the results demonstrated that the organisation had indeed developed the maturity to run these two narratives concurrently, to take pride in what had been achieved, but also to recognise that there was more expected (see Figure 12.4). Despite the physical and emotional impacts on a large majority of the staff, and some minor slippages into defensive styles, the constructive cultural gains seen through the previous exercise were maintained in the updated results.

Figure 12.4 Comparison of Organisational Cultural Inventory assessment between 2012 and 2014

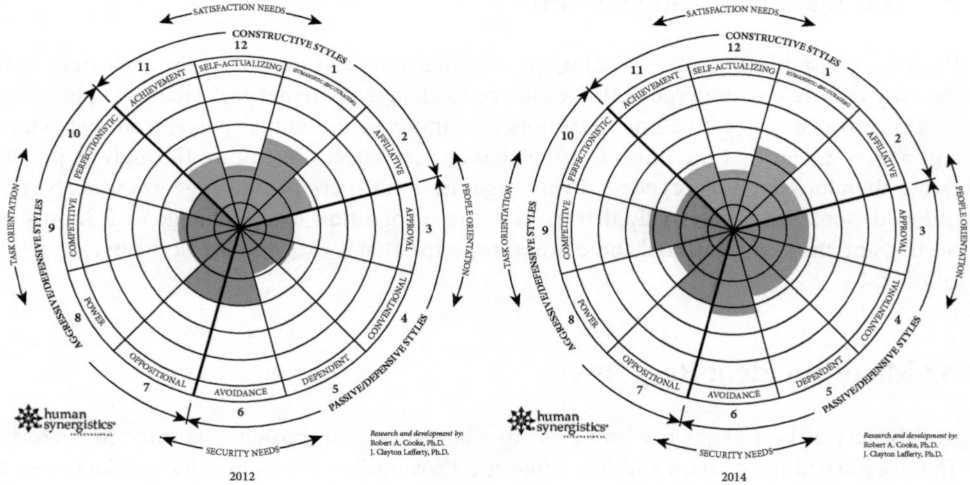

2012   2014

As may be expected with an incident of such significance, an inquiry was announced soon after to evaluate the response and to seek to identify what could have been done better. The approach taken by EPA Victoria was consistent with the internal narrative, with early acknowledgement both in written and verbal testimony that despite its efforts, the regulator had not met the community's expectations. This willingness to acknowledge the failure and not seek to explain away or defend decisions ultimately provided a strong supportive response both from the inquiry, who recommended significant investment in building a permanent capability for such response, and importantly from the community who sought out direct involvement with EPA Victoria in an ongoing effort to rebuild trust in both the regulator and the quality of their environment.

C. Change of Leadership

Towards the middle of 2014, the departure of the CEO and subsequently a number of the executive team signalled a new set of changes for the organisation. The test of the resilience of a culture, and to what extent it is truly embedded in the organisation or simply driven by leadership, is the ability to withstand change at the top of the organisation. With the establishment of a new executive, staff will watch eagerly for indications and signs of any change in direction, and often behaviours will regress as individuals seek security in periods of uncertainty.

With a new executive, the aforementioned totems and norms became redundant from a leadership perspective. Where there has been no involvement in the creation of such arte-facts it is unrealistic to expect that they simply be carried forward. Indeed, there is a real risk that their continued use may be seen as disingenuous by staff as they relate to a previous journey.

One of the important observations made by the incoming CEO, and early in the forma-tion of the new executive, was that while the overall cultural journey had made important progress, some parts of the internal narrative were potentially blocking the next level of achievement. The focus and resultant improvements in 'humanistic-encouraging' and 'affili-ative' styles was identified as potentially masking some defensive styles. These styles are often misunderstood as being 'nice' and always consulting on decisions. However, this char-acterisation in a defensive sense can play out as people feeling that they need to agree with others, and lead to group think ('approval') and to continually seek inputs and fail to take action, which in turn can discourage accountability ('avoidance').

A new narrative was developed that acknowledged the importance of culture and the journey thus far, but introduced a challenge to give equal focus on delivery and perfor-mance; this was formed around the framing of demonstrating the public value that the regulator offered. The linkage back to the OCI tool was that the two constructive segments that had made the least progress were 'achievement' and 'self-actualising'. Through the development of the new narrative as a conscious transition that at the same time challenged the story that the organisation had constructed, the new executive was able to establish its own narrative and a new set of totems. This provided a smooth transition to a new leader-ship and charted a new course without a significant disruption to the existing cultural gains (see Figure 12.5).

D. Government Inquiry

In November 2014 there was also a change of government in Victoria. As part of its election platform, the incoming government committed to a ministerial inquiry into EPA Victoria. Unlike previous inquiries, this was not directly focused on any particular failures, although reference was made to the mine fire response, but was in recognition that the community

Figure 12.5 Comparison of Organisational Cultural Inventory assessment between 2014 and 2015

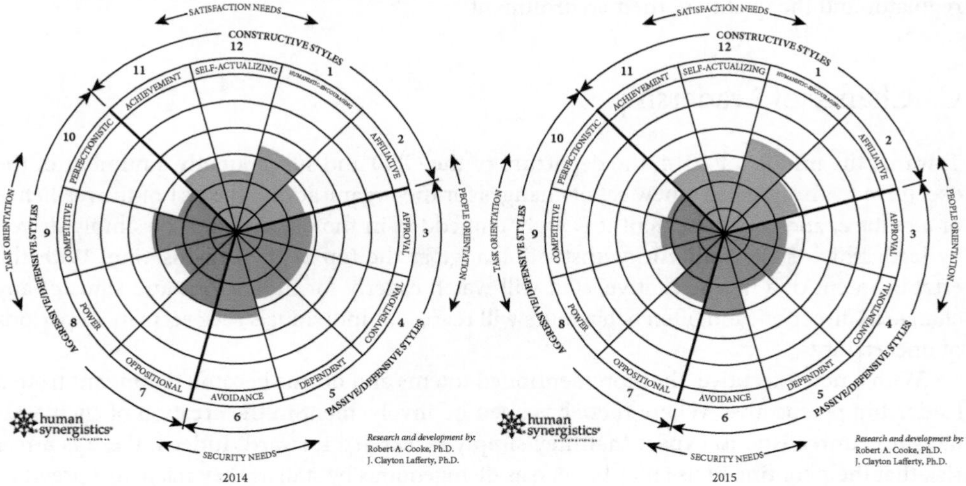

and business needed a regulator that reflected the current and future needs for environmental protection. It was the first comprehensive look at all aspects of the regulator, including its base legislation, in its 45-year history.

There was some degree of trepidation among the staff, as might be expected from a regulator that had been involved in a sequence of inquiries over recent times that, while ultimately responsible for driving positive change, were unavoidably critical of individual and collective efforts. This was especially the case given that the scope of this inquiry covering all aspects of the organisation, right down to the core purpose of the regulator, and minimal limitations on what recommendations it could make.

However, the response, in line with the culture, was to provide an open, transparent and accessible approach. To the extent EPA Victoria's views were sought by the panel, answers given were objective, honest and in some cases necessarily self-critical. It is not unusual in such circumstances that an agency will seek to make its best case. In contrast to this, the philosophy taken was to provide an open and frank account when asked, and to acknowledge the criticism of others when it became evident and not seek to dispute or correct others' accounts. If the exercise were to truly seek to set up the regulator for the next four decades, then only an honest account of the present would suffice.

To what degree this approach informed or influenced the final outcome cannot be demonstrated nor measured. The resultant set of recommendations, in keeping with the terms of reference, have provided a huge change platform with a corresponding significant investment by government in order to implement the change. This provides an enormous challenge for the organisation, to deliver on such a comprehensive rebuild, but also to maintain the cultural journey and deliver on the internal and external experience of the regulator.

At the time of writing this study, a further OCI survey is underway. The results cannot be forecast, and once again there are significant factors that can drive the experience of working for the regulator either way. There is confidence, however, based on previous history and recent performance, that the result will demonstrate that the strong foundations are still in place, but there will always remain the journey to improve.

E. Final Reflection on the Role of Culture

For any regulator, one of the most important influences on legitimacy is the external experience of interaction with its people. In turn, the greatest indicator of the likely external experience is to understand how the organisation is being experienced internally. Whether the expectation is certainty, decisiveness, willingness to exercise judgement, confidence in ambiguity or simply a bias to act, a strong constructive culture will enable these behaviours which in turn drive high performance internally, and a positive experience externally.

Building a strong culture starts with the recognition of its importance, continues through a journey of growing honesty and self-awareness and is constantly tested and refined through the navigation of prevailing circumstance. The role of a regulator by necessity is subject to constant scrutiny and criticism, the challenge to maintain legitimacy and mandate, with the responsibility to develop programmes to drive fundamental social change that can span generations. Any long-term strategy for the success of the regulator must have at its heart a drive toward a strong, resilient and constructive culture.

Practices: Outcome Measurement

13

Outcome Measurement

GRAHAM RUSSELL AND HELEN KIRKMAN

The preceding chapters of this book have explained the first domain of the Regulatory Delivery Model – the three elements that are considered within the model as prerequisites for good regulatory delivery. Contributions from a range of countries with diverse contexts have illustrated the practical aspects of improving the conditions for good regulatory delivery through a focus on Governance Frameworks, the Accountability of regulatory agencies and Culture.

In the following chapters, we shift our focus to the second domain of the Regulatory Delivery Model. This domain is concerned with the day-to-day planning, policies and processes that ensure that regulatory agencies are making the right decisions to deliver their role in the most efficient and effective ways – referred to in the model as their 'practices'. The three practices considered in the model establish a strong focus on outcomes and the purpose behind the regulatory requirements, as well as the use of data to make risk-based decisions about where to allocate resources and the most appropriate type of 'intervention' to use if the desired outcomes are to be achieved.

As explained in chapter two, each of the six elements of the Regulatory Delivery Model merits examination in its own right. However, there is additional value, when considering the performance of a regulatory agency, in exploring the interaction between the elements. This is particularly true of the dynamic relationship between the three practices. At multiple levels, the regulatory agency needs to identify the outcomes it is aiming to deliver, identify and prioritise the risks to their outcomes and choose the right interventions to tackle those risks. Effective measurement of its progress towards outcomes enables an improvement cycle of refining outcome identification, risk assessment, prioritisation and the selection of appropriate interventions (see Figure 13.1). These themes will be drawn out in this chapter, which introduces the first of the three practices – Outcome Measurement – and in subsequent chapters, which will examine Risk-based Prioritisation (chapter sixteen) and Intervention Choices (chapter twenty). Although we have addressed the three practices in this order, there is no single correct starting point and a mature approach will work across and between the practices as matters are identified, addressed and resolved.

However, there are also significant interactions to be noted here in relation to the prerequisites examined in earlier chapters. Proper governance of the regulatory agency is dependent on the measurement of progress towards outcomes – enabling appropriate monitoring, reporting and management of resources and performance. Effective accountability relies on clear, well-communicated outcomes and transparency around the regulatory agency's delivery against those outcomes, and this is further explored through this chapter.

Figure 13.1 The Regulatory Delivery Model: practices

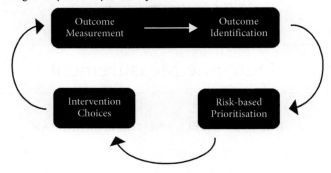

This chapter will first explain what we mean when we talk, in the Regulatory Delivery Model, about the practice of Outcome Measurement and will explore the importance for regulatory agencies of identifying their outcomes, understanding their contribution to those outcomes and measuring progress towards them. We will consider the constituents of an outcome-focused approach: the identification of appropriate impacts and outcomes; understanding the regulatory agency's contribution to impacts and outcomes; and measuring its progress. And we will look at the dynamic relationship between Outcome Measurement and the other elements of the Regulatory Delivery Model, in particular the remaining practices: Risk-based Prioritisation and Intervention Choices.

I. Defining 'Outcomes'

Terms such as 'outcomes', 'impacts', 'goals', 'objectives' and even 'outputs' are often used inter-changeably. For the purposes of this chapter, we have chosen to use the terms 'outcomes' and 'impacts' as they are defined and used in the Impacts and Outcomes Toolkit[1] that was developed for use by local regulatory services in the UK, as described in chapter fourteen. The toolkit established the following definitions:

> Outcomes are the intended and unintended results and consequences of your activities, and tend to be categorised into short-, medium- and longer-term results. In this context, impacts are considered to be long-term outcomes with a wider impact on the community or environment. They include changes in economic and financial conditions, in social conditions (eg reduced violence or increased cooperation) or in environmental and political conditions (eg participation and equal opportunities).

This concept of outcomes as the intended and also, importantly, the unintended results and consequences of the activities of a regulatory agency is very broad. Often, in this chapter, where we talk about an 'outcome-focused' approach, we are more narrowly focused on the regulatory agency's desired outcomes: the results and consequences that they hope or aim to

---

[1] 'Impacts and Outcomes Toolkit: Summary' (Local Better Regulation Office, 2010). Note: the Local Better Regulation Office is a predecessor organisation to the Office for Product Safety and Standards.

achieve. We also use the term 'objectives', limiting its use to the discussion of very short-term goals such as those that are identified as the focus of activity over an annual planning cycle.

We reserve use of the term 'outputs' for the direct products of a regulatory agency's activities. Referring again to the Impacts and Outcomes Toolkit,[2] 'Outputs are the direct product of an activity and typically are tangible and countable. Outputs generally refer to what is being done or what is being produced.'

II. The Importance of an Outcomes-focused Approach for Regulatory Agencies

It should be self-evident that any organisation needs to know what its intended outcomes are and to be able to understand whether it is making progress towards them. Well-communicated outcomes – a strong sense of what the organisation is trying to achieve – are equally important both within the organisation and externally. Internally, they give the organisation's staff a clear direction and sense of purpose (the importance of which is discussed in chapter ten, in relation to the regulatory agency's culture). Externally, transparency about the regulatory agency's intended outcomes and its performance improve stakeholder understanding, establishing a foundation for trust and confidence in the agency (see chapter seven on accountability).

Without an informed knowledge and understanding of what it is trying to achieve, and the extent to which it is succeeding, the regulatory agency will struggle to build confidence amongst its different audiences that it is acting with purpose and achieving the right results. Its inability to articulate where it is heading, and what progress is being made, will inevitably impact adversely on partnership working and on credibility and public trust. This contributes to disengagement and risks leading to a failure to build a mandate, one consequence of which – though by no means the only one – can be an adverse impact on resourcing of the organisation's activities. This is particularly significant in an environment of austerity, with the funding of all public agencies subject to challenge (as discussed in chapter fourteen, in relation to local regulators in the UK).

A recent report by Michael Barber for the UK Government takes a value-for-money approach to the question of how government spends its money to get the right outcomes and how it can deliver the improvement in public services that citizens expect. The report argues for a much stronger emphasis on the outcomes that public services are delivering and challenges the accepted wisdom that the data needed to enable effective monitoring of the outcomes being delivered is not available. The preface to the report highlights the key role that measurement of results plays:

> If we can't measure results, people will talk about what they always talk about: money. We need to track how we turn public money into results for citizens. We need to understand the impact each pound spent has. And we need to prioritise to ensure that resources are allocated to where they will be most effective.[3]

---

[2] ibid.
[3] Michael Barber, 'Delivering Better Outcomes for Citizens: Practical Steps for Unlocking Public Value' (HM Treasury, 2017).

The report draws on the thinking of Mark Moore, a professor at the Harvard Kennedy School of Government, who has been influential in the field of improving public sector outcomes. Moore views the conditions for maximising the public value of a service as being:[4]

- outcomes are clearly defined and being delivered;
- the resources allocated to it are being used efficiently in pursuit of the authorised goals;
- the beneficiaries of the service and the citizens/taxpayers perceive it to be effective and run broadly in accordance with society's values; and
- the institution or service concerned is well managed, resilient and capable of delivering in the long run as well as in the short run.

The report proposes a Public Value Framework for use by public bodies. This framework is based on four pillars, the first of which – 'pursuing goals' – effectively sets out an outcomes-focused approach, encouraging consideration of three areas: 'Understanding goals and indicators; Degree of ambition; Progress towards indicators and goals'.

The maximisation of public value is as important for regulatory agencies as it is for other public bodies. Regulation is never an end in itself – it exists to deliver one or more defined outcomes that are of sufficient importance to society for policy-makers to have determined that regulation is needed. The regulatory agency is tasked because society cares about whether or not the law delivers the defined outcomes and it stands to reason, therefore, that the regulatory agency should be expected to be able to demonstrate progress towards those outcomes.

Where the regulatory agency understands and measures the impact of its activities – both intended and unintended – it is then able to make informed decisions, shifting resource allocation to those activities that are contributing effectively and efficiently, in preference to those that are less effective or less efficient. In contrast, where the regulatory agency fails to challenge itself on whether its strategies are effectively delivering, it may fail to target the most significant risks to the desired outcomes or may unintentionally act in a way that emphasises one outcome over another. There is also a tendency for it to continue to allocate resources to activities that may not be delivering any progress towards desired outcomes or may even be counterproductive.

III. Constituents of an Outcomes-focused Approach

The drivers for an outcomes-focused approach are multiple, as noted above, and the consequences of failing to take such an approach are significant. To this extent, anyone championing an outcomes-focused approach runs the risk of being charged with preaching 'motherhood and apple pie'. Nevertheless, regulatory agencies do not all follow outcomes-focused approaches as a matter of course and, in many areas, good evaluation is the exception rather than the norm. A 2012 study of complementary approaches to environmental inspections noted that 'Evaluation of any forms of environmental inspections (traditional or otherwise) and of complementary or alternative approaches has been undertaken rarely.'[5]

[4] Mark Moore, *Recognising Public Value* (Harvard, Harvard University Press, 2013).
[5] Chris Booth, 'Exploring the Use and Effectiveness of Complementary Approaches to Environmental Inspection for Ensuring Compliance' (European Union Network for the Implementation and Enforcement of Environmental Law, 2012).

This is perhaps unsurprising as experience shows that despite the deceptive simplicity of the concept of focusing on outcomes, putting the concept into practice can be immensely challenging. Some of the reasons for this are explored through the remainder of this chapter, which addresses three constituents of an outcomes-focused approach: the identification of appropriate impacts and outcomes; understanding the regulatory agency's contribution to impacts and outcomes; and measuring its progress.

A. Identifying Appropriate Outcomes

The regulatory agency's desired outcomes might reasonably be expected to reflect the policy impacts and outcomes of the laws that they are tasked with enforcing. The defined policy impacts and outcomes tend towards the medium and long-term and are generally social, economic, environmental or a combination of these three. Figure 13.2 below is useful in helping regulators to conceptualise their impact at this higher level, focusing not on assessment against specific regulatory requirements but on the impact on the environment, the economy and society. This is part of the process of moving from 'Does this inspection improve compliance?' to 'How do my interventions protect people and places and support employment?' Regulators will not necessarily see their work in these terms, but these are the impacts that budget-holders and opinion-formers see as important.

Figure 13.2 Areas of policy impacts and outcomes

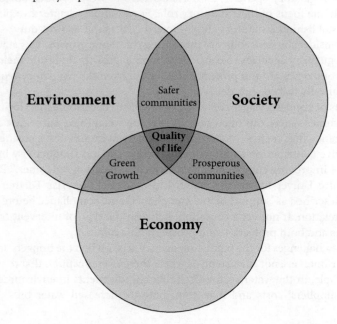

When thinking about impact with regulators it can be helpful to ask them to identify the purpose of their activity and probe further into their answer with a series of 'why' questions. This will generally lead to an answer that can be positioned on this diagram in terms of environment, society or economy. It is particularly useful to identify the 'overlaps', recognising that the most important outcomes are often those that contribute to safer communities, more prosperous communities, green growth or – ultimately – to improvements in quality of life.

As a regulatory agency seeks to focus on these larger outcomes, there are some areas of challenge that it may have to confront.

Focusing on outcomes might create conflicts with narrow policy aims of specific laws and regulations; for example, the legal framework may fail to establish clear outcomes but focus on prescriptive rules. Chapter twenty-five provides examples of the challenges faced through the regulatory reform programme in Mongolia, where a lack of clear outcomes for regulatory activity was a contributory factor in the regulatory agency's failure to focus resources on the areas of greatest regulatory risk. The agency had to establish a new authorising environment empowering it to work on an appropriately broad set of outcomes.

Another potential area for conflict can arise when a regulatory agency identifies or is tasked with outcomes that reflect wider priorities. For example, the regulatory agency may seek to build public confidence in the regulated market, the law and the regulatory agency itself. Perhaps more controversially, it may need to reflect wider government or local priorities in relation to economic growth. Experience shows that some regulatory agencies feel unable to consider wider outcomes as they see their role as being bounded by the outcomes they were established to deliver; by their statutory powers; or by the need to enforce prescriptive rules. As noted in chapter three, government is able to refine or amend the statutory role or purpose of regulatory agencies, authorising them to work towards outcomes that were not previously the focus of their statutory role. For example, chapter five points to the UK example of establishing a statutory duty – referred to as the 'growth duty' – for regulatory agencies to consider the desirability of promoting economic growth. This statutory duty has enabled all regulatory agencies to consider economic growth alongside their consideration of the policy outcomes around protection that stem from the regulatory requirements that they are specifically tasked with delivering.

The efforts of regulatory agencies will in many cases contribute to a (legitimately) broad range of outcomes. There can often be mutuality between these outcomes. For example, a regulatory agency that creates a coherent, consistent environment for businesses is likely to make a positive contribution to growth of employment and productivity but must, at the same time, be improving compliance and therefore protection outcomes.[6] Recent research by Staffordshire University for the Staffordshire Local Enterprise Partnership compares approaches described as 'support before compliance' and 'compliance before support', identifying a correlation, if not yet a causation, between the type of interventions a regulatory agency makes and both protection and prosperity outcomes.[7]

One of the challenges for the regulatory agency arises when the impacts and outcomes to which it contributes are not consistent, or where there is a perception that they are inconsistent. For example, in the water sector, desirable improvements in environmental outcomes can add to suppliers' costs and may contribute to increased water bills for consumers.

---

[6] HOST Policy Research, 'Economic Development and Regulation' (Better Regulation Delivery Office, 2014).
[7] Staffordshire University, 'Measuring the Impact of Regulation', study for Stoke-on-Trent and Staffordshire Enterprise Partnership (forthcoming).

There is a trade-off here in terms of the water regulator's desired outcome of affordability, particularly for vulnerable consumers. In the UK, the economic outcome of growth – articulated in the Regulators' Code and the statutory Growth Duty – has been seen as challenging for certain regulators. For example, the UK's Gambling Commission noted that

> there is a risk that the concept of the desirability of economic growth becomes confused or conflated with the promotion of the commercial interests of specific economic sectors. If it appears to the public that it is any part of the Commission's role to promote the industry – as opposed to permitting the industry to promote itself and grow so far as is compatible with consumer protection, the likely outcome is a reduction in public confidence and a consequent reduction in the public acceptance of gambling as a main stream leisure activity.[8]

These are real challenges faced by regulatory agencies across the world which must be resolved if the agency is to be sustainable and successful in the medium term. Resolution begins with engagement with stakeholders to understand their objectives and concerns and the search for win-win solutions. Conflicts cannot always be completely resolved. When that isn't possible, the strength of the agency's authorisation, the confidence its leaders and staff show in their strategy and the track record of delivery that the agency has established will be important.

A genuinely outcomes-focused approach requires the regulatory agency to be clear about its desired outcomes at all levels, from a strategic level, looking across its areas of responsibility, to the operational level, for example in relation to its interactions with individual regulated entities. Whilst the regulatory agency will need to maintain a focus on the long-term impacts that policy-makers seek, it will also need, in defining its desired outcomes, to take account of the immediate public and political imperative and the medium-term financial/capital cycle that drives business decision-making. Effective regulatory agencies find ways to articulate desired outcomes that are visible in the short term while remaining aligned with long-term goals. The inherent difference in these timeframes is a core challenge for regulators and can be seen as one reason why regulatory agencies have tended to turn to 'proxies' for regulatory outcomes – whether these are outputs such as the 'number of inspections', or alternative outcomes which may be shorter term and easier to measure, such as improved levels of awareness or understanding of the regulatory requirements.

There has been a historical emphasis on quantifying and reporting on the regulatory agency's inputs and outputs, which can lead to these being equated to a measure of achievement or a job well done. In the absence of evidence of what makes a difference, the temptation can be to argue that more resources will allow for more activity, in the hope or belief that more activity will mean that more is being achieved. Measures such as the number of inspectors, inspection levels or frequencies, or numbers of prosecutions or other sanctions, when taken as proxies for outcomes, have a perverse effect. They encourage a focus on quantity over quality and incentivise poor choices. By misdirecting effort, they actually reduce the protection afforded to beneficiaries and can contribute to a disproportionate administrative burden being experienced by regulated entities. For example, the administrative burden that businesses may suffer in connection with inspection can be disproportionate where the

---

[8] Gambling Commission written submission and oral evidence to the Joint Committee on the Draft Deregulation Bill, available at www.parliament.uk/documents/joint-committees/draft-deregulation-bill/JCDDBVolume1 Evidence.pdf (pp 550–51).

business has a very good compliance record but is inspected despite this because the regulatory agency is focused on achieving a particular number of inspections. Chapter twenty-five highlights the difficulties of moving to a risk-based approach to inspection targeting in a context where the performance of inspectors was measured against the number of inspections carried out and the amount of fines collected.

Alternatively, shorter-term or intermediate objectives can prove valuable as stepping stones towards the regulatory agency's longer-term outcomes. However, it is important that these are always aligned with longer-term impacts and outcomes and do not distract from them. Compliance with regulatory requirements is a valid outcome of a regulatory officer's interventions with individual businesses, but an exclusive focus on compliance as the regulatory agency's desired outcome can lead to ineffective use of effort. For example, it might lead the regulatory agency to expend too much effort on non-compliance with administrative requirements – which are often more easily resolved – at the expense of allocating resource to non-compliance that has a more significant impact on regulatory risk (see chapter sixteen for further discussion on this point). The OECD, in its best practice principles for regulatory enforcement,[9] suggests that 'improvements in the number of businesses that are "broadly compliant" with the requirements should be used only as a complement to outcome indicators'.

A further challenge arises where maximising the regulatory agency's contribution to its desired outcomes risks an adverse impact on the outcomes of another regulatory agency. This issue is explored by Stephen Breyer,[10] who notes examples of regulatory agencies 'ignoring one program's safety or environmental effects upon another, which suggests a need for inter-programme coordination'. In addition to these examples of a lack of coordination, Breyer points to a more positive example in which a regulatory agency, in 1992, took a wider view:

> The Federal Aviation Administration declined to require child safety seats on airliners, reasoning that such a requirement, entailing that families would have to buy an extra ticket to accommodate the seat, would lead families to travel by road instead, where the danger of death is significantly greater.

B. Understanding the Contribution

The regulatory agency can face particular challenges in identifying the contribution that it makes to long-term impacts and outcomes. Some of the most significant aspects of this challenge are explored here – the indirect nature of the regulatory agency's contribution; the multiplicity of contributors; and the time lapse between activities and outcomes together with the difficulties in answering the counterfactual question – before going on to introduce some ways in which these challenges can be addressed.

---

[9] 'Regulatory Enforcement and Inspections, OECD Best Practice Principles for Regulatory Policy' (OECD, 2014).

[10] Stephen Breyer, 'Breaking the Vicious Circle: Toward Effective Risk Regulation' (Harvard University Press, 1993).

i. An Indirect Contribution

Desired outcomes will almost always involve factors beyond the regulatory agency's control. The challenge, referred to here as the indirect nature of the regulatory agency's contribution, has been clearly articulated by the UK's National Audit Office, in its 2016 review of performance management by regulatory agencies:[11]

> [P]erformance measurement by regulatory services is particularly complex, because their intended outcomes are generally delivered by the organisations that they regulate. Their effectiveness is basically a function of their ability to influence the outcomes that are delivered by the regulated entities.

The law usually sets out to control or change the behaviour of regulated entities. In most situations, the regulatory agency's role is limited to encouraging or supporting that change, monitoring the behaviour of regulated entities, and acting where their behaviour does not align with the regulatory requirements. It is the decision-makers in the business, subject to other influences, both internal and external, who directly drive the outcomes. While they may be willing to comply with regulatory requirements, they might nevertheless fail to comply on occasion. While the reasons for failure to comply are obvious for some regulated entities – they have neither the intention nor the capability to comply, indeed their business model is predicated on criminality – when others fail it can be for a variety of reasons, ranging from a lack of understanding or a genuine difference in interpretation of a regulatory requirement to a simple mistake by an employee in following instructions that should have enabled the business to achieve compliance. Engaging with the causes of non-compliance, and closing that compliance gap, will generate the outcomes intended for the regulatory requirements, even if the impact of the regulatory agency is indirect.

There are some cases where the regulatory agency has powers to tackle specific risks to the desired outcomes and, in these limited circumstances, the regulatory agency could be said to be making a more direct contribution to short-term outcomes. For example, a regulatory agency may have powers to close premises that pose an immediate risk to human health or to seize non-compliant products to prevent them entering the supply chain, thereby reducing the risk of further consumer detriment. These activities are also important, but they seldom contribute more than a small percentage of the agency's impact.

ii. A Multiplicity of Contributors

The regulatory agency will often be one of a number of organisations[12] – including other regulatory agencies, public bodies and others – that have a shared interest in the desired impacts and outcomes. This is likely to be particularly true of longer-term impacts and outcomes. A clear example of this can be seen in relation to environmental regulation that aims to reduce emissions of greenhouse gases. In the UK, numerous regulatory requirements have been implemented and responsibility for delivering these rests with a number

---

[11] 'Performance Measurement by Regulators' (National Audit Office, 2016).
[12] Cary Coglianese, 'Measuring Regulatory Performance: Evaluating the Impact of Regulation and Regulatory Policy' (OECD, 2012).

of different regulatory agencies. At the same time, a large number of other bodies are active in this area and have an interest in what is being achieved. For example, public and private sector bodies are promoting energy conservation and efficiency measures. It will never be possible to confidently and accurately attribute any progress in reducing the UK's greenhouse gas emissions to each of the many contributors.

Where outcomes are jointly owned with a number of different partners the regulatory agency is trying both to identify its own potential to contribute to the desired outcomes and to understand this in the context of other measures that contribute to the same outcomes. As an example, a product-safety regulator might choose to focus its efforts, in the period before Christmas, on the safety of seasonal goods such as Christmas tree lights. At the same time, a popular television drama might feature a storyline about the tragic consequences of a fire caused by faulty lights. The contribution of each of these events to consumer and business behaviour and, ultimately, to safety outcomes can't easily be distinguished or separately measured. This challenge has been recognised by the OECD in the best practice principles referred to earlier in this chapter:

> It is acknowledged that properly assessing the effectiveness of enforcement and inspection agencies is difficult, because improvements or worsening outcomes (health, safety etc.) cannot directly be attributed to their activities because of the vast number of other, often more important, factors. Nonetheless, it remains crucial to monitor such outcomes in order to judge whether enforcement is having any positive contribution.

iii. Time Lapses

The time that lapses between the regulatory agency's activities and changes in the behaviour of regulated entities can be significant. However, the gap between those changes and resultant outcomes can be much more substantial. For example, the widespread use of asbestos in construction and elsewhere in the UK from the 1950s onwards is known to have a strong association with incidence of malignant mesothelioma. However, the time lapse between initial exposure to asbestos and the manifestation of mesothelioma is typically at least 30 years[13] meaning that the impact of work by local and national regulatory agencies in Great Britain from the 1970s onwards to address the risks of occupational exposure to asbestos could not be seen for several decades.

These time lapses exacerbate the challenges associated with the indirect nature of the regulatory agency's influence on outcomes and the multiplicity of influences.

iv. Counterfactual

Each of these difficulties in establishing the contribution made by a specific regulatory agency contributes to the overall challenge and makes it more likely that the focus will revert to the measurement of inputs and outputs. In principle the challenge can be resolved through understanding what might have happened if the regulatory agency had not acted,

---

[13] Mesothelioma mortality in Great Britain 1968–2016 (London, Health and Safety Executive, 2018), available at www.hse.gov.uk/statistics/causdis/mesothelioma/mesothelioma.pdf.

or if it had acted differently. Gathering data relating to the regulatory agency's activities and analysing it over time can help the agency to identify useful trends, for example in levels of non-compliance identified, but in the absence of control data, the data has limited value in evidencing whether the agency's activities contributed to the trends identified. Generating control data is, however, difficult where public policy has determined that regulatory protections are required and UK Government analysts work to specific guidance to deal with the frequent absence of control data in public policy.[14]

Traditional enforcement models have tended to be based on the assumption that delivery of compliance is achieved simply through enforcement against breaches of the relevant rules that are created under the regulatory regime, and that enforcement (generally taken to mean prosecution in the courts) has both a direct and a wider deterrent effect. Inspection is therefore seen as a means of identifying non-compliance that the regulatory agency can then deal with through enforcement. The number of inspections, number of non-compliances identified and number of prosecutions (or other sanctions) can be viewed, in this model, as measures of success. In order to understand what the regulatory agency is actually achieving in terms of outcomes, it is necessary to challenge the assumptions that sit behind this model and ask what would have happened if the regulatory agency had taken a different approach – perhaps focusing less on inspection or dealing with non-compliance in other ways. A number of countries have used caps on inspection numbers or moratoria on inspections, for example of small or medium-sized enterprises, as part of efforts to fundamentally reform the approach to inspection in the context of perceived burdens on business associated with 'over-inspection'. Evidence from these countries of the outcomes of such measures could provide a valuable counterfactual.

Chapter fifteen summarises the enlightening work of Florentin Blanc in comparing and contrasting high-level, long-term data on accidents in three European countries, enabling him to draw conclusions about the effectiveness of the different approaches taken by occupational health and safety regulators in those countries. Further studies looking at different regulatory areas, comparing different countries or using different time periods might help to generate the sort of data that would enable regulators to show the impact of their contribution, however indirect, contributory or long term it might be.

v. Telling the Story

The Barber report mentioned earlier in this chapter articulates the challenge in demonstrating the contribution of public services, using hospitals as an example:

> A hospital might deliver a large number of medical appointments with the funding allocated to it, but if those appointments do not translate into improved health outcomes for patients then the service is not improving the lives of those it serves.[15]

This message will resonate with regulatory agencies, with their historic reliance on reporting their performance in terms of the inputs, activities and outputs that they can actually manage. As highlighted above, the causal links from these can be unusually

---

[14] 'The Magenta Book. Guidance for evaluation' (HM Treasury, 2011).
[15] Barber, 'Delivering Better Outcomes for Citizens' (2017).

diffuse and remote from the desired impacts and outcomes. For example, a regulatory agency might employ a number of inspectors and deploy them to inspect a proportion of the entities that have obligations under the law but if these inspections do not shift the behaviour of the regulated entities in the right direction – improving their compliance with the requirements – then the regulatory agency will be hard-pressed to demonstrate that it is making a contribution to the intended outcomes of the law. Even where the regulatory agency has a positive influence on regulated entities, it may still struggle to show a substantive contribution to longer-term impacts and outcomes. For example, regulation in the UK prohibits the sale of alcohol and tobacco products to young people under the age of 18. Local regulatory services (Trading Standards) have committed significant resources to enforcing this regulatory requirement, employing a range of interventions, from educating businesses and supporting them to comply, to sending underage volunteers into retail premises to test whether the retailer will sell to them, and then taking punitive action where this happens. Over a period of years, local Trading Standards services have been able to point to data showing that the proportion of retailers that refuse to sell to underage volunteers has risen.[16] Whilst this is a positive message, in terms of the regulatory agency using its influence to improve compliance, it does not necessarily follow that any change in the number of young people drinking or taking up smoking can be attributed to the fact that more retailers are complying with the law.

The following chapter outlines the development of a tool that can be used by regulatory agencies to identify the pathways by which their activities contribute to the desired impacts and outcomes through the use of logic chains. The Local Better Regulation Office (see Annex 1) commissioned the research and subsequent development of this tool[17] by RAND Europe to assist local regulatory services in the UK in demonstrating their contribution to outcomes – by using logic chains to tell their story from inputs through to long-term impacts. The research conducted as a precursor to developing the tool identified that, at that time, only 55 per cent of the local authority services that were surveyed collected any information on the wider impacts of their regulatory services.

The Office for Product Safety and Standards and its predecessor organisations have made extensive use of this logic-modelling approach – both with other regulatory agencies and internally, with our own staff who are performing a role in delivering regulation. It has proved extremely valuable in allowing regulatory agencies to explore the question 'What impact are our activities having?' and to work out how they can begin to answer this question. The logic-modelling approach encourages the regulatory agency to challenge its own assumptions about the causal links between its inputs, activities, outputs and outcomes. For example, an assumption that a particular set of activities will raise compliance levels can be explored.

An example of a logic-modelling approach is summarised in brief in Figure 13.3. This particular example was developed in a workshop by one of our own enforcement teams,

---

[16] 'Youth Alcohol Action Plan' (Department for Children, Schools and Families, The Home Office, Department of Health, 2008), available at www.gov.uk/government/uploads/system/uploads/attachment_data/file/238735/7387.pdf.

[17] Jan Tiessen, Claire Celia, Lidia Villalba-van-Dijk, Anaïs Reding, Christian van Stolk and Tom Ling, 'Impacts and Outcomes of Local Authority Regulatory Services: The Toolkit' (Local Better Regulation Office, 2009a) and Jan Tiessen, Claire Celia, Lidia Villalba-van-Dijk, Anaïs Reding, Christian van Stolk and Tom Ling, 'Impacts and Outcomes of Local Authority Regulatory Services: Final Report' (Local Better Regulation Office, 2009b).

responsible for delivering regulation of timber imports. The team mapped the links between its inputs, activities, outputs and outcomes through to long-term impacts such as stronger markets for sustainable timber, reduced illegal logging and deforestation, and reductions in CO_2 emissions. It is worth noting that each item in a column of Figure 13.3 may contribute to one or more of the items in the next column along. For example, all of the outputs listed in the Outputs column may play a part in encouraging 'More responsible business practices in sourcing timber'.

Figure 13.3   An example of a logic modelling approach used by the Office for Product Safety and Standards to identify our contribution to outcomes and impacts

Inputs	Activities	Outputs	Outcomes	Impacts
Legal mandate: powers to enforce	Advice and guidance activities	Information and guidance documents	Improved compliance	Stronger market for sustainable timber
Competent staff	Developing compliance tools for businesses	Tailored advice delivered	Confidence and certainty in business community	Reduced illegal logging and deforestation
Technical expertise	Training businesses	Businesses trained	A level playing field for UK businesses importing timber	Improved governance in timber supplying countries
Funding	Verifying licences for timber imports	Licenced timber enters the country	More responsible business practices in sourcing timber	Conservation and safeguarding of biodiversity
Data and intelligence	Inspections and other checks on compliance measures	Sanctions for non-compliance	Consumer confidence in UK timber products	Reductions in CO_2 emissions
	Receiving allegations of non-compliance	Regulatory reports		

A similar logic modelling approach has recently been recommended to regulatory agencies in the UK by the National Audit Office.[18]

C. Measuring Progress

Because measuring outcomes is difficult, performance management is challenging for regulators, particularly where they have historically relied on key performance measures

---

[18] National Audit Office, 'Performance Measurement' (2016).

relating solely to inputs, activities and outputs. However, following the maxim that 'what gets measured gets done', regulators must find ways to measure progress towards the desired impacts and outcomes that they have identified.

Malcolm Sparrow,[19] advocating a shift towards increased use of problem-solving regulatory approaches, proposed that the change in measurement and reporting practices that would need to accompany such a shift could usefully draw on a simple classification of 'business results' into four categories, which he refers to as 'Tier 1. Effects, impacts and outcomes'; 'Tier 2. Behavioural outcomes'; 'Tier 3. Agency activities and outputs'; and 'Tier 4. Resource efficiency'. These four categories map readily to the logic-modelling approach proposed to regulators in the UK,[20] as shown in Table 13.1 below.

Table 13.1 Classification of business results[21] mapped against RAND Europe's logic-modelling approach

	Inputs	Activities	Outputs	Outcomes	Impacts
Tier 1 Effects, impacts and outcomes (such as environmental results; health effects; decline in injury rates)					
Tier 2 Behavioural outcomes (such as compliance and noncompliance rates; adoption of best practices)					
Tier 3 Agency activities and outputs (such as enforcement actions; inspections; education and outreach)					
Tier 4 Resource efficiency (with respect to use of agency resources; regulated community's resources; State authority)					

[19] Malcolm Sparrow, *The Regulatory Craft: Controlling Risks, Solving Problems, and Managing Compliance.* (Washington DC, Brookings Institution Press, 2000).

[20] Tiessen et al, 'The Toolkit' (2009a) ch 14; National Audit Office (n 11).

[21] Sparrow, *The Regulatory Craft* (2000) Table 8-1, 119.

Sparrow notes that 'the precise contents of the four tiers are less important than the overall shape, which reveals the aspirations of regulatory agencies with respect to reporting their accomplishments.'

Any shift from a reliance on measuring solely activity and outputs requires the regulatory agency to commit resources to the development of an appropriate measurement framework and the means to use it on an ongoing basis, both in terms of sourcing and collating the data that will be needed and in terms of analytical capacity. It also requires a commitment to publicising the results of what is done; in Sparrow's phraseology, 'telling people about the problems you have fixed'. Without that commitment, and the confidence it builds in the regulatory agency and its communities, the simpler, more comfortable nostrums of inspections ticked-off, prosecutions 'won', and fines banked will return.

i. A Performance Measurement Framework

The regulatory agency's performance measurement framework should bring together a portfolio of appropriate indicators that span its activities and that are capable, when taken together, of painting a holistic picture of the way that the agency is working and what it is achieving. These indicators should include measurement of reductions in risks to the agency's desired outcomes and impacts but will not be limited to these. They are also likely to include the more traditional indicators of regulatory activity and outputs, measures of customer satisfaction and indicators relating to shorter-term or intermediate objectives that the regulatory agency has identified as stepping stones towards its longer-term outcomes. The UK's National Audit Office, in its good practice guide for regulatory performance measurement, pointed to the use by some regulatory agencies of indicators that distinguish outcome measures from measures relating to the regulatory agency's own performance in influencing those outcomes:

> [T]he Pensions Regulator separately lists Key Performance Indicators (KPI), which provide details of performance against indicators for the year under review; and Key Outcome Indicators (KOI), setting out how they link to the Pensions Regulator's statutory objectives, and an indication of longer-term trends in those indicators. This distinction also reflects the fact that some objectives can apply over longer than a single reporting period.

The tool developed by RAND Europe,[22] referred to earlier in this chapter and explained in detail in chapter fourteen, advises regulators to identify a 'long list' of potential indicators that could be useful in measuring the key elements of the pathways that they have developed to demonstrate their contribution to outcomes. This list can then be prioritised, and the priority indicators assessed to determine their viability and importance.

As noted in chapter seven, some countries have chosen to establish common key performance indicators for regulatory agencies with the aim of improving transparency and accountability. The Australian Regulator Performance Framework,[23] implemented in 2015, is an interesting example of this approach. It established a framework of six key performance indicators (see Box 13.1) underpinned by 'measures of good regulatory performance'.

---

[22] Tiessen et al (2009a).
[23] 'Regulator Performance Framework' (Australian Government, 2014).

Regulatory agencies are required to assess themselves against these key performance indicators and to publish their self-assessment.[24]

Box 13.1 Australian Regulator Performance Framework key performance indicators

1. Regulators do not unnecessarily impede the efficient operation of regulated entities
2. Communication with regulated entities is clear, targeted and effective
3. Actions undertaken by regulators are proportionate to the regulatory risk being managed
4. Compliance and monitoring approaches are streamlined and coordinated
5. Regulators are open and transparent in their dealings with regulated entities
6. Regulators actively contribute to the continuous improvement of regulatory frameworks

---

ii. Data

Measurement of progress is heavily reliant on the availability of good quality, comparable data (both historical and current). All too often, the data that is most readily available relates to inputs, activities and outputs, while the data required to measure progress in terms of long-term impacts and outcomes is scarce and intangible. If this data exists at all, it is likely to come from external sources. For example, public health data on prevalence of smoking in children, hospital admissions for food poisoning[25] or days of work lost due to work-related injuries.[26] Partnership working is likely to be key for the regulatory agency in accessing useful data of this nature.

In relation to shorter-term or intermediate outcomes, such as the 'Tier 3 Behavioural Change' referred to by Sparrow, the regulatory agency's own recording of compliance and non-compliance rates is likely to be an important data source. However, the OECD best practice principles for regulatory enforcement and inspections[27] counsel caution in respect of data that is generated internally by the regulatory agency, advocating the use of data that is collected independently:

> As a rule, data that is directly the result of an agency's processes (eg number of prosecutions or sanctions, which is a number the agency can directly influence based on changes in enforcement policy) should never be used to assess compliance levels, because it is by no means 'independent' data, and it creates negative incentives. More broadly, any data that is recorded or produced by the agency should be treated with caution in terms of evaluation, because of the potential for conflict

---

[24] For example, see Comcare's 2016/17 self-assessment against the Regulator Performance Framework, available at www.comcare.gov.au/Forms_and_Publications/publications/services/laws_and_regulations/laws_and_regulations/comcare_regulatory_performance_framework_2016-17.

[25] Ginger Zhe Jin and Phillip Leslie, 'The Effect of Information on Product Quality: Evidence from Restaurant Hygiene Grade Cards' (2003) 118 *The Quarterly Journal of Economics* 409.

[26] UK data collected by the Office for National Statistics is available at www.hse.gov.uk/statistics/lfs/index.htm#allinjuries.

[27] OECD 'Regulatory Enforcement and Inspections' (2014).

of interest and there may be incentives for the inspectorate to alter the data so as to improve its apparent performance.

Rich sources of data will usually exist within the regulated community and this data will often have the potential to contribute to a more complete picture. Various contributors to this book point to the value of data that is collected by regulated entities and shared with the regulatory agency – none more so than the UK's Chief Inspector of Drinking Water. In chapter nineteen, Marcus Rink describes an increasingly data-driven approach, in which the analysis of industry data is being used to identify risks and to track progress in tackling those risks. One clear example relates to the use of company data to identify a persistent issue with unacceptably high levels of a particular pesticide in drinking water supplies. A collaborative approach, encouraging the water companies to work with farmers in their catchment areas, saw the number of failures of the pesticide standard attributed to this particular pesticide decrease dramatically over a three-year period.[28]

Christopher Hodges and Ruth Steinholtz discuss in chapter twenty-two the importance of establishing relationships of trust between regulatory agencies and those they regulate which enable data to be shared and checked. They draw on the example of civil aviation safety, where a collaborative, open culture is encouraging individuals and organisations to share full and timely information that can be used to identify and reduce risks.

The regulatory agency will also find it valuable to gather data on perceptions within the regulated community, including those it has interacted with. Surveys and other research methodologies can be helpful in generating data about the quality of the regulatory agency's interventions or the success of particular activities in achieving the desired objectives. For example, in the context where the regulatory agency has formed the view that low compliance rates are in part attributable to a lack of knowledge or understanding of the regulatory requirements, a survey before and after an educational campaign could help to establish whether the campaign has raised levels of awareness and understanding and might also give some indication as to whether business approaches to the regulatory requirements have changed.

iii. Analytical Capacity

We live in an information- and data-rich world, with the potential for this information and data to be used in increasingly sophisticated ways. The regulatory agency needs to make available the time and resources for analysis and interpretation of data and to invest in the necessary analytical expertise and tools.

Benjamin Franklin said, 'By failing to prepare, you are preparing to fail' and Winston Churchill more famously modified the advice to 'Failing to plan is planning to fail'. Analytical capacity, properly deployed, can steer us away from these risks. However, the shift required should not be underestimated. To be a truly intelligence-led organisation, using data effectively to prepare interventions and plan their execution, requires more than a lone analyst, locked in a room down a disused corridor. Regulatory agencies have a particular dependency on analytical capacity and the question of how much resource should be given

---

[28] See http://dwi.defra.gov.uk/about/annual-report/2016/index.html.

to analysis is often asked. While this is a great question – and reveals that the agency is thinking along the right lines – the answer has to depend on the context. As a rule of thumb a ratio of 3:1 for operational and analytical resourcing is a fair guide. In other words, 25 per cent of a regulatory agency's deployable enforcement resource would be committed to analytical and intelligence work. Regulatory experts will explain that, however desirable this may be, it is unachievable in practice: 'no-one could take that amount of resource away from the frontline'. But those experts will also be able to recount tales of wasted effort, misapplied operations and projects frustrated by poor intelligence. If intervention choices are to achieve the intended outcomes, then they must be well directed.

Of course, having sufficient staff resources allocated to the task is only part of the challenge. They must be properly trained and deployed, supported by the right hardware and systems, effectively led and nurtured in a supportive environment. Analysts who see their reports 'filed' by operational staff too busy 'doing' to take time to 'think' will not give their best. If a tiny fraction of the money spent installing the latest data analysis and handling systems was spent improving relationships between analysts and frontline officers, they might all see more fruit from their labours.

And regulatory agencies must think about the mix of analytical skills they will need. In the Office for Product Safety and Standards we employ social researchers, statisticians and economists as well as intelligence analysts. Each has a different and valued contribution. The mix required will depend on the challenges facing an agency, its context and the risks it seeks to mitigate. Regulatory agencies making market interventions will need more economists than those deploying social researchers to understand citizen behaviour or those using intelligence analysts to track patterns of criminal activity.

In making a commitment to analysis the regulatory agency is opening the door to the opportunities presented by data science, not least in relation to strengthening risk models (see chapter sixteen), but should be aware that there can be hidden hazards associated with the latest trends in 'big data'. Data scientist Cathy O'Neil[29] cautions against the risks that she sees as inherent in the blind use of algorithms, rule-based processes for solving mathematical problems, that appear compelling but can be formulated on the basis of bias and powerful interests:

> A regulatory system for 'Weapons of Math Destruction' would have to measure such hidden costs, while also incorporating a host of non-numerical values … Though economists may attempt to calculate costs for smog or agricultural runoff, or the extinction of the spotted owl, numbers can never express their value. And the same is often true of fairness and the common good in mathematical models. They're concepts that reside only in the human mind, and they resist quantification. And since humans are in charge of making the models they rarely go the extra mile or two to even try. It's just considered too difficult. But we need to impose human values on these systems, even at the cost of efficiency … Mathematical models should be our tools, not our masters.

Analytical expertise is important if the regulatory agency is to make the best use of scientific evidence, risk analysis and intelligence in decision-making and is to achieve a meaningful

---

[29] Cathy O'Neil, *Weapons of Math Destruction: How Big Data Increases Inequality and Threatens Destruction* (US Crown Publishers, 2016). See also the announcement of an investigation into the potential for bias in algorithmic decision-making by the UK's Centre for Data Ethics and Innovation, available at www.gov.uk/government/news/investigation-launched-into-potential-for-bias-in-algorithmic-decision-making-in-society.

assessment of its progress towards its desired outcomes and the factors that are contributing to or impeding progress. But this expertise must be focused in the right direction, be implemented in accordance with the values of the organisation and assessed in terms of its contribution. The decades-long search for 'evidence-led policy' has shown policy-makers that a powerful tool must be used wisely. Regulators seeking to use analytical tools to become intelligence-led will need to be equally wise.

IV. Key Lines of Enquiry

As discussed in chapter two, we have developed key lines of enquiry in respect of each element of the Regulatory Delivery Model that can be used to assess and understand the current picture in respect of that element. These questions, presented in Box 13.2 in respect of Outcome Measurement, are intended as a starting point on which a regulatory agency or a third party can build in order to give a sense of where strengths and weaknesses lie and to highlight potential for improvement.

Box 13.2 Key lines of enquiry: outcome measurement

Identification

- Has the regulatory agency identified appropriate impacts and outcomes, from strategic to operational?
- Are these communicated and understood, both internally and externally?
- Do they include short- and longer-term societal impacts as well as broader outcomes, such as confidence- and capacity-building?
- How does the agency deal with conflicts (perceived or otherwise) between its outcomes?
- Is the agency aware of positive and negative impacts it has on outcomes targeted by other regulatory agencies, and vice versa?

Contribution

- How does the regulatory agency understand its (indirect) contribution to impacts and outcomes through the (direct) activity of regulated entities?
- Does the agency understand how it contributes to impacts and outcomes shared with other regulators and other state and non-state actors?
- What methodologies does the agency use to understand its contribution over time?
- How well does the agency articulate its contribution, both internally and externally?
- Does the agency use counterfactuals to assess its contribution and tell the story of its impact?

Measurement

- Does the regulatory agency have a culture of measurement and evaluation with regards to its impacts and outcomes?

- Does the agency have appropriate indicators that span its activities?

- Does the agency have adequate and appropriate capacity to analyse data effectively, in ways that drive performance and build confidence in its impacts and outcomes?

- What performance measurement framework does the agency use? Does the framework cover impacts and outcomes as well as inputs and outputs?

- Is use of the framework well established and are staff confident and competent in its use?

- Does the agency have access to the data required for assessment of its impact? If not, is it taking appropriate steps to secure continuous improvement in its access to relevant data?

V. Summary

This chapter set out to explain what is meant, in the Regulatory Delivery Model, by Outcome Measurement and to explore the importance for regulatory agencies of identifying their outcomes and measuring progress towards them. We considered the constituents of an outcome-focused approach, exploring some of the challenges for regulatory agencies in implementing and maintaining such an approach, and looking at potential ways forward. We have begun to consider the dynamic relationship between Outcome Measurement and the other practices of the Regulatory Delivery Model: Risk-based Prioritisation and Intervention Choices.

The next two chapters illustrate two particular themes that we have touched on in this chapter: the need for effective tools to identify and measure impacts alongside better ways to tell the story of regulatory impact and the search for evidence of what works, and why. In chapter fourteen, Christian van Stolk and Tom Ling discuss their work to better assess the impact of local regulatory services and their development of a tool that has been touched on in this chapter. In chapter fifteen, Florentin Blanc and Giuliana Cola present research into the outcomes of the activities of occupational health and safety regulators in three countries and discuss what the research tells us about the impact of inspections.

14

The Impacts and Outcomes Toolkit, Getting to the Outcomes of Regulatory Services

CHRISTIAN VAN STOLK AND TOM LING

Many regulatory services[1] operate in a changing policy environment shaped by the extension of the better regulation agenda to all levels of government, the prevalence of fiscal austerity in many governments around the world and a shift to streamlined, more outcome-oriented and joined-up performance management systems. However, most regulatory services operate in contexts where they interact with other strong drivers of behaviour and they are targeted on outcomes that may be influenced by many other factors. Consequently evaluating both the immediate effects of regulation on behaviour and apportioning attribution is often challenging.

In this chapter, we will discuss our work on a tool to better assess the impact of regulatory services. In 2010, RAND Europe embarked on a project with the then Local Better Regulation Office in the UK (now Office for Product Safety and Standards; see Annex 1) to measure the outcomes of local delivery of regulation in England and Wales by local authorities and fire authorities ('local regulatory services'). This tool tried to assist local regulatory services to build systematic narratives on how their activities contribute to outcomes. This required understanding what their activities are and how they logically contribute to outcomes. It also required some thought on what can be measured and what should be measured to build these narratives. In the end, the tool had to be practical and allow local regulatory services to track their performance over time. In this chapter, we reflect in some depth on what was developed, elaborate on some of the reasons we chose a certain evaluation approach, and offer some observations on how the tool worked and on the wider applicability of the tool.

I. Measurement is Challenging but Important

Understanding what the outcomes of local regulatory services are is critical on a number of levels. At the outset, local regulatory services can lack visibility in government and among decision-makers in both their own local authorities and in central government. Having a good understanding of the outcomes that local regulatory services contribute to can help in

---

[1] This chapter is focused mainly on regulatory enforcement at the local or municipal level. This is where the authors have most experience. The chapter probably has wider relevance or applicability.

justifying appropriate funding. This observation goes directly to the value that government and local decision-makers place on regulatory services. A 2008 survey at the local level in the UK found that local regulatory services represent slightly less than one per cent of total local authority expenditure, which is equal to about £1.24 billion.[2] Furthermore, funding of regulatory services often comes from multiple sources, which means that funding can be put at risk as policy-makers redirect funding to other areas. This is especially important in a climate where governments are looking to make efficiency savings. Moreover, the benefits of local regulatory services are often not visible in terms of the contribution they are making to society and the economy. They often become more visible only when there are regulatory failures or unintended outcomes. So, they face both the perception of being part of unnecessary administrative burdens restricting economic and societal activities as well as being in the news when failures occur and wider society wonders why intervention did not occur earlier.

The better regulation agenda (see Annex 1) also means that regulatory services increasingly need to be prepared to measure their impact on stakeholders and demonstrate that their activities create benefits and outcomes for businesses, communities and the general public.

Finally, performance management frameworks used in local government for accountability and value for money purposes require regulatory services to have a better knowledge of the outcomes to which they are contributing and how they can help in achieving performance targets.

For all these reasons it is important for those with responsibility for delivering regulation (as well as for those designing it) to have a clear understanding of outcomes. However, there are many challenges in getting to, and measuring, these outcomes. Local regulatory services, like so many government bodies, are embedded in complex governance arrangements at the local, national and at times the regional and supra-national level. Looking at the UK in particular, the regulatory landscape is diverse and comprises a wide range of other actors from the national to the local level such as:

- government departments;
- national regulatory agencies;
- supra-national regulators;
- local regulatory services (local authorities and fire authorities);
- sector organisations and non-departmental public bodies; and
- professional bodies and national agencies.

In addition, there is a lot of partnership-working taking place at the local and national level, including the police, the health service and so on, creating a need for a further level of governance.

If a regulation enforced at the local regulatory services level, such as food hygiene legislation, is very effective in reducing food-borne diseases, to which level should the impact be attributed? Are the positive outcomes the result of a well-designed regulation (EU) and reasonable national transposition (UK Government), clear strategy and direction

---

[2] 'Mapping the Local Authority Regulatory Services Landscape' (Local Better Regulation Office, 2009). Quoted financial data is for 2006–07.

(Food Standards Agency) or of excellent enforcement on the ground (local regulatory services)? At the same time, it is clear that for a regulation to succeed, all the elements of the chain need to be working together to achieve the desired outcomes. The 'problem of many hands' is familiar to evaluators, but can be hard to resolve.

This speaks to designing better approaches to assess the impacts and outcomes of regulatory services. This is what the project that RAND Europe undertook in 2010 with the then Local Better Regulation Office in the UK tried to do.

II. Selecting What to Measure is Key

In understanding the impact of regulation, and specifically of regulatory delivery, it is important to understand how regulation affects the targeted behaviour. For instance, in improving food safety in restaurants and food outlets we would want to know how the regulation contributes to improved hygiene in establishments and then understand the additional outcomes (intended and unintended outcomes of this regulation). As a result, we need to understand the full cycle of regulation from regulatory proposals, to policy design and eventual implementation and delivery. This requires an understanding of the intervention logic of a regulation and mapping the outputs and outcomes of each activity. We will comment on establishing the intervention logic of local regulatory services later on in the chapter.

In terms of understanding what to measure, there are two main considerations. The first is what the focus of measurement is.[3] There are a number of possibilities. Measurement could focus on the impact of a regulatory intervention and seek to understand how much the intervention influenced the targeted behaviour. To take our earlier food safety example, it may be helpful to know what the cost is of each regulatory intervention aimed at improving food hygiene in restaurants and food outlets. It could look at cost-effectiveness and try to analyse what the unit cost is of each intervention type. To take our example further, we may want to know what the unit cost of improving food hygiene is in each of the food outlets. Moreover, an examination of net benefits may be helpful. This speaks to monetising the outcomes in addition to the previous option and understanding the cost–benefit ratio of a regulatory intervention, which can be compared across interventions. In our example, there may be three regulatory interventions to improve food hygiene and by comparing the costs and benefits of each it is possible to arrive at the net benefits of each and subsequently the preferred option. Finally, a further consideration is equity, or how fairly the net benefits and costs are distributed across society. Taking our example further, there may be concern if there are substantial distributional effects. These effects could arise if small to medium size enterprises are disproportionally affected, or food outlets owned by specific minority groups, or food outlets in specific geographical areas, and so on.

Clearly, the focus of measurement is linked to some of the factors identified in this chapter that are driving local regulatory services to engage more with outcome measurement. Each of these factors, be it the better regulation agenda, an increased focus on outcome-oriented performance management or the climate of fiscal austerity, drives the need for

---

[3] This section has been adapted from Cary Coglianese, *Measuring Regulatory Performance: Evaluating the Impact of Regulation and Regulatory Policy* (OECD, 2012).

greater accountability in local regulatory services. As such, the focus of measurement can change as the context in which local regulatory services operate change over time.

A further consideration is the art of the possible. When looking at different ways to measure the value added of local regulatory services, a main limitation is what 'can be' or 'has been' measured. In terms of the former, it is useful to think about methodologies that assist in measuring the impact of a regulation such as standard cost modelling, cost–benefit analysis, etc. Understanding what methodologies can achieve then also helpfully informs what key decision-makers in local regulatory services can achieve in any analysis of outcomes and analysis.[4] A key challenge in any evaluation is a possible misalignment between the questions asked and what the methodologies could possibly provide in terms of answers given the nature of the regulatory intervention and the context in which it takes place. It is for instance futile to try to measure what cannot be measured. In terms of the latter, it is helpful to understand which outcomes and impacts have been associated with local regulatory services in previous studies, which ones have been measured, and understand how good the measurement has been. Furthermore, shaping the routine administrative data collected as part of well-managed implementation can also provide a valuable and inexpensive source of data.

In RAND Europe's work on the impact on local regulatory services (involved in implementation and enforcement activities in areas as diverse as fire safety, food hygiene, trading standards, waste management etc) in England and Wales,[5] we tried to classify impact and outcomes in economic, social and environmental areas and sort them by affected stakeholders. Official reports and documents, for instance the Rogers Review,[6] formed the basis of this analysis. An initial list of 75 impacts was identified and aggregated into a final list of 48 impacts where we felt that there was good evidence of impact and better measurement. These may be summarised by type of impact and stakeholders affected.

Both negative impacts (costs) and positive economic impacts may be observed for a wide range of stakeholders. Directly or indirectly, local regulatory services contribute to:

- the administrative burden placed on business from regulatory requirements;
- compliance costs of business;
- productivity increases in the local economy;
- reduction of unfair competition;
- reduction in healthcare costs; and
- reduction in environmental cleaning costs.

These economic impacts are, however, not distributed evenly across the different categories of stakeholder. Businesses appear to carry most of the direct and short-term economic burden of local regulatory services activity through administrative and compliance costs, while the longer-term benefits appear to accrue to wider society and the public. Nevertheless, local businesses also stand to benefit economically through, for instance, increased

---

[4] Claudio Radaelli and Oliver Fritsch, *Measuring Regulatory Performance: Evaluating Regulatory Management Tools and Programmes* (OECD, 2012).

[5] For all relevant publications associated with the project, see www.rand.org/randeurope/research/projects/local-regulation.html.

[6] Rogers Review, 'National Enforcement Priorities for Local Authority Regulatory Services' (TSO, 2007).

productivity related to reduced work-related ill health or less unfair competition. A closer look at the economic beneficiaries shows that local authority and government services in particular benefit from the activities of local regulatory services, through:

- reduced waste removal and cleaning costs for the local authority;
- reduced healthcare costs; and
- reduced costs from anti-social behaviour for the police authorities.

Finally, the general public also stands to benefit from local regulatory services activity in economic terms, mainly as consumers who would be less exposed to scams and frauds.

The social impacts of local regulatory services are focused on the likely positive health effects of their activities, but also include less tangible aspects. Through the impact matrix the following social impacts have been identified:

- safer food;
- increased consumer confidence;
- less anti-social behaviour, crime and violence;
- reduction in infectious diseases;
- healthier workforce;
- reduced alcohol-related harm; and
- better standards of living and health in homes in multiple occupancy (HMO).

These benefits mostly accrue to the general public as a whole and can sometimes be attributed to specific subgroups. Our review identified children, consumers and employees as being impacted on in particular by local regulatory services activities.

An example of a social and health impact is enforcing hygiene standards in food businesses. The size of the problem was estimated for 2009 to be at 500,000 cases of food-borne disease in the UK.[7]

Finally, environmental impacts were identified through the use of the impact evaluation matrix. Specifically these are:

- improved air quality;
- reduced contamination of land;
- increased cleanliness of public streets and spaces; and
- decreased noise pollution.

The whole local community benefits from cleaner air, land and water. Enforcing waste removal regulation is a typical example of how local regulatory services are having an environmental impact at the local level.

This mapping exercise offered a comprehensive way to look at the possible impacts and outcomes of local regulatory services. However, it did not associate specific impact and outcomes with specific regulatory activities.

---

[7] Sarah O'Brien, Tricia Larose, and Goutam Adak, on behalf of the Foodborne Disease Attribution Study Group, 'Modelling Study to Estimate the Health Burden of Foodborne Diseases: Cases, General Practice Consultations and Hospitalisations in the UK' (2009) *BMJ Open* 2016; 6:e011119.

III. Deciding How to Measure

The next important step is to try and understand how regulatory activities contribute to specific outcomes and impacts. The main aim is to uncover the intervention logic of regulatory services or how regulatory policies and activities are associated with specific outcomes and impacts. This approach sits within the 'theory of change' family of evaluations. Such an approach takes into account the difficulties of measuring the attribution of a single policy, actor or intervention on a complex, multifaceted and multicausal problem. It replaces the need for making a clear statement of attribution with an approach that demonstrates the contribution to a given outcome or impact of an intervention, action or policy by establishing a causal chain (or a theory of change that might be thought of as a series of 'if-then' statements) for how a specific intervention will result in (desired) behavioural or systemic changes. By providing information along each step of the causal chain, this approach develops a plausible argument that a specific intervention had, or had not, contributed to a specific outcome (intended or unintended).[8]

Replacing a statement of *attribution* with a statement of *contribution* has, however, consequences for the inferences that can and should be made.[9] This could be important for accountability purposes. Cost–benefit analysis typically requires a clear attribution of actions to a specific outcome or impact. This applies to determining the costs and benefits that result from regulatory services, actions and policy. Statements of cost–benefit should therefore be made with caution in relation to these pathways. Nevertheless, the pathways are an important step towards such an analysis. Only by identifying impacts and outcomes in the first place can they form the basis for further analysis.

Logic models[10] enable us to produce a graphic representation of how a regulatory policy, intervention or action is intended to work – that is, how resources are converted into programme activities, and how those activities in turn produce the results intended. Therefore, logic models generally allow a researcher to analyse the relationship between inputs and outputs, and between inputs and outcomes. Logic models provide an opportunity within the 'accountability area' to measure results, correct problems and identify successes.[11] They also ensure a shared understanding of the intervention and help uncover any implicit disagreements and confusions. An abstract version of a logic model is shown in Figure 14.1.

Logic models usually stop short of formulating specific links between the elements within each category. A logic model would, for example, list a number of activities as well a number of outputs, without linking the specific activity to a specific output and then a specific outcome. A further issue is that in a complex system often the various interactions between partners are not depicted. For the purpose of developing the pathways, it is therefore helpful to supplement the logic models with elements known from process-mapping, by indicating links between the elements of the logic model and highlighting interactions with key partners.

---

[8] ibid.

[9] For more information on contribution analysis, see eg John Mayne, 'Contribution Analysis: An Approach to Exploring Cause and Effect' (2008) 16 *ILAC Brief*.

[10] Kellogg Foundation, Logic Model Development Guide, available at www.wkkf.org/Pubs/Tools/Evaluation/Pub3669.pdf.

[11] David Osborne, and Ted Gaebler, *Reinventing Government: How the Entrepreneurial Spirit is Transforming the Public Sector* (Reading, MA, Addison-Wesley Publishing Co, 1992).

Figure 14.1 Outline of a basic logic model

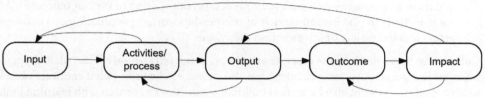

Source: RAND Europe.

This approach takes as its starting point the argument of Weiss that:[12]

> The concept of grounding evaluation in theories of change takes for granted that social programs [in this case regulation activities] are based on explicit or implicit theories about how and why the program [regulation activities] will work ... The evaluation should surface those theories and lay them out in as fine detail as possible, identifying all the assumptions and sub-assumptions built into the program. The evaluators then construct methods for data collection and analysis to track the unfolding assumptions. The aim is to examine the extent to which program theories hold ... the evaluation should show which of the assumptions underlying the program are best supported by the evidence.

This is an approach rather than a methodology (its successful delivery requires the harnessing of a range of methodologies such as mapping of outcomes, process mapping and others). The approach proposed in this chapter conceptually has six elements:

1. It requires an evaluator not only to look at the outcomes of the regulatory activities, but also to pay close attention to the processes leading to these outcomes. This is often more akin to exploring causal chains using mixed methods and contrasts with more classical evaluation approaches, which tend to look at outcomes first and then to address attribution by quantifying how often, and how far, A follows B.
2. It requires a more 'embedded' evaluator working closely with regulators, practitioners and end users to understand and elaborate a sometimes changing theory of change. This should be easier for evaluators working with those involved in the regulatory activity than for external evaluators. Without losing independence, this embedded evaluator will understand the world of the policy-makers, practitioners and service users, including what motivates their behaviour.
3. It requires an ability to reconstruct and represent the sequence of events connecting actions to each other and how these contributed to the outcomes identified.
4. It is sensitive to the possibility that during the lifetime of a regulation, activities may change in response to learning or to exogenous events. In building a long-term understanding of the impacts of local regulatory services this is likely to be relevant and important.
5. It will also be sensitive to the fact that different and potentially conflicting theories of change might be simultaneously pursued within different local services.

---

[12] Carol Weiss, 'Nothing as Practical as a Good Theory: Exploring Theory Based Evaluation for Comprehensive Community Initiatives for Children and Families' in James Connell, Anne Kubisch, Lisbeth Schorr and Carol Weiss (eds), *New Approaches to Evaluating Community Initiatives: Concepts, Methods and Contexts*. (Washington, The Aspen Institute, 1995) 66–67.

6.   It is sensitive to the fact that the regulatory activity does not take place in a vacuum but occurs in a complex system with multiple actors contributing to various outcomes. As such, it needs to understand models of partnership working, feedback loops between actors and the variety of actors within the system.

Collectively, these six elements describe an interest in not only *causal effects* (what happens when an independent variable changes) but also *causal mechanisms* (what connects causes to their effects). It might also be seen as building a regulatory approach with learning built into its operation.

The approach taken in looking at the outcomes and impacts of local regulatory services has been to encourage practitioners to focus on understanding what Mayne calls the 'contribution story';[13] that is, to understand why practitioners believe that their use of resources (money, authority, expertise, time, etc) will contribute to public benefits and what side-effects and unintended outcomes they envisage. Data collection is then driven by the need to support or challenge these narratives. This allows us to narrow down the potential range of questions posed by a more general (and sometimes abstract) theory of change approach and to focus on the things service users, practitioners and policy-makers most need to know. In practice, we therefore need a tool for developing and understanding the 'contribution story' which we can use to make sense of the (sometimes varying) claims made.

Broadly, in order to make the contribution approach manageable in practice, the approach taken with local regulatory services was to come up with a toolkit. This was intended to assist both evaluators and practitioners in getting closer to the impact and outcomes of local regulatory services. There are three main steps: mapping the intervention logic using logic models; identifying and defining indicators; and presenting the findings in a dashboard.[14] These are discussed in turn below.

A.   Mapping the Intervention Logic Using Logic Models

This activity is typically undertaken with the people from regulatory services involved in designing and conducting regulatory activities. The aim here is to identify the inputs, activities, outputs and outcomes that are involved in a regulatory intervention. We suggest using logic models to achieve some initial clarity about the contribution story. It usually takes the shape of a workshop with officers and managers from the local regulatory service and seeks to achieve consensus around the components of a logic model. Typically, a process-mapping exercise managed by evaluators or by someone in the regulatory service with a background in evaluation that will look at partnership working and more specifically at the links between activities and outputs and outcomes will be an input to this session. The output is a logic model that those involved in the regulatory activities see as their contribution story or narrative. However, logic models carry dangers that should be guarded against. First, they can be excessively linear and homogenising, and distract attention from feedback loops and the uneven pattern and pace of implementation. Secondly, they can focus too

---

[13] John Mayne, 'Contribution Analysis: An Approach to Exploring Cause and Effect' (2008) 16 *ILAC Brief* 9.
[14] See Jan Tiessen, Claire Celia, Lidia Villalba-van-Dijk, Anaïs Reding, Christian van Stolk and Tom Ling, 'Impacts and Outcomes of Local Authority Regulatory Services: Final Report' (Local Better Regulation Office, 2009).

strongly on intended outcomes and fail to identify unintended outcomes and side-effects. Thirdly, in our experience they can be alienating for those being evaluated, who find their complex world being recategorised and redefined as inputs, processes, outcomes, etc. If evaluators are unaware of this effect, this may be an unhelpful way to understand the causal chain and become a barrier to understanding the motivations and behaviour that drive it. However, despite these limitations, the process is very helpful in surfacing unexamined or unshared assumptions and building, possibly for the first time, a clear and shared narrative of the high-level contribution story that can be debated and discussed by those with a really detailed knowledge of its operation. In our experience, these benefits were considerable.

B. Identifying and Defining Indicators

At a very pragmatic level, it is important to collect performance indicators along the logic model to understand and illustrate the relationships between inputs, activities, outputs and outcomes. These data allow the service to move beyond debating assumptions and focus on collecting data that make sense of what is known. This is a function of mapping the possible impact and outcomes and the 'art of the possible'. Considerations are what is feasible, suitable and acceptable to collect. It is unlikely that data can be collected on all aspects of a logic model. However, going through this exercise has two benefits. Firstly, it establishes the 'art of the possible' and solid reflections on what can be collected. This data provides some evidence in what really brings about change in behaviour and outcomes and is not unlike the 'process-tracing' approach of George and Bennett (2005).[15] Here, we advocate that their approach of drilling down into individual behaviour should be supported with strong statistical evidence of costs and consequences where data can feasibly be collected. Marshalling evidence to help assess the contribution story requires us to use a set of comparator data (trends before and after a change in regulatory practice, different outcomes associated with different regulatory practices, and so forth). Without a convincing comparator the contribution story becomes less persuasive. Secondly, it assists in prioritising what should be collected and reported on. In other words, it is also a prioritisation tool. Figure 14.2 shows a matrix approach to deciding which indicators should be included – along the axes of how central or marginal the indicator is to a convincing contribution story, and how easy or difficult the indicator is to collect.

Figure 14.3 gives an example logic model for trading standards in the UK. Trading standards is a local regulatory service responsible for delivering regulation in the areas of consumer protection and unfair trading. In this example, an interested party can read the graphic depiction from left to right or right to left. So, if one is interested in particular impacts (eg consumer savings, safer communities), the graphic allows you to trace back how outcomes, outputs and activities connect to these. Similarly, one could start with basic activities such as education, advice and inspections and see what outputs they produce and how these contribute to outcomes and eventually impacts. Finally, those involved in the local regulatory service can also then establish how easy it is to collect some of this information. In this example, we identified that the then Office of Fair Trading, a national regulatory

---

[15] Alexander George and Andrew Bennett, *Case Studies and Theory Development in the Social Sciences* (Cambridge MA and London, MIT Press, 2005).

Figure 14.2 Prioritisation matrix for selecting indicators

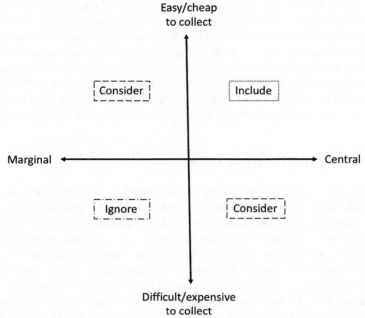

Source: RAND Europe.

agency, already provided some information on some of the impacts, but few other impacts were being assessed. In this example, similar to many examples, most of the data will relate to inputs, activities and outputs and some to outcomes and impacts.

C. Presenting the Findings in a Dashboard

This provides a visual representation of how the logic model is progressing giving decision-makers a quick and easy means to identify progress and potential problems. Once the prioritisation has taken place, those involved can decide to present these indicators in a dashboard, which allows them to monitor their activities, present some of the findings for accountability purposes, and evaluate how their services and actions develop over time and impact on society, the economy and the environment. Figure 14.4 gives an example for a trading standards service in the UK.

IV. Some Observations on the Process

This tool still presents a relatively comprehensive and complex process, which may be beyond the technical and financial resources of a range of local regulatory services. This involved evaluators doing background research, facilitating workshops with local regulatory services, designing process maps, data analysis and assisting in the development of logic models and performance frameworks. Building on the case studies that were undertaken

Figure 14.3   An overview of a logic model pathway focusing on local trading standards in the UK

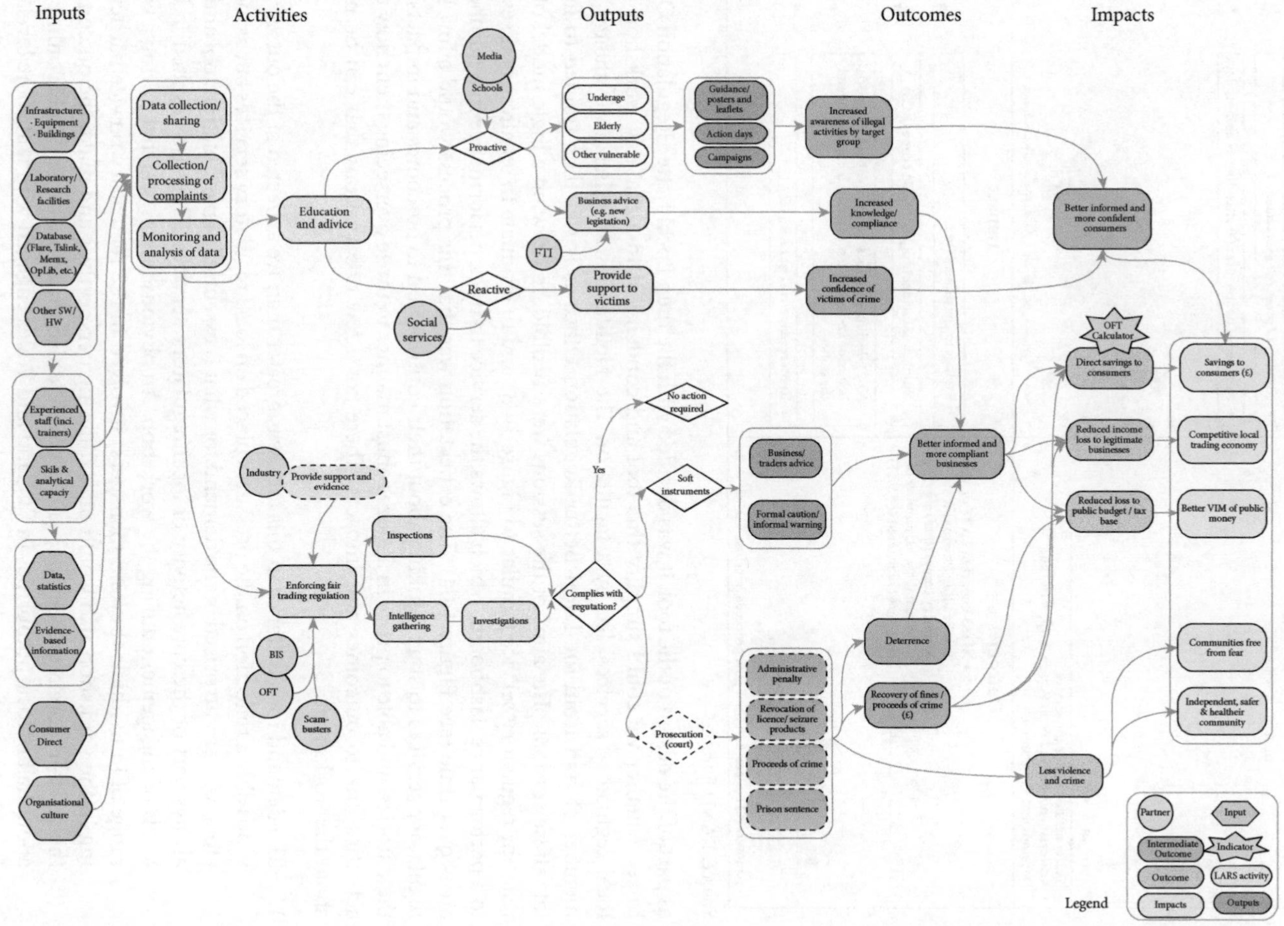

Source: RAND Europe.

Figure 14.4 Example of a dashboard for trading standards

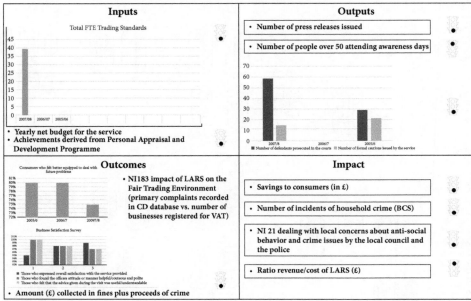

Source: RAND Europe.

as part of the design of the tool, it was decided with the then Local Better Regulation Office to see whether we could simplify this tool and condense it to a one-day workshop with local regulatory services, led by a facilitator. The facilitator was either an evaluator or a member of staff from the Local Better Regulation Office as it was then trained to facilitate these sessions. The aims of the sessions were twofold: to draw up a logic model of the relevant regulatory service (similar to Figure 14.3) and to graduate in an afternoon session to a performance dashboard, which allows the service to track performance in a number of areas over time (see Figure 14.4). The expectation was that this process would allow local regulatory services to start thinking about their contribution to outcomes and impacts, tell their stories, and able to prove in a more robust manner to those overseeing them how their activities link to outcomes and impacts. There are a few observations that can be made about the workshops:

1. The demand for assistance in this area was greater than we expected at the outset. This is possibly a reflection on the pressures placed on local regulatory services but as evaluators we were surprised in the demand for what is essentially an evaluation tool and not always part of the core activity of local regulatory services. This also resulted in high levels of engagement during the workshop. An obvious lesson was that having a wider range of individuals (beyond managers) involved in the regulatory service participating in the workshop also would offer differing perspectives and make the outcome of the session more representative and useful. We also made the tool available online and about half of local authorities in England and Wales engaged with it at some level.

2. It was striking that a wide range of regulatory services had never reflected on what they were doing and for what purpose and how they could envision doing things differently within the current regulatory frameworks. There was a considerable appetite for

learning about how regulatory activities fitted within the wider relationships which together brought social benefits. Often, activities existed in isolation and those involved in regulatory services had had few opportunities to reflect on how these specific activities were linked to other services and impacts. There were also interesting discussions around the weight of activities or trade-offs between activities. For instance, in some local fire authorities, it is clear that the prevalence of fires is decreasing and also that the risks presented by modern workplaces are different from the past. As such, one could expect those fire services to reduce the number of regulatory inspections of workplaces (within the scope of national regulation) and put more resources into education and advice. We found that in some services the resources dedicated to those specific activities had stayed more or less the same over a long period of time leading to lack of capacity in providing fire safety education and overcapacity (and potentially needless activities) in the other. These discussions were particularly helpful in the context of some services having to make cuts in resources and of course ensuring that services respond to current and future trends.

3. Many services were apprehensive about measurement. They often had little capacity and where capacity to collect data and undertake evaluation had existed these posts were often vulnerable at a time of fiscal austerity after the crisis of 2008. This work established that quite a bit of data was already collected for different purposes by national regulatory agencies, policy-makers and local regulatory services. However, it was not always brought together in a systematic manner. As such, the burden around data collection was less than some of the services anticipated at the outset. Much of these routine and administrative data could be repurposed and could feed into the performance dashboard (in Figure 14.4).

4. In the end, the workshops may have been more helpful in educating local regulatory services and promoting an evaluation culture among local regulators than rigidly arriving at a performance framework for each local regulatory service at the end of the day. In this way, there was potentially a more diffuse set of benefits that we may not have fully anticipated at the outset of the project.

V. Some Final Observations

A few final observations can be made on the basis of the project undertaken with the then Local Better Regulation Office in 2010, and these in our view remain relevant today. Firstly, at the time about 50 per cent of local regulatory services collected data on their performance in the UK.[16] In many of these cases, it was not clear what they were collecting and for what purpose. Secondly, as outlined before, there was a huge demand for better assessment of impacts and outcomes. This possibly speaks to the accountability and budgetary pressures placed on regulatory services at the local level in the UK. As mentioned earlier, such services are not always visible and the value added may not be clear to national and local decision-makers. Thirdly, the costs of regulatory services and the burden that they impose are at times easier to establish than their intrinsic benefits. Fourthly, when undertaking the logic-modelling workshops, it became clear that many services had had very few opportunities to

---

[16] See Tiessen et al, 'Final Report' (2009).

reflect on what activities they undertook, why they undertook these activities and what the likely outcomes and impacts of their activities were. In some ways, the activities had been mandated or substantial path dependencies existed around how services were organised.

In this sense, the exercise that was undertaken had a range of benefits. On a strategic level, it allowed those involved in the planning and delivery of local regulatory services to reflect on what they were doing, the design of their regulatory activities, partnership working and the linkages between different actors in the regulatory landscape, and the effectiveness of their actions. Moreover, it allowed them in a more robust manner to establish how their activities contribute to a range of outcomes and impacts. This was important for account-ability purposes and improving the visibility of these services. In addition, it showed that it was possible across a range of services to establish how these regulatory services contribute to outcomes. Finally, the work met a wider demand from local regulatory services given the difficulties in conceptualising and measuring outcomes and impacts and fostered an evaluation culture among those working in regulatory services. As such, this work struck a chord with local regulatory services often facing accountability pressures and lacking the resources and capacities to start telling their contribution stories in a systematic manner.

15

The Impact of Inspections, Measuring Outcomes from Occupational Safety and Health Inspections

FLORENTIN BLANC AND GIULIANA COLA

I. Introduction

Assessing the impact of regulation, and specifically of regulatory delivery, is complex – *what* should be measured and *how*, and with what reliability to meaningfully reflect performance? Enforcement should not be a self-referential activity, whose outcomes are measured merely as finding and punishing violations, where enforcement would be its own goal. Rather, to the extent that a regulation has instrumental goals, achieving them should be seen as the goal of regulatory delivery. Because there is no such thing as optimal design of legislation, not all rules will have the same relevance to regulatory goals, and a degree of discretion is necessary.[1] If measuring outcomes in terms of desired public welfare is difficult, measuring compliance levels may be an acceptable substitute, assuming that compliance correlates with positive outcomes (even though this is imperfectly the case at best). Measuring compliance, however, is also problematic, and is very different from counting the number of violations or sanctions.

Existing literature has attempted to answer the question of the goal of regulatory delivery, but not completely satisfactorily.[2] Recently Mintz, regarding environmental enforcement,[3] has returned to the distinction of outputs and outcomes. The outcome would measure the result of regulatory delivery with respect to public health and the environment – and not only to compliance.[4] It remains to be seen whether, and to what extent, this is possible. Mintz, for instance, indicates that measuring environmental improvements as a result

---

[1] See Colin Diver, 'The Optimal Precision of Administrative Rules' (1983) 93 *The Yale Law Journal* 65; Robert Baldwin, *Rules and Government* (Oxford, Clarendon Press, 1995).

[2] Neil Gunningham, 'Enforcement and Compliance Strategies' in *The Oxford Handbook of Regulation* (Oxford, Oxford University Press, 2010) indicates at p 169 that enforcement strategies will have to balance 'these sometimes competing criteria of effectiveness, efficiency and legitimacy'.

[3] See inter alia Joel Mintz, 'Assessing National Environmental Enforcement: some Lessons from the United States Experience' (2013) 25 *The Georgetown International Environmental Law Review* 1 and 'Measuring Environmental Enforcement Success: the Elusive Search for Objectivity' (2014) *Environmental Law Reporter* 107.

[4] Mintz, 'Measuring Environmental Enforcement Success' (2014) 107.

of enforcement efforts is difficult (eg because variations in weather conditions, entirely unrelated to enforcement can have a strong impact on air and water quality).[5] He also sees problems in using compliance rates as a second-best solution: one is that compliance rates are frequently not measured; the second is that a compliance rate of eg 90 per cent may look excellent, but can be dramatic when the remaining 10 per cent non-compliance leads to the highest degree of environmental harm – so one would need to 'weight' non-compliances according to risk or harm, which again is complex.[6]

In fact, though measuring outcomes may be difficult and limited by uncertainty, we will show in this chapter – by presenting a case study of regulatory delivery performance in occupational safety (covering Britain, France and Germany) – that it is, at least in some cases, possible. Before doing so, however, we will briefly discuss why we consider reporting on activity volume profoundly inadequate, and reporting on compliance levels a poor proxy for outcomes.

A. Measuring Outputs

Many regulatory delivery institutions around the world use outputs, and particularly inspection numbers, as a performance indicator. It is, however, a circular reference: increasing the volume of work will automatically lead to assuming performance has increased if the two are equated, and will miss the purpose to assess whether the work was effective not its quantity.

In fact, output measures provide no information as to the timeliness of an enforcement intervention.[7] Measuring only outputs means that the more an agency produces 'activity', the higher its 'rating' will be, even if it completely fails at its mission. However, this often happens in regulatory delivery, based on an assumption among many that 'more' automatically means 'better', that more inspections and sanctions will *ipso facto* create higher compliance, and better outcomes.[8] This is anchored in purely deterrence-based models of compliance, and in the assumption that better compliance is identical with better outcomes (eg safety). There is, however, much work suggesting that compliance drivers are considerably more complex,[9] and that the links between compliance and outcomes are also less than straightforward.[10] Some studies even show an inverse correlation between increased

---

[5] ibid.

[6] Mintz (2014) (n 3) 107.

[7] ibid.

[8] See Steve Tombs and David Whyte, *Regulatory Surrender: Death, Inquiry and the Non-Enforcement of Law* (London, Institute of Employment Rights, 2010); and Steve Tombs and David Whyte, 'Transcending the Deregulation Debate? Regulation, Risk and the Enforcement of Health and Safety Law in the UK' (2013) 7 *Regulation & Governance* 61. for illustrations of the assumption that more inspections and enforcement are necessarily better (and, conversely, fewer inspections and enforcement are worse).

[9] See Florentin Blanc et al, *Understanding and Addressing the Risk Regulation Reflex. Lessons from International Experience in Dealing with Risk, Responsibility and Regulation* (The Hague, Netherlands Ministry of Internal Affairs, 2015) 66–69; Christopher Hodges, 'Corporate Behaviour: Enforcement, Support or Ethical Culture?', Oxford Legal Studies Research Paper No 19/2015 5–6.

[10] See Doreen McBarnet and Christopher Whelan, 'The Elusive Spirit of the Law: Formation and the Struggle for Legal Control', (1991) 54 *The Modern Law Review* 848–73; Neil Gunningham, Robert Kagan and Dorothy Thornton, *Shades of Green: Business, Regulation and Environment*, (Stanford, Stanford University Press, 2003);

controls and increased compliance.[11] In any case, as we have seen with the example of occupational safety and health in Britain and Germany, practice also shows that there are many cases where more 'intense' inspections and enforcement correspond to *worse* rather than *better* outcomes. Moreover, giving incentives to inspectorates to inspect (and use enforcement measures) as much as possible distracts them from considering actual outcomes – both in terms of the public welfare goals they are supposed to help achieve, and of the social and economic impact of their activities. We thus conclude that this approach should be excluded to the benefit of more outcomes-focused measurement.

B. Measuring Compliance

Measuring compliance levels, and using their variations to assess regulatory delivery performance, would appear to directly relate to regulatory mandates and the aim of delivery activities. However, it can be problematic. First, as discussed, is the imperfect link between compliance and desired outcomes – itself linked to the impossibility of designing rules of 'optimal precision':[12] only 'prescriptive' technical norms would seem to give the certainty that what is required from the business corresponds to the intent of the regulation, but these norms leave business uncertain as to *how* to reach the desired result, and put inspectors in a difficult situation too, because of time-lags or third-party effects.[13]

The compliance–outcomes mismatch is highest when regulations have been inadequately drafted, and tends to increase as technological changes accelerate, or when third-party effects increase. This disconnect is consequential for inspections,[14] and one of the reasons some advocate for increasing inspectors' discretion.[15] Even in environmental protection, where many rules are 'target'-based, the impossibility of considering in advance all side-effects and all types of impacts means that compliance is never a fully satisfactory measure.[16]

The second problem is the difficulty of obtaining reliable compliance data. Kagan, Gunningham and Thornton write that 'the regulatory agency databases that researchers use to measure noncompliance vary in quality, while researchers who rely on those databases

Gwyn Bevan and Christopher Hood, 'What's Measured is what Matters: Targets and Gaming in the English Public Health Care Systems' (2006) 84 *Public Administration* 517.

[11] See Katharina Gangl, Benno Tongler, Erich Kirchler, and Eva Hofmann, 'Effects of Supervision on Tax Compliance: Evidence from a Field Experiment in Austria' (2014) 123 *Economics Letters* 378.

[12] See Colin Diver, 'Optimal Precision' (1983); Robert Baldwin, 'Why Rules Don't Work' (1990) 59 *The Modern Law Review* 321 and *Rules and Government* (1995); Anthony Ogus, *Regulation: Legal Form and Economic Theory* (Oxford, Clarendon Press, 1994).

[13] Many effects from hazards covered by regulation may only occur years or decades later, and likewise the results of effective (or not) regulation may only be seen much later (time-lag). The hazards and harms that regulation seeks to address are influenced by many other factors and third-parties, eg economic forces, natural circumstances, social and cultural conditions – meaning that establishing the precise contribution of regulation and regulatory delivery is very difficult.

[14] See for instance in occupational safety and health Ann Bartel and Lacy Thomas, 'Direct and Indirect Effects of Regulation: A New Look at OSH's impact' (1985) 28 *Journal of Law and Economics* 1.

[15] See *Wetenschappelijke Raad voor het Regeringsbeleid* (2013) available at www.wrr.nl/publicaties/rapporten/2013/09/09/toezien-op-publieke-belangen.-naar-een-verruimd-perspectief-op-rijkstoezicht.

[16] Gunningham et al, *Shades of Green* (2003).

often differ in what they treat as significant noncompliance'[17] – both being understatements. Lehmann, Nielsen and Parker go further:

> [T]o the extent that data are available from individuals inside firms or from records collected by regulatory agencies, the data will be filtered and biased according to what those who collected it saw as relevant and important to compliance and what they see as socially and politically desirable to share with the researcher.[18]

A raw compliance rate is not enough in any case, as it should be corrected by the level of risk or harm created by different violations.[19]

Levels of compliance, whether reported by businesses or by inspectors, are unreliable. Businesses have an imperfect understanding of what full compliance would be, and a reluctance to report fraud and violations. Inspectors have a number of incentives to report compliance levels that may differ from reality (not necessarily better – policy priorities may also mean that reporting lower compliance than actually found makes career sense), and of course never have a full view of the level of compliance in any given business, even one that they inspected. They also have less information on non-visited businesses. While one may assume that the 'imperfect information' issue may be relatively constant, and thus not excessively skew evaluations of *relative* effectiveness,[20] the same is not true of pressure from inspectors' management, policy makers, etc. Research in crime and law enforcement has repeatedly shown major issues with how police forces register and report crime levels (including under-registration of crimes that the police would be unlikely to solve, so as to increase the rate of success – or systematic enforcement against petty crime in order to make 'activity' statistics look up, making it appear as if there were a surge in some violations, etc).[21] Similarly, Bardach and Kagan have shown that, when inspectorate management emphasises a 'looking tough' approach and penalises inspectors who appear to have lower activity and enforcement numbers, this produces a more legalistic and aggressive enforcement practice,[22] with considerable side-effects (what the authors call 'unreasonableness'), without this reflecting on the real level of compliance and safety.

A third reason for caution is that maybe full compliance with all regulations is not always a desirable goal. Though it may theoretically be so, achieving full compliance may lead to excessively high enforcement and compliance costs. For Stigler, the goal of enforcement actions is not to achieve compliance at all costs (for the marginal costs of

---

[17] Robert Kagan, Neil Gunningham, and Dorothy Thornton, ' Fear, Duty and Regulatory Compliance Lessons from Three Research Projects' in Christine Parker and Vibeke Nielsen (eds), *Explaining Compliance: Business Responses to Regulation*, (Cheltenham, Edward Elgar Publishing, 2011).

[18] Christine Parker and Vibeke Nielsen (eds), Explaining Compliance: Business Responses to Regulation (Cheltenham, Edward Elgar Publishing, 2011) 6.

[19] Mintz (2014) (n 3) 107.

[20] Although more qualified and professional inspectors tend to be better at detecting violations, as noted by Soren Winter and Peter May in 'Motivation for Compliance and Environmental Regulation' 20 *Journal of Policy Analysts and Management* 675.

[21] There is a vast amount of literature on this issue eg Wesley Skogan 'Measurement Problems in Official and Survey Crime Rates' (1975) 3 *Journal of Criminal Justice* 17; 'Crime Statistics: An Independent Review, Carried out for the Secretary of State for the UK Home Department' (November 2006).

[22] Eugene Bardach and Robert Kagan, *Going by the Book: The Problem of Regulatory Unreasonableness* (Philadelphia, Temple University Press, 1982) 76–77.

achieving full compliance might be higher than its marginal benefits), but rather to aim at optimal compliance.[23] Building further on 'optimal compliance', recent literature in law and economics has advocated 'cost-effective compliance'.[24] Less than full compliance can be 'optimal' because of the high costs of achieving full compliance. In legal terms, this amounts to applying a proportionality test to regulatory delivery activity.

C. Measuring Outcomes

A third approach holds that regulatory delivery should not just be cost-effective, but reach the regulatory goals, eg avoidance of environmental harm or improvement of environmental quality. As noted, while measuring outcomes poses real challenges, attributing changes in compliance to regulatory delivery is no less problematic[25] – even assuming reliable compliance data, which is rarely (if ever) available.

Focusing on outcomes follows the 2014 OECD principles for regulatory enforcement[26] and corresponds to an instrumental perspective on regulation. There are other legitimate ways to assess regulatory systems,[27] and there are critics of the instrumental perspective,[28] but it fits best with concerns about 'effectiveness'. Outcomes, however, are not easy: how to define them, how to measure them, and what relationship exists between the outcomes and regulatory delivery activities (the problem of attribution)?

Defining outcomes is comparatively easy. For each regulatory delivery area, key indicators can be identified relating to a regulatory mandate. The Environment Agency of England (EA), for instance, has a 'corporate scorecard'[29] organised around priority areas such as 'increasing the resilience of people, property and businesses to the risks of flooding and coastal erosion' or 'protecting and improving water, land and biodiversity'. These, in turn, include specific indicators such as 'reduce the risk from flooding for more households' or 'fewer salmon rivers in the "at risk" category'. Other indicators include 'number of water bodies at good ecological status' or reduction of 'serious and significant pollution incidents'.

---

[23] George Stigler, 'The Theory of Economic Regulation' (1971) 2 *Bell Journal of Economics* 3.

[24] See inter alia Anthony Ogus, Michael Faure and Niels Philipsen, *Best Practices for Consumer Policy: Report on the Effectiveness of Enforcement Regimes* (OECD, 2006); Michael Faure and Katarina Svatikova, 'Enforcement of Environmental Law in the Flemish Region' (2010) 19 *European Energy and Environmental Law Review* 69; Michael Faure and Katarina Swatikova, 'Criminal or Administrative Law to Protect the Environment? Evidence from Western Europe' (2012) 24 *Journal of Environmental Law* 253.

[25] See Don Dewee, David Duff and Michael Trebilcock, *Exploring the Domain of Accident Law: Taking the Facts Seriously* (Oxford, Oxford University Press, 1996) 307–15.

[26] 'Regulatory Enforcement and Inspections, OECD Best Practice Principles for Regulatory Policy' (OECD, 2014).

[27] See Wim Voermans, 'Legislation and Regulation' in Ulrich Karpen and Helen Xanthaki (eds) *Handbook of Legislation* (Oxford, Hart Publishing, 2017) for an overview of the other uses of legislation. See Keith Hawkins, *Law as Last Resort – Prosecution Decision-making in a Regulatory Agency* (Oxford, Oxford University Press, 2002) at 3–4 for the application to occupational health and safety.

[28] eg Karen Yeung, 'Better Regulation, Administrative Sanctions and Constitutional Values' (2013) 33 *Legal Studies* 312.

[29] UK Environment Agency, 'Corporate Scorecard 2014–2015', available at www.gov.uk/government/uploads/system/uploads/attachment_data/file/457335/LIT_10170.pdf.

A greater challenge is to link indicators to regulatory delivery activities, considering the number of factors that drive environmental outcomes (eg technology, climate, market pressure, macro-economic situation). It is not just a problem of attribution, but also of political 'risk' to commit to improvements in certain indicators. This can in part be addressed by 'hedging' against externalities in the way indicators are formulated or assessed (eg targeting an improvement 'barring exceptional circumstances' and explaining these if and when they occur). This is also why institutions such as the EA also retain some 'compliance' indicators, such as 'improve business compliance through supporting legitimate business to comply and tackling the deliberately non-compliant', measured by a reduction in 'sites in lowest compliance bands'. By contrast, the EA does not have targets for air pollution (an area where factors beyond its control vastly exceed those that it can influence), even though it does report on specific air pollution indicators.

Even if the indicators correspond to the regulatory goals and improvements are achieved, attribution of outcomes to regulatory delivery is still problematic. Outcomes such as environmental protection or worker safety ultimately depend on the economic actors themselves (enterprises, managers, workers, and in some cases – eg food safety – consumers as well), and inspectors only play an indirect role by incentivising improved compliance and outcomes (or attempting to do so).[30] Determining precise attribution of changes is, in most cases, an impossible quest, which would require data of a level of quality and detail that is simply absent. Looking at trends can be an acceptable substitute, but to ascertain the effect of inspections and enforcement specifically would require the comparison of trends between sufficiently similar jurisdictions to see whether the evolution of specific outcomes appears to vary significantly in parallel to differences in regulatory delivery practices. Indeed, improvements in key safety outcomes (eg food safety, environmental pollution) in many cases pre-date the set-up of agencies in charge of delivering regulations in these areas. Thus, only a marked acceleration in the improvement trend would provide some evidence of the specific effectiveness of inspections and enforcement.

Additional challenges have been well illustrated for occupational health and safety by Hawkins. Indeed, 'it is very difficult for regulatory agencies to exhibit their effectiveness in terms of the number of injuries or deaths that did not occur'.[31] While reporting on *trends* may help to address this issue, the problem of time lag ('when a period of industrial activity may be generating a problem which is not recognisable for a number of years') remains, particularly for rare or latent events.[32] Overall, while measuring outcomes is the most relevant way to evaluate enforcement effectiveness, the complexity of the causal chains means that this can never be a simple exercise and requires the consideration of trends (and changes in trends), comparisons across different jurisdictions, and external factors at play.

---

[30] See Keith Hawkins, *Law as Last Resort – Prosecution Decision-Making in a Regulatory Agency* (Oxford, Oxford University Press, 2002) 9.
[31] ibid, 8.
[32] ibid, 10.

II. Case Study: Regulatory Delivery and Outcomes in Occupational Safety – Britain,[33] France and Germany

There were several reasons to select occupational safety, and these three countries. First, this field had been specifically studied in Britain and Germany already.[34] Second, data is easy to access and harmonised (by Eurostat)[35] – and reliable, for fatal accidents. Third, a significant extent of shared regulation exists, through EU Directives. Interestingly, these three countries were the first worldwide to create labour safety laws and inspectorates but have ended up with very different practices and systems in this sphere, giving potential for an enlightening comparison. We first discuss the British approach to occupational safety and health (OSH) in some detail, because it sharply differs from comparators, and has been the subject of controversies to which this case study may help respond.

A. Context – Consolidation of 'Risk-Based Approaches' in Britain

Regulatory delivery in OSH includes primarily guidance and inspections, as there is no permitting system. OSH inspections are shared between the Health and Safety Executive (HSE), a national body, and Local Authorities (LAs). The former is responsible for slightly under half of business premises, LAs for the rest – but in recent years LAs have been conducting over two-thirds of inspections.[36] The dual structure is historical, and HSE is, broadly speaking, responsible for 'high-risk' and 'major hazard' areas (in particular those covered by EU directives). In recent years, the HSE has taken a stronger role in guidance to LA officers (although not direct authority).[37]

The existence of a specific profession of environmental health officers (EHOs), with a broad perspective on environmental health risks rather than a narrow technical focus,

---

[33] The case study focuses on Great Britain and not the United Kingdom, because Northern Ireland has its own body in charge of occupational safety and health. Some statistics, however, are for the United Kingdom as a whole and on the basis this does not impact the overall analysis we have used them where needed without further comments.

[34] eg Hawkins, *Law as Last Resort* (2002) and Laura Tilindyte, *Enforcing Health and Safety Regulation. A Comparative Economic Approach* (Maastricht, Intersentia, 2012).

[35] Eurostat ensures not only uniformity of definitions, but standardisation of incidence rates to correct for differences in economic structure.

[36] See 'The Role of the Health and Safety Commission and the Health and Safety Executive in Regulating Workplace Health and Safety: Third Report of the Session (House of Commons Work and Pensions Select Committee, 2008), and Better Regulation Executive, 'Improving Outcomes from Health and Safety (Department for Business Enterprise and Regulatory Reform, 2008) at 59 indicating a 55/45 split LAs/HSE. For a variety of reasons 'health and safety' has been particularly targeted by efforts to reduce regulatory costs (for the state) and burdens (for businesses and citizens); one possible explanation for this decline is political but this would not explain why the HSE in particular has been under constant pressure to reduce inspections, more (or so it appears) than other regulatory areas.

[37] This is underpinned by the HSE's regulatory function. It was strengthened following presentation to the UK Parliament of a report in 2011 (the Löfstedt Review: Reclaiming health and safety for all: an independent review of health and safety legislation). This report also highlighted the 'twin peaks' problem (some premises with actually higher risk tended not to be inspected at all (or insufficiently) because they were in the HSE's remit, and some premises with in fact lower (though not inconsequential) risk were being inspected far more intensively by LAs) and called for a much narrower focus on high-risk premises.

as well as the large share of this profession employed in the regulatory sphere, are a British specificity. Elsewhere, inspectors would stem from distinct technical fields, not linked to regulatory issues. There has been a succession of policy steps to achieve greater consistency in regulatory delivery, not only in OSH (eg 2005 Hampton Review, 2008 and 2014 Regulators Code; see chapter 1 and Annex 1). In OSH specifically, the HSE formalised its approach through an 'Enforcement Policy Statement'[38] and an 'Enforcement Management Model'.[39]

The Löfstedt Review recommendations were translated into the 2013 National Local Authority Enforcement Code[40] issued by the HSE and applicable to all LAs; enforcement activities relating to health and safety. Its purpose was summarised by the Government as: 'local authorities are being banned from unnecessary health and safety inspections' and 'will instead target proactive council inspections on higher risk activities in specified sectors or when there is intelligence of workplaces putting employees or the public at risk.'[41] The LA Enforcement Code emphasises the importance of

> choosing the most appropriate way of influencing risk creators and by targeting their interventions, including inspection, investigation and enforcement activity, on those businesses and sectors that represent a higher level of risk to the health and safety of workers and the public.[42]

It stresses the importance of proportionality and instructs LAs to follow the HSE's Enforcement Management Model, as well the importance of the Primary Authority scheme as a way to provide more guidance and consistency, and more risk focus. In conclusion, following the adoption of the LA Enforcement Code, a relatively unified model of risk-based inspections applies, at least in theory, to all health and safety inspections in Britain.[43]

As Hawkins has shown, prosecution has already long been a 'last resort' for HSE inspectors. In fact, this went back to the nineteenth century – even though in principle health and safety violations are to a large extent 'criminalised', ie can be subject to prosecution and (in case of conviction) criminal penalties. As a far more frequent alternative, in cases judged serious enough for more than simple advice, inspectors can issue improvement notices (mandating the resolution of a given violation in a set time period) and prohibition notices (adding the prohibition to use a given piece of equipment, facility, establishment etc).

Critics of the changes in health and safety enforcement in Britain in the past 15 years have spoken of a complete collapse in enforcement – *Hazards* magazine speaking of a 'neutered watchdog'.[44] Notices, however, have continued to increase and decrease irrespective of the government in place and of reform trends (see Figure 15.1).

---

[38] Enforcement Policy Statement (2015), Health and Safety Executive, available at www.hse.gov.uk/enforce/enforcepolicy.htm.

[39] Enforcement Management Model (2013), Health and Safety Executive, available at http://www.hse.gov.uk/enforce/enforcement-management-model.htm.

[40] See the HSE website for an introduction and the full text, available at www.hse.gov.uk/lau/la-enforcement-code.htm.

[41] Taken from the Government website's summary page on the Code; see www.gov.uk/government/news/new-code-curbs-unnecessary-council-safety-checks.

[42] www.hse.gov.uk/lau/la-enforcement-code.htm, p 4.

[43] See detailed statistics on LA inspections at www.hse.gov.uk/lau/enforcement-lae1-returns.htm.

[44] (2010) 111 *Hazards*, available at www.hazards.org/votetodie/neutered.htm.

Figure 15.1 Number of enforcement notices issued by HSE including both improvement and prohibition notices

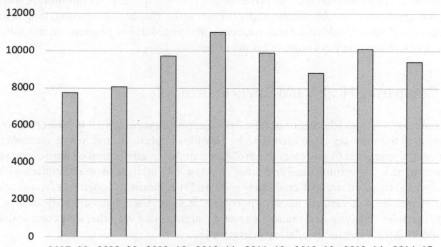

Sources: HSE Annual Reports 2011–12 and 2014–15.

Researchers have found that, quite logically, HSE tends to focus its prosecutions on cases that not only meet the evidential and public interest tests of the Code for Crown Prosecutors[45] but among these, on those where it assesses that the chances of successful conviction are maximal.[46] Indeed, the conviction rate has been around 95 per cent for the past few years. While a high conviction rate does suggest an efficient use of resources, the fact that HSE annual reports feature the conviction rate as one of the indicators[47] may introduce a bias in incentives. Performance indicators and targets have an impact on staff behaviour, and experience in other law-enforcement bodies eg public prosecutor offices and police departments suggests that using such indicators can, over time, discourage officers from attempting prosecutions that are relevant, but have a lower chance of success, because they would decrease the rate of convictions.[48] Per Tilindyte, there are 'several sets of explanations put forward' by HSE management for the decrease in prosecutions, in particular the 'rebalancing of resources towards more advice and guidance' but also the fact that 'the criminal justice system is seen as increasingly time consuming'.[49] In fact, HSE staff seems to have become increasingly focused and efficient at maximising their enforcement effect: the percentage of convictions and the average penalty per conviction are clearly on an upwards trend, as is the ratio of notices per inspection.[50]

Thus the assertion that there has been a collapse in enforcement, and a trend of 'under-enforcement' does not hold up to scrutiny – even less, we would argue, the same authors'

---

[45] 'Code for Crown Prosecutors' (London, Crown Prosecution Service, 2018).
[46] See Hawkins (2002); Tilindyte, *Enforcing Health and Safety Regulation* (2012).
[47] HSE 2017–18 annual reports, table 2 (p 29), see: www.hse.gov.uk/aboutus/reports/ara-2017-18.pdf.
[48] See Mark Ramseyer, Eric Rasmusen and Manu Raghav, 'Convictions versus Convictions Rates: the Prosecutor's Choice' (2009) 11 *American Law and Economics Review* 47.
[49] Tilindyte (n 34) 143.
[50] ibid, 149 and 238.

even more radical claim of 'regulatory surrender'.[51] Still, their point that there has been a tendency to resort less to criminal prosecutions is not disputed. The question is whether such an approach – less inspection visits overall, more risk-based targeting, emphasis on guidance and advice, risk-based enforcement with limited use of prosecution but substantial use of notices – delivers positive results or not.

B. Comparing Health and Safety Outcomes

The only way to assess whether or not the British approach is effective is to look at outcomes. Because of the time-lag issue identified by Hawkins,[52] occupational health outcomes are particularly complex. In any case, the problem remains of attribution of improvements to enforcement, or to technological and other changes.[53] To address these difficulties, we have opted to: (a) focus on occupational safety only, and specifically by looking at fatal accidents only, as problems of variable under-reporting of non-fatal accidents are well-known; and (b) to consider relative performance of several countries that are otherwise comparable, to try and look for a specific regulatory delivery effect.

i. The Complex Issue of 'Comparability'

Saying that several jurisdictions are 'comparable' is difficult and involves looking at a number of variables. Differences between Britain, Germany and France are real – but the average differences are in many cases smaller than the intra-country differences (eg on GDP per capita, where the gap between south-east and northern England or between Bavaria and Sachsen-Anhalt is larger than the aggregate Britain–Germany difference). All three are advanced economies, with comparable GDP levels and technological development, some of the earliest to have industrialised and have created a health and safety regulatory system (Britain being first on both counts). The population size and enterprise population are both also relatively similar (Germany is larger on both counts, but all are within the same 'group' among EU countries). Different employment structures (sectors, size of businesses, etc) are corrected for by Eurostat. The question of different 'cultures' is more complex and disputed.

Many sweeping generalities and unfounded assumptions circulate on the different cultures and their characteristics (and effects), but few (if any) hold true when confronted with careful examination of facts and data. As Chang reminds us, the stereotypes that cast Germans as more hard-working and more respectful of rules were reversed in the nineteenth century, when British writers found them to be 'lazy' and 'lying'.[54] The recent Volkswagen emissions scandal is, from this perspective, a welcome reminder that stereotypes have little

---

[51] Steve Tombs and David Whyte, 'A Crisis of Enforcement: The Decriminalisation of Death and Injury at Work', Briefing 6 (Centre for Crime and Justice Studies, 2008), 8, available at: www.crimeandjustice.org.uk/sites/crimeandjustice.org.uk/files/crisisenforcementweb.pdf.

[52] Hawkins (2002) 10.

[53] ibid, 9.

[54] Ha-Joon Chang, *Bad Samaritans. The Myth of Free Trade and the Secret History of Capitalism* (London, Bloomsbury Press, 2007).

to do with reality. From our perspective of making 'modest' comparisons, not attempting to model or draw strict quantitative inferences, the similarities between the three appear large enough, with a long history of state building, public administration, legal compliance, social services, etc.

Assessing how similar cultures are in relation to safety is difficult. At the highest level, mortality rates by age group are an important indicator – but of course they reflect a number of factors, with income level the most important, including eating habits and healthcare systems, meaning that a specific impact of 'safety culture' is difficult to spot.[55] Road safety is again an indicator that is influenced by factors such as geography (larger, more rural countries with more secondary roads traffic, such as France, typically get worse safety outcomes). Looking at mortality from *all* accidents, and not just accidents at work, appeared the most suitable way to assess overall comparability.

Eurostat statistical series on fatal accidents are broken down by age and cause/type of accident.[56] Beyond the many variations that can be observed, the data at least does not suggest that one of the three countries would be safer 'across the board'. Figures 15.2 and 15.3 show both the aggregate data (overall mortality rate from accidents) as well as the age breakdown and some of the breakdown by cause of accident. Figure 15.2 shows that average mortality is similar in Germany and the UK (both performing better than EU average). While accidental mortality is higher in France, it is not consistently so across all categories; rather, France's under-performance is driven primarily by accidents affecting people over 65 years of age. Working-age accidental mortality in France is in line with the EU average, and close to Germany and the UK.

Considering the cause of accident (see Figure 15.3) shows that there is no consistent over- or under-performer among the three countries – each has at least one type of cause for which it is performing much better, or much worse, than average. While the UK, for instance, has less mortality from falls or transport accidents, it has a higher rate of poisoning. France's overall under-performance is primarily driven by 'others', a Eurostat category that consolidates a large number of sub-categories from the WHO ICD-10 classification, making it impossible to pinpoint where the divergence comes from.[57] We can at least conclude that: (a) Germany's and the UK's situation in terms of accidental deaths overall is similar; (b) while the situation in France overall is worse, the difference is much smaller when considering the age groups under 65 years; and (c) even in France, accidental mortality is not consistently higher (in some areas it is lower than in Germany and/or the UK).

This suggests that, if cultural factors are at play, they are not uniform – none of these countries appears to have a worse 'safety culture' in general, but each has some specific safety weaknesses. This at least validates the possibility of singling out occupational safety data and regulatory delivery, and seeing what differences exist. Based on the overall accident

[55] See Ira Helsloot, *Veiligheid als (bij)product – Over beleidsontwikkeling in ineractive tussen* (Nijmegen, Radboud Universiteit, 2012).

[56] Data sources – see summaries at http://ec.europa.eu/eurostat/statistics-explained/index.php/Accidents_and_injuries_statistics and https://ec.europa.eu/health/sites/health/files/data_collection/docs/idb_report_2013_en.pdf – detailed data comes from the Eurostat database, indicator 'Causes of death – standardised death rate by residence [hlth_cd_asdr2]'.

[57] Available at www.who.int/classifications/icd/en.

Figure 15.2 Standardised mortality rate from accidents (per 100,000 inhabitants) in 2014 in Germany, UK, France and the EU: totals and by age group

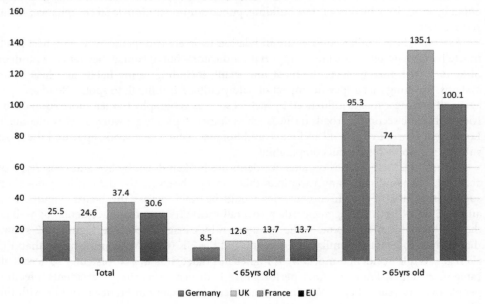

mortality data, we could expect that all three countries should perform no worse than the EU average, and that the differences between them should be limited, given that occupational accidents include a large number of causes, and could at first be expected to behave in

Figure 15.3 Standardised mortality rate from accidents (per 100,000 inhabitants) in 2014 in Germany, UK, France and EU: by type of accident (under 65s only)

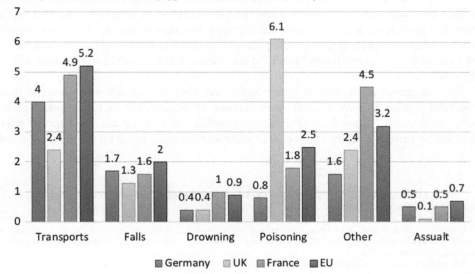

line with 'overall accidents for under 65'. As we will see further, however, this is not the case and differences in fatal occupational accidents are much stronger.

ii. Health and Safety Outcomes in Britain, Germany and France

As already stated, we rely here on fatal occupational accidents only. Because fatal accident rates are low, a change of a few units from year to year can lead to important changes in percentage points – thus it is important to compare averages over a longer period than a single year. The Eurostat definition since 2008 includes

> all accidents in the course of work, whether they happen inside or outside the premises of the employer […] in public places or during transport (including road traffic accidents or accidents in any other mean of transportation) and at home (such as during teleworking)

though it excludes 'accidents on the way to or from work'. Statistics are also held 'excluding transport', and these are the ones the HSE generally reports for Britain, as transport is not within its mandate.[58,59] We will consider here both statistical series.

As pointed out by Tombs and Whyte, the exclusion of traffic accidents involving 'at work' vehicles is important – it increases the overall mortality rate, and affects the difference between British, German, and French fatal injury rates, as well as part of their evolution.[60,61] While Britain performs better overall than Germany and consistently better than France, the difference is far sharper when excluding traffic accidents, and is slightly reversed in some recent years when including them.[62]

In any event, Britain's performance in occupational safety, using fatal injuries as a proxy, is much better than the EU average, even using EU-15 only, ie the 'oldest' (and wealthiest) members. It is vastly better than France's (2008–14 average of 3.8 including traffic accidents or 2.68 excluding them; see Table 15.1). For Germany, excluding traffic accidents, the gap is constantly in favour of Britain and has remained remarkably constant (33 per cent lower during 1998–2014, 29 per cent lower for 2008–14, and 32 per cent in 2014). In recent years, including traffic accidents, Britain's performance appears to have plateaued (and even worsened in recent years), whereas Germany's improved markedly.

While their performance is similar on average over 2008–14 (Britain's rate being five per cent lower), there are important year-on-year swings and Britain's rate veers from 60 per cent lower in 2008 to 60 per cent higher than Germany's in 2013. Overall, swings in data including traffic accidents seems to be substantially stronger, possibly linked to a higher number of factors that could influence the overall rate, and the potential for 'catastrophic' road accidents having an influence on the data. Crucially, Britain performs

---

[58] Available at www.hse.gov.uk/statistics/european/european-comparisons.pdf.

[59] Available at www.hse.gov.uk/statistics/pdf/fatalinjuries.pdf.

[60] Available at www.hse.gov.uk/statistics/european/european-comparisons.pdf.

[61] Available at http://www.hse.gov.uk/statistics/pdf/fatalinjuries.pdf.

[62] All standardised incidence rates for fatal accidents are per 100,000 workers. For the methodology, see Eurostat (2013), 'European Statistics on Accidents at Work (ESAW) – Summary Methodology', available at http://ec.europa.eu/eurostat/en/web/products-manuals-and-guidelines/-/KS-RA-12-102. Pre-2008 data excludes traffic and transport accidents (even if work-related or during work time), while data since 2008 includes them (but Eurostat also offers tables for incidence rate without these).

Figure 15.4 Standardised rates of fatal occupational injuries 2008–14 excluding traffic- and transport-related[63]

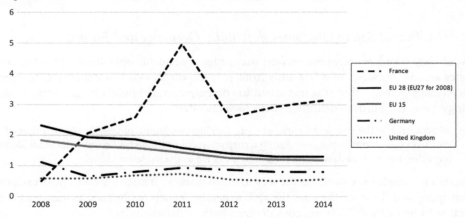

Figure 15.5 Standardised rates of fatal occupational injuries 2008–14 including traffic- and transport-related[64]

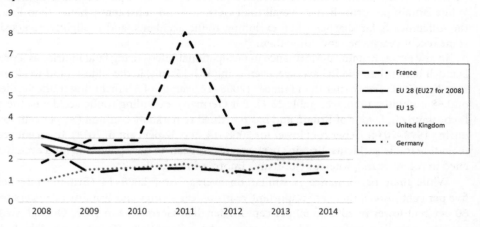

far better in areas where the HSE has competence (excluding transport) than where it is not active (transport-related).

France has a rate of fatal occupational accidents (including transport) that is very high: a 2008–14 average of 3.8, more than 50 per cent above the EU-15's and 2.5 times more than Britain's or Germany's. The gap with Britain and Germany is even greater when excluding traffic accidents. France has the seventh worst average over 2008–14 in both indicators. It seems to be sliding in relation to the performance of other 'old Member States': over

---

[63] Eurostat data.
[64] Eurostat data.

Table 15.1 Average standardised rates of fatal occupation injuries 1998–2014

	Average (excluding traffic- and transport-related fatalities)			Average (including traffic- and transport-related fatalities)
	1998–2007	*2008–14*	*1998–2014*[65]	*2008–14*
United Kingdom[66]	1.41	0.6	1.07	1.54
Germany	2.14	0.85	1.61	1.62
France	2.97	2.68	2.85	3.8
EU-15	2.56	1.44	2.11	2.31
EU-28 (EU-27 until 2008 included)	NA	1.67	NA	2.55

the period 1998–2007, four of the EU-15 had worse performance while since 2008 only Portugal (and Austria, if traffic-related accidents are included) has worse performance.

Over the period 2008–14, Britain retains on average the lowest fatal injury rate in the EU (excluding traffic accidents), with Slovakia, Germany, and the Netherlands coming close (in that order), and the Scandinavian countries close behind. For 1998–2008, the best performance was Sweden's, followed by Britain, the Netherlands and Finland. Including traffic-related accidents, the United Kingdom is third and Germany fourth over 2008–14.[67]

As for Germany, while it was performing relatively badly in the 1990s, its OSH results have improved very markedly and it reached the 'leading group' inside the EU in the past ten years.

iii. Health and Safety Inspection Numbers in Britain, Germany and France

Having considered outcomes, let us look at OSH regulatory delivery practices: inspections numbers; targeting methods; enforcement 'style'; and compliance promotion. As Tilindyte has shown, the structures and practices in Britain and Germany differ significantly, and France is equally different (though in some ways closer to Germany). Structural differences mean that comparisons are imperfect, because the scope covered differs in each country.

OSH inspections in Germany are conducted by two sets of bodies: state officials working for the federated states (*Länder*) in the Enterprise Supervision services (*Gewerbeaufsicht*),

---

[65] Due to change in methodology in 2008, this average is only for informational purposes.

[66] Eurostat data from 1998 to 2007 refer to Great Britain and not the United Kingdom, as for the timeframe 2008–14.

[67] The best ranked country including traffic accidents, is Greece. The small difference between the rate excluding and including them may suggest under-reporting of the labour-related character of some road accidents (as its general road safety level has improved enormously but remains worse than most of the OSH 'good performers'). Over 1998–2007, Greece's OSH performance is far worse, suggesting that its excellent rating post-2008 may be (in a paradox frequently observed in OSH) linked to the brutal economic crisis (the more 'marginal' businesses close, activity is lower and more time available, construction practically shuts down, etc).

and employees of the mandatory insurance providers (*gesetzliche Unfallversicherungen*). The latter focus exclusively on occupational safety and health issues (checking compliance with norms meant to reduce accidents and illness, and thus insurance payments) while the former have a broader, looser mandate. In some *Länder*, the *Gewerbeaufsicht* are assigned other missions such as environmental or product safety, while in some their organisation has been devolved to the local (municipal) level.[68] These inspectors also control legislation relating to child labour, work time, etc, but not 'provisions of collective agreements, and they do not enforce legislation in relation to social security and employment contracts, such as the payment of wages or dismissal'.[69]

In France, The Labour Inspection (*Inspection du Travail*) is responsible for all labour-related legislation: OSH; vulnerable categories; work time; wages; holidays; dismissals; etc.[70] While the majority of its visits to enterprises correspond to 'controls' (inspections), a number of them are conducted to respond to labour disputes. Like in Germany, however, additional inspections purely on health and safety at work, are conducted by insurance bodies – the *CARSAT* (*Caisses d'Assurance Retraite et de la Santé Au Travail* – Pension and Occupational Health Funds), one per region. This similarity with Germany is due to France's imitating (and adapting) the Bismarckian model in 1945. The Labour Inspection itself is structured nationally, but operational work is planned at the regional level, and inspectors have very high autonomy vis-à-vis their hierarchy.

In short, while the German and French 'insurance' structures are focused solely on OSH, the state inspections look at other issues, and therefore a certain percentage of their inspection time and regulatory delivery efforts are not OSH-related. This means the comparison of numbers has to be corrected somewhat; on the other hand, HSE is mandated to look at 'health and safety' in a holistic way, going beyond the occupational angle, and is also responsible for major hazards facilities (EU *Seveso* Directive), which falls to other bodies in France and Germany, thus the correction goes both ways. In addition, in Britain, local authority EHOs conducting non-OSH visits (eg focusing on hygiene) can also look 'on the side' at OSH issues, thus conducting a form of monitoring that may improve the overall coverage and ability to identify risks. As we will see, the extent of the difference in numbers means that all these nuances are unlikely to affect the general trend (see Figure 15.6).

In France, OSH inspections seem to suffer from sustained problems in relation to data: a significant (but not quantified) number of inspectors refuse to record inspection visits in the Labour Inspection's information management system, meaning that the number of visits (and of enforcement measures) is only an estimate. An internet search on the previous or latest IT systems (Cap Sitere, then Wiki'T) shows mainly trade union calls to boycott. Large year-on-year variations may thus, in addition to changes in internal organisation and variations in available staff, reflect serious variations in the level of under-reporting. The Ministry of Labour publishes yearly reports to the International Labour Organization that include inspections and enforcement statistics,[71] but they repeatedly point out

---

[68] Tilindyte (n 34) 166–67, 175.

[69] ILO's summary page on Labour Inspection Structure and Organization in Germany, available at www.ilo.org/labadmin/info/WCMS_209470/lang--en/index.htm.

[70] See *Direction Générale du Travail* (2015) at 9–26, available at http://travail-emploi.gouv.fr/IMG/pdf/l_inspection_du_travail_en_france_en_2015.pdf.

[71] See *Direction Générale du Travail* (2000–15).

the data-quality problems.[72] There seems to be a general trend of a decreasing number of inspections in all three countries (see Figure 15.6), but it is less clear in France over 2000–15, with numbers going up or down repeatedly (which may be an illusion due to varying rates of reporting).

Comparing between countries requires the adjustment of the number of inspections proportionally to the population being controlled. Ideally, inspection rates should be normalised correcting for different economic structures, but only German data would potentially be detailed enough to allow this. Correcting for differences in population requires a decision as to which indicator to use. To reflect the focus of OSH inspectors on enterprises with employees, we have decided to use the number of employees, taking the figure for businesses to more than ten employees. This indicator is nearly identical with the total population ratio. The ratios for total active population or for number of businesses would have been very different, reflecting different employment dynamics and enterprise structures, but these would fit less with the focus of OSH work.[73] Figure 15.6 shows these standardised inspection numbers corrected for business population, with Germany 2011 as 100.

Figure 15.6 Standardised number of inspections in 2011–15 (corrected for business population; Germany 2011 = 100)[74]

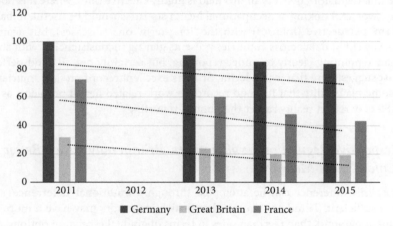

For the past ten years, OSH inspections have been roughly three to four times more frequent in Germany, and twice more in France than in Britain. The gap with Germany has increased in recent years, while the unreliability of French statistics makes the

---

[72] See in particular *Direction Générale du Travail* (2000) [*L'inspection du Travail en France en 2000 – les chiffres clés. Rapport au Bureau International du Travail*, Ministère de l'emploi et de la solidarité, Paris, 2000]. This report indicates that all statistics on inspections published in the 1990s are essentially worthless because of erratic reporting rates and low reporting accuracy (190).

[73] Löfstedt has recommended not inspecting businesses with no employees except when their type of activity could pose a significant risk to outsiders. This policy, while not having the force of law, is widely implemented in Britain (and in fact was most probably widely implemented already before the report). French labour inspectors focus on salaried workers, likewise, and not on the self-employed.

[74] For details of methodology see Florentin Blanc, *From Chasing Violations to Managing Risks: Origins, Challenges and Evolutions in Regulatory Inspections* (Cheltenham, Edward Elgar Publishing, 2018).

trends unclear. The downward trend is clear in Germany as well, but it is stronger in Britain. While the many imperfections in data would lead to discounting small differences, ratios of two or three times (and more) clearly show that OSH inspections are significantly less frequent in Britain than in the two comparators.

Three times more frequent inspections (and more) for outcomes that have been in the long term generally far worse and (at best, if taking the most favourable indicator) are now equivalent appears like a strong indication that inspections and enforcement practices in Germany are clearly less efficient than in Britain.[75] This example clearly shows that the naïve assumption that 'more inspections' will automatically mean 'better outcomes' is mistaken; it also leads us to ask what makes British regulatory delivery so much more effective.

C. Understanding Results: Looking at Regulatory Delivery Practices

On the most reliable indicator (fatal accidents), Britain has generally been performing significantly better than Germany (though the latter has improved its results in recent years), and many times better than France. British performance is worse in areas where OSH regulators are not involved (traffic-related accidents), but this only strengthens the evidence that regulatory delivery in this field is highly effective (and, where it is not present, results are worse). Looking at occupational health statistics would be useful, to balance the 'short-term' perspective (injuries) with the 'long-term' one (diseases), but again Labour Force Survey (LFS) data across countries presents glaring inconsistencies, with some good performance pointing clearly to under-reporting, but certainly not *all* good performance. Let us just suggest here that, considering Britain's excellent record on fatal injuries, there is at least some plausibility that its good record on work-related health problems as reported by the LFS may reflect reality rather than under-reporting.[76]

i. A 'Responsive Regulation' Explanation – Britain may have a Better Set of Enforcement Measures

Explaining this difference can be attempted through a traditional 'deterrence' angle, but it seems insufficient. Tilindyte suggests that British inspectors may have a more adequate 'enforcement pyramid' than German ones in terms of gradual escalation options, considering not only the letter of the law but the actual practice.[77] Although the HSE only has notices at its disposal, their publication of enforcement notices (public registers)[78] adds a powerful 'naming and shaming' effect. She concluded that the strength and flexibility of notices was such that HSE inspectors and management showed little interest in using new administrative penalties in addition to existing options of criminal prosecution and notices.[79]

---

[75] One could even use this as a possible indication that OSH outcomes have no relation at all to inspections and enforcement practices. For the many reasons exposed in earlier chapters and sections, we believe this would be an excessive claim – but surely this example shows once again that there is no direct correlation between more inspections and better outcomes.

[76] See 'European Comparisons – Summary of UK Performance' (Health and Safety Executive, 2017) 4.

[77] Tilindyte (n 34) 230–74.

[78] Available at www.hse.gov.uk/notices.

[79] Tilindyte (n 34) 249–50 and 257–66.

German inspectors have in theory more varied and powerful administrative sanctioning tools, but in practice (perhaps due to complexity of procedures, ignorance of the option to impose corporate rather than individual sanctions, 'culture') use them very rarely.[80] Concerning criminal sanctions, she likewise concludes that both probability and potential severity are somewhat higher in Britain – and that the lack of corporate liability could be a significant limitation in Germany.[81] These relative weaknesses are important, though we doubt they can explain the scale of the difference in efficiency, particularly considering numerous research results showing the limited role of deterrence in shaping compliance[82] (see also chapter twenty-two).

Evidence from France is likewise mixed for a deterrence-based explanation to the divergence between enforcement efforts and outcomes. In recent years, French labour inspectors have indeed made less use of formal sanctions, at least to the extent that data is correctly reported (which, as indicated above, is far from certain). Following legal changes in 2014, French labour inspectors now have significant powers to inflict administrative fines – including in the OSH sphere since 2016 – but it is still unclear how much they are using them for labour safety.[83] The vast majority of follow-up measures after labour inspections are official letters (warnings) that are not a formal enforcement measure and carry no penalty. The numbers in Table 15.2 (again, affected by significant under-reporting) show that this is very frequently used. Labour inspectors can also use improvement notices (including prohibition notices), like in Britain, and these powers (as well as investigative ones) have been again increased in 2016.[84] In recent years, based on reported data, improvement notices seem to have been used far less frequently than in Britain – even more so considering that at most two-thirds of these would have been OSH-related.[85] The highest level of sanction is the *Procès-Verbal* (PV), through which the inspector formally notifies the Public Prosecutor of the violation. It is again unclear if the reported numbers are correct, but in any case they need to be deflated because not all of them are actually taken up by prosecutors. Criminal prosecution is marked by very long delays (sometimes several years), so complete data is only available with a long time-lag.

Overall, between under-reporting by labour inspectors and prosecutors' offices, complex codification (detailed statistics itemise the number of violations recorded and points of law quoted, which are far higher than the number of economic operators actually sanctioned), delays in procedures, etc it is difficult to have certainty, but Table 15.2 is as good an approximation as can be obtained based on public data.[86]

---

[80] ibid, 270–71.

[81] ibid, 269–70.

[82] See Tom Tyler, *Why People Obey the Law* (Yale, Yale University Press, 1990); Tom Tyler, 'Procedural Justice, Legitimacy and the Effective Rule of Law' (2003) 30 *Crimes and Justice*, 283; Tom Tyler 'The Psychology of Self-Regulation Normative Motivation for Compliance' in Christine Parker and Vibeke Nielsen (eds) *Explaining Compliance: Business Responses to Regulation* (Cheltenham, Edward Elgar Publishing, 2011); Christopher Hodges, 'Corporate Behaviour: Enforcement Support or Ethical Culture?', University of Oxford Legal Research Paper, Series no 19/2015 and Christopher Hodges, *Law and Corporate Behaviour: Integrating Theories of Regulation, Enforcement, Compliance and Ethics* (Oxford, Hart Publishing, 2015).

[83] *Direction Générale du Travail* (2015) 102–291: fines in the first half-year after the legal changes, but all of these relating to illegal work. No data yet on its use in OSH.

[84] For further information see the CHSCT website at https://espace-chsct.fr/toutes-les-actualites-du-chsct/inspection-du-travail-les-amendes-administratives-sont-generalisees.

[85] See *Direction Générale du Travail* (2015) 85.

[86] Sources: *Direction Générale du Travail*, in particular Annexes to the 2013 and 2015 report editions.

From Table 15.2, we can tentatively estimate that there are around 1,000 OSH-related prosecutions per year in France, which is higher than the 600–650 reported in Britain.[87] The British number is, however, more reliable, procedures are significantly faster, and anecdotal evidence suggests penalties may be higher, at least in recent years. The number of improvement notices (5,700) and prohibition notices (2,900) is also far higher in Britain (2015 data).[88,89]

From this uncertain and complex data, we can probably draw conclusions somewhat similar to Tilindyte's concerning Germany: while in theory French inspectors have quite significant instruments, in practice British ones probably have a more adequate 'enforcement pyramid'. The high number of PVs, and the relatively high number of prosecutions undertaken as a follow-up, can be seen as a rather heavy-handed response, but their effectiveness is limited by the long duration of proceedings. Formal improvement notices are used far less than in Britain, even though inspections are far more frequent.

The situation may change now that inspectors have new powers to issue administrative fines, but many studies have suggested that fines are often of limited effectiveness.[90] Increased powers to suspend operations in case of imminent danger can be expected to have a positive impact.

Overall, even though OSH inspections in Britain are less frequent than in France, and far less than in Germany, the share that results in official notices is higher, and the 'responsive' character of the enforcement response (more potential for graded response, more immediate response, more credible threats of escalation)[91] probably makes it more effective. Thus, with a lower inspection burden, and fewer administrative sanctions, the HSE and LAs may nonetheless achieve a higher compliance effect, through 'responsive deterrence'.

ii. Risk Focus in Targeting and During Inspection Visits

Another element of explanation concerns targeting of interventions. Tilindyte presents historical data on inspections, 'deficiencies' identified (for Germany), and enforcement measures.[92] The data is partial (only HSE Field Operations Directorate for Britain,[93] and only *Gewerbeaufsicht* for Germany) but enlightening. While, for the periods considered,

---

[87] HSE, Annual Report 2014–2015 (HSE, 2015) 28.

[88] ibid, 25.

[89] Directly comparing the number of prohibition notices is impossible because French inspectors' powers to suspend operations used to be mostly restricted to construction sites (they were expanded in 2016), and otherwise they had to use a provisional relief judicial procedure, which happened only a few dozen times per year. The number of suspensions on construction sites is not reported as such. Extrapolating from available data, it is probably at least a few hundred per year.

[90] See Tilindyte (n 34); Christopher Hodges, 'Corporate Behaviour' (2015) and Christopher Hodges *Law and Corporate Behaviour* (2015); Erich Kirchler, *The Economic Psychology of Tax Behaviour* (Cambridge, Cambridge University Press, 2007).

[91] Ian Ayres and John Braithwaite, *Responsive Regulation: Transcending the Deregulation Debate* (Oxford, Oxford University Press, 1992).

[92] Tilindyte (n 34) 238–39.

[93] Which is HSE's largest directorate, by far; see www.hse.gov.uk/fod.

Table 15.2 Numbers of Enforcement Actions of Different Types by the French Labour Inspection Body, Extrapolated to Account for Under-reporting, and Estimates of Enforcement Actions Relating to OSH

France Labour Inspection	2000	2004	2005	2006	2007	2008	2009	2010	2011	2012	2013	2014	2015
Number of *Procès-Verbal*		4,950	5,084	4,889	5,777	6,094	7,071	7,506	8,456	7,644	6,708	5,795	4,035
OSH related		1,733	1,839	1,851	2,233	2,354	2,556	2,672	2,978	2,725	2,041	2,028	1,412
% OSH		35%	36%	38%	39%	39%	36%	36%	35%	36%	30%	35%	35%
Follow up known and concluded		3,329	3,009	2,513	3,114	3,094	3,238	3,414	3,325	2,535	1,600	756	129
% known and concluded		67%	59%	51%	54%	51%	46%	45%	39%	33%	24%	13%	3%
Prosecutions – known		1,896	1,668	1,344	1,518	1,433	1,380	1,450	1,406	1,029	743	314	46
Prosecutions – extrapolated		2,819	2,818	2,615	2,816	2,822	3,014	3,188	3,576	3,103	3,115	2,407	1,439
Prosecutions – known – OSH estimate		664	603	509	587	554	499	516	495	367	226	110	16
Prosecutions – extrapolated – OSH estimate		987	1,019	990	1,089	1,090	1,089	1,135	1,259	1,106	948	842	504
Alternatives to prosecution – known		525	508	354	583	638	807	870	835	655	355	190	28
Alternatives to prosecution – extrapolated		781	858	689	1,082	1,257	1,762	1,913	2,124	1,975	1,488	1,456	876
Alternatives to prosecution – known – OSH estimate		184	184	134	225	246	292	310	294	234	108	67	10
Alternatives to prosecution – extrapolated – OSH estimate		273	310	261	418	485	637	681	748	704	453	510	307
Improvement notices (OSH estimate)	6,020				3,261				4,272	3,585	3,494	1,994	1,589
Official letters (non-formal enforcement) [recorded]					161k				226.3k	163k	183.5k	131.6k	119.3k

HSE FOD conducts only 12–13 per cent as many inspections as the *Gewerbeaufsicht*, it issues 55–66 per cent as many notices, and initiates from two to seven times as many prosecutions (although the German authorities also have the ability to impose direct administrative penalties). In other words, German inspectorates visit far more premises, but seem to find problems that are sufficient to warrant enforcement action only very rarely. The numbers presented in the previous section suggest the situation is similar in France (twice as many inspections; far fewer notices). This should be considered also in light of the number of 'OSH deficiencies' identified in Germany, on average 1.5–1.6 per inspection. Thus, inspectors find a vast number of 'deficiencies', but consider most of these to be too mundane for enforcement, or enforcement not to be the adequate response. The same is again true in France: 338,552 legal infringements found in the OSH sphere in 2015,[94] but only a few thousand formal responses.

There are several ways to interpret such findings, including that this may represent 'reluctance' to adopt a formal approach, but there is also a distinct possibility that this reflects a 'net cast far too wide'.[95] German and French inspectors may be over-inspecting, ie visiting a large number of premises where the risk level is low, then identifying 'deficiencies'[96] that reflect a large set of very prescriptive and detailed rules (which make non-compliance likely by their very nature), but declining to enforce because they clearly see that it would be disproportionate (and would likely trigger backlash from their own management or from the public, even if their own professional judgement did not discourage them from enforcing). This means not only that too many premises are inspected, but that too many issues of limited relevance are controlled during the inspection – whereas the HSE not only seeks to inspect only the highest-risk premises, but also to selectively control the aspects of operations that present the most risk, rather than all applicable rules.

In order to improve its regulatory targeting capability, so as to secure the greatest impact on reducing work-related risk, the HSE has developed an IT system (Find-It) which is explained in chapter eighteen. The system has improved efficiency, reduced the time needed to plan, and increased the ratio of serious violations on total inspections (which, given that safety outcomes have not worsened, indicates better detection and not worsening compliance overall).[97] By contrast, inspections in Germany are planned based on a variety of different and non-connected systems.[98] In France, not only is there much resistance to increased use of information management systems (as seen above), but the 'generalist' competence of the inspectorate, and the considerable share of efforts that go into controlling labour legislation in general, may mean that inspectors have less technical competence in OSH, and less time to focus on it.[99]

The fragmentation of the German system goes together with a somewhat weaker management of information, and a less formalised risk-based planning system. German authorities

---

[94] Annexes to *Direction Générale du Travail* (2015) 40.

[95] Tilindyte (n 34) 239.

[96] Which do not necessarily amount to an offence; ibid, 191.

[97] See World Bank Group study, 'Inspections Integration Models' (New York, World Bank Publications, 2018).

[98] Tilindyte (n 34) 182–84.

[99] See *Direction Générale du Travail* (2015) 9–10. This broad competence has been repeatedly reaffirmed in the past 15 years.

used to have regular, 'individualised' supervision of businesses largely independently of risk, before the reduction in resources and change in approach led to more targeting.[100] Much of the targeting is done 'in the absence of *formal* models or comprehensive risk assessment models', with some targeting based on sectors, other on issues, and many cases simply on the inspectors' 'personal experience and expertise'. Formalised models exist so far only in some *Länder*.[101]

Britain adopted risk-management as the foundation for OSH early on: the 1974 Health and Safety Act made risk assessment the norm for all workplaces. Rather than prescribing standards, the 1974 Act emphasised outcomes and left flexibility on how best to achieve them. By contrast, in Germany, OSH remained essentially based on sector-specific, detailed standards-based regulations. The 1989 EC Directive on health and safety at work (89/391/EEC), which introduced 'general principles of prevention'[102] based on risk led to significant changes in the German legal order (but very little in Britain, as the Directive had similar principles to the 1974 Act).[103] The Directive was translated into German law with the 1996 Occupational Health and Safety Act.[104] While the current system (in particular mandatory insurers' requirements) is still largely based on pre-1996 principles, including detailed sector-specific rules, and the uptake of risk assessment by businesses has been slow,[105] this legal change had important consequences. In any case, improvements in OSH outcomes in Germany correlate with the introduction of systematic risk-assessment and risk-management.

iii. Compliance Promotion

Interestingly, professional attitudes between German and British inspectors have some similarities, at least in terms of emphasis on advice and 'informal' rather than formal enforcement.[106] It does not appear to be a 'lack of advice' overall that could explain the relative under-performance of German inspections. In fact, that both Britain and Germany rank among the best performers in terms of OSH in the EU (and globally) suggests that 'informal enforcement', targeted use of sanctions and emphasis on advice and guidance may together be effective. Tilindyte quotes the EU's Senior Labour Inspectors Committee (SLIC) as reporting in 2005 a 'widespread, seemingly institutionalised, assumption that advice is more effective and preferable to [formal] enforcement'[107] and suggests that this, at least, in 'tension' with the SLIC principles which, while they foresee the use of 'informal enforcement', also put some emphasis on adequate powers and formal enforcement.[108]

---

[100] Tilindyte (n 34) 182, 183.

[101] ibid 183, 184.

[102] ibid, 92–96.

[103] The process was contentious. The Directive imposes mandatory prescriptions and does not use any language comparable to the British 'So Far As Reasonably Practicable' (SFARP). 'SFARP' was challenged before the CJEU in 2005 by the European Commission, but the CJEU found in favour of the UK (Tilindyte (n 34) 108), leaving the foundation of British OSH regulation unchanged.

[104] Tilindyte (n 34) 165–66.

[105] ibid, 183.

[106] ibid, 193–94 and 239–40.

[107] Tilindyte (n 34) 239.

[108] ibid 98, 99.

However, the performance of systems that have traditionally put less emphasis on advice and seen more conflict-prone relations between inspectors and businesses, is significantly worse.

France indeed has a high rate of fatal accidents, and a relatively high number of inspections (at least compared to Britain). Relations between inspectors and businesses also tend to be difficult; incidents and the need for police or other protection are reported at length in each report to the ILO.[109] While incidents are reported only in one to two per cent of visits at most, and have decreased in recent years, this appears to be specific to France and not similarly present in Britain or Germany. This may be due in part to the general approach and institutional culture of the inspectorate (with inspectors traditionally seeing themselves as protecting workers against employers, rather than as 'promoting safety', for instance) – and to the fact that inspectors also control employment law, the source of many conflicts. Thus, it could be that a generally more conflict-prone relationship due to labour law controls and the role of the inspectors as 'protectors of workers against employers' results in their recommendations on OSH issues being less frequently heeded, even though they formulate a large number of recommendations each year.

A key difference between the HSE's practices and advice provided by German inspectors (or, even more so, by French ones) appears to be the degree to which, in the UK, advice is provided pre-emptively and with a broad outreach effort, in a way that is designed to be easy to understand and implement. Whereas German inspectors (and French ones)[110] seem to primarily provide ad hoc advice based on their findings and their own experience and understanding, the HSE (and, increasingly, LAs) provide guidance. This guidance is not provided only when an inspection reveals problems, but proactively, to everyone who requests or looks for it (and efforts are made to publicise it). In past years, the HSE also sought to have staff from a variety of communities working in high-risk sectors, so as to be able to tune their messages and delivery style to their audience and achieve higher trust. The HSE has made particular efforts to change communication style and channels to reach audiences that were less receptive to inspectors' advice, eg farmers (one part of the farm safety campaign specifically targeted farmers' wives, for instance).[111]

As Tilindyte points out, advising businesses on how to comply with OSH regulations is a duty of the German state authorities.[112] As she underlines, inspectors 'see themselves primarily as consultants, service providers' assisting with compliance, and this is 'particularly true for inspectors of the accident insurers'.[113] In fact, as we have seen, the SLIC's assessment considered that, if anything, the German system was too far on the side of 'advice' and not enough on the 'enforcement' side. As Tilindyte underlines, changes that started around 10 years ago strengthened the 'service-oriented' advice component of German OSH activities; this change may have contributed to the improvement in outcomes. Still, the primary vehicle of advice in German OSH remains the inspection visit. A (non-exhaustive) look at different government websites covering OSH suggests that significant efforts have

---

[109] See *Direction Générale du Travail* (2015) 55–65.

[110] A more thorough review of information efforts on OSH in France would be needed but to start with there is no Labour Inspection website or a specific page on the Ministry's website. It is also very difficult to find any guidance documents and usually the Ministry signposts back to sector-specific professional associations.

[111] See www.hse.gov.uk/campaigns/index.htm.

[112] Tilindyte (n 34) 190.

[113] ibid, 190.

been made to improve availability and accessibility of guidance, but improvements are still required.

The German system's fragmentation may be part of the problem, as there is a mix of federal and state-level websites to consider, each with a different structure and focus. We reviewed the information available on two state-level websites (Niedersachsen[114] and Nordrhein-Westfalen,[115] the first as an example of a mid-size state with significant manufacturing industry and a centralised OSH service, making research easier, and the second being the most populous and industrial state in Germany), the website of the Federal Ministry for Labour and Social Affairs,[116] and that of the Federal Agency for Labour Protection and Occupational Medicine.[117] In comparison, for Britain, we have only had to peruse the HSE website, which acts as a comprehensive portal for health and safety issues. The German websites appear often inadequate for the needs of business operators, managers and workers, having fragmented information, complex documents, lack of practical examples, etc. It is also difficult to know which portal to use. When real efforts are made to make the information easier to find and to use (as in Nordrhein-Westfalen), this is done at the Land level, and thus likely to be ignored in other parts of the country. Each Land duplicates the others' efforts, and best results are not shared.

A more thorough review of information efforts on OSH in France would be needed, but to start with there is no Labour Inspection website or specific page on the Ministry's website. There is, however, a specific section on 'occupational health tools'. There, many guidance documents can be found, some of which appear excellent in both the quality of advice and how it is given in a concrete, relevant way. There are, however, a number of 'dead links', and the status of these guidance documents is somewhat unclear – there is no certainty for the reader that they provide authoritative, assured guidance, ie that inspectors would be fully satisfied if they are implemented. Some documents are too schematic to be really useful,

---

[114] *Gewerbeaufischt* for Niedersachsen (Lower Saxony), available at http://www.gewerbeaufsicht.niedersachsen.de. There are a number of specific pages eg on OSH organisation in the workplace, protection against specific hazards. The portal also links to practical tools, in particular a safety inspection checklist focusing on hazardous installations (available at www.gewerbeaufsicht.niedersachsen.de/download/30099/Ausfuellbares_Pruefschema_fuer_Sicherheitsberichte.pdf), and (for the same type of safety visits) safety inspection guidelines (available at www.gewerbeaufsicht.niedersachsen.de/download/81617/Niedersaechsischer_Inspektionsleitfaden_2012_zur_Durchfuehrung_der_jaehrlichen_Vor-Ort-Inspektion_entsprechend_16_Stoerfall-Verordnung.pdf). Practical, easy-to-use guidance is, however, rare, and mostly missing eg for construction.

[115] Portal for occupational safety in Nordrhein Westfalen (North-Rhine-Westfalia), at www.arbeitsschutz.nrw.de. The portal is well structured and includes sound guidance on risk assessment and management (eg www.arbeitsschutz.nrw.de/themenfelder/arbeitsschutzsystem_gefaehrdungsbeurteilung/index.php). It has tips, eg on lifting heavy weights, but these are more conceptual than practical (see www.arbeitsschutz.nrw.de/themenfelder/arbeitsplaetze_arbeitsstaetten/heben_und_tragen/index.php). It has tips for builders (www.arbeitsschutz.nrw.de/themenfelder/baustellen/pflichten_des_bauherren/index.php), but is light on practical recommendations.

[116] *Bundesministerium für Arbeit und Soziales*, available at www.bmas.de/DE/Startseite/start.html; pages on labour safety issues, eg www.bmas.de/DE/Themen/Arbeitsschutz/inhalt.html, and for legislation in this area see eg www.bmas.de/DE/Service/Gesetze/arbstaettv.html. On OSH, the website has primarily (a) general descriptions of issues and policy activities in different areas and (b) federal legislation. Practical guidance, if any, is very limited. There is also no easy collection of links to other institutions.

[117] *Bundesanstalt für Arbeitsschutz und Arbeitsmedizin (BAuA)*, available at http://www.baua.de. The portal is heavy on research papers and legislation, but also has guidance documents on topics that can be very useful, eg on handling heavy weights, but these documents tend to be very complex and break down the assessment and recommendations in many components. It targets specialists rather than operators.

some others excessively detailed. Gaps ('dead links') are often in particularly critical areas (eg construction). Overall, considerable efforts have clearly been made to develop these tools, but it is unclear to what extent these guidance documents are taken into account by inspectors and are able to provide 'assured advice' to businesses.[118]

In Britain, by contrast, the HSE website is a single portal for all things 'health and safety'. One of the site's main tabs is 'Guidance'[119] – which then leads into several clear sections eg 'Industries' and 'Topics'. There is a specific section on 'Risk Management'[120] including a set of interactive tools and checklists for different types of premises. There are clear, detailed and practical brochures for a number of key types of risks, eg working with weights,[121] 'slips and trips' (one of the most frequent causes of accidents),[122] or types of establishments such as construction.[123] The guide to 'absolutely essential' health and safety advice in construction has practical, clear, visual explanations. Information is more accessible in Britain, and more usable. The HSE's efforts not only follow a long tradition, but are also part of a cross-government effort to make guidance accessible, clear and authoritative.[124]

iv. Enforcement Predictability and Consistency

Finally, it is plausible that the way enforcement is structured, and discretion framed, influences outcomes. British OSH inspectors' discretion is exercised within a particular set of institutions, practices and cultures that have been formalised in an 'enforcement management framework' that improves transparency and predictability and links the exercise of discretion to risk assessment and responsive regulation.[125]

Enforcement discretion exists in Germany, within the limits of Administrative Procedures Law (*Verwaltungsverfahrengesetz*), and depending on the wording of the law being enforced, but there are no specific guidelines to help inspectors take decisions, and make these more transparent.[126] There are a number of general principles, notably 'equal treatment', 'proportionality', 'necessity', etc.[127] All of these, however, require interpretation, and leave considerably more leeway and uncertainty than the very specific guidance included in the HSE's Enforcement Management Model (EMM).

In France, there is a strong tradition of complete autonomy and full discretion of labour inspectors. Their decisions can of course be reviewed by administrative courts, and general legal and constitutional principles will apply, but this is a longer-term remedy. Since 2015, a reform aiming to introduce more consistency has required enforcement decisions to be

---

[118] See http://travail-emploi.gouv.fr/sante-au-travail/outils-et-guides.
[119] Available at www.hse.gov.uk/guidance/index.htm.
[120] See www.hse.gov.uk/risk/index.htm.
[121] See www.hse.gov.uk/pubns/indg143.pdf (brochure with clear, visual guidance), www.hse.gov.uk/pubns/indg383.pdf (detailed version with assessment charts), www.hse.gov.uk/pubns/indg398.pdf (guidance on use of handling aids).
[122] See www.hse.gov.uk/slips/index.htm including a number of assessment tools, practical tips and brochures, etc.
[123] See www.hse.gov.uk/construction/index.htm, and 'absolutely essential' health and safety brochure, available at www.hse.gov.uk/pubns/indg344.pdf.
[124] Sarah Anderson, *The Good Guidance Guide: Taking the Uncertainty out of Regulation* (London, Department for Business, Enterprise and Regulatory Reform, 2009).
[125] Hawkins (2002).
[126] Tilindyte (n 34) 187–88.
[127] Ibid, 188.

made in a collegial way and endorsed at the level of the 'territorial unit'; and introduced more national level coordination to improve consistency.[128] These changes have, however, faced major resistance from inspectors' trade unions. Thus, predictability and consistency of OSH enforcement in France are only at very early stages of development.

There are two ways in which the clarity, predictability and transparency introduced by the EMM could support safety outcomes. First, through a positive procedural justice effect, by making it clearer for duty-holders how they will be assessed, and how decisions will be taken – resulting in an increased likelihood of voluntary compliance.[129] Second, because the EMM emphasises the importance of risk assessment and of the 'risk gap', it pushes businesses to focus on critical issues. In other words, businesses are incentivised to maximise the safety outcomes for a given 'percentage' of compliance. By contrast, German and even more so French businesses are left with far more uncertainty on what inspectors expect, are more likely to try and increase compliance in all directions, or focus on points that appear clear but may have less impact. Further research could test this hypothesis and assess the impact of these differences.

III. Conclusion

A. Transport-related Accidents – Additional Evidence for Effectiveness

The above discussion suggests two things: that higher inspection numbers do not automatically produce higher compliance; and that higher compliance seems correlated with a more comprehensive approach to better regulatory delivery. It nonetheless does not mean that 'fewer inspections are always better'. First, OSH inspection numbers in the United States are again (pro-rated to the population) several times lower than in Britain, and this time the outcomes are significantly worse. While there are many reasons for this, very low inspection coverage cannot be ruled out as one.[130] Looking at the difference between fatal accident rates including or excluding transport-related ones strengthens the point that more inspections does not (always) help, but regulatory delivery efforts probably do.

Because Britain performs much better excluding transportation-related accidents than including them, we can deduce that its performance solely on transportation-related OSH accidents is relatively poor (since it worsens its average). The source of the problem is regulatory. Under the Reporting of Injuries, Diseases and Dangerous Occurrences Regulations (RIDDOR) which govern occupational accidents reporting, work-related accidents on public roads are not reportable to HSE, since responsibility for investigating them lies with the police. HSE would only get involved if the police identify any serious management failings that they feel led to the accident and as a result refer it to the HSE. Such referrals are,

---

[128] See *Direction Générale du Travail* (2015) 31–32, 34–37, and particularly 38–41.

[129] Tom Tyler, 'Procedural Justice, Legitimacy and the Effective Rule of Law' (2003) 30 *Crimes and Justice* 283; E Allen Lind and Christiane Arndt, 'Perceived Fairness and Regulatory Policy: A Behavioural Science Perspective on Government-Citizen Interactions' in *OECD Regulatory Policy Working Papers*, no 6 (2016).

[130] See Blanc, *From Chasing Violations* (2018).

in practice, quite rare.[131] Even when work-related transport is taking place on public roads, health and safety law still applies and employers are under a duty to manage occupational road risk in the same way as any other risk. HSE and LA inspectors could include this risk in their preventive and inspection work; in practice, however, given limited resources, they rarely do.

This issue has been known for a long time: the Royal Society for the Prevention of Accidents (RoSPA) has been lobbying for a greater focus on road accidents 'at work' for many years, and laid out findings and recommendations in a 2002 report. This report estimated that between one-quarter and one-third of road fatalities in Britain may be work-related, and that 'at-work' road accidents may make up more fatalities than all other occupational injuries (Eurostat data indeed suggests the two to be roughly equivalent, or road accidents possibly a bit more numerous than all other types). It suggested that 'car and van drivers who cover 25,000 miles a year as part of their job' were working in the equivalent of 'acknowledged high hazard sectors such as construction and quarrying'.[132] It found, however, that 'health and safety law is not applied on the road' in spite of existing legal duties.[133] More than a decade afterwards, however, none of these recommendations has been implemented, and the additional resources the report called for have given way to a sharp reduction in resources.

This is doubly interesting for our case. First, this is an illustration of the well-known adage 'what gets measured gets done'. The HSE and local authorities achieve excellent safety results in spite of limited resources, but the lack of attention to transport-related safety leads to worse performance on 'at-work' road accidents that are on par with countries that overall have far worse OSH performance than Britain. Second, it shows that Britain's high OSH performance is not a given, not an automatic result of a 'better culture of safety'. Its better results appear clearly correlated with areas of intervention of the HSE and local authorities, and thus with their active efforts to promote compliance through guidance, risk-focused inspections, risk-proportional enforcement. When these efforts are absent, results worsen (and the somewhat less-well-structured, but nonetheless real, efforts of German OSH inspectors have better results than the regulatory delivery 'gap' in Britain).

B. Reduction of Proactive Inspections and 'Fee for Intervention' – Challenges for OSH in Britain

This case study suggests that there is no automatic correlation between the number of inspections and regulatory outcomes, and that a comprehensive, risk-based and compliance-focused approach to regulatory delivery seems to deliver better results. This does not mean, as seen through the issue of transport-related accidents, that 'no inspections' or 'no regulatory delivery' is better. Thus, while reducing the number of inspections up to a certain level may leave outcomes constant (or even improved, as in Germany), there may be a limit to such an evolution. Some evolutions, decided without proper evidence base, cause concerns.

---

[131] Author's interview with experienced health and safety inspectors in Britain.
[132] See p 1 at www.rospa.com/rospaweb/docs/advice-services/occupational-safety/morr-story-so-far.pdf.
[133] ibid.

In order to reduce burden on compliant businesses, recent UK governments have driven a move towards less proactive inspections. This is very problematic, as proactive inspections are widely considered to be more effective, more efficient, as opposed to reactive ones. The latter appear low-cost (requiring no targeting or intelligence-gathering and relying on accidents, complaints or findings of previous visits). A proper risk-based approach can, however, not be primarily based on reactive inspections, and reactive approaches have a poor effectiveness record as by definition they intervene too late. In fact, HSE has constantly conducted far more proactive than reactive inspections, but the published data shows a sharp reduction in proactive inspections by LAs. Reactive inspections may appear 'justified' in a 'punitive' vision of inspections, but they are simply not the most effective from a risk-based prevention perspective.

A valid question would be whether reducing OSH inspections in Britain, at this stage, makes sense – from a burden perspective, and from an effectiveness and efficiency one. We have seen that OSH inspections in Britain are several times rarer than in Germany or France. They may be close to the point where too-rare visits make it difficult to maintain a robust risk-based targeting system[134] (though there may be solutions in sharing data with other regulators). How, then, do health and safety inspections compare to other types of inspections within Britain, when they are thus singled out for reduction? Considering the data compiled under the Focus on Enforcement initiative of the Department for Business Innovation and Skills – the latest available year being 2012–13 – four agencies[135] conducted most 'business inspections': the EA, the HSE, the Food Standards Agency (FSA) and the Animal Health and Veterinary Laboratory Agency (AHVLA). But OSH inspections were dwarfed by the number of food safety visits: more than 540,000 for the FSA, and over 100,000 for AHVLA. Most of these visits were in fact conducted by third parties and reported by the national regulator (for the FSA, these third parties are LAs). Thus, in 2012–13, OSH inspections made up fewer than 140,000, and broadly 'food-safety related' ones over 640,000. In this perspective, it is not clear that targeting a reduction of OSH inspections made sense even from a pure burden-reduction angle.

It may be that food safety issues warrant a higher level of control from a risk perspective (this would require detailed research on the prevalence of OSH and food risks in Britain, which is beyond our scope), but it may also be that food safety inspection numbers are 'shielded' from reduction by a combination of popular perceptions of risk (food safety being usually high among public concerns), EU regulations, and the fact that nearly all inspections are done by LAs. By contrast, it appears that 'health and safety' gets targeted for reductions because of a combination of mistaken beliefs ('health and safety myths'), limited support from the HSE's parent department (Work and Pensions), and possibly the vagueness of the term ('health and safety' is so broad that many people may attribute regulations and controls to HSE that are completely unrelated to its activities). Whatever the causes, in any case, it seems reducing what is already clearly a very 'lean' inspection number is unlikely to have positive results.

---

[134] See Julia Black and Robert Baldwin, 'Really Responsive Risk-based Regulation' (2010) 32 *Law and Policy* 181.
[135] 2012–13 Regulator Data is available on the government archive 'Focus on Enforcement' pages at https://webarchive.nationalarchives.gov.uk/20160106103952/http://discuss.bis.gov.uk/focusonenforcement/business-focus-on-enforcement-2.

i. Conclusion – Evaluating Regulatory Delivery Outcomes, Both Feasible and Necessary

From the above, we can conclude that evaluating regulatory delivery outcomes is not impossible, and that comparative assessment of methods and results is a useful approach. Achieving a higher level of confidence in results or comparing other domains with less readily available safety data, may of course be more difficult, and require more resources. What this also shows is that this evaluation work is essential. In our case, the two countries with the higher volume of control had worse results, and in the best-performing country, a question remains about how far is too far. Looking more systematically at resources, costs, results and methods of regulatory delivery structures, and doing so in a comparative way, may be an excellent way to improve public administration, and achieve better outcomes by challenging conceptions or approaches that are mistakenly taken for 'obvious' simply because they are traditional, or chime in with prevailing ideologies.

Practices: Risk-based Prioritisation

16

Risk-based Prioritisation

GRAHAM RUSSELL AND HELEN KIRKMAN

In chapter thirteen, we examined the importance for a regulatory agency of being clear about the outcomes that it is working towards and pointed to the challenges that face a regulatory agency in delivering progress towards identified regulatory outcomes within the limitations of scarce resources. In deploying its resources, a regulatory agency needs to make choices about both where it should focus its efforts and how it should do so. At the same time, it will need to be mindful of the importance of making fair, proportionate decisions.

This chapter addresses the question of where the regulatory agency chooses to direct its resources – a practice that is framed within the Regulatory Delivery Model in terms of 'Risk-based Prioritisation'. The closely related question of how the regulatory agency makes decisions about the most appropriate strategies to use to reduce the risks that it has chosen to target – its 'Intervention Choices' – is addressed in chapter twenty.

This chapter will first explore what we mean by risk in the regulatory delivery context and explore its importance for regulatory agencies. We will consider the constituents of risk – 'hazard' and 'likelihood of harm' – and explain what we mean when we talk about the practice of Risk-based Prioritisation. We have noted in previous chapters the dynamic relationship between the elements of the Regulatory Delivery Model, and the particular inter-dependencies between the three practices – Outcome Measurement, Risk-based Prioritisation and Intervention Choices. Risk-based prioritisation relies on the identification of risks to the regulatory agency's outcomes and informs its activities. By understanding and measuring the impact of those activities, in terms of the contribution to desired outcomes, the regulatory agency is then able to review and amend its risk-based prioritisation and the strategies that it uses.

I. Defining 'Risk'

The term 'risk' is used in many different ways in everyday life and this presents a challenge which must be addressed in order to avoid confusion. Dictionaries define risk as 'the chance or possibility of a danger, loss, injury or other adverse consequence'[1] and this sense of danger or loss invariably underpins use of the word. However, it is important to recognise that understanding of the word is context-dependent, as is the extent to which it is seen as

---

[1] Oxford English Dictionary definition.

quantifiable. The public at large may use the term quite loosely and the media will often use it to elicit emotional responses. In contrast, in commercial organisations, risk is often carefully defined, in terms of, for example, financial risk, physical risk or reputational risk. In the UK, risk management by central government is addressed in guidance which defines risk in terms of uncertainty:

> It is a matter of definition that organisations exist for a purpose – perhaps to deliver a service, or to achieve particular outcomes. In the private sector the primary purpose of an organisation is generally concerned with the enhancement of shareholder value; in the central government sector the purpose is generally concerned with the delivery of service or with the delivery of a beneficial outcome in the public interest. Whatever the purpose of the organisation may be, the delivery of its objectives is surrounded by uncertainty which both poses threats to success and offers opportunity for increasing success.

Risk is defined as this uncertainty of outcome, whether positive opportunity or negative threat, of actions and events.[2]

Just as risk is understood in many different ways across society, its use in relation to regulatory delivery is equally understood in different ways, and a plethora of terminology has developed to describe risk-based approaches to regulation. For this reason, the terminology used in this chapter is carefully defined.

The role of a regulatory agency involves managing risks to regulatory outcomes by reducing their likelihood or their impact. Within the Regulatory Delivery Model we talk about 'risk-based prioritisation'. This phrase recognises that the role of reducing risk requires the regulatory agency to ensure that its decision-making, at all levels, is based on an informed assessment of risk and that it prioritises on the basis of that assessment.

In the regulatory context, the concept of risk is two-dimensional, and is a way of classifying or explaining the combination of the magnitude of a hazard and the likelihood that the hazard will cause harm. For the purposes of this chapter, this is referred to as 'regulatory risk'. The concepts of 'hazard' and 'likelihood' are explored further later in this chapter.

II. The Importance of Risk-based Prioritisation to Regulatory Agencies

Regulatory agencies exist, and their continued existence is resourced, because there is a risk of harm that public policy has identified that would not be properly managed without their intervention. Over time the purpose of the regulatory agency is to manage that risk by reducing its likelihood or its impact, or both.

As noted above, a regulatory agency must determine how it can best use its finite resources to achieve its purposes. In making decisions about resource allocation, the regulatory agency faces the challenge of assessing and comparing different threats, and potential threats to the regulatory outcomes that it is working towards. An alternative to a market mechanism for allocation of scarce resources is required but, while risk is widely assumed to be the appropriate alternative, in practice it is poorly understood and seldom comprehensively applied.

---

[2] *The Orange Book: Management of Risk – Principles and Concepts* (HM Treasury, 2004).

The concept of regulatory risk provides regulatory agencies with a currency, or a means of assessing different challenges to their desired regulatory outcomes. It provides a structured way of thinking about relative impacts, positive or negative, and comparing them so that the regulatory agency can direct its efforts in proportion to the risk. We say that 'risk is the currency of regulation' because, like a currency, it allows comparison between different hazards. So, just as I can choose whether to spend £10,000 on a car, a luxury holiday or as the deposit for a house, so risk allows comparison between options with wholly different costs and benefits. Regulatory outcomes can be positive or negative. Financial detriment and physical harm are both losses whilst healthier communities and thriving businesses are benefits. Risks are expressed in terms of harms which can be the prospect of a loss or the failure to achieve a benefit.

Effective regulatory delivery uses risk at every level of decision-making. At the strategic level the question might be: do we in this country need to focus more resources on regulation of financial institutions or food safety? Used in this way, risk can support long-term economic planning, comparing for example the hazards to domestic consumers and to the confidence needed for international trade in the context of the economy's strategic priorities and recognising the role of regulation in establishing confidence in the business environment. At the opposite extreme risk informs operational decision-making: should an inspector use their time to work with a business on their control of fire safety or environmental impact? Used at this level, risk allows assessment of impact and imminence between the immediate hazard of loss of life and property in a fire which, while unlikely, might happen at any time, with the ongoing and certain harm being caused by environmental pollution. This comparison allows prioritisation of action. Whatever the level at which choices need to be made, the challenge is to compare opportunities and impacts which differ not only in the type of harm (human life, environmental degradation or financial detriment) but also over different timespans and territorial effect. By identifying and analysing regulatory risk a regulatory agency can make, or enable others to make, more informed decisions.

It should be acknowledged that risk is not the only way of prioritising and other bases have been proposed. For example, it is argued that the most regulatory resource should be allocated to those operators with the highest propensity to change, the contexts where regulatory activity will have most impact. There is some merit in this approach, particularly if a regulatory agency needs to establish its credibility when new – or following a set-back – by making a visible difference. However, if these choices are not guided by risk, they can lead to a view that the agency focuses on the trivial or headline-seeking which ultimately reduces confidence in the regime or that the agency targets the 'willing' and thereby rewards others for their negative attitude. Others argue that regulatory resource should be focused on the areas of highest hazard. Again, this can have merit, ensuring that the real harms are addressed, but regulators who have pursued this course, without a synthetic view of risk which incorporates likelihood as well as hazard, have spent long years with little to show for their efforts. Both of these arguments, that resource should be focused on areas where change can be most readily achieved or where hazard is highest, can more safely be addressed by transparently considering the loading within the risk framework and treating different shapes of risk differently – something we will return to later in this chapter.

Most regulators will find themselves at some point in a position where resources are allocated on the basis of immediate political priorities or public concerns rather than in line with a thorough-going assessment of risk and comparison of options. This has been considered in the work on risk-reflex reactions discussed in chapter one and is part of the wider challenge of establishing an appropriate interaction between the role of regulation in addressing the urgent concerns of society, expressed through elected politicians or otherwise, and its role in setting and delivering government's long-term goals. The regulatory agency that has confidence in its evidence-based approach to outcome measurement and risk-based prioritisation offers opinion formers and policy-makers valuable tools, including insight into the consequences of the decisions they make.

Other criticisms of risk-based prioritisation are rooted in concerns about resource constraints. 'Risk-based regulation' is sometimes misleadingly aligned with 'light-touch enforcement' and perceived as an excuse for not inspecting every regulated entity or investigating every incident. However, in a finite world resource constraints are an inescapable reality. While risk-based prioritisation is and should be overt and transparent, decisions are always being made about allocation of scarce resources. Operating on the basis of marginal adjustments to established norms may be 'safer' for the reputation of the regulatory agency and preserve a view that everything is being covered but it is neither honest nor forward-looking. In practice the view that the agency could or should be looking at 'everything' is likely to lead to regulators spreading their resources so thinly that they achieve little or no long-term impact.[3]

A. Applying Risk-based Prioritisation at Every Level

The question of targeting of resources and effort in order to maximise the regulatory agency's impact is important on at least four distinct levels:

(a) **In determining priorities between regulatory areas.** This question is most often applicable in terms of the allocation of resources between regulatory agencies and will often sit beyond the control of each individual regulatory agency. However, there are situations in which a regulatory agency has responsibility for multiple regulatory areas – this is the case, for example, for local authorities in the UK. They have responsibility for a wide range of regulation and must determine how they will allocate their resources between consumer protection, food safety, occupational health and safety, and so on. This is challenging – when assessing, for example, the relative negative impact of business practices that leave workers at risk of serious injury, and those that cause significant financial detriment to consumers – and requires a robust use of risk to enable comparison.

(b) **In determining regulatory priorities within a regulatory area.** This is a strategic question for all regulatory agencies, regardless of whether their area of responsibility is narrow – for example, focused on a specific topic or business sector – or broad – regulating across a wide range of sectors. So, for example, how does an occupational health and safety regulator allocate its resources? As noted in chapter eighteen, the UK's Health and Safety Executive regulates an estimated one million businesses in

---

[3] As discussed in ch 1, the approach that says regulators should look at everything also presupposes that such inspection activity is effective. In contrast, having an inspector permanently present tends to reduce the operator's sense of responsibility and can therefore reduce protection.

the UK and is unable to directly intervene with each of them. It prioritises particular sectors and activities on which it then focuses its efforts.

(c) **In determining, in relation to the regulatory priorities identified, the individual regulated entities, premises or activities that should be targeted at an operational level.** For example, a regulatory agency with responsibility for food safety may have identified production of meat products as one of its regulatory priorities. Faced with a defined number of producers – businesses of different sizes producing a diverse range of meat products in differing volumes – the regulatory agency will need to decide which of these it will target for direct interventions, including but not limited to inspections.

(d) **In being clear, at the level of an individual regulated entity or premises, where the focus of any checks on compliance should be.** This requires the regulatory agency's frontline staff to have an understanding of the regulatory agency's strategic priorities and the reasons for operational targeting of the particular regulated entity. It is impor-tant that frontline officers remain mindful of their primary purpose of controlling regulatory risk, recognising that securing compliance with specific regulatory require-ments is, at best, a 'means to an end'. This understanding should inform how the officer focuses their effort, both in terms of the amount of time committed to a particular inspection and the proportion of time spent, during the inspection, on different aspects of compliance. It should also inform the officer's response to any non-compliance iden-tified. A consideration of the seriousness of a compliance breach, in particular how much risk has been created by the failure to comply, is critical to the selection of a proportionate response. Other factors are also important in making these decisions – as they are at the other levels identified here – and these are explored further when we discuss the final element of the Regulatory Delivery Model – Intervention Choices (see chapter twenty).

At all of these levels, risk-based decision-making is important to regulatory agencies. It allows them to prioritise in a robust and comparable manner, ensuring that the regulatory agency's scarce resources are used effectively and that it is able to defend its decisions.

Risk-based decision-making also forms the foundation for proportionate behaviour by the regulatory agency and for this reason, amongst others, it is important to regulated enti-ties. Interactions with regulatory agencies invariably involve a cost to regulated entities. This may be a direct financial cost, for example the payment of fees. Equally, it may be a cost in terms of staff time spent in preparing for and dealing with an inspection or a regulatory agency's request for information. For many regulated entities, particularly small businesses, these costs can be significant. Whatever the benefits that interaction with a regulatory agency brings, there is a direct cost and time spent with an inspector is time away from the business of making money. Proportionality, or lack of proportionality, underpins percep-tions as to whether these costs are fair and justified. It also influences a regulated entity's general view as to whether the regulatory agency behaves fairly.

The UK's Risk and Regulation Advisory Council considered the role of 'risk actors' who, through their actions and interactions, shape perceptions of and responses to public risk, contributing to distorted perceptions of risks which can encourage poor policy-making and decisions.[4] It is important to recognise that regulatory agencies play a part in shaping

---

[4] 'Response with Responsibility: Policy-making for Public Risk in the 21st Century' (Risk and Regulation Advi-sory Council, 2009).

perceptions of risk. They are, themselves, risk actors – not merely passive recipients of the risk environment. The culture of the regulatory agency (see chapter ten) is significant here. For example, where the regulatory agency is risk-averse it is more likely to impose burdens on those it regulates, for example by requiring or encouraging them to take steps that are disproportionate to the level of risk. Where an agency lacks confidence in its future, it will want to raise awareness about negative events in the hope that this will sustain the perceived need for its function. Such approaches influence public perceptions of the risk, leading to a self-perpetuating cycle.

III. Risk Identification and Assessment

The identification and assessment of regulatory risks is complex, and the challenges involved are different for each regulatory agency, depending on the area of regulation that they are responsible for, the regulated entities that they oversee and the context in which they are operating. Former US Secretary of Defense Donald Rumsfeld is widely quoted, and indeed misquoted, but in regard to assessing regulatory risk he was surely right:[5]

> [T]here are known knowns; there are things we know we know. We also know there are known unknowns; that is to say we know there are some things we do not know. But there are also unknown unknowns – the ones we don't know we don't know.

Regulatory risk is not necessarily visible or easily quantified. The visible risks, and the risks articulated by the 'worried well' do not always reflect the true risks to society or to those whose voices are less heard. Risk can and does shift over time, requiring the regulatory agency to review its approach. One of the principal professional skills of a regulatory officer is the ability to identify, define and assess risk.

In attempting to assess regulatory risks, the regulatory agency must consider both dimensions of risk – hazard and likelihood – and these two dimensions are explained below.

A. Hazard

A 'hazard' is anything that has the potential to cause harm, and the hazards with which regulatory agencies are concerned are diverse and far-reaching. They might, for example, involve an adverse impact on individual citizens – perhaps personal injury or financial detriment – or on the environment – for example, through contamination of land or destruction of natural resources. Equally, the harm may be to businesses, for example, through unfair competition.

The magnitude of a hazard is determined by both the nature of the harm that it can cause and the potential scale or extent of that harm. For example, the magnitude of an environmental hazard would be assessed by considering the nature of the associated harms, such as release of toxic substances, and the potential scale of the harm in terms of the area of land and waterways that might be contaminated, the number of people that might be affected, etc.

---

[5] US Department of Defense news briefing, 12 February 2002, available at http://archive.defense.gov/Transcripts/Transcript.aspx?TranscriptID=2636.

In considering the nature of the harm, it is important that the regulatory agency takes into account the concept of 'reversibility of harm', that is, the potential for the harm caused by the hazard to be reversed. For example, in thinking about the regulatory protections afforded to employees, a distinction can be drawn between the hazards addressed by employment law, such as low pay or loss of holiday pay, where the harm might, theoretically be reversed through compensation measures, and those addressed through occupational safety law, which might, at the extreme, cause loss of life. Alongside the size and shape of the risk, this assessment of the hazard creates a sense of different 'colours of risk' – differentiating risks that might otherwise look the same but have considerably different impacts.

Assessment of the level of hazard is an objective activity that involves gathering relevant information and data from a range of sources. This will usually include:

• information about the types of harm and their scale;

• information about the regulated entities with which the hazard might be associated, including their number, locations, nature, etc; and

• data relating to incidents of harm that have resulted from exposure to the hazard, and any identified causes, for example, injuries, fires, cases of food poisoning, consumer complaints, accidents, environmental pollution incidents, etc.

It is important that both the nature and the scale of the harm created by the hazard are considered. For example, at the level of individual food businesses, contamination of a food product with a bacterium such as *E coli* 0157 is clearly a hazard as consumption of the contaminated food product can cause intestinal infection. Taking the example of two food producers – both producing similar food products – the nature of the harm that could be caused by exposure to *E coli* is the same, but the scale of the harm could be very different. For example, it is likely to be lower for a small food producer that sells only within its neighbourhood than for a larger business that supplies high volumes of food products across the country.

At the level of individual regulated entities, regulatory agencies sometimes apply a rule of thumb that says that there is a bigger hazard associated with larger businesses as the potential scale of any harm that they may cause is likely to be greater. However, this rule should be treated with caution. A more accurate assessment of the potential severity of a hazard would involve looking not only at the size of the business but also at the level of relevant activity and at the supply chains in which it is involved. To take again the example of the food producer, two producers may, on the face of it, be of a similar size in terms of turnover or staff numbers but the first may produce relatively small quantities that it supplies directly to members of the public, for example through local markets, while the second may produce larger quantities that it is supplying to catering businesses for incorporation into the meals that they produce. The second business represents a bigger hazard because any contamination of its products will impact on a much larger number of consumers. Further examination of the supply chain might enable the regulatory agency to further refine its assessment of the level of hazard. For example, in the UK, young children and elderly people (the 'under 5' and 'over 75' groups) are known to be particularly vulnerable to *E coli* 0157.[6] Food producers and caterers that supply these vulnerable groups, for example

---

[6] Hugh Pennington, 'The Public Inquiry into the September 2005 Outbreak of E.Coli 0157 in South Wales: Summary' (The Stationery Office, 2009).

through meals in nurseries, schools, care homes and hospitals, might therefore be considered to represent a greater level of hazard.

A second approximation sometimes applied by regulatory agencies, is that the level of hazard associated with a regulated entity will not generally change significantly. However, this rule should also be treated with caution: as businesses grow, diversify and innovate, both the nature of the harm that may be caused and the potential scale of harm may require re-examination. Perhaps a better approach is to assume that the level of hazard associated with a regulated entity is less likely to immediately or directly respond to a regulatory agency's interventions; this is significant in relation to the choices that the regulatory agency makes in allocating its resources, as discussed later in this chapter. For example, in the absence of significant changes to external factors, the level of hazard associated with a large chemical plant will generally remain constant because both the nature of the harm that may be caused and the potential scale of that harm will tend to remain the same. Over time, the level of hazard may be reduced by capital investment such as technological solutions that allow the use of less toxic chemicals and reduce emissions of pollutants. Or the level of hazard could be increased if poor control over zoning allows residential dwellings to be built in the vicinity of the plant. The regulatory agency's interventions may increase the likelihood of technological improvements, for example by providing the business operating the plant with the knowledge and confidence to make such investment, or may influence zoning decisions by good data-sharing with the appropriate decision-makers.

B. Likelihood of Harm

The 'likelihood' of a hazard causing harm is often explained in regulatory contexts in terms of the likelihood of non-compliance although this tends to draw the agency into consideration of operational risk rather than strategic risks where occurrence is not solely related to compliance. As explained earlier, the regulatory agency's role is ultimately to reduce regulatory risks and even at the operational level this is not always achieved by focusing exclusively on reducing non-compliance, simply because not all non-compliance is equal. For example, regulations will often place obligations on regulated entities which are largely administrative in their nature, such as reporting requirements or some labelling requirements. Whilst these requirements may be important – and will often improve efficiency by making the role of the regulatory agency easier – a failure to comply with them does not necessarily result in increased likelihood of harm to the intended beneficiaries of the law. The UK's Health and Safety Executive, in guidance to its officers on enforcement decisions, draws this distinction clearly, noting that some legal duties on employers – such as a requirement to report incidents – do not directly result in control of risk.[7] The guidance considers non-compliance with such requirements, referred to as 'compliance and administrative arrangements' – separately from risk-based issues and states that 'In cases where both risk and compliance issues exist, inspectors should decide on action principally in relation to the control of risk'.

Assessing likelihood tends to be harder than assessing hazard. In regard to operational risk good assessment is heavily dependent on the knowledge and skills of frontline officers,

---

[7] 'Enforcement Management Model' (Health and Safety Executive, 2013), available at www.hse.gov.uk/enforce/enforcement-management-model.htm.

who need to be able to make an informed judgement as to the ability of the management of the regulated entity to achieve and maintain compliance, referred to as assessing 'confidence in management'. The professional skills required to assess the likelihood of non-compliance and to use risk assessment accurately and fairly should be valued by the regulatory agency and incorporated into its competency framework (see chapter ten for further discussion of competency frameworks).

Officers are able to build up a picture of the likelihood of non-compliance by considering a range of information and using their professional judgment to reach a conclusion. This will usually involve consideration of:

- evidence of current and previous levels of compliance, such as data from inspections;
- enforcement actions, internal or third-party audits;
- evidence of awareness and understanding of the regulatory requirements;
- evidence of attitudes to compliance, eg the attitude of management; and
- the existence of robust systems to manage the hazard(s).

An assessment of the likelihood of non-compliance is important both at the level of a market, industry or sector, and at the level of individual regulated entities. This assessment, particularly those aspects of it that inform the regulatory agency's understanding of the capacity of the regulated entity – its ability to change – are essential to the design of effective interventions (see chapter twenty).

C. Risk Rating

The quantification of regulatory risk involves carefully combining assessments of both hazard and likelihood of non-compliance – ignoring one or other of these dimensions of risk can cause the regulatory agency to focus its efforts in the wrong areas. For example, some activities will always represent a high hazard but the risk associated with some high hazard activities can be controlled by good management, often equated by regulators to 'compliant behaviour'. Where the likelihood of a hazard causing harm is disregarded by a regulatory agency, and high hazard activities are equated with high risks, the regulatory agency can misdirect its resources. So, for example, a large chemical plant represents a high hazard as it has the potential to cause harm to people and the environment on a huge scale. However, a well-managed plant equipped with the most up-to-date technology and a strong safety culture will represent a lower regulatory risk than a plant that has outdated technology and less robust management processes. Categorising both plants as 'high risk' may result in the regulatory agency committing the same resource to each. This is likely to cause frustration on the part of the well-managed plant and will also mean that the regulatory agency cannot commit sufficient resource to effectively address the issues presented by the poorly managed plant.

The quantification of relative regulatory risks is often achieved by using a 'risk framework' (sometimes called a 'risk matrix'). A risk framework allows for a 'risk rating' or 'risk score' to be allocated to a particular regulated entity relative to other regulated entities. Equally, it may be used to rate a particular sector or market relative to other sectors or markets. A proper risk assessment model is an important part of the regulatory agency's governance framework (see chapter three).

Risk frameworks vary in their degree of sophistication and may use numerical scoring to a greater or lesser degree but will usually result in the allocation of regulated entities to a small number of 'risk bands' or categories that the regulatory agency can then consider. In the UK, a common approach to categorising regulatory risk was proposed in 2012.[8] This common approach establishes four levels of hazard (High, Upper Medium, Lower Medium, and Low) and five levels of likelihood (Very High, High, Medium, Low, and Very Low), which are combined in the risk framework shown in Figure 16.1 below.

Figure 16.1 Regulatory risk framework

Likelihood of non-compliance

		Very low	Low	Medium	High	Very high
Level of hazard	**High**	Lower Medium	Upper Medium	Upper Medium	High	High
	Upper medium	Lower Medium	Lower Medium	Upper Medium	Upper Medium	High
	Lower medium	Low	Lower Medium	Lower Medium	Upper Medium	Upper Medium
	Low	Low	Low	Lower Medium	Lower Medium	Upper Medium

This risk framework enables a regulatory agency to divide regulated entities into four risk bands: High, Upper Medium, Lower Medium, and Low.

A risk framework can generally be seen to be working well where the proportion of regulated entities falling into the 'High risk' band is small and the proportion falling into the 'Low risk' band is large (see Figure 16.2). This will be the case where a large number of entities or operations are being considered. In sectors with small numbers of operators, or dominated by particular aberrant behaviour, different shapes can emerge, but this is unusual and needs to be well evidenced and monitored over time. There is a temptation for a regulatory agency to take a cautious 'safety first' approach which results in its risk assessments drifting upwards so that the majority of regulated entities are allocated to the 'Upper Medium' and 'High' risk bands. This is unhelpful as it devalues the risk assessment as a tool to assist the regulatory agency in appropriate resource allocation. The regulatory agency's assessment needs to be rigorous and remain focused on relative risks.

---

[8] 'Common Approach to Risk Assessment' (Better Regulation Delivery Office, 2012). Note: the Better Regulation Delivery Office is a predecessor organisation to the Office for Product Safety and Standards.

Figure 16.2 'Risk pyramid' showing the typical shape when you display the number of regulated entities across the risk bands

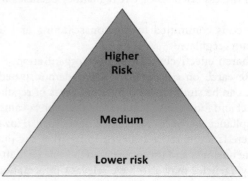

As outlined earlier in this chapter, consideration of regulatory risk needs to take place at multiple levels. A risk framework may be used by a regulatory agency in determining its priorities, for example in relation to particular markets, sectors, premises or products. It may also be used to establish a profile of the individual regulated entities, to inform its operational targeting. For example, the risk rating may be used to determine an intervention frequency.

IV. Data, Information and Intelligence

The proper assessment of both hazard and likelihood of non-compliance is fundamentally reliant on the use of good-quality, relevant information. This improves decision-making and can contribute to the regulatory agency's effectiveness. The OECD Best Practice Principles for Regulatory Enforcement and Inspections emphasise the importance of IT systems in this respect: 'Information and communication technologies should be used to maximise risk-focus, coordination and information-sharing – as well as optimal use of resources.'[9] (see chapter twenty-five, which reports on the benefits delivered through the development of an inspection database in Mongolia).

Within the Regulatory Delivery Model, the examination of the practice of Risk-based Prioritisation involves a careful consideration of how regulatory agencies are gathering, accessing and analysing data, information and intelligence in order to make informed assessments of regulatory risk at all levels. Experience shows that the following factors are common to regulatory agencies that are making good use of data to inform their risk assessment:

1. Adequate resource is devoted to analytical capacity. This means that available infor-
    mation can be collated, analysed and interrogated, generating the intelligence that is
    needed by decision-makers (this argument is developed further in chapter thirteen

---

[9] 'Regulatory Enforcement and Inspections, OECD Best Practice Principles for Regulatory Policy' (OECD, 2014).

looking at Outcome Measurement in terms of how much analytical resource is required, and in the experiences of UK regulatory agencies in chapters eighteen and nineteen).

2.   Adequate resource is committed to horizon scanning and understanding developments in the sectors regulated.

3.   Data is being shared effectively with partner organisations, including other regulatory agencies. Research on risk in the UK has demonstrated that the likelihood of non-compliance can be similar across different areas of regulation, for example environmental impact and food safety, and there is therefore a value to sharing information about non-compliance between regulatory agencies.[10] However, the research also suggests that there is a difference between things that the public can see and things that matter to the business and those that aren't visible or matter less to the business.[11] Other regulatory agencies may also have relevant information on whether there has been a change in management or whether the business is in financial difficulties that may lead it to cut corners.

4.   The sources of information and data being used are diverse, including, for example:

   • data that the regulatory agency gathers itself, such as, records of inspection findings and regulatory advice requested;
   • data that is shared by other regulators;
   • details of complaints about regulated entities and allegations of non-compliance which may be from consumers, employees or other members of the public;
   • incidents that have taken place such as fires, food poisonings, pollution, accidents;
   • market trend analysis; and
   • public health data.

In recent years there has been massive growth in the data available and ever more sophisticated tools are being developed to analyse data and put it to use. The rate of change in the area of data science presents both a challenge and an opportunity for regulatory agencies. Recent work by the UK's Behavioural Insights Team provides a powerful example of the way in which data science could strengthen risk models, helping regulatory agencies to improve their targeting.[12]

V. Using Risk Assessment

Regulatory agencies will need to use their risk assessments sequentially and at multiple levels in order to decide what they will focus on. At each level, the regulatory agency needs to consider the risk profile that has been generated by its risk framework for example, a% 'High risk'; b% 'Upper medium risk'; c% 'Lower medium risk'; d% 'Low risk'. However, a good

---

[10] See 'What is the Value in Regulators Sharing Information: Research Results' (Better Regulation Delivery Office, 2013).

[11] Paul Sanderson, Daniel Banks, Simon Deakin and Chihiro Udagawa, 'Encouraging Inter-regulator Data Sharing: the Perceptions of Regulators: A Report for the Better Regulation Delivery Office' (University of Cambridge Centre for Housing and Planning Research, 2015).

[12] 'Using Data Science in Policy. A report by the Behavioural Insights Team' (Behavioural Insights Team, 2017).

understanding is also needed of a range of other factors, some of which are less tangible. These might include, for example, cultural factors that may increase the impact of certain hazards, perhaps in particular localities or communities or may affect public perceptions of hazard. For example, the risks associated with the consumption of certain raw or semi-cooked foods are higher where safe handling of such foodstuffs is not habitual and not so well understood. Public perceptions and concerns can, in some regulatory areas, mean that the regulatory agency needs to be mindful of the importance of maintaining public confidence. This might, for example, involve a higher level of inspection in certain areas than the regulatory agency might otherwise feel is required, in order to provide public reassurance.

Consideration also needs to be given to the differing shapes and colours of regulatory risk and routes to risk. An understanding of these factors is key to identifying where and how the regulatory agency can have the greatest impact. These factors are examined below, in relation to how they influence decisions on resource allocation.

In determining its resource allocation, the regulatory agency will inevitably need to be clear about those regulatory risks that are not current priorities and will not therefore be resourced. However, it is important that a watching brief is maintained on areas that are identified as 'low risk'. This provides a sense check on the accuracy of the regulatory agency's risk assessment methodology and also ensures that the regulatory agency is not taken by surprise by developments in these areas. Without this, as time goes on there is a tendency for 'low risk' to become 'unknown risk'.

A. Shapes, Colours and Routes to Regulatory Risk

'Shapes of risk' is a term used to explain the differentiation of regulatory risks that have been allocated to the same risk band by virtue of their assessments in different dimensions: hazard or likelihood. At an operational level, for example, in the risk framework shown in Figure 16.3 below, both businesses have been rated as 'Upper medium risk'. Business A has been assessed as having a low likelihood of non-compliance but if non-compliance does arise, the impact would be high. Conversely, Business B has been assessed as having a very high likelihood of non-compliance, but the impact of that non-compliance is low.

It is important to remember that the hazard score is primarily a function of the nature of the business and it is often unlikely that action by the regulatory agency will reduce this, whereas effective action by the regulatory agency may have a significant impact on the likelihood of non-compliance. The regulatory agency's aim is to achieve meaningful reductions in regulatory risk and a judgment-based decision is required to determine the appropriate allocation of resources between Business A and Business B. At best effective regulatory action might shift Business A from 'Upper medium risk' to 'Lower medium risk' whereas sustained change could see the risk associated with Business B move from 'Upper medium' to 'Low'.

At a more strategic level, events in the box occupied by Business B are sometimes called 'Black Swans'[13] – rare but high-impact events. Risk mitigation strategies generally call for proportionate precautions to reduce the impact of such events rather than trying to reduce what may already be an ultra-low likelihood.

---

[13] Nassim Nicholas Taleb, *The Black Swan: the Impact of the Highly Improbable* (London, Penguin, 2007).

Figure 16.3 Example of businesses with different 'shapes of regulatory risk'

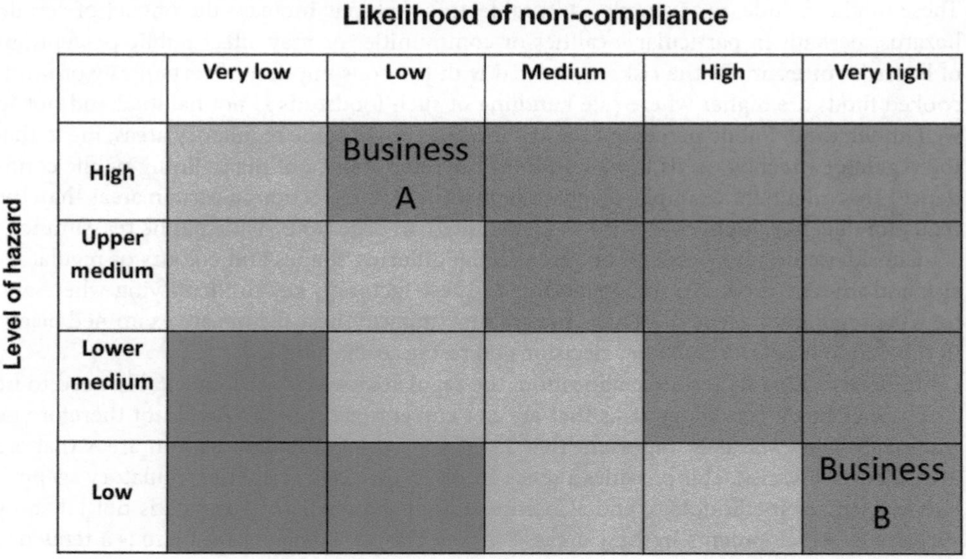

Likelihood of non-compliance

	Very low	Low	Medium	High	Very high
High		Business A			
Upper medium					
Lower medium					
Low					Business B

(Level of hazard — vertical axis label)

'Colours of risk' (discussed earlier) is a phrase used to assert the differences in impact that different types of harm can have on victims, depending on the harm and their vulnerability, and is important to prevent a regulatory agency taking a monochrome view.

The question of the best approach for the regulatory agency to take, in addressing different shapes and colours of regulatory risk, is explored further in chapter twenty, where the additional question of distinguishing businesses that arrive at a similar 'likelihood of non-compliance' for different reasons (sometimes referred to as 'routes to regulatory risk' or 'routes to likelihood') is also examined.

B. 'Earned Recognition'

A review of five large regulatory agencies in the UK in 2008[14] considered their progress towards the use of risk-based approaches, concluding that:

> Regulators accept the need for risk-based regulation and, in most instances have established mechanisms to assess risk and direct resources accordingly. Regulators use risk assessment at both the strategic level to set overall priorities and allocate resources and at the frontline to decide whom to inspect.

However, the review team also noted that, while some of the agencies had made some progress, there was more to do both with regard to the systems and their recognition by regulated entities:

> Some businesses interviewed for the reviews nevertheless believed the regulatory attention they received was not sufficiently related to their actual performance. These businesses felt that the

---

[14] 'Regulatory Quality: How Regulators are Implementing the Hampton Vision' (National Audit Office, 2008).

regulatory effort was targeted at dealing with the inherent risk of a business activity and ignored firms' own capabilities for managing the risk and history of compliance.

Recent years have seen an increased focus in the UK on the use of risk-based prioritisation to deliver what is sometimes called 'earned recognition',[15,16] or more recently, 'regulated self-assurance'.[17] This means that assessments of regulatory risk take proper account of the way in which individual regulated entities, or indeed regulated sectors, are managing their own compliance. For example, where a business is investing heavily in compliance and is committing resource to demonstrate its own compliance, for example through an accredited third-party audit arrangement, this should be recognised by the regulatory agency (see chapter twenty-three). This might mean, for example, that the regulatory agency adjusts its risk rating for the business and consequently intervenes less frequently.

C. Transparency

Transparency around the regulatory agency's risk-based approaches is a powerful means of enhancing accountability (see chapter seven). Where stakeholders recognise that the regulatory agency's priorities are based on risk and understand the manner in which they have been determined, the conditions are created for improved confidence and trust in the agency. Similarly, an understanding of the risk assessment frameworks that are being used to drive operational targeting enables stakeholders to hold the regulatory agency to account and this improves confidence. This applies both to regulated entities – with regard to their own behaviour and their confidence that their own investment in compliance will not be undermined by unfair competition – and to beneficiaries, who need to know that decisions about priorities are soundly based and can be challenged. The UK's Regulators' Code (see chapter five) acknowledges the importance of this understanding, setting an expectation that regulatory agencies will involve stakeholders in the design of their risk frameworks: 'Regulators designing a risk assessment framework, for their own use or for use by others, should have mechanisms in place to consult on the design with those affected, and to review it regularly.'[18]

A lack of transparency around risk-based targeting can contribute to:

(a) a lack of trust in the regulatory agency, which impedes partnership working;
(a) a failure to build a mandate for the ongoing resourcing to deliver the regulatory agency's activities; and
(a) a failure, on the part of the regulatory agency, to target the most significant risks and thereby achieve the desired outcomes.

Transparency can also act as a driver for behaviour change, contributing to risk reduction by regulated entities. For example, transparent communication of the risk framework and

---

[15] 'Government Response to the Consultation on Transforming Regulatory Enforcement' (Department for Business, Innovation and Skills, 2011).
[16] Richard Macdonald, 'Striking a Balance: Reducing Burdens; Increasing Responsibility; Earning Recognition. Report on Better Regulation in Farming and Food by the Independent Farming Regulation Taskforce' (Defra, 2011).
[17] 'Regulatory Futures Review' (Cabinet Office, 2017).
[18] 'Regulators' Code' (Better Regulation Delivery Office, 2014).

of the risk score derived from it in relation to an individual regulated entity can motivate the regulated entity to improve, with the aim of reducing its risk score. This is particularly evident where there is a direct and visible correlation between the risk score and the activity of the regulatory agency, or the costs that it charges to the regulated entity. (See chapter seventeen for details of the Environment Agency's risk-based approach to charges under which activities that present a lower risk face lower charges and higher risk activities attract a higher charge).

Equally, transparency of risk scores can drive improvements where regulated entities can see an associated cost–benefit, such as improved confidence for their customers, as is clearly demonstrated in the example of food hygiene ratings explored in chapter twenty-one.

VI. Key Lines of Enquiry

As discussed in chapter two, we have developed key lines of enquiry in respect of each element of the Regulatory Delivery Model that can be used to assess and understand the current picture in respect of that element. These questions, presented in Box 16.1 in respect of Risk-based Prioritisation, are intended as a starting point on which a regulatory agency or a third party can build in order to give a sense of where strengths and weaknesses lie and to highlight potential for improvement.

Box 16.1 Key lines of enquiry: risk-based prioritisation

Identification and assessment

- Does the regulatory agency understand and articulate risks to its outcomes at strategic and operational levels?
- Does the agency effectively identify and assess risk?
- Does the agency understand its risk context in terms of shape, colour and routes to risk as well as level of risk?
- Does the agency have access to, and use, sufficient capable resources for horizon scanning and understanding changes in risk?
- Does the agency recognise its own role in shaping perceptions of risk?

Data, information and intelligence

- Is the regulatory agency's assessment of risk (in terms of both hazard and likelihood of harm) informed by effective use of all available data?
- Does the agency have access to, and use, sufficient capable resources for risk analysis?
- Does the agency take a proactive approach to identifying and closing data gaps?
- Does the agency share data with other regulatory agencies effectively?

Using risk

- Does the regulatory agency make use of risk frameworks? Are these developed in consultation?
- Does the agency prioritise and deprioritise on the basis of risk at all levels?
- Does the agency's use of risk underpin a culture of being intelligence-led?
- Does the agency maintain a 'watching brief' on low risk?
- Is the risk-based prioritisation process transparent to regulated entities and to beneficiaries?
- Does the agency's use of risk assessment allow regulated entities to engage with their own risk score, earning recognition for their compliance activities?

VII. Summary

This chapter set out to explain the concept of risk as a decision-making tool, both for the effective use of scarce regulatory resources and as a way of ensuring proportionality. We considered the constituents of risk and the ways in which risk-based prioritisation can be used. We have also considered the dynamic relationship between risk-based prioritisation and other elements of the Regulatory Delivery Model.

The next three chapters illustrate various aspects of risk-based approaches rooted in the experience of the authors, which bring to life the ways in which regulatory agencies are using risk.

In chapter seventeen, Paul Leinster and Simon Pollard describe the leading role taken by England's Environment Agency in developing and implementing risk-based approaches to environmental permitting. In chapter eighteen, David Snowball, Joseph Januszewski, Mike Calcutt, Michael Bone and Phil Preece report on the Health and Safety Executive's development of 'Find-IT', an IT-based data intelligence tool that is used by the agency to inform risk-based operational decisions about where to direct its proactive interventions. In chapter nineteen, Marcus Rink, the UK's Chief Inspector of Drinking Water, explains the data-driven approach used to regulate the quality of drinking water supplied by companies in England and Wales.

17

Effective Environmental Regulation, the Use of Risk-based Permitting, Compliance Approaches and Associated Charging Schemes

PAUL LEINSTER AND SIMON POLLARD

I. Introduction

Over recent years governments and their regulators have sought to improve the design and implementation of regulation using risk-based approaches, targeting regulatory effort towards the greatest risks.[1] The UK Regulators' Code[2] and OECD Best Practice Regulatory Principles[3] both stress that regulation should be risk-based. Risk is a combination of the severity of the hazard and the likelihood of the hazard occurring.

Many governments have also sought to reduce administrative costs to businesses and facilitate economic growth. As part of this, a concept of 'better regulation' has been widely promoted that seeks to achieve policy and regulatory outcomes at lower cost for all involved in the delivery of the regulatory requirements. Hampton considered that better regulation should not compromise regulatory outcomes.[4]

II. The Environment Agency and Better Regulation

The Environment Agency (EA) was established in 1996 to protect and improve the environment. Within England, the EA's responsibilities include regulating major industry and waste, water quality and resources, flood risk management, fisheries, and conservation and ecology. Its stated priorities include working with businesses and other organisations to

---

[1] For example: Andy Gouldson, Alec Morton and Simon Pollard, 'Better Environmental Regulation Contributions from Risk based Decision-making' (2009) 407 *Science of the Total Environment* 5283; Philip Hampton, 'Reducing Administrative Burdens: Effective Inspection and Enforcement' (London, HM Treasury, 2005); Christopher Taylor, Simon Pollard Sophie Rocks and Andy Argus, 'Selecting Policy Instruments for Better Environmental Regulation: a Critique and Future Research Agenda' (2012) 22 *Environmental Policy and Governance* 268.

[2] 'Regulators' Code' (Birmingham, Better Regulation Delivery Office, 2014).

[3] 'Regulatory Enforcement and Inspections, OECD Best Practice Principles for Regulatory Policy' (OECD, 2014).

[4] Hampton, 'Reducing Administrative Burdens' (2005).

manage the use of resources, protecting and improving water, land and biodiversity, and improving the way they work as a regulator to protect people and the environment and support sustainable growth.[5]

III. Risk-based Regulation

The EA has been developing and utilising risk-based regulatory approaches ever since it was formed in 1996, as an important contribution to its intent of being a better regulator. This programme included the incorporation of proportionate, risk-based, targeted, outcome-focused approaches within the design, development and implementation of regulations. The EA's model for regulation is based on defining the outcomes to be achieved and the risks to be managed and then targeting action and resources accordingly to ensure people and the environment are properly protected and where necessary improvements are made.[6]

The EA has also taken a leading role in the development and implementation of better regulation approaches. Better regulation relies on balancing rights and responsibilities – between protecting people and the environment, the right of industry to operate with minimal interference, and empowering those who enforce rules to do so in an efficient and effective manner.[7]

To increase efficiency and effectiveness, wherever possible, regulatory approaches within the EA are standardised and simplified both within and between business sectors, across geographic areas, and over time. This helps to provide consistency and a level playing field for all businesses in a sector, and certainty and continuity for planning and investment purposes.

The risks to people and the environment arising from a particular activity will depend on a range of factors including the nature and complexity of the activities, where they are located, and how well they are being managed. Within a risk-based approach to regulation, the degree of effort required to address a particular activity and the choice of interventions should take account of: the magnitude of the risks, the potential impacts posed by an activity, the management and technical systems employed to maintain the risks at an acceptable limit, and the level of confidence the regulator and society have in the organisations and people responsible for the activity, including their management of the associated risks. More time and effort should be spent on individuals or companies carrying out activities that have the highest hazards and those that pose the highest risks because of poor management of compliance with environmental requirements.

The EA has over the years sought to write regulations and guidance in a way that makes it as easy as possible for businesses to do the right thing and also that provides incentives for good performers. This allows the EA to reduce inspections at well-run sites and focus more of their effort on: (a) the highest hazards because of the consequences if control measures are compromised; (b) the highest risks; (c) persistent poor performers; and (d) those who deliberately decide not to comply.

Over time, the body of environmental legislation and regulations the EA implements was added to and modified. Periodic review of the legislation is therefore necessary to

---

[5] See www.gov.uk/government/organisations/environment-agency/about.
[6] See 'Delivering for the Environment: A 21st Century Approach to Regulation' (Environment Agency, 2015).
[7] Peter Kellett, 'Is the Better Regulation Agenda Producing Better Regulation?' (2008) 20 *Environmental Law and Management* 221.

ensure the overall regulatory requirements are coherent and consistent and that they are compatible with effective and efficient regulatory approaches that minimise administrative costs and bureaucracy whilst maintaining the necessary protections for people, wildlife and the environment.

The Environmental Permitting (England and Wales) Regulations 2007 which came into force on 6 April 2008 are a product of such a review. These regulations replaced over 40 pieces of unconsolidated legislation with a single set covering: who needs a permit and who needs to register an exemption; a single permitting and compliance system; and how European Directives and domestic policy requirements are delivered through permits and compliance. The Environmental Permitting Regulations delivered the same outcomes at one-third of the length of previous legislation. This reduction enabled further simplification in guidance, procedures, forms, IT systems and the training needed to understand and deliver the system. The Environmental Permitting Regulations 2007 also improved the structure of legislation, so it is easier to follow, in particular by separating the procedure from the substantive environmental protection requirements.[8] Subsequently the Environmental Permitting (England and Wales) Regulations 2016 further widened the scope of the existing environmental permitting and compliance system in England and Wales.

IV. Environmental Permitting

Permitting is an important component of the overall regulatory approach to protecting and improving the environment in many jurisdictions. An environmental permit allows specified activities that have a potential impact on the environment and the health of the public, to be carried out within a prescribed set of conditions. There are many factors that determine the conditions the EA places within a permit including the environmental standards set in European and national legislation, process standards (such as best available techniques (BAT)) and local site considerations. Permit conditions applied by the EA are of two types: operating standards required to protect people and the environment; and conditions that deliver improvements. The conditions can include emission limits for discharges to air and water and are set at levels to ensure people and the environment are properly protected. The EA has developed a hierarchy of permit types which it then applies as appropriate to different situations, as follows:[9]

- *Bespoke permit* – a custom-designed permit tailored to specific circumstances. These are used for higher-risk activities or where there is a site-specific need. However, even bespoke permits can be standardised as far as possible to minimise unnecessary effort. In many situations the improvement programme will be the most site-specific aspect.
- *Standard rules permits* – these are used for defined, less complex, lower hazard activities as a simpler, quicker and cheaper alternative to bespoke permits. However, it is not possible to vary the standard permit requirements and there are no rights of appeal against the conditions. A single overarching risk assessment is undertaken for a specified activity which is then used to set the conditions within the standard rules permit.
- *Registrations* – the details and locations of certain activities which are deemed to be low-risk must be registered with the EA. The rules to be adhered to can be laid down in legislation or in a set of requirements published by the regulator. Any conditions attached to registrations must be complied with.

---

[8] Kellett, 'Better Regulation' (2008).
[9] 'Regulating for People, the Environment and Growth' (Environment Agency, 2013).

In addition, in certain circumstances there are 'general binding rules' which are legally binding requirements set out in regulations that set the minimum standards or conditions which apply to a particular activity.

Greater resources are required to review an application and then determine the conditions to include within a bespoke permit compared with other permit types. However, even with bespoke permits, the standardised application and permit templates the EA has developed reduces the time required to apply for and in the determination of the permit.

Where the proposed activities meet all the requirements of a particular standard rules permit, except for certain location requirements, an operator can request that the EA treat the regulated facility as a standard facility, subject to a simple specific risk assessment. A charge is made for reviewing this risk assessment. Currently this only applies to a limited number of standard rule sets in relation to some conservation criteria.

The EA reviews existing permits on a periodic basis to ensure they keep pace with changing circumstances and remain protective of people and the environment.

V. Operational Risk Appraisal

One of the predecessor bodies that was merged to form the EA, Her Majesty's Inspectorate of Pollution, and subsequently the EA itself, developed an appraisal system called Operational Risk Appraisal (Opra) to assess risks to people and the environment for activities requiring permits under the Environmental Permitting Regulations.[10,11] It provides a systematic way of assessing risks from permitted activities which are then used as the basis for targeting regulatory effort. Opra enables the EA to target regulatory effort better, reduce inspections and charges for good performers and reduce environmental risks for people and the environment in the vicinity of the activity.

Both the nature of the hazard, the control systems and the capability of those operating an activity are taken into account. This ensures people and the environment are protected in an efficient and effective way, while minimising the burden of regulation on good performers. The Opra system is based on five attributes:

- *Complexity* – of the activities covered by the permit; substances used; what could be released from the site; the work the regulator needs to do to ensure compliance.

- *Emissions and inputs* – releases to air, water and land; waste coming on to and being transferred from the site.

- *Location* – the state of the environment around a site; proximity to where people live, work and play; proximity to special sites; flood risk; surface and ground waters; potential for direct release to water; proximity to an area which a local council is targeting to improve air quality.

---

[10] 'Operator and Pollution Risk Appraisal (OPRA)' (London, Her Majesty's Inspectorate of Pollution, 1995); 'The Application of Risk Assessment and Risk Management to Integrated Pollution Control', Centre for Integrated Pollution Control, Report 1 (Her Majesty's Inspectorate of Pollution, 1995).

[11] 'Operator and Pollution Risk Appraisal (OPRA)' Version 2 (Environmental Agency, 1997) and 'Environmental Permitting Regulations Operational Risk Appraisal (OPRA for Environmental Permitting Regulations)' Version 3 (Environment Agency, 2017).

- *Operator performance* – including management systems and procedures in place and enforcement history.
- *Compliance rating* – based on how well the operator has kept to the conditions required in the permit; any enforcement activity.

Each of the first four attributes above is scored and then placed into one of five bands, A to E, where A-rated activities pose the least hazard or risk depending on the attribute and E the highest. For the compliance rating attribute six bands are used, A to F. Activities in the highest bands require more regulatory effort because of the higher hazard or risk and the greater level of management needed by the operator to comply with permit conditions.

Opra helps the EA plan its use of resources, report on how the activities it regulates are performing and allocate charges. How the EA does this is outlined in the following sections.

VI. Compliance Assessment

The EA's role is to assess whether operators are complying with their legal requirements including as expressed through their permit conditions. It is the responsibility of operators to take ownership of their environmental impacts and to comply with legal requirements. The inspection and compliance approaches adopted by the EA are designed to ensure there is a high probability that non-compliance will be detected and addressed appropriately. The experience of the EA is that the vast majority of businesses in England comply with their environmental permit conditions.[12]

Within the EA compliance assessment resources are allocated on the basis of the Opra band profile which is used as a measure of the risk posed to people and the environment by the activity. The EA takes care to maintain a clear distinction between its regulatory role and site management processes.

The essence of the compliance assessment activities the EA undertakes on a site with a permit is to check performance against specified conditions. On complex sites this can require considerable interpretation and judgement by the EA inspector. Overall environmental performance of a site or of an activity will also be reviewed to identify areas for further improvement.

Compliance assessment activities undertaken by the EA comprise the appropriate mix of: site visits, in-depth audits and review of procedures; scrutiny of reports, monitoring data and progress of improvement programmes; check-monitoring; and responding to incidents and complaints. The EA uses announced and unannounced site inspections to identify items which indicate system or process failures for subsequent audit or review and issues not covered by the existing permit that should be incorporated. They also check to ensure that no activities are being carried out that should not be and to identify potential weaknesses in environmental control measures.

To obtain a particular environmental outcome can require different approaches with individual companies dependent upon factors such as company culture, state of

---

[12] 'Regulating for People, Environment and Growth: 2015 Evidence Summary' (Environment Agency, 2017).

environmental awareness and maturity of control systems. The EA uses the Opra appraisal system to target time and effort and tailor its approach to compliance, inspection and enforcement activities. It helps the EA distinguish between an operator that has on a rare occasion strayed into non-compliance, one where standards have slipped over a period of time, and the deliberately non-compliant.

The EA's interventions seek to ensure levels of compliance are maintained on good sites and improved on poorly performing sites. Where the EA finds consistently good management by operators of their activities with associated compliance with permit conditions they are then able to reduce their level of oversight.

Operators not complying with permit conditions can then receive increased oversight and scrutiny by the EA so that activities return to being in compliance. This can include the use of proportionate enforcement action. Appropriate enforcement activities including prosecutions and enforcement undertakings are used to address non-compliant and illegal activities. Continued poor performance can result in refusal to issue a permit, or revoking an existing permit. Persistent, deliberate wrong-doing is likely to result in prosecution via the courts.

In recent years the EA has been more proactive in revoking permits if an operator persistently breaches its permit conditions over a prolonged period or, in refusing to issue a permit where operators have convictions for environmental offences, a lack of technical competence or inadequate financial resources. It may also suspend an environmental permit if it considers that operation of the facility poses a risk of serious pollution or initiate a permit variation to improve standards.

VII. Environmental Management Systems

Compliance assessment by the EA takes account of the underpinning management systems for an activity as well as environmental performance. Non-compliance can often be an indicator of a problem with the management systems not just an isolated incident of poor performance. Good management systems that are fully implemented and inform day-to-day practices can help ensure that compliance standards are maintained although they are not a guarantee that this will happen. Dahlström et al found that, although businesses who had elected to adopt the ISO 14001 environmental management standard exhibited better environmental management processes than those who had not, this did not appear to reduce the likelihood of environmental incidents or complaints.[13]

An environmental management system (EMS) is a structured approach which can help an organisation identify and manage its environmental impacts and improve its environmental performance. It provides a methodical approach to planning, implementing and reviewing an organisation's environmental impacts and associated management processes.

---

[13] Kristina Dahlström, Chris Howes, Paul Leinster and Jim Skea (2003) 'Environmental Management Systems and Company Performance: Assessing the Case for Extending Risk-based Regulation' 13 *European Environment*, 187.

An effective EMS can also help an organisation: save money by preventing and reducing waste and pollution; meet legal requirements and other environmental obligations; control environmental risks and reduce liabilities; ensure staff are competent to deliver their environmental responsibilities; and improve relations and reputation with customers and stakeholders. A robust EMS can also drive improvements that may not be directly covered in permit conditions, such as procurement and product lifecycle issues.

EMSs are taken into account by the EA in the operator performance attribute of an activity's Opra score. However, the regulatory approach at any site is informed by the observed standards of environmental protection and management not just what is documented within a system.

VIII. Charges

The costs associated with complying with regulations comprise both the measures that have to be implemented to meet the standards and the associated administrative costs. Typically, implementation costs far exceed the administrative costs. However, administrative requirements are often viewed as unnecessarily bureaucratic and burdensome.

The EA has developed a risk-based approach to charges (Unified Charging Framework) which links to the Opra system.[14] The objective is to make the level of regulatory effort proportionate to the environmental risk of the permitted activity, to encourage good performance and for this to be reflected in the charges. The charging scheme is designed to recover permitting and compliance costs fully. Applications which take more resource to determine attract a higher charge than those which can be dealt with simply.

In this way, well-managed/low-hazard activities present less of a risk and are charged less, with higher risk activities being charged more. All activities associated with permitting and compliance such as permit determination, variations and surrenders are covered by the charging scheme.

The Unified Charging Framework is based on the same three permitting tiers (bespoke, standard, registrations) used in Opra. Currently Tier 1 is not used for any charges within the Environmental Permitting Regulations Charging Scheme.

Tier 2 charges generally apply to permits subject to standard conditions and a specific group of lower-risk bespoke permits. Tier 2 activities have fixed charges for permit applications, variations, transfers or surrender. The Opra compliance rating attribute may be used to adjust yearly subsistence charges.

Tier 3 activities relate to bespoke permits. The complexity, emissions and inputs, location and operator performance attributes are used to work out application, variation, surrender and closure charges. The subsistence charge is based on all five attributes (including the compliance rating).

The average application fee for a standard permit is around 40 per cent of the fee for a bespoke permit. In 2015, 77 per cent of the waste permits issued were standard rules permits.

---

[14] 'Environmental Permitting Charging Scheme and Guidance' Version 5 (Environment Agency, 2016).

Subsistence charges should cover all the costs the regulator incurs in the ongoing regulation of a facility.

An annual compliance rating is calculated for each permitted activity based on the EA's Compliance Classification Scheme (CCS).[15] Permit non-compliances are allocated CCS points depending on the nature of the breach. More serious breaches score a greater number of points. The points from each event are summed to give an annual total. The points allocated reflect the additional work typically having to be taken in dealing with the permit breach. For Category 1 breaches (the most serious) some costs are recovered through subsequent legal action, for example costs awarded following prosecution.

For Tier 2 and Tier 3 permits the compliance rating is then used to assign regulatory effort and the associated charges. The compliance ratings range from A for those activities with no permit breaches to F for activities assigned more than 150 CCS points.

Operators in compliance rating band F are the poorest performers and are charged three times the base charge. A review is carried out halfway through the following year of all band F-rated activities and if operational staff consider there has been a significant improvement in compliance with permit requirements and performance has improved to the extent that the half-year score is less than 50 points, an adjustment may be made to the second half-year charge to bring it into line with a band E performance. This is equivalent to 1.5 times the base charge.

IX. Third-party Assurance

In some circumstances it can be appropriate for a regulator to rely on a third-party assurance scheme (see also chapter twenty-three). The EA introduced such a scheme in 2010 for intensive pig and poultry farms regulated under the Environmental Permitting Regulations.[16] The scheme is targeted at the larger pig and poultry producers who are achieving a high standard of compliance with their environmental permit, and was developed with the National Farmers Union and the Red Tractor Farm Assurance (previously known as Assured Food Standards) scheme, with the support of the National Pig Association, the British Poultry Council and the British Egg Industry Council.

For farms that join the scheme the certification body carries out one permit compliance assessment visit each year and the EA visits the farm once in every three years.

The EA remains responsible for regulation, but the information the certification body collects on their behalf helps them assess whether a farm is complying with the permit conditions. The certification body provides the EA with a visit report. A copy of the report is also provided to the farmer. If the farm is complying with its permit, no further action is taken until the subsequent inspection, unless a complaint or an incident is reported. Any areas of non-compliance will be followed up with the operator.

Some farmers don't want to join the scheme and are happy to remain with the standard EA approach. Farms that are not in the scheme continue to be inspected by the EA at least once a year.

[15] ibid.
[16] 'Regulating for People' (2013).

Because participants in the scheme receive only one EA visit every three years the annual subsistence fee is reduced by just over a third. The certification body will charge for carrying out their visit, but this is likely to be less than the EA's charge reduction.

X. The Use of Opra to Inform Regulatory Practice

Opra profiles are publicly available. The EA publishes information on compliance with permit conditions on an annual basis for the more than 14,000 sites with permits that are given performance ratings.[17] Bands A, B and C represent acceptable performance and bands D, E and F unsatisfactory compliance with permit conditions. Communities can use the information to challenge poor performance by operators.

In 2015, 97 per cent of the sites were rated A, B or C for permit compliance. The number of sites in band A increased by 12 per cent between 2014 and 2015 (8,078 to 9,051). Compared with 2014 there was a slight decrease (0.9 per cent) in the percentage of those rated D, E or F. Operators that have a D, E or F Opra permit compliance rating for two consecutive years are considered to be persistent poor performers. The number of persistent poor performers for the two years 2013 and 2014 was 229. The number for the years 2014 and 2015 was 213, a seven per cent decrease.

The number of poor performers (D, E, Fs) has remained stubbornly around three per cent or slightly higher for the last few years. Some of these appear to be recalcitrant, persistently poor performers. The nature of regulation and regulatory approaches that will be effective for such operators is unlikely to be the same as for the consistently good and well-motivated performers. In 2015, 44 permits were revoked and 22 were refused.

It is particularly noteworthy that the waste sector has the largest number of operators in the persistently poor category although it is recognised that there are many more permitted waste activities than any other sector. In 2015, 89 per cent of the persistent poor performers were in the waste sector. However, waste is the only activity where there is a large amount of illegal activity.

The skills, experience and motivations of regulators who are able to deal effectively with the largely compliant businesses are not necessarily the same as those who are able to deal with the persistent poor performers, the deliberately non-compliant and the organised crime fraternity.

The profiles also allow regulatory options to be explored. The full range of Opra banding data enables benchmarking to be undertaken within and between sectors to assess potential impacts and standards of management. The data is also useful for multi-site companies for their internal purposes and also to inform account management discussions between companies and the EA. The information can facilitate strategic discussions about improving environmental performance across a business.

The EA also uses sector-based approaches to take account of the different characteristics and environmental impacts associated with individual business sectors and to improve the efficiency and effectiveness of the regulatory process. Personnel in the EA with particular

[17] '2015 Evidence Summary' (2017).

expertise and experience in specific sectors are then better able to understand and communicate priorities and be more responsive to both innovation and areas of concern within a sector.

Systems have been introduced in the EA to ensure there is consistency in the decisions made by officers in different areas of the country and to ensure businesses have ready access to regulators to clarify regulatory requirements.

XI. Role of Business

For risk-based earned recognition systems to work businesses have to take full responsibility for their activities and visibly demonstrate this including through the implementation of necessary improvement and investment plans. It may be appropriate as part of an earned recognition system to introduce annual compliance statements that are signed off by a board-level director.

If regulators are to offer reduced levels of oversight then businesses have to ensure that local communities and the public retain confidence in their commitment and ability to provide the necessary high levels of control.

It is important that companies establish effective communications with communities in the vicinities of their sites, including setting up, where appropriate, liaison panels and providing transparent and accessible environmental performance data. This is particularly important if there are high levels of public interest in particular sites. The primary route of communication should be between the site operator and the community and not via the regulator.

18

The Find-IT Tool, an Approach to Evidence-Led Targeted Interventions

DAVID SNOWBALL, JOSEPH JANUSZEWSKI, MIKE CALCUTT,
MICHAEL BONE AND PHIL PREECE

I. Introduction

The Health and Safety Executive (HSE) is the UK's national regulator for workplace health and safety, focusing on preventing work-related death, injury and ill-health. The HSE's work ranges from influencing behaviours across whole industry sectors, through campaigns and guidance, to targeted interventions on individual businesses including inspections and enforcement action.

The HSE's strategy for improving standards across the health and safety system is called Helping Great Britain Work Well.[1] This sets direction and guides the HSE in working with others who can influence outcomes, including suppliers, trade associations, professional bodies and trade unions. Where appropriate, the HSE works closely with other regulators whose activities overlap, sharing relevant information and intelligence to amplify impact.

Operationally, the HSE's action is targeted, consistent and transparent. It enforces the law proportionately, taking into account both the level of risk and the seriousness of a breach and follows the principles set out in the UK Regulators' Code[2] (see chapter five). Its actions are framed by its Enforcement Policy Statement[3] and Enforcement Management Model.[4]

The HSE assigns resources to problems at sector level through 19 sector-based plans[5] and a series of cross-cutting health strategies.[6] For each sector, the plans define the key health and safety issues that need to be tackled and a tailored approach in each case.

---

[1] 'Helping GB Work Well' (Health and Safety Executive, 2016), available at www.hse.gov.uk/strategy/strategy-document.htm.

[2] 'Regulators' Code' (Better Regulation Delivery Office, 2014).

[3] 'Enforcement Policy Statement' (Health and Safety Executive, 2015), available at www.hse.gov.uk/enforce/enforcepolicy.htm.

[4] 'Enforcement Management Model' (Health and Safety Executive, 2013), available at www.hse.gov.uk/enforce/enforcement-management-model.htm.

[5] 'Sector Plans' (Health and Safety Executive, 2017), available at www.hse.gov.uk/aboutus/strategiesandplans/sector-plans/index.htm.

[6] 'Health Priority Plans' (Health and Safety Executive, 2017), available at www.hse.gov.uk/aboutus/strategiesandplans/health-and-work-strategy/index.htm.

This chapter outlines how the HSE is using its scientific expertise to develop an IT-based data intelligence tool to inform operational decisions about how best to apply proactive intervention effort. The chapter explains our Find-IT tool, how we use it, what impact it is having, its wider application to other regulators and how we plan to develop it further. Throughout, we refer to 'duty-holders' to define those who have duties under health and safety legislation.

II. Risk-based Interventions

The guiding principle in UK health and safety legislation, embodied in the 1974 Health and Safety at Work Act, is that whoever creates a risk is responsible for managing it. We use a variety of techniques to inform, persuade or, if necessary, compel duty-holders to comply with the law and to protect their employees and others from work-related risks. We do not need to directly intervene with all of the estimated one million businesses that we regulate in Great Britain, so we concentrate our face to face regulatory efforts where we want to have the biggest impact.

We target those sectors and activities where we expect to find:

- the most serious risks;
- poor standards of risk control; or
- both.

Face-to-face intervention by a trained HSE inspector is an effective but resource-demanding way to address the management of workplace risk and to drive behaviour change. An inspector can gather first-hand evidence – through observation, questioning workers and scrutinising paperwork – to enable them to judge how well a business is managing risk and, importantly, take immediate action to remedy any serious defects that emerge.

Any business being inspected equally has a reasonable expectation that the inspector can explain why they have been selected for attention. This theme is common to a range of recent UK Government reports addressing risk prioritisation, including: the Hampton review;[7] Good Health and Safety, Good for Everyone;[8] the Löfstedt review of health and safety legislation;[9] and the Regulatory Futures review[10] (also see chapter sixteen on risk-based prioritisation).

We visit around 20,000 duty-holders each year in sectors or activities where we expect to find serious risks or poor controls. Our key challenge is to ensure we select the duty-holders who warrant this attention and whose health and safety performance will benefit most from

---

[7] Philip Hampton, *Reducing Administrative Burdens: Effective Inspection and Enforcement* (London, HM Treasury, 2005).

[8] 'Good Health and Safety, Good for Everyone' (Department for Work and Pensions, 2011).

[9] Ragnar Löfstedt, 'Reclaiming Health and Safety for All: An Independent Review of Health and Safety Regulation' (The Stationery Office, 2011).

[10] 'Regulatory Futures Review' (Cabinet Office, 2017).

face-to-face contact with an inspector. There are several high-level questions the HSE needs to address:

- What is the scale of workplace activity that could give rise to injury and ill-health?
- What sites/duty-holders are active?
- Which of those sites/duty-holders operate in sectors with high(er) health and safety risks?
- Which sites/duty-holders have a record of poor(er) health and safety performance?
- Where is resource best deployed to greatest (risk-reducing) effect?
- When and how should we plan to focus our regulatory attention to achieve impact on risk and non-compliance?

A. Overview of the Find-IT Tool

Find-IT is a tool that enables us to combine and interrogate a wide range of data sets. It helps inspectors exercise their discretion in selecting duty-holders and is more than a simple list of suitable sites. It allows us to bring both aspects together to fine-tune our targeting choices.

Our experience has shown that disparate data sources each have their own strengths, weaknesses and unique characteristics, but if we can match and link them, we can build a more complete picture by evening out differences and exploiting commonalities in ways that let us usefully interrogate the material.

Figure 18.1 Interrogating layers of geographical data can provide insights about business premises

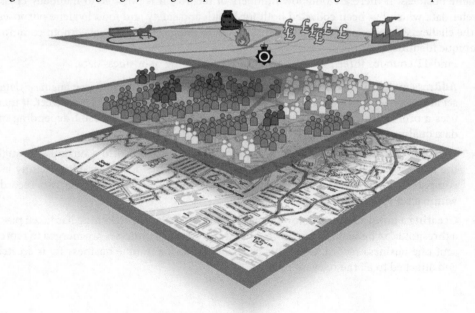

As well as the HSE's regulatory data and any statutory information which duty-holders are required to report to the HSE, we currently draw data from:

- commercial data sets providing information about companies;
- public registers of companies and mapping information (Ordnance Survey);
- other regulators (eg those covering environmental safety, food safety, and fire services), whether available publicly or by special agreement.

Specifically, we can combine and interrogate diverse data sets to reveal new insights about individual businesses which would not otherwise be possible (Figure 18.1 illustrates this). Find-IT gives us ways both to analyse data and to apply the resulting knowledge to identify, with greater confidence, duty-holders who warrant inspection within the scope of our planned priorities.

Find-IT consists of two elements:

- a data engine that contains a variety of algorithms to join disparate data sets without the need for unique identifiers; and
- a customisable digital platform that allows users to interrogate and exploit the combined data.

i. Data Engine

Find-IT's data engine uses algorithms to match and link disparate databases within and across organisations. When data about a business is shared there is rarely a unique identifier that makes it possible to establish or confirm that data from different sources relate to the same business. If there are only low numbers of records, it is possible to manually cross-refer data which has been collected both for health and safety and food hygiene purposes. The challenge is more pronounced when we want to merge large datasets without common unique identifiers.

Find-IT contains three processes to automate matching of business data:

- **Address matching** – This programme loads unstructured data from any business dataset and matches it to a geographical location such as a building name and street. It then uses a probabilistic matching technique to find the best possible result depending on data quality.
- **Organisation matching** – Once a location has been attributed to a business through the address-matching process all data points within a defined geographic vicinity are compared. This process provides a score that represents how probable two records within a set vicinity refer to the same business.
- **Creating a unique record** – Now the address and organisation matching has taken place a threshold can be set to define at what point two similar businesses are merged to represent one business record. Once this has been defined, a unique business ID is created and attached to all the relevant records.

ii. Web-based Platform

Once the data has been matched the combined data sets can be interrogated via an intuitive and customisable digital interface. This interface has multiple such customisable views and allows the user to quickly and easily identify and extract valuable business information. Three of the key views are:

- The **filter** view allows the user to create a bespoke filter to rapidly query the data held in Find-IT and to ask complex questions. A relevant example (shown in Figure 18.2) for HSE might be: 'Show me all woodworking businesses that have not been inspected in the last three years and which have experienced more than one accident and a recent prosecution'.

Figure 18.2 Find-IT search screen

- The **map** view can be used at any point within the Find-IT tool. If the map view has been populated by a query, the map will show the spatial clustering of results (ie the (1) icons in Figure 18.3). It can be accessed through the businesses record, used directly to browse businesses by location or display results from the filter view.

- The **results** view returns a selection of businesses from a query run by the user in the filter view. This provides simple overviews and acts as a gateway to more detailed information. The initial information shown about each record (see Figure 18.4) provides salient information about a business and easy access to explore further detailed information about historic performance (see Figure 18.5).

Figure 18.3 Map view of Find-IT query results

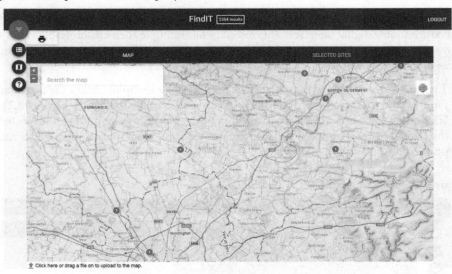

Figure 18.4 Results view showing query results by duty-holder performance

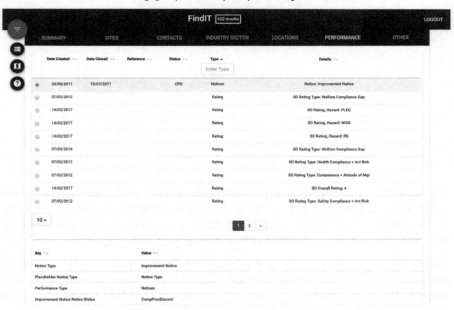

Figure 18.5 Results view showing summary screen for a specific duty-holder

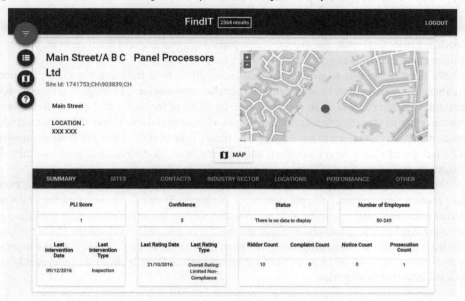

To ensure that Find-IT delivered the HSE's business objectives an agile approach to developing the tool was used. This focused on capturing, prioritising and delivering business and the range of user requirements (including inspectors, intelligence officers, administrative support staff and senior operational leaders).

The ability to prioritise our requirements meant that certain developments could be delivered early allowing for continuous improvement, flexible scheduling and the ability to realise the biggest benefits at an early stage of the project. For example, the results view was delivered to support work planning before the map view to improve the user interface; functionality for wider use by inspectors is being developed after concluding developments for intelligence officer users.

In practice this also allowed the software development and operational teams to work more collaboratively, focusing on the highest priorities. Continuous development through an agile approach meant that there were no surprises when the tool was delivered to users and this was a key part in ensuring that targeting processes using Find-IT capability were successfully implemented.

B. Using Find-IT

The tool is designed to be used by field-based staff. A typical HSE team consists of six to eight inspectors and is led by a principal inspector responsible for delivering planned activities by distributing reactive and proactive workloads, scheduling the workflow to balance the volumes with other development, coaching and managerial tasks. An intelligence officer works alongside support teams to provide Find-IT expertise.

C. Preparation for Inspection Visits

Preparation for inspections involves assembling the key information at the right time to provide inspectors with the relevant company background and intervention history to inform their face-to-face contacts.

We need to be able to provide a reliable workflow to deliver the objectives in annual business plans. They have to align with our parallel information campaigns and longer-term strategies while enabling us to resource investigations of incidents and concerns. However, the currency of targeting information and pre-visit material can decay if it is not acted on promptly. Inspectors need to have access to a timely flow of viable inspection visits for which sufficient checks have been completed and relevant briefing material has been assembled to inform their day-to-day activities.

Working together, the principal inspector and the support team agree on the necessary lead-in time to create the planned work packages. They need to account for delivering current strategic and operational priorities, supporting the scheduling of campaigns, and securing any specific information requirements for particular duty-holders. Once the needs of a team are known, the intelligence officer can interrogate Find-IT to estimate the numbers of businesses that will be in scope for inspection both nationally and locally. Typically they will fall into three categories:

- higher-risk sectors (HRS) – such as woodworking or sheet-metal fabrication – where inspection is justified on the basis of generic accident and ill health data;
- any duty-holder in any sector where a visit can be justified on the basis of a record of poor past performance; and
- a single, cross-sector priority topic – such as legionella – where the HSE has decided to take action.

D. Refining and Refreshing Targeting Information

After their interventions, inspectors complete an IT-based record confirming what they have seen and what action they have taken, including their professional assessment of the duty-holder's competence to manage risk. This data populates Find-IT with professional feedback, judgement and local knowledge about active workplaces.

The intelligence officer can adjust the search criteria to widen or narrow the selection process and add other criteria to prioritise future targeting lists in more detail.

Principal inspectors can apply their own judgement and further refine the Find-IT lists to:

- Apply local knowledge and regulatory judgement to sense-test the choices (eg to remove multiple sites for the same duty-holder if there is already engagement at head office level).
- Add other viable workplaces based on local experience if the intelligence threshold is met.

- Explore what further information might be obtainable to give greater definition to the available proactive work. This might arise if, for example, another regulator can provide previously unavailable data.

Box 18.1 describes the way data is able to be used to improve targeting.

Box 18.1 Quicker, more responsive targeting

Before Find-IT, administrative support staff had to manually check a number of disparate and poor-quality data sets and notifications (eg accident notifications, worker complaints). This was time-consuming and could lead to sites suitable for inspection not being identified. Find-IT brings the various performance indicators together and provides a clear overview of a site, its location, performance and intervention history. A simple scoring system is used with each performance indicator given a value. Sites with the greatest number of different performance indicators and therefore highest scores are prioritised for inspection. This consolidation of data and performance overview allows new intelligence to be assessed quickly against existing site knowledge and evidence-based decisions about the use of inspector resource can be made.

E. Making Use of Real-time Intelligence

Principal inspectors also monitor information about duty-holders that comes to the HSE's attention from external sources including:

- reported injuries and ill health (required under UK accident reporting legislation);[11]

- concerns or complaints reported by employees and the public to the HSE Concerns team;[12]

- reports arising from unsatisfactory statutory insurance examinations (in the UK it is a legal requirement to inform the regulator in such cases);[13] and

- information on a range of topics that might come from other regulators. Research undertaken within the UK has demonstrated that premises which are poorly managed in one area of regulation are likely to also be poorly managed in other areas of regulation.[14]

---

[11] The Reporting of Injuries, Diseases and Dangerous Occurrences Regulations 2013 (referred to as RIDDOR) puts duties on employers, the self-employed and people in control of work premises to report certain serious workplace accidents, occupational diseases and specified dangerous occurrences (near misses).

[12] See www.hse.gov.uk/contact/concerns.htm.

[13] Where there is a defect which is or could become a danger to people, the person undertaking the examination or inspection reports this to the duty-holder immediately *and* notifies the relevant enforcing authority with a copy of the report (eg for lifting equipment liable to fail or a pressure system that may rupture).

[14] See www.gov.uk/government/publications/risk-assessment-information-sharing.

The research also indicated that businesses manage each business critical activity to the same or a similar level.

This is another part of the developing intelligence jigsaw. Regardless of how tactically useful the detail is, it provides evidence that a company is still in business and may highlight those previously unknown to the HSE. While each item is not automatically indicative of a serious health and safety failure, it is of value to Find-IT to inform a balanced judgement about how a business is managing risk. In some cases, though, the new information may justify a proactive inspection. Our intelligence officers therefore regularly search for higher priority workplaces that are within the scope of the current priorities.

Box 18.2 National industry inspection campaign

Premises and performance data is provided by other government departments and regulatory agencies to support specific campaigns and is data-matched against site information already held in Find-IT. Where no record of the site exists, a new premises record is created, increasing the data set available to search for sites for inspection against set priority indicators. For example, sites which have been given a poor performance rating by the HSE and another regulator are prioritised for inspection, followed by sites with a poor performance rating from another regulatory agency and previously not known to the HSE. This maximises the use of data previously collected and ensures sites with a poor performance history are identified.

F. Outcomes and Benefits

Combining the data analysis enabled by Find-IT with a more focused and developed approach to targeting inspections has significantly improved our ability to deal with serious risks though proactive interventions.

We have increased the number of visits where we have taken action to control serious risks, both in absolute terms and as a proportion of the total number of visits. Against a baseline of approximately 20,000 visits each year we took action in more than 9,000 visits in 2016/17 compared to 7,800 in 2015/16 and 7,200 in 2014/15. These all represent improved risk reduction for the employees in those workplaces and correlates with significant development of our targeting processes and Find-IT capability over the past four years.

By sharpening the focus of our interventions both on specific industries and on specific risks *within* those industries, we are increasingly able to track progress and impact on health risks identified in our sector and health plans (eg silica dust in stone-working; musculo-skeletal disorders in food manufacturing).

Our inspectors have reported there are fewer 'wasted' visits to premises which are either unoccupied or are not active in the 'target' industries, because of our targeting processes and the currency of the Find-IT intelligence.

Box 18.3 Increasing operational efficiency

Inspectors carry out a mixture of reactive investigation work and proactive inspection of sites identified and prioritised for inspection. Find-IT is used to find and prioritise sites for inspection which are geographically located close to sites where reactive work is being undertaken. As with all sites identified through Find-IT, they can be shown on a map to visualise geographical locations. This increases the efficiency of operational activity and deployment of inspector resource and reduces travel costs.

Our preparation and planning work can be done to a consistent pattern from any location. This gives us flexibility when balancing or transferring workloads between geographically dispersed offices.

We can better estimate the available proactive workload and use Find-IT to show operational managers the numbers, types, sizes and geographical distribution of workplaces in scope for inspection based on their planning discussions.

We can use new or improved sources of intelligence to refine, refresh and reprioritise our plans and the workplaces targeted throughout the year. We have been able, for example, to provide focused support to joint initiatives with other regulators to maintain our involvement without excessive diversion of scarce resources.

We have an increased capability to explore patterns of company structures and networks to cross-match poorly performing businesses under common ownership. This also has implications for better joined-up regulatory action.

We can see similar opportunities for developing insights into how supply chains involving common duty-holders function.

We are more confident in explaining the basis for our targeting decisions and answering challenges about the basis on which we make our choices.

G. Lessons Learned

Find-IT started life as an attempt to generate accurate intelligence about viable duty-holders to replace time-consuming manual data-handling. It has grown into a much wider set of self-challenges for the HSE.

Some significant consequences are already evident:

- HSE inspectors develop an enhanced appreciation of the challenges facing duty-holders through their day jobs. They accumulate local knowledge and insight which is valuable in informing targeting decisions. An essential part of embedding Find-IT has been in briefing inspectors face-to-face in all our main office locations to encourage buy-in to what might otherwise look like top-down direction about where to go.

- Whilst Find-IT is very good at cross-matching datasets, our targeting remains dependent on the quality of the source data. We can mitigate some of this risk by using multiple datasets to triangulate information, but we still carry out some focused checks to filter out inactive businesses.

- The information that inspectors collect at each visit about duty-holders and their performance further improves the effectiveness of our targeting. We routinely review how much information we record (seeking to minimise it as far as practicable), but Find-IT has reiterated the importance of making sure we record only what is truly essential to meet our operational needs.

- The feedback from our targeted activity has opened new lines of operational research activity including how to benchmark the impact we are having on risk reduction over time. This is an important area for future development.

- Find-IT has helped us to improve liaison with other regulators but more work is needed to improve the data sharing between organisations (see below). Some of this relates to concerns about data security, but, more generally, there is not yet a commonly-held view about the benefits of such sharing across government.[15]

H. Wider Impact and Future Development beyond the HSE

Find-IT is readily transferable to other areas of regulation. We have delivered a number of intelligence projects for other government departments ranging from predicting non-compliance on farms, using machine learning, through to delivering software applications that share data between local and national regulators.

Two examples are noteworthy.

i. Intelligent Regulatory Information System

HSE worked with the Office for Product Safety and Standards to explore the possibilities of extending Find-IT to include multi-agency data. The Intelligent Regulatory Information System (IRIS)[16] has been developed to explore the benefits of sharing data between multiple local and national regulators. The key challenge has been the probabilistic data matching between 12 different datasets covering regulation of:

- workplace health and safety;
- care quality;
- food hygiene;
- fire protection; and
- food standards.

---

[15] Paul Sanderson, Daniel Banks, Simon Deakin and Chihiro Udagawa, 'Encouraging Inter-regulator Data Sharing: the Perceptions of Regulators: A Report for the Better Regulation Delivery Office' (Cambridge, University of Cambridge Centre for Housing and Planning Research, 2015).

[16] 'Evaluation Report of Data Sharing Through the Intelligent Regulatory Information System (IRIS)' (Health and Safety Laboratory, 2015).

For a six-month pilot period, four regulators working in one of the UK's county areas shared certain data they held on business premises within the area, to mutually assist with the targeting of their regulatory activities. The work combined general information about the premises regulated, regulatory data (such as enforcement action taken and confidence in management scores) and third-party data, giving wider insight into company activities. The cross regulatory aspect of this work meant that multiple users had to be able to do two things with the data: easily interpret unfamiliar material and flexibly interrogate/query it. The delivery team mapped all the activity, functions and compliance information from the different regulatory areas to common scales to produce a 'Confidence in management rating'.

As with the HSE Find-IT tool, IRIS is sufficiently flexible to allow the user to access data through a mapping interface to apply geography to decision choices. Evaluation of the pilot found that IRIS was successful at identifying legal gateways to sharing data and providing a tool to help match and expose shared data to the regulators. The general consensus of those involved was that the experience of sharing data for regulatory purposes was beneficial, the two key benefits being:

- improved risk-based targeting of inspections; and
- reduced operational risk concerning unknown premises.

Positive outcomes from the pilot included identification of a number of sites which were in need of regulatory action, and the delivery of seminars to a group of poor performers operating in a particular sector within the county.

ii. Regulatory Intelligence Hub

The concept of a UK regulatory intelligence hub has been developed on the back of IRIS and through working with other government departments. This remains work in progress but potentially offers the prospect of developing best practice guides, better sharing of intelligence solutions and bespoke analytical work for regulators who cannot access dedicated intelligence resource.

The following elements give a flavour of the issues:

- **Data sharing** – The hub will need to understand fully the legal gateways for data-sharing to provide best practice and help unpick issues that are commonly experienced when regulators look to acquire or share data.
- **Security understanding and expertise** – Security of data and information is of paramount importance when dealing with intelligence. A regulatory intelligence hub will need to understand end-to-end security of systems and data to help advise and undertake intelligence related tasks.
- **Regulatory policy** – To make sure that intelligence and data analytics are embedded appropriately within regulatory areas there needs to be regulatory domain expertise within the hub to help lead projects and inform policy-makers within wider government of the potential benefits of certain approaches to intelligence.
- **Software and analytical capabilities** – At the centre of the hub there will need to be an analytical capability to demonstrate best practice and undertake or mentor departments on high profile projects.

III. Next Steps

Find-IT has involved close working between scientific and operational staff in the HSE and is enhancing the insights that can be extracted from regulatory data.

We are developing a user interface for HSE inspectors to use in their day-to-day work. Workplaces that require their attention, whether for targeted inspection or a reactive investigation, should be visually accessible via maps on a smartphone or other mobile device. Inspectors will be able to make real-time decisions about how to minimise their travel, increasing efficiency.

The return on investment in Find-IT will continue to increase. We foresee a future approach to proactive work where we are much better able to align the strategic needs of the organisation with the real-time and tactical insights that will come from the thousands of daily interactions we have with duty-holders. The HSE has always been able to gather information and intelligence from many sources, simply as a function of its role as a regulator. Find-IT will help us continue to improve on how it extracts as much useful insight and operational benefit from it as possible.

19

Regulating Quality Outputs, an Approach Based on Provision of Data to Drive Behaviour

MARCUS RINK

The Drinking Water Inspectorate (DWI) regulates water quality in England and Wales.[1] The regulated activity covers delivery of almost 15 billion litres a day to almost 55 million people.[2] There are 17 appointed regional water companies in the DWI's jurisdiction, each operating across specific geographical areas and a further nine small water companies that supply water within the regional water company areas in England and Wales.[3] In addition, around two per cent of water is supplied to users through a private supply, eg by bed and breakfast and restaurant-owners. The primary regulator for such 51,546 private suppliers is the local authority, and the DWI gives advice, guidance and training to local authorities.

The DWI is a business unit in the Water and Flood Risk Management Directorate of the Department for Environment, Food and Rural Affairs. Whilst reporting to the Director, the Chief Inspector of Drinking Water, appointed by the Secretary of State, has a statutory role and powers, as established by legislation – currently the Water Industry Act 1991.[4] The DWI has wide enforcement powers, including powers[5] that have been delegated by Ministers to the Chief Inspector and provisions concerning proceedings against undertakers and others who 'supply water unfit for human consumption' that are vested directly in the Chief Inspector.[6]

The DWI is a small regulatory body, with a staff of around 40 people, three-quarters of whom are technically qualified inspectors, with a significant proportion of these having previously had experience of working in the regulated industry. Full cost-recovery was introduced in 2013/14[7] and the budget for 2016/17 was under £2.5 million.

---

[1] See www.dwi.gov.uk.
[2] See The Drinking Water Inspectorate Business performance report 2016/17 (DWI 2017).
[3] See www.ofwat.gov.uk/regulated-companies/ofwat-industry-overview/licences.
[4] The DWI was established under s 60 of the Water Act 1989 which was consolidated into the Water Industry Act 1991, subsequently amended by the Water Act 2003 and the Water Act 2014.
[5] Water Industry Act, s 68.
[6] Water Industry Act, s 70.
[7] Currently under the Water Quality and Supply (Fees) Order 2016.

The DWI was established in January 1990 at a time of fundamental change to the water industry in England and Wales. The Water Act 1989 privatised the 10 existing regional water authorities in the wake of several major water supply public health emergencies, most notably the Lowermoor Treatment Plant incident at Camelford in 1988 (where aluminium sulphate was mistakenly tipped into the wrong part of a plant and contaminated extensive drinking supplies) and the Oxford/Swindon Cryptosporidium outbreak in 1989.

Parliament was clear at the time of privatisation that the regulation of drinking water quality – with its significant implications for public health – needed to be separated from the responsibility for managing water resources and the responsibility for economic regulation of the newly privatised water companies that deliver water supplies to customers.

The DWI was established with responsibility for the Water Supply (Water Quality) Regulations 1989[8] which implemented the 1980 EU Drinking Water Directive as well as setting the framework for the drinking water monitoring to be undertaken. The legislation and regulations stipulated the principal requirement that water shall be 'good, clean and wholesome'.

For the period 2015–20 the DWI has the aim to secure safe, clean drinking water for all consumers through the following four strategic objectives:

1.   Water suppliers deliver water that is safe and clean.
2.   The public have confidence in their drinking water.
3.   Drinking water legislation that is fit for purpose and implemented in the public interest.
4.   The Inspectorate is a progressive and trusted organisation.

The DWI operates within a regulatory framework which encompasses Ofwat (the economic regulator of the water sector), the Environment Agency (which has responsibility for water resources in England), Natural Resources Wales (which has similar responsibilities in Wales) and the local authorities that regulate private water supplies. It states its policy as:[9]

> The Inspectorate applies the principles of better regulation by promoting self-regulation in the form of risk assessments for those we regulate, and identifying regulatory failure through risk analysis of the data we receive. We will continue to engage and promote constructive dialogue with our fellow regulators: Ofwat; local authorities; the Environment Agency; Consumer Council for Water; and the representative of the water industry, Water UK; as well as Defra and the Welsh Government.

I. A Staged Strategy to Improving Effective Delivery

The water industry in England and Wales is a mature industry that shares the goal of 'good, clean and wholesome' drinking water with the regulator.

The regulator has a staged strategy to improving the effectiveness of the regulation through an approach that relies heavily on the analysis of data to inform risk-based prioritisation and targeting of its resources. It is committed to proportionate approaches to

---

[8] Subsequently replaced by the Water Supply (Water Quality) Regulations 2016 (England) and The Water Supply (Water Quality) Regulations 2010 (as amended).
[9] See The Drinking Water Inspectorate Business Performance Report 2016/17 (DWI, 2017).

driving improvement, working collaboratively with companies that show a willingness to improve, through the agreement of a Transformation programme, and taking firm enforcement action where this is justified.

In developing his thinking, a key moment was when the Chief Inspector reflected on a BBC radio interview with the chief inspector of another regulated sector. The first question was how the inspectorate changed behaviour, the answer being through 'Recommendations'. The second question was 'What does the inspectorate do with the Recommendations?' and that elicited no convincing answer. Under the new DWI system, '*we* score them, and this focuses on *our* behaviour. We want to look at *how* we move them out of the red zone.'

The DWI's message to companies is that it has no surprises or secrets, it tells people how it operates, so they can see predictability, fairness and consistency, and what they have to do. To encourage a culture of sharing and no surprises, the DWI has a secondment programme of company staff, so they can see how things work from the inside. They can also realise what the response will be if they get it wrong. There is a great deal of dialogue with companies and Water UK at all levels.

There is full transparency on the system and the metrics on which it is based. From 2017 all metrics have been given to the industry. From this, they can see what the DWI will do, and what they can do to achieve a good score and improve from a low score. This process goes beyond trying to achieve quick wins on individual issues, and adopts a permanent performance and improvement culture. It has changed the balance of emphasis from focusing just on individual non-compliances.

The DWI has taken a 'problem-solving' approach to addressing compliance challenges. The introduction of a 'source to tap' risk assessment methodology focuses companies on the whole supply chain from catchment to tap. For example, catchment management aims to reduce pollution challenges from sources where water is abstracted, by considering how these arise and how they may be mitigated. This will range from, for instance: naturally arising hazards such as algae growing in impounding reservoirs; microbiological contaminants from animal origin; geogenic contaminants arising from sources such as those naturally high in metals; to contaminants of anthropogenic origin such as pesticides. If the challenges to water treatment are reduced through improving the quality for abstraction, then the treatment process requires less intervention, invariably reducing the cost of treatment. As an example of this strategy, the DWI addressed persistent issues with unacceptably high levels of a particular pesticide, metaldehyde, which is widely used to kill slugs in agriculture and horticulture and is extremely difficult to remove from water without very expensive advanced processes. A methodology of undertakings, which are informal non-legally binding agreements, between the DWI and the water companies set out the methodology of catchment management to reduce the occurrence of the pesticide in areas directly affecting water abstracted for supply. This encouraged the water companies to take steps such as managing their abstraction regimes and working with farmers within their catchment to encourage the replacement of metaldehyde with an alternative pesticide. This collaborative approach has seen the number of failures of the pesticide standard attributed to metaldehyde decrease from 365 in 2013 to 47 in 2016[10] without the need for direct enforcement.

---

[10] See http://dwi.defra.gov.uk/about/annual-report/2016/index.html.

The DWI is aimed at changing companies' thinking into one of 'driving down risk' by using methodology which focuses on consequential outcomes such as compliance failures or events to promote proactive action. This is being delivered in a multi-staged strategy over a number of years, the first step was completed by introducing the source to tap risk assessment for companies to identify and mitigate their own risk. The second step focused upon the actions taken by companies following first-level regulatory intervention in the form of recommendations by, for instance, compliance failures or events where things have not always gone to plan. For this the DWI developed a mathematical model of behavioural response to understand the risk of continued or repeated failures by companies through their actions or lack of action. The continuing development of this strategy moves away from simple number counting and percentage statistics and expands into formal risk measures in the form of the Compliance Risk Index (CRI) and the Event Risk Index (ERI) to measure the impact of failures on consumers. It goes beyond simple compliance because it recognises the already high standards achieved within England and Wales since 1991 (achieving about 99.96 per cent compliance in 2016 with the standards for water quality) and that the water industry has to enter the next level of attainment to advance beyond the plateau of the past 10 years (see Figure 19.1).

The strategy of driving effective long-term changes in behaviour to reduce risk requires alignment of cross-regulatory objectives to avoid conflicting priorities in an industry where there are multiple regulators who may need to focus on the same or similar outcome. Ofwat, the economic regulator of water, regulates water companies in England and Wales in order to provide consumers with a good quality and efficient service at a fair price. The delivery of economic regulation in securing water companies properly carry out their statutory function requires a financial framework which includes the provision of wholesome drinking water through planning for the efficient use of resources and assets. This framework and methodology is known as the price review; a five-year cyclical process which determines the price limits water companies can charge to consumers based upon a company's business plan and their performance throughout the period employing agreed measures and incentives. The current periodic review will set out in 2019 the price limits for the period between 2020 and 2025.

The strategy of the DWI rests on the premise that by sharing its water quality indices with Ofwat, any framework intended to deliver on the periodic review objectives for water quality will act synergistically to deliver the best outcome for both regulators, the water companies and most importantly the consumer. Therefore, even though there is a regulatory and legal requirement to meet water quality standards, the alignment of financial incentives removes any conflict for companies to meet separate objectives set within the review process. To achieve this aim, DWI accelerated the CRI and ERI strategy by embedding them in the Ofwat 2019 final methodology[11] which sets out how water prices are set. Not to do so would delay the implementation of an aligned strategy until the next periodic cycle of 2025–30 losing any realistic change in company behaviour for at least another five years. As these measures are now set within the business plans, the strategic objectives of the companies are financially incentivised to deliver improving performance for CRI and ERI now and for the future. This in turn begins to drive down the risk of compliance failures

---

[11] 2019 Price Review: Final Methodology, available at www.ofwat.gov.uk/regulated-companies/price-review/2019-price-review-final-methodology.

further improving water quality at the tap and equally reducing high impact events caused by the failure of company assets thereby improving their resilience and the consumer experience and trust. This long-term planning strategy focused on water quality will improve the service for future generations by continually aspiring towards a very low risk.

II. A Data-Driven System

The regulatory task for drinking water quality is based upon technical legislation which requires compliance with clear standards; it is therefore approached as a technical matter. This approach requires the assessment and analysis of considerable amounts of data using a robust mathematical approach; not to do so would ignore the fundamental principle of technical regulation and evidence-based and defensible decision-making. This is important when decisions are made concerning enforcement and particularly so if criminal proceedings were to be taken.

Under the regulatory system, water companies are required to submit certain data and information to the regulator, as specified in The Water Industry (Suppliers' Information) Direction 2017. This includes, but is not limited to:

- routine reporting, on a monthly basis, of the results of daily tests that they are required to carry out on samples of drinking water; and
- self-reporting of any event that may give rise to a significant risk to public health, affect the quality or sufficiency of a supply or might cause concern to the supplier, consumers or other authority.

In 2016 the DWI assessed over four million pieces of analytical data submitted by the regulated companies, the results of over 500 post-incident investigations by the DWI, and its findings from 47 proactive audits of company sites. It evaluated 2,936 risk assessment reports, issued 153 legal notices, closed 24 Notices, approved 144 products for use in contact with drinking water and handled over 1,250 enquiries from local authorities, consumers and organisations.

A. Compliance Data

Daily testing by the companies provides a clear picture of water quality and allows the DWI to monitor performance and analyse trends.

Each company has a specific number of tests, and in 2016 companies in England carried out 3,877,030 individual tests (against a stipulated target of 3,879,888) and in Wales 280,903 (against a target of 281,000).[12] Fifty-two parameters of water quality are specified and companies are required to record failures against each parameter.

Results are published for each company[13] as part of the Chief Inspectors Report. In 2016, the reports for England recorded a total of 586 failures to meet EU and national standards,

---

[12] See 'Drinking Water 2016. Summary of the Chief Inspector's Report for Drinking Water in England' (DWI, 2017).
[13] See http://dwi.defra.gov.uk/about/annual-report/2016/index.html.

the most frequent being taste and colour (139), coliform bacteria (125), iron (96), lead (69) and pesticides (54).

The daily compliance data is submitted by companies up to six weeks after analysis on a rolling monthly basis. The DWI adopts a systematic approach in analysing these data initially using database look-up tables automatically identifying the majority of the four million test data which is compliant with the regulatory standards and separating them from all non-compliant data. The non-compliant data (around 1,200 per year when including all indicator parameters) are then assessed individually by the DWI for compliance with the regulations. The regulations require an investigation by the company to determine the cause and extent of the failure, what the failure is attributable to, and the steps taken to protect public health. Where these requirements are not met or where it cannot be concluded that the failure is unlikely to recur, the DWI will take regulatory action such as in the form of recommendations to the company or if it considers necessary further action such as enforcement.

The performance of the water industry and companies has, since 1991, been measured by the percentage of those tests which failed the standard compared to those which were compliant. In 2004 this was modified to an index of overall drinking water quality referred to as MZC per cent (Mean Zonal Compliance) that comprised the average of 39 specified parameters that are tested to establish the quality of water at consumers' taps. Other indices were used to demonstrate compliance at water treatment works or service reservoirs. Between 1991 and 2015, regulatory compliance improved from about 98.4 per cent to 99.96 per cent or in actual reduction of failures from about 50,000 failures to about 800 failures (Figure 19.1).

Figure 19.1 Industry regulatory compliance 1991–2015

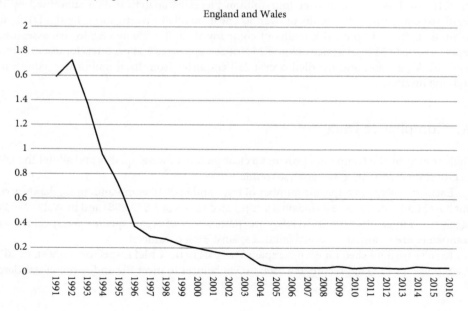

In August 2015 the Chief Inspector recognised that a new drinking water quality measure was required to replace the current MZC Index for a number of reasons, including provisions in amended regulations which permitted companies to move away from the current monitoring programme (based on sample numbers) to a risk-based monitoring methodology to assess compliance. The new Compliance Risk Index (CRI) is a measure designed to illustrate the risk arising from treated water compliance failures, and it aligns with the current risk-based approach to regulation of water supplies used by the DWI. All compliance failures are assessed by the DWI using the provisions of the Water Industry Act 1991.[14] In doing so, the DWI has regard to its published Enforcement Policy,[15] and it also follows the principles of 'better regulation' to scrutinise company performance on the basis of its risk of failing to meet the requirements of the Regulations.

This new measure includes elements relating to the significance of the parameter failing the standards in the Regulations, the cause and the manner of the investigation of the failure by the company, any mitigation put in place by the company and the location of the failure within the supply system, taking into account the proportion of the company's consumers affected. Integrated into the regulatory assessment and databases of the DWI since January 2016, the methodology uses a complex mathematical calculation to grade failures for their seriousness scoring the potential hazard the failure poses together with the outcome of the assessment (using a standard '5×5' grid principle – see Figure 16.1 in chapter sixteen).

Compliance failures for different parameters do not pose equal risk to consumers. The standards in the Regulations are based on different criteria: whilst some are set on a human health basis, others are based on aesthetic concerns, as indicators or for other reasons. This means that the risk posed from non-compliance with a parameter standard varies depending on the reason for the standard. All compliance failures are assessed to ensure that the wellbeing and interests of consumers were protected by best practice in management of compliance failures. Obviously, a well-managed compliance failure with appropriate and speedy mitigation action poses a lower risk to consumers. The DWI also considers the root cause of the failure and whether the company's actions led to, or increased, the likelihood of the failure, and whether further remedial action is necessary. Finally, the impact score accounts for the likely impact of the compliance failure, the data used varies depending upon where in the supply chain the failure occurs. For company assets this impact element relates to the size of the asset (output of water treatment works and capacity of service reservoirs). For failures occurring in water supply zones the impact depends upon the population affected and defaults to the population of the relevant water supply zone.

This may be seen in the equation below:

$$CRI = \frac{\text{Seriousness. Assessment. Impact (Population or WTW volume or SR capacity)}}{\text{Population of the company or WTW volume or SR capacity}}$$

[14] See www.legislation.gov.uk/ukpga/1991/56/contents.
[15] See www.dwi.gov.uk/about/enforcement-pol/dwi-enforcementv2.pdf.

The compliance risk scores for each of the companies is calculated by summing the individual values from all treatment works, service reservoirs and zones and these can be viewed as a company score or by the specific part of the supply system. A national CRI is calculated taking the population of England and Wales which is then incorporated into the national graph of performance to provide a standard against which companies can measure themselves. The results for 2016 published by the Chief Inspector in his report on the industry performance in 2017 are shown in Figure 19.2.

Figure 19.2 Industry overview of Compliance Risk Index 2016

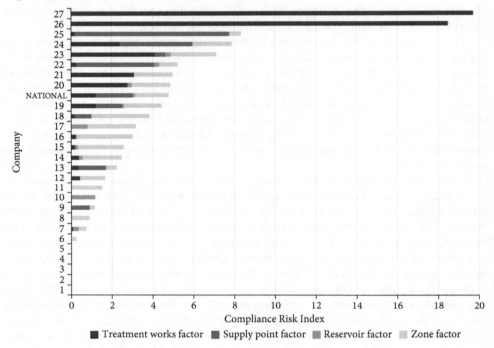

The national CRI for England and Wales in 2016 was 4.85 and this figure provides a key comparator, year on year, in driving down risk in the water supply industry or a single company as well as an understanding of the relative performance between companies within the overview. In 2016, for instance, companies 6 and 7 (in Figure 19.2) had a lower then average compliance risk whilst companies 26 and 27 were much higher. Furthermore, it can be identified that the majority of risk for company 16 derived from distribution while that from company 25 was almost entirely catchment-related. The CRI sets a national benchmark, enabling the company and the DWI to focus its investment and regulatory efforts where they are most needed. As part of a better regulatory strategy by the DWI, the focus would be most on those companies that exceed the national average but also on those companies which have notable bias in any particular area of their CRI, for example distribution for companies 16 and 17, treatment works for companies 23, 26 and 27 and catchment for companies 22, 24 and 25.

Figure 19.3 National overview of Compliance Risk Index 2016

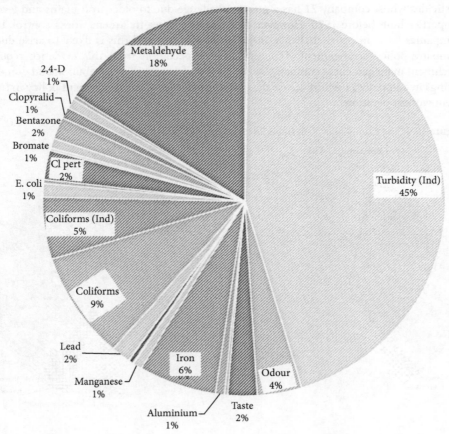

Exploring a breakdown of the CRI by parameter (see Figure 19.3) enables the DWI to identify the overall industry challenges nationally. In 2016, turbidity at works constituted 45 per cent of the CRI; 16 per cent was due to a pesticide used in agriculture to reduce slugs; nine per cent from coliforms detected at service reservoirs and works; and six per cent from iron arising from distribution. Importantly, the analysis is also able to discriminate risks in the domestic supply and identifies two per cent of the national risk is caused by the presence of lead. A national regulatory strategy has been developed by the DWI to reduce the risk by providing evidence for policy, research, financial investment and technical regulatory intervention in these specific areas.

This analysis is explored in greater detail for the individual company at parameter level using the same methodology. Figure 19.4 identifies the key contributing parameters to the CRI as an example in each of two companies. This example examines company 21 and company 24 which are in geographically distinct areas in England but are under the same ownership and management structure. Company 24 is located in an arable area where pesticides are more widely used and this contributes to about 45 per cent of the CRI by two pesticides whilst company 21 has a greater challenge due to older iron mains and lead in properties built before 1970. However, in respect of water treatment works control, both companies have an equal challenge in turbidity at works and this is likely to arise due to company policy arrangement. The regulatory expectation from this evidence requires catchment management at company 24 but conversely a focus on distribution and domestic fittings in company 21 whilst across the two companies senior management policy in treatment works operations.

Figure 19.4 The Compliance Risk Index 2016 for companies 21 and 24

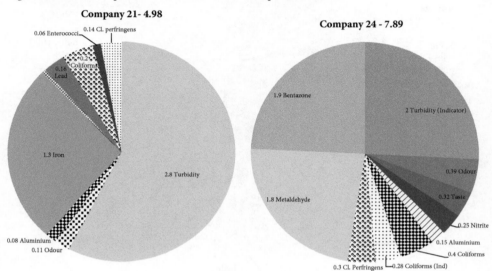

B. Reporting Events

As noted above, the companies are also required to self-report any event that may give rise to a significant risk to public health, affect the quality or sufficiency of a supply or might cause concern to the supplier, consumers or other authority. Such events must be reported as soon as possible after occurrence and are categorised by the DWI into minor, significant and serious/major categories.

There are usually about 500 such reports a year and the number of incidents for 2015 and 2016 are shown at Table 19.1.

The DWI has developed a new drinking water quality measure for events, based on similar thinking to the development of the CRI. This allows companies to move away from the current event response categorisation to a risk-based methodology to assess the impacts of events on consumers and to promote proactive risk mitigation. The Event Risk Index (ERI) is a measure designed to illustrate the risk arising from water quality events, and it aligns with the current risk-based approach to regulation of water supplies used by the DWI.

Table 19.1 Industry reported events 2015 and 2016

	Risk assessment category (DWI)					
	Minor*		Significant		Serious/major**	
Nature of event	2015	2016	2015	2016	2015	2016
Air in water	5	1	3	1		
Chemical	34	37	4	2	1	
Discoloured water	18	19	45	35		
Inadequate treatment	9	5	30	22	2	
Loss of supplies/poor pressure	37	38	29	26		1
Microbiological	50	47	22	39	3	3
Taste/Odour	36	32	13	12		1
Health concern	9	2	10		1	
Public concern	95	114	34	19	1	2
Other	15	7	17	8	2	
England	**308**	**302**	**207**	**164**	**10**	**8**
Wales	**16**	**21**	**16**	**10**	**0**	**0**
England and Wales*	**322**	**323**	**223**	**174**	**10**	**8**

*Minor category numbers include all not significant and minor events.
** Serious category numbers include all serious and major events.

Significant events must be reported by companies as soon as reasonable, followed by an initial written report within three days and as necessary a further report at 20 days. The reported events are allocated an initial score of 1–5 (5 is most severe) by a DWI inspector, on the basis of a mathematical calculation. A score of 1 would be assigned to an event where there is no health risk but consumers may have been dissatisfied or inconvenienced such as aeration; for 3 this would be an aesthetic or confidence outcome where consumers are likely to, or did, reject the water and for 5, this would equate to a health risk where consumers actually, or potentially, suffered harm. All reports are assessed on a graduated scale, category 1 events attracting little or no assessment and category 5 events result in a large response immediately mobilised which may include site visits.

The inspector's assessment of an event will result in a report. This is sent to the company and may include suggestions (eg 'We have seen the following better practice elsewhere and you should consider this'), recommendations ('this is a likely or actual breach of the regulations and there will be an expectation that the company will take steps to bring it back into compliance') or another graduated form of enforcement such as a warning letter or legal action. The DWI expects companies to give a formal response to the report.

The DWI adopts the same approach with ERI as it does with CRI, using the '5×5' grid principle – where the categorisation represents the seriousness of the event (hazard) and the assessment represents the likelihood of recurrence. The individual risk score is adjusted by taking into account the population affected by the event and the duration of the event together with the company size. Like CRI, ERI measures risk, calculating a value which takes into account the consequence of the event, any potential health risks and the assessed actions of the company in response.

This may be seen in the equation below:

$$ERI = \frac{\text{Seriousness. Assessment. Impact (Population. Time)}}{\text{Population of the Company}}$$

For example: a treatment works supplying 500,000 consumers has failed allowing undisinfected contaminated water (Cat 5), to be supplied for 10 hours to consumers by a company who supplies five million consumers and where legal action was taken, (Assessment 5), would attract a score of 25. If the same works in the same company supplied aerated water (Cat 1) to the same consumers and there were no suggestions, recommendations or other actions (Assessment 1), this would attract a score of 1.

The sum of all the events divided by the company population would be the ERI for that company and the sum of all the events in England and Wales divided by the population of the two countries would be the national ERI.

C. Developing Robust New Measures

The new approach for both CRI and ERI has been developed quickly to be aligned with the five-year price-setting cycle set by the financial regulator. The current Chief Inspector redesigned the system, and colleagues developed the advanced mathematics, which were tested on previous years' data and proved to be robust and reliable. Initial conversations were opened with industry in August 2016 and continued through 2017 and into 2018. The strategic objective is to drive long-term company behaviour based upon the principle of reducing risk the outcome of which is to reduce events and compliance failures in the expectation of delivering wholesome and acceptable water to consumers. This system relies on a perception of risk, the perception being that of the regulator.

By aligning quality and financial regulation this promotes the removal of potentially conflicting measures upon which companies react in the short term such as those seen with MZC. That artificial construct is considered to be unhelpful to safety/quality performance as it does not direct minds to strategic matters. A target approach involving only an average of failures versus those which do not fail leads companies to focus on compliance failures resolving the quick wins and saying that they only have 0.04 per cent of a problem, which misleads the public because the greatest impact on consumers is when there is an event which causes major disruption, discontent and distrust of the company. Developing the new system involved a great deal of discussion fully involving companies and especially the trade association, Water UK, on what the system was designed to achieve and how it was going to operate.

The first outputs of the new regulatory strategy were published in 2016. It was described as follows:[16]

> [It] seeks to develop further risk-based analysis of company performance. This builds upon the
> principles of better regulation by analysing information in a proportionate, consistent, equitable

---

[16] Drinking water 2016. Summary of the Chief Inspector's report for drinking water in England (DWI, 2017), 18.

and transparent way. The Inspectorate has consulted and worked with the Water Industry to seek a methodology which recognises and encourages best practice in the industry whilst eliciting the best outcome for consumers. ...

This strategy seeks to understand which companies are most likely to breach Regulations through failure to respond to previous occurrences and apply learning. ...

[In relation to the Event Risk Index,] understanding the risk behaviour of water companies to the mitigation and management of events is a critical strategic concern of the Inspectorate. The expectation of the Inspectorate is for companies to become resilient through their people, processes and procedures. Companies should also check their supply arrangements to ensure firstly, that incidents are reduced or, should there be an incident, that their response is such that there is no discernible effect on consumers. ...

The Inspectorate's strategic programme seeks to ensure that companies consider water quality risks and objectives upon which business plans can build for the long-term, driving continued confidence in the industry by consumers and all those who have vested interests. It is nonsensical to drive short-term polarised measures when the industry is asset heavy and long-term investment in those assets as well as collaboration with stakeholders, such as those associated with catchment and domestic systems, are key to maintaining quality. Focusing on and reducing risk in the facing challenges of resource, pollution, changing demographics and demands over the coming decades requires planning to achieve the far objectives.

Early data on the outcome of this strategy may be seen in Figure 19.5. The unadjusted data of company 23 for CRI between 2014 and 2016 indicates the effect on the company behaviour clearly produces improvements over the three-year period, most notably in the improvement at water treatment works.

Figure 19.5 The Compliance Risk Index 2014–2016 for company 23 (preliminary data)

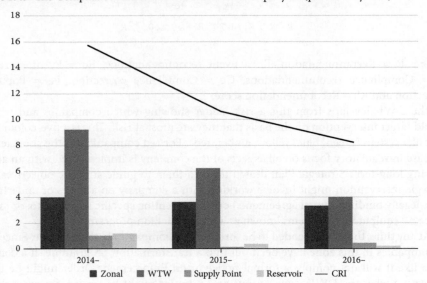

The strategy of the DWI seeks to go beyond the use of risk metrics directed at the regulated companies and to identify those companies most at risk of regulatory failure and the necessary focus by the regulator. Recommendations are more long term about how the regulator and the regulatory system works, based on the lowest level or first stage of regulatory intervention, in effect what's happening under the iceberg. They are made by the regulator in response to a breach or potential breach of the regulations under which companies meet their obligations. Typically they may arise from events, compliance, consumer complaints, audits or any other area where regulatory intervention occurs.

The objective is to get companies to take action themselves: they should be regarded as self-regulatory partners in this respect. Whilst observing this position, the DWI verifies that this model is operating by evidence should the need for further intervention be required. In this manner all recommendations made by the DWI are recorded and scored again utilising the 5×5 risk matrix of seriousness and likelihood. The seriousness of the breach graduates from 1 which represents a simple technical breach, 3 a serious breach of the regulation and up to the most severe where 5 represents a repeat of a similar breach with confidence or public health implications. All responses returned by the company are then assessed, where an assessment of 1 is satisfactory and those which are unacceptable, have no evidence to substantiate action by the company or no response and therefore likely to recur, are categorised as 5. Each recommendation will then produce a score between 1 and 25 from which a complex mathematical calculation sums each subgroup (events, compliance, complaints, etc). These are corrected on a linear graduated scale of all companies before taking the grand sum and applying a company population adjustment producing a final company risk value. As a long-term measure, recommendations are summed over a number of years on a diminishing scale:

This may be seen in the following equations of the Recommendations Likelihood Index:

$$\Sigma^R = \frac{\Sigma^{Er}}{E_C} + \frac{\Sigma^{Cr}}{C_C} + \cdots \cdots \frac{\Sigma^{Xr}}{X_C} \ and \ RS = \frac{\Sigma^R}{P_C}$$

$$R = R_1 + R_2 + 0.5^{3-2} \ R_3 + \cdots \cdots \cdots 0.5^{y-2} R_y$$

Where: R = Recommendation, Er = Event recommendations, Ec = Event correction, Cr = Compliance recommendations, Cc = Compliance correction, Pc = Population correction and RS = Recommendation score.

The DWI develops from this a risk ladder showing which companies and where it should target intervention on the basis that they are most at risk. This is a five-colour traffic light like system (green, blue, yellow, amber, red). For red companies, in the short term an increase in regulatory focus on all aspects of the company is implemented with an accompanying long-term Strategic Plan drawn up with them to guide strategic objectives. Such strategic intervention might involve working with a company on a series of undertakings (non-legally binding mutual agreements) on implementing specific upgrades to, or maintenance of, equipment or systems known as a transformation programme.

At any time, there have tended to be three or four companies in the red zone. Since 2015, all companies in this zone have been put into a transformation programme. If a company looks like it will not comply, a formal notice or an Enforcement Order might be issued, stipulating what the DWI's expectations are. A notice might be served, for example, at a treatment works where there is a risk of a contaminant being present for a company to mitigate this risk by eg installing UV treatment, or to stop supply. If it is felt that a company is negligent or reckless, the DWI may prosecute (the legal trigger being that water supplied is unfit or injurious to health, or that the treatment process is inadequate). Notwithstanding this focused approach, review of a proportion of events by those companies at the lower end of the risk ladder, in the green or blue areas, is necessary for assurance that the methodology remains robust and appropriately targeted.

III. Enforcement

The DWI's Enforcement Policy[17] is subject to the UK Government's overarching better regulation policy, and states the following:

> DWI recognises that the best way to achieve compliance with the law is to ensure, by guidance and advice, that those carrying out regulated activities understand the nature and extent of their responsibilities and comply voluntarily.
>
> However, there are times when conformity with the law needs to be sought by formal enforcement action. Formal enforcement is about securing compliance with regulatory requirements. To this end there is a spectrum of civil and criminal sanctions available to us. These include statutory undertakings to take remedial action, statutory notices (where in some instances an offence is committed if not obeyed) and criminal prosecution before the courts.
>
> ...
>
> The effective use of enforcement powers in regulatory schemes is important to secure compliance with the law and, where necessary, to ensure that those who have not complied may be held to account. Enforcing authorities need to take into account the need to maintain the balance between enforcement and other advisory activities when allocating resources.

The DWI has a wide range of enforcement powers. Prosecutions are rare, perhaps one or two a year.[18] The DWI's view is that they are a last resort and constitute failure of other controls. In 2017 there were two: Company 13's construction works at a site were carried out by cutting corners so as to finish on time after delays and ended up being reckless. They were fined £400,000 for the supply of water unfit for consumption and £80,000 for using non-approved materials in contact with water.[19] Company 19 had to issue a 'boil notice' in 2015 to over 700,000 consumers when a small protozoan parasite was found in the supply and were fined £300,000.[20]

Two recent cases illustrate the change in approach. Company 23 had a serious incident in 2016 caused by a faulty valve, in which 3,700 properties received water with elevated chlorine, resulting in a 'Do Not Use' notice to customers for 26 hours. The Inspectorate's investigation concluded that this serious event was avoidable and that there were a number of missed opportunities to identify and rectify the problem before the event and to mitigate its impact. This could have led to a prosecution. However, the company was in a Transformation Programme with the DWI at that time, which had been agreed after it had been prosecuted for a series of breaches between 2012 and 2014. The CEO had committed to

---

[17] 'Securing Safe, Clean Drinking Water for All. Enforcement Policy' (DWI, 2016).
[18] See www.dwi.gov.uk/press-media/incidents-and-prosecutions/pros-caut.html.
[19] Press release, 25 August 2017, www.dwi.gov.uk/press-media/press-releases/20170825_srn_sentencing.pdf.
[20] See www.dwi.gov.uk/press-media/press-releases/20171010_uut_sentencing.pdf.

an investment programme, which was being implemented, and it was recognised might take five or 10 years to complete. The DWI was satisfied that the company was moving satisfactorily through the Transformation Programme, as the metrics during 2017 showed that the previous trend was being reversed both for CRI (Figure 19.5), and the Recommendations Index (Figure 19.6). So the DWI decided not to prosecute for this breach. It thought that such a move would lead to company personnel feeling embittered and would adversely affect motivation to improve. A caution was issued instead.[21] This produced a notably positive reaction from the CEO and the staff of the company alike.

Figure 19.6 The Recommendations Index 2016–2017 for company 13 and company 23

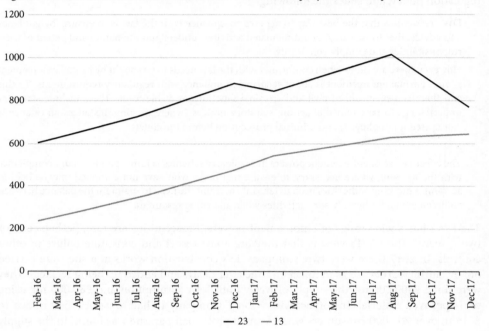

In contrast, company 13's Southampton construction works event was being considered around the same time. Whilst the company apologised and pointed out that its board had changed since the event and had started to formulate a Transformation Programme, the company was subject to Notices and Enforcement Orders following necessary regulatory interventions which were in doubt of being complied with. Furthermore, when considering the regulatory response and the company response to recommendations (Figure 19.6), evidence was lacking that the company had changed or turned around. The company's first objection to its prosecution was that it was unfair when compared with company 23. However, after the DWI pointed out that the two companies were in different spaces, that objection was dropped.

---

[21] Press release, 23 June 2017, www.dwi.gov.uk/press-media/press-releases/20170623-svt-caution.pdf.

Practices: Intervention Choices

20

Intervention Choices

GRAHAM RUSSELL AND HELEN KIRKMAN

The Regulatory Delivery Model identifies three inter-related practices considered as being fundamental to a regulatory agency's ability to achieve progress towards its regulatory outcomes. Chapter thirteen explored Outcome Measurement and chapter sixteen the question of how regulatory agencies can best decide where to direct their finite resources through Risk-based Prioritisation.

This chapter examines the third of these practices: the question of how a regulatory agency, being clear on its outcomes and having decided where to direct its resources, should best use them. The regulatory agency's approach to this question is considered within the Regulatory Delivery Model in terms of its 'Intervention Choices'.

We have explored the interactions between Intervention Choices and the other practices of the Regulatory Delivery Model in chapters thirteen and sixteen. There are also clear links between the capacity and motivation of regulatory agencies to make effective intervention choices and the prerequisites of the Regulatory Delivery Model. Where regulatory agencies have effective accountability mechanisms in place (see chapter seven), these shape their intervention choices, including by enabling them to accurately assess when it will be appropriate to use interventions that are relationship-based. In addition, a more proactive, positive culture within a regulatory agency (see chapter ten) will tend towards use of a wider palette of intervention choices. Acceptance of an over-prescriptive governance framework (see chapter three), potentially arising from a risk-averse culture or even weak leadership, will both limit the options available to the agency and, crucially, its capacity to challenge that lack of flexibility and discretion.

In this chapter we first consider the importance of the regulatory agency's intervention choices before considering the shape and range of the interventions that are available to regulatory agencies. We then explore how, in selecting from this range of interventions, the regulatory agency can ensure that it makes the right choices – selecting those interventions that will be most effective. We also reflect on ways in which regulatory agencies can make use of different relationships within the regulatory landscape, and the question of the regulatory agency's intervention style.

I. Why are Intervention Choices Important?

The task of regulatory agencies, while often expressed in terms of mitigating risk or ensuring compliance with regulation, is fundamentally about changing the behaviour of regulated entities. While some agencies do have direct authority to mitigate risks themselves, even in these cases most of their impact is achieved by changing the way others act. Behaviour of regulated entities matters not just because it determines compliance and non-compliance but because it contributes to wider outcomes of reducing regulatory risks. The primary question for a regulatory agency is therefore what it can do that will be most effective in delivering the desired behaviour change amongst those it regulates. A secondary question of relevance to many regulatory agencies will be what else they can do that will contribute to risk reduction.

In our work with diverse regulatory agencies, we have found it helpful to break these questions down into two constituents and to address them separately. These constituents – 'what interventions are available to the regulatory agency?' and 'which intervention(s) will be most effective?' – are explained later in this chapter. Where a regulatory agency is able to address both elements of this question it is well placed to make considered decisions on whether and how to intervene. Its intervention choices will be more appropriate, and this is likely to be beneficial in two specific ways. First, its interventions are more likely to change behaviour, with resultant improvements in compliance and reductions in regulatory risks. Secondly, where appropriate intervention choices are being made, the regulatory agency's behaviour is inherently more proportionate. As noted in chapter sixteen, proportionality is prized by regulated entities and colours their perception of regulatory fairness. The power imbalance between regulatory agencies and those they regulate is almost always, particularly in the case of smaller businesses, tilted towards the agency and choices can, from the perspective of regulated entities, appear capricious or unfair, necessitating even more care from the regulatory agency in making its intervention choices.

Regulatory interventions will always have an impact and it is important for the regulatory agency to do what it can to understand this impact so that informed choices can be made. This involves consideration of the costs of the intervention – to the regulatory agency, to regulated entities and to society – and the benefits to the same three parties. These costs and benefits are variable and hard to quantify and will seldom be aligned. Equally, consideration should be given to the potential unintended consequences that can be associated with particular interventions. For example, high levels of intervention by the regulatory agency can result in a situation where regulated entities become over-reliant on regulatory oversight and fail to take responsibility for compliance, seeing the responsibility for compliance as being owned externally to the regulated entity.

In *The Regulatory Craft*,[1] Malcolm Sparrow highlights the importance for regulatory agencies of identifying problem areas or patterns of non-compliance and designing interventions that are effective in controlling or reducing them – in his words, 'to pick important problems and fix them (and tell everyone)'. He emphasises the role that a wide range of tools plays in equipping a regulatory agency to respond effectively to problems and points to the importance of being open to innovative practice.

Where a regulatory agency uses a narrow range of interventions, perhaps those that it has traditionally relied on, it is less likely to be effective. For example, a heavy reliance on formal enforcement actions to coerce or punish, particularly those that involve the judicial system, is costly and this cost has traditionally been justified by pointing to a deterrent effect

---

[1] Malcolm Sparrow, *The Regulatory Craft: Controlling Risks, Solving Problems, and Managing Compliance* (Washington DC, Brookings Institution Press, 2000).

on the wider regulated community. However, increasing evidence shows that the alleged 'deterrent' effect of enforcement actions has limited sustained impact on compliance levels, as noted by Christopher Hodges and Ruth Steinholtz in chapter twenty-two. Similarly, many regulatory agencies have traditionally focused a significant proportion of their resources on inspection activity but have not always questioned whether other approaches might deliver greater benefits. Florentin Blanc's research into different approaches to occupational health and safety enforcement (see chapter fifteen) has shown that higher inspection rates do not necessarily equate to better outcomes and can correspond to worse outcomes. The research conducted for Staffordshire Local Enterprise Partnership mentioned in chapter thirteen compares approaches described as 'support before compliance' and 'compliance before support' in terms of their impact on food hygiene ratings and finds that starting with assessing compliance through inspection may be more costly and less likely to lead to better outcomes of either protection (in terms of food hygiene ratings) or prosperity (in terms of business survival).[2] None of this research suggests that sanctions or inspections are unimportant or ineffective, but it does point towards something that is fundamental to the impact of any regulatory agency – whether it has access to and confidence in the use of a full range of intervention choices.

Informed comparisons and choices between interventions should be enabled by any available evidence of the effectiveness of different intervention strategies – whether these have been previously used by the regulatory agency itself or by other regulatory agencies. As noted in chapter thirteen, the ongoing assessment of performance and evaluation of progress towards regulatory outcomes will highlight where the tools being used are effective and where they may need to be modified.

II. Regulatory Shape

There are various ways in which the intervention choices available to regulatory agencies can be categorised and one of these concerns the question of the way in which the 'regulatory shape' has been designed. It is important that careful consideration is given to intervention choices at every stage, from policy design to frontline delivery. Consideration of interventions made by regulatory agencies has tended to focus on operational decisions, but this is both too narrow and too late. At the policy design stage, the focus is rightly on what behaviour is to be expected from those subject to the regulatory requirements but equal attention is merited for the design of the relationship that they will have with the regulatory agency and what sort of regulator the agency should therefore be.

It is at the policy design stage that a 'strategy' is chosen, whether implicitly or explicitly, that defines the balance of regulatory effort between points in the regulatory lifecycle. The choices made establish a 'regulatory shape' or approach to intervention which allocates regulatory intervention resources between three regulatory phases: before regulated activity commences, for example, through business registration or licensing (pre-entry authorisation); during the undertaking of the regulated activity, for example through market surveillance or inspection (in-service supervision); or after the regulated activity

---

[2] Staffordshire University, 'Measuring the Impact of Regulation', study for Stoke-on-Trent and Staffordshire Enterprise Partnership (forthcoming).

has resulted in an incident for example, through investigation (post-event investigation). In terms of risk this can be expressed as: before a risk can exist; while the risk exists; and after it has been realised.

This is illustrated in Figure 20.1. Approach A has relatively high levels of regulatory oversight in relation to market entry and relatively lower regulatory resource is allocated to market surveillance, inspection and investigation. In Approach B, pre-entry oversight is lower but businesses in the market are subject to higher levels of ongoing supervision while Approach C focuses primarily on investigation of what has already 'gone wrong'.

Figure 20.1 An example of contrasting regulatory shapes

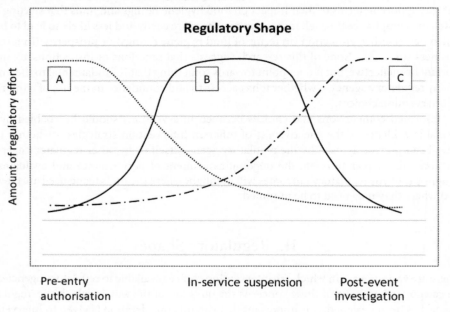

A comparison across various countries indicates that very different solutions have been selected, both between countries and between regulatory areas within a country. While it is not always possible to trace an intentional decision-making process behind the design or shape, links can be drawn to the risk appetite and culture of the society from which they arise. Assessing the causality of these links is a step too far at this point, but we can talk with more certainty about the impacts of the alternatives on the agency and on the outcomes for beneficiaries and regulated entities. The amount of regulatory effort, and potentially the cost to the state, may be similar in different approaches but the impact on regulated entities is very different.

The shape of the regulatory approach, in the economy generally or for the regulatory areas within one agency's mandate, will have a direct effect on the relationship between the regulatory agency and those it regulates, in terms of opportunities to build trust, share data and build outcomes. Whatever the extent of its role in creating that shape, the regulatory agency will need to respond to it, ensuring that it is capable of delivering what is required. Where the emphasis is on in-service inspection and supervision, the agency will need to internalise a level of technical skill and competence in its officers which is different from the assessment skills required by a regulatory agency that is administering a licensing system in which it is the applicant business that is required to present proof of competence through, for example, third-party certification. The relative absence of barriers to entry in an approach shaped around interventions during the undertaking of the regulated activity places greater emphasis on the ability of the officer to understand and drive the motivation of the regulated entity. Conversely, where the emphasis is on post-event investigation, the skills of the officers will need to be more forensic, reconstructing causes and effects, and allocating responsibility.

For the regulated entity, an emphasis on post-event investigation may be attractive. The entity will receive few, if any, interventions unless they cause harm and they can see because only the 'polluter pays' they gain benefit from their investment in compliance. However, it can be a high-risk position for them, as well as for the regulatory agency. The distance between regulator and regulated will grow and, to the extent that early interventions drive compliance, the likelihood of non-compliance will increase. Equally significantly, the consequences of non-compliance are also likely to rise. Not only regulatory consequences – sanctions and remedial costs – but impact on customers and on reputation. For these (and less well-founded reasons) established, incumbent businesses may prefer a system rooted in pre-entry authorisation, and conversations in various countries have shown a remarkable attachment on the part of businesses to onerous licensing regimes. (This in itself is a reason to search out and engage with 'nearly companies' and start-ups if the regulatory agency is to fully understand the impact of a licensing regime.)

The impact of the different regulatory shapes on beneficiaries takes us back to the questions of the nature and 'colour' of risks discussed in chapter sixteen. Pre-entry authorisation approaches deliver the 'precautionary principle' and may be appropriate where the hazard is high, risks would be very costly to remedy, or the harm is irreversible, provided that entry barriers focus on capability for compliance. In-service supervision can be less bureaucratic than a licensing regime whilst still addressing a broad spectrum of harms and it can build confidence when it is important that something is seen to be being done (the regulatory equivalent of 'visible policing' known in the UK as 'bobbies on the beat'). Post-event investigation can still satisfy a need for attribution and retribution and provide learning that shapes future action, even if restoration is not possible.

Even this brief assessment suggests some grounds for intentional decision-making about regulatory shape at the design or strategy stage. Opening up such a discussion about appropriate intervention choices would not only increase the likelihood of the regulatory agency achieving multiple goals, it would also equip it with the confidence to make those choices in all its activities.

III. The Range of Interventions

To return to the question posed earlier in this chapter as to what a regulatory agency can do that will be most effective in delivering the desired regulatory outcomes. The first constituent of this question relates to the range of interventions required of and available to the regulatory agency: 'What interventions are available to the regulatory agency?'. This question can be considered by first examining the regulatory agency's governance framework, which sets out the interventions required of the regulatory agency and empowers the regulatory agency to use certain interventions, and then by examining the range of interventions that the regulatory agency may choose to use in the absence of specific powers, including the option not to intervene. We will also consider how regulatory agencies can extend the range of interventions available to them by working with and through others in 'co-production' approaches.

A. 'Required' Interventions

For many regulatory agencies, the question of regulatory shape is wholly or largely pre-determined by legislation. Solutions chosen at the policy design stage may mean that the regulatory agency is required to use specific interventions. For example, the legislation may establish a licensing requirement for businesses and a role for the regulatory agency in administering the licensing process.

In some countries, legislation may direct the regulatory agency to employ specific supervisory interventions, for example, mandating inspection as part of licence application processes or in response to consumer complaints or imposing a requirement that every incident is reported and every report investigated. In the UK, while not all work-related injuries are investigated, there will be an investigation for all that result in a fatality.[3] Chapter twenty-five highlights the Mongolian experience of moving from mandatory inspection towards a risk-based approach to responding to consumer complaints.

B. 'Powers' to Intervene

For some regulatory agencies, the legislative framework affords them discretion to design or significantly influence the shape of regulatory interventions. For example, the regulatory agency may have a discretionary power to establish a pre-entry registration or licence requirement. Where the regulatory agency has this discretion, it is important that its approach is deliberate and considered, reflecting the regulatory risks that it seeks to control and the needs of the market being regulated.

A risk-based approach to selecting and using the right regulatory shape can ensure that regulatory effort is focused at the point in the regulatory lifecycle where it is most needed and that the related burdens on business are proportionate. For example, while it might be appropriate to have pre-entry requirements for food-processing businesses, the requirements can be proportionate to risk: low-risk businesses might be required only to register; businesses presenting a medium risk would need a licence or permit; while only the highest risk businesses would be required to present specialist proof of competence relating to the business operation.[4]

---

[3] 'Incident Selection Criteria – Revised' (Health and Safety Executive, 2014), available at www.hse.gov.uk/enforce/incidselcrits.pdf.

[4] As an example, UK food businesses are subject to pre-entry authorisation requirements which differ depending on the business activities, from a requirement to register premises with their local authority to a requirement to apply for approval by their local authority or (where veterinary controls are required) by the Food Standards Agency.

The legislative framework will usually grant a range of powers to the regulatory agency in relation to in-service supervision of businesses (for example, the power to inspect goods or premises or to require production of documents) and sanctioning powers, enabling it to deal with non-compliance through prosecution or other enforcement actions.

C. Other Interventions

The legislative frameworks within which regulatory agencies operate can vary enormously, requiring or empowering the regulatory agency to take a relatively narrow or a very broad range of actions. It is important for each regulatory agency to look beyond these specific actions and to avoid being unnecessarily constrained by its statutory powers: a variety of 'tools' or 'interventions' should be considered.

A wide range of other interventions are available to most regulatory agencies that can be used in conjunction with or as alternatives to traditional licence, inspection or investigation-based approaches. These might include, for example: initiatives to raise awareness and understanding of the regulatory requirements amongst those they regulate; oversight of industry compliance initiatives; partnership working through intermediaries; and initiatives to empower the beneficiaries of regulation, particularly those most at risk. These types of initiatives are further explored later in this chapter.

D. Non-intervention

In considering its intervention choices, it is also important for a regulatory agency to recognise that there are situations in which the most appropriate choice is to not intervene. The OECD's best practice principle of selectivity for regulatory agencies emphasises this:

> Promoting compliance and enforcing rules should be left to market forces, private sector and civil society actions wherever possible: inspections and enforcement cannot be everywhere and address everything, and there are many other ways to achieve regulatory objectives.[5]

The regulatory agency may choose not to intervene where, as recognised by the OECD principles, others are best placed to do so. Alternatively, intervention may not be needed because acceptance of the requirements is high, and the risk of non-compliance is extremely low. For example, laws introduced in England in July 2007 to make virtually all enclosed public places and workplaces smoke-free achieved very high compliance rates from the outset,[6] with little need for regulators to intervene, and these high levels of acceptance have since established 'smoke-free' as a social norm.

The regulatory agency might equally identify situations where the risk is high, but its intervention has little or no merit because further risk reduction is not possible. For example, where the hazard associated with an activity is inherently high but is being well managed by the regulated entity, further regulatory intervention may not deliver any benefit.

---

[5] Principle 2, 'Regulatory Enforcement and Inspections', OECD Best Practice Principles for Regulatory Policy (OECD, 2014).
[6] 'Smokefree England – one year on' (Department of Health, 2008).

In any situation where a regulatory agency decides not to intervene there may be a need to maintain a presence, both to monitor the risk situation, for example through a low level of random sampling, and to maintain confidence in the sector and amongst beneficiaries.

E. Co-production Approaches

Regulatory agencies have traditionally focused on their own interactions with regulated entities. However, there is increasing recognition that whilst direct intervention by the regulatory agency may be the most appropriate tool in some circumstances, this will not always be the case. Regulatory agencies can use the various relationships within the regulatory landscape, as shown in Figure 20.2, whether in addition to or instead of more traditional interventions, to drive regulatory outcomes.

Figure 20.2 Relationships between parties in the regulatory landscape

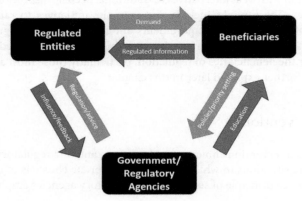

Regulatory agencies may, through co-production models, be able to achieve cost-effective and sustainable changes in the behaviour of regulated entities by exploiting other influences on the regulated entity. For example, the behaviour of regulated entities can be influenced by a wide range of third parties, with the most obvious of these often being the beneficiaries of regulation. There are many times more citizens, workers and consumers than businesses, other regulated entities and inspectors. This means that there can be potential, in the right circumstances, for lots of influence, multiplying the impact of the regulatory agency. Direct involvement of beneficiaries and their representatives can contribute to intelligence assessment, create a demand for regulated information, increase the likelihood of informed choices and motivate businesses to improve. Graham has discussed, in the introduction to this book, Staffordshire County Council's establishment of a consumer watchdog scheme, putting into practice the concept of 'armchair auditors' or 'citizens as inspectors' in the consumer protection field. Similar examples exist in the areas of environmental regulation, where citizens can play a role in notifying the regulatory agency of environmental violations[7] and in the contribution of trade unions to labour market regulation.

---

[7] Chris Booth, 'Exploring the Use and Effectiveness of Complementary Approaches to Environmental Inspection for Ensuring Compliance' (European Union Network for the Implementation and Enforcement of Environmental Law, 2012).

There can also be potential for a business to be influenced towards more compliant behaviour by its commercial customers, insurers, trade associations and professional bodies, legal and financial advisers, consultants, competitor businesses, etc. As with beneficiaries, this requires the regulatory agency to have an understanding of the capacity and capability of third parties to drive change. Where this exists, the regulatory agency can build regulatory partnerships. The possibility of harnessing beneficiaries may require the regulatory agency to take responsibility for building suitable capacity and can be dependent on a relationship of trust between beneficiaries and the regulatory agency, which creates the potential to use co-production models.[8] This can sound daunting to regulatory agencies unused to working in this way, but the resources required to build the capacity for successful citizen empowerment approaches can deliver multiple benefits. Where such approaches are successful, they not only contribute to reductions in regulatory risks, but can also release regulatory resource which can be used to target persistent and deliberate non-compliance.

The Better Regulation Delivery Office worked with UK researchers, regulators and citizen representative organisations in 2013 to develop an approach to exploring the possibilities for citizen empowerment, and to using it effectively where appropriate. This approach focuses initially on the question of whether citizen empowerment can work in a specified regulated market as it is clear that it will work better in some markets than others and there are contexts where it is not appropriate. For example, when considering the relationship between consumers and regulated businesses in order to understand the potential for using citizen empowerment, the regulatory agency needs to establish the extent to which consumers are able to make choices and how much influence they can exert, through these choices or otherwise.

Having established that there is potential for citizen empowerment approaches to work in a regulated market, the regulatory agency will need to consider how it can maximise the effectiveness of those approaches. The research[9] identified a five-step pathway to empowerment to help regulatory agencies identify areas for action on a particular issue. The steps are designed to apply across a range of issues and incorporate the perspective and considerations of each party at every step. While the specific considerations at each step will differ by issue, the aim of each step remains constant. The five steps can be summarised as:

1. **Awareness** – The first question is whether beneficiaries know that the risk exists and whether it is visible to them. Where appropriate, the regulatory agency can then determine what action could be taken to raise awareness of the risks, considering how the action can be designed so that it is effective for the groups being targeted.
2. **Information** – The next question is what information can be provided that is a proxy for compliance and how the regulatory agency can ensure that the information is reliable. As with awareness raising, the regulatory agency can then determine what action could be taken to disseminate appropriate information, considering how the information will be accessed by the groups being targeted.

---

[8] Paul Sanderson, 'The Citizen in Regulation. A Report on the Evidence Base for the Local Better Regulation Office' (Centre for Housing and Planning Research, 2011).

[9] 'Growing Empowered Economies: A Guide for Local Regulators' (Research by Quadrangle in partnership with the Better Regulation Delivery Office, unpublished). Also ICF GHK in association with Quadrangle, Targeting regulatory decision-making to empower citizens and incentivise business compliance: 'Literature and Evidence Review – Final Report' (unpublished, available from authors on request).

3. **Understanding** – Here we ask whether the relevant beneficiaries are able to process the information in order to form a robust basis for decisions about whether and how to act. Where appropriate, the regulatory agency may consider whether action is required to raise capability and capacity or to format the information so that it is accessible for the groups being targeted.
4. **Engagement** – It is important to understand whether the audience are sufficiently motivated to become engaged. This can depend on factors such as whether it is relevant to them or those they care about, whether they assume someone else will do something about it, and whether they believe their actions can make a difference.
5. **Action** – In order for beneficiaries to act in a manner that will reduce regulatory risks, they need to understand what actions are available to them. The likelihood that they will act may depend on how easy it is to act and what barriers to action exist.

In relation to consumer protection, where consumers are the intended beneficiaries of regulation, there are a growing number of examples, in the UK and elsewhere, of regulatory initiatives to empower consumers. One clear example of the benefits of empowering consumers to make better purchasing decisions can be seen in the development of food hygiene rating schemes in various countries over the past 20 years, as explored in chapter twenty-one. Improved purchasing decisions in relation to safe food reduce the regulatory risks associated with poor food hygiene for those consumers making more informed decisions and have a positive influence on business behaviour.

IV. Designing Effective Interventions

The second constituent of the question posed earlier as to what a regulatory agency can do that will be most effective in delivering the desired regulatory outcomes relates to the choices that the regulatory agency makes in selecting from the range of interventions available to it. The regulatory agency should be selecting each intervention or combination of interventions on the basis of how effective it will be, actively considering the potential to reduce risks and improve outcomes.

Risk assessment is valuable in helping the regulatory agency to determine where it should best allocate its resources (see chapter sixteen) and can also act as a helpful starting point for the agency when considering intervention choices. For example, as noted earlier in this chapter in relation to the design of regulatory shape, risk can inform decisions on the most appropriate type of pre-entry intervention. This might range from registration where the risk is relatively low, through to proof of competence for the highest risks. Similarly, risk can inform the design of appropriate in-service supervision interventions, which might involve occasional random checks on a sample of lower-risk premises or products, routine, generic inspection of medium risk premises or products, and frequent interventions by specialist inspectors where the risk are highest, for example at key points in supply chains. Investigations might always follow where harm caused is above a prescribed threshold.

However, it is important that a risk score is not the sole factor that guides decisions on the appropriate regulatory intervention. The OECD's best practice principles for regulatory agencies note the importance of a responsive approach: 'Enforcement should be based on "responsive regulation" principles: inspection enforcement activities should be modulated depending on the profile and behaviour of specific businesses.'[10] Responsive regulation is a concept identified by Ian Ayres and John Braithwaite to describe an enforcement strategy in which regulators take account of the motivations and general performance record of those regulated when they decide how to respond to a breach of the law.[11] The ability of the regulatory agency to make sound 'responsive' choices depends on a deep understanding of the environment and the market it regulates, including the culture, risk appetites and attitudes to compliance amongst the regulated entities. This enables the agency to unpick the risk score, considering how the risk has been generated.

As considered in chapter sixteen, the shape of regulatory risk differs; the same risk score may, for example, be allocated to two regulated entities but for very different reasons. For example, one business may be managing a high-hazard process quite well and this combination of a high hazard and low likelihood of non-compliance place it in an 'Upper medium' risk band. Another business in the same risk band has a very high likelihood of non-compliance but the impact of its non-compliance is low (see Figure 16.3). It is unlikely that the same regulatory interventions will be appropriate for each of these businesses. It is key to remember here that the hazard score is primarily a function of the nature of the business or the activity it is undertaking and it is generally less likely that, in the short term at least, regulatory intervention will reduce this. One specific exception to this general approach is worth noting at this point. Capturing data about the nature of a harm – its type, location and scale and the extent of mitigating action taken – has been a purpose in some inspections, for example in regard to fire safety to ensure that future fire-fighting can be carried out with minimum risk to citizens and fire officers. In designing future intervention strategies this need shouldn't be ignored, but alternative means of capturing the data may be available.

A. Reasons for Non-compliance

If interventions are unlikely to quickly change a hazard rating, action by the regulatory agency is more likely to have a significant impact on the likelihood of non-compliance. Even here, it is important to recognise that regulated entities may be assessed by a regulatory agency as presenting a similar likelihood of non-compliance but for quite different reasons. This concept is referred to as 'routes to regulatory risk', or sometimes 'routes to likelihood' and the distinction here between different routes relates primarily to the regulated entity's attitude to complying with the requirements and its capacity to achieve compliance, although other factors may also have an influence. For example, where regulatory requirements are new, lack of awareness and understanding of the requirements across the sector may mean that the sector demonstrates a high likelihood of non-compliance. A skilled regulatory agency will acknowledge the underlying reasons for a high likelihood of non-compliance and will select or design interventions that are appropriate to the circumstances. It can be helpful for a regulatory agency to assign regulated entities with a high likelihood of

---

[10] Principle 4, 'Regulatory Enforcement and Inspections', OECD Best Practice Principles for Regulatory Policy (OECD, 2014).

[11] Ian Ayres and John Braithwaite, *Responsive Regulation: Transcending the Deregulation Debate* (Oxford, Oxford University Press, 1992).

non-compliance to a small number of conceptual 'behaviour' groups. The regulatory agency might, for example, categorise the approach to compliance as:

- 'low intention' – at the extremes, this behaviour may be described as criminal;
- 'low attention' – careless; and
- 'low capacity' – incompetent or ignorant.

An OECD[12] report on regulatory compliance proposes that explanations for non-compliance fall into three categories:

> The degree to which the target group knows of, and comprehends the rules;
>
> The degree to which the target group is willing to comply; and
>
> The degree to which the target group is able to comply with the rules.

Categorisation such as these can be valuable in terms of providing a structured way of thinking about appropriate interventions across a market or sector, as shown in Figure 20.3. Where the regulatory agency diagnoses that low levels of awareness or understanding are contributing to non-compliance across a sector, these causes can be addressed, for example, through the provision and promotion of guidance or through targeted information campaigns. Trade associations and other trusted intermediaries can be a crucial connection point, enabling the regulatory agency to reach larger numbers of businesses. Trade associations are also well placed to assist the agency in designing meaningful communications and practical tools to support business compliance.

Where the diagnosis is that there are issues with a lack of motivation to comply, the regulatory agency needs to understand the reasons for this in order to address them. Motivation to comply can be determined by the extent to which the regulatory requirements align with the financial interests of the business. For example, regulations that protect consumers from immediate harm might be closely aligned with business interest, whereas issues such as the energy consumption of products may be less visible to consumers, and consequently may not generate the same interest from the business. It is critical for the regulatory agency to understand the extent to which the intent of regulations aligns or conflicts with business interests in order to understand the potential for compliance to be achieved largely through business or consumer pressure. Regulators can also influence motivation to comply through a range of means. For example, regulators can promote the positive benefits of compliance such as reduced waste, or improved customer satisfaction. Alternatively, motivation may need to be stimulated by highlighting the risks of non-compliance to business; for these audiences, evidence of powerful enforcement action can have a deterrent impact.

A categorisation based on awareness, motivation and capacity can be equally helpful in relation to variation between individual regulated entities. This again requires the regulatory agency to have a good level of understanding of those it regulates, and the behavioural influences and drivers that are at play. However, it is important to recognise that these categories do not have clearly defined boundaries and regulated entities may exhibit behaviours that fall into more than one category. This can be the case at a point in time – with a business exhibiting different attitudes to compliance in respect of different regulatory

---

[12] 'Reducing the Risk of Policy Failure: Challenges for Regulatory Compliance' (OECD, 2000).

Figure 20.3 Choosing appropriate interventions across a regulated sector

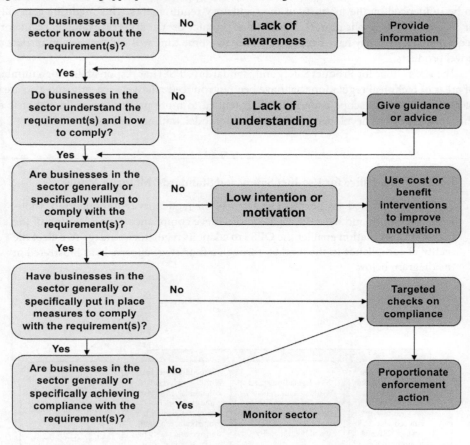

requirements – and over time, in particular as the business moves from a start-up phase to maturity.[13]

B. Maturity of Regulation

Recognition of awareness, motivation and capacity is significant for the regulatory agency in terms of ensuring compliance, but is equally important in the development of regulatory policy. An approach to policy development in which businesses are fully consulted on forthcoming regulations including the evidence base for them and the assessment of their impact can help to raise awareness of requirements, assist in building acceptance and therefore motivation to comply, and can also help to ensure that the resultant rules are practical for business to implement.

---

[13] 'Compliance Advisory Service. A Feasibility Study for EMDA' (Faster Futures Ltd and Enterprise Research and Development Unit, University of Lincoln, 2008).

As this develops, the categorisation of business approaches to compliance will continue to be influenced by the maturity of the regulatory requirements. This might be generally, or in terms of its application to a particular product or activity. For example, regulatory requirements that may have been in existence for some time will still feel new in respect of novel products.

The UK's Office for Product Safety and Standards (OPSS) has responsibility for a number of areas of technical regulation that have been introduced relatively recently and also areas of regulation whose scope is periodically extended to more product areas. In response to this, the agency has developed its own Maturity Model, outlined in Box 20.1.

Box 20.1 The Office for Product Safety and Standards' Maturity Model

To comply regulated entities must be aware of the regulatory requirements, be motivated to comply, and have the capacity to achieve compliance. Consideration of the maturity of legislation enables the OPSS to adapt its regulatory strategy to reflect the reality of compliance in the market, through a four-stage approach, as illustrated in the diagram below.

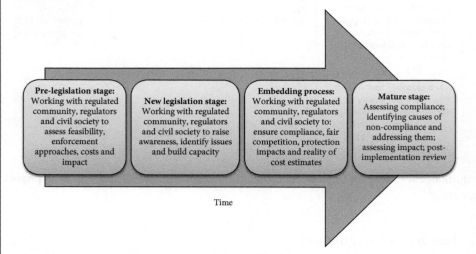

Pre-legislation stage: Working with regulated community, regulators and civil society to assess feasibility, enforcement approaches, costs and impact

New legislation stage: Working with regulated community, regulators and civil society to raise awareness, identify issues and build capacity

Embedding process: Working with regulated community, regulators and civil society to: ensure compliance, fair competition, protection impacts and reality of cost estimates

Mature stage: Assessing compliance; identifying causes of non-compliance and addressing them; assessing impact; post-implementation review

Time

In some cases, otherwise mature regulations are extended to new areas. For example, energy efficiency requirements are regularly extended to include new product categories. In these situations, the market includes businesses that can be expected to be aware of the rules, as well as businesses to whom the requirements will be new. OPSS will target awareness raising and support activity towards the newly included businesses, whilst maintaining focus on checking compliance for the more mature areas.

Equally, technological change can also result in mature regulations being applied to new situations and this may require the regulatory agency to revert to an early phase approach to support business. For example, the UK's regulations dealing with the metering of electricity date back to the 1980s. However, significant technological change is underway in this market including, for example, rising demand for electric vehicle recharging solutions. This is resulting in significant innovation and an increased need for business support in the interpretation of regulatory requirements.

Stage 1. Pre-legislation

Once legislation is proposed, OPSS undertakes analysis to understand the types of businesses and other entities regulated, what they will need to do to achieve compliance, and how they can best be reached. At this early stage OPSS's focus will be on raising awareness with regulated entities and engaging with the relevant sectors to understand and address potential barriers to compliance whilst informing impact assessments and design options.

Stage 2. New legislation

Awareness and understanding of regulatory requirements may be low when they are first enacted and will build over time. Depending on risk factors such as the nature of the hazard being addressed, a focus on awareness raising and supporting compliance typically dominates OPSS's approach for the first few years of new requirements being enacted.

Capacity to comply will be dependent, in part, upon the complexity of the compliance task and the resources of the regulated entity. In general, smaller businesses will be less likely to have access to regulatory specialists and therefore will tend towards a lower capacity for compliance. OPSS carefully considers the capacity of target businesses to comply with new requirements and where necessary develops tailored support products to strengthen capacity.

Stage 3. Embedding requirements

As the requirements are embedded, the balance of OPSS activity will shift towards assessing compliance and the associated action to secure compliance. It is important to recognise, however, as noted earlier, that awareness-raising and support must be maintained at some level to meet the needs of new businesses entering the market.

Stage 4. Mature regulatory framework

As legislation matures, many regulatory areas reach a state of sustained high levels of compliance. At this stage, the strategy of OPSS will again be adjusted to ensure that compliance is monitored and maintained, whilst maximising regulatory efficiency. A key consideration here is the extent to which motivation to comply and capacity to comply will be maintained with a reduced level of regulatory input. One example of this is OPSS's responsibility to ensure that UK retailers provide facilities for consumers to return depleted batteries to stores. Compliance with the requirement is straightforward, necessitating the provision of a collection bin and a disposal contract. A sustained period of awareness raising followed by inspection of larger businesses had been implemented in order to address very low levels of compliance. Compliance is also driven by consumer behaviour, with sufficient numbers of consumers accustomed to returning batteries to apply pressure on businesses to provide facilities. By 2016, inspections of multi-site retailers were confirming that compliance was being achieved at around 95 per cent of stores.[14] In this environment OPSS suspended routine regulatory checks, maintaining limited sampling to verify that compliance overall is being maintained.

In relation to mature regulation, therefore, a 'watching brief' is maintained and ongoing dialogue with the regulated community remains important. This dialogue ensures that OPSS is alerted to developments in the sector and informs its horizon scanning.

C. Approaches to Building Compliance

As explored though this and earlier chapters, questions of risk-based prioritisation and the design of regulatory shape will determine where the regulatory agency focuses its efforts and, in particular, its own interactions with those it regulates. These interventions with regulated entities are likely to span a wide range of activities, whether these involve registration and licensing, direct checks on compliance (eg data requirements and inspections), the provision of support for compliance (eg awareness-raising initiatives, advice and guidance) or their responses to compliance failures, through investigation and sanctioning. The agency's interventions with and through others will have an even wider span, ranging from education to empowerment, and must be rooted in a sound understanding of behavioural insights.

Historically, in many countries and in many regulatory contexts, there has been an emphasis on what are now seen as the traditional tools of regulatory agencies: namely, high levels of inspection to detect non-compliance and the deterrence of non-compliance through sanctions. However, the evidence for the impact of inspection on behaviour is mixed and, similarly, in respect of traditional approaches to enforcement, recent analysis suggests that, for most businesses, deterrence has, at best, limited impact. The OECD report on regulatory compliance mentioned earlier in this chapter explores responses to 'overly legalistic regulation' and reports research that establishes that unreasonable and unresponsive regulation has negative effects on compliance rates. Similarly, enforcement styles which rely on 'strict, coercive strategies' can impact on the goodwill and motivation of those businesses that were already willing to be socially responsible, adversely affecting compliance and increasing resistance to the enforcer. One example given is research in which businesses were interviewed about environmental and health and safety regulation: 'Where the

---

[14]'Enforcement and Market Surveillance Annual Report 2016–17' (Office for Product Safety and Standards, 2018).

businesses felt that regulators were being overly legalistic in the application of rules and imposition of fines they would tend to respond by scaling down their efforts to comply with the intent of the law'.[15]

Research into the likelihood of compliance indicates that businesses respond most when they see impact on reputation and profitability.[16] Alternative approaches that improve compliance whilst also improving the confidence or control the business has or the confidence that consumers have in the business are seen to have more impact.[17]

Increasingly, there is recognition that the most effective approach for most regulatory agencies is to 'sell' the benefits of compliance to those they regulate, encouraging and supporting the majority of businesses to voluntarily comply. In this context and for a given risk profile, they need to use the 80:20 rule to maximise compliance amongst the willing majority, leaving the scarce resources of the regulatory agency to focus on the criminal, the careless and the incompetent. The OECD's best practice principles for regulatory agencies encourage compliance promotion, including through the use of appropriate materials such as regulatory guidance and compliance toolkits.[18]

In the UK, the influence of the Hampton review,[19] discussed in chapter one, has been significant in encouraging the use of a wider range of regulatory tools, in particular in embedding supportive approaches by regulatory agencies. Hampton focused on the interaction between regulators and individual businesses and promoted the benefits of business advice and education as an effective regulatory tool. The provision of regulatory advice, guidance and information was subsequently incorporated into the governance framework for UK regulators through the Regulators' Code, explained in chapter five.

Numerous local authority-led projects in the UK over the past 20 years have demonstrated the potential benefits of a supportive approach. In an early example, a 2004 collaboration between Bolton Metropolitan Borough Council and Salford University aimed at improving food hygiene standards in ethnic catering businesses demonstrated that directed training support to businesses that had not previously responded well to a traditional inspection regime was very effective in raising compliance levels: 65 per cent of the premises targeted in the first phase of the project showed significant improvement.[20]

The importance of a wide range of regulatory tools and the ability to use these tools flexibly is particularly marked where the regulatory agency is faced with non-compliance. Traditional enforcement models have often been based on the detection and prosecution of individual breaches of the law, with an underlying belief that the imposition of a sanction for the most serious non-compliance would deter the offender, who would comply in future, but would also have a deterrent effect on other regulated entities. Fresh understandings,

---

[15] Eugene Bardach and Robert Kagan, *Going by the Book: The Problem of Regulatory Unreasonableness* (Philadelphia, Temple University Press, 1982) cited in OECD (2000).

[16] See for example 'Drivers of Compliance and Non-compliance with Competition Law' (London, Office of Fair Trading, 2010); 'Qualitative Research Exploring Regulation Cultures and Behaviours' (Social Science Research Unit, Food Standards Agency, 2012); 'Regulation and Growth' (Local Better Regulation Office, 2012).

[17] 'Food Safety Management Evaluation Research Report' (Food Standards Agency, 2007).

[18] Principle 10, 'Regulatory Enforcement and Inspections', OECD Best Practice Principles for Regulatory Policy (OECD, 2014).

[19] Philip Hampton, 'Reducing Administrative Burdens: Effective Inspection and Enforcement' (HM Treasury, 2005).

[20] 'Improving the Public Image and Risk Assessment of Ethnic Minority Food Retail Businesses – the 'Bolt' Project'. Presentation to Food Standards Agency workshop, 2004 (unpublished).

such as from behavioural science and experience, have updated thinking through insights into human and organisational behaviour. The critical insight is to separate actions that impose sanctions in response to anti-social behaviour (backward-looking), from responses aimed at affecting future behaviour (forward-looking). Sanctions imposed for past behaviour should not be seen as being the way to affect future behaviour – one needs a different approach for that.

D. Use of Sanctions

Accordingly, regulators need an array of tools, ranging from punitive sanctions to the discretion to support businesses to improve, make changes and get things right. It is not effective or proportionate to seek to affect future behaviour by responding to every breach by imposing a punitive sanction on every offender, irrespective of their motivation or history. What is effective is to use the right tools in response to the circumstances. The effectiveness of the regulatory agency in pursuing its regulatory objectives can be undermined equally by under-penalisation and over-penalisation.

In the UK, while the Macrory review[21] recognised the importance of effective sanctions as a deterrent and as a catalyst to ensure regulatory compliance, Richard Macrory placed deterrence last on his list of objectives. His report asserted that many UK regulators were over-reliant on criminal prosecution, which was not the most appropriate tool for ensuring that non-compliance is addressed and that any damage is remedied or behaviour changed. The review proposed a shift towards a more flexible and proportionate approach with a broad range of sanctioning options which would better allow regulators to respond to individual cases. It recommended six principles that regulatory agencies should have regard to:[22]

> A sanction should:
>
> 1. Aim to change the behaviour of the offender;
> 2. Aim to eliminate any financial gain or benefit from non-compliance;
> 3. Be responsive and consider what is appropriate for the particular offender and regulatory issue, which can include punishment and the public stigma that should be associated with a criminal conviction;
> 4. Be proportionate to the nature of the offence and the harm caused;
> 5. Aim to restore the harm caused by regulatory non-compliance, where appropriate; and
> 6. Aim to deter future non-compliance.

The UK has subsequently seen the introduction of more flexible sanctioning powers – referred to as 'civil sanctions' – particularly in the area of environmental regulation, which allow the regulatory agency to select a response that is proportionate to the circumstances. The civil sanctions include the options of accepting a formal undertaking from a regulated entity that commits to taking appropriate corrective action (requiring remedial action to prevent further non-compliance or requiring the regulated entity to restore the position, so far as possible, to what it would have been if no offence had been committed)

---

[21] Richard Macrory, 'Regulatory Justice: Making Sanctions Effective' (Cabinet Office, 2006).
[22] ibid.

or financial penalties. Access to these new powers is accompanied by a requirement for transparency as to their use, both in terms of providing guidance as to how they will be used and publishing details of the cases in which they have been used.

Research by Christopher Hodges[23] has identified a shift in the UK towards a more responsive approach to non-compliance. This involves consideration by the regulatory agency of a wide range of factors in determining how it will respond to non-compliance. These factors fall into two broad categories relating, first, to the nature of the non-compliance and, secondly, to the underlying reasons for the non-compliance.

In the first category, the regulatory agency considers how serious the non-compliance is, in particular, how much risk has been created by the failure to comply, recognising that some non-compliance – sometimes referred to as technical or administrative non-compliance – does not directly lead to significant regulatory harm. While this issue needs to be considered carefully (sometimes what can be dismissed as technical was created to provide a trip wire before the cliff edge), attention should be given to whether the non-compliance resulted, or is likely to result, in any actual harm and, if so, how serious this harm is.

In the second category, the regulatory agency considers the regulated entity's approach to compliance; for example whether it had taken suitable steps to achieve and maintain compliance, whether it had shown a reckless disregard in the face of known risks, whether it was deliberately seeking to gain economic advantage, and its compliance history, for example, whether non-compliance had previously been identified and, if so, what steps had been taken to prevent reoccurrence. Consideration should also be given to the regulated entity's relationship with and response to the regulatory agency; for example, whether it is open and cooperative or has attempted to deceive or obstruct the agency.

All of these factors, relating to both severity and approach, should be set out in the regulatory agency's enforcement policy with the intent that both regulated entities and beneficiaries should understand the process that is followed.

In selecting appropriate and proportionate responses to non-compliance, the regulatory agency should not be constrained by the actions that it has statutory powers to deploy, particularly where these statutory powers are primarily punitive. A hierarchy of responses to non-compliance will often include actions that are not based in statutory powers. For example, a regulatory agency may respond to a single instance of non-compliance by providing compliance advice or guidance, where there is good reason to believe that the business will act on the advice or guidance. Additional assurance can be obtained by the use of agreements – sometimes referred to as business improvement plans or voluntary undertakings – between a business and the regulatory agency.

V. Key Lines of Enquiry

As discussed in chapter two, we have developed key lines of enquiry in respect of each element of the Regulatory Delivery Model that can be used to assess and understand the current picture in respect of that element. These questions, presented in Box 20.2 in respect of Intervention Choices, are intended as a starting point on which a regulatory agency or a

---

[23] See discussion on enforcement policies in Christopher Hodges, *Law and Corporate Behaviour: Integrating Theories of Regulation, Enforcement, Culture and Ethics* (Oxford, Hart Publishing, 2015).

third party can build in order to give a sense of where strengths and weaknesses lie and to highlight potential for improvement.

Box 20.2 Key lines of enquiry: intervention choices

Range and shape

- Does the regulatory agency respond appropriately to the shape of its regulatory environment?
- Does the agency have the capability to choose interventions effectively?
- Does the agency use all of the interventions made available to it in legislation, including its discretionary powers?
- Does the agency use, as appropriate, all other intervention options available to it (including not intervening)?
- Does the agency have an effective methodology for understanding when and how beneficiaries and other actors can be equipped to intervene to improve outcomes?
- Does the agency work effectively with partners in its deployment of intervention choices?

Building compliance

- Is the regulatory agency able to understand and assess the impact of alternative intervention choices?
- Does the agency assess the characteristics of the entities it regulates in ways that enable it to understand which intervention choice will be most effective (responsive regulation)?
- Does the agency deploy this thinking to understand the sector and, where appropriate, individual businesses, in terms of awareness, motivation and capability?
- Does the agency respond effectively to the maturity of the regulatory requirements it enforces and the sectors it works with?
- Does the agency assess the impact of the interventions it makes and modify its behaviour accordingly?

Use of sanctions

- Does the regulatory agency have access to an adequate range of sanctions?
- Does the agency use the sanctions available to it to drive appropriate outcomes?
- Does the agency monitor the use of sanctions, including those issued by the agency and through courts and other means, to assess their impact?

VI. Summary

This chapter set out to explain the final practice of the Regulatory Delivery Model: Intervention Choices. We have explored the importance of good intervention choices and have discussed the shape and range of interventions that are available to regulatory agencies, along with the factors that influence their selection. We have also considered some of the interactions between Intervention Choices and other elements of the Regulatory Delivery Model.

The next two chapters bring the very different interests and experience of the authors to bear on the question of choosing interventions that work. In chapter twenty-one, Erica Sheward and Mariam Shkubuliani consider how the provision of compliance-related information by a regulatory agency can empower consumers, drawing on examples from the regulation of food safety. In chapter twenty-two, Christopher Hodges and Ruth Steinholtz propose that regulatory agencies should take account of whether the behaviour of businesses they regulate is based on ethical values and should be looking for opportunities to build relationships of trust with those businesses.

21

Consumer Empowerment, Providing Information from Food Inspections in Ways that Enable Consumer Behaviour

ERICA SHEWARD AND MARIAM SHKUBULIANI

I. Introduction

Historically, in the UK, as in other developed countries around the world, regulatory agencies have recognised that the influences on businesses to achieve compliance are wider than the regulator's own direct interactions, as outlined in the previous chapter.

It could be argued that rules alone cannot, and have never been able to, change the behaviour of society. Harnessing the aspirations of society through 'co-producing' regulatory outcomes with both citizens (as the beneficiaries of regulation) and the business they regulate offers different opportunities for regulators to change the behaviour of the careless, the incompetent and the criminal. In consideration of appropriate and effective interventions, regulatory agencies should consider both the challenges and opportunities arising from co-production approaches. Encouraging regulators to consider regulatory outcomes which are broader than 'compliance' per se is essential in the conception and development of such approaches.

The rate at which innovative and disruptive business models continue to emerge challenges the ability of regulatory agencies to keep pace. Regulatory agencies seeking to develop the flexibility to respond to disruptive business technology need to develop and encourage citizen empowerment mechanisms including digital approaches. In striving for flexible, innovative regulatory delivery options many are using the principles of citizen empowerment to craft both supplementary as well as replacement interventions.

As noted in chapter twenty, co-produced approaches have relevance for all regulatory agencies and the principles of citizen empowerment also have applicability, although there is always a need to consider the features of the regulated market and assess how likely it is that citizen empowerment can be effective. In this chapter, we focus on the application of these principles in relation to consumer protection regulation, using the area of food safety regulation to draw out examples of how the principles are being applied in practice in one area.

II. The Use of Consumer Empowerment as a Regulatory Tool

Regulatory theory increasingly places emphasis on the role of information-sharing between consumers and the state with a view to encouraging and allowing consumers to protect themselves and promoting a competitive economy. Increasing the information available to consumers is undoubtedly beneficial although some authors, such as Howells,[1] have cautioned that the limitations of consumer protection through information also have to be recognised as consumers may not always respond to information provided as rationally as advocates of such approaches would sometimes have us assume.

Inevitably, there are challenges to the legitimacy of co-producing regulatory outcomes, with a focus on the wider detriments sustained by consumers at either end of the social strata, ie that the co-production model empowers the articulate and aware at the expense of the poor and disadvantaged, and that it is immoral for the state to expect citizens to do its job for it. However, despite the detractors, co-regulatory approaches to the delivery of regulatory outcomes have become more widespread and, increasingly, regulatory agencies have innovated, using the empowerment of consumers to support the reduction of regulatory risks.

The contribution that consumer empowerment makes to minimising regulatory risk has two aspects. First, the active involvement of citizens or their representatives in encouraging or lobbying businesses to improve compliance can raise standards. Secondly, the provision of information can enable citizens to make choices that minimise the risk to themselves. This protects the individual consumer that makes the informed choice and can indirectly lead businesses to improve because they see an economic benefit.

The provision of 'regulatory' information to enable consumers to make informed decisions (theoretically 'empowering them') has a long history and can be separated into two strands:

Strand 1: The regulation requires the business to provide information to the consumer. For example, in food regulation, this might include ingredients labelling, allergen warnings, etc. The regulatory agency's primary role is in ensuring that business complies with the regulation, providing the required information. However, the regulatory agency might also choose to take an active role in explaining the required information to consumers or promoting to them the importance of considering the information.

Strand 2: The regulatory agency itself provides information to consumers. This could take a number of forms:

(a)   Ad hoc publicity, which is almost always negative publicity about a poorly performing business. For example, a press release about a business closure (prohibition notice) or prosecution.[2]

(b)   Routine, ongoing publication of information about the regulator's activities with regard to individual businesses. For example, publication of a register of enforcement actions;[3] inspection reports etc.

---

[1] Geraint Howells, 'The Potential Limits of Consumer Empowerment by Information' (2005) 32 *The Journal of Law and Society* 349.

[2] See, for example, publicity issued by Croydon Borough Council, a local authority in London, to raise awareness of its prosecution of restaurant owners for food hygiene and health and safety failings, available at http://news.croydon.gov.uk/doctor-and-ex-wife-fined-more-than-90000-for-filthy-eatery.

[3] See, for example, the database of food law prosecutions made available by the UK's Food Standards Agency, available at https://data.gov.uk/dataset/17206153-70bf-4205-803e-93d30c0d2fc6/fsa-successful-prosecutions.

(c) Publication of details of businesses that are in regulator-run schemes that 'recognise' businesses that meet a certain standard or make a certain commitment. For example, 'trusted trader'-type schemes.[4]

(d) Publication of 'league tables' that purport to show the relative performance of different regulated entities subject to inspection or other forms of enforcement.

The focus of the academic literature in relation to consumer empowerment through provision of information by the regulatory agency has largely been around the 'ad hoc publicity' approach, with less attention being given to the other forms of information provision until relatively recently.

'Naming and shaming' is the most widely understood term for an intervention that embraces public opinion and consumer demand in the achievement of compliance, what is sometimes termed 'governance through publicity'. This type of intervention allows for businesses to be subject to a degree of adverse publicity following contraventions of the law. Naming and shaming as an intervention relies on the premise that empowering consumers with information about non-compliant individuals and businesses will lead to a semi-surveillance culture amongst the beneficeries of regulation upon whom a shared responsibility for promoting and supporting compliance will inevitably fall.

Naming and shaming as an intervention is examined in the Ayres and Braithwaite 'responsive regulation' literature.[5,6] Responsive regulation regards corporate compliance as not primarily the result of fear of legal sanctions, but as a result of a combination of the intrinsic motivation to behave responsibly, combined with external influences, such as stakeholder pressure. As a catalyst for third-party action, adverse publicity plays an important role and shaming has value in changing future behaviour.

In the UK, regulatory agencies have been designing and delivering consumer empowerment approaches for a while. Historically, the emphasis has been on the provision of regulated information by business (strand 1 above) and on the use of ad hoc publicity (strand 2a above). However, recent years have seen significant progress in the development of consumer empowerment approaches in which the regulatory agency makes information available to consumers on an ongoing basis, for example, making information about the compliance status of all businesses available to consumers, be it good and bad, rather than merely publicising prosecutions. Clearly the usefulness of this approach depends on the market being regulated, including the capacity of consumers to make informed choices and the extent to which providing compliance information will impact on the regulated entity's behaviour. This progress has happened at a time of increased emphasis on transparency, both as one of the UK's Principles of Good Regulation (see chapter five) and, more widely, through legislative measures to promote openness by public bodies in the UK to public scrutiny.[7]

The UK's national Food Hygiene Rating Scheme (FHRS) provides an interesting example of an approach to consumer empowerment to achieve regulatory outcomes which are

[4] See, for example, Local Authority Trader Schemes, available at www.traderregister.org.uk/website_selection.php.

[5] Ian Ayres and John Braithwaite, *Responsive Regulation: Transcending the Deregulation Debate* (Oxford, Oxford University Press, 1992).

[6] John Braithwaite, *Crime, Shame and Reintegration* (Oxford, Oxford University Press, 1989).

[7] The Freedom of Information Act 2000 and the Environmental Information Regulations 2004.

perceivably broader than compliance alone. The context, development and operation of the scheme will be explored further in this chapter to illustrate the potential benefits of such approaches.

A. The Importance of Food Hygiene to Public Health

The food industry is a huge global business and one of the key driving forces in the area of economy and social life. Inevitably, food has a profound significance on people's wellbeing. WHO defines food-borne disease as 'any disease of infectious or toxic nature caused by or thought to be caused by the consumption of food or water'. Measuring the global incidence of food-borne illnesses is a difficult task, but according to the World Health Organisation,[8] 2.1 million people died as a result of diarrhoeal diseases in 2000. Food-borne diseases pose problems not only in developing countries but can sporadically affect masses of the population in any country, regardless of its stage of development. Even with effective food hygiene and safety legislation, enforcement and consumer awareness, people still face serious problems relating to food-borne illnesses.[9]

Food-borne disease is not a new public health problem. There are age-old diseases affecting humans since the dawn of time and in some developing countries food-related incidents are so common that they have become a fact of everyday life.[10] Even though there are food-borne disease statistics available, public authorities have realised that the cases reported often represent only a small part of the whole problem. Many victims suffer in silence; their symptoms are undiagnosed or unreported making the number of incidents higher than those reflected by official statistics.[11]

In the UK, it is estimated that each year about a million people suffer from some kind of food-borne illnesses, of whom around 20,000 receive hospital treatment and about 500 die.[12] The trend of eating away from home – in restaurants, cafes and other food establishments – is rooted in people's changing lifestyles. In the UK, it is mostly a result of improved economic stability. Greater disposable income equates to the potential for consumers to spend more money when eating outside the home while enjoying a diversity of cuisine and different restaurant experiences.[13] However, with these benefits can come risks, ie being exposed to poor hygiene practices resulting in incidences of food-borne illness.

Across the UK poor hygiene practices are one of the main causes of food poisoning cases, which lead to severe illness or even death. In particular, it is vulnerable groups such as children, the elderly, or immune-compromised people who are more susceptible to

---

[8] 'Foodborne Diseases; a Focus for Health Education', 53rd World Health Assembly (World Health Organisation, 2000).

[9] Fritz Kaferstein, Yasmine Motarjemi and Douglas Bettcher, 'Foodborne Disease Control: A Transnational Challenge' (Geneva, 1997), 503–506.

[10] Yasmine Motarjemi and Fritz Kaferstein, 'Food Sfety, Hazard Analysis and Critical Control Point and the Increase in Foodborne Diseases: a Paradox?' (1999) 10 *Food Control* 325.

[11] VK Lim, 'Foodborne Diseases in Malaysia' (2002) 57 *Medical Journal of Malaysia* 1.

[12] 'Foodborne Disease Strategy 2010–2015, An FSA Programme for the Reduction of Foodborne Disease in the UK' (Food Standards Agency, 2011).

[13] Nadiatul Shahid and John Whisson, 'Effectiveness of the Tees Valley Food Hygiene Award Scheme towards Food Business Operators and Consumers in the Middleborough District' (2012) 4 *Procedia – Social and Behavioural Sciences* 368.

such illnesses.[14] Safe food prepared in a hygienic environment is a basic human right, but this is not always achieved.[15] Food safety is a challenging issue and there is often confusion amongst consumers about what is healthy and safe to eat. Consumers need to understand what is good for them and what can be hazardous.[16]

When people eat outside of the home they expect good-quality food with acceptable standards of food hygiene and safety. In order to preserve consumer trust, it is the responsibility of a food establishment to maintain and where necessary improve food hygiene procedures and practices, which in turn should reduce incidences of food-borne illnesses. Furthermore, this helps businesses to achieve compliance and protect their reputation.

B. Food Hygiene Regulation in the UK

In the UK there is a longstanding history of legislating to address issues of food quality and food-borne illness, dating back to the twelfth century.[17] More recently, food safety regulations have been focused on the implementation of specific management systems designed to raise food hygiene standards in food businesses. Prior to joining the EU in the early 1970s, food safety was regulated under public health legislation. 1968 saw the introduction of a very important change within food law: the Medicines Act 1968 divided the legislation relating to food and control of medicines for human and veterinary use for the first time. The next major change came with the introduction of the Food Act 1984, subsequently replaced by the current Food Safety Act 1990.

The Food Safety Act 1990 provides the framework for food regulation in the UK and comprises four key sections ensuring both food safety and consumer protection. These include: rendering food injurious to health; selling food not complying with food safety requirements; selling food not of the nature, substance or quality demanded; and falsely describing or presenting food. Significant changes within food law have been introduced over the last 20 years, most notably with the implementation of the EU's General Food Law Regulation,[18] which established new requirements on safety, traceability, withdrawal and recall requirements.

Responsibility for food hygiene and safety enforcement in the UK is shared between central and local government. Central government creates the policy and deals with EU requirements. The central competent authority in the UK for the implementation and oversight of food law enforcement is the Food Standards Agency (FSA). The FSA has authority to set performance standards and monitor local authorities' enforcement activities. It collects and inspects data on enforcement activity and this data is reported to the

---

[14] Clare Hughes, Ian Gillespie and Sarah O'Brien, 'Foodborne Transmission of Infectious Intestinal Disease in England and Wales, 1992–2003' (2007) 18 *Food Control* 766.

[15] Solomon Oranusi, O Oguoma and E Agusi, 'Microbiological Quality Assessment of Foods Sold in Student's Cafeterias' (2013) 3 *Global Research Journal of Microbiology* 1.

[16] Jenny Leach, Heather Mercer, Graham Stew and Stephen Denyer, 'Improving Food Hygiene Standards – a Customer Focused Approach' (2001) 103 *British Food Journal* 238.

[17] The Assize of Bread and Ales was developed in Medieval English Law to regulate quality. From 1266 to the 19th century, the focus of food regulation was on adulteration of food. By the early 20th century, laws such as the Milk and Dairies Act 1914 were being introduced to address food-borne illness.

[18] The General Food Law Regulation (Regulation (EC) No 178/2002).

European Commission and made publicly available, providing transparency around the operation of the enforcement regime.[19] The FSA delivers food hygiene and safety regulation directly only in relation to abattoirs and meat-cutting plants. However, it has responsibility for ensuring the local authorities are delivering enforcement of food safety and hygiene effectively and for ensuring that outcomes are being achieved.

The FSA issues statutory guidance to local authorities, known as the Food Law Code of Practice,[20] and local authorities delivering food safety and hygiene enforcement are required to have regard to this guidance. The FSA also requires local authorities to report to them the number of inspections carried out and the level of compliance achieved by each food business they regulate.

Local authorities[21] have responsibility for delivering food safety and hygiene regulation in relation to all food businesses other than the abattoirs and cutting plants overseen by the FSA. They deliver their responsibilities under the oversight of the FSA, as the national regulator.

Local authority enforcement of food hygiene and safety legislation is undertaken by environmental health officers (EHOs) and food safety technical officers (FSOs), whose responsibilities go beyond the inspection of food production, catering and retail premises in relation to food safety. EHOs also inspect housing standards, environmental pollution, health safety and noise control.[22] The delivery of food safety regulation in the UK by specialist regulators – EHOs and FSOs – is in contrast to the rest of the EU where the delivery of food hygiene regulation is largely the responsibility of veterinarians. The technical competency of EHOs and FSOs is ensured by a framework overseen by the FSA.

There are a number of enforcement interventions that local authority regulators can use to ensure compliance with food hygiene legislation which include inspection, audit, monitoring and surveillance, advice and guidance, education and the provision of information. EHOs are described by some authors as a combination of 'touchy-feely teacher and tough enforcer' as they try to achieve a balance between providing advice to businesses and taking enforcement action in the interest of consumer protection. They not only help businesses to comply with the minimum standards of food safety legislation but also push businesses to adopt better practices.[23] EHOs and FSOs may take enforcement action against those businesses that are non-compliant. Depending on the level of risk to human health enforcement actions can range from issuing improvement notices to premises closure or prosecution of the business. Local authorities set out their enforcement strategy in a policy which should be consistently applied across their activities.

---

[19] The Food Standards Agency publishes data annually. For example, see 'Annual Report on UK Local Authority Food Law Enforcement 1 April 2016 to 31 March 2017', available at www.food.gov.uk/about-us/local-authorities#monitoring-local-authority-activity.

[20] 'The Food Law Code of Practice 2017' (Food Standards Agency, 2017).

[21] The structure of local government in the UK is complex. In Scotland, Wales and some parts of England, local government is by a 'unitary' and single-tier authority which will have responsibility for the enforcement of both food safety and hygiene legislation and food standards legislation. In some parts of England, local government rests with two-tier local authorities – most commonly an upper tier authority referred to as a 'county' and lower tier authorities referred to as 'districts'. In this case, the enforcement of food safety and hygiene legislation is the responsibility of the districts while the enforcement of food standards legislation lies with the county.

[22] Bridget Hutter and Clive Jones, 'From Government to Governance: External Influences on Business Risk Management' (2007) 1 *Regulation & Governance* 27.

[23] Christopher Griffith, 'Are we Making the Most of Food Safety Inspections? A Glimpse into the Future' (2005) 107 *British Food Journal* 132.

III. Considering New Approaches to Food Safety Regulation in the UK

It is well recognised in all areas of regulation that regulatory relationships between businesses and regulators are complicated, and the enforcement of food hygiene regulations is no exception. Enforcement is a relationship between food businesses themselves and those who regulate them, influenced by varying forces and motives for compliance. Enforcement officers strive to ensure businesses are complying with the law which potentially should equate to an indication of safe food. However, businesses often struggle to understand what it is that they need to do to comply; they may have difficulty in understanding the legal requirements and as a result find themselves on the wrong side of the law. This may happen because businesses (particularly small businesses) can be ill-equipped with technical knowledge or lack financial resources to seek out professional advice. It is well documented that small food businesses in the UK also face challenges in complying with a range of other regulated activities such as health and safety, employment law and financial regulation.[24]

Unlike businesses, regulators often view compliance as an organic and holistic process integral to the food safety culture of the business and not just something done only during inspections. Research suggests that small and medium food businesses have a contrasting approach and view compliance as a reactive process which is performed at a particular point in time, ie as accomplishing everything EHOs tell them to do during inspections.[25]

There has been much conjecture about which interventions deliver the best regulatory outcomes within a given sector. In the UK there is a statutory responsibility on local regulators to make sure that they do not impose unnecessary regulatory burdens during the course of their enforcement interactions with businesses and that, in line with that, they adopt risk-based approaches at every stage of their decision-making processes. They are obliged to demonstrate, if challenged, that their regulatory approach is consistent, risk-based, proportionate and transparent to those they regulate.[26]

Early research by the FSA, shortly after its creation in 2001, identified a number of issues which collectively brought about the right conditions for the creation of a new approach to achieving outcomes. Following a series of high-profile food scares (including outbreaks of BSE and foot and mouth, to name but two) a dearth of consumer confidence in central government as an effective regulator of food safety matters arose. This situation was exacerbated by wider evidence that food safety inspections as the intervention of choice as well as EU mandate, were not on their own delivering the desired improvements in food business compliance. This combination of factors resulted in the FSA looking to learn from the experiences of others, both domestically and internationally.

Throughout the UK there was localised development of food hygiene ratings schemes. The development of a number of different scheme formats at local authority level throughout the early 2000s – the most popular of which was the 'Scores on The Doors Scheme' – ultimately supported the harmonisation of approaches through the development of a national scheme led by the FSA as the national regulator.

---

[24] Robin Fairman and Charlotte Yapp, 'Assessing Compliance with Food Safety Legislation in Small Businesses' (2005)107 *British Food Journal* 150.

[25] ibid.

[26] 'Regulators' Code' (Better Regulation Delivery Office, 2014).

Research commissioned by the FSA in 2005 indicated that schemes designed to measure and numerically or symbolically express the level of food hygiene compliance of a food business based on standardised assessment criteria developed by a regulator (food hygiene rating schemes) could be an effective tool in helping consumers to access information on the food safety performance of food businesses.[27] The provision of this information in theory helps consumers to exercise choice on where to eat away from home.

A. Examples of Food Hygiene Rating Schemes

The FSA research was designed to draw upon international examples of existing food hygiene ratings schemes to provide an evidence base for the design of a potential UK-wide scheme. The research centred on ratings schemes operating in countries which were relatively similar to the UK in terms of their economic development.

A number of variations and formats of food hygiene rating schemes were found to be in evidence internationally; however, there was no universally agreed method of communicating inspection results to consumers. The basis of these schemes is predicated on the assumption that giving consumers such information – and as such 'empowering' them – is likely to affect their behaviour, ie they will avoid eating at places they believe are unhygienic.[28]

Types of rating schemes cited in the FSA research included a letter grading scheme; a 'smiley face' scheme; a 'traffic light' scheme; gold/silver/bronze schemes; and two-tier schemes using simple ratings of 'pass' or 'improvement required'. Examples of these approaches are presented below.

1. **Letter-grading schemes** – The Los Angeles letter-grading scheme was the first found to be developed, as early as 1998, following a television programme where hidden cameras were used to detect unhygienic food-handling practices in some restaurants. Regular inspections, the frequency of which is determined on the basis of risk, are documented in the Food Official Inspection Report and scored. The letter grades used are 'A' for a score of 90–100, 'B' for scores of 80–89 and 'C' for scores of 70–79. Businesses that are awarded a score below 70 points receive a score card indicating that the business has poor food-handling practices. The business is required to display the grade awarded and inspection results are also available to the public through the Department of Public Health website.[29,30]

   New York City subsequently launched a similar scheme,[31] following the letter grading formula adopted in Los Angeles.

---

[27] Greenstreet Berman, 'Scores on the Doors: Consumer and Business Views, Report for the Food Standards Agency (FSA, 2006).

[28] Ginger Zhe Jin and Phillip Leslie, 'The Effect of Information on Product Quality: Evidence from Restaurant Hygiene Grade Cards' (2003)118 *Quarterly Journal of Economics* 409.

[29] Available at https://ehservices.publichealth.lacounty.gov/servlet/guest?service=1&enterprise=1.

[30] Ginger Zhe Jin and Phillip Leslie, 'The Case in Support of Restaurant Hygiene Grade Cards' (2005) 20 *The Magazine of Food, Farm, and Resource Issues* 97.

[31] 'Public Recognition and Use of Grades Trends in Restaurant Sanitary Conditions and Foodborne Illnesses', available at www1.nyc.gov/assets/doh/downloads/pdf/rii/restaurant-grading-18-month-report.pdf.

2. **'Smiley face' schemes** – The Danish Government introduced a 'smiley scheme' in 2001,[32] using a smiley face to provide a convenient and easy way of interpreting food hygiene inspection results. A big smile indicates high standards of food hygiene, a regular smile indicates satisfactory standards, a face with no smile indicates unsatisfactory standards and a frowning face indicates highly unsatisfactory standards.

    Food establishments are inspected regularly and subsequently receive an inspection report showing the inspection results, the smiley awarded and the results of the preceding three inspections, which gives consumer an opportunity to see how the food establishment has performed over time. Beneath the smiley face further information is provided explaining why the establishment received the corresponding scores. All food establishments are required to display the scores in a prominent place and inspection results are also published on a national website.[33] To encourage and reward good performance, the Danish Government introduced an 'elite smiley', which is awarded to those businesses that consistently receive top ratings.[34]

3. **Traffic light schemes** – The Toronto (Canada) DineSafe scheme was also introduced in 2001 and required all businesses to display inspection ratings based on a traffic light scoring system, ie businesses are required to display either a green sign (meaning 'pass'), a yellow sign (meaning 'conditional pass') or a red sign (meaning 'closed'). Consumers can acquire inspection results on the city's website[35] or via a hotline.[36]

Whilst the FSA's research focused on examples of ratings schemes in developed countries, it is interesting to note that there are also more recent examples of such schemes being introduced in less advanced economies, where regulatory delivery frameworks are not so well developed and regulatory interactions may be less frequent. The use of a hygiene rating scheme to inform consumers can, in this context, be perceived to be essential in assisting them to make good choices about where they eat and drink to assure their safety. One example of this genre of schemes is the Nepalese food safety sticker scheme. This scheme was developed specifically for roadside hotels and takeaways in Nepal, where business activities can be high-risk, robust, frequent regulatory oversight is challenging, and the customers are predominantly foreign tourists.

The development and operation of the food safety sticker scheme is the responsibility of the Department of Food Technology and Quality Control. On inspection, businesses are awarded a score that indicates the level of food safety at the premises. This is displayed as a coloured sticker, with green indicating a good score; yellow-green indicating a generally satisfactory score, yellow indicating that improvement is required and red indicating that urgent improvement is necessary. Improving the business environment to enable private-sector-led economic growth has been a key priority for the Government of Nepal and tourism has been seen as a priority sector for a number of years. Nepal has a growing reputation as a tourist destination, but tourism services have perceivably been of general low quality with limited regulation or standards enforcement. It was decided along with assistance from international donors to explore how approaches that use citizen choices as

---

[32] Annemette Nielsen, 'Contesting Competence – Change in the Danish Food System' (2006) 47 *Appetite* 143.
[33] See www.findsmiley.dk.
[34] 'Facts' (The Danish Veterinary and Food Administration, December 2015).
[35] Dinesafe Toronto, available at www.toronto.ca/health/dinesafe/index.htm.
[36] 'Food Premises Inspection and Disclosure System. Evaluation Report' (Toronto Public Health, 2002).

an alternative to regulation could be used in Nepal and made the food safety sticker scheme a reform priority.

In 2014, the Nepalese Government recognised that strengthening the inspection criteria which underpinned the food safety sticker scheme would benefit the business environment in the short term by improving the consistency, proportionality and transparency of the inspection process for businesses, and in the longer term by providing an incentive for businesses to meet food safety standards, leading to a reduction in food poisoning cases amongst tourists, improved ability for Nepal to attract higher-income tourists and therefore more potential for private sector development in the tourism sector.

B. UK Approach to Developing a Food Hygiene Rating Scheme

Following scrutiny of other food hygiene rating schemes and extensive research with consumers, businesses and local regulators in the UK, the FSA embarked on the creation of its own scheme. As noted earlier in this chapter, measures to promote greater transparency and accountability of public bodies, encouraging scrutiny and oversight by citizens, were influential in supporting a business case for the FSA to explore the benefits of a rating scheme.

The FSA had introduced a pilot scheme in 2004 to make inspection information on food businesses available for public viewing, based on the original local authority schemes, and referred to as 'Scores on the Doors'. The inspection results were translated into symbols to simplify and make it understandable for consumers. Different local authorities adopted different symbols during the pilot period, such as stars or smiley faces (as in the Danish example), or a simple two-tiered 'pass' or 'improvement required'.[37]

Following the trial of a number of ratings scheme formats, the FSA commissioned an evaluation in 2007 of the impact of the local authority schemes. The research with businesses, consumers and local authority officers identified evidence that 'Scores on the Doors schemes encouraged businesses to improve hygiene standards and may have led to measurable improvements in hygiene inspection scores'.[38] Businesses also gave positive reasons for displaying Scores on the Doors certificates, including increasing customer confidence in their business and reputational benefits.

This research informed the FSA's decision to launch a national food hygiene rating scheme (FHRS) with the aim of ensuring consistency and eliminating variations across different local authorities, which were creating inefficiencies for regulators and confusion for consumers. Some local authorities were still in favour of operating their own hygiene rating scheme, with many wishing to retain Scores on the Doors but, from the national perspective, the availability of a national scheme was thought to prevent confusion and maintain consistency.[39]

In the face of concerns from local authorities and businesses about the creation and administration of a national scheme, the FSA ran a public consultation in 2008, before

---

[37] 'Information Note: Food Hygiene Information System in Selected Places' (Legislative Council Secretariat, 2008).

[38] Greenstreet Berman, *Evaluation of Scores on The Doors Final Main Report for the Food Standards Agency* (FSA, 2008).

[39] Denise Worsfold, 'Consumer Information on Hygiene Inspections of Food Premises' (2006) 17 *Journal of Foodservice* 23.

launching the single scheme. Consultation packages were sent to a number of interested parties and 414 responses were received: 279 from stakeholders in England; 66 in Scotland; 41 in Wales; and 28 in Northern Ireland. Of these responses, 45 per cent were from enforcement stakeholders, 52 per cent from industry stakeholders and four per cent from consumers.

Summarising the results of the consultation, the FSA decided that:

- in England, Wales and Northern Ireland a six-tier system should be in place as the previous schemes were based on this design;
- Scotland should retain a two-tier system as most of the stakeholders favoured this system;
- the display of the scores should be voluntary;
- mechanisms for re-inspection/revisits for rescoring, and appeals should be in place;
- a support package, including guidance, training and an IT platform, should be in place for local authorities; and
- a UK-wide steering group comprising local authority, food industry and consumers should be established in order to oversee the development of the two schemes with a view to shared learning and commonality of approach.

Following the outcomes from the consultation, a steering group was set up to develop the FHRS. The steering group included local authorities, the Chartered Institute of Environmental Health, the food industry, consumers and government. All local authorities were then encouraged by FSA to abandon any existing schemes and participate in the national FHRS.

By 2016, all English local authorities had adopted the national FHRS. This followed the post-consultation format of a six-tier scheme covering hygiene ratings in England, Wales and Northern Ireland.

IV. Operation of the FSA's Food Hygiene Rating Scheme

The FHRS currently operates on a voluntary basis in England and on a statutory basis in Wales and Northern Ireland. Following the establishment of a separate national regulator for food hygiene in Scotland in 2015 (Food Standards Scotland) the Scottish ratings scheme has continued as a two-tier version.

Local authorities in England operate the FHRS scheme on the basis of guidance issued by the FSA, referred to as the 'brand standard'.[40] In Wales and Northern Ireland, the operation of the FHRS scheme is very similar to that in England, although legislation has been introduced to put the scheme on a statutory footing and local authorities follow guidance issued under the relevant legislation.

The scheme provides consumers with information about a business based on the assessment made by a local inspector at the time that the business is inspected to check compliance with legal requirements on food hygiene.

---

[40] 'The Food Hygiene Rating Scheme: Guidance for local authorities on implementation and operation – the Brand Standard' (FSA, 2018).

In England, the scope of the FHRS extends to food businesses that supply food direct to consumers (although certain businesses are not given a rating where specific circumstances apply). In Wales, the scope of the scheme was extended in 2014 to other types of food businesses, such as manufacturers and wholesalers.

A. Ratings

The calculation of the food hygiene rating scores that form the basis of the FHRS is set out in the Food Law Code of Practice[41] – the statutory guidance to local authorities that includes guidance on inspection of food businesses. The score is assessed based on three criteria:

- the current level of compliance with food hygiene and safety procedures (including temperature control, food handling practices);
- the current level of compliance with structural requirements (including layout, ventilation, lighting, general cleanliness of the premises); and
- confidence in management/control systems (including the business' history of compliance and management-personnel approach towards hygiene and food safety).

A numerical value is given for each of the above-mentioned areas, from 0–25 for compliance with hygiene and structural requirements and 0–30 for confidence in management (where 0 is the best score).

The numerical scores awarded on inspection are translated into FHRS ratings of 0 to 5, with 0 representing very poor hygiene standards where urgent improvement is necessary and 5 representing very good standards of food hygiene, as shown in Table 21.1. The Brand Standard includes extensive and detailed guidance on scoring, to ensure that scoring practice between different local authorities and different inspectors is as consistent as possible.

Table 21.1 Mapping of intervention rating scores onto FHRS ratings

Total intervention rating score	0–15	20	25–30	35–40	45–50	> 50
Additional scoring factor	No individual score greater than 5	No individual score greater than 10	No individual score greater than 10	No individual score greater than 15	No individual score greater than 20	
Food hygiene rating	5	4	3	2	1	0
Descriptor	Very good	Good	Generally satisfactory	Improvement necessary	Major improvement necessary	Urgent improvement necessary

Source: FSA's Brand Standard.

---

[41] 'The Food Law Code of Practice 2017' (FSA, 2017).

Converting food hygiene scores into symbols to make the scheme easier for consumers to understand is challenging and, as noted earlier in this chapter, a variety of symbols are used in different schemes. The symbols adopted by the FSA for the national FHRS are based on a representation of the numerical rating awarded which also shows the 0–5 scale.

B. Publication and Display

All ratings awarded by local authorities are compiled by the FSA and published on a national database.[42]

In England, where the operation of the FHRS by local authorities is on a voluntary basis, there is no legal requirement for businesses to display the rating that they receive. In contrast, in Wales, following continued devolution of food safety responsibilities from the UK Government to the Welsh Assembly, the Food Hygiene Rating (Wales) Act 2013 was passed, requiring that all food businesses in Wales within its scope were subject to the mandatory display of food hygiene ratings. A transition period of two and half years was proposed, making it a legal requirement for a food business to display its rating from November 2016. There have been calls for a similar requirement to be introduced in England.[43]

C. Consistency and Accountability

In setting out the framework for the FHRS, the FSA's Brand Standard seeks to ensure consistency and fairness in the implementation and operation of the scheme. It establishes the rules by which local authorities should operate the scheme and also recognises that the implications of the scheme for business are significant, establishing accountability mechanisms that enable businesses to challenge or respond to ratings. Table 21.2 summarises the requirements of the Brand Standard for local authorities implementing the FHRS scheme.

Table 21.2 Summary of the requirements of the FSA's Brand Standard

Formal partnership agreements	Formal sign-up is an agreement based on the Brand Standard for the FHRS signed by the FSA and each local authority wishing to adopt the scheme. This agreement demonstrates the local authority's commitment and serves to safeguard credibility and integrity of the scheme.
Use of FHRS branding	Proper use of the FHRS branding, comprising FHRS logos and stickers, is very important to maintain the credibility and integrity of the FHRS.
Use of the FHRS IT platform	The IT platform that comprises a central database, a portal and an online search facility are important tools for transferring local authority data to the national database as well as providing transparency for consumers

(continued)

---

[42] Available at http://ratings.food.gov.uk.

[43] Local Government Association press release, (September 2017), available at www.local.gov.uk/about/news/councils-displaying-food-hygiene-ratings-must-be-made-mandatory-after-brexit.

Table 21.2 *(Continued)*

Establishing and operating a consistency framework	A consistent framework (ie in implementation and operation of the scheme) is important in order to gain all benefits the scheme is offering. This section should include monitoring and auditing procedures in order to ensure consistent application of the guidance.
Appeals	Local authorities are required to make available an appeal procedure giving businesses 21 days to dispute the rating awarded if they think that it does not properly reflect hygiene standards of their premises.
'Right to reply'	The 'right to reply' procedure gives businesses an opportunity to make comments on the rating awarded, for example to explain what action has been taken to improve standards or to explain any particular circumstance affecting their scores during the inspections. The business's reply must be published alongside its rating.
Requests for re-inspections/ revisits for re-rating purposes	The opportunity to request a revisit gives businesses that have improved their hygiene standards a chance to gain an improved rating without waiting for the next planned inspection.
	Local authorities are entitled to charge a fee for such visits on a cost-recovery basis. The fee charged can be set at the discretion of the local authority operator. There is no mandatory requirement to charge for re-inspections, but most local authorities do so.
	Take-up of revisits has been seen to be quite high for businesses not achieving ratings of 3 and above, but equally quite high for businesses achieving a 4 rating when previously they had been awarded a 5.[44]

There are inevitably challenges in ensuring consistency of food hygiene rating practice between different officers and between different local authorities. The FSA Brand Standard seeks to address this by setting out detailed and robust requirements by which the FHRS must be operated by each local authority. This includes inter-authority monitoring and consistency exercises and reporting of ratings data in relation to appeals and complaints to local authorities from businesses back to the FSA. Ultimately the Brand Standard provides for the FSA the power to withdraw the operation of the scheme from a local authority if it believes that the scheme is not being operated in line with the requirements of the Brand Standard and is unfair to business. It is interesting to note that withdrawal of the right to operate the scheme from a local authority by the FSA has never happened to date despite a number of complaints from business that it was not being operated correctly.

Some businesses have been seen to argue that despite all of the safeguards for business built into the scheme ie ratings appeals, requests for revisits and the right to reply, these

[44] Sandra Vegeris, 'The Food Hygiene Rating Scheme and The Food Hygiene Information Scheme: Evaluation findings 2011–2014' (Policy Studies Institute, University of Westminster, 2015).

mechanisms have serious limitations. The British Hospitality Association food safety technical committee have continued to argue that its members are exposed to the inconsistent application of food hygiene ratings and that because appeals have to be made to the local authority which awards the rating, and not the FSA itself, the appeals mechanisms are ineffective and lack independence.

V. The Impact of Food Hygiene Rating Schemes

The success of any food hygiene scheme that embraces consumer empowerment as an alternative intervention tool without unduly disadvantaging compliant businesses broadly relies on a number of factors:

- that consumer awareness of the scheme is at a level whereby they will make decisions about where they do or do not eat based on published hygiene ratings;
- that consumers understand what ratings mean and can correlate them with their own perceptions of what they consider to be appropriate standards of premises hygiene based on their own/societal norms;
- that the award of hygiene ratings will motivate businesses to improve compliance, and that there are clear actions businesses can take to improve compliance;
- that businesses are not unfairly treated by the publication of ratings which are not reflective of the actual hygiene conditions; and
- that improvements in the compliance of food businesses will lead to a reduction in the incidence of food poisoning.

A. Consumer Views

Surveys undertaken in the US and Canada indicated that the public are in favour of using a simple hygiene reporting system. According to research, 77 per cent of the public in Toronto felt safer eating in places that had a hygiene rating scheme in place than eating in food establishments which had not been rated. Seventy-five per cent of the respondents were aware of the ratings posted in businesses and 85 per cent understood what green/pass sign meant in both the US and Canadian schemes.[45]

Worsfold suggested that consumers in the UK in general did not have a clear idea of who inspected food premises and how the hygiene standards were assessed. Furthermore, they had unrealistic views with regard to the frequency of inspections and regulatory oversight in general and appeared to believe that enforcement officers undertook far more interventions than they actually did.[46] However, people who regularly ate away from home claimed that the hygiene of food premises was very important factor for them when deciding where to dine. Consumers believed that they should be entitled to have access to information on

[45] 'Food Premises Inspection' (2002) 1–39.
[46] Worsfold, 'Consumer Information' (2006).

hygiene inspection results and they were in favour of a reliable system which enabled them to judge hygiene standards of catering premises in particular. However, Worsfold also found that if there is to be a greater transparency with regard to hygiene standards of food establishments then the public should be well educated about the inspection and enforcement processes for them to be effective.

The success of rating schemes as 'regulatory nudge' exemplars is an example of the way that public policies can be designed to shape consumer behaviour. However, success also relies on consumers actively using the ratings given by regulators to influence their behaviour when eating out ie choosing to patronise premises with better ratings and avoid those with poorer ones. It also relies on the fact that consumers can easily access ratings information and can interpret what the ratings mean.

B. Improved Food Hygiene Performance

From a business point of view, improvements in compliance are potentially driven up in two ways: businesses fear a bad rating so strive to improve in advance of being inspected; and also poorly rated businesses are likely to suffer a loss of business as consumers decide not to eat there. Losing trade is allegedly what motivates businesses to gain better ratings and evidence suggests that they compare their scores with competitors, such competition driving businesses to achieve better ratings.[47]

In relation to the UK experience of the FHRS scheme, there is no doubt that the ratings of food businesses in general have continued to improve. Initial scheme evaluation findings published data between 2011 and 2014 which showed that the FHRS effectively improved broad compliance (equivalent to a FHRS rating of 3 or above) among food premises by 2.0 percentage points in the first year of operation.[48] By the end of the second year, the scheme increased the proportion of fully compliant food premises (equivalent to a FHRS rating of 5) by 3.3 percentage points. At the same time, the FHRS reduced the number of poorly compliant food premises (equivalent to a FHRS rating of 0 or 1) by 1.9 and 1.7 percentage points over the first two years of operation respectively. Early evidence from FHRS predecessor schemes also showed improved compliance.[49]

Nowhere are improvements in food business compliance in evidence more than in Wales, where ease of access to information for consumers is even more pronounced via mandatory display of ratings. Following the introduction of mandatory display the proportion of businesses scoring a zero rating fell from 0.6 per cent in 2013 to 0.2 per cent in 2017, and the proportion of businesses achieving a score of 3 and above rose from 87 per cent to 95 per cent in 2017.[50]

---

[47] Sandra Vegeris and D Smeaton, 'Evaluation of the Food Hygiene Rating Scheme and the Food Hygiene Information Scheme: Process Evaluation – Final Report' (Policy Studies Institute, University of Westminster, 2014).

[48] Vegeris, 'The Food Hygiene Rating Scheme' (2015).

[49] 'Scores on Doors Food Hygiene Scheme Proves a Success in Westminster', *The Caterer* (2008), available at www.thecaterer.com/articles/323877/scores-on-doors-food-hygiene-scheme-proves-a-success-in-westminster.

[50] 'Review of the Implementation and Operation of the Statutory Food Hygiene Rating Scheme in Wales and the Operation of the Appeals System, A Report for the National Assembly for Wales' (FSA, 2018).

VI. Lessons Learned from the UK Experience

Today consumers are more concerned about the safety and wholesomeness of food products than previous generations. Consumer empowerment is viewed as an important tool in improving business compliance and as a sustainable way of improving food safety standards in both developed and developing countries.

Consumers' need for more information when making purchasing decisions which could impact their safety, is influencing many to harness the consumer desire for information in the co-creation of state and citizen approaches to regulation. The UK national FHRS provides an excellent example of how good regulatory governance through accountability and transparency can assist improved compliance of businesses.

Ultimately the success of the scheme relies on the fact that consumers understand it and use it to vote with their feet when making decisions about where they eat out and, as we have seen, requires that regulators are competent and consistent in the application of ratings to ensure fairness to business. Failure to deliver consistency continues to be a challenge in the eyes of businesses in terms of whether the FHRS empowers consumers with information or names and shames businesses. Making a choice based on information which is incorrect (ie the wrong rating being applied or a misunderstanding of what the rating means) could result in significant detriment to both consumers and businesses. There has been some suggestion that the current six-tier scheme is too complicated for consumers to understand and that they may be making decisions about where they eat based on incorrect assumptions.[51]

These challenges are best addressed by ensuring that the development of these types of interventions are done in conjunction with all relevant stakeholders – citizens, regulators and businesses – to ensure good governance and appropriate levels of accountability. Understanding the difference between making inspection data available for the purposes of empowering consumers to make the right choices when eating out, and simply naming and shaming non-compliant businesses through publicity, is an important distinction to make in the maintenance of the principles and practices of good regulation.

What is clear from the UK FHRS example is that it is possible to drive changes in both consumer and business behaviour simultaneously by using alternative intervention choices albeit linked to an existing inspection-based activity. This adds value to what is already being done in a way that separate or distinctly different interventions activity could not and makes it possible for all stakeholders to be accountable to each other in a way that they had not been before.

---

[51] Mariam Shkubuliani, 'Consumers Understanding of the National Food Hygiene Rating System' (unpublished research, 2015).

22

Ethical Business Regulation, a New Understanding of the Power of Trust-Based Relationships

CHRISTOPHER HODGES AND RUTH STEINHOLTZ

The culture of any entity profoundly affects how it operates, and how successful it will be in achieving its aims. The same is true for public and business organisations.

This chapter builds on that understanding by explaining how a recognition of business culture and behaviour can help to inform a regulator agency's choice of intervention. It proposes a model that enables both business and regulatory organisations to maximise achievement of their respective aims, through a relationship of trust built on evidence that both sides operate with a shared understanding of the importance of ethical business practice – the Ethical Business Regulation (EBR) model.

The fundamental basis of EBR is that one or a group of businesses should commit to operating based on ethical values in all its activities; this is known as Ethical Business Practice (EBP). Businesses must produce, on an ongoing basis, evidence of that commitment

Figure 22.1 The EBR relationship

and its various manifestations in their activities. A commitment to developing and maintaining an appropriate culture should be evidenced by both the business and the regulatory agency and the accumulated evidence enables the two sides to engage in a relationship of trust (EBR) working together to achieve the goals of their respective organisations as expected by the society in which they operate. The position is illustrated in Figure 22.1.

I. Basis of the Ideas

The EBP and EBR model is based on extensive research and experience.[1] Some of the major strands of knowledge come from understanding how humans think and act (behavioural psychology) and from empirical evidence on how many regulators have learned to operate in encouraging compliance and in responding to breaches of rules, that has built up over 50 or so years. We will summarise some of the thinking on those two areas.

A. Behavioural Psychology

Research in the past century has illuminated how humans act and make decisions.[2] The findings of behavioural psychology show that most human beings aim to do the right thing, want to be seen by others to do the right thing, although they can break rules surprisingly often and then rationalise to themselves that their actions are ethical. Thus, strategies to maximise compliant outcomes include emphasising acting based on reference to ethical values rather than trying to remember (often many) rules. Since humans working in groups are significantly influenced by the actions of others, the strategy includes encouraging checking what others think before making decisions. But this checking must go outside an immediate closed group to avoid internal bias and group-think (such as in criminal gangs). People will not break rules where they genuinely perceive (if they are thinking about it) that the risk of being identified is high – however, humans are also not particularly good at assessing risk. Hence, transparency and discussion about the right thing to do in a particular circumstance is important, but it should not relate only to the risk of being identified. Major sources of such transparent checking should include colleagues, staff, suppliers, customers, and superiors (government and regulators).[3]

This way of thinking does not assume, as some historical legal and economic theories have done, that all decisions are based on objective rational assessment of costs and benefits based on cost-maximisation, or that outcomes are solely caused by individuals who can be blamed and held responsible, and whose future behaviour can be affected by imposition of punishment that will deter all wrongdoing. Some actors may indeed deserve strong

---

[1] A summary of the thinking is in Christopher Hodges and Ruth Steinholtz, *Ethical Business Practice and Regulation: A Behavioural and Ethical Approach to Compliance and Enforcement* (Oxford, Hart Publishing, 2017). A large compendium of evidence is contained in Christopher Hodges, *Law and Corporate Behaviour: Integrating Theories of Regulation, Enforcement, Culture and Ethics* (Oxford, Hart Publishing, 2015).

[2] Accessible books include: Tom Tyler, *Why People Obey the Law* (Yale, Yale University Press, 1990); Dan Ariely, *Predictably Irrational: The Hidden Forces That Shape Our Decisions* (New York, HarperCollins, 2008); Daniel Kahneman, *Thinking, Fast and Slow* (London, Allen Lane, 2011); Jonathan Haidt, *The Righteous Mind. Why Good People are Divided by Politics and Religion* (London, Penguin Books, 2012); Dennis Gentilin, *The Origins of Ethical Failures. Lessons for Leaders* (Abingdon and New York, Routledge, 2016); Richard Barrett, *The Values-Driven Organisation* (Abingdon and New York, Routledge, 2013).

[3] The actions of sociopaths and psychopaths are not based on normal ethical considerations, so they have to be identified and removed from positions where they can have damaging influence on others.

sanctions, because they have behaved unethically; removing them from circulation, removing their ability to act badly in future, and removing their proceeds of crime may be the only effective response. But imposing sanctions proportionate to historic behaviour will not necessarily affect future behaviour.

Further, if strong sanctions are imposed on people who believe that they are trying to do the right thing, they will resent it, and their willingness to act ethically and comply with any rules will be reduced. So, a public regulator – and a business employer – should have a toolbox of enforcement measures that provides a wide range of options, but should be careful to select the response that is proportionate to the ethical motivation and understanding of someone who has broken a rule.

The science referred to above has been applied (under the title of 'behavioural economics' or 'nudge') by governments to influence actions by citizens and consumers (paying tax on time, not exceeding road speed limits, eating more wisely, sensible consumption, etc).[4] The EBP and EBR concepts merely apply the same thinking to decisions by people in business organisations (compliance) and to the relationship between the state and businesses (regulation).

The experience of how to achieve safety in the civil aviation sector illustrates the general approach. It challenges many existing assumptions about 'how to enforce'. 'Simply stated, a regulatory "compliant" airline is not necessarily a safe airline.'[5] Regulators and businesses realised that aviation safety simply cannot be achieved without a close working relationship between authorities and airlines, and the people involved. Relevant information is constantly shared and checked.[6] It is regarded as vital to maintain a collaborative 'no blame' culture throughout the sector, between all individuals, and between and within all the organisations. If people fear being blamed, they will not share full or timely information. The approach is not to blame an individual for making a mistake, but to identify why any human in a similar situation might make the same mistake, and so as to be able to reduce that risk. This 'open culture', as it is called, is supported and enforced primarily by social rather than legal or authoritarian means. It recognises that mistakes will occur, and the response to an adverse event must be to share all the relevant information immediately and react to it, but never to conceal it. Aviation talks about maintaining *performance* rather than compliance.[7] Compliance is an outcome, not an approach.[8]

The aviation safety world has redefined the concepts of accountability and responsibility. Accountability is maintained by constantly, visibly contributing to the group.[9] The worst thing a pilot, engineer, air traffic controller or other person can do is to fail to be open and sharing. Rather like the City of London's 'my word is my bond' mentality, the trust is essentially social, rather than imposed or produced by sanctions or threats. The enforcement policy of the Civil Aviation Authority clearly differentiates responses to operators.[10]

---

[4] Richard Thaler and Cass Sunstein, *Nudge. Improving Decisions about Health, Wealth and Happiness* (Yale, Yale University Press, 2008); David Halpern, *Inside the Nudge Unit. How Small Changes can Make a Big Difference* (London, WH Allen, 2015).

[5] Bill Yantis, 'SMS Implementation' in Alan Stolzer, Carl Halford and John Goglia (eds), *Implementing Safety Management Systems in Aviation* (Farnham, Ashgate Publishing, 2011).

[6] 'Keeping the Aviation Industry Safe: Safety Intelligence and Safety Wisdom 16 Aviation Industry Senior Executives Reflect on how they Run a Safe Business in a Commercial Environment. A Future Sky Safety White Paper' (European Commission, 2016).

[7] 'The Transformation to Performance-based Regulation' (Civil Aviation Authority, 2014) 1.

[8] Ruth Steinholtz, 'Ethics Ambassadors: Getting under the Skin of the Business' (2014) 3–4 *Business Compliance* 16.

[9] See the Safety Management Manual of British Airways.

[10] 'Civil Aviation Authority Regulatory Enforcement Policy' (Civil Aviation Authority, October 2012).

By way of contrast, we might look at the state of thinking about how to regulate financial services. In that sector, the regulatory approach in the decade since the 2008 crisis has been to deploy two tools: first, extensive specification of what banks should do (many rules, requirements and systems); and, second, a tough enforcement approach, aimed at deterring wrongdoing. These tools have tended to inhibit actions by the majority while not eradicating the risk that some individuals will continue to act unethically. The problem is that it can now be seen that, overall, behaviours and cultures have not improved much in banking. Bankers feel they are drowning in rules, constricted in actions, and frightened of unfair enforcement. As we note below, thoughtful central bankers are returning to the idea that the answer to behaviours in the industry lies in the culture of organisations.[11]

B. Developments in Regulatory Practice

The second strand of empirical research has looked at how regulators work. A 2017 OECD publication on examples of the application of behavioural insights by 60 public bodies in 23 countries noted that 'governments are searching for simple and effective regulatory solutions to promote more efficient outcomes without resorting to additional rules or sanctions'.[12]

Research has shown that many UK regulatory authorities have adopted a supportive approach in their daily engagement with businesses, and only a minority adopt a simple deterrent approach.[13] The majority do appear to be more effective in achieving compliance.

UK government policy has stressed the need for regulators to adopt a positive and proactive approach towards ensuring compliance, notably in the 2014 Regulators' Code,[14] described in detail in chapter five, which requires that:

(1) Regulators should carry out their activities in a way that *supports those they regulate to comply and grow*; and
(2) Regulators should ensure clear information, guidance and advice is available to *help those they regulate meet their responsibilities to comply*.[15]

An example of this is the 2018 statement by the Office for Product Safety and Standards, whose service standards on what businesses can expect of it emphasise that it carries out all its activities 'in a way that supports those we regulate to comply and grow', and includes the following statements (which, it will be seen, are a long way from an approach based on deterrence):[16]

Helping you to get it right

We want to work with you to help your business to be compliant and successful and it is important to us that you feel able to come to us for advice when you need it. We won't take enforcement action just because you ask us a question or tell us that you have a problem. ...

---

[11] 'Supervision of Behaviour and Culture: Foundations, Practice & Future Developments' (DeNederlandsche-Bank, 2015).

[12] 'Behavioural Insights and Public Policy. Lessons from Around the World' (OECD, 2017).

[13] See Hodges, *Law and Corporate Behaviour* (2015); and Figure 10.1 in Hodges and Steinholtz, *Ethical Business Practice and Regulation* (2017).

[14] 'Regulators' Code' (Birmingham, Better Regulation Delivery Office, 2014); introduced as the 'Regulators' Compliance Code: Statutory Code of Practice for Regulators' (Department for Business Enterprise and Regulatory Reform, 2007), made under the Legislative and Regulatory Reform Act 2006, s 22(1).

[15] 'Regulators' Code' (2014), provisions 1 and 5.

[16] 'What you can Expect of the Office for Product Safety and Standards' (Office for Product Safety and Standards, 2018).

Responding to non-compliance

Our aim, when dealing with non-compliance, is to deliver fair and objective enforcement in a manner consistent with the intentions of the legislation and the necessity of delivering a robust and credible enforcement regime. Where we identify any failure to meet legal obligations, we will respond proportionately, taking account of the nature, seriousness and circumstances of the offence, including taking firm enforcement action when necessary.

The concept of 'earned recognition' has been a stage in the evolution of a risk-based approach, also a requirement of the UK's Regulators' Code.[17] In its 2017 review of the 'direction of travel' in regulatory structures, the UK Government highlighted moves in various regulated sectors towards a 'regulated self-assurance' model, in which responsible businesses take ownership for controlling their risks, and regulators support those businesses who do that.[18] That model evolves away from the extremes of either an authoritarian 'command and control' approach or an uncontrolled 'self-regulatory' approach. At the heart of the new approach is engagement between businesses and regulators on an ongoing adult basis so as to achieve both compliance with society's regulatory goals and business growth. The importance of EBP was stressed by the review team:

> In practice this means that businesses who 'do the right thing' should be regulated with a very light touch. As part of this, regulators should encourage more ethical business practices. However, where regulated entities do not 'do the right thing' and do not follow ethical business practices, redress should be sought.

An example of an approach based on these ideas is the Food Standards Agency (FSA), which, following discussions with stakeholders in 2016, published its plan[19] for future regulatory delivery, that set out the five principles that are shown in Box 22.1. The principles clearly place responsibility for food safety on the commercial enterprises, and state that those who 'do the right thing' should be recognised.

Box 22.1 The FSA's five principles

1. Businesses are responsible for producing food that is safe and what it says it is, and should be able to demonstrate that they do so. Consumers have a right to information to help them make informed choices about the food they buy. Businesses have a responsibility to be transparent and honest in their provision of that information.
2. FSA and regulatory partners' decisions should be tailored, proportionate and based on a clear picture of UK food businesses.
3. The regulator should take into account all available sources of information.
4. Businesses doing the right thing for consumers should be recognised; action will be taken against those that do not.
5. Businesses should meet the costs of regulation, which should be no more than they need to be.

---

[17] 'Regulators' Code' (n 14), provision 3.
[18] 'Regulatory Futures Review' (Cabinet Office, 2017).
[19] 'Regulating Our Future: Why Food Regulation Needs to Change and How we are Going to Do it' (FSA, 2017).

The FSA's 2016 strategy builds on studies that suggest that the audit data collected by food businesses could potentially be used by local authorities to assess compliance with food hygiene standards.[20] Given the fact that major food businesses typically have extensive and professional quality control and scientific testing operations, a relationship of trust should reduce unnecessary duplicative testing and inspections. In a different example of a collaborative programme between the FSA and the major retailers and processing plants, laboratory reports of the campylobacter bacteria on chickens were reduced by 17 per cent, with a direct saving to the economy of over £13 million in the cost of days off work and NHS costs.[21]

II. Relationship and Trust

Regulated self-assurance and EBR require a relationship between regulator and regulated entities. Further, desired outcomes will be maximised where the relationship is one of full mutual engagement to achieve shared outcomes.

Such a relationship is easiest to establish, manage and grow when it exists within a structure that enables cooperation and discussion. An excellent example of such a structure is the Primary Authority scheme, which is based on partnerships, agreements on allocated responsibilities, and the expectation that issues can be raised and will be answered without allocating blame (see chapter nine).[22] Above all, the formal, statutory structure of the Primary Authority model, involving defining responsibilities of Local Authorities and participating businesses in agreed protocols, has created engaged relationships between regulators and businesses, and between authorities themselves. The scheme supports development of consistent good practice.

A critical component is the ability of businesses to seek clarification of what they should do to comply with the rules. The resultant assured advice brings the consequence that compliance with it would not trigger enforcement action. The model has been an outstanding success. At January 2019, there were over 2,400 individual businesses of all sizes in Primary Authority partnerships with local authorities. A further 73,600 were able to receive robust guidance on which they could rely as a result of a primary authority partnership between their trade association or other coordinating body and a local authority.[23] The basis of Primary Authority, and the benefits that it is delivering for local regulators, businesses and those that the regulation is intended to protect, are explored in detail in chapter nine.

Case studies such as those of the FSA, Primary Authority model and civil aviation safety illustrate the fundamental point that regulatory relationships must be built on trust if they

---

[20] 'Regulating Our Future Audit Data Research Published', press release (London, FSA, 2017); Yvonne Robinson and Darryl Thomson, 'Report on the Regulating our Future Pilot to Test the Consistency between Local Authority Interventions and First and Second Party Audit Processes' (Bristol City Council, Food Standards Agency, Mitchells & Butlers, NSF, 2017); F Kirby and Y Robinson, 'Report on Pilot Study: Sharing of Industry Audit Data to Inform the Local Authority Interventions' (FSA and Tesco, 2017).

[21] 'Latest Figures Reveal Decline in Cases of Campylobacter', press release (FSA, 2017).

[22] 'Primary Authority Statutory Guidance' (Regulatory Delivery, 2017).

[23] Office for Product Safety and Standards internal data.

are to be effective. Trust is increasingly regarded as critical by many regulators[24] and by companies.[25] The OECD recognised the importance of maintaining trust of the regulated by regulators as an important principle in the governance of regulators,[26] and has recently issued 'Guidelines on Measuring Trust'.[27]

The EBR model aims to provide evidence of trust from both sides. It challenges businesses to provide evidence of their commitment to ethical values through structures, statements, evaluations and other relevant evidence and regulators to demonstrate their willingness and ability to engage with businesses that provide such evidence and to regulate them differently.

III. Ethical Business Practice and Ethical Culture

Consistently ethical behaviour is most likely as the product of an ethical culture in an organisation or society. All of the major reports on the causes and responses to the 2008 global financial crisis have concluded that culture is the ultimate key to the misbehaviour of financial firms: extensive papers by financial regulators,[28] corporate regulators[29] and business leaders[30] have stressed the importance of culture, so as to provide confidence in the long-term stability and reliability of financial services, investment, pensions and trade. Culture is the missing link to the industrial and economic strategy of a modern nation, and can be transformative.[31] Figure 22.2 illustrates the framework of EBP and EBR, showing the multiplicity of forces which shape an organisation's culture.

[24] Pete Lunn, *Regulatory Policy and Behavioural Economics* (OECD, 2014) 11; 'The Governance of Regulators, OECD Best Practice Principles for Regulatory Policy' (OECD, 2014); 'Standards of Conduct. Treating Customers Fairly. Findings from the 2014 Challenge Panel' Ofgem, March 2015); 'Food We Can Trust: Regulating the Future' (FSA, 2016); 'Keeping the Aviation Industry Safe: Safety Intelligence and Safety Wisdom. 16 Aviation Industry Senior Executives Reflect on how they Run a Safe Business in a Commercial Environment. A Future Sky Safety White Paper' (European Commission, 2016).

[25] 'Corporate Governance and Business Integrity. A Stocktaking of Corporate Practices' (Paris, OECD, 2015); 'Final Draft: The UK Corporate Governance Code' (London, FRC, 2016); 'Corporate Culture and the Role of Boards. Report of Observations' (Financial Reporting Council, 2016); Peter Montagnon, 'Stakeholder Engagement Values, Business Culture & Society' (Institute of Business Ethics, 2016).

[26] Pete Lunn, 'Regulatory Policy and Behavioural Economics' (OECD, 2014, quoting 'OECD Best Practice Principles for the Governance of Regulators' (OECD, 2013).

[27] 'OECD Guidelines on Measuring Trust' (OECD, 2017).

[28] 'Toward Effective Governance of Financial Institutions' (Group of 30, 2012); 'A New Paradigm. Financial Institution Boards and Supervisors' (Group of 30, 2013); 'The FCA's Approach to Advancing its Objectives (London, Financial Conduct Authority, 2013); 'The Salz Review of Barclays' Business Practices report to the Board of Barclays PLC' (2013), para 2.4; 'Report of the Collective Engagement Working Group' (Collective Engagement Working Group, 2013); 'A Report on the Culture of British Retail Banking' (New City Agenda and Cass Business School, 2014); 'Supervision of Behaviour and Culture: Foundations, Practice & Future Developments' (DeNederlandsche-Bank, 2015); 'Promoting Integrity by Creating Opportunities for Responsible Businesses' (B20 Cross-Thematic Group, 2017); 'Annual Review 2016–2017' (Banking Standards Board, 2017).

[29] 'Final Draft: The UK Corporate Governance Code' (London, FRC, 2016), para 4.

[30] 'Investing in Integrity. The Lord Mayor's Conference on Trust and Values (City Values Forum, October 2012); Annual Review 2016–2017' (2017).

[31] 'Good Work. The Taylor Review of Modern Working Practices' (HM Government, 2017) (emphasis on fair working is at the heart of a successful workplace).

Figure 22.2 EBP and EBR Frameworks

Source: Hodges and Steinholtz, 2017.

The initial formal step of creating EBP within an organisation has to come from business. An ethical culture cannot be imposed from outside:

> The conclusion that culture matters is a problematic one for regulators because it involves a qualitative approach. They cannot force companies to have a 'good' culture because they cannot define exactly what that means and measure compliance on an objective basis.[32]

An individual business must decide if it wishes to adopt EBP, and then to produce sufficient evidence that it can be trusted. For some businesses, removing false incentives (eg over-reliance on commercial targets and remuneration based on income) may initially present some challenges. However, it must be accepted that some incentives can generate either good or bad behaviour, often as an unintended consequence. Some examples are; placing short-term business needs above social or other considerations; having large pay differentials between senior and junior workers; and paying bonuses based solely on financial targets.

---

[32] 'Report of a Senior Practitioners' Workshop on Identifying Indicators of Corporate Culture' (International Corporate Governance Network, IBE, Institute of Chartered Secretaries and Administrators, held on 17 December 2015).

Firms will need both a cultural and leadership framework and a values-orientated ethics and compliance framework.[33] These specify the fundamental beliefs, principles and policies as well as aspects of the ethos, systems and processes, which will create an effective ethical culture, or 'high cultural capital'[34] and therefore give rise to evidence on the extent to which an organisation can be expected to be operating ethically. The presence or absence of such information will, therefore, be telling. A major component of EBP and EBR is the use of sophisticated tools that measure the culture in an organisation, and the extent to which the culture itself may be increasing the risk of misconduct through the existence of various types of dysfunction.[35]

IV. Appropriate Culture for Regulators

The EBR model raises a series of challenges for regulators. For example, it is critical that regulators have an appropriate culture that enables them to engage with businesses interested in EBR. This will include being open, flexible, results-orientated, and trusting but not foolish.

EBR distinguishes those businesses that can produce evidence that they are consciously striving to act ethically and treats them accordingly. Regulatory agencies must be able to make that judgement. The evidence on which to base a decision on whether a business deserves trust may come from many different sources. Evidence of a company's efforts to comply with the law is a starting point, and many businesses will also have compliance and quality systems, and evidence from their system records, audits, complaint handling and so on, to show that they can be expected to comply with legal requirements. Some more sophisticated businesses will be able to supply metrics related to their values and how they inform their culture. The fact that a certain number of errors or complaints are identified might not, depending on the circumstances, be that significant, but it will be highly relevant to know how the business responded to any adverse event or information. EBR does not presume perfection; rather it looks for honesty in admitting errors and a learning attitude to dealing with them.

It can be seen that the regulator's culture can either support or inhibit its own mode of operation and behaviour, and its interactions with the outside world. Equally, the regulator can support or impede the desired behaviour of regulated bodies. In order for EBR to succeed, regulators must understand their own cultures and what values are deemed important and what types of behaviours this generates. Businesses that are concerned with continuous improvement and effective compliance will be more likely to engage with a regulator who is open to exploring together with the business the root causes of non-compliance, rather than responding by automatically punishing the business. The latter will be a barrier to openness from the business. This may require changes to the culture of the regulator and the attitudes of its employees, and additions to their skills.

---

[33] Hodges and Steinholtz (n 1) chs 13, 14 and apps 1 and 2.
[34] Stephanie Chaly, James Hennessy, Lev Menand, Kevin Stiroh and Joseph Tracy, *Misconduct Risk, Culture, and Supervision* (New York, Federal Reserve Bank of New York, 2017).
[35] Leading examples are the Barrett Values Centre's Cultural Transformation Tools and the Denison Organisational Culture Survey.

At the root of the desire to engage with EBR is a recognition both that blame, punishment and deterrence have not produced the desired outcomes in the past and that a narrow focus on compliance with rules at a point in time may distract the business and the regulator from a focus on the real risks that affect their outcomes.

As we have said, regulators should respond fairly to businesses that produce evidence of their effective ethical culture based upon EBP, and who desire to enter into an EBR relationship. The EBR relationship should ideally be a common journey between the relevant organisations. Regulators should be consistent between themselves in adopting this new approach. It will not be fair if some work with businesses to solve problems and others impose large fines on those same businesses. The relationship should, of course, guard against complacency and capture, but it is inherent in EBR that the roles and authority of all parties is respected.

A fundamental question is whether a regulator *wants* to work together with others. There is some risk in this for the regulator, who may have concerns over loss of authority, or capture, or simple distrust of business. Those considerations should be balanced with issues of whether a regulator is able to do its job effectively without understanding the practical challenges business faces in complying with regulation, and with balancing all other considerations. On the business's side, distrust of the reaction of the regulator, wider consequences for the business and fear of public exposure bringing damage to reputation could inhibit cooperation.

A second question is whether a regulator is *able to engage* in the relationship space. Assessing the culture of the regulator will improve the chances of success, as it will introduce the regulator to the language of culture and shed light on any changes that are needed within their own organisation. There may be too much distrust on either or both sides. Regulatory officers, particularly those that have played a traditional enforcement role, may be cynical as a result of years of dealing with non-compliance, thereby seeing all businesses as unethical. A deeper understanding of what causes people to do bad things would help to address this cynicism.

Even if there is reluctance to engage in EBR, it needs to be recognised that the attitude and actions of a regulator can either destroy or support an ethical culture in the businesses that it oversees. For example, many businesses treat competition authorities as the enemy, since their approach to increasing compliance is based essentially on enforcement by imposing deterrent penalties.

V. Implementing EBR

A regulator that decides to adopt an EBR policy will need to make a sequence of decisions, including the following. First, how is the new policy to be announced, so as to provide an explanation that will command the support of the public and the regulated community, especially in providing consistency and predictability in decisions? It will be important to explain the goals of the change in approach, not least that the policy is justified as being best able to achieve results, because people are encouraged to learn from mistakes and enabled to improve, so that general levels of compliance and performance are increased, risks identified are reduced, and economic growth is supported.

Second, how will its operational procedures, including its procedures for making enforcement decisions, need to be amended to take account of its EBR policy? The regulator's written Enforcement Policy, which specifies aggravating and mitigating factors considered in making its enforcement decision, should be able to justify taking account of EBP on the basis of pre-existing trust and the likelihood that the EBR relationship will produce positive change. Does the policy clearly explain the basis for differentiating between ethical and other businesses, and for a differentiated response to breaches of law?

Third, who is going to be the prime mover in initiating discussion about establishing the relationship and what it might entail? Will a move be seen as a sign of weakness? It should be interpreted as a sign of strength, a willingness to engage. Although the ultimate decision to engage with EBR must come from the business; the invitation to do so could come from the regulator.

Fourth, how do the parties define what they need to do and not do to establish and maintain effective engagement? What actions, and what evidence of internal ethical culture might be expected or deliverable? Should the EBR relationship be recorded in a written protocol, that clarifies roles, evidence, and expectations of behaviour?

Fifth, how will the regulator in fact react to infringements that may occur despite the EBR relationship? And how will it react to external social or political pressure to blame and punish someone? EBR does not mean that EBP businesses might not do some things seriously wrong, and not deserve appropriate proportionate sanctions. But it does mean that the selection of proportionate sanctions should recognise motivations, root causes, openness to improvement and the overall culture. A good example of this distinction is given at the end of chapter nineteen by Marcus Rink, of the UK's Drinking Water Inspectorate, who was able to rely on transformation programmes agreed with individual water companies and on clear empirical data to distinguish different water companies and impose sanctions appropriately.

EBR represents an additional tool in the regulatory toolbox, to deal with the famous problem, recognised by Abraham Maslow, that 'if the only thing you have is a hammer, everything looks like a nail'. Since every act of misconduct is not motivated by the same calculation, every act of enforcement should not use the same sanctions.

Details of how EBR should operate in different sectors are currently being developed. One of the areas of enquiry is what attitudes may need to be addressed and what skills improved or introduced in order for EBR to take root and succeed. A number of pilot studies are now under way, to learn how EBP works best in different settings. The Scottish Government has adopted EBR as a core policy in delivering its political goal of a fair Scotland.[36] Interest has been indicated by the United Nations Commission for Trade and Development (UNCTAD),[37] OECD,[38] the European Commission[39] and regulators from Singapore to Ontario, Canada to the UK. It is intended that a great deal of learning about this approach and the capabilities required to make it work can be shared widely.

---

[36] 'Competition and Consumer Policy, Delivering Better Outcomes for Consumers and Businesses in Scotland', (Scottish Government, 2016).

[37] Draft 'Manual on Consumer Protection' (UNCTAD, 2016) ch 6.

[38] 'OECD Events on Behavioural Insights 11–12 May 2017. Key Messages & Summary' (Paris, OECD, 2017).

[39] 'Opportunity Now: Europe's Mission to Innovate' (European Commission, 2016) 40.

23

Standards-based Regulation, the Role of Standards and Accreditation in Regulatory Delivery

SCOTT STEEDMAN, MATT GANTLEY AND RICHARD SANDERS

This chapter sets out how standards and accreditation can be used by regulatory agencies as aspects of intervention choices that support consumer protection and enable businesses to innovate and thrive. We explore how these tools can provide confidence to regulatory agencies in business compliance which in turn provides opportunities to reduce burdens on compliant businesses, inform risk-based targeting and achieve stronger protections. We look at how the National Quality Infrastructure system of standards and accreditation works, and consider how it can be used, not just as a tool for policy-makers but as an intervention choice for regulatory agencies. We explore four of the intervention models that standards and accreditation can support – self-regulation, earned recognition, information and education, and co-regulation – before looking in more detail at two examples from the UK.

I. Introduction to Standards and Accreditation

Trading relationships rely on an important structure of standards, agreements, codes and regulations designed to ensure that when businesses and consumers buy something, they get what they expect. For these to carry weight, they must be developed, maintained and implemented rigorously and consistently. The National Quality Infrastructure (NQI) comprises the institutions and systems a country has in place to deliver this. The NQI has four core components:

- **Standardisation** – creates the national and international standards that describe good practice in how things are made and done.
- **Accreditation** – ensures that those who carry out conformity assessment, testing, certification and inspection are competent to do so.
- **Measurement** – implementation of specifications and standards to ensure accuracy, validity and consistency.
- **Conformity assessment** – testing and certification to ensure the quality, performance, reliability or safety of products meet specifications and standards before they enter the market.

These four core components must be aligned with the overarching regulatory framework and underpinned by effective market surveillance. Consumer organisations also play an important part.

The four core components of the NQI support and facilitate international trade. The outputs of the NQI underpin World Trade Organisation rules on eliminating technical barriers to trade by the acceptance of international standards and the mutual recognition of conformity assessment results and regulatory equivalence. Figure 23.1 shows some of the key aspects and relationships within an NQI, noting that standards are also widely used by businesses for purposes other than certification, eg to support the improvement of business performance, to demonstrate social responsibility and to strengthen business to business relationships.

Figure 23.1 A National Quality Infrastructure[1]

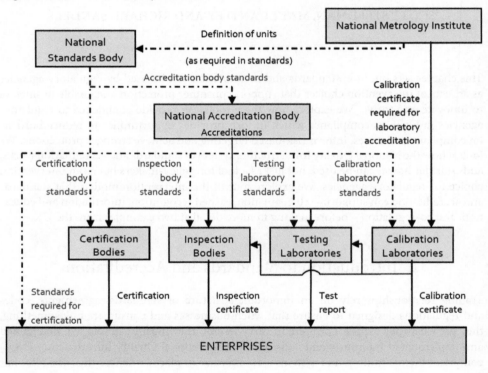

A. Benefits of a Trusted National Quality Infrastructure

The benefits of a well-regarded and trusted National Quality Infrastructure include:

- standards which enable the creation of better, safer, more sustainable products, promote consumer protection and foster trust in supply chains;

---

[1] Reproduced with permission from J Luis Guasch, Jean-Louis Racine, Isabel Sánchez and Makhtar Diop, *Quality Systems and Standards for a Competitive Edge* (Washington DC, World Bank, 2007).

- knowledge from standards and measurement techniques to enable more innovation and faster commercialisation of innovation,[2] creating new markets at home and abroad for businesses;[3]

- increased exports through reduction in technical barriers to international trade[4] and confidence in markets: an additional £6.1 billion of additional UK exports per year can be attributed to standards;[5]

- improved business performance and productivity, increasing domestic commercial activity and competitiveness in international markets: 37.4 per cent of UK productivity growth can be attributed to standards;[6] and

- removal of the need for duplications of standards, tests, regulations and accreditations, thus reducing the costs of international trade.

The United Nations Economic Commission for Europe (UNECE) trade recommendations promote the use of standards and accreditation by policy-makers as a tool for reducing technical barriers to trade, promoting increased resilience to disasters, fostering innovation and for good governance.[7]

B. Standards

Standards are market-defined solutions that capture current good practice and encourage its use throughout the economy. They are developed on the basis of consensus of all interested parties, are subject to unrestricted open consultation and undergo systematic review to ensure their continuing validity. Standards are of themselves voluntary, in that there is no obligation to apply them or comply with them; in a few cases their use can be made mandatory by regulatory instruments. They are tools devised for the convenience of those who wish to use them, and the approach allows for innovation. Standards help to facilitate international trade (particularly by reducing technical barriers), provide a framework for economies of scale and interoperability, enhance consumer protection and confidence and, where appropriate, offer effective alternatives to regulation.

The UK's National Standards Body is the British Standards Institution (BSI). BSI is the world's first National Standards Body, founded in 1901 as the Engineering Standards Committee. BSI's status as the National Standards Body is formally codified in a Memorandum of Understanding (MoU) with the Department for Business, Energy and Industrial Strategy (BEIS) which also recognises BSI's status as the UK member of the international and

---

[2] See Databuild, 'National Measurement System Customer Survey: Final Report for NPL' (National Physical Laboratory, 2015).

[3] See Peter Swann, *The Economics of Standardisation* (Manchester, University of Manchester, 2000); Marion Frenz and Ray Lambert, 'The Economics of Accreditation: Final Report for BIS' (Department for Business, Innovation and Skills, 2013); see also a range of case studies available at www.publicsectorassurance.org.

[4] For example Peter Swann, 'International Standards and Trade: A Review of the Empirical Literature', OECD Trade Policy Working Papers, No 97 (OECD, 2010).

[5] The Centre for Economics and Business Research, 'The Economic Contribution of Standards to the UK Economy' (BSI, 2015).

[6] ibid.

[7] See www.publicsectorassurance.org/supporting-material/unece-trade-recommendations-reference-accreditation.

European standards organisations (ISO, IEC and CEN, CENELEC and ETSI[8] respectively). BSI is also a signatory to the Code of Good Practice for the preparation, adoption and application of standards, Annex 3 to the WTO TBT Agreement.

C. Conformity Assessment

In many circumstances, market regulators and customers generally expect or require that suppliers provide some evidence of compliance with standards. This is termed 'conformity assessment' and refers to the processes used to demonstrate that a product or service meets relevant requirements. Often a self-declaration will be sufficient, the obligation to meet the requirements in the standard being set down in the contract between supplier and customer. Conformity assessment providers such as certification or inspection bodies offer a wide range of testing, inspection, calibration, verification, validation and certification services. Conformity assessment can be conducted or commissioned by the supplier (self-assessment), by the customer, or by a third party independent of the outcome of the assessment. Regulations may include requirements on what approach to conformity assessment is required. Where higher levels of assurance are needed, third-party conformity assessment is more likely to be required. Conformity assessment aims to provide assurance to regulatory agencies and the market that claims of conformity are legitimate. In this chapter, discussion on the role of standards and accreditation is taken to include conformity assessment where this is appropriate or required.

D. Accreditation

Accreditation determines the technical competence and integrity of organisations offering conformity assessment. Accreditation is an ongoing process to establish that the evaluator is impartial and technically competent, that resources and facilities are appropriate and that the evaluator's performance meets the required standard and can be sustained. Accreditation is referenced in the WTO TBT agreement (Article 6) as the credible means of delivering confidence in conformity assessment results.

UKAS is appointed by the UK Government as the sole national accreditation body to assess organisations carrying out conformity assessment activities against internationally recognised standards.[9] UKAS operates under an MoU[10] with the Government, through the Secretary of State for Department for Business, Energy and Industrial

---

[8] ISO – International Organisation for Standardisation; IEC – International Electrotechnical Commission; CEN – European Committee for Standardization; CENELEC – European Committee for Electrotechnical Standardisation; ETSI – European Telecommunications Standards Institute.

[9] Under the Accreditation Regulations 2009 (SI No 3155/2009) and the EU Regulation (EC) 765/2008 on accreditation and market surveillance.

[10] 'Memorandum of Understanding between BEIS and UKAS' (May 2017), available at www.gov.uk/government/publications/memorandum-of-understanding-between-department-for-business-innovation-and-skills-and-united-kingdom-accreditation-service--4.

Strategy. UKAS is a non-profit-distributing company limited by guarantee with over 50 years' experience.

UKAS is regularly reviewed by international peers to demonstrate its competence to be a signatory to European and international accreditation multilateral mutual recognition agreements. These agreements reduce the need for multiple assessments of suppliers, and as a consequence help to reduce barriers to trade for organisations which hold UKAS accredited test reports or certificates.

II. Standards and Accreditation as an Intervention Choice

Standards and accreditation are used by policy-makers across a range of policy areas to support regulatory frameworks. They can produce benefits for all parties, with a cheaper and more effective basis for the adoption of best practice. For policy-makers, using standards and accreditation helps keep technical detail on how to comply out of legislation, thus avoiding legislation being overly prescriptive or quickly outdated by scientific or technological advances, which can lead to the exclusion of innovative approaches and products from the market. Enabling businesses to use recognised standards to demonstrate how they meet legislative requirements provides confidence to businesses and maintains protections. Requiring assessment by accredited conformity assessment bodies provides public and government confidence that standards are being met.

A. Standards and Accreditation as a Policy Tool: EU Harmonised Product Requirements

One example where standards and accreditation have been used in regulatory policy design is the European regulatory system for ensuring the safety and performance of non-food products. As part of the single market in goods, the EU has harmonised product requirements through the New Legislative Framework (NLF). The approach taken is that of laying down only the broad essential requirements in the legislation, predominantly entailing essential health and safety requirements (EHSRs), but not exclusively so. The scope of the laws tends to be rather broad, eg 'machinery' and 'low voltage equipment', so that there is as much simplicity as possible for manufacturers. The expressions of scope are, if at all possible, generic, ie they do not comprise a list of, say, machinery with a tower crane, a backhoe loader or such and such a power tool, but, instead, 'equipment with a drive mechanism', etc. This is very important as it future-proofs the legislation as much as possible, enabling innovation and minimising the need for revision through the legislative processes. The products in scope are then typically divided up further – once again, generically if possible – according to the conformity assessment procedures they are required to undergo by the legislation, the degree of third-party intervention being determined by the level of risk presented. Dependent on risk, conformity assessment ranges from 'internal production control' (self-assessment) to third-party conformity assessment by accredited bodies.

To help manufacturers comply, the principle was established that the essential require-ments would be expressed in risk-based terms and that an independent standardisation process would offer a means of meeting the requirements through a technical explanation set down in standards, in line with the latest developments in the state of the art (which standards experts are much better equipped than the mainstream lawmakers to take on board). A standard can be harmonised through a Commission process of requesting its development in support of regulatory outcomes, and its subsequent citation in the EU Official Journal means following the standard confers a 'presumption of conformity' to the essential legal requirement. The manufacturer can therefore demonstrate the compliance of a product by addressing the requirements of the standard which indicates that they have also addressed the requirements of the legislation. As such, it will generally provide a more straightforward route through the conformity assessment process. Nearly 4,000 European standards can be used to provide presumption of conformity with these laws. These are the voluntary means providing the detail and which are readily available to manufacturers to comply with the broad legal requirements.

B. Standards and Accreditation as a Regulatory Delivery Tool

Standards and accreditation are not just a policy-making tool. Regulatory agencies can and do use these approaches as an intervention choice. Standards and accreditation can:

- reduce the cost to the taxpayer by moving the delivery of inspection to the private sector – the burden of checking compliance is placed on industry rather than government or regulatory agencies;
- support risk-based regulation by providing information to help target a regulatory agency's intervention where it is most needed; and
- reduce the regulatory burden on society and lower the inspection costs incurred by regulatory agencies, whilst at the same time ensuring robust outcomes in terms of compliance and behaviours.

By using market actors to deliver the desired levels of conformity assessment through certi-fication bodies (which may be notified bodies[11] in the context of EU regulation), evidence[12] suggests that the costs are outweighed by the significant economic advantage that busi-nesses derive from the increased capacity and flexibility that the market can provide, whilst enabling regulatory agencies to maintain appropriate levels of oversight.

For regulatory agencies, standards and accreditation intervention choices fall into four broad categories: 'self-regulation'; 'earned recognition'; 'information/education'; and 'co-regulation' (see Figure 23.2).

---

[11] A notified body is an organisation designated by an EU country to assess the conformity of certain products before being placed on the market.

[12] See for example the collection of research and case studies available at www.business-benefits.org.

Figure 23.2 Models of regulatory delivery where standards and accreditation can play key parts

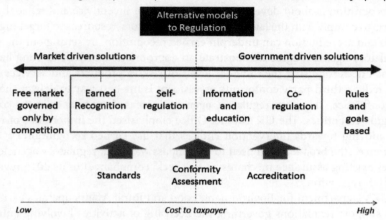

i. *Self-regulation*

Self-regulation is an approach where businesses voluntarily agree to meet certain standards. For example, an industry or profession might choose to develop and adopt its own code of practice promoting ethical conduct. In order for regulatory agencies (and the public) to have confidence that self-regulation is effective, standards and accreditation can be used as part of a self-regulatory regime. Regulatory agencies can encourage the use of standards to deliver regulatory outcomes, or indeed may wish to sponsor the creation of a standard for a particular purpose. Regulatory agencies might also work with an industry to develop a code of practice or a means of determining compliance that involves other parties in setting standards and authorising the activity. Examples include customer charters, codes of conduct, approved or recognised codes and voluntary agreements. Standards developed in support of self-regulation can be supported by accredited conformity assessment if greater assurance of compliance is required, eg if there are serious health and safety implications.

For example, the UK Health and Safety Executive (HSE)-approved code of practice on the control of Legionella requires employers and landlords to carry out a risk assessment, undertaken by a 'competent person'. BSI has developed a standard for Legionella risk assessment (BS 8580: 2010). Businesses use BS 8580 to ensure that they comply with the HSE code of practice. UKAS accredits inspection organisations to assess against BS 8580. Businesses and HSE can have confidence in the risk assessments carried out by accredited inspectors. We will explore self-regulation further later in this chapter when we consider the way the HSE regulates the safety hazard from asbestos.

ii. *Earned Recognition*

Earned recognition is where businesses can 'earn' recognition from regulatory agencies, in the form of reduced costs or inspections, for demonstrating high levels of compliance. Demonstrating compliance with standards or participating in an accredited assurance scheme can be one effective mechanism to support earned recognition. Regulatory agencies use the evidence of compliance to inform risk ratings and tailor interventions accordingly. Earned recognition is about developing approaches that incentivise and reflect businesses' own efforts to comply with the law and releasing regulators' resources to target higher risks. Standards and accreditation can underpin earned recognition, by setting out the standards that regulatory agencies agree demonstrate an appropriate approach to compliance. This should include recognising the different levels of risk in products and services to decide when accredited third-party conformity assessment is the best way to deliver the required level of confidence. This gives regulatory agencies increased confidence in the compliance of the regulated entities. The UK Cabinet Office emphasised the importance of regulatory agencies moving towards intervention choices that use earned recognition or 'regulated self-assurance' (the broader term used to encompass ways that regulatory agencies can use businesses existing assurance mechanisms to 'check' compliance) in its 2015 review of the future of UK regulation.[13]

The UK's Department for Environment, Food and Rural Affairs operates earned recognition to support regulations governing the licensing of activities involving animals. The regulations[14] cover activities such as dog breeding, dog and cat boarding, selling animals as pets, hiring out horses and keeping or training animals for exhibition and require establishments which operate these activities to be licensed by the local authority in which they operate. The licences will need to be renewed each year unless the establishments are assessed as low risk when licences can be issued for two or three years. Establishments that are certified by a UKAS accredited body for activities which fall within the scope of the regulations will be regarded as low risk and will therefore qualify for a longer licence. For example, the Kennel Club's Assured Breeders Scheme.[15]

Later in this chapter we explore in more detail the use of earned recognition underpinned by standards and accreditation by the Food Standards Agency (FSA) in relation to regulating the farming industry.

iii. *Information and Education*

Information and education is one of the tools that regulatory agencies use frequently. But in some circumstances the impact of information and education interventions by regulatory agencies can be improved with the use of standards and accreditation. One of the benefits of the standards-making process is its collaborative approach to building consensus amongst stakeholders to reach an agreed way of doing things. Standards developed by the National Standards Body can also be influential with businesses. Regulatory agencies can use this existing mechanism to develop codes of practice or fast-track standards through the standards-making process, securing stakeholder buy-in and using an approach familiar to businesses.

In the UK, regulatory agencies (as well as trade associations, industry, government or other bodies) can fund the development of a BSI PAS, which is a fast-track document (akin to a formal standard but usually developed in less than one year) developed on the basis of

---

[13] 'Regulatory Futures Review' (Cabinet Office, 2017).
[14] The Animal Welfare (Licensing of Activities Involving Animals) (England) Regulations 2018.
[15] See www.thekennelclub.org.uk/breeding/assured-breeder-scheme.

wide stakeholder engagement, open public consultation and consensus. For example, the Department for Business, Energy and Industrial Strategy commissioned BSI to develop a code of practice on consumer product safety-related recalls and other corrective actions.[16] This followed on from an independent review that identified that consumer product recalls typically only recover about 10–20 per cent of targeted goods. BSI brought together key stakeholders including regulatory agencies, manufacturers and consumers to document good practice. The resulting code of practice PAS includes guidance for manufacturers, importers and distributors on how to put in place plans to manage large-scale product recalls. It also provides advice to regulatory agencies on working with businesses to support product recalls and is already in use around the world.

iv. Co-regulation

Co-regulation is where government sets the top-level regulatory requirements and leaves the sector to define how these general principles are met in terms of technical solutions.[17] In some cases, the use of standards is referenced in regulation as a way of achieving compliance. In others, the market itself may decide to develop standards for their own guidance on the technical state of the art and thus assist with compliance. The EU's approach to technical harmonisation through the New Legislative Framework approach discussed earlier is an example of co-regulation using standards and accreditation, which has proved successful in enabling the creation of the EU single market and now covers the majority of household products available in the UK.

Another example is the way Trust Service Providers are regulated. Trust Service Providers are bodies providing digital certificates which create and validate electronic signatures, essential for the integrity and trust in electronic transactions. The eiDAS Regulation (Regulation (EU) 910/2014) requires auditing of Trust Service Providers by a certification body accredited by UKAS to the requirements of the international standard for organisations certifying products, services or processes (ISO/IEC 17065).[18] BSI brought together key stakeholders to represent the UK's interest in developing the standard and UKAS worked with the Information Commissioner's Office to produce guidance for the implementation of eiDAS in the UK. UKAS accredits certification bodies to certify Trust Service Providers under the relevant European Telecommunications Standards Institute standards which were designed to meet eiDAS. This means that government and consumers can have confidence in Trust Service Providers without direct government intervention.

Another example of coregulation is the way the Forensic Science Regulator has regulated the quality standards that apply to forensic science in England and Wales. UKAS assesses laboratories undertaking forensic analysis against a broad range of forensic examination and testing activities including fingerprint comparison, digital forensics and scenes of crime. UKAS accreditation not only provides authoritative assurance of the technical competence of an organisation to undertake specified activities but also reviews particular

---

[16] 'PAS7100:2018 Code of Practice on Consumer Product Safety Related Recalls and other Corrective Actions', (London, BSI, 2018).

[17] Here we use the definition given by the Cabinet Office in 'Regulatory Futures Review' (2017).

[18] 'ISO/IEC 17065: 2012 Conformity Assessment – Requirements for Bodies Certifying Products, Processes and Services' (ISO, 2012).

aspects relevant to the criminal justice system, for example, continuity of evidence, management of case files and storage of exhibits. Accreditation determines the competence of staff, the validity and suitability of methods, the appropriateness of equipment and facilities, and the ongoing assurance and confidence in outcomes through internal quality control.

We will now look in more detail at two examples of how regulatory agencies have used standards and accreditation as an effective regulatory delivery intervention: firstly earned recognition in the farming industry, and secondly self-regulation for materials containing asbestos.

III. Earned Recognition through Farm Assurance Schemes

A. Introduction

In the UK one area where earned recognition underpinned by standards and accreditation is used is in farming regulation. This case study focuses on the Red Tractor scheme run by Assured Food Standards, and how the FSA has developed a mechanism for members of the Red Tractor scheme to earn recognition for their compliance efforts.

A number of third-party food and animal feed assurance schemes were set up in the UK in the 1990s in response to food safety scares such as salmonella, E coli and BSE.[19] Retailers wanted a better way to assure themselves of consistently applied food standards through the supply chain without each retailer having to conduct audits, and the industry wanted to bolster consumer confidence in British food products.

The Red Tractor scheme was established in 2000 and is now the UK's biggest farm assurance scheme. The scheme covers food safety, traceability, animal welfare and environmental protection throughout the food production chain across a range of food types including meat, poultry, dairy, fruit and vegetables and crop-based products such as flour, breakfast cereals and beer. The Red Tractor logo can be applied to products which are fully traceable back to farms meeting Red Tractor standards, and where businesses in the supply chain have met relevant standards. Red Tractor is run by representatives from across the food chain: the National Farmers' Unions; the Agriculture and Horticulture Development Board; Dairy UK; and the British Retail Consortium. In 2018 there were 78,000 Red Tractor farmers selling food to over 700 companies licensed to use the logo on their packaging, assuring £13 billion-worth of food products annually.[20]

The drivers of the scheme are to protect the reputations of businesses using commercial pressure to drive responsible practice. Industry takes control of its own destiny and is pre-competitive – everyone is in it together. The industry recognises that loss of trust in one business equals loss of trust in the sector and that managing reputations is a catalyst for good practice.

---

[19] M Wright, G Palmer, A Shahriyer, R Williams and R Smith, 'Assessment and Comparison of Third Party Assurance Schemes in the Food Sector: A Common Framework. Final Report for the Food Standards Agency' (Greenstreet Berman, 2013).

[20] www.redtractor.org.uk.

B. How Red Tractor Works

The standards underpinning the Red Tractor scheme are developed and maintained by panels of experts from across all sections of the food and farming industry. They incorporate legal requirements plus additional criteria covering good agricultural practices, good manufacturing practices, food safety, animal health and welfare, and traceability.

Conformity against the scheme standards[21] is assessed and monitored using certification, carried out by commercial and independent certification bodies accredited to ISO 17065 by UKAS. Approximately 60,000 audits[22] are carried out every year. Failure to maintain certification has serious commercial impact on the members and is thus a driver to continued compliance.

Standards should be developed by experts who work to reach consensus. National standards (British Standards, managed by BSI in its role as the National Standards Body) are developed and maintained following a formal governance process that is consistent with the requirements of the international and regional standardisation organisations. Certification schemes such as Red Tractor make use of standards developed specifically for the purpose of the scheme. The governance of these standards will be determined by the scheme owner. A certification scheme may make use of national standards as well as requiring compliance with its own standards or other documents.

C. Developing an Earned Recognition Approach

The Government's approach to regulating the farming industry came under scrutiny in the 2010s following complaints from the industry about the cumulative inspection burden from multiple government agencies and the National Audit Office's conclusion that farm inspections were not delivering value for money.[23] A key theme of the 2011 Macdonald Farming Regulation Task Force[24] was 'earned recognition', where consistently high standards in farming practice could be rewarded with less frequent inspection by including accredited third-party information into risk models. As part of the response to the Task Force, the Government assessed the potential for using earned recognition in a number of areas of farming regulation[25] and regulatory agencies were tasked with exploring this intervention choice further.

Regulatory agencies commissioned research to establish an evidence base for whether farm assurance schemes were adequate for use in an earned recognition approach, in terms

---

[21] Scheme standards are standards developed for, and associated with, a specific conformity assessment certification scheme. Scheme standards are therefore different from formal standards (eg national standards managed by the National Standards Body), which are developed and maintained with full stakeholder engagement and open public consultation independently of any certification scheme offered in the market.

[22] Figures from www.redtractor.org.uk (December 2018).

[23] 'Streamlining Farm Oversight' (National Audit Office, 2012).

[24] Richard Macdonald, 'Striking a Balance: Reducing Burdens; Increasing Responsibility; Earning Recognition. Report on Better Regulation in Farming and Food by the Independent Farming Regulation Taskforce' (Defra, 2011).

[25] 'Farming Regulation Task Force Implementation Earned Recognition Plan' (Defra, 2013).

of the type of requirements (standards) and checks in place for areas that they regulate.[26] Comparisons of farm assurance scheme data and regulatory inspection data found some evidence that members of a farm assurance scheme were more likely to be compliant with animal health and welfare and food and feed regulations.[27]

Having established that farm assurance schemes such as Red Tractor could in theory provide the necessary assurance for regulatory agencies to have confidence in the scheme, a practical mechanism was required for earned recognition to be applied. Here we discuss the approach of the FSA to demonstrate the steps a regulatory agency can take to have confidence in this intervention. Other UK regulatory agencies also operate earned recognition for farmers that are members of assurance schemes.

The FSA's approach involves first assessing whether the assurance scheme is sufficiently robust. Any assurance scheme can apply to be approved by the FSA; and approval brings earned recognition. A set of criteria exist for approval which include the standards-setting process, the process for compliance and certification (eg using UKAS accreditation against the requirements of ISO 17065), the assessment process (eg frequency and type of checks), the competence and authorisation of assessors and mechanisms for sharing data with the regulatory agency. Six of the Red Tractor schemes are currently approved by the FSA (beef and lamb, crops and sugar beet, dairy, fresh produce, pigs, and poultry) for earned recognition in relation to feed, dairy hygiene and food hygiene in the context of primary production. Several other food assurance schemes are also approved by the FSA for an earned recognition approach.[28] The FSA reviews and reverifies the approval status of assurance schemes regularly using data and intelligence from the schemes and enforcement authorities. This includes checks on a percentage of assurance scheme members to verify compliance.

Following approval, an MoU between the FSA and the assurance scheme is agreed which sets out the framework for delivery of earned recognition.[29] Where local authority regulatory agencies enforce the relevant regulations, FSA publishes guidance on how members of approved assurance schemes should be treated. For example, for Red Tractor, the Feed Law Code of Practice Guidance includes detailed guidance for local regulatory agencies on what action they should take to implement earned recognition, such as how to adjust the frequency and type of planned intervention with primary producers that are members of Red Tractor-approved schemes.[30] There is also guidance for local regulatory agencies on how to deal with notifications from Red Tractor inspections highlighting issues with non-compliance and how to remove earned recognition from businesses that are found not to be maintaining a satisfactory level of compliance.[31]

---

[26] For example, see Wright et al, 'Assessment and Comparison of Third Party Assurance Schemes' (2013) and University of Warwick, 'Does membership of a Farm Assurance Scheme affect compliance with Animal Welfare Legislation and Codes. Final Report to Defra' (Defra, 2010).

[27] For example. Corinna Clark, Ron Crump, Al Kilbride and Laura Green, 'Farm Membership of Voluntary Welfare Schemes Results in Better Compliance with Animal Welfare Legislation in Great Britain' (2016) 25 *Animal Welfare* 461, and Glyn Jones (Fera) and John Paul Gosling (University of Leeds), 'Study on Farm Assurance Scheme Membership and Compliance with Regulation under Cross Compliance. Report to Defra' (Defra, 2013).

[28] 'Earned Recognition – Approved Assurance Schemes' available at www.food.gov.uk/business-guidance/earned-recognition-approved-assurance-schemes.

[29] See, for example, 'Memorandum of Understanding for Earned Recognition between the Food Standards Agency and Assured Food Standards' (FSA, 2017), available at www.food.gov.uk/sites/default/files/media/document/MOU%20Red%20Tractor%20Nov%202017.pdf.

[30] 'Feed Law Practice Guidance England' (FSA, 2018) 72.

[31] 'Guidance on Food Standards Agency Approved Assurance Schemes in the Animal Feed and Food Hygiene at the Level of Primary Production Sectors' (Food Standards Agency, 2018).

Membership of the Red Tractor scheme reduces dairy hygiene inspections from every two to 10 years and feed hygiene inspections from 25 per cent being inspected annually to two per cent of Red Tractor farms.[32]

D. Benefits of Earned Recognition

Earned recognition by regulatory agencies aims to incentivise and reflect businesses' own efforts to comply with the law and works with existing industry-led compliance checks which are often supply chain requirements. For businesses, a reduction in inspection frequency from regulatory agencies saves the costs of participating in an inspection. Compliance with Red Tractor standards ensure they maintain a recognised consumer quality mark, can satisfy retailers of their compliance and satisfy regulatory agencies using the same approach.

From the regulatory agency's perspective, earned recognition means the cost of checking compliance is (in part) moving from the regulatory agency to the regulated, freeing up resource to focus elsewhere. There remain some ongoing costs in ensuring that the route to earn recognition is adequate, and to conduct ongoing monitoring, but this supports confidence in the intervention choice, for regulatory agencies and ultimately citizens. The use of a standards-making process accompanied by using conformity assessment as a means to give confidence in compliance checks forms the basis of these assurance checks by the regulatory agency.

In practice there remain improvements that can be made to the use of earned recognition through Red Tractor and other farm assurance schemes. A 2016 FSA audit[33] of local regulatory agency feed inspections found that earned recognition mechanisms put in place by the FSA had not been implemented effectively by some local regulatory agencies, meaning some members of Red Tractor and other assurance schemes were not fully benefitting from reduced inspections. Reasons for this included the use of out-of-date processes for inspection scheduling and ineffective tagging of businesses that were part of an approved assurance scheme.

There have been high-profile food safety scandals at Red Tractor certified meat-processing plants, affecting confidence in the brand.[34] Whilst meat-processing is not an area subject to earned recognition by regulatory agencies, it highlighted the need for Red Tractor to be continually evaluating its approach and sharing data effectively with regulatory agencies.[35] In fact, Red Tractor and regulatory agencies are looking at the same questions around the effectiveness of interventions, including how they target interventions, how they apply risk ratings, how they can use technology and data-sharing to better effect and how to improve levels of non-compliance.[36] If earned recognition schemes do not use intelligent

---

[32] Glenys Stacey, 'Farm Inspection and Regulation Review' (Defra, December 2018).

[33] 'An Assessment of Local Authority Official Controls on Feed of Non-Animal Origin (FNAO) and Feed Establishments, including Primary Producers in England' (Food Standards Agency, 2016).

[34] For example see 'Trust the Tractor? The Evidence is not Exactly Reassuring' (2018) *The Grocer*, 3 August 2018, available at https://m.thegrocer.co.uk/570200.article?mobilesite=enabled.

[35] Environment, Food and Rural Affairs Committee, 'Inquiry into 2 Sisters and Standards in Poultry Processing' (House of Commons, 2017).

[36] For example, see 'Assured Food Standards Red Tractor, Information for Pig, Dairy and Poultry Members: Risk Based Approach to Inspections', available at https://assurance.redtractor.org.uk/standards/member-rules.

approaches to inspection and other data-gathering exercises then they can become a more costly alternative than the original regime.

Nevertheless, regulatory agencies and the industry remain committed to making the earned recognition approach work for third-party assurance schemes. The Environment Agency reduces inspection frequency of intensive pig and poultry farms that are members of the Pig and Poultry Assurance scheme from every year to every three years and reduces its fees.[37] The Animal and Plant Health Agency uses membership of UKAS accredited farm assurance schemes as part of its risk model to determine frequency of welfare inspections.[38] The FSA has made earned recognition one of the key components of its Regulating our Future strategy[39] and is committed to expanding the role that private assurance schemes can play in effectively and efficiently achieving positive regulatory outcomes. The Stacey Review on Farm Inspection and Regulation in 2018[40] also encourages the expansion of earned recognition approaches to reduce the regulatory burden for farmers whilst maintaining confidence in regulatory compliance.

IV. Self-regulation: Asbestos Surveys

Another example of how standards and accreditation have been used to deliver regulatory outcomes concerns the control of asbestos, as part of a broader self-regulation approach. Asbestos is a naturally occurring mineral and was used extensively in the building industries for about 150 years until the late 1990s. It is hazardous to human health and has been banned for many years, but is still present in many buildings. For example, in 2002, it was estimated that about half a million non-domestic premises in the UK still contained some form of asbestos.[41]

In the UK, the HSE introduced regulations to protect workers and other from the risks of exposure to asbestos. Amongst other requirements, the Control of Asbestos Regulations require surveying and in certain circumstances testing for the presence of asbestos. In terms of intervention choices, the regulatory agency does not take responsibility for the surveying or testing. It is neither efficient nor effective for the regulatory agency to do this as it requires highly specialist knowledge and potentially expensive testing facilities.

The regulations require testing for the presence of asbestos to be carried out by a laboratory that is accredited by UKAS against the requirements of ISO/IEC 17025, the international standard for test laboratories.[42] This requirement means that HSE can be assured that material containing asbestos can be reliably identified and therefore the exposure risks managed. HSE also recommends (but does not mandate) that, where surveys are carried out for the presence of asbestos, they should be carried out by accredited inspection bodies.

---

[37] Pig and Poultry Assurance Scheme (Environment Agency, 2018).

[38] 'Farming Regulation Task Force Implementation Earned Recognition Plan' (Defra, 2013).

[39] 'Regulating our Future: Why Food Regulation Needs to Change and how we are Going to do it' (Food Standards Agency, 2017).

[40] Glenys Stacey, 'Farm Inspection and Regulation Review' (Defra, December 2018).

[41] Health and Safety Executive, 'Post Implementation Review of the Control of Asbestos Regulations 2012' (The Stationery Office, 2017).

[42] 'ISO/IEC 17025: 2017 General Requirements for the Competence of Testing and Calibration Laboratories' (ISO, 2017).

In terms of surveying, the regulations require owners and occupiers of non-domestic premises to carry out a 'suitable and sufficient' assessment of whether asbestos is likely to be present. Different levels of survey are required, depending on whether the premises is in 'normal' use (eg occupation) or whether the premises are being refurbished or demolished where there is a higher risk of disturbing any asbestos present. Use of an accredited surveyor is not a legal requirement. This means regulated entities have a choice on how to comply, and the regulatory agency an opportunity to consider what intervention could achieve the best outcome. HSE recognises that accreditation gives the regulatory agency confidence in the competence and impartiality of surveyors and therefore confidence that exposure is being managed effectively. HSE's guidance on managing asbestos[43] provides information about when a surveyor would be required and where the duty-holder might be able to conduct a survey themselves (eg if the premises are simple and straightforward and no refurbishment/demolition work is planned). It also provides guidance on how to choose a competent surveyor[44] which strongly recommends using an accredited surveyor. HSE has also partnered with UKAS to promote the use of UKAS accredited asbestos surveyors as the best method for regulated entities to ensure they are legally compliant.[45] There are more than 100 asbestos inspection bodies currently accredited by UKAS against the requirements of ISO 17020,[46] the international standard for bodies performing inspection. UKAS checks that the organisation has technically competent staff, appropriate resources and facilities, is impartial and is performing to the required standard.

Use of international standards in this way provides a recognised benchmark against which the competence, impartiality and consistency of the test laboratories and inspection bodies can be assessed. Accreditation by UKAS provides independent confirmation that the requirements of the standards have been met by the organisations carrying out the activity. Accreditation as a process provides further assurance to the regulatory agencies (in this case the HSE) that the laboratories and inspection bodies have the necessary competence to carry out the tasks designated to them without the HSE having to undertake assessments or investigations of its own.

A recent review[47] of the UK asbestos regulations concluded that the fall in exposure to asbestos between 1980 and 2015 will lead to 25,700 fewer deaths from mesothelioma and lung cancer in the 100 years between 2001 and 2100. The report concludes that not all the deaths prevented can be attributed to the regulations, but that evidence suggests that the measures required by the regulations have been very influential in controlling exposures.

V. Conclusions

In this chapter we have highlighted ways in which regulatory agencies can use the established approaches within the National Quality Infrastructure to their benefit. Improving

[43] See www.hse.gov.uk/asbestos/surveys.htm.

[44] See www.hse.gov.uk/asbestos/surveyors.htm.

[45] 'Who should you Commission to Carry Out your Surveys for Asbestos?' (UKAS, 2012).

[46] 'ISO/IEC 17020: 2012 Conformity Assessment – Requirements for the Operation of Various Types of Bodies Performing Inspection' (ISO, 2012). This has been adopted as a national standard in the UK where it is known as BS EN ISO/IEC 17020. UK input to ISO/IEC 17020 is managed through BSI as the UK member of ISO and IEC.

[47] 'Post Implementation Review of the Control of Asbestos Regulations 2012' (The Stationery Office, 2017).

protection, prosperity and efficiency by improving outcomes for citizens and workers, reducing costs to business whilst increasing choice and lowering the costs for the regulatory agency. These approaches can enable earned recognition and other alternative approaches to regulatory delivery, by giving regulatory agencies confidence as to which businesses are likely to be compliant. This information can be incorporated into risk-based targeting schemes, improving the efficiency and effectiveness of the regulatory agency, and working with the grain of compliance regimes that industry uses.

PART THREE

International Best Practice Examples

24

Regulatory Delivery in Brazil: Past and Future

MARCELO PACHECO DOS GUARANYS

I. Introduction

This chapter presents important efforts to drive change in regulatory delivery in Brazil over the last two decades. The modernisation of legislation in different sectors and the establishment of regulatory agencies in the 1990s created a new environment, but there is still much to be done in order to change Brazil's culture on how to intervene in the economy to better achieve the outcomes citizens want.

The chapter describes the current situation for regulatory delivery in Brazil and the initiatives that are being implemented by federal government, from the improvement of the governance, accountability and culture prerequisites of the Regulatory Delivery Model to the development of the instruments used to evaluate, prioritise and choose regulatory options.

II. History and Culture

First, it is important to provide a little background about Brazil's history and culture regarding the relationship between the Government and the economy and, as a consequence, the impact on regulatory delivery.

In 1500, the Portuguese arrived in what is now the Brazilian territory. Brazil was a Portuguese colony until 1808, when the Portuguese royal family moved to Brazil, escaping from the attack of Napoleon Bonaparte, and transferring the Portuguese kingdom's capital to the country.

Brazil became an independent country in 1822 and a republic in 1889. However, some important cultural heritage remains: the presence of the Government in the economy has always been strong, with direct provision of services, bureaucratic controls and a need to request permission from the state to carry out many commercial activities. At the same time, citizens expect that the Government will solve their problems and provide their basic needs, ie they have a great demand for public policies.

Another important feature of Brazil's culture is the lack of information about the costs of public policies or regulation. Maybe due to its colonial past, people are used to paying taxes without knowing what the destination of their money is. Because of the complexity of the Brazilian tax system it is not easy for citizens to have the right information about government expenditure. We can say the same about rule-making: citizens are not used to expressing their view on the impact of regulation, and, often, even regulators are not.

III. State Organisation and Regulation

Brazil is currently the sixth largest country in the world with a population of approximately 207 million people. It is a federal presidential republic composed of three levels of federation: the Union (federal government); 26 states and the Federal District (home to Brasilia, the capital city); and 5,570 municipalities. The Federal Constitution establishes separated powers to each level of the federation entity, but some powers are exercised by all three levels.

The power to regulate sectors may be exercised at only one level or by all of them, depending on the sector. Each federal level is free to organise themselves and create their own agencies or organisations. For example, all three levels have the power to regulate land transportation. Federal government regulates transportation between states and may create an agency to regulate it. States regulate transportation between cities inside each state and each state may create an agency to regulate it inside its territory. And municipalities regulate transportation inside each municipality territory and each municipality may create an agency to regulate it in its territory.

IV. Brazilian Federal Regulatory Agencies

Brazil only really started what could be thought of as a modern era for regulatory delivery in the mid-1990s. In fact, it was during that decade that the most important public utilities were privatised or granted to the private sector, requiring a better business environment. Long-term contracts needed an environment that would provide protection from political interference and from significant fluctuations in regulation when there is a change of president or ministers. It was also important to improve the transparency of rulemaking.

As a response, the first federal regulatory agencies were created with better governance and transparency in order to deliver better public services. Since then, 11 federal regulatory agencies have been created, as set out in Table 24.1.

Table 24.1 Federal regulators in Brazil

Federal regulator	Area regulated	Year created
National Electricity Agency (ANEEL)	Electricity	1996
National Agency for Oil, Natural Gas and Biofuels (ANP)	Oil and gas	1997
National Agency for Telecommunications (ANATEL)	Telecommunications	1997
Health Regulatory Agency (ANVISA)	Health	1999

(continued)

Table 24.1 *(Continued)*

Federal regulator	Area regulated	Year created
National Agency for Private Health Insurance and Plans (ANS)	Health insurance	2000
National Water (ANA)	Water	2000
National Agency for Land Transportation (ANTT)	Land transportation	2001
National Agency for Water Transportation (ANTAQ)	Water transportation	2001
National Film Agency (ANCINE)	Audiovisual industry	2001
National Civil Aviation Agency (ANAC)	Civil aviation	2005
National Mining Agency (ANM)	Mining	2017

It is important to note that not all the federal regulatory agencies are responsible for public utilities: ANCINE, for example, is responsible for regulating the audio-visual industry. These federal agencies are only one part of the regulatory framework in Brazil. There are dozens of other federal organisations and countless state and municipal organisations that are also responsible for delivering regulation and do not have a specific framework.

Although the sectors these agencies regulate are quite different, the agencies all have a common institutional and organisational framework. They are all responsible, in their own fields, for technical regulation, economic regulation, certification and inspection, and were created so that regulated entities could have a stable business environment. Their main characteristics are as follows:

- **Autonomy**: agencies are independent bodies and have their own budgets; they must follow the law and specific policies of each sector, but, although they are all linked to a minister responsible for policy-making, there is no relationship of hierarchy; they are responsible for final technical decisions in each field that can only be reviewed by the judiciary (not by the minister). Directors are appointed by the President and submitted for approval by the Senate; they have four- or five-year terms and can only be removed from office in case of criminal or administrative disciplinary conviction.

- **Governance**: decisions and regulations are not made by only one person, but by a board of directors.

- **Transparency**: all important regulation must be submitted to public consultation before being presented to the board; all board meetings whose agenda previews the consideration of a new rule or decision of interest of any person shall be open to the public.

- **Staff specialisation**: each regulatory agency has a specific profession of regulatory specialist in order to attract and develop technical knowledge to the government.

V. First Initiatives for Improving Effectiveness of Regulatory Agencies

As seen above, regulatory agencies were a new step in Brazil. However, despite the common structure, each agency was created within a different context and by different laws, which has not allowed a homogenous implementation of the regulatory culture. In 2004, the Federal Government identified that the recently created agencies needed to have their institutional framework under the same law,[1] so that the accountability between government and regulators could be strengthened in all areas. It was also important to establish a clear separation between policy-making and rule-making, in a way that each minister should be responsible for setting out policies in its field and agencies should follow these policies and establish necessary rules.[2]

Three initiatives deserve mention in relation to strengthening the way regulatory agencies operated in a consistent way:

1. the proposal of a general law for regulatory agencies in 2004;
2. the establishment of analytical opinions on regulatory rules by the Ministry of Finance; and
3. the creation by the Presidency of the Programme for Strengthening Institutional Capacity for Management in Regulation (PRO-REG).

The first initiative, the bill for regulatory agencies, was originally presented to National Congress[3] in 2004 and contained several interesting objectives in relation to increasing social participation and improving the effectiveness of agencies. However, it was also focused on stronger governance of the agencies with more control by ministries and on the separation between political and regulatory powers. Due to this, it was interpreted as an undue interference by the Federal Government in the autonomy of regulatory agencies and faced strong resistance from defenders of the agencies' autonomy and was withdrawn in 2014.

The second was an embryonic attempt to start a regulatory oversight body within the Ministry of Finance, which is responsible for the advocacy of competition and best regulatory practices.[4] In 2006 the Ministry of Finance Secretariat of Economic Monitoring (since January 2019, SEAE: Secretariat for Competition Advocacy and Competitiveness) started to form analytical opinions on the impact of every significant regulation proposed by all agencies and make these publicly available. These analytical opinions were non-binding and lightweight instruments which do not need to be followed by the agencies, but they must be made publicly available on the internet.

The third initiative, and the one with the best results, was the implementation of PRO-REG in 2007. It was conceived as a partnership between the Inter-American Development Bank and the Government, represented by the Civil House of the Presidency of the Republic. The main objective of PRO-REG is to strengthen the quality of federal

---

[1] Law 9986/2000 deals with all agencies, but only on aspects related to human resources and the directors' mandate.

[2] All regulatory agencies, with the exception of ANAC and ANM, were created during President Fernando Henrique Cardoso's administration. In 2003, President Lula took office and questioned some characteristics of these agencies.

[3] National Congress is the Brazilian Parliament. In Brazil, the federal legislative branch is a bicameral system formed by the Federal Senate and the Chamber of Deputies.

[4] The Brazilian System for Competition Defence is composed of: the Administrative Council for Economic Defence (CADE), an independent agency reporting to the Ministry of Justice, responsible for investigating and deciding, ultimately, on competition issues, as well as responsible for fostering and promoting the culture of competition in Brazil; and the Secretariat for Competition Advocacy and Competitiveness (SEAE) at the Ministry of Economy, responsible for promoting competition advocacy inside and outside the Government.

government regulatory delivery by strengthening coordination among participating organisations, improving mechanisms of accountability and promoting participation of citizens and regulated entities.[5]

To ensure better coordination among different institutions, PRO-REG was created with a steering committee, with the participation of representatives from cross-cutting federal government departments (Civil House of the Presidency of the Republic, the Ministry of Finance and the Ministry of Planning, Development and Management), and an advisory committee, composed of the representatives of the federal regulatory agencies, their responsible ministries,[6] the Ministry of Justice and the Administrative Council for Economic Defence (CADE, the Brazilian competition agency). Together, both committees aim at defining the strategic direction and the priorities of PRO-REG.

Since its beginning, PRO-REG has developed a series of actions, focused on understanding the Brazilian regulatory environment and on training regulators in order to improve the impact of regulatory activity. Studies were carried out on relevant topics. At the same time, a series of training events on legal and economic tools were organised for public servants working in the federal regulatory system. PRO-REG has also published books on topics related to regulation, all available online.[7]

Over the last three years, the programme has adopted a more strategic approach, seeking to map and consolidate the advances already achieved and to promote the effective adoption and systematisation of the best practices observed at the federal level and internationally for effective regulatory delivery. Some initiatives that deserve to be highlighted are: the use of regulatory impact analysis as a tool to improve regulatory delivery; the improvement of the management of existing regulation; and the promotion of mechanisms of transparency and accountability in the scope of the regulatory process. Throughout its implementation, PRO-REG has also been developing a series of partnerships with government entities and civil society in order to establish a joint culture of focusing on regulatory delivery.[8]

VI. Recent Developments

Brazil is an emerging economy and has shown significant annual economic growth since 1991. However, in 2015 and 2016, the Brazilian economy experienced a sharp downturn, emerging from an economic boom to a deep recession. The economy shrank 3.8 per cent

---

[5] Information from PRO-REG available at www.regulacao.gov.br/acesso-a-informacao/institucional.

[6] The responsible ministry is the one responsible for policy-making in the same sector as the regulatory agencies. For example, the Ministry of Transport is the responsible ministry for ANAC, ANTT and ANTAQ, the agencies for civil aviation, land and water transportation.

[7] See www.regulacao.gov.br/central-de-conteudos/biblioteca-menu.

[8] At the national level, partnerships were established with the Brazilian Association of Regulatory Agencies (ABAR), the Brazilian Institute for Consumer Protection (Idec), the National Forum of Civil Entities for Consumer Protection (FNECDC), the National Consumer Defence School (ENDC), the National Confederation of Industry (CNI), Brazil – United States Chamber of Commerce (Amcham Brazil) and, more recently, Foreign Trade Chamber (CAMEX) and National School for Public Administration (ENAP). At the international level, PRO-REG established partnerships with the US Office of Information and Regulatory Affairs (OIRA), the UK Government, the European Commission and the Latin American countries through the Latin American Network for Regulatory Improvement.

in 2015 and 3.6 per cent in 2016 meaning two consecutive years of decline in gross domestic product, the worst result for the economy ever recorded in the official statistics.

With the economic crisis it became clear that there was a need to improve public policies to make spending more efficient. In the same way, the importance of improving the instruments of evaluation of the regulation with the intention of reducing unnecessary costs for society was reinforced.[9]

In order to make the economy grow again, the Government prioritised short- and long-term spending cuts through the establishment of a cap on public spending and the promotion of social security reform. In addition to these measures, the analysis carried out with organised civil society, through the Economic and Social Development Council[10] pointed to the need for public policies with four objectives:

1.   improvement of the business environment;
2.   reinforcement of stability and regulatory quality;
3.   reduction of bureaucracy; and
4.   increase in productivity and competitiveness.

As a result, other structural reforms were promoted, such as labour reform and tax reform. Oil and gas, electricity, mining and telecommunications regulatory frameworks were also reviewed in order to allow more investments and returns to the Brazilian population.

Regulatory agencies became the centre of discussions again. Complaints were focused on the lack of criteria for directors' appointment, the absence of transparency and assessment in the regulatory decision-making process and the deficiency of communication with citizens, leading to a crisis of legitimacy. It was clear that government should look again at public policies to reinforce the prerequisites of regulatory delivery: governance; accountability; and culture.

It is important to keep in mind that any institutional change in Brazil can take considerable time in view of the complexity of our administrative political system, with three levels of federation. In this context, institutional changes can vary at each level in their implementation times. In general, they start at the federal level through federal public policies and are gradually implemented by states and municipalities.

VII. New Measures to Improve the Business Environment

In May 2016, the Federal Government decided to restart the debate on the bill for regulatory agencies, which had been dropped in 2014. After a series of meetings with all the federal agencies and the Ministry of Finance and the Ministry of Planning (the main actors of PRO-REG governance), a new proposal was taken to the Senate.[11] The main objective

---

[9] The Global Competitiveness Index 2017–2018 edition published by the World Economic Forum ranked Brazil 80th in 140 countries. Specifically, Brazil was ranked 136th in 'burden of government regulation' and 133rd in 'efficiency of government spending'.

[10] The Economic and Social Development Council was a collegiate body composed of representatives of civil society that was responsible, from 2003 to 2018, for directly advising the President of the Republic in all areas.

[11] The Bill for Regulatory Agencies is PL 6621/2016, available at www.camara.gov.br/proposicoesWeb/fichadetra mitacao?idProposicao=2120019.

of this new proposal was the implementation of agencies' autonomy with standardisation of aspects related to management, governance, decision-making and accountability. At the time of writing the bill has been approved by the Chamber of Deputies, but still needs to be approved by the Senate.

Taking into consideration the prerequisites of regulatory delivery, we can say that this bill aims directly at governance and accountability in order to shape regulatory culture. The general idea is to increase the technical level of the directors by raising the criteria for the selection process. With that, it becomes possible to increase the independence of the board. However, with more independence, it is important to have more transparency and accountability. The most important aspects of the bill are presented below.

1. **Increasing autonomy**: In the current model, federal regulatory agencies have autonomy and independence, but there are some aspects of management that require the approval of the ministry responsible. The bill changes this scenario, giving agencies the right to negotiate their budget and staffing needs directly with the Ministry of Planning, without having to pass through the responsible minister. This aims to resolve the issue that ministers can use agencies' administrative needs to influence their behaviour.

2. **Selection of directors**: Each federal regulatory agency has a board of directors. Currently each director must be appointed by the President and approved by the Senate. The problem with this is that political interests can be higher than technical interests when choosing the directors. As a way to avoid this, the bill presents new requirements to be a director, based on academic knowledge and professional and management experience. Also, there are new restrictions to be appointed as a director, preventing politicians, trade unionists and people with conflicting interests from taking office.

    Another innovation is the public pre-selection process of agencies' directors. Currently there is no selection process for choosing who will be appointed, which leads to a lot of pressure from different stakeholders for names to be considered. The bill proposes the creation of a commission that will be responsible for conducting public selection for each position of director. Candidates will attend a public call, and the commission will analyse them and select a list of three candidates to be submitted to the President. The President will choose one person from the list and send him or her to be approved by the Senate.

3. **Governance**: Currently, all federal regulatory agencies are directed by a board, but each one varies in the number of directors and the duration of their term. The rules on whether directors can be reappointed is also something that varies between each agency.

    The bill establishes five-year terms for directors in all agencies, with no possibility of being reappointed. And, in order to minimise abrupt changes in the understanding of the board, the terms end at different times so that there is no more than one director changing in any one year.

4. **Decision-making and transparency**: All board decisions concerning introducing new regulations or changing existing regulations will have to be agreed by an absolute majority. Board meetings will be open to the public, recorded and made available on the internet for anyone to view.

Agencies will be obliged to publicly consult on draft regulations whenever they are of general interest to businesses or citizens. Public consultations will have to contain a regulatory impact analysis explaining what regulatory options were considered and the effects of the option that was chosen.

5.   **Accountability**: New rules for accountability are presented in the bill focused on improving the communication between federal regulatory agencies and government, regulated entities and citizens. The key is to have a transparent means of planning agencies' activities so that citizens and the Government can monitor their performance and results. In this context, four documents are very important and will be demanded from all agencies:

(i)   **Strategic Plan**: presented every four years, in line with the planning cycle for the Federal Government. It will contain the objectives, targets and strategic results related to regulation, inspection and management of each agency. It must also indicate external factors that may significantly affect its effectiveness.

(ii) **Annual Management Plan**: this must be connected to the Strategic Plan and will specify the targets and objectives that will be addressed during that year. It will estimate budgetary resources and the expenditure plan for the year. It must also contain the Regulatory Agenda.

(iii) **Regulatory Agenda**: this sets out the plans for reviewing and changing regulatory requirements, contemplating the set of priority topics that will be under discussion during its duration. It can be for one or more years, but it is important to specify which regulations will be discussed in each year so stakeholders can be prepared to participate in the rule-making process.

(iv) **Annual Report**: this is the reporting instrument that will demonstrate the agency's compliance with the Strategic Plan, the Annual Plan and the Regulatory Agenda in each year.

All these instruments must be approved by the board of directors and sent to the Federal Senate, the Chamber of Deputies, the Brazilian National Accounting Office and government ministers. They have to be available online and, once a year, each agency's president must attend a public session at the Senate to report on the performance of the agency and present an assessment of relevant public policies.

6.   **Ombudsman**: Although almost all federal regulatory agencies already have an ombudsman, powers and features are not the same. The bill presents new characteristics that reinforce the autonomy of the ombudsman, making him more similar to a director: appointed by the president, approved by senate and with a three-year mandate.

The ombudsman will have a degree of autonomy – being part of the agency structure but independent from the board. The ombudsman will be responsible for:

*   ensuring the quality of the services provided by the regulatory agency and its compliance with standard time limits;
*   receiving complaints about the performance of the regulatory agency;
*   preparing an Ombudsman's Annual Report analysing the performance of the agency, that will also be sent to the Senate, the Chamber, the Brazilian National Accounting Office and government ministers.

7.   **Relationships with different government organisations**: To avoid conflicts and to develop an institutional environment that allows an effective operation of different

government organisations, the bill sets out certain rules for the integrated actions of the regulatory agencies themselves and with three groups of regulatory agencies: the competition authority; the consumer protection and environmental protection agencies; and state and municipal regulatory agencies.

One kind of conflict that used to be common in Brazil relates to the roles of the competition authority and federal regulatory agencies. With this in mind and with a view to promoting competition and effective enforcement of competition law in regulated markets, the bill establishes that competition authorities and regulatory agencies shall act in close cooperation and exchange intelligence. In the exercise of their duties, regulatory agencies are responsible for monitoring market practices of businesses in order to assist the competition authority in enforcing competition law. On the other hand, the competition authority is responsible for the enforcement of competition law even in regulated sectors, having exclusive powers to analyse mergers and to investigate possible competition law violations.

Among federal regulatory agencies, two or more may establish joint regulation acts about issues relevant to them, for instance electricity and oil. They shall be approved by the board of each regulatory agency involved and must contain rules for monitoring results and to solve conflicts from their application. Regulatory agencies may set up committees for the exchange of experiences and information among themselves and with the competition agency, in order to establish common guidelines and procedures for the exercise of regulation in their fields, as well as allowing mutual consultation when editing standards that imply changes in the competition conditions of each sector.

Regulatory agencies will also be allowed to set up cooperation agreements with consumer and environmental protection agencies. This will allow for different ways of enforcing these regulatory areas with the agencies working in partnership, reducing conflicts in their application and making inspections more efficient.

Finally, with regard to state and municipal regulatory agencies, federal regulatory agencies will be able to decentralise activities such as inspection and arbitration, through cooperation agreements.

VIII. Guidelines for Regulatory Impact Analysis

The Regulatory Agencies Law is still under discussion in the National Congress with final approval expected by the middle of 2019. Meanwhile, federal government seeks to implement measures that anticipate the benefits of the institutional changes not only for the regulatory agencies, but to all government entities that are responsible for delivering regulation.

The Regulatory Agencies Law is focused on the prerequisites, while the initiatives that will be explained from this point aim at improving the practices of regulatory delivery: risk-based prioritisation; intervention choice; and outcome measurement. In this context, even before the law comes into force, the Government decided to elaborate the guidelines to start changing regulators´ culture.

Under the PRO-REG initiative, the Government developed general guidelines for regulatory impact analysis, so-called General Regulatory Impact Assessment Guidelines. As mentioned before, Regulatory Impact Assessment will be obligatory in the regulatory agencies' decision-making process whenever there is regulatory change of general interest to citizens or regulated entities with potential to influence their rights or obligations. The following are Regulatory Impact Assessment objectives as set out in the guidelines:[12]

- to guide and support the decision-making process;
- to provide greater efficiency for regulatory decisions;
- to provide greater regulatory coherence and quality;
- to provide greater technical robustness and predictability for relevant regulatory decisions;
- to increase the transparency and understanding of the regulatory process as a whole, raising the awareness of market players and the general public regarding regulatory problems, analysis steps, techniques used, alternative solutions envisioned and the criteria considered to support relevant regulatory decisions; and
- to contribute to the continuous improvement of regulatory action outcomes.

In summary, it can be said that the guidelines are the standardisation of Regulatory Impact Assessment in all regulatory agencies, introducing better practices and more developed and organised instruments. For some agencies, it will be a big step forward, since, as mentioned, evaluation of regulation is not something that has been consolidated in Brazilian culture.

It is not the guidelines' intention to be totally prescriptive; rather, to make regulators organise the way to approach an issue, the possible solutions, their costs and effects. It is not necessary to have a complex analysis in every case. More complete analysis will be required in more complex cases.

Regulators will be asked to initiate an impact assessment as soon as the agency starts designing new regulation to solve an identified regulatory problem. A regulatory impact assessment will be considered by the board of directors and will have to be submitted to public consultation. The intention here is to allow citizens to understand why a specific option of regulating a situation may be adopted instead of other possible options.

The guidelines also require that, whenever the regulatory agency adopts a regulation to address an identified regulatory problem, the regulation must include a revision deadline, for a future regulatory stock review. More complex regulation shall undergo a Regulatory Outcome Evaluation, making the ex post analysis obligatory too.

Regulatory Impact Assessment Guidelines will be implemented initially in regulatory agencies, but others will be encouraged to follow them. This will form part of the new policy on public governance.

IX. New Policy on Public Governance

In order to improve public governance in federal government, another bill was prepared in 2017 and submitted to National Congress.[13] Based on best practices recommended by

---

[12] Objectives taken from www.regulacao.gov.br/agenciasreguladoras/consulta-publica/consulta-publica-001-2017/diretrizes_e_roteiro_analitico_ingles_17-10.pdf.

[13] The Bill for Public Government is PL 9163/2017, available at www.camara.gov.br/proposicoesWeb/fichadetramitacao?idProposicao=2163153.

the OECD, a new policy was designed presenting improvements in three pillars: strategy; leadership; and control. The objectives are to improve the integration of long-, medium- and short-term planning, and to establish better governance and control to each government programme. It is expected to increase the quality of public management, reducing the risks of failure.

At the same time, an Inter-ministerial Committee on Governance[14] was created, composed of the ministers at the centre of government, with powers to set governance directives and approve manuals and guidelines for public policies. In 2018, four guides were approved by the Committee: Public Governance; Public policies ex ante analysis; Public policies ex post analysis; and the General Regulatory Impact Assessment Guidelines. The latter was approved along with a recommendation that ministries should start Regulatory Impact Assessment pilot projects. The intention was to apply the same regulatory framework to agencies and other regulators while taking account of the different stages of institutional development. It will be up to the ministers to determine if Regulatory Impact Assessment will be requested for all regulators from the start or if it will be implemented in phases. Whatever the decision, Brazil is facing a revolution in terms of changing the culture of policy-making.

X. Improving Regulatory Delivery in Trade

As already mentioned, the 11 regulatory agencies subject to detailed reforms described earlier are only one part of the regulatory landscape in Brazil. There are at least 20 other federal government organisations that are also responsible for delivering regulation and do not have a specific framework.

In order to improve the effectiveness of its activities, the Federal Government has been conducting an important capacity-building programme for regulatory delivery and PRO-REG has been considering these entities in its policies and programmes. Regulators other than the 11 federal regulatory agencies are being encouraged to follow best regulatory practices. One of the main steps towards this was the approval of General Regulatory Impact Assessment Guidelines, introducing regulatory impact analysis and social participation in the development of regulation in organisations where it is practically non-existent.

Other initiatives are in place. In trade, the Federal Government Chamber of Foreign Trade (CAMEX),[15] responsible for implementing and coordinating policies and activities related to foreign trade in goods and services, is a nice example. With the assistance of a

---

[14] Created by the Presidential Decree 9203/2017, available at www.planalto.gov.br/ccivil_03/_ato2015-2018/2017/decreto/D9203.htm.

[15] CAMEX is responsible for formulating, adopting, implementing and coordinating policies and activities related to foreign trade in goods and services, promoting foreign trade, investments and the international competitiveness of the country. CAMEX Council of Ministers is the highest and final deliberation body and, by the end of 2018, was composed of the following ministers: Civil Cabinet of the Presidency of the Republic; Foreign Affairs; Finance; Agriculture; Industry, Foreign Trade and Services; Planning, Development and Management; and General-Secretary of the Presidency of the Republic. This composition will change during 2019 due to the fact that the new Ministry of Economy is the result of the merger of Ministry of Finance, Ministry for Planning, Development and Management, Ministry of Industry, Foreign Trade and Services and Ministry of Labour.

regulatory working group, the Chamber published the first foreign trade regulatory agenda in a pioneering initiative to coordinate the activities of 27 regulators that impact this activity.

In order to develop the agenda, these 27 regulators were asked to identify laws and regulations related to foreign trade that, in their opinion, should be a priority to be reviewed, changed, or repealed, as well as new areas that they thought it necessary to start to regulate. This draft regulatory agenda was submitted to public consultation so that it could be evaluated by regulated entities and citizens, who also were encouraged to suggest new actions.

As a result, the Foreign Trade Regulatory Agenda consists of a planning tool that identifies and organises the strategic regulatory issues that will be monitored by CAMEX. It promotes transparency and predictability, since it will make public the priority actions of all the regulators, allowing stronger participation of companies and citizens.

This is the first initiative to improve regulatory delivery in Brazil outside of the 11 federal regulatory agencies reforms. It is also the first time that there has been an attempt to organise and plan the joint work of several different organisations. The Foreign Trade Regulatory Agenda inaugurates a new era of regulatory practices. Regulators will be incentivised to compile and revise rules to provide more transparency and improve the business environment. At the same time, obsolete rules should be eliminated and new proposals must follow the same process of regulatory impact assessment and public consultation faced by regulatory agencies.

By the end of 2018, CAMEX approved a Resolution for Good Regulatory Practices, that determined that 26 of the 27 regulators that impact on foreign trade[16] should carry out a regulatory impact assessment before introducing new regulations and hold public consultations. This is an important step for implementing a good regulatory culture across all regulators.

Brazil is also leading a very important regional initiative. Mercosur is a South American trade bloc, whose full members are Argentina, Brazil, Paraguay and Uruguay,[17] with the purpose of promoting free trade and the movement of goods, people and currency. The Common Market Council is the highest-level agency of Mercosur. Member states preside over the Council in rotating alphabetical order, for six-month periods. At the end of 2017, acting as temporary president of Mercosur, Brazil presented the Protocol of Regulatory Coherence, with the objective of strengthening and encouraging the regulatory bodies of the members of Mercosur to adopt regulatory coherence policies, ultimately promoting the establishment of a transparent and predictable regulatory environment for both citizens and economic operators.

Regulatory coherence refers to the use of good regulatory practices in the process of planning, drafting, adopting, implementing, monitoring and reviewing regulations in order to facilitate a business environment with less bureaucracy and to improve regulatory cooperation, promoting international trade, investment, economic growth and job creation. Through the protocol, members of Mercosur reaffirm their commitment to facilitate trade in goods and services, as well as the flow of investment between them as a result of the adoption of good regulatory practices. For example, the establishment of internal mechanisms that facilitate coordination between institutions, associated with the creation and revision of

---

[16] The only exception is the Secretariat for Federal Revenue.
[17] In 2016 Venezuela was suspended from Mercosur.

regulations (like CAMEX is doing with the regulatory agenda), and the use of public consultation and regulatory impact assessment by the competent regulatory authority.

XI. Conclusion

Recently emerged from the greatest economic crisis in its history, Brazil now seeks to adopt measures that will stimulate the economy and improve the business environment, allowing the resumption of economic growth and job creation. In this context, improving the delivery of regulation is one of the key elements in order to achieve these goals, and Brazil has a long way to go.

In the context of the Regulatory Delivery Model, all components need to be strengthened. Starting from the prerequisites, federal regulatory agencies appear to already have some good level progress towards best practices when governance and accountability are analysed, and the latest reforms have been working to strengthen these areas. However, the culture of policy-makers and regulatory agencies is not currently strong on considering whether they are delivering the right outcomes for businesses or citizens, and there is room for a lot of improvements to match citizens' and businesses' demands.

Regulatory delivery instruments are what need more attention from policy-makers. Since Brazil's regulatory agencies have only just begun thinking about regulatory delivery, subjects such as outcome measurement, risk-based prioritisation and intervention choices have always been far from the public policy priority agenda. In fact, Brazil has always performed poorly in measuring public policies in general, and only in the last two years has the public policy assessment system begun to give more visible results to society. The set of initiatives presented in this chapter aim at changing the institutional framework of regulation in Brazil, improving the regulatory culture and allowing more solid foundations for the country's development.

25

Lessons from Creating a Consolidated Inspection Agency in Mongolia

JIGJIDMAA DUGEREE, GIULIANA COLA, FLORENTIN BLANC
AND GIUSEPPA OTTIMOFIORE

I. Introduction

Mongolia presents an interesting experience of transformation from a burdensome and ineffective regulatory framework, firstly through the consolidation of most of its inspectorates into one agency and then through reform of its practices. In a global landscape where experiences of single inspections agencies have been rare and sometimes disappointing, Mongolia offers one of the most positive and stimulating results.

Only a few countries have actually created a single inspectorate, although internationally this is discussed frequently. Some examples include: Croatia, which was never completely 'single' and split again after more than 15 years of existence; Bosnia and Herzegovina, which has been more successful; and Mozambique, which is in its very early stages. The idea of a single inspectorate has also been raised in the Netherlands (see chapter eleven).

In Mongolia not only have the institutions formally changed but, perhaps more importantly, inspection practices have changed as well. Of course, this did not happen immediately, and required considerable efforts. Mongolia has specific challenges – its vast size, low population density, and its limited ability to attract suitable candidates to the job of reforming a public agency, especially with the competition from a rapidly growing private sector in the jobs market.

This chapter focuses on the process that led to change through the establishment of a sound governance framework through amendments to the legislation governing inspection practices, to the efforts to start taking a risk-based approach and the approaches taken to creating the leadership needed to drive cultural change in the context of frequent management turnover.

A. Mongolia – An Outline

Between the Mongolian revolutions of 1921 and the 1990s, Mongolia was closely associated with the Soviet Union and followed its political, economic and institutional set-up. The history of regulatory inspections in Mongolia began in 1930, with the creation of a unit that controlled and inspected state budget expenditures and the exploitation of state assets.[1] The first institution for hygiene and health inspections[2] was also established in the 1930s, as were veterinary controls.[3]

During this period, Mongolia was going through a transformational change, from a pastoral, livestock dominated country with virtually no processing into a more diversified economy. The country was starting to urbanise: modern housing and government office buildings appeared, and major construction projects were underway, with roads, railroads, bridges, border posts and large processing mills and factories being built. The growth in construction created a need for proper institutions for planning, control and inspections. From 1942, Mongolia established regulatory controls on cargo under the Ministry of Transport and a Building Control Unit was constituted in 1956 under the Ministry of Construction.

Until 1991, Mongolia received substantial assistance (both financial and technical) from the Soviet Union and its Eastern European allies. Accordingly, its regulatory system was developed along the lines of the Soviet and post-Soviet system, with laws and regulations supported by a large number of mandatory standards (GOST[4] -type standards) and very prescriptive, detailed, mandatory requirements – mostly 'specification-based' requirements indicating exact characteristics and parameters to follow for a given process, product etc.

B. Consolidating Regulatory Agencies

With the collapse of the Soviet Union at the beginning of the 1990s and national pro-democracy movements that marked the end of the socialist era in Mongolian history, the country faced the tough challenge of creating new political structures and institutions that would develop democracy and an open market economy. After more than 70 years Mongols regained the right to have their own assets and private businesses started to emerge.

Between 1999 and 2002, the Government conducted a review of the functions of its existing regulatory bodies. This included those where inspections were under a ministry's direct remit and it was tasked with verifying compliance with sector-specific laws, as well as internal inspections of these ministries on compliance with applicable rules on state budget, procurement and expenses. There was recognition of the challenges associated with 'inspecting your own minister', including subordination issues, and the possibility of pressure being exerted on inspectors. The review identified that the number of regulatory agencies was

---

[1] This unit – the Financial Control Department – went through multiple reorganisations and reporting lines over time and was eventually, in 2003, brought into the consolidated inspection agency – the State Specialized Inspection Agency, later General Agency for Specialized Inspections.

[2] The Bacterium Research Centre, formed in 1933, subsequently evolved into the State Hygiene Inspections Department and then the Health Inspections Department of the Ministry of Health.

[3] Following the introduction of veterinary controls in 1937, there were several changes to veterinary and phytosanitary inspection functions which followed institutional changes at ministerial level based on economic goals laid out in the five-year plan modelled on the Soviet Union's.

[4] GOST standards are regional technical standards administered by the Euro-Asian Interstate Council for Standardisation, Metrology and Certification (EASC). Previously, GOST standards were developed by the Soviet Union as part of its national standardisation programme.

substantial, given the small size of the economy, and that there were many areas of duplication and overlap between them. Moreover, private businesses were complaining about numerous visits by inspectors from different agencies, reporting that these could happen on a weekly basis, disrupting normal operations.

In response to this review, the Government acted to reduce the number of its regulatory agencies. January 2003 saw the establishment of the first consolidated inspectorate,[5] the State Specialized Inspection Agency. At the same time, the consolidation of other regulatory agencies also occurred, creating the General Agency for State Emergency (responsible for fire safety, state emergency reserves and civil protection) and the Agency for Land Administration and Management, Geodesy and Cartography.

This chapter presents a case study of the experiences of the State Specialized Inspection Agency – which was renamed in 2013 as the General Agency for Specialized Inspections (GASI) – as a consolidated agency implementing major reforms in Mongolia.

II. Identifying the Need to Reform Regulatory Practice

The creation of the inspectorate (referred to as 'the Agency') in 2003 brought together more than 20 government agencies, responsible for more than 30 surveillance fields.[6] These ranged from regulatory areas with a very broad scope, including labour, environment and health, to very narrow technical fields, such as radiation and IT. The Agency's mandate was to enforce laws and regulations, to create a favourable business environment and to serve the public interest in a less burdensome way.

The Agency became Mongolia's largest inspection body (outside of revenue agencies) and it continued to grow, as it was given responsibility for new areas of regulation. For example, when Mongolia introduced a policy on self-sufficient production of vegetables and plants, the Agency broadened its existing scope in the agricultural field introducing potato inspectors. Similarly, the Agency responded to Mongolia's Law on Tourism – which required inspectors to control the foreign language proficiency of tourist guides and their knowledge of the politics, economy, history and traditions of Mongolia – by establishing a central tourism inspection unit and adding more inspection functions for its local field inspectors. However, the lack of focus on risks in these laws and the absence of guidelines on enforcement and compliance meant that inspectors were often not given any clarity or capability to enforce the laws adequately or consistently, and so more inspections just added more burden and no benefit.

By 2008, five years after the establishment of the Agency, questions were being asked about whether the creation of a consolidated agency had been the right decision. The MPs who had been instrumental in establishing the Agency and had served as ministers in the Cabinet at that time, concluded that the consolidation had not delivered the expected

---

[5] By virtue of the adoption of the Law on State Inspections and Control; the Parliament of Mongolia Resolution No 58, and consequently the Resolution No 162 and the PM Order No 94.

[6] The legislative framework as at the end of 2017 consisted of 106 laws, in turn implemented by other laws, 23 parliamentary resolutions, 42 international agreements and conventions, more than 300 cabinet resolutions, 434 rules and regulations and 1200 standards and technical regulations.

outcomes in terms of a reduction in the number of inspections and the associated regulatory burden. On the contrary, they felt that the Agency had increased its enforcement pressure, relying on heavy sanctions and creating considerable burden. In addition, new forms of duplication had emerged between different branches of the Agency, which were based centrally, at the provincial level and covering Ulaanbaatar city.

The 2003 Law on State Control and Inspections, an overarching law introduced as part of the reforms that consolidated Mongolia's regulators, was focused on the powers and duties of government authorities and inspectors. It granted them extensive rights but was silent on the inspections process in general and on inspection objectives and outcomes. Equally, it did not address the rights of businesses subject to inspection or impose any duty on inspectors to report. In addition, most of the sector-based laws under which the Agency was acting specifically required it to conduct inspections 'to enforce the legislation', but did not clearly set out the focus, objectives or process for inspections. Taken together, the overarching law and sector-based laws allowed for the unfettered exercise of discretion by inspection units or individual inspectors with no constraints on subjective opinions and decisions during the inspection process. The lack of guidelines for inspectors contributed to inconsistencies in their interpretation of laws and regulations. In addition, it was felt that the Agency could too easily take on 'new' inspection responsibilities without consideration as to what inspection in this area would achieve.

The Government decided to call upon the World Bank Group, with its international experience and knowledge of regulatory and inspections reforms, to help reform the Agency and in 2009, the International Finance Corporation, a member of the World Bank Group, embarked upon a seven-year technical assistance project. The Mongolia Business Inspections Reform Project ('the project') aimed to help the Agency to adopt best practice in risk-based approaches, so that regulatory reform could fit the structure of the Agency. Finally, in order to build a more efficient inspection system, it became clear that additional work was necessary and undertaken to change the mentality and culture of the Agency as well.

There were several critical issues to deal with and the following sections describe how the World Bank Group project supporting the Agency, and the Agency itself, tackled these issues and achieved improvement. The rest of the chapter is structured around reform themes rather than taking reforms in historical order and so at this point it may be helpful to set out the structure of the Agency as of 2016, noting that some of this structure (such as the Risk Management Unit) was introduced during the project's period of reforms.

The 30 or so surveillance areas in the Agency's responsibility are split into seven departments: Food and Agriculture; Environment, Geology and Mining; Health, Education and Culture; Infrastructure; Border; Occupational Safety; and Nuclear-Radiation. Later references to 'inland' relate to all these departments of the Agency except 'Border'. There are also two key cross-cutting departments:

- Risk Management, Strategy and Planning Unit ('Risk Management Unit') – with overall responsibility for risk assessment, strategic and operational planning, and consolidating data on inspections.[7]

---

[7] Noting that prior to 2014, there was a risk assessment unit, but that this was part of the general administration department.

- Administration Department – including monitoring and evaluation, HR, finance and law units.

The Agency is also split by geographical locations. There is Central GASI, based in Ulaanbaatar, consisting of senior management, cross-cutting departments and administration, and local GASI offices for each *Aimag* (administrative sub-division). The local structure includes Ulaanbaatar City GASI, which consists of a central headquarters and nine district offices throughout Ulaanbaatar. Figure 25.1 sets out the structure of the Agency. In 2016 the Agency's inspection cadre consisted of 1,800 staff across all these different elements of the organisation, out of which 1,250 were inspectors and 550 were managers and staff other than inspectors. The Chairman of the Agency is appointed by the Cabinet and reports to the Deputy Prime Minister.[8]

Figure 25.1 Structure of the Agency

Chairman Deputy Chairman								
Central GASI–Cross-cutting functions		*Central GASI –Regulatory Area Specialist Departments*						
Administration (HR, finance, legal, evaluation)	Risk Management Unit	Food and Agriculture	Environment, Geology and Mining	Health, Education and Culture	Infra-structure	Occupational Safety	Nuclear and Radiation	Border
		Frontline staff including inspectors are within Local GASI as below Local GASI branches are administratively attached to the city/local authority						
		City GASI – Ulaanbataar local branch HQ and nine district offices			Provincial GASI – 21 *Aimag* branches			

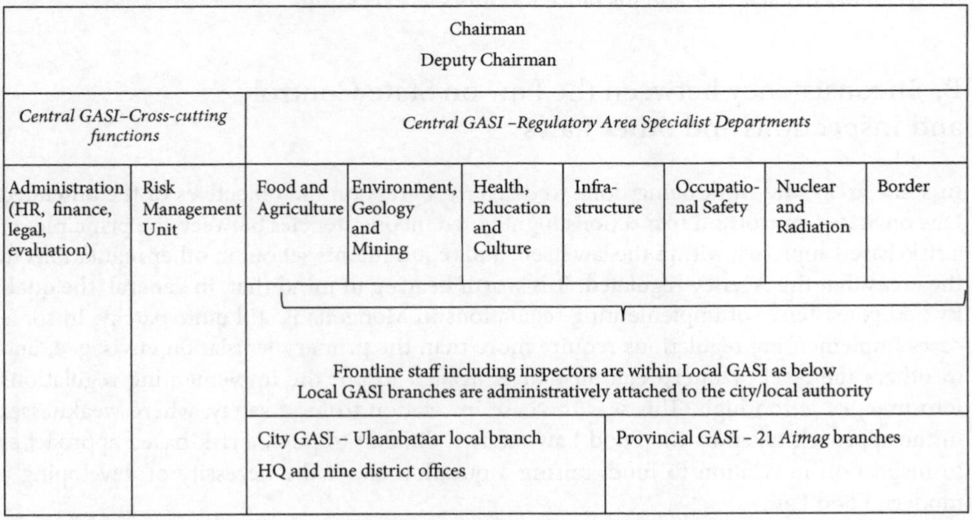

III. Governance – Establishing a Sound Framework

A. Amending the Law on State Control and Inspections

The project started the reform process by amending the 2003 Law on State Control and Inspections to set the principles for an improved approach, introducing a risk-based approach and new tools for inspections such as risk criteria and checklists. The subjective powers of inspectors were limited by introducing a more streamlined process for inspections and granting rights to the businesses subject to inspection. The amendments to the Law on State Control and Inspections were adopted on 10 June 2010.

---

[8] This section was adapted from an internal World Bank Group report prepared by Donald Macrae.

The project subsequently assisted the Agency in developing and adopting regulations to implement the requirements of the amended Law on State Control and Inspections. These prescribed the detail in relation to annual planning of inspections, the inspection process (for example requiring advance notice of some inspections), frequency of inspections, checklist development and risk assessment development.

The development of these implementing regulations involved not only lawyers, but inspectors and administration staff who tested or piloted certain draft provisions through simulation of inspections, piloting checklists, and consulting with businesses, using history of previous cases and best practices from other countries such as the UK, Lithuania, Bosnia and Herzegovina, the Netherlands and Serbia. There are different requirements for adoption and amendment of these implementing regulations, some are approved by the Agency's Chairman (for example updates to checklists), and some require higher level approval by the Cabinet – for example the Deputy Prime Minister adopts the annual plan of inspections in December of each year and his office monitors its execution.

B. Inconsistency between the Law on State Control and Inspections and other Laws

In some areas, the work being done to deliver progress on the objectives of the amended Law on State Control and Inspections highlighted inconsistencies between the principles of a risk-based approach within the law itself, and requirements set out in other regulations in the areas that the Agency regulated. It is worth bearing in mind that, in general, the quality and consistency of implementing regulations in Mongolia is still quite patchy. In some cases implementing regulations require more than the primary legislation envisaged, and in others the level of interpretation that is needed to put the implementing regulations into practice is too high. This was the case in relation to food safety, where weaknesses in the approach taken by the Food Law made it difficult to pursue risk-based approaches to inspection in relation to food, raising a question about the necessity of developing a modern Food Law.

In 2011, the Agency's Risk Management Unit approached members of Parliament with an interest in food safety issues, the Office of the President and food businesses, in order to evaluate the situation and assess the demand for new legislation. At the end of a two-year intensive collaboration with relevant stakeholders and study tours to the UK and Lithuania, Mongolia's Parliament adopted the Food Product Safety Law in 2013. The law contains a chapter on inspections process in line with international good practice, definitions of risks and hazards, and very clear requirements on food safety. The law was in some ways revolutionary in that it shifted responsibility for ensuring safety. This had previously been seen as primarily the responsibility of the state, but the new law placed responsibility with food business operators, making them accountable for managing risks from the beginning of the food production process, following the 'From Farm to Fork' concept.

However, it remains the case that the regulatory framework in Mongolia has a number of inconsistencies between laws, as well as laws that are unclear on the purpose or requirements, which poses a problem for the Agency as the body responsible for enforcing these laws. The Agency has attempted to tackle this issue in several ways. Firstly, it has been proactive in making recommendations to relevant ministries of the areas of legislation that are inconsistent with revised practices and are therefore difficult or impossible to enforce. Largely this has not resulted in changing the legislation. In parallel, the Agency has also worked internally to find a way to clarify areas where there are conflicting requirements, for example, by using a risk-based approach to checklist developments to filter out criteria – which, while a requirement of the law, may not reasonably be considered to be a risk that needs managing. This has evolved over time, as the organisation has moved towards understanding its role more as to improve safety rather than merely to enforce all laws equally.

C. Accountability: Multiple Reporting Lines and Conflicting Objectives

There are some issues related to the lack of clarity of purpose of the Agency's work between the central Agency and the local branches (Ulaanbaatar and Aimag units). They arise from the functional attachment of the city and provincial branches of the Agency to the local authorities, Ulaanbaatar city and provincial governors' offices. This means that as well as national priorities in safety and enforcement of national laws and regulations, the city and provincial branches have to deliver against the governors' local objectives, which include collection of fines that go into the central budget (with targets specified in the Budget Law) and enforcing local regulatory acts. These objectives do not always align with national priorities and can often result in inspections that are not necessarily risk-focused.

For example, local units of the Agency have been involved in inspection raids or local campaigns which involve all local enforcement agencies and in general increase burden for businesses and do not add value in protecting people from harm, or even collect evidence and data for future analysis. These types of inspections are generally focused on finding irregularities and taking more stringent measures including closing premises and imposing penalties rather than taking a risk-based approach. Typical campaigns happen before major holidays such as New Year, Lunar New Year, and the Naadam summer festival. Setting plans for collection of fines under the Budget Law is in fact against the provisions of the Law on State Control and Inspections. But politically this issue hasn't been addressed, probably because performance of inspectors is measured against the number of inspections and amount of fines collected. There are signs that inspectors themselves are unhappy with this approach though, a perceptions survey of inspectors conducted in 2016[9] ('staff survey') asked about performance indicators for future application to inspectors' work. The traditional indicators – numbers of inspections, number of violations and imposed penalties – only amounted to 16.6 per cent of the answers. Three indicators summed to 82 per cent: 'risk reduction and prevention' came top with 30.4 per cent, followed by 'increasing compliance' with 25.4 per cent, just a little ahead of 'reduction in violations' at 24.9 per cent.

---

[9] 'GASI Internal Survey of Inspectors' (unpublished, 2016). 803 out of 1,800 staff participated, including 728 inspectors and other specialists, and 75 managers.

IV. Embedding Risk-based Approaches

A. The Need for Risk-based Approaches

The reform programme began in 2008, at a time when the legal and regulatory environment in Mongolia lacked any risk focus. As already mentioned, there were no clear objectives for inspections stipulated by law. As the scope of the Agency's regulatory responsibilities is very broad, the shift to a risk-based approach posed multiple challenges. The previous approach had resulted in a high number of inspections (58 per cent of respondents reported being inspected by the Agency in 2009),[10] but with no method of differentiating which of those inspections had the potential to do more good, by being targeted at a business that was a higher risk. The same approach was taken to responding to complaints – all complaints were treated equally, usually resulting in an inspection, no matter how serious the allegation. It was also seen that the inspections themselves did not focus on the areas of the business practice most likely to cause harm. The fact that legislation in Mongolia is often not in itself risk-based meant that inspections against the legislative requirements with no way of prioritising matters more likely to cause harm were unlikely to be effective, because they treated all matters of non-compliance as equal.

When considering the reforms of the Agency, it is important to remember that the Agency is a relatively new regulator in a small developing country with limited resources, compared to well-established ones in developed countries. Mastering the skills of efficient and purposeful inspections and perfecting analysis will undoubtedly take several years. However, clear progress is being made and some examples of it are presented below.

B. Risk-based Approaches Mandated

The changes made to the Law on State Control and Inspections in 2010 and the implementing regulations included a number of requirements aimed at creating a risk-based approach. The Law states that the 'risk level of the subject of inspection shall be classified as low, medium and high, considering likelihood of damage and consequences to human life, health, environment, and social safety'.[11] Criteria for risk classification are determined by the Government.

The Government Resolution on Risk Categorization Criteria[12] outlines 29 areas for risk categorisation and specifies more detailed risk criteria and a scoring system for the food safety area. The other 28 areas of regulation are left to the Deputy Prime Minister to provide details in subsequent Decrees ('a list of inspection objects and inspection frequency').

Risk criteria and results from inspections based on checklists are then used by the Agency to determine the risk level of each business entity, and plan inspections based on the frequencies recommended in the relevant decrees.[13] The inspection frequency rates for all

---

[10] 'Business Inspections in Mongolia. Netherlands IFC Partnership Program' (International Finance Corporation, 2010) 7.

[11] Mongolia's 2003 State and Inspection Law as revised in June 2010, Arts No 5.1 and 5.2.

[12] The Government Resolution on Risk Criteria and Indicators for Risk Categorization of Inspection Objects, No 23 of 30 January 2012.

[13] This section was adapted from an internal World Bank Group report prepared by Donald Macrae.

sectors that the Agency inspects are set by an Order of the Deputy Prime Minister. Depending on the sectors of the economy, and levels of risks, businesses are checked at different frequencies – such as in the food sector where high-risk businesses are inspected once every six months, medium-risk businesses once every 12 months, and low-risk businesses once every 18 months. The Agency develops an annual plan of inspections based on risk levels and frequencies, and by considering the available number of inspectors. Checklists used for inspectors are available at the Agency's website.[14]

C. Towards a Risk-based Approach to Planning Inspections

Since 2014, the Agency's annual plan of inspections has allocated most of its resources to inspection of high-risk and medium-risk businesses. In 2016, the Agency assigned high risk to 14,277 businesses, medium risk to 48,034 and low risk to 33,819.[15] Represented graphically, these are far from the shape of the expected 'risk pyramid' which due to the goal of risk-based prioritisation, would tend to show a large number of businesses categorised low risk and a small number of high risk (see chapter sixteen and in particular Figure 16.2). However, comparing data from 2011 and 2016, we can see that gradual prioritisation is taking place, as shown in Figure 25.2. For businesses where information was unavailable, initial risk ratings (particularly in the food sector) were set as 'high', and gradual rollout of risk assessment means they were often reclassified to 'medium'. Though the process remains incomplete, the initial progress is in stark contrast with the tendency observed in many post-Soviet countries, where most businesses are assigned to 'high risk' and little evolution takes place.

Figure 25.2 Distribution of businesses in each risk category ('risk profile') in 2011 and 2016[16]

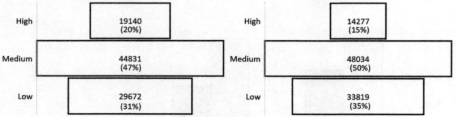

The Risk Management Unit uses the risk rating as a guide to planning inspections, to try to target resources on the higher-risk businesses. In 2015 planned inspections (excluding those in reaction to a complaint) were split as low risk 37 per cent of total inspections, medium risk 45 per cent and high risk 18 per cent. This is recognised as not yet in line with moving inspection resource to focussing on the high-risk businesses, but is a work in progress. The reform is one of those that requires a certain amount of time so that transformation happens

---

[14] See www.inspection.gov.mn.
[15] Because the assignment of risk categories covers different inspection functions, totals shown exceed the number of businesses in scope of the Agency – as eg one business may fall into different risk categories for different inspection functions, producing aggregate figures that include some double counting.
[16] Internal GASI data obtained in 2012 and 2017.

in practice and not only on paper. It is impossible to decree that, from the next day, all inspections will be risk-based, but rather an implementation period is needed to conduct training, develop methods and take into consideration social and cultural aspects and roles and responsibilities of different actors and stakeholders.

The Agency has been going through a learning process regarding the practice of effective risk-based approaches. Barriers include difficulties with unclear objectives of regulations, as well as the significant number of small new businesses entering the market that may have low capacity to comply (eg poor knowledge of rules and regulations, limited financial resources), which in turn creates additional risks. Business capacity is also often limited because of lack of experience, as the very existence of a private sector in Mongolia only started 25 years ago, which further increases the pressure and expectation on the GASI.

However, possessing systematic data covering inspected businesses is substantial progress for the Agency, a fact which enables it to set a goal of modelling the future risk profile to the pyramid shape. More recently, the Risk Management Unit have been undertaking detailed analysis to try to identify potential deviations from agreed approaches to risk assessment. For example, by analysing trends in numbers of high-risk businesses for each *Aimag* to identify regions with fluctuations and then working with inspectors to understand whether this is legitimate.

Over the period 2009 to 2015, the share of businesses inspected by the Agency per year decreased from 58 per cent to 43 per cent, as shown in Figure 25.3. The only one of the seven regulatory departments where the proportion of regulated businesses that received an inspection did not decrease was the Border Department, where there was a small increase.

Figure 25.3 Percentage of businesses regulated by the Agency that received one or more inspections[17]

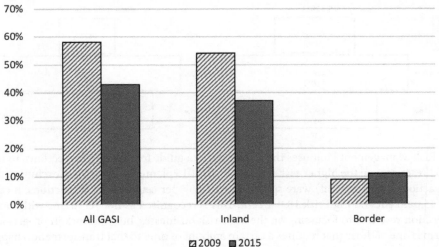

[17] 'Business Inspections in Mongolia' (2010) and 'Mongolia Inspections Reform Project – 2009–2016. Evaluation Report on Reform Outcomes' (World Bank Group, 2016, unpublished).

While a decrease in the number of inspections may not always indicate a risk-based approach, in the case of the Agency it demonstrates that the changes have resulted in targeting inspection effort on a smaller number of businesses. It is also worth looking at the average number of inspections for those businesses that did receive an inspection. Figure 25.4 shows that there was an increase in the average number of inspections per year (from 4.6 in 2009 to 5.3 in 2015), but that this was mainly driven by a big increase in the average number of inspections for those inspected at least once by the Border Department.

Figure 25.4 Average number of inspections, for those businesses that received at least one inspection (an inspection by the Border Department is an inspection of a product, not a premises)

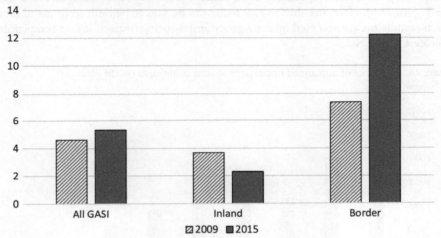

■ 2009 ■ 2015

D. Responding to Complaints about Regulated Entities

A vivid example of the Agency's effective use of risk-based approaches to address regulatory gaps can be seen in the significant changes to the way the Agency responds to consumer complaints.

At the beginning of the reform the Agency was overwhelmed by high volumes of consumer complaints relating to various problems such as poor quality mobile phones, noisy neighbours, food smells emanating from cafés and restaurants in housing areas, food poisoning and rogue businesses. Complaints were being channelled to the Agency from visitor centres and the city and national government hotlines without proper screening.

Government agencies are under a duty[18] to respond to consumer complaints and to report on the measures taken and there is an expectation that this will be done quickly. This required the Agency to conduct a large number of unplanned, reactive inspections

---

[18] Under the Law on Consumer Protection and the Law on Citizens Complaints.

that absorbed almost half of its resources on often lower-risk issues and provided little useful data for risk assessment. It also created an overlap between the Agency and the Consumer Protection Agency, which has primary responsibility in some of the areas of complaint. In addition, the legislation had developed such high public expectations that citizens thought that the Agency could inspect anywhere at any time.

The Agency's management took several steps to lower the number of complaints to which they needed to respond, by publishing a list of areas that are not the responsibility of the Agency[19] and by filtering complaints through specific criteria based on their mandate. Complaints falling outside these criteria were returned to their source or referred to the relevant authority, and this has led to a substantial decrease in the number of unplanned, reactive inspections in response to complaints – from 59,198 in 2009 to 2,370 in 2017 (see Figure 25.5). Here, the shift in risk focus can be said to be both in terms of focusing which complaints are accepted by the Agency and focusing inspections on complaints that indicate a higher risk.

Figure 25.5 Number of unplanned inspections against complaints (GASI data)

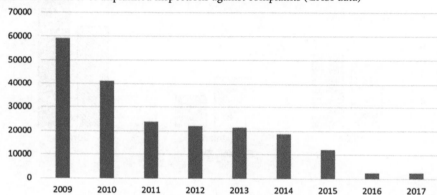

E. Risk-based Inspectors – Checklist-based Inspection

The revised Law on State Control and Inspections required the use of checklists in planned inspections, as a way to curb the excessive discretion previously afforded to inspectors during inspection, to focus their checks on the areas of highest risk, and to give businesses clarity of what to expect of an inspection. By 2016 the Agency had checklists for all of its departments (see Table 25.1).

It is acknowledged that the current checklists are not perfect. As the Agency has had to develop checklists based on the current laws and regulations, it is difficult to avoid replicating the problems stemming from the fact that current legislation is not risk-based.

---

[19] A list of issues that are outside of the Agency's scope is regularly updated by order of its Chairman (eg Order #149 of 2017 stated 107 areas of regulation that are not within the scope of the Agency).

Table 25.1 Number of checklists

Inspection area	No. of checklists
Food and Agriculture	40
Environment, Geology and Mining	23
Health, Education and Culture	31
Infrastructure	57
Border and Quarantine	24
Occupational Safety and Social Security	10
Nuclear and Radiation	6

For example, the Law on Tourism required guides to prevent tourists from accidents, and the Agency has full mandate to inspect guides on their actions to prevent accidents, but there was no clarity on how to inspect guides' actions appropriately (except for the fact that certain safety guidelines are expressly stated). Luckily for guides and tour operators, the Agency's risk focus 'ignored' those legal requirements that do not impact on the safety risk to tourists.

Recognising the issues with checklists, the Agency undertook a major exercise in having checklists and risk criteria revised through 2015 and established a practice to review checklists on an annual basis. This work is done under a special working group, which includes inspectors, businesses, professional associations and other interested stakeholders. All inspectors from different levels and units, and more than 1,000 businesses had an opportunity to participate in discussions and provide their feedback in 2015. Many thoughtful comments were received from professional associations and non-governmental organisations. Thus, as a result of these efforts, all the checklists were revised in 2015 and approved by the Agency's Chairman. Similarly, 30 risk criteria were also reviewed and revised.

Findings from a survey of businesses conducted by the World Bank Group in 2016 (the 'business survey') show that compliance with the requirement to use checklists at inspections was high by 2015: 80 per cent of businesses surveyed indicated that the Agency's inspectors consistently used checklists during visits.[20]

Mechanisms were also put in place to conduct internal monitoring of inspectors' work. The Risk Management Unit conducted checks of inspectors' reports, analysing trends in inspection reports for similar high and medium-risk businesses to identify inspections where there was a possibility that the inspection process had not been followed. Having identified these, an inspector from the monitoring team was sent to reinspect the business. This allowed tracking of the quality of inspections and the authenticity of data as well as guarding against the development of 'cosy' relationships between an individual inspector and a business, in which non-compliance is not recorded.

---

[20] Survey of 1,000 private businesses in Mongolia about their experience with state inspections in 2015, see 'Business Inspections in Mongolia' (n 10) and 'Mongolia Inspections Reform' (2016).

F. Risk Management Strategy

A recent important document is the Risk Management Strategy (RMS).[21] The strategy sets out that risk management principles are to be applicable across all parts of the Agency, 'to fully incorporate risk management principles into the entire function of GASI and ensure its effective and prudent implementation in compliance with relevant laws and policies'. It also states that 'all operations and functionalities including structural change, staff recruitment and human resource development, action plan and inspections shall be based on principles of risk management', recognising alignment of allocation of resources, operational plans and even the Agency's structure with a risk-based approach. Box 25.1 outlines the key principles of the RMS; the approach to implementation is discussed further in the leadership section.

Box 25.1: General principles of the Agency's RMS

Principle 1 – Risk will be applied throughout the Agency's operations:

- GASI exists to manage risk on behalf of the public therefore risk is at the heart of all operations.
- Public risks will be assessed on the basis of scientific data and other evidence.
- Public risks will be managed through the four strategies of Avoid, Reduce, Share or Accept.

Principle 2 – GASI will work with partners to provide more effective management of public risks:

- GASI will work with businesses through compliance support and will also balance safety with legitimate commercial concerns.
- GASI will work with consumers to drive market competition and standards through better informed buying decisions.
- GASI will work with other institutions and agencies, such as providing epidemiological data to Ministry of Health.
- GASI will work with the public by advice on effective management of some common risks, but will also seek acceptance that some risks are too low to need scarce GASI resources.

Principle 3 – GASI will be accountable to the public for delivering risk reduction:

- GASI will publish at the start of the year its plans for what it intends to do to manage specific dangers over the coming year.
- GASI will publish risk indicators that it will use to measure progress.
- GASI will publish the results of its work against the plans set out at the start.

---

[21] Risk Management Strategy, approved by Deputy Prime Minister Order No 87 of 3 December 2014.

G. Refocusing Effort in the Tourism Sector

The tourism sector is an example of where the Agency's risk approach is starting to shape the way it regulates a sector. The Law on Tourism is not clear on the purpose and objectives of inspections, so in practice the Agency used to inspect tourism service providers (mainly tourist camps, motels, hotels and restaurants) alongside local authorities, police and representatives from the Ministry of Tourism. Absence of clear process and objectives of inspection mandates broadened the scope of controls and impacts on the effectiveness of enforcement. Local authorities' interest were mostly in hygiene, employment and social security, the police were interested in alcohol sales after permitted hours and prostitution. This regulatory uncertainty on enforcement used to allow the Agency to join inspections raids run by local authorities and police without checklists and without following the inspections process outlined in the Law on State Control and Inspections. This did not help the Agency in its accountability on enforcement.

As the Agency has gradually shifted to be more risk-focused, the unit in charge of tourism inspection was dissolved at the central level, and the work of the inspectors visiting hotels and restaurants is now focused on hygiene and safety requirements.

H. Intervention Choices: A Shift Towards a More Supportive Approach

The Agency now includes the provision of advice, guidance and training for low-risk businesses in its annual plan. In 2016, the Agency planned to provide such 'consultancy' services to 6,366 businesses and it reached 5,336. The provision of advice, guidance and training is a new function for inspectors. At the beginning of the reform, inspectors were opposed to advising businesses as they were afraid of becoming 'a toothless tiger' – or of becoming 'ordinary consultants' instead of 'powerful inspectors'.

The 2016 business survey identified that 73 per cent of business respondents considered that the Agency's inspections had improved their operations. Focus group meetings organised by the project team echoed general trends of improvement, with businesses feeling that inspectors were less prone than before to sanctions and were gradually becoming more focused on supporting businesses – in particular, they more frequently gave advice on how to comply. The same survey showed that 64 per cent of respondents from Ulaanbaatar and 44 per cent from rural areas had seen improvement in inspectors' skills and attitudes.

There remains a scepticism amongst some inspectors about businesses attitudes towards compliance with the staff survey showing that more than a third of inspectors thought that the majority of businesses do not care about harming others, but equally 44 per cent of staff believed that businesses were either generally compliant, or would be compliant if they had the resources, capacity and knowledge to be so. In order to build core competencies in giving advice and consulting, the Agency produced guidelines on advice and consultancy covering frequently asked questions and non-compliance examples for use by inspectors.

I. Challenges and Drivers of Introducing Risk-based Approaches

To assist inspection departments with development of risk criteria and checklists, the Agency's Risk Management Unit found it needed to speak the inspectors' 'technical language' and understand their priorities. Big changes to inspection processes, such as introducing risk-based planning and the use of checklists, created some tensions and conflicts amongst Agency inspectors and central teams. This was observed in particular at early stages of the reform process, and each time new management was appointed. These points frequently prompted Agency staff to begin questioning the whole reform process and often lead to a greater degree of resistance to change, or more emphasis being put on any failures by the Agency (eg food poisoning cases) rather than on the successes (eg broader food safety or occupational issues that the Agency had successfully resolved).

As the reform accelerated, and more importantly, when inspectors and the Risk Management Unit started to see emerging trends of non-compliance by conducting analysis, belief in the risk-based approach increased.

The move towards a risk-based approach based on results of inspections using checklists was affected by a number of difficulties. But overall, the Agency's ability to deliver as the consolidated inspection agency had increased. After having practised risk-based inspections for three years, the Agency gradually came to the realisation that the risk-based approach is about a lot of 'desk job' rather than just physical checks. Learning from each other during debates and collaborative work on review of checklists and analysis, getting training based on real cases, centralised administration and risk assessment resources and other advantages of being a consolidated agency (including budget and a centralised channel of decisions and orders by the Chairman) have helped the Agency to transform from a purely policing agency into more of a thinking organisation driven by data, evidence and analysis. The culture was shifting from 'Catch all crooks' to 'Target based on analysis and enforce proportionately based on evidence'.

J. Further Reform – Developing IT Solutions

The Agency's Risk Management Unit had been using spreadsheets to record all inspection results, a manual and labour-intensive approach, but one that had enabled them to become much more data-driven. However, having visited other countries on study visits and seen the possibilities of a dedicated inspection database, the Agency embarked on creating its own IT solution.[22] In parallel, politicians were concerned about the lack of transparency from the Agency, and so the Prime Minister ordered the development of an IT system. The objectives were to help with analysis and data collection, internal and external reporting, business profiling including information on violations and risk ratings. In addition the requirement was for businesses to have secure private access to their inspection reports.

---

[22] This is an example of technology and IT solutions giving opportunities for longer-term reform. The requirement to set up an IT system originally came from the draft of a Supervision Law that was being debated in Parliament (and stalled), but the Prime Minister used the IT-specific contents of this law to draft and adopt the Ministerial Decree No 159 in 2015, thus providing a basis for long-term development of an information management solution for inspections.

The architecture of the system was based on learning from the Republic of Srpska Inspectorate (Bosnia and Herzegovina) and enhanced by new ideas stemming from the reform experiences, international best practices and a general drive to tighten up the risk-based approach. One of the objectives of IT development was to avoid the reform being reversed because of government and management swings. The Glass Inspection Portal was fully developed by December 2016 and the Head of the IT and Planning Department of the Republic of Srpska Inspectorate evaluated it as one of the most functional inspection management systems in the world.

Businesses are able to access the inspection database with a unique ID and password. They can review all inspections reports, filled out checklists, measures taken, assigned risk levels, and they can provide comments on the inspection report or express disagreement with the conclusions and measures taken by an inspector. If a complaint against an inspector is then made, the system will notify the senior inspector or chief inspector for them to review the case and reply to the business.

The IT system allows the Agency to plan 'joint' inspections – inspections that cover more than one regulatory area. The team of inspectors is usually led by the inspector in charge of the dominant sector in which the business operates – eg for mining businesses the lead is either a mining or an environmental inspector – but if the company has a previous history of non-compliance in occupational safety, the lead is the occupational safety inspector.

Furthermore, the system allows the time spent on conducting the inspection to be tracked, by both the inspector and the business. Businesses can even upload the amount of time their employees spent on an inspection, its duration, and how much it cost them.

The combination of the IT system together with the consolidated structure of the Agency makes it possible to achieve many goals at the same time: (i) better transparency; (ii) more efficiency in targeting violations and non-compliance; (iii) data analysis and safe data storage; (iv) one annual plan for the entire Agency; (v) better coordination between the Agency's inspection departments and between the Agency and its local branches; and (vi) monitoring, evaluation and reporting. Additionally, management changes now have fewer negative effects on the operations of the Agency itself – new managers cannot simply reverse the reform, because it is backed by a new regulatory environment, operational procedures and practices, IT and more knowledgeable inspectors and staff. This last point brings us to consider the capacity-building issues the project was faced with, as the Agency embarked on the reform path with almost zero-base in risk, and the leadership that was created by the Risk Management Unit.

V. Changing the Culture of the Agency: Leadership through Instability

It took almost six years to build not only a new risk-based and a more transparent process of inspections but also to sustain it, as the agency faced frequent management changes. As well as eight chairmen in seven years, there was also a high turnover of staff due to political changes at the central government level cascading into local levels. These challenges to creating leadership within the Agency are discussed in this section.

In summer 2012, the Democratic Party came to power and subsequently took a decision to dissolve the Agency, returning to smaller inspections agencies – such as a Food and Drug Administration – attached to their line ministries. Uncertainty around this proposed change continued for just over a year. The Agency's management, staff and inspectors were hesitant to work on the reform agenda, as they lost motivation and were concerned about their own future. The project team's priority at this point was to explain the expected outcomes and comparative advantages of the consolidation reform of 2003 and the ongoing reform programme to the Prime Minister and the chief of the Cabinet secretariat. The most convincing point in relation to keeping the Agency in its existing form was that, if the Agency were to dismantle, it would create 19 additional agencies under different ministries. The creation of 19 new agencies would have increased administrative burden and probably impacted negatively on the business environment.

While debates and discussions continued, the Parliament (where democrats and their coalition outnumbered opposition to certain changes in the regulatory environment) moved the responsibility for financial inspections from the Agency to the Ministry of Finance. It was probably the toughest time for the Agency and the project team with a lot of uncertainty and no political support from the leaders of the country. However, from 2014 to 2016, the reform was back on track at full speed. The new Prime Minister, Saikhanbileg Chimed, who served as the chief of the Cabinet Secretariat in the previous office, gave the green light and started championing the reforms – including the Glass Inspection Portal's development.

A. Mitigating the Effects of Changes in Agency Management

Poor governance and lack of strategic management capacities are issues that the Agency was not able to avoid. For the Government, lack of public sector capacity in Mongolia is a core obstacle in building efficient and strong government institutions with clear objectives and noticeable results, not just an issue for the Agency.

The project did not directly deal with governance issues as these were not the main objective of the inspection reform, which mainly focused on regulatory aspects. However, ignoring governance issues could have had significant drawbacks on the overall impact of the regulatory reform, and the project team had to find a way to come up with solutions to overcome the issues relating to governance. As the top management of the Agency had changed frequently, and it was paramount to maintain a certain speed of reform to avoid paralysis, the project worked across all levels:

- with Parliament to create top-level reform champions;
- with the Cabinet, especially the Deputy Prime Minister's office, to strengthen the latter's role as guiding and overseeing the Agency's operations;
- with top and middle management of the Agency directly;
- set up the Risk Management Unit – the special unit created to sustain reform efforts; and
- worked directly with frontline inspectors.

Such broad horizontal and vertical operations carried out by the project were able to create 'pockets of resistance' when paralysis or regression of the reform threatened.

It is worth reiterating that during the previous seven years, the inspectorate saw eight chairmen at the top with around 60 per cent turnover amongst middle management and to a lesser degree amongst inspectors and support staff. Top managers (especially chairmen) were appointed by the political elite of the ruling party, or other political parties as for a typical 'spoils system'. The pressure on chairmen was high: they were constantly juggling the reform priorities with fulfilling political interests, such as replacing the existing inspection staff with new ones that were politically affiliated with the party to which the chairman belonged. However, there were also chairmen, younger and more ambitious in their careers, who championed ongoing reforms. These efforts opened doors for some of them to become MPs, a position from where they continued providing some support to sustain the reform from the parliament level.

B. The Agency's Risk Management Unit: Creating a Champion

The implementation of risk assessment, as set out in the revised Law on State Control and Inspections and its implementing regulations, was difficult for the Agency and was lacking consistency and management leadership. In addition, the speed of the implementation of reforms was slower than desired, on occasion no progress being made due to management change and different interpretations of what a risk-based approach meant. Rotation of staff, inspectors, heads of departments and chairmen also made it impossible to put into practice the knowledge and skills gained through the numerous training sessions and other practical work carried out by the Risk Management Unit (which was then part of the administration department). Therefore, the unit itself perceived the urgent need for a strategy, covering the main principles of risk management, risk reduction, and collaboration with different stakeholders.

The risk management unit discussions with several top managers and the overall observation of the reform process led to the conclusion that a high turnover of management made the unit itself weak as leaders. Consequently, the core of the Agency (which is mainly frontline inspectors) became not only more resistant to backward change when newly appointed chairmen tried to 'push back', but also reluctant to escalate the reform to the next stage when a more progressively thinking chairman took office.

The solution took the form of a policy paper. Almost one year after initial discussions, the Agency's Risk Management Strategy was adopted by an Order of the Deputy Prime Minister in December 2014 (see Box 25.1 above for the key principles of the strategy). As part of the commitment to the Risk Management Strategy, the risk assessment unit became its own central department in late 2014. The creation of the Risk Management Unit and the adoption of the Risk Management Strategy increased the risk management staffs' 'power' to lead the reform, as it set them as equals to the inspection departments in the hierarchical structure of the Agency, allowing them to discuss, negotiate or require actions from the Agency's inspections departments. In addition, the Risk Management Unit developed new reporting lines in the local units of the Agency by having designated focal points for each local unit, responsible for dissemination of information, collection of data, assistance with training and being the spokesperson for risk management.

The Risk Management Unit had become the core department at the centre of the reform, stronger than others in pursuing the reform agenda in times of management change.

Inspectors actively took part in risk management, through a very tight collaboration between the Risk Management Unit and frontline inspectors in developing and amending checklists, collecting data and discussions on risk management-related issues. In March 2015, as part of the Risk Management Strategy's implementation, the seven Inspection Departments were asked to produce a first draft of a medium-term action plan covering three years of activities. The process took almost a year. During this period, it was very encouraging to see the level of commitment, technical knowledge of senior inspectors and some department heads being translated into well-defined objectives and new indicators corresponding to overall objectives in risk management. It is important to point out that the Agency used to operate on an annual basis for planning, and that this work on longer-term three-year action plans was very new. The process also benefited from the consolidated structure of the Agency. All inspection departments worked in parallel and learned from each other. By the end of 2016, the Food Production and Services Inspection Unit had adopted its first three-year plan to implement the Risk Management Strategy.

During the process of Risk Management Strategy design and implementation, inspectors were frustrated that the frequent change of heads of departments was setting back the new approach, each change requiring yet more time spent (on average six months) explaining the risk-based approach and getting them to support the reform. But equally this showed that the reform was now supported by some inspectors and that the application of the risk-based approach was infiltrating across the functions of the Agency. Inspectors were becoming more skilful in their inspection practices and more knowledgeable, thanks to the analysis of data and evidence. Overall, this made them more powerful. In Spring 2016, a newly appointed Chairman visited several *Aimags* to get introduced to the staff and understand the local situation. When he pointed out the need to inspect as much as possible at one of the big meetings with inspectors, the answer was: 'inspectors' work now is based on risk assessment; this was introduced several years ago and they are selective in inspections based on analysis'.

C. Embedding New Ways of Working: Training and Competency

People are the driving engine of change. But they can also stop and reverse it. It is crucial to create enough momentum, so that change does not stop, but instead opens the way to reach the ultimate goal. It is extremely difficult to train people in something new when they believe that they already have the right knowledge and are experienced in working for a prestigious state organisation such as the Agency – for which inspectors proudly display their badges and uniforms. But it is also very tough to meet their expectations of training, as it is unlikely that they would trust the capacities of trainers and specialists to understand the unique position of Mongolia and the specifics of local matters. Therefore, it was important to train those inspectors and even more to train the engine itself – the Risk Management Unit staff, middle managers and advisors to the Prime Minister and Deputy Prime Minister. Training was given not only in classrooms, but through practice (eg developing checklists and simulating inspections), individual sessions with the Deputy Prime Minister and the Prime Minister, well-crafted study tours for middle management and key staff, but also participating in international forums and workshops, and online.

As previously mentioned, the reporting lines between central GASI and its local branches were weak, which required the Risk Management Unit to widen outreach to include the local branches in *Aimags* and Ulaanbaatar directly. Targeted training either for specific *Aimag* branches with the poorest performance or regional training with representatives of 4–5 *Aimag* branches and their businesses was arranged. Training usually started by sharing non-conformities that inspectors had found at business premises observed during visits the previous day. This practice of relating the training to local conditions helped the inspectors being trained to understand how the training could be applied. The Risk Management Unit brought along central inspectors and staff to convey important policies and recent decisions, conduct training on risk assessment based on real cases and hear feedback and problems that local inspectors experienced in practice. This specific training for frontline inspectors and local businesses filled up some gaps in leadership of the reform process at local levels.

It is worth remembering that Mongolia is not only the eighteenth largest country in the world, but the most sparsely populated, meaning that population centres are few and far between. Distances between *Aimag* centres (of which there are 21) and some of their *sums* (smaller administrative units) range from 200 km to 800 km (mostly off-road). Distances are compounded by relief, limited transportation network, and the harsh climate. Getting to the most remote centres can take a couple of days from Ulaanbaatar. Organisation of training in local areas absorbs substantial time for preparation and long-distance travel; some of the specific *Aimag* training required travelling more than 1000 km off-road to reach a destination. Despite the difficulties with logistics, over five and a half years of implementation the project organised 111 different forms of training for a total of 6,609 people.

It is quite difficult to measure the impact of training. For some training sessions trainees were given short tests before and after the training. The number of correctly answered questions increased by 35–40 per cent after training was completed. On one occasion, a larger test was also organised to look at the average level of knowledge of food inspectors in food microbiology, food chemistry and plant protection and quarantine. The purpose of the test was to identify the current knowledge base and any gaps among inspectors. Some inspectors were offended by this test, as their technical knowledge had not previously been questioned during their time with the Agency. Nevertheless, the test was done, and results were shared confidentially with each inspector (whose name was replaced by an ID number). A report on the score of inspectors was given to the Chairman for him to decide on further steps. At the end, inspectors started trusting the consultants delivering training (professors and doctors in food safety, food microbiology, leading international experts in regulatory reforms, etc) and the relationship became more productive. The trust and respect were translated into awards to the consultants from the Agency (eg honorary medals and diplomas) as a symbol of both recognition and incentive. Participation and learning from international workshops, in particular those organised by the UK Government, helped the Agency's Risk Management Unit to discover new ideas to be used during the next steps in deepening the reform and improving their reform design and implementation skills.

VI. Towards Better Outcomes

A. Shifting Towards an Outcome Focus

The Agency's traditional focus has been on output indicators, based on activities. The introduction of the Risk Management Strategy brought with it emphasis on consideration of outcome indicators and on being accountable to the public for delivering public benefits, rather than just conducting inspections. The Risk Management Strategy states the Agency's mission is 'to prevent and reduce risks … and ensure public safety while supporting economic growth'. This in itself is a significant shift in how the Agency presents itself.

For example, the Food Department's Medium-Term Action Plan, published to implement the commitments within the Risk Management Strategy includes measures such as a five per cent reduction in the numbers of businesses categorised as high risk by increasing business compliance through guidance, and provision of training for businesses based on an assessment of the issues they have. The latter example shows a consistent shift within the Agency from an enforcement approach focused solely on finding and punishing infractions to a culture more focused on building compliance and giving advice. If you look back across the reforms, during the middle of the reform journey the Food Department was graded as the poorest performer because they collected the lowest amount of penalties, which was the measure of success. However, the same unit was later a pioneer in developing, testing and improving checklists, improving their inspection technique through training and simulated inspections, training businesses and getting their feedback. By having long-term planning as part of implementation of the Risk Management Strategy including concrete objectives and indicators, the Agency's operations are now less able to be influenced by management change.

B. Reduction in Burdens for Business

An evaluation of the impact of Mongolia's inspection reform project in 2016 estimated cumulative compliance costs savings for businesses of more than US $2.6 million over four years as a result of the substantial decrease in 'inland' inspections by the Agency. The business survey from 2016 showed a significant decrease in the number of inspections by the Agency, by 26 per cent.[23]

The business survey also identified that businesses were experiencing the benefits of some of the reforms to inspection process that had been implemented. For example, four out of five respondents reported that 'inland' inspectors consistently used checklists. There was also a significant decrease in the proportion of inspections that resulted in a sanction or follow-up inspection, reflecting a change of approach from 'chasing and punishing violations' towards more 'supporting and promoting compliance and risk-management'.

C. The Inspectors' Perspective

The staff survey revealed that there was still a lack of confidence in applying a risk-based approach as there was felt to be no institutional shield against unforeseen risks, and inspectors feared they might be heavily blamed by the management and general public in case of incidents. This was also supported by various discussions held with the frontline inspectors:

---

[23] World Bank Group (2016); Mongolia Inspections Reform Project (2016).

a change in mentality was needed too and the reform, top-down and driven from outside the Agency did not always have inspectors' support. Every reform agenda should pay attention to the human factor and engage the staff from the onset.

The fear of not being able to manage risks is also rooted in what is an inadequate professional level of inspectors. Frequently changing management weakened the professional pool of inspectors by bringing its own circle of political affiliates that gradually pushed professional inspectors out of the Agency. Hence, it was not a big surprise to see polarity of inspectors' opinions in regard to methods and volumes of inspections given such background: 41 per cent of inspectors were in favour of strict inspections; 32 per cent wanted to have as many inspections as possible; and only 27 per cent wanted to have focus on high-risk entities. Out of a total of 731 surveyed inspectors and staff, 46 per cent had worked at the Agency for under five years.

VII. Lessons Learned and Future Priorities for the Agency

The project team's experience of the six-year Mongolia Business Inspection Reform Project enabled it to identify key lessons in relation to implementing sustainable improvements in regulatory practice.

A. Leadership

Reforming business regulation requires strong political will from the country's most senior leaders and is also dependent on this political will being sustained over a sufficiently long period of time (at least 10 years).

Where regulatory agencies are consolidated, the consolidated agency will require a prolonged period to establish itself. During this period, appetite for the consolidation might decrease at the government level and other reform priorities may emerge. It is important to have a mechanism for ensuring that momentum is maintained to realise the benefits of a single agency. Establishing a reform committee with a specific mandate, objectives and goals reporting to the top of government, that would survive political cycles, can help to maintain this momentum. The committee should oversee the consolidation process from its start (eg assessing the pros and cons of consolidations, working with involved agencies) to reach full implementation.

B. IT

The Agency is a large institution (more than 1,800 staff and inspectors) of a country with a population of 3.1 million, that is spread widely in organisational and geographical terms. Its mandate is to conduct inspections in 29 fields, using more than 189 different checklists. All of these require a strong and efficient management system and a risk-based focus in the laws and regulations that it enforces. Having a custom designed IT system is essential for risk management and internal operations.

C. Competency and Performance Management

Performance management should be in sync with the objectives of a risk-based approach. Inspectors should be encouraged to accept certain risks, and the organisation should not be blamed for occasional incidents that could not have been anticipated by looking at existing trends. A new set of behavioural and non-monetary incentives could be introduced to reward high performers and people with innovative ideas. The cultural shift from 'policing' to more 'consulting' (plus bringing more transparency and accountability) dramatically decreases subjectivity and individualism in the inspections process where inspectors enjoy and leverage their powers. New incentives should encourage professionalism and competency of inspectors, and their career should be based on merits. Unfortunately, not many inspectors and staff had been promoted to managerial positions during the seven years of the reform.

Capacity-building requires resources: good trainers and funding. There should be a plan of training with assigned budget, with a curriculum designed for specific needs based on an assessment of knowledge. The Agency only had an annual budget of US $1,500 for training, which is very low.

D. Communications

Communications between the public and the rest of government are essential. Some questions about the Agency were included in an 'omnibus' survey of the general population in the third quarter of 2015 ('citizens survey').[24] Over 50 per cent of respondents to the citizens survey expected the Agency to protect the population against harm 'wherever it comes from', and the percentage was notably higher among respondents who had an incorrect perception of the Agency's mandate (68 per cent in this category). Only slightly less than 50 per cent of respondents of the citizens survey thought that the Agency had responsibility for 'contributing to improve environmental protection, construction and workplace safety'. The citizens survey shows that the Agency needs to do more public education on their responsibilities and communicate more through their Risk Management Strategy.

Specific outreach can be developed through intra-agency communication channels and reporting to the ministries and local government on delivery, enforcement and compliance of the relevant laws and regulations.

VIII. Conclusions

In his book *The Regulatory Craft*,[25] Malcolm Sparrow defined three core elements of reforms:[26]

1.   clear focus on results;

---

[24] References upon request.
[25] Malcolm Sparrow, *The Regulatory Craft. Controlling Risks, Solving Problems, and Managing Compliance* (Washington, DC, Brookings Institution Press, 2000).
[26] ibid, 100.

2.   adoption of problem-solving approach; and
3.   an investment in collaborative partnerships.

If we were to assess the Agency's progress on the reform path using the above elements, it is still in the process of defining more focused objectives and expected results. The work on developing the three-year planning to implement the RMS was transformational in terms of linking a risk-based approach with operational planning and setting new indicators and activities to reach targets.

An excellent base for a problem-solving approach was laid out by implementing the risk-based approach, conducting analysis on data collected from checklists and other sources to develop annual and three-year plans. Introducing new functions such as giving advice and guidance enabled the Agency to understand business compliance in a better way. At the same time, the risk-based approach allowed the Agency to impose sanctions based on evidence and proportionate to the degree of harm caused by the offence. When required, the Agency can take firm stances by using its enforcement 'sting'.

The Agency is still in the process of realising value from collaborative partnerships with other public institutions, and this should ideally be led by top management. However, it was encouraging to see how the Risk Management Unit worked with consumers and business associations to raise awareness about the risk-based approach, explain checklists and get feedback.

26

Harmonising Delivery at National
and Local Levels in the Philippines

ARIEL FRANCISCO FARAON AND NESTOR IAN FAVILA FIEDALAN

I. Introduction

This chapter introduces a powerful insight into the complexities of regulatory delivery reform in an ambitious growing economy. It explains first the culture, law and practice overseeing the framework for regulatory policy and delivery, then explains some of the challenges businesses face in practice and the way local and national bodies work to implement regulation. Finally, it offers an application to the area of food safety.

II. The Legal Framework for Regulatory Governance in the Philippines

The 1987 Philippine Constitution provides the political governance and serves as a basis for defining the power and general structure of the Government. It follows a presidential system of government with three democratic governance structures composed of the executive, legislative and judiciary branches of government. The executive power is vested upon the elected President who heads the executive branch of government. The different executive departments are headed by the appointed secretaries and their immediate subordinates manning the different departments. They are supported by a bureaucracy mandated to implement government policy directives and programmes to deliver public good and services.

The Philippine legislature is composed of two houses: the House of Representatives, composed of elective representatives of congressional districts and party-list groups; and Senate, composed of 24 members elected at large. An independent Supreme Court has jurisdiction over the judiciary branch of government and supervises all types of courts, including regional trial courts, Court of Appeals, etc. The country has an independent judicial infrastructure and independent constitutional bodies (Commission on Audit, Commission on Elections, and the Civil Service Commission) and a fairly well-developed civil society.

Local governments at the provincial, municipal and city levels enjoy local autonomy following the enactment of the 1991 Local Government Code that decentralised and devolved certain powers and responsibilities, for example the delivery of healthcare services, to local governments. Local officials, for example the provincial governor, city or municipal mayor, are elected at the local level. At the local level, municipal, city and provincial governments enjoy autonomy but have remained partly dependent on the national Government's fiscal transfers to finance local development expenditure. The 1991 Local Government Code devolved and decentralised taxing, borrowing, and service delivery powers to local governments. With respect to regulation, local governments impose tertiary rules or regulations such as licences and permits on firms through local requirements presented and approved at local councils.

The form of government has a bearing on how regulation is developed and implemented in the country. In the Philippines, the executive implements the laws enacted by Congress. It can issue regulations in the form of Executive Orders, Circulars and Presidential Proclamations, which direct the behaviour of businesses and individuals concerned, but these issuances may be revoked, amended or changed by the succeeding President (Chief Executive). On the other hand, laws enacted by Congress have the full force of law and they are implemented by the Chief Executive, who can neither amend nor revoke them. Laws can only be changed, revoked or amended by an Act of Congress.

A number of institutions performing regulatory functions exist. The source of government regulation is generally the legislature which has the power to enact laws, subject to the limitations imposed by the 1987 Philippine Constitution. It possesses the power to make the law, which includes the determination of its subject, scope, and operation. In the Philippines, 'regulations' are executive issuances to implement particular executive decisions or laws enacted by Congress. The Government also issues Implementing Rules and Regulations (IRRs), which are the legal instruments used to implement a law enacted by Congress. The IRRs are analogous to the 'secondary regulations to implement primary laws' mentioned by the OECD as a type of regulation under its comprehensive definition.[1]

Thus, in the Philippine context, certain regulations can be issued through executive decisions, which are implemented by the concerned government department. Local government regulation passes through an approval process at local councils. On the other hand, other regulations can only be issued by Congress but are implemented by the Government. This is an important distinction because in the former case, the executive has a wide latitude for regulatory reform, while in the latter case the Government has to work with and through Congress to change, amend, or revoke existing regulation, or enact new regulation.

In this chapter we discuss the reforms to regulations including rules, permits and licences controlled and implemented by the national Government, local governments and regulatory bodies. These impact investment, production and consumption behaviour on a daily basis and can be more easily modified or revoked by regulatory bodies than primary laws.[2] In relation to these areas of regulation Figure 26.1 shows the different levels of government and regulatory bodies involved.

---

[1] See 'Regulatory Policy and the Road to Sustainable Growth' (OECD, 2010).
[2] Gilberto Llanto, 'Toward an Effective Regulatory Management System: Philippines', PIDS Discussion Paper Series, No 2015-32 (Philippine Institute for Development Studies, 2015).

Figure 26.1 The layers of government which impose or enforce secondary/tertiary regulatory requirements on regulated entities (businesses or in some cases other entities)

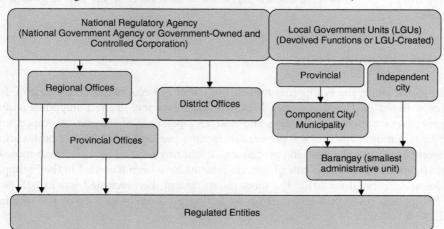

It is undeniable that regulations are implemented for varying objectives. In the Philippines, a number of state policies are adhered to in the imposition of rules and regulations. Ultimately the core objective of regulation is the protection of public interest and the promotion of the greater good of the people. A common notion is that regulations restrict certain business practices for the public wellbeing. Yet, it can be said that regulations are also passed to enable business activities to commence and flourish. Hence, regulation per se does not always imply obstruction and restriction of business activity. Only when it is imposed to interfere in the proper interplay of market forces will it become unfavourable to the business community. However, when regulation is put in place to advance and protect the interests of the business sector and the public, and these interests are balanced successfully, then regulation facilitates growth and development.

III. Business Perceptions of Regulation and Delivery

Businesses deal with regulation throughout their daily operations. At a minimum, before they start their operations, permits and licences are required by some regulatory agencies. To sustain operations, compliance with regulatory requirements is also necessary, and this will include a number of rules and regulations that aim to protect public security and health.

The level of difficulty of regulatory compliance varies by industry. The Government may have good intentions when enacting and implementing new laws and regulations, but regulatory burden may bring adverse effects to businesses. Excessive regulation affects business in different ways including but not limited to the market, pricing, or product quality.

Over-regulation is not uncommon for industries like telecommunications. Some barriers to competition are institutionalised, which can be in the form of prohibitive bureaucratic requirements, arbitrary fees and permits, or inconsistency and inequity arising from poorly conceived and managed use of discretion on the part of government officials.[3]

A. Global Comparisons

In the global arena, the Philippines ranked 170 out of 189 economies on the ease of doing business. Based on Doing Business 2014, starting a business in the Philippines required 15 procedures, which took 35 days and cost 18.7 per cent of income per capita and a paid-in minimum capital of 4.6 per cent of income per capita. While economies around the world have been streamlining procedures, instituting reforms to make them more efficient and easier for business enterprises, no reforms have been recorded in the Philippines by Doing Business since 2012. The most recent reform then recorded was in 2011 when the Philippines eased business start-up by setting up a one-stop shop at the municipal level.[4]

B. Comparisons between Major Cities in the Philippines

To enter a market and stay in business, an entity has to comply with rules and regulations. Just like in every undertaking where benefits can be derived, costs are incurred. In a study conducted by the World Bank Group,[5] regulation in starting a business was evaluated in 25 cities across the Philippines. Four parameters were measured:

1. procedures[6] to legally start and operate a company;
2. time required to complete each procedure;
3. cost[7] required to complete each procedure; and
4. the paid-in minimum capital.[8]

The World Bank 'Doing Business' research revealed that the extent of business regulations varies per city.[9] The study covered local regulations that enhance and constrain business activity along the areas of starting a business, dealing with construction permits, and

---

[3] Philippine Broadband, 'A Policy Brief' (Arangkada Philippines Publication, February 2016).

[4] 'Doing Business in the Philippines 2011' (World Bank, 2010).

[5] ibid.

[6] Procedures mean 'any interaction of the company with external parties' from such as government agencies, lawyers, auditors or notaries involving pre-registration, registration and post-registration. See ibid 32.

[7] Cost pertains to 'all official fees and fees for legal or professional services if such services are required by law' (ibid 32).

[8] Paid-in minimum capital is the 'amount that the entrepreneur needs to deposit in a bank or with a notary before registration and up to three months following incorporation' (ibid 33), which must at least be 6.25% of the corporation's authorised capital stock (25% of the subscribed capital) but not less than Php5000 (The Corporation Code of the Philippines, 1980). Altogether, these are the costs borne by a company to start operations.

[9] The World Bank's study showed that 'starting a business is easiest in General Santos, where it takes 22 days and costs 15.3% of income per capita to comply with the 17 requirements. It is more difficult in San Juan, where it requires 21 procedures that take 39 days and cost 26.3%. Dealing with construction permits is easiest in Davao

property registration. As the 2010 World Bank study noted, while public interest may be a sound rationale in imposing regulations, undesirable results ensue and those likely to bear such burden are the businesses being regulated. Sometimes, regulations determine the survival of an entity or an industry. At times, it is the development of the industry which is affected.

IV. Harmonising Delivery of National and Local Regulations

With weak institutional arrangements, it has been observed that instead of playing an enabling and supportive role, national regulatory agencies still intervened in the way Local Government Units (LGUs) managed the implementation of devolved tasks, policies and programmes. The absence of a clear regulatory framework permitted and encouraged the existence of a two-track delivery system, where both national government agencies and LGUs can initiate devolved activities.[10] There is also a need to address conflicting laws and policies that affect the environment. For instance, an environmental dispute exploded when the same piece of public land was declared on the basis of overlapping policies as a protected area, an ancestral domain, and a mining zone.[11]

With several institutions performing regulatory functions, it is not unlikely that regulators enact conflicting laws concerning a particular industry. Regulations imposed by local government units may be contradictory to national laws enacted by the legislature. This situation happened in Southern Mindanao, with regard to the Tampakan mine project managed by Sagittarius Mines, Inc,[12] where implementation was delayed because the environmental compliance certificate[13] could not be issued due to a ban on open-pit mining imposed by the local government. The business behind the project brought the matter to the courts contesting that the ban was in conflict with the provisions of the Philippine Mining Act of 1995, which allows open-pit mining and asserting that national regulations take primacy over local government regulations.[14]

Various studies refer to serious gaps in carrying out the devolution of environmental functions contemplated under the Local Government Code. On many occasions, national

---

City, where it takes 57 days, but more cumbersome in Manila, where it takes 169 days. Local requirements remain responsible for the variation in the number of steps required to build a warehouse. It is easiest to register property in Valenzuela and Navotas and more difficult in Cagayan de Oro and General Santos–differences are mainly driven by the performance of national government agencies'.

[10] Rosario Manasan, 'Devolution of Environmental and Natural Resource Management in the Philippines: Analytical and Policy Issues' (2002) 29 *Philippine Journal of Development* 53.

[11] Alex Brillantes, 'Philippines' in P'an-sŏk Kim (ed), *Public Administration and Public Governance in ASEAN Member Countries and Korea* (Seoul, Daeyoung Moonhwasa Publishing Company, 2009) 183–224.

[12] Sagittarius Mines, Inc was developing the Tampakan Copper-Gold Project, an open-pit mine and processing facility, located approximately 50 km north of General Santos City on the Philippine island of Mindanao. If developed, the mine would be the largest in the Philippines and among the largest copper mines in the world. The proposed mine site covers an area of approximately 10,000 hectares.

[13] An Environmental Compliance Certificate is a prerequisite for obtaining a permit to operate the mine.

[14] See 'Indophil remains committed to Tampakan mine project', *The Philippine Star*, 20 April 2012, available at www.philstar.com/business/2012/04/30/801644/indophil-remains-committed-tampakan-mine-project.

government agencies still maintain the power to control, supervise and review many of the devolved services even though LGUs are held responsible for them. This results in administrative confusion, overlaps and duplication of functions. The level of decentralisation achieved in the environment and natural resources sector has been described as partial if not insignificant.[15] The effective involvement of LGUs in environmental efforts had been hampered by numerous challenges in the mobilisation of human, financial and organisational resources. For instance, the resources and personnel transferred to LGUs were not commensurate to the cost of the devolved functions. Among the national government agencies with devolved functions, the Department for Environment and Natural Resources has the lowest number of personnel devolved to LGUs at around 4.2 per cent.[16]

National government agencies form part of the local regulatory regime most especially in the business licensing system, due to their functions as defined by national laws or executive orders. They grant certificates, licences, or clearances to businesses before they can engage in activity in the locality. This situation has caused conflicts in the implementation of laws at the local level and standardisation of the implementation process is a continuing challenge. Specifically, the process of devolution of powers to the LGUs, pursuant to the constitutional mandate of ensuring their autonomy, has bred jurisdictional tension between the LGUs and the state. For example, a case to determine rightful jurisdiction of regulatory power in the operation of cable television between the National Telecommunications Commission and Local Legislative Council was referred to the High Court. The court declared that in the absence of constitutional or legislative authorisation, municipalities have no power to grant franchises and LGUs must be reminded that they merely form part of the whole.[17]

Although local government works within this wide legislative framework, it can ensure that the framework is oriented towards local or community interests. Local government can influence the structure of regulation at the policy formulation stage. It can lobby with the national government and act in collaboration with other agencies in the shaping up of policy structures. Once the policy is decided and the policy framework determined, it can exercise a key role in disseminating the policy and in explaining the effects of the regulatory requirements to the community.

In enforcing regulation, the primary concern of the local government is to ensure that regulatory requirements are consistently applied. It also has to carry out enforcement activities such as inspections and see to it that performance standards are met. Good governance is critical to poverty reduction, economic development and human development. It ensures the judicious and transparent use of public funds, promotes the growth of a productive and competitive private sector, enhances the effective delivery of public services, and upholds the rule of law. Good governance is particularly important for businesses: when regulations are simple, transparent and predictable, transaction costs are lower. Entrepreneurs do not have to waste precious resources on red tape. The playing field levels out, enabling anyone to do business without having to resort to connections or informal payments.

---

[15] Francisco Magno, 'Decentralization and Environmental Governance in the Philippines', Working Paper Series No 130 (Southeast Asia Research Centre, The City University of Hong Kong, 2012).

[16] 'Asian Development Bank Annual Report 2004' (Asian Development Bank, 2005).

[17] 'Batangas CATV vs Court of Appeals', available at http://sc.judiciary.gov.ph/jurisprudence/2004/sep2004/138810.htm.

V. Improving Delivery

Through the years, there have been a number of attempts to harmonise national and local regulations aimed at improving quality of service delivery. Process improvements aimed at making the business registration and renewal process as simple and efficient as possible have been undertaken. These involved reviewing the current processes and determining which steps are necessary and which ones can be eliminated.

There are two types of business permit applications: starting a new business and renewal of existing business. They differ in terms of documentary requirements, number of steps and processing times. A new business permit application takes longer since it entails more documentary requirements and involves more steps including transactions with other government agencies. Application for a business permit renewal, on the other hand, takes a shorter time since a number of reforms have already been instituted by LGUs to speed up the process, such as the institutionalisation of the Business One-Stop Shop.

Many LGUs have implemented process improvement initiatives. This is to simplify long processes that are often accompanied by inconveniences such as long queues, uncomfortable office surroundings or long distances between offices. Simple business registration and renewal processes attract more businesses to register. This translates to more revenue for the LGU and results in a better-quality service in the eyes of the clients as well as those of other stakeholders.

Simplifying the business registration process in an LGU can greatly ease the burden of applicants and make the process of doing business with the LGU more convenient. The performance of the business permits and licensing office in an LGU can be gauged by the improvement in the following key performance indicators:

- number of businesses that applied/renewed an application for a business permit;
- time allotted to secure a business permit;
- number of steps (including signatures) required to secure a business permit;
- number of documentary requirements; and
- revenue generated from business registration.[18]

Although the Local Government Code covers the business registration process to some extent, its efficiency and effectiveness is largely dependent on the LGU's ability to create and apply approaches that make the process more customer-friendly and convenient, thus ultimately increasing business registrations. However, there is a need to review the process in order to address areas for improvement. Some of the most frequent complaints of business permit applicants/customers are:

- long waiting times and difficulties in obtaining clearances from non-LGU entities (eg barangay, Bureau of Fire Protection, City Health Office, City Engineer's Office, and the Social Security System);
- too many or repetitive steps; lack of clear and standard systems, requirements, and calculation of fees; slow processing time due to manual procedures; proliferation of

---

[18] 'Streamlining Business Registration in LGUs: Good Practices' (Department of Trade and Industry, 2006).

illegal fixers who charge exorbitant fees; use of connections and grease money to facilitate processing; and lack of information on process flow and requirements, time frames and laws governing LGUs;

- too many requirements of national government agencies, and difficulty obtaining the necessary signatures;

- lack of personnel or staff who are competent, ethical, and customer-oriented, and uncomfortable physical environment – lack of space and ventilation; and

- distance to barangay hall, inaccessibility of signatories in barangay; and scattered geographic location of offices needed for transactions.[19]

The cities of Ormoc, Bacolod, Iligan, Ozamiz, General Santos, Zamboanga, Surigao and Malaybalay conducted a time and motion study and, based on the results, identified how their BPL process could be streamlined. Another approach adopted was the conduct of advance inspections (fire, sanitation, building, etc) prior to the renewal period. These inspections are held from February to November of each year. Still, other LGUs issue either temporary permits or the final/approved documents even if the applicant does not have or has not completed submission of the required clearances or necessary documents, in which case, the applicant is given a period from one to six months to submit these requirements.[20]

VI. Examples of City-based Reforms

A. Davao City

Davao City introduced a single assessment of all business permit fees at the City Treasurer's Office, instead of requiring visits to different agencies. In addition, Davao City now allows businesses to start operations without waiting for an inspection from its City Planning and Development Office and its Bureau of Fire Protection; these inspections now take place after a business is up and running. As a result of its business reforms, Davao City cut seven procedures, speeding up the start-up process by an average of 16 days.

B. Valenzuela

Valenzuela introduced similar reforms and cut eight procedures and seven days from the business start-up process.

C. Pasay

Pasay no longer requires separate applications for its zoning clearance and electrical and mechanical permits; an entrepreneur can obtain a copy of these clearances and permits from the owner of the building and submit them with their business permit application.

---

[19] ibid.
[20] ibid.

As a result, two procedures were eliminated and an entrepreneur saves PHP 956 (US $21), on average.

Other cities could learn from these successful examples of business reforms on the local level. Local business reforms are also making it easier to obtain construction permits in some Philippine cities. In Davao City, officers from its Bureau of Fire Protection are now stationed at city hall to facilitate applications and payments for fire-safety evaluation clearances. In certain instances, however, changes at the national level do not support the cities' efforts to improve efficiency. The recent national amendment of the Fire Code is an example. In December 2008, Congress enacted the Fire Code of the Philippines or Republic Act No 9514, updating the previous Fire Code of 1977 (Presidential Decree No 1185). The new Fire Code mandates a fire safety inspection from the Bureau of Fire Protection as a prerequisite to any permits or licences issued by local governments. In line with international good practice, an inspection of new construction is necessary to ensure that an establishment will be safe from fire hazards and is mandatory to obtain the certificate of occupancy. However, the Implementing Rules and Regulations of the Philippines' new Fire Code require any new business to secure a Fire Safety Inspection Certificate as a prerequisite to a business permit, even when the new business is leasing space in a building that has a certificate. This adds an unnecessary burden to an entrepreneur who wants to start a business legally.

D. National Reforms to Drive Better Local Delivery

National level reforms can also promote better business regulation approaches at the local level. In 2007, Congress passed the Republic Act No 9485, otherwise known as the Anti-Red Tape Act, requiring local and national government agencies to draft their Citizen's Charter, which is an official document that describes the procedures for obtaining a particular service and the guaranteed performance level that the public may expect. A Citizen's Charter is intended, in part, to avert corrupt practices. While many cities, such as Pasay, have drafted their Citizen's Charters and display them at City Hall, implementation is inconsistent from city to city and a national mechanism for enforcing the charter remains to be established.

While the power of local governments to regulate commercial activities is subject to certain limitations prescribed under the Local Government Code and other national laws, the national government can only supervise local governments to ensure that they do not exceed their powers, according to the constitution. As a result, national government initiatives to institute uniform standards and best practices in cities cannot simply be imposed top-down. National initiatives must be implemented with buy-in from the local governments, which requires considerable time and effort.

On 28 May 2018, Republic Act No 11032 on the Ease of Doing Business and Efficient Government Service Delivery Act was signed into law by the President. The enactment of the new law is expected to significantly reduce complaints on delayed government transactions. It aims to reduce processing time, cut bureaucratic red tape and eliminate corrupt practices.[21] The law institutionalises the many reform initiatives that were implemented to ease doing business in the country in order to attract investments.

Now we turn to an example of reform in the area of food safety.

---

[21] 'The Ease of Doing Business under RA 11032', available at: https://pia.gov.ph/news/articles/1013993.

VII. Food Safety: A Worked Example of Reform

One of the most complex areas of regulation in the Philippines is the food safety control system. The system is overseen by two central departments – the Department of Agriculture and Department of Health – and involves different regulatory agencies and local government units. With the devolution of some health-related regulatory functions to the local government units, the delineation of functions between the national agencies mandated to implement food safety regulations and local government was unclear and the delineation of regulatory functions related to food safety between relevant local government units was also unclear. This posed threats to public safety and health and prompted the national government to institute appropriate institutional reforms to address the issues. These complexities did not only require administrative simplification in order to improve regulatory delivery. They required institutional changes and major changes in laws and administrative issuances. The passage of the Food Safety Act addressed the issues of overlapping and conflicting regulatory functions between and among relevant national regulatory agencies, and between these regulatory agencies and local government.

A. The Philippines Food Safety Control System before the Food Safety Act

Before the passage of the Food Safety Act of 2013, the Philippines food safety control system was characterised by overlapping, unclear delineation of functions between relevant regulatory agencies of the Department of Agriculture, Department of Health and the LGUs. This imposed burdens of compliance on the regulated entities, (especially those who were importing agricultural products) and resulted in poor regulatory delivery and problems in regulatory compliance.

Some of the bodies involved included:

- The Food and Drugs Administration – mandated to ensure the safety of foods, drugs and other household substances and to regulate the supply of processed foods and imported food products.

- The Bureau of Quarantine – mandated to implement the food safety relevant provisions of the Quarantine Act of 2004.

- The Centre for Health Developments (regional) – mandated to implement food safety related issues in the Code on Sanitation.

- The Bureau of Animal Industry – mandated to promote the development of the livestock and poultry industries and to regulate the import, export and supply of animals and animal products.

- The Bureau of Plant Industry – mandated to promote the development of the plant industry and to regulate the import and export of plants, plant products and regulated articles.

- The Bureau of Fisheries and Aquatic Resources – mandated to promote the development of the fishery industry and to regulate the import and export of fish and fishery products.

- The National Dairy Authority – mandated to ensure the accelerated development of the dairy industry through policy direction and programme implementation.
- The National Meat Inspection Service – mandated to harmonise the meat inspection laws with international standards to enable the domestic meat processing industry to participate in global trade.
- The Sugar Regulatory Administration – mandated to promote the growth and development of the sugar industry through greater participation of the private sector and to improve the working conditions of the labourers.
- The Philippine Coconut Authority – mandated to develop the industry to its full potential in line with the new vision of a united, globally competitive and efficient coconut industry.

There were also other Department of Health units with mandates on food safety including the National Epidemiology Centre, the Research Institute of Tropical Medicine and the National Centre for Disease Prevention and Control. Even within the Department of Health, the food safety regulatory function was scattered across several operational units.

While there were noted strengths in the structure of the country's food safety control system including:

- the existence of food safety control laws and standards;
- documentation of experiences, lessons learnt and best practices;
- involvement of private partner assistance in the implementation of the food safety control system; and
- industry and consumer confidence in the country's food safety control system,

there were also weaknesses, including:

- overlapping jurisdictions in specific areas leading to overextension or duplication of services;
- unclear enforcement mandates hand in hand with inefficient control structures;
- weak risk analysis/management applications; and
- issues related to the devolution of functions to the LGUs.

Overall the quality of regulatory delivery was challenged by the identified weaknesses and problems in the levels of compliance were noted, endangering public safety and public welfare.

B. Institutional Reforms to Harmonise Regulatory Delivery

To address the issues and gaps in the design and institutional arrangements in the implementation of food safety requirements, the Food Safety Act of 2013 (Republic Act No 10611) was passed into law in 2013. This legislation rationalised the country's food safety control system and provided for:

- a legal framework for the development and implementation of food safety requirements to achieve a high level of consumer health protection in the consumption of food sold in markets and in ensuring fair trade;

- the establishment of national standards on food safety and the adoption of international standards such as the Codex Alimentarius Commission;
- a legal basis for policies for the development and implementation of regulations to which secondary legislation can be harmonised;
- a structure for food safety regulation that brings the fragmented food safety system to a higher level of coordination;
- the use of science and risk analysis when developing and implementing food safety regulations; and
- programmes for strengthening effectiveness and capabilities of stakeholders.

The law adopts a farm-to-fork preventive approach for the control of hazards in the food chain and is designed using the food chain approach to food safety that argues food safety and quality is the responsibility of everyone along the food chain. In the absence of adequate scientific data for analysing risks, it provides for the adoption of precautionary measures until data can be established. It emphasises that primary responsibility for food safety is with the private sector (food business operators) for safe food.

The law has three main objectives:

- protect the public from food-borne and water-borne illnesses and unsanitary, unwholesome, misbranded or adulterated foods;
- enhance industry and consumer confidence in the food regulatory system; and
- achieve economic growth and development by promoting fair trade practices and a sound regulatory foundation for domestic and international trade.

i. Coordination of Regulatory Functions

In order to achieve the food chain approach to food safety it was important to link regulatory functions of relevant regulatory agencies with each other. This required a mechanism for coordination and accountability to ensure that the whole food safety control system was functioning efficiently and effectively. The Food Safety Act provides the framework for coordination among the food safety regulatory agencies through the creation of the Food Safety Regulation Coordinating Board that serves as a coordinating mechanism for effective implementation.

Under the Act, LGUs are mandated to assist in the implementation of food safety. Central ministries have responsibilities to ensure capacity through provision of the necessary technical assistance in the implementation of their food safety functions under their jurisdiction, in periodically assessing the effectiveness of these training programmes in coordination with the Department of Interior and Local Government, and in monitoring the presence of contaminants in food to determine food safety hazards in the food supply chain.

To strengthen the scientific basis of the regulatory system, the Food Development Centre is responsible for providing scientific support in testing, research and training. The Centre for Food Regulation and Research of the Food and Drugs Administration is responsible for participating in Codex and other international standard-setting bodies, communicating risks and developing information-sharing among stakeholders, establishing laboratories for food safety and strengthening the capabilities of existing laboratories, developing a database for food safety hazards and food-borne illness from epidemiological data, strengthening the scientific capabilities on product safety and quality standards, and providing certification of food safety inspectors.

C. Food Business Operator Responsibilities

One of the best features of this law is the emphasis on private sector participation in the regulatory delivery process. The law provides that the capability of farmers, fishermen, industries, consumers and government personnel in ensuring food safety should be improved. The responsibilities of the food business operators as well as consumers are defined in the law, making regulatory delivery as far as safety regulations are concerned, a collaborative process. Food business operators must ensure that food satisfies the requirements of food law relevant to their activities in the food supply chain and that control systems are in place to prevent, eliminate, or reduce risks to consumers.

The primary responsibilities of food business operators include ensuring safety of their food products and compliance with legal requirements and ensuring the prevention or minimisation of food safety hazards. Farmers and fishermen as well as food business operators in small and micro industries are assisted by the Department of Agriculture and the Department of Health in coordination with the LGUs to implement the standards and codes of practice. Food business operators are encouraged to implement a HACCP-based approach or an equivalent food safety control programme in their operations and designate a competent food safety compliance officer.

VIII. Conclusion: Opportunities for Further Improvement

In his first State of the Nation Address in 2016, the Chief Executive, President Rodrigo Roa Duterte emphasised that one of his administration's development priorities was to ensure competitiveness and promote ease of doing business. He carried with him his experience from when he was the mayor of Davao City. His policy pronouncement has made continuing systems and process reforms in the delivery of frontline services a nationwide imperative.

There are several regulatory reform initiatives ongoing in the Philippines. One of the major aims of these reforms is to ease doing business in the country and promote sustainable and inclusive growth especially in the countryside. However, economic development is sometimes hampered by how regulation is delivered at the local and national levels. Ease of doing business is usually dictated by how business-related regulations are delivered.

Further development will lie in better organisation such as agreement between the various links in the service chain, good utilisation of information technology and media, and in researching the possibilities of providing a more decentralised service. Improvements start with good analysis and mapping of the expectations of citizens. Attention to training and study opportunities for staff also improves performance.

As a developing nation, regulatory agencies in the Philippines should extend due consideration to the interests of business enterprises, in line with the aim of protecting public welfare. The country will not progress from its current state if laws are so restrictive that they hamper industrial growth. Foreign ownership restrictions, embodied either in statutes or the Philippine Constitution, need to be reviewed, considering that the country only has limited investible funds to finance huge capital-intensive business projects. Furthermore, the consequences of any pricing regulation must be evaluated extensively before it is implemented. Reforms that would ease the requirements of starting a business also need to be passed. In the enactment of laws, rules and regulations, the phraseology must be clear enough to avoid conflicting interpretations but broad enough so as not to be too restrictive in their application. National and local regulations should be unified or at the very least remain consistent, in order to prevent business disruptions.

Last but not least, the acceptance of and commitment to the importance of good friendly service delivery by administration and management and a (local) government that is more responsive to citizens and businesses is essential in improving the capacity of local governments. This demands a customer orientation and the realisation that the service delivery has left much to be desired. Old systems were more focused on keeping citizens under control and the government organisation was mainly based on internal questions. Customer orientation is a mix of customer-friendly behaviour by government workers and the need to be steered by the demands of citizens as a customer, even when you know citizens are not really eager to request licences, permits and other often complex documentation.

Improving service delivery is not an isolated process. The strengthening of citizens' participation, the fight against corruption and improving the skills of management and the administration are ongoing elements in improving regulatory delivery.

PART FOUR

Reflections

27

Reflections on Regulatory Delivery: Evolution and Future

CHRISTOPHER HODGES

This final chapter reflects on the significance of the detailed information and analyses that have been set out in this book, with the aim of putting the Regulatory Delivery Model and related developments in wider contexts. One context is that of evolution in regulatory theory and practice, another is that of socio-political evolution. It ends by suggesting some thoughts for possible future evolution.

I. Regulatory Professionalism

It is rare that the day-to-day activities of regulatory professionals are illuminated. There have been some – but all too rare – academic socio-legal studies into what regulators do, and how they aim to achieve 'compliance'; for example by scholars such as Hawkins, Braithwaite, Grabosky, Hutter and recently Blanc.[1]

This book is particularly valuable in providing illumination by regulatory professionals themselves on how they frame their roles, and how they aim to perform them. It is also valuable in demonstrating regulators' concern that their roles and activities should be considered within a framework that is rational, has political and social acceptability, and justification, to produce outcomes that benefit the society within which they operate.

Most of the authors of this book are, or have been, officials. They write from their very practical standpoints of having to make regulation work. They write not from the perspective of ideological, theoretical or political conceptions of what regulation should be, but from practical understanding of what regulators actually do across a wide range of

---

[1] Leading works include: Keith Hawkins, *Environment and Enforcement: Regulation and the Social Definition of Pollution* (Oxford, Clarendon Press, 1984); John Braithwaite and Peter Grabosky, *Of Manners Gentle: Enforcement Strategies of Australian Business Regulatory Agencies* (Oxford, Oxford University Press, 1987); Ian Ayres and John Braithwaite, *Responsive Regulation: Transcending the Deregulation Debate* (Oxford, Oxford University Press, 1992); Bridget Hutter, *Compliance: Regulation and Environment* (Oxford, Clarendon Press, 1997); Bridget Hutter, *Regulation and Risk: Occupational Health and Safety on the Railways* (Oxford, Oxford University Press, 2001); Keith Hawkins, *Law as Last Resort* (Oxford, Oxford University Press, 2002); Florentin Blanc, *From Chasing Violations to Managing Risks. Origins, Challenges and Evolutions in Regulatory Inspections* (Cheltenham, Edward Elgar Publishing, 2018).

specialisms, such as occupational safety, trading standards, food safety, consumer protection, water quality, environmental protection and so on. Many of the expert contributors also have the advantage of having overviews of numerous regulatory regimes, not only of different subjects, but also in different countries. They are familiar with the broad development of theories of regulation, but are strongly influenced by extensive self-scrutiny based on practical experience of what works – and does not work – in achieving long-term reduction of risk and promotion of performance that maximises compliance with society's standards.

One challenge to comprehending the structures and constraints within which regulators operate is the diversification in the number of regulatory agencies and increasing complexity of the regulatory frameworks and rules that now apply in different sectors and types of regulatory activity. This diversification and complexity leads to the fact that many regulatory regimes are now so sophisticated and complex that they present a considerable degree of impenetrability, and expertise tends to be generated in individual silos (such as financial services, energy, communications, pharmaceuticals, workplace safety, environmental protection, food standards, consumer protection, competition and so on) and few practitioners are fully aware of the architecture, detailed rules or working practices outside the one silo with which they are familiar.

Hence this book should provide much-needed illumination into the world of regulatory agencies and assist their work and that of their regulated communities, in addition to providing wider public and scholarly understanding.

II. The Significance of Regulatory Delivery

The book makes a significant claim. It is that both the design of regulations and of regulatory regimes have all too often lacked an essential dimension – that of the concept of regulatory delivery. Without a rigorous approach to delivery, regulatory regimes will fail to deliver fully. Few regimes have been subject to an initial delivery assessment (asking: Will it work? How will it work? How well will it work?) or post-implementation assessment (How is it working? etc). As a result, traditional modes of enforcement are frequently too narrow. The idea that compliance will be created solely by imposing deterrent sanctions on whoever is identified as having committed a breach of a rule is no longer credible. Instead, it is necessary to engage with a range of choices, with deep capacity, to bring systemic oversight and data-driven interventions aimed at achieving practical improvements in activities, operations and culture so as to reduce risk. The paradigm has shifted from rules, enforcement and deterrence to one of responsiveness, compliance support, culture and ethical behaviour, reserving firm sanctions for those who intentionally, grievously or repeatedly offend.

It is the absence of a coherent approach that the creators of the Regulatory Delivery Model have sought to remedy. The model elaborates the prerequisites (Governance Frameworks, Accountability and Culture) and practices (Risk-based Prioritisation, Intervention Choices and Outcome Measurement) for successful regulatory delivery. These six elements might strike some observers as obvious and others as irrelevant to the success of regulation. But the evidence set out in this book shows the fundamental importance of regulatory delivery and therefore of these factors as requirements for success. The approach is an evolution but is truly revolutionary and will transform outcomes if adopted seriously.

III. Stages of Understanding of Regulation

The concepts of regulatory delivery and the Regulatory Delivery Model are the latest developments in long journeys of conceptualising and practising regulation. It may be helpful here to provide a short review of some of the major stages in these journeys, not least to see how far we have come, what has been discarded, and what the model contributes to our understanding.

It is well known that the evolution in regulatory theorising is often depicted as a journey from the concept of 'command and control' to 'responsiveness'. We now add 'culture' as a critical element.

The authoritarian model is based on the exercise of power and the theory that this deters certain future behaviour. This state of mind is often accompanied by failure to think about why and how those subject to regulation can or will comply with the requirements, and what barriers they may face in trying to do so. A default position of authoritarianism can characterise all those who break the rules as having malicious intent, criminals who deserve punishment, and assume that punishment will prevent future law-breaking. The fact that such an attitude may be unsupported by the evidence of continuous law-breaking, in other words that as a theory of how to maximise future compliance it constantly fails, is ignored. Too often in this approach, success may be measured by the size of the fine, or total fines, imposed. Such supposed metrics of success may bring instant public recognition in media headlines and meet arbitrary revenue (or even income) targets imposed by the Ministry of Finance. They may also bring some peer recognition and ranking amongst the regulatory community. However, these metrics and recognitions all turn out to be unfortunate drivers of the wrong kind of regulatory behaviour.

Understanding motivation begins to enable development of soundly based relationships which are the basis first of confidence in the system and then trust in the people who operate it. Consideration of the value of trust in regulatory relationships has been developed into a key vision in the journey to date of a cooperative model based on trust between the public and private parties. This concept is crystallised in the concepts of Ethical Business Practice and Ethical Business Regulation, explained in chapter twenty-two. The underlying idea of cooperation is strikingly similar to the Dutch *polder* concept introduced by Rob Velders in chapter eleven. It is also strongly democratic. Humans work best when they work together, rather than against each other, even if some competition between groups can provide benefits.

A further milestone in the journey is that of increasing professionalism amongst regulators. There has been much discussion of issues such as risk-based regulation, principles-based regulation, metrics-based regulation and recently outcomes-focused regulation. The development of the Regulatory Delivery Model is a product of serious thinking about how to do regulation by its professionals. As an internally generated model it reflects the profession's concern to take a holistic view of the factors that shape the delivery of good outcomes for society.

Another important milestone in thinking is the realisation that most businesses predominantly comprise of honest citizens who do not go to work to break society's laws, but that rules may sometimes be broken for many different reasons. Small businesses, for example, may be unaware of the rules, their detailed requirements, or of how to comply. Larger organisations may face so many issues and have such internal complexity that compliance is crowded out. Huge advancements in behavioural science have illuminated how people think and act, and how honest people can fail to comply with all of the rules all of the time. This science has equally illuminated how to support improvements in culture and performance that result in rule-compliance – and the fact that zealous, hard enforcement will tend to diminish compliance rather than increase it.

These thoughts lead to another milestone, which is the emergence of more sophisticated thinking about how regulated entities might be able to comply and what barriers they face in doing this. This leads to thinking about how to support businesses, rather than 'enforce' against them, which has become a strong feature of (some) regulators in the UK in recent decades. This line of development has been given impetus by the adoption by politicians of official policy that regulators should support business compliance, enshrined in the Regulators' Code, as described in chapter five. The development of Primary Authority, as described in chapter nine, embodies these principles in the UK. Analysis suggests Primary Authority is based upon three fundamental premises: firstly, that there should be efficient communication channels to raise and resolve problems of interpretation and application; second, that issues could be raised through these channels by either regulators or businesses, in the latter case with an expectation that the response would be supportive rather than punitive; and third, that head offices, trade associations and related bodies can amplify compliance messages in relation to their outlets and members. Hence, the architecture, lines of communication and cooperation can all be simplified and made more efficient and effective if the relevant key personnel all play their part in the integrated system. The Primary Authority mechanism has been spectacularly successful, but is still too little-known to people who are not involved in it.

The lines of thinking referred to above led logically to the concept of regulatory delivery; in other words, whether the systems and activities of regulation in fact lead to delivery of desired outcomes. This concept inherently requires thought about what regulators do and what regulated entities do, how both of them do it, and ultimately why they do it. This book therefore represents the fruits of a period of intense self-scrutiny. One that has been led by regulators themselves – and it is significant that it is those professionals who have done this and not external theorists or those responsible for policy. There is no political or theoretical dogma here. The ideas in this book derive from extensive practical experience. The reality is that the approaches identified here themselves have implications for what should be good regulatory policy.

The development of these ideas led to a focus not just on the purpose of the regulatory regime but that of the underlying activity, namely the business or other social activity (the primary activity). Regulation does not exist to prevent lawful activity; its purpose is to shape the way in which the activity is undertaken, limit its ancillary impacts and enable the activity to produce its desired social and economic benefits. This has led to the UK idea of regulators being subject to a growth duty – consideration of whether their activities have beneficial, supportive or unnecessarily limiting effects on the primary activity.

So, this journey has led to focus on the Regulatory Delivery Model, a structured way to evaluate the constitutional and architectural requirements for regulatory delivery to operate effectively. It is no accident that the three prerequisites of the model – Governance Frameworks, Accountability and Culture – concern not only internal optimisation but also ultimately the ways a regulatory agency relates to, and engages with, the society in which it operates. The essential requirement is that the agency should not become a self-regarding, internalised world that exists with no honest relationship to the outside world, which includes politicians, other regulators, the regulated community, those who benefit from the primary activities, and society generally. The Regulatory Delivery Model postulates a fundamentally engaged series of relationships, forming a connected society.

The development in ideas on regulatory delivery described above has a fascinating parallel in the evolution of thinking about human behaviour. Maslow, Laloux and Barrett are particularly relevant. The psychologist Abraham Maslow identified a hierarchy of seven levels of human needs through which individuals should develop if they are to reach full potential.[2] Fernand Laloux applied the same thinking to identify stages in the development of how humans group themselves into different organisations, depending on the development of their ideas and social, economic and political needs.[3] He argues that the most recent stage has developed features of meritocratic empowerment, values-driven culture and inspirational purpose, a multiple stakeholder perspective with no hierarchy among stakeholders and the family as the guiding metaphor. Laloux also considers that humanity is currently going through a transformation stage in which fear is replaced by collaboration. Richard Barrett further applied Maslow's categorisation by proposing seven levels of organisational consciousness (survival, relationship, self-esteem, transformation, internal cohesion, making a difference and service) each of which are necessary to form the foundation of an effective culture.[4] From this, Barrett developed a Cultural Values Assessment tool that diagnoses culture throughout an organisation and indicates from the issues identified what remedial action is necessary to provide a full complement of the seven levels.

These developments also parallel the evolution in thinking about corporations, which has been undergoing a major readjustment from the narrow 'maximising shareholder value' of late-twentieth-century economic theory[5] to the holistic 'maximising stakeholders' value'.[6] The latest thinking in the theory of corporations is that all organisations need to have – and be governed by – a single social purpose.[7] This is echoed in the 2018 amendments of the UK's Corporate Governance Code to require boards of directors to establish a company's purpose and ensure that culture promotes integrity and openness, values diversity and is responsive to the views of shareholders and wider stakeholders.[8]

---

[2] Abraham Maslow, *Motivation and Personality* (New York, HarperCollins, 1987); *Toward a Psychology of Being*, 2nd edn (New York, Van Nostrand Reinhold, 1968); *The Farther Reaches of Human Nature* (London, Penguin, 1993).

[3] Fernand Laloux, *Reinventing Organizations: A Guide to Creating Organizations Inspired by the Next Stage of Human Consciousness* (Massachusetts, Parker Nelson Publishing, 2014).

[4] Richard Barrett, *The Values-Driven Organization: Cultural Health and Employee Well-Being as a Pathway to Sustainable Performance*, 2nd edn (Abingdon and New York, Routledge, 2017) 63.

[5] Milton Friedman, *Capitalism and Freedom* (Chicago, University of Chicago Press, 1962).

[6] John Mackey and Ray Sisodia, *Conscious Capitalism. Liberating the Heroic Spirit of Business* (Harvard, Harvard Business Review Press, 2014).

[7] Colin Mayer, *Prosperity* (Oxford, Oxford University Press, 2019).

[8] 'The UK Corporate Governance Code' (Financial Reporting Council, 2018).

IV. Applicability of the Model

Is the Regulatory Delivery Model limited to the UK or certain other countries, and if so, which, and why? Or is it of general application?

We argue that the principles can and should be universally applicable. Graham noted in his Introduction that the Regulatory Delivery Model emerged from comparative work that he and his team undertook in a number of contrasting countries, and from thinking about the prerequisites and practices that are central to regulatory delivery. Further, this book includes examples from a wide range of countries where elements of the model have been successfully applied. These considerations appear to indicate that the lessons and model are applicable widely.

Chapters five and six of this book constitute a fascinating comparison of approaches to changing the behaviour of regulatory agencies in common law and civil law jurisdictions, the UK and Lithuania. The former adopted a statutory requirement for agencies to observe a code, whereas the latter included all requirements in the law. The UK's Code states principles, whereas the Lithuanian law is both more concrete and more general. Both approaches seem to have delivered significant change, although considerably more empirical evaluation could be undertaken in both jurisdictions, which could also give an interesting comparative view.

If an understanding of regulatory delivery, enabled by a use of the Regulatory Delivery Model, has wide potential application, are there some states or situations in which there may be extraneous barriers to success?

The need for predictability and trust to be present, or at least able to be adequately spread, in society has been referred to above. On the other hand, discussions are currently underway on how delivery concepts like Ethical Business Regulation can be applied as a specific means of providing a vision that will enable business and state relationships to escape from a corrupt regime. This points to an important characteristic, one that is not often recognised in regulatory design – the extent to which successful implementation is predicated on an absence of corruption in the regime and society. The Regulatory Delivery Model asserts that the prerequisites – Governance Frameworks, Accountability and Culture – enable understanding of the system including the extent and impact of corruption.

A related debate concerns the concept of regulatory capture. It is striking that capture is referred to extensively in, for example, American regulatory literature, but features less in British or Dutch works. One reason for this involves the fact that capture of regulators may have different meanings in different situations. In the context of the United States of America, concern is expressed that a public authority may be captured politically by those who appoint the head of an agency or those who vote through financial budgets, as well as the risk of being too close to the industry that is regulated. In Western European states, by contrast, capture-by-the-regulated is the more discussed phenomenon. Public authorities anywhere may bemoan a lack of resources, but the causes in Europe in the recent decade have been austerity rather than political dogma. In either case we argue that the Governance Frameworks and Accountability elements of the Regulatory Delivery Model, together with transparency, are specifically designed to provide protection. Overall, the strength of any of these elements of capture will vary depending on local factors, not least the local political and architectural context.

The ideas that regulators should understand their regulated communities and the problems that they face, and adopt a responsive, proportionate approach, involving exercise of appropriate flexibility and discretion – all ideas that are inherent to the success of regulatory delivery – challenge the over-riding fear of regulatory capture and its use as a justification for a lack of engagement. Use of the Regulatory Delivery Model should help to guard against such risk. The model encourages assessment of the effectiveness of engagement and cooperation, sometimes in close discussion and debate.

It is also important to recognise that any responsive regime has to endow the regulatory authority with discretion and the flexibility to select different interventions so as to respond to particular circumstances. Two points arise here. First, differentiation in response can be principled and justified. But the paradigm needs to be understood. Second, predictability and consistency in response and intervention can be achieved through the existence of publicly stated criteria, such as an approved regulatory and enforcement policy, evidence that differentiates between different actors, and the availability of oversight through mechanisms such as judicial review or Parliamentary accountability.

These points are illustrated by the approach to enforcement adopted by the UK's Drinking Water Inspectorate (DWI) referred to in chapter nineteen. The DWI publishes its objectives, approach to inspection and intervention, and the data on performance of all the water companies. One company objected that it was prosecuted and had a large and unfair fine imposed while another company that had committed a different infringement only received an improvement notice; the DWI responded that the stated goals are for companies to demonstrate that they are seeking to improve performance – perhaps over 10 years and through agreement with DWI of a transformation programme – and whereas the second company was striving to improve, the first company had demonstrably not improved. It is no longer solely individual breaches that drive sanctions, but evidence of engagement to deliver real improvements in performance.

V. Looking to the Future

Advances in regulatory delivery challenge an approach that is based on design of the regime and rules alone. The question of delivery cannot be ignored. And its understanding will be advanced through the six elements of the Regulatory Delivery Model. What might important next steps be? We suggest three particular steps that could logically be taken.

Firstly, it would be logical for individual states and business sectors to use the model to review their regulatory approaches, national architectures, approaches, culture, techniques and outcomes. Many questions arise, of which the following are only some. Are the landscapes and regulatory regimes consistent with successful regulatory delivery? What is the evidence of successful delivery or of its failure? Does such evidence exist, or does it need to be collected? Do certain techniques – such as reliance on inspection or public grading of organisations – achieve good outcomes? Do public authorities escape exposure to adoption of best regulatory practice eg because they claim to be enforcement bodies and not regulatory bodies? Might use of the Regulatory Delivery Model by all the public authorities in a state, or across a region, lead to adoption of the same approach to, for example, culture and intervention? Are businesses subject to significantly different regulatory or enforcement regimes from different authorities, leading to confusion and inconsistency? How can ethical cultures be created?

Second, it may be useful to create national and international communities of practice on regulatory delivery. These would provide fora for discussion, comparison, mandating research and benchmarking. They might also go further and provide a mechanism to review and stimulate all public regulatory bodies or provide some oversight of performance. Some national models already exist, but all could be developed further. These include Canada's Community of Federal Regulators, the Inspection Council of the Netherlands (see chapter eleven), and to some extent the UK's Regulators' Network. Illuminating questions to ask are whether all individual regulatory bodies in the country adopt best practice, or the same practice, and whether such bodies ever shrink their activities or cease to exist. In the international sphere, an independent authoritative community of practice may be beneficial. International review mechanisms exist under the auspices of the OECD and the Financial Action Task Force.

The authors of this book have created the International Network for Delivery of Regulation (INDR) to provide exactly such a community of expertise and discussion.[9] Major objectives of the INDR are to map current best practice, to research current practice so as to provide empirical evidence of what works and what does not, and to fill in gaps in knowledge. For example, one topic for research will be to identify how states set out requirements for interventions in law; whether they enable discretion for the regulator to respond to individual circumstances and how, if at all, they make control provisions transparent for example by requiring an accessible Enforcement Policy, as UK agencies are required to have under the Regulators' Code.

Third, the importance of the culture of organisations – both regulators and the regulated – has emerged as a profound but transformative insight. It appears that it is particularly significant in the regulatory space, for reasons explored in this book. Into this arena, Ethical Business Regulation has been presented as a recent concept but examples of elements of it exist widely and can now be drawn together into a consistent and powerful new tool. Across various countries and in an interestingly varied set of sectors and industries innovators are engaged in applying or scoping Ethical Business Regulation and results so far are very encouraging. Much more work can be done here.

This book will have succeeded if it is read widely by regulatory, political and business interests and leads to fresh approaches to regulatory delivery. It has been said above that the concept of regulatory delivery and thus the ubiquity of the Regulatory Delivery Model is intensely practical and non-political. If the ideas in this book are correct, various consequences should follow from a new focus on delivering effective regulation and desired outcomes. Following the formulation of outcomes of regulatory delivery in chapter one – Protection, Prosperity and Efficiency – we can say first that compliance should be maximised, the vulnerable should be protected and the rule of law will be upheld. Second, economic activity should be healthy, entrepreneurs should thrive and prosperity should flow as innovation is encouraged and productivity rises. Third, that relationships between regulated entities and the state should be engaged and collaborative, costs to the state should fall whilst information to drive evidence-based decision-making should flow. Is all of this rational and will it occur? That will call for evaluation in a future book.

---

[9] See www.law.ox.ac.uk/centres-institutes/centre-socio-legal-studies/indr.

Annex 1: UK Regulatory Reform Key Dates

Date	
1948	Harold Wilson – President of the Board of Trade and later Prime Minister announces '**bonfire of controls**' See *Hansard*, HC (series 5) Vol 457, cols 112–120 (4 November 1948)
1974	**Health and Safety at Work Act** created what is now the Health and Safety Executive as a risk-based regulator Available at www.legislation.gov.uk/ukpga/1974/37
1980s	**Deregulation units** set up in government departments **Compliance Cost Assessments** (1985) **Deregulation White Papers** Creation of **arm's length bodies**, providing regulatory agencies with some independence from government
1990s	**Regulatory Impact Assessments** in widespread use See www.gov.uk/government/collections/impact-assessments-guidance-for-government-departments
1994	**Deregulation Taskforce** (renamed Better Regulation Taskforce in 1997)
1994	**Bonfire of red tape** promised by Michael Heseltine See www.independent.co.uk/news/heseltine-lights-flames-of-change-promised-bonfire-of-red-tape-aims-to-widen-choice-for-consumers-1407992.html
1997	The UK's **Principles of Good Regulation** were established as a pillar of the regulatory simplification programme Available at http://webarchive.nationalarchives.gov.uk/20100407173247/http://archive.cabinetoffice.gov.uk/brc/upload/assets/www.brc.gov.uk/principlesleaflet.pdf
1998	**Enforcement Concordat**, a voluntary code setting out what businesses can expect from enforcement officers Available at webarchive.nationalarchives.gov.uk/20021025163013/http://www.cabinet-office.gov.uk:80/regulation/publicsector/enforcement/enforcement.htm
2000	**Food Standards Agency** established to build confidence in the safety of food See www.food.gov.uk
2005	**Hampton Report** on Effective Inspections and Enforcement Available at http://webarchive.nationalarchives.gov.uk/20130221080106/http://www.hm-treasury.gov.uk/d/bud05hamptonv1.pdf

2006	**Legislative and Regulatory Reform Act 2006** established the principles of good regulation in respect of regulators' activities and empowered ministers to issue a statutory code of practice for regulators (see Regulators' Code) Available at www.legislation.gov.uk/ukpga/2006/51/introduction
2006	**Better Regulation Commission** – superseded by the Better Regulation Executive (2008)
2006	**Macrory Report** on sanctions Available at https://webarchive.nationalarchives.gov.uk/20121205164501/http://www.bis.gov.uk/files/file44593.pdf
2006–2010	**Hampton Implementation Reviews** See www.nao.org.uk/wp-content/uploads/2008/03/HIR_Guidance.pdf
2007	**Rogers Review** on priorities for local regulators Available at www.regulation.org.uk/library/2007-rogers_review.pdf
2007	**Local Better Regulation Office** (LBRO), created to improve consistency in local authority regulatory services (environmental health, fire safety, licensing and trading standards) to drive economic prosperity and community wellbeing. LBRO was given a statutory basis by the Regulatory Enforcement and Sanctions Act 2008. Guidance to the Act: http://webarchive.nationalarchives.gov.uk/+/http://www.berr.gov.uk/files/file47135.pdf See: Archive LBRO website http://webarchive.nationalarchives.gov.uk/20090326192449/http://www.lbro.org.uk/Default.aspx?id=2 LBRO was followed by: • The Better Regulation Delivery Office in 2012 • Regulatory Delivery in 2016 • The Office for Product Safety and Standards in 2018
2008	**Regulatory Enforcement and Sanctions Act** See www.legislation.gov.uk/ukpga/2008/13/contents
2008–2009	**Risk and Regulation Advisory Council** established See https://webarchive.nationalarchives.gov.uk/20100104183913/http://www.berr.gov.uk/deliverypartners/list/rrac/index.html
2009	**The Anderson Review** published the Good Guidance Guide Available at https://webarchive.nationalarchives.gov.uk/20090609052836/http://www.berr.gov.uk/files/file49881.pdf
2009	**Retail Enforcement Pilot** launched See www.gov.uk/government/publications/local-regulation-retail-enforcement-pilot
2009	**Regulatory Policy Committee** created See www.gov.uk/government/publications/costs-and-benefits-of-new-regulation-regulatory-policy-committee-opinions-since-may-2015; deregulatory proposals; and regulatory agencies' submissions in respect of the government's Business Impact Target
2009	**Primary Authority** established See https://assets.publishing.service.gov.uk/government/uploads/system/uploads/attachment_data/file/664316/primary-authority-overview.pdf

2011	**Red Tape Challenge** launched See: http://webarchive.nationalarchives.gov.uk/20150507103821/http://www.redtapechallenge.cabinetoffice.gov.uk/home/index
2011	**One-in, One-out** regime launched in the UK See https://assets.publishing.service.gov.uk/government/uploads/system/uploads/attachment_data/file/31617/11-p96a-one-in-one-out-new-regulation.pdf
2012	**Better Regulation Delivery Office** (BRDO) created after a 2010 review of LBRO led to its functions being brought into government, with the establishment of BRDO (now the Office for Product Safety and Standards) as a directorate of what is now the Department for Business, Energy and Industrial Strategy, with a wider remit, taking responsibility for engagement with businesses and regulatory agencies at a local and national level to improve government understanding See 'Delivering Better Regulation: Government Response to the Consultation on the Future of the Local Better Regulation Office' (Department for Business, Innovation and Skills, November 2011). Available at www.gov.uk/government/uploads/system/uploads/attachment_data/file/197614/11-1388-government-response-to-consultation-future-of-lbro.pdf
2012	**Focus on Enforcement** reviews launched Further information available at http://webarchive.nationalarchives.gov.uk/20160106103937/http://discuss.bis.gov.uk/focusonenforcement
2014	**Regulators' Code** published Available at www.gov.uk/government/uploads/system/uploads/attachment_data/file/300126/14-705-regulators-code.pdf Previously the Regulators Compliance Code: 'Regulators' Compliance Code: Statutory Code of Practice for Regulators' (Department for Business, Enterprise and Regulatory Reform, 2007). Available at http://webarchive.nationalarchives.gov.uk/20081112123923/http://www.berr.gov.uk/whatwedo/bre/inspection-enforcement/implementing-principles/regulatory-compliance-code/page44055.html
2016	**Regulatory Delivery** superseded the Better Regulation Delivery Office (BRDO) in 2016. Regulatory Delivery combined BRDO and the National Measurement and Regulation Office to focus on regulation and enforcement. The launch of Regulatory Delivery brought together policy expertise and practical experience for the effective delivery of regulation.
2016	**Cutting Red Tape Reviews** launched
2017	**Regulatory Futures** report published by Cabinet Office Available at www.gov.uk/government/publications/regulatory-futures-review
2017	**Growth Duty** launched 'Growth Duty: Statutory Guidance' (Department for Business, Energy & Industrial Strategy, March 2017). Available at www.gov.uk/government/uploads/system/uploads/attachment_data/file/603743/growth-duty-statutory-guidance.pdf
2018	**Office for Product Safety and Standards** superseded Regulatory Delivery in 2018, continuing the work of Regulatory Delivery, with additional responsibilities as the national regulator for product safety See www.gov.uk/government/organisations/office-for-product-safety-and-standards

ACKNOWLEDGEMENTS

Acknowledgements – Graham Russell

I will always be grateful that I was raised in a loving family and nurtured by the sage counsel of my father, the practical wisdom of my mother and the competitive edge sharpened by my siblings. The loss of my father, Peter Russell, is a source of daily sadness but he lives on in his stories and in his faith for a better life beyond.

I want to thank all those who have contributed to this book, directly by contributing to the case studies, and indirectly by shaping the journey towards Regulatory Delivery. There are far too many to name but I have tried to mentioned some of the key people as they arise in the story told in the Introduction. Others include Len Swift and Mike Mottershead, who first introduced me to the world of Trading Standards, Councillor Sandra Hambleton who showed me the value of public service and Ron Gainsford who was, and is, an inspiration. If I have seen anything it is because, to paraphrase Isaac Newton, I have stood on the shoulders of such giants.

More recently, it has been my privilege to have worked with outstanding regulators in a rich variety of places. That wouldn't have been possible without the ambition and drive of Florentin Blanc and the organisational flair of Stewart Gibbon and Tamsin McSorley. Many of the missions were made possible through our partnership with the IFC/World Bank. Apart from those contributing to this book, Fred Zake, Vaanii Baker, Jemel Liverpool and Kimani Kimotho in Africa, Fatima Toktosunova in Kyrgyzstan and Lars Grava, Wafa Aranki and Peter Ladegaard in Washington deserve my thanks.

I have particular respect for those who have brought different backgrounds and experience into the regulatory environment. Tim Leese and Gemma Hume created an awareness of consumer potential in Staffordshire Trading Standards. Loris Strappazzon and Rachel Holloway brought a policy perspective to LBRO while Gordon Maddan opened our understanding of business. Today OPSS is enriched by the diverse perspectives of our highly talented and motivated teams.

This book would not have been started without the encouragement of Chris Hodges and Erica Sheward and would never have been finished without the diligence of Helen Kirkman, Jenny Nobes, Joanna Ivey and Charmaine Cole. The inspiration is theirs, but the errors remain mine. My office wouldn't have functioned for the last twelve years without the good humour of Vanessa Philips, my longsuffering PA, the passion for people of Helena Bailey and the diligence of Lynne Howard. I owe them all my thanks, and to my leadership team Amy Newland, Duncan Johnson, Kate Fletcher, Rebecca Bradfield, Sarah Smith and Will Creswell who shape our culture and ensure our outcomes.

Finally, and most importantly, I am grateful to my wonderful, beautiful, creative and caring wife, Jane. Since I left a 'proper job' in Trading Standards in 2007 she has wondered what I do. We both hope that this book may provide an answer!

Acknowledgements – Christopher Hodges

Chris would like to thank the multitude of regulatory experts whom he has had the privilege to observe and work with for over forty years. It has been a pleasure to push the boundaries of effective regulation with Graham Russell and all his outstanding team at OPSS. Warm thanks are due to them and to all the contributors to this book. Chris would also like to thank Charmaine Cole for the laborious task of wonderfully accurate editing.

Graham and Chris are very grateful to the team at Hart Publishing for their support and understanding throughout, especially Sinead Moloney, Roberta Bassi, Tom Adams, Emma Platt and Richard Cox.

This book has been a collaborative effort over three years, and as such some of the regulatory delivery initiatives described by contributors will have developed further since the time the content was drafted.

Views and opinions expressed in this book do not necessarily reflect the official policy or position of authors' affiliate organisations.

INDEX

NB – page locators followed by '*f*' indicate information in figures, '*t*' indicates information in tables and '*b*' indicates information in boxes.